Reasonableness and Risk

Reasonableness and Risk

Right and Responsibility in the Law of Torts

GREGORY C. KEATING

Oxford University Press is a department of the University of Oxford. It furthers the University's objective of excellence in research, scholarship, and education by publishing worldwide. Oxford is a registered trade mark of Oxford University Press in the UK and certain other countries.

Published in the United States of America by Oxford University Press
198 Madison Avenue, New York, NY 10016, United States of America.

© Gregory C. Keating 2022

All rights reserved. No part of this publication may be reproduced, stored in a retrieval system, or transmitted, in any form or by any means, without the prior permission in writing of Oxford University Press, or as expressly permitted by law, by license, or under terms agreed with the appropriate reproduction rights organization. Inquiries concerning reproduction outside the scope of the above should be sent to the Rights Department, Oxford University Press, at the address above.

You must not circulate this work in any other form
and you must impose this same condition on any acquirer.

CIP data is on file at the Library of Congress

ISBN 978-0-19-086794-2

DOI: 10.1093/oso/9780190867942.001.0001

Printed by Integrated Books International, United States of America

Note to Readers

This publication is designed to provide accurate and authoritative information in regard to the subject matter covered. It is based upon sources believed to be accurate and reliable and is intended to be current as of the time it was written. It is sold with the understanding that the publisher is not engaged in rendering legal, accounting, or other professional services. If legal advice or other expert assistance is required, the services of a competent professional person should be sought. Also, to confirm that the information has not been affected or changed by recent developments, traditional legal research techniques should be used, including checking primary sources where appropriate.

(Based on the Declaration of Principles jointly adopted by a Committee of the American Bar Association and a Committee of Publishers and Associations.)

You may order this or any other Oxford University Press publication by visiting the Oxford University Press website at www.oup.com.

For Carol, Lindsay, and Emily

Contents

Preface	xi
Acknowledgements	xv

1. Wrongs, Harms, and Costs	1
I. The Elusiveness of Tort	3
II. The Asymmetry of Harm and Benefit	9
III. Harm in the Law of Torts	13
IV. Judgments of Value	16
2. The Priority of Responsibility over Repair	19
I. The Academic Turn in Tort Theory	20
II. Moving Forward	24
A. Corrective Justice	24
1. Sovereign and Subordinate Corrective Justice	25
2. Regulating the Future and Rectifying the Past	28
a. Putting Flesh on the Principle	30
3. Adjudicative Practice	32
B. The Unity of Right and Reparation	35
1. The Priority of Rights over Reparation	36
a. Enforcing Rights	39
b. Repairing Injuries	41
c. Relating and Distinguishing Legal Institutions	42
2. Wrongful Losses and Primary Rights	45
a. Wandering the Law Looking for Wrongs to Repair	46
b. Irreparable Injuries and Wrongs without Losses	48
C. The Structure of Primary Norms	51
1. The Omnilaterality of Primary Obligation	51
2. Primary Wrongs	53
3. Looking Forward and Backward	58
D. Putting Primary Norms First	59
1. Making Sense of Tort Law	61
a. Safeguarding Individual Agency	61
E. Summing Up	67
3. The Importance of Interests	69
I. Ideas of "Private Law"	71
A. "Private Law" as Form—And Substance	73
B. Interpretive and Philosophical Challenges	77

    II. Torts without Interests   83
        A. Wrongly Taking Charge of Another   88
        B. Damaging Means   93
        C. Assimilating Disregard to Domination   95
        D. Balancing Security and Liberty   99
        E. Strict Liability   101
    III. The Permeability of Modern Tort to "Public Law"   104
    IV. Tort and the Domains of Justice   111
    V. Background and Foreground Justice   115
    VI. Form and Substance   120

4. Fairness and Fault   123
    I. Reasonableness and Rationality in Negligence Theory   125
        A. Reasonableness as Social Rationality   129
            1. The Hand Formula   130
            2. Reasonableness as Rationality—The Economic Interpretation   134
        B. Reasonable Care as Fair Precaution   142
            1. The Priority of Physical Harm and the Domain of Negligence Law   144
            2. Precaution and Proportionality: Revisiting the Hand Formula   150
            3. Ineliminable Risks and Inefficient Precautions   155
            4. The Specter of Paternalism   160
            5. Jury Adjudication   162
        C. Reasonable Persons   164
            1. The Irrelevance of Subjective Valuation   167
            2. The Role of Normalizing Assumptions   173
        D. The Template of Reasonableness   175
            1. Reasonable Expectations and Salient Precautions   175
            2. Subordinate Doctrines of Due Care   179
        E. Taking Negligence Law Seriously   182

5. From Reparation to Regulation   185
    I. Harm beyond Repair   185
        A. Possibilities, Limits, and Lessons   187
        B. Damages for Wrongful Death   189
    II. Safety as a Primary Good   193
    III. Three Standards of Precaution   199
        A. The Safe-Level Standard   200
            1. The Significance of a Risk: Quantity and Quality   200
        B. The Feasibility Standard   202
            1. Technological Feasibility   203
            2. Economic Feasibility   205
        C. The Cost-Benefit Standard and Its Claims   209
    IV. Myth or Reality: Three Applications   210

	A. The Safety Standard: Consumer Expectations	211
	B. The Feasibility Standard: Rescues	214
	C. Cost-Justification and Commensurability: Private Necessity	217
V.	Judgments of Value	218
	A. Consumer Choice: Valuing Other People's Lives	220
	B. From Efficiency to Fairness and Equal Right	223
	C. Tying the Threads Together	226

6. Strict Responsibilities — 229
   I. Sovereignty and Strict Liability: Harms to Autonomy Rights — 240
   II. Harm-Based Strict Liabilities: Responsibility without Fault — 247
   III. Correcting Corrective Justice Theory — 257
   IV. Indeterminacy and Morality in Harm-Based Strict Liability — 260

7. Enterprise Liability: Collective Responsibility and Commutative Justice — 265
   I. The Significance of Enterprise Liability — 267
   II. The Justice of Enterprise Liability — 268
      A. What Is Enterprise Liability? — 271
         1. Features of the Form — 272
         2. Why Enterprise Liability Is Most Fully Realized through Strict Liability — 273
         3. Objections — 275
      B. Policy, Principle, and Responsibility — 278
         1. The Policies of Accident Avoidance and Loss-Spreading — 278
         2. The Principle of Fairness — 281
      C. Fairness in the World of Organized Risk — 282
         1. The World of Acts and the World of Activities — 285
      D. Fate, Fortune, and the Facets of Fairness — 288
         1. Three Facets of Fairness — 288
         2. Relaxing Causation — 290
      E. Enterprise Liability beyond Tort — 291
         1. Advantages of Administrative Alternatives — 292
         2. Limits and Exceptions: The Resilience of Negligence Liability — 297
            a. Property Rights — 298
            b. When Risk Is Essential to an Activity — 299

8. The Heterogeneity of Tort — 301

Bibliography — 313
Index — 333

Preface

Torts is among the most intuitive of legal subjects. Everyday interactions gone awry—cars that crash, products that maim, drugs that addict and harm—are its domain. Bread and butter tort cases therefore attract instinctive judgments of responsibility, shaped by lifelong experience and learning about what we do and do not owe to others to avoid impairing their persons and interests. First-year law students do not walk into their torts classes with fully formed answers to the myriad legal questions raised by injurious modern activities—such as texting while driving, or marketing ostensibly harmless but highly addictive electronic cigarettes—but they do walk into class with inchoate ideas of wrong, harm, and responsibility. And those inchoate ideas enable them at least to situate tort law's more refined analyses. Like the fish in David Foster Wallace's famous 2009 commencement address "This is Water," first-year law students experience the peculiar surprise of learning that they have been swimming in tort law's waters all along.

If the topics of tort law are intuitive, putting one's finger on the heart of the field is surprisingly hard to do. The classic definition of Torts is both formal and negative. Torts, we are told, are civil wrongs not arising out of contractual relations. The problem here is not merely definitional. Ever since modern tort law emerged in the latter half of the nineteenth century, the academic literature has been haunted by the worry that Torts is neither an inherently necessary, nor a well-formed, legal field. The diversity of topics and themes that fall under the umbrella of tort law fuels these fears. For one thing, the primary obligations imposed by diverse torts are remarkably heterogeneous: some have to do with intentional wrongs, others with accidental wrongs; some protect tangible interests in our persons and property, others protect intangible interests in our reputation, privacy, and economic engagements. For another, tort law embraces two competing general principles of responsibility: negligence (or fault) liability and strict (or no fault) liability. For a third, the law of torts sometimes settles on individual persons as the basic locus of responsibility—on the natural persons who text and drive, for example. Other times, though, tort law latches onto institutions as the basic locus of responsibility—on the firms whose defective products inflict harm, for instance. Finally, the realm of Torts seems uniquely vulnerable to eclipse by other legal institutions. The modern administrative state often encroaches upon tort law's domain, sundering its characteristic unity of right and remedy and replacing tort law with two distinct institutions—one concerned with regulating risky conduct and the other concerned with providing compensation for injury or loss.

Faced with this formidable heterogeneity, leading modern schools of tort theory have come to place great weight on tort law's remedial apparatus as the key to the subject. Important and influential views insist that the importance of tort law lies primarily in enacting corrective justice, or in empowering civil recourse. These views have considerable merit up to a point; recourse and reparation certainly are basic aspects of tort law. But this emphasis on tort law's secondary norms of recourse and repair comes at a cost. In searching for the essence of the legal field in its response to completed wrongs, tort theory is in danger of turning its gaze away from the heart of its subject, namely, the primary obligation-imposing norms that articulate what we do and do not owe to one another in the way of obligations not to interfere with or impair each other's persons, property, and interests, intentionally or accidentally. Maddeningly heterogeneous as these primary obligations are, their breach is the predicate that brings into play tort law's powers of recourse and obligations of repair.

This book thus adopts the view that tort law's ever-evolving norms articulating our primary responsibilities not to interfere with or impair one another in diverse ways are the heart of the subject. From this perspective, the law of torts—broadly understood to encompass its administrative and statutory alternatives along with the common law subject—is a fundamental and necessary legal field. Just as there must be a law of contract governing obligations arising from agreements, and a law of property governing obligations pertaining to the ownership and use of external objects, so too there must be a law articulating the obligations that persons owe to one another simply as beings with vulnerable bodies, fragile lives, urgent interests, and important projects. The domain of tort law may, no doubt, be constructed in diverse ways. It may vary over time as values and social relations change, and as new sources of risk and harm emerge. It may expand and contract relative to contract and property. But any legal system worthy of the name must articulate what it is that we owe to one another in the way of coercively enforceable responsibilities not to impair or interfere with each other.

By spelling out what we owe in the way of obligations to respect each other's persons, property, and intangible interests, the primary norms of tort law help to establish the terms of our mutual security as members of civil society. When the law of torts extends its protections to a previously unprotected interest—to an interest in emotional tranquility, say—it safeguards that interest against injury. It obligates all of us not to impair the interest in question in ways that tort law now proscribes, and empowers those we wrongly harm to require that we repair any harm that we do them by breaching that obligation. John Stuart Mill put his finger on the importance of such protection when he remarked that rights which establish our security safeguard "the very groundwork of our existence."

We depend on security "for all our immunity from evil and for the whole value of all and every good" because only "the gratification of the instant could be of any worth to us if we could be deprived of everything the next instant."[1] Because the core of the law of torts safeguards the very groundwork of our existence, the primary rights and responsibilities of tort law specify important, and often overlooked, norms of basic justice.

This book thus places tort law's primary obligation imposing norms—and its competing principles of fault and strict responsibility—at the center of its account of the subject. It also examines the regulatory and administrative institutions with which the common law of torts cooperates and competes, treating these as part of the same family of institutions concerned to establish what we owe to one another in the way of obligations not to impair or interfere with each other's persons and projects. By doing so, it hopes both to develop a particular point of view on its subject, and to bring the preoccupations of tort theory closer to the preoccupations of tort law.

---

[1] John Stuart Mill, Utilitarianism 53 (Hackett, 1979) (1861).

Acknowledgements

The seeds of this book were sown during my earliest days as a law student. Like many first-year law students before and since, I had no idea what tort law was when I entered law school. I soon found myself deeply fascinated. My interest was sparked both by the subject and by Morton Horwitz's passionate and masterful Socratic teaching. Later in law school, I encountered Lewis Sargentich. Ever since, I have been a lucky beneficiary of his thinking about torts, law, and legal theory. But for many illuminating discussions with Lew, I would not have developed the views that I articulate in this book concerning the relation of tort to direct regulation of risk and administrative schemes that displace the common law of torts. The bookend to having learned so much from my teachers is that I have also learned from my students. Their diverse and subtly different responses over time to cases, doctrines, and issues have led me to see aspects of tort law that would not otherwise have caught my eye.

The ideas in this book have developed, in fits and starts, over many years. I have therefore benefitted from the help, the comments, the work, the collegiality, and the friendship of many people. When I first began to teach at USC, I had the good fortune to have Dick Craswell as my colleague. Dick was an ideal senior colleague. Without his endlessly patient tutoring, I would not have acquired whatever appreciation of economic analysis I do have. Conversations with Dick made me see the power, range, and subtlety of the economic analysis of torts. Later, I learned enormously from more infrequent, but always edifying, discussions with Guido Calabresi. Professor Calabresi's views about tort law and the pricing of human life have been a powerful stimulus to my thinking. Without that stimulus, I would not have developed the view that prominent American regulatory norms do, in fact, prescribe more than efficient precaution and register the special value of human life in a compelling way. Indeed, the economic analysis of torts has had a powerful, formative impact on the agenda of this book. Without the additional provocation of Louis Kaplow's and Steve Shavell's forceful and uncompromising defense of welfarism, I would not have been driven to recognize the significance of the harm-benefit asymmetry for tort law, or to defend the view that non-consequentialist moral considerations justify standards of precaution more stringent than cost-justified precaution.

It has been my equal good fortune to have had colleagues and friends whose orientation towards questions of risk and responsibility is, like my own, decidedly non-economic. At the beginning of my career, Barbara Herman was a wonderfully intelligent, perceptive, and supportive senior colleague and mentor. Since then, I have had the great luck of having Gary Watson and Gideon Yaffe as my colleagues at USC. They have shaped my thinking in ways too pervasive to describe. I have also had the good fortune to have Seana Shiffrin as my colleague across town. Seana's own work on harm, and many helpful conversations over many years, have had a deep impact on the way that I have come to think about harm. Jules Coleman and Arthur Ripstein, whose views I criticize in this book, have both had profound impacts on my thinking, through their work and our many conversations. The same is true of the work, and the colleagueship, of John Goldberg and Ben Zipursky. We first began discussing questions of tort, private law, and legal theory more than two decades ago and have continued to do so ever since.

At the USC Gould School of Law, where I have been fortunate to spend my career, I have been blessed by many talented and generous colleagues in addition to Barbara and Dick, Gary, and Gideon. Those whose intelligence, instruction, and support I have benefitted from include: Scott Altman, Jennifer Arlen, Scott Bice, Rebecca Brown, Alex Capron, Marshall Cohen, Sam Erman, Ron Garet, Tom Griffith, Ariela Gross, Gillian Hadfield, Felipe Jimenez, Ehud Kamar, Ed Kleinbard, Dan Klerman, Andrei Marmor, Ed McCaffery, Marcela Prieto, Jon Quong, Bob Rasmussen, Mike Shapiro, Larry Simon, Matt Spitzer, Nomi Stolzenberg, Chris Stone, Eric Talley, and Catherine Wells. I am also lucky to have had deans—Scott Bice, Matt Spitzer, Ed McCaffery, Bob Rasmussen, and Andrew Guzman—who have supported my scholarship generously and made USC a good place to work.

I am also lucky to have had the assistance and stimulation of an intellectually vibrant community of torts scholars, private law scholars, and legal theory scholars, in this country and beyond. I have learned from many members of this community in both formal and informal ways. Some of those from whom I have learned much are: Ken Abraham, Larry Alexander, Lisa Austin, Ronen Avraham, Christine Beuermann, Ellie Bublick, Alan Calnan, Martha Chamallas, Nico Cornell, Hanoch Dagan, Avihay Dorfman, Nora Engstrom, Chris Essert, Benjamin Ewing, Jim Fleming, George Fletcher, Samuel Freeman, Barbara Fried, John Gardner, Mark Geistfeld, Andrew Gold, John Goldberg, Mark Grady, Mike Green, Tom Grey, Alon Harel, Jeffrey Helmreich, Scott Hershovitz, Ori Herstein, Heidi Hurd, Keith Hylton, Aaron James, Frances Kamm, Larissa Katz, Erin Kelly, Doug Kysar, Alexi Lahav, Brian Lee, Daniel Markovits, Paul Miller, Michael Moore, Sophia Moreau, John Oberdiek, Gideon Parchomovsky, Dennis Patterson, James Penner, Stephen Perry, Dan Priel, Robert Rabin, Arthur Ripstein, Chris Robinette, Steven Schaus, Tony Sebok, Cathy Sharkey, Ken Simons, Henry Smith, Lionel Smith, Steve Smith, Jane Stapleton, Sandy Steel,

Rob Stevens, Martin Stone, Rebecca Stone, Victor Tadros, Cristina Tilley, Jeremy Waldron, Ernest Weinrib, Ted White, John Witt, and Richard Wright.

Although the ideas in this book began to germinate early in my career, the book itself did not come into sharp focus for me until the past few years. It might not have come together at all without the benefit of a year as Fellow-in-Residence at the Edmund and Lily Safra Center for Ethics at Harvard. I am grateful to my dean, Andrew Guzman, for supporting that year, to Danielle Allen, the Center's Director, for creating a warm and congenial place to work, and to my colleagues at the Center—especially Dick Fallon, Meira Levinson, Tim Scanlon, and Dennis Thompson—for companionship, edification, and stimulation. Tim's commentary on a workshop paper predecessor to Chapter Three of this book was invaluable.

I have also had a great deal of help in producing this book. David Lipp, my editor at Oxford, has been a most helpful sounding board and source of guidance. My supremely competent administrative assistant, Hannah Pae, and a succession of excellent research assistants—Shauli Bar-On, Joseph Harper, Michelle Kim, Isaac Maycock, Remy Merritt, and William Wilson—have helped with thankless but important tasks, have provided valuable feedback on the book's chapters, and have offered good editorial advice as well. Suzanne Greenberg has gone beyond the call of friendship in going over every chapter in intense and meticulous detail, providing expert editorial advice and tightening up the book and its arguments. My colleague and friend Ariela Gross gave me characteristically wise and helpful advice as I was bringing this book to a close.

My greatest debt is to my spouse, Carol McCleary, and to our out daughters, Lindsay and Emily, for their love and support, and their interest in this book simply because it is my project.

1
Wrongs, Harms, and Costs

Shortly after the turn of the twenty-first century, the Oregon Supreme Court handed down a decision which cited both Edward Coke's *Institutes* and Blackstone's *Commentaries on the Laws of England*.[1] The Court's appeal to these ancient authorities was prompted by the application of a recently enacted Oregon statute to bar the plaintiff's tort claim against his employer. The plaintiff alleged that exposure to toxic fumes at his workplace had caused him to suffer from severe respiratory problems. As applied, the plaintiff argued, the statute stripped him of rights guaranteed by a clause in Oregon's Bill of Rights:

> [E]very man shall have a remedy by due course of law for injury done him in his person, property, or reputation.

The Oregon Constitution was adopted in 1859—more than two hundred years after Coke wrote and more than ninety years after Blackstone published the first of his *Commentaries*.[2] The Court reached back far beyond Oregon's founding because it took "injury" and "remedy" to be terms of art whose meaning was fixed long before Oregon ratified its constitution. The same was true, the Court thought, of the role and importance of the law of torts itself.

Coke's commentary on Chapter 29 of the Magna Carta of 1225 thus explained that the common law had evolved to protect individuals in two broad respects. The first was a shield against arbitrary government actions involving a person's life, liberty, or property. The second was a guarantee to every subject that a legal remedy was available for injury to goods, land, or person by any other subject of the realm.[3]

---

[1] Smothers v. Gresham Transfer, Inc. 25 P.3d 333 (Or. 2001) overruled in part by Horton v. Oregon Health and Sci. U., 376 P.3d 998 (Or. 2016). Edward Coke, The Second Part of the Institutes of the Laws of England (1797 ed.). William Blackstone, Commentaries (1766).

[2] *Id.* Coke's four *Institutes* were published between 1628 and 1644.

[3] *Smothers*, 25 P.3d at 342. The state constitutional clause that *Smothers* was interpreting is commonly called a "remedy" clause. These are common in state constitutions. See John C.P. Goldberg, The Constitutional Status of Tort Law: Due Process and the Right to a Law for the Redress of Wrongs, 115 Yale L.J. 524 (2005).

Reasonableness and Risk. Gregory C. Keating, Oxford University Press. © Gregory C. Keating 2022.
DOI: 10.1093/oso/9780190867942.003.0001

For Coke, the protections conferred by the common law of torts were thus coequal to those conferred by constitutional law. Constitutional law secures us against wrongful treatment at the hands of the State, whereas the law of torts secures us against wrongful treatment at each other's hands.

The lesson here is simple, but often overlooked. It is as much a requirement of basic justice that citizens have rights against one another as it is that they have rights against the state. Any mature legal system must contain a body of law addressing what we owe in the way of obligations to respect each other's physical and psychological integrity, property, privacy, freedom of action, reputation, and so on. If people were free to injure and interfere with one another as they pleased, we would still be in a state of nature.

The legal universe that Coke and Blackstone inhabited was, of course, very different from our own. In our world, criminal law, not tort, may come to mind as the primary legal institution that protects us against harm at each other's hands. There are, to be sure, deep affinities between criminal law and the law of torts. Both deal with wrongs, and their domains overlap. In many cases, an action is both a wrong punishable in a criminal prosecution by the state and a wrong subject to redress in a civil lawsuit by an individual. In other cases, though, only one of these legal fields applies. Notwithstanding their affinities, the primary concerns of tort and crime are now different, and those differences are reflected in the wrongs that most preoccupy them. Criminal law is primarily concerned with the claims and interests of the public at large. It aims to suppress and to punish intentional conduct that endangers all of us. Partly because it doles out punishment, criminal law cares a great deal about the blameworthiness of criminal defendants.

The law of torts, by contrast, is primarily concerned with what we owe directly to each other. Tort law focuses much more on whether the defendant wronged the plaintiff than it does on the defendant's blameworthiness, and it is preoccupied with repair, not punishment. Modern tort law recognizes a variety of intentional wrongs, but it is centrally and distinctively concerned with accidental wrongs. Consequently, much of the conduct that attracts the attention of modern tort law is seriously harmful, but not egregiously wrongful. A split second of carelessness behind the wheel of a car, for example, is not especially blameworthy, but it can do devastating harm. Such lapses of care are a fundamental preoccupation of the law of torts, and of almost no interest to criminal law. Because modern tort law is centered on accidents, it addresses wrongs and harms that both matter and normally lie beyond the reach of criminal law.

Our accident-centered tort law is a child of the latter half of the nineteenth century. Since that time, the field has proven to be remarkably plastic. Its scope and its content have changed greatly. Product accidents have migrated from contract law to tort law, and the duties owed to entrants onto real property are now spelled out by tort law, not by property law. Psychological integrity and privacy have gained a measure of legal protection that they did not have a hundred years ago. Perhaps because it is both relatively young and strikingly prone to transformation, modern tort law has seemed to scholars both especially elusive and enduringly fragile.

I. The Elusiveness of Tort

Fundamental legal categories often appear easy to encapsulate. Contract and property seem to be. Torts is not. Torts scholars seem to be mired in a modest version of the predicament that St. Augustine found himself in with respect to time. They know what their field is; they just can't seem to explain their subject to anyone else.[4] Compact descriptions of the subject, intended to orient students, provoke deep disagreement. The fourth and final edition of William Prosser's classic hornbook begins with the traditional definition of a tort as "a civil wrong, other than breach of contract, for which the law will provide a remedy in the form of an action for damages." But Prosser rejects "even this vague statement [as] inaccurate since one important form of remedy for a tort is an injunction, granted in a court of equity, before any damage occurs. Another is restitution... and still another is self-help by the injured party."[5] Piling on, Prosser points out that this traditional definition is "of no value to the layman" because he "wants to know the nature of those breaches of duty which give rise to an action for damages."[6] Having dispatched the traditional definition, Prosser's treatise proposes its own: "The common thread woven into all torts is the idea of unreasonable interference with the interests of others."[7]

Prosser's definition, too, has failed to attract universal assent. Its open-ended terms—"interests," "interference," "unreasonable"—might be regarded as placeholders into which the treatise will pour content. But the phrase "unreasonable interference" might also be read to invoke the particulars of the tort of nuisance, thereby imposing the mold of one particular tort on the entire field.[8] To confuse matters further, it is common for economically inclined scholars to treat the relevant subject as the "law of accidents."[9] The implication is that the intentional torts are insignificant relics of an earlier age. The extent of this

---

[4] "What, then, is time? If no one asks me, I know; if I want to explain it to someone who does ask me, I do not know." Augustine, The Confessions 242 (Michael P. Foley, ed., Hackett, 2006). H.L.A. Hart thought that the "concept of law" (and other legal concepts) provoked the same kind of inarticulateness. H.L.A. Hart, The Concept of Law 13 (Oxford, 3rd ed., 2012) (1961).

[5] W. Page Keeton et al., Prosser and Keeton on Torts § 1, at 2 (West Group, 5th ed., 1984).

[6] Id. § 1, at 1, n.2.

[7] Id. § 1, at 6.

[8] John C.P. Goldberg & Benjamin C. Zipursky, Torts as Wrongs, 88 Tex. L. Rev. 917, 920 (2010).

[9] See, e.g., Guido Calabresi, The Costs of Accidents (Yale, 1970); Steven Shavell, Economic Analysis of Accident Law (Harvard, 1987).

disagreement has led two prominent tort theorists to lament that "academics have lost their feel for [a] basic legal category."[10] The assumption that American academics once had a confident grasp of the category is itself debatable. One hundred and fifty years ago, Oliver Wendell Holmes opined that "[t]orts is not a proper subject for a law book."[11] Holmes soon changed his mind, but the view of the subject that he settled on has been disputed down to this day.[12]

The law of torts is heterogeneous in diverse ways. For one thing, it is divided between intentional and accidental wrongs. For another, the domain of intentional torts is itself internally diverse. Some intentional wrongs safeguard our interests in the physical and psychological integrity of our persons. Others protect property rights, privacy, contractual rights, and intangible interests. And some intentional torts simply plug holes elsewhere in the legal system.[13] A further, and deeper, source of heterogeneity is the fact that liability for accidental harm is split between competing principles of fault and strict responsibility. The dominant principle of negligence imposes responsibility for inflicting harm *because* that harm should have been avoided. The exceptional principle of strict liability imposes responsibility for harm that should *not* have been avoided on the ground that the unavoidable harm in question should be borne by the party responsible for its infliction. The intimate entanglement of the accidental branch of modern tort law with direct regulation of risk and administrative alternatives to the law of torts proper is another increasingly important source of heterogeneity. Often, the "private" law of torts must be understood in relation to bodies of "public" law with which it competes and cooperates. Last, individual and collective forms of responsibility compete for control of the terrain of accidental injury, both within and beyond the law of torts proper. Negligence law is framed largely in terms of individual wrongdoing, but other domains of tort law, including vicarious liability and products liability, are fairly regarded as imposing responsibility more on enterprises than on individuals.

Notwithstanding the diversity of its primary norms and forms of responsibility, modern tort law does have a distinctive domain. The law of torts as we know it took shape in the latter half of the nineteenth century in response to the emergence of accidental physical harm as a pressing social problem. To this day, tort law continues to be preoccupied with accidental injury, and that

---

[10] Goldberg & Zipursky 2010, *supra* note 8, at 919.
[11] Oliver Wendell Holmes, Book Review, 5 Am. L. Rev. 340, 341 (1871) (reviewing C.G. Addison, The Law of Torts (1870)). For discussion, see Thomas C. Grey, Accidental Torts, 54 Vand. L. Rev. 1225, 1232 (2001). As Grey notes, Holmes overcame his doubts and published *The Theory of Torts*, two years later. See Oliver Wendell Holmes, The Theory of Torts, 7 Am. L. Rev 652, 653 (1873).
[12] See, *e.g.*, John C.P. Goldberg & Benjamin C. Zipursky, Recognizing Wrongs 359 (Harvard, 2020).
[13] Dan B. Dobbs et al., Hornbook on Torts §§ 1.3, 1.5, 1.6, 38.1 (West, 2000). For examples of idiosyncratic torts see *id.* at §§ 39.2 (malicious prosecution), 39.13 (abuse of process), and 44.4 (spoliation of evidence).

preoccupation gives tort theory its principal subject. It is no surprise that the first great book advancing the economic analysis of tort was entitled *The Costs of Accidents*.[14] Accidents are the heart of modern tort law, and the domain of accidental harm is where administrative schemes and direct risk regulation sometimes complete and sometimes displace the law of torts. The preoccupations of modern tort law and tort theory are the preoccupations of this book. Its core concern is with the legal regimes that govern the infliction of accidental physical harm, taking them to be attempts to devise reasonable standards of precaution and principles of responsibility with respect to the imposition, avoidance, and repair of such harm.

Risk, one of the terms in this book's title, is thus a fundamental subject of the book. But why reasonableness? References to reasonableness appear throughout the law of torts, and the term signals something important. The law of battery protects us against unauthorized contacts with our persons that offend a "reasonable sense of personal dignity."[15] The use of deadly force in self-defense is only justifiable when the person using it *reasonably* fears grievous bodily harm.[16] To be actionable, an assault must arouse apprehension "in the mind of a reasonable person."[17] The figure of the reasonable person may be the most important trope in the law of negligence, and references to "reasonable care" and "reasonable precaution" are too numerous to count. An important form of strict liability in nuisance law is described as liability for "unreasonable harm."[18]

"Reasonable" might be read simply as a synonym for "justifiable." Reasonable risks are risks whose imposition is justified; reasonable self-defense is self-defense that is justified. This interpretation captures something true and important, but the word "reasonable" has resonances that "justifiable" does not, and those resonances are relevant here. Unlike the concept of rationality with which it is sometimes equated—especially in economic approaches to tort—reasonableness is a morally freighted concept.[19] Reasonable people give

---

[14] Calabresi 1970, *supra* note 9.
[15] Brzoska v. Olson, 668 A.2d 1355, 1361 (Del. 1995) (citing Restatement (Second) of Torts § 19 (1965)); Keeton 1984, *supra* note 5, § 9 at 42.
[16] See, *e.g.*, Hattori v. Peairs, 662 So.2d 509 (La. App. 1995); 13 Am. Jur. Proof of Facts 3d 219 (1991).
[17] Cullison v. Medley, 570 N.E.2d 27, 30–31 (Ind. 1991); Keeton 1984, *supra* note 5, § 10 at 43–47. The Second and Third Restatements mark a partial departure from an objective standard applied to the apprehension of the assaulted person, applying a reasonable person standard only to assaults committed with words alone and not accompanied by overt acts. Restatement (Second) of Torts § 31 (1965); Restatement (Third) of Torts: Intentional Torts to Persons § 103 Discussion Draft, cmt. g (2014).
[18] See, *e.g.*, Wheat v. Freeman Coal Mining Corp., 319 N.E.2d 290, 295–96 (Ill. App. Ct. 1974); Restatement (Second) of Torts § 826(b) (1979).
[19] For an example of collapsing reasonableness into rationality, see, *e.g.*, Richard A. Posner, A Theory of Negligence, 1 J. Legal Stud. 29, 32–33 (1972). For the distinction between reasonableness and rationality, see W.M. Sibley, The Rational versus the Reasonable, 62 Phil. Rev. 554 (1953); John

appropriate weight to the interests of others and constrain their conduct accordingly. Reasonable people act in ways that are justifiable to those who are affected by their conduct. Acting rationally, by contrast, is merely a matter of prudence. It requires pursuing one's own interests in an instrumentally intelligent way. When rationality is extended from a single person to society at large, the aim in view is the prudent pursuit of society's interests. When socially rational conduct is cashed out in economic terms, the end in view is minimizing the combined costs of accidents and their prevention in order to maximize wealth. This collapsing of the claims of distinct persons into the interests of a single rational actor cuts the moral heart out of tort law. We are distinct persons with separate lives to lead, and what we owe to each other in the way of care and repair is tort law's subject. Tort law's rhetoric of reasonableness signals that it takes our relations to one another to be a matter of morality, not prudence.

This book thus takes tort law's relentless use of the word "reasonable" to imply a deontological outlook. Tort is about what we owe to each other in the way of coercively enforceable obligations not to impair or interfere with each other's urgent interests as we go about our lives in civil society. By taking a deontological view of tort as a law of wrongs, rights, and relational responsibilities, the book plunges into an ongoing, fundamental debate in the field. The law of torts was the first great topic of the economic analysis of law, and modern tort theory began life as the offspring of the economic analysis of law. Ronald Coase's *The Problem of Social Cost* illustrated its thesis with examples drawn from trespass and nuisance law.[20] Guido Calabresi's and Richard Posner's enduring contributions to our thinking about negligence, strict liability, and tort law more generally, followed shortly after Coase published his great paper.[21] These contributions gave birth to the conception of tort as a shadow price system—a price system whose role is to minimize the combined costs of accidents, their prevention, and the costs of operating the tort system itself, so as to maximize wealth. The economic conception replaced the idea of torts as wrongs done by one person to another with the idea of torts as jointly created "social costs"; replaced the intrinsically moral idea of reasonableness with the prudential idea of social rationality; eclipsed both the distinctions and the relations among persons by treating social choice as individual choice writ large; and spelled out the idea of justified precaution as cost-justified precaution. These ideas have had immense influence in the American Legal Academy, migrating far beyond the law of torts.

Rawls, Political Liberalism 48–53 (Columbia, rev. ed., 2005); Thomas M. Scanlon, What We Owe to Each Other (Harvard, 1998), at 189–247.

[20] Ronald Coase, The Problem of Social Cost, 3 J.L. & Econ. 1 (1960).
[21] See, *e.g.*, Calabresi 1970, *supra* note 9; Posner 1972, *supra* note 19.

In true dialectical fashion, the emergence of economic analysis spawned the rise of corrective justice theory in its modern form. Theorists of tort as corrective justice—preeminently Jules Coleman and Ernest Weinrib—argued that the economic analysis of tort could not offer a plausible account of the formal structure of ordinary tort lawsuits. Economic analysis regards it as irrational to fixate on the sunk costs of the past, and therefore regards tort lawsuits as forward-looking efforts to minimize future accident costs. Yet ordinary tort lawsuits are backward-looking inquiries into whether the defendant wronged the plaintiff, not forward-looking searches for cheapest cost-avoiders. Leveraging this point, corrective justice and civil recourse theorists now defend robust theories of torts as a law of wrongs, rights, and responsibilities. By emphasizing tort law's remedial and adjudicative aspects, corrective justice and civil recourse theorists have powerfully revived the traditional idea of torts as a law of wrongs, preoccupied with noneconomic questions of who did what to whom.

Corrective justice theory's insistence on the importance of backward-looking repair to the law of torts is an enduring contribution to our understanding of the subject. To be real rights, not paper ones, the legal rights that persons have against one another require remedies that are generally effective. Without remedies, rights are not effectively instituted. They cannot be enforced, and the harms done by their violation cannot be mended. And, unless they are effectively instituted, legal rights are legal rights in name only. Moreover, the law of torts does involve a particular approach to rights: it empowers those whose rights have been violated to seek redress from those who have done the violating. That redress usually takes the form of reparation for harm done. Tort law's remedial structure enforces the field's primary rights in a distinctive way.

But corrective justice theory also gets something important wrong—namely, the relative priority of remedial and primary responsibilities. For corrective justice theory, the failings of the economic theory of tort are essentially conceptual. Economics cannot adequately explain or justify the backward-looking, bilateral, structure of tort law. But tort also contains forward-looking, action-guiding, primary norms of right and responsibility. Placing proper weight on these rights and responsibilities brings to the fore a different conception of the subject and a different set of concerns about the economic theory of tort. Economics conceives of tort law as an instrument for minimizing the combined costs of accidents and their prevention so that social wealth and welfare are maximized. The claims that persons have against one another not to be interfered with or impaired are merely conduits designed to steer us toward the maximal production of wealth and welfare. Taking the primary rights that tort law recognizes—preeminently, rights to the liberty and security of our persons and our property—on their own terms, however, suggests that the economic analysis of torts misreads the fundamental values that the law of torts embodies.

Rights are institutional mechanisms that protect essential interests of those who hold them. The role of tort law is to spell out what various rights—to the liberty and integrity of our persons, to a measure of emotional peace, to a sphere of privacy, to reputation, and so on—require in the way of coercively enforceable duties not to impair or interfere with each other in various ways. The particular wrongs and rights that tort law recognizes, however, cry out for justification in larger moral and political terms.[22] The claim that tort law's rights and responsibilities are not merely devices designed to induce people to behave in ways that minimize the combined costs of accidents and their prevention is purely critical. Moving forward requires that we articulate an alternative to the economic conception, not just find fault with its assertions. Fortunately, an alternative lies latent in the law itself. Tort law protects people against diverse forms of interference and impairment, but the core of the law of torts confers protections that are important background conditions *for persons* to be able to pursue the ends and projects that give meaning to their lives. Tort law's morality is deontological. Tort, that is, spells out what people owe to each other in the way of reciprocal responsibilities not to interfere with, or impair, essential interests that we have as persons. Tort is a fundamental legal institution because it establishes an essential form of justice among persons. It helps to create and to sustain an essential part of the security that we all need to lead decent and independent lives. In Rawlsian terms, safety is a kind of primary good—something that everyone needs if they are to pursue their ends and purposes as equal and independent members of civil society.

The chapters that follow develop this deontological conception of tort in connection with diverse topics. We begin by examining the present state of tort theory and then turn to the field's fundamental principles of responsibility—fault and strict liability—both within and beyond the law of torts. Chapters Two and Three orient us by engaging leading noneconomic accounts of tort law. Chapter Two addresses corrective justice theory in the robust incarnation that regards corrective justice as the master principle of the legal field. Chapter Three investigates the view that "tort is private law"—that tort law's substance tumbles out of its form—and argues that we must attend to substance as well as to form. Making the best sense that we can of tort law requires recognizing that tort's rights and responsibilities protect urgent interests. Chapter Four addresses the main doctrines of negligence law, arguing that negligence law means what it says when it speaks not of socially rational care, but of reasonable care. Chapter

---

[22] On an "interest theory" of rights, for example, the task will be to show that the interest of the right-holder is sufficient to justify imposing coercively enforceable duties on others. See Charles R. Beitz, The Moral Rights of Creators of Artistic and Literary Works, 13 J. Pol. Phil. 330, 335–37 (2005) (and sources cited therein).

Five addresses prominent regulatory standards that require more than cost-justified precaution against risks that ripen into devastating and irreparable injury. Chapters Six and Seven address legal domains that impose responsibility for repairing harms whose infliction should not be avoided. Chapter Six takes up traditional strict liabilities in tort. Chapter Seven addresses the more modern idea of "enterprise liability." Enterprise liability affirms a collective conception of responsibility; it asserts that, in our social world, many accidental harms should be addressed as the inevitable byproducts of enduring productive activities. Chapter Eight, the concluding chapter, returns to the topic of tort law's heterogeneity. It suggests that we should view the fact that tort law is torn between individual and collective conceptions of responsibility, and between fault and strict liabilities, as more a source of the field's vitality than a sign of its disarray.

Throughout these chapters, the discussion emphasizes a pervasive contrast between the view developed in this book and the economic analysis of tort. The moral significance of harm is at the center of that contrast. Modern tort law is both a law of wrongs and a law of harm. It is a law of wrongs because torts are civil wrongs—violations of one person's rights committed by another person, natural or artificial. It is a law of harm, because modern tort law is distinctively preoccupied with accidental physical harm. Modern tort law arose in the latter half of the nineteenth century—hand in hand with the emergence of an industrial society—and it is especially concerned with the physical harms that modern productive activities inflict. Physical harm has no special significance within the economic analysis of tort law, but it does have special negative significance within a theory that places persons, their separateness, and their relations to each other at its center. The special negative significance of harm plays a central role in the accounts of negligence, risk regulation, and strict liability, which this book develops. Conversely, the fact that harm has no special significance within an economic framework explains why it is that economic analysis is usually critical of stringent standards of precaution—such as the "safety" and "feasibility" standards deployed in major federal statutes—that this book regards favorably. The special significance of harm from a deontological point of view therefore merits explicit discussion as a grounding for the specific topics that follow.

II. The Asymmetry of Harm and Benefit

The contrast between the significance that deontology and orthodox economic analysis assign to harm is nicely illustrated by the economic understanding of negligence. Orthodox economic analysis conceives of reasonable precaution as cost-justified precaution. Accidents should be avoided when it costs less to avoid them than to let them happen.[23] Cost-benefit analysis, the parent of cost-justified precaution, is regarded by economically inclined legal scholars as the master method for evaluation of all questions of risk and precaution.[24] Within cost-benefit analysis, harm has no special significance, and its avoidance has no special priority. Harm is just one possible cost in a calculus of cost and benefit, and costs and benefits are minuses and pluses on the same scale. "From an abstract perspective there would seem to be little reason for harms and benefits to be treated differently. Decades of cost-benefit analyses suggest that the two categories are interchangeable: reducing by one dollar damage that would otherwise occur is equivalent to providing a dollar's worth of new goods or services."[25]

This claim of symmetry is at odds with our ordinary intuitions and our law. In both morality and law, our obligations to avoid harming others are stronger than our obligations to benefit them. We can be compelled to refrain from battering our neighbors, but we cannot be compelled either to love or to help them. Tort is robust, whereas restitution is anemic. The U.S. Constitution contains a takings clause, but not a "givings" clause. For cost-benefit analysis, the harm-benefit asymmetry is a puzzle at best and an irrationality at worst. If avoiding a dollar's worth of damage "is equivalent to providing a dollar's worth of new goods or services," then we ought to treat harms and benefits symmetrically.[26] If we take off the lenses of cost-benefit analysis, however, we can see the sense in the asymmetry. Harm is a morally freighted word. Harms are presumptively bad for anyone to suffer. Harms impair essential conditions of human agency. Physical harms—death, disability, disease, and the like—rob us of normal and foundational powers of action. Physical harm comes close to being unconditionally bad.[27]

Few benefits, by contrast, are unconditionally good. Benefits enhance lives, but their power to do so is much more contingent than the badness of physical harm. The power of benefits to enhance lives depends significantly on the details of the life in question. Many benefits are good for *someone* but of no use to most people. Extraordinary visual-spatial processing skills, for example, are of great value to football quarterbacks and of little use to law professors. The gifts that make for mathematical genius may be wasted on someone whose passion is painting. Unusually low levels of anxiety may be indispensable to elite mountaineers and

---

[23] See, *e.g.*, Posner 1972, *supra* note 19.
[24] See, *e.g.*, Cass R. Sunstein, The Cost-Benefit Revolution (MIT Press, 2018).
[25] Wendy T. Gordon, Of Harms and Benefits: Torts, Restitution, and Intellectual Property, 21 J. Legal Stud. 449, 451 (1992).
[26] Gordon 1992, *supra* note 25, at 451.
[27] In some cases, the physical harm suffered may avoid a greater physical harm. In others, the harm may enable the realization of some value or good to whose realization the harmed person is deeply committed. These are exceptional cases, however, and even in these cases the harm suffered is still, in itself, bad. A broken arm may be worth suffering if it avoids death by drowning, but it is still a harm.

an impediment to a journalist who needs to take a "do or die" attitude toward a deadline. Whether some benefit—great wealth, or great musical talent, or great athletic skill, or great mathematical brilliance, for example—plays a valuable role in someone's life depends greatly on their aspirations and projects. Even extraordinary wealth is not an unalloyed good. Great wealth is necessary to major philanthropy, but it may impair the pursuit of authentic relationships. The capacity of wealth and its pursuit to get in the way of pursuing valuable ends is, in fact, considerable. Winning the lottery turns out to be anything but an unqualified good.[28] Being born rich may undermine drive and achievement.

Harms and benefits stand in very different relations to our powers of agency in general and to our wills in particular. Harms impair our normal powers of human agency. Benefits enhance our lives only if they are congruent with ends and projects to which we have committed ourselves. To thrust an unsought benefit upon someone and demand compensation from them for the value conferred is to impose upon them.[29] Unsought benefits stand in the same relation to our wills as harms do. They subject us to conditions that we have not chosen; they sever the link between our wishes, our wills, and what we do with our money and our time. If I can demand the market value of my services from you simply by playing beautiful music outside your open bedroom window, I have the power to force you either to close your window and forgo the pleasures of lovely evening air, or purchase from me a service you have not chosen to consume. You are presumptively entitled to open and close your windows as you see fit and to determine how you spend your time and money. Choosing how to spend them is an important part of your power to govern your life in accordance with your will. To have benefits forced upon you is to be harmed.

These assertions rest, of course, on conceptions of harm and benefit. The concept of a benefit, for its part, is broad, straightforward, and relatively uncontroversial. A benefit is an advantage; something that promotes or enhances well-being.[30] The philosophical literature on "harm," by contrast, is divided between dueling conceptions. The preoccupations of tort, however, are illuminated most by a conception that takes harm to be a condition of impairment.[31] In contrast to

---

[28] See, *e.g.*, Philip Brickman et al., Lottery Winners and Accident Victims: Is Happiness Relative?, 36 J. Personality & Soc. Psychol. 917 (1978).
[29] See, *e.g.*, Lee Anne Fennell, Forcings, 114 Colum. L. Rev. 1297 (2014) (discussing forced ownership of property by the government).
[30] See Seana Shiffrin, Harm and Its Moral Significance, 18 Legal Theory 357 (2012).
[31] Preeminently, this conception is advanced by Judith Jarvis Thomson, The Realm of Rights 262–68 (Harvard, 1990), and by Shiffrin 2012, *supra* note 30. See also Judith Thomson, More on the Metaphysics of Harm, 82 Phil. & Phenomenological Res. 436 (2011). A third conception of harm, championed by Matthew Hanser, takes harms to be events that injure basic human goods, not the ensuing conditions of impairment. Basic goods are "those goods [the] possession of which makes possible the achievement of a wide variety of the potential components of a reasonably happy life. . . . [The] basic goods . . . include certain fairly general physical and mental powers and abilities.

the more prominent interest account of harm, the impairment account focuses on the condition or state of being harmed, not on the relation of that position to an antecedent or alternative condition. Suffering excruciating pain, for example, is harm—even if the alternative is death and even if you prefer agonizing pain to death. Core harms in this conception are conditions that compromise normal functioning. Deafness, for example, is a harm because hearing is a normal human power, a part of normal human functioning. This is true even if the person in question is born deaf and so never suffered the loss of hearing—never underwent any worsening of position.[32]

The concept of an "impairment of normal functioning" is, to be sure, a broad one. Anything that can function normally can have its proper functioning impaired. A toy robot can be harmed by having its motor damaged. Tort law, though, is preoccupied with a narrower set of impaired conditions—with physical disabilities, broken, deformed, and severed limbs, chronic pain, and serious developmental disabilities. Broken bones, severed limbs, defects of sight and hearing, diseased organs, and disfigured body parts all compromise the basic capacities through which we act. Powers of sight, hearing, speech, thought, mobility, and so on play central roles in normal human lives. When we are seriously ill—or disabled, or in great pain—we are denied our normal lives. When we are in any of these impaired conditions, we are deprived of the normal capacities through which we shape our lives and our worlds in accordance with our wills.[33] We draw upon our wills when we act, and the exercise of our wills makes us aware of our own persons as beings capable of bringing possibilities into existence by choosing to do so. I can, for example, bring words into existence on a page by typing on a keyboard. Physical harms, chronic pain, and developmental disabilities rob us of normal forms of mastery over ourselves, our experience, and some portions of the external world by driving a wedge between our wills and our lives.[34] If all the bones in my hands were broken, try as I might I could

The power of sight, for example, is a basic good for human beings." Matthew Hanser, The Metaphysics of Harm, 77 Phil. & Phenomenological Res. 421, 440–41 (2008).

[32] Deafness is, in some ways, a difficult case. In important part, being deaf is bad for someone who suffers from it because speech is a basic form of human communication. When this social condition is mitigated, the harm of deafness is mitigated. For a fascinating study of this possibility, see Nora Ellen Groce, Everyone Here Spoke Sign Language: Hereditary Deafness on Martha's Vineyard (Harvard University Press, 1988). Whether residual harm remains depends on how we appraise the significance of not being able to hear music, conversation, words spoken in poetry, literature, plays, and so on. And there is the further complication that the harm of deafness might be counterbalanced by enabling forms of human interaction and experience not available to persons with normal hearing.

[33] See Shiffrin 2012, *supra* note 30, at 383. In sharpening the concept of harm in this way, Shiffrin is, in part, criticizing Raz's conception as too broad. See *id.* at 389, n.48. By contrast, she is further articulating Thomson's conception, though Thomson might not accept the sharpening. See Thomson 1990, *supra* note 31, at 227–48, 250–51, 253–71; Thomson 2011, *supra* note 31 at 436.

[34] Seana Shiffrin, Wrongful Life, Procreative Responsibility, and the Significance of Harm, 5 Legal Theory 117, 123 (1999).

not bring words into existence on the screen of my computer by typing on my keyboard.

III. Harm in the Law of Torts

One point in favor of the "impaired condition" conception of harm is that it maps remarkably well onto our law of torts. Tort law distinguishes between a broad conception of tortious wrongdoing as conduct which invades "legally protected interests" (or rights), and a narrower conception of physical harm as the suffering of an impaired condition.[35] Physical harm is an element of a standard negligence claim, and of many intentional torts and strict liabilities, too. The way in which physical harm is understood, therefore, plays a fundamental role in the law of torts. And the law of torts understands physical harm in terms of impairment. The *First Restatement of Torts*, for example, defined bodily harm as "any impairment of the physical condition of another's body or physical pain or illness."[36] The *Second Restatement* refined this definition, describing "bodily harm" as "any physical impairment of the condition of another's body" and explaining that "an impairment of the physical condition of another's body [exists] if the structure or function of any part of the other's body is altered."[37] The *Third Restatement* now defines "physical harm" as "the physical impairment of the human body ('bodily harm') or of real property or tangible personal property . . . [such impairment] includes physical injury, illness, disease, impairment of bodily function, and death."[38]

Statutes and case law also commonly embrace an impaired condition conception of harm. Michigan's codification of the standard common law rule in the automobile accident context, for example, defines "serious impairment of bodily function" to mean "an objectively manifested impairment of an important body function that affects the person's general ability to lead his or her normal life."[39]

---

[35] See, *e.g.*, Restatement (Second) of Torts §§ 7, 15 (1965).

[36] Restatement (First) of Torts § 15 (1934).

[37] Restatement (Second) of Torts § 15 cmt. a (1965). Section 7 distinguishes "bodily harm" from "injury" with "injury" covering cases in which a "legally protected interest" is invaded, but no harm is done. A harmless trespass would be an injury in this sense. *Id.* at § 7.

[38] Restatement (Third) of Torts: Liability For Physical & Emotional Harm § 4 (2010). The *Third Restatement* extends the idea of harm as an impaired condition to include the impairment of property. The philosophical conception of harm is concerned only with harm to persons. The most straightforward way to extend the philosophical conception of harm to cover damage to property is to draw upon the fact that we have rights in property. Rights to property extend our powers of agency and give rise to claims against others that they neither interfere with nor damage the property in question. Such damage impairs the agency of the owner.

[39] MCL 500.3135(1) ("A person remains subject to tort liability for noneconomic loss caused by his or her ownership, maintenance, or use of a motor vehicle only if the injured person has suffered death, serious impairment of body function, or permanent serious disfigurement."). A recent Michigan Supreme Court case, *McCormick v. Carrier*, 795 N.W.2d 517 (Mich. 2010), applies this

A body of case law grappling with the slowly unfolding consequences of exposure to asbestos overwhelmingly holds that identifiable subclinical damage to human cells will not support a tort claim. "The threat of future harm, not yet realized, is not enough."[40] Functional impairment must be shown.[41] Without such impairment there is no physical harm even though exposure to asbestos imposes very real financial and psychological costs when it results in subclinical cellular damage.[42]

Because physical capacities play central roles in normal human lives, physical harm is the central case of harm under the impaired condition conception.[43] Blindness is, for example, a serious harm, because sight is a normal human capacity and its loss usually diminishes a person's life. Being blind denies someone access to an important range of normal human activities. Other things equal, a person whose sight is normal has access to a richer life than a blind person does. A broken leg is a serious harm because a person whose leg is broken is unable to engage in a range of normal activities, beginning with walking. Loss of a leg is a more serious harm than a broken leg because loss of a leg is permanent, whereas a broken leg, properly treated, will heal.[44] On an impaired condition conception,

concept of impairment in an instructive manner. The plaintiff's foot was broken and bruised when the defendant's truck ran it over. The foot healed, though it continued to ache occasionally. With the healed foot, the plaintiff could perform the same work he performed prior to the injury but the post-injury foot hampered his fishing and other recreational activities. The court found impairment because the plaintiff's ability to lead his normal life was adversely affected.

[40] Burns v. Jaquays Mining Corp, 752 P.2d 28, 30 (Ariz. Ct. App. 1987) (quoting W. Page Keeton et al., Prosser & Keeton on the Law of Torts § 30, at 165 (West, 5th ed., 1984)). Pleural thickening, a condition in which the lining of the lung thickens, may be the most common form of cellular damage, which does not, by itself, count as physical harm. Because the harms of asbestos exposure are progressive, pleural thickening is a harbinger of asbestosis and mesothelioma.

[41] In addition to *Burns*, illustrative decisions include *Owens-Illinois, Inc. v. Armstrong*, 604 A.2d 47 (Md. Ct. App. 1992); *In re Hawaii Federal Asbestos Cases*, 734 F. Supp. 1563 (D. Haw. 1990). *Verbryke v. Owens-Corning Fiberglas Corp.*, 84 Ohio App. 3d 388 (1992) holds that pleural thickening does constitute bodily harm, but it is abrogated by *Ackison v. Anchor Packing Company*, 120 Ohio St. 3d 228 (2008).

[42] Medical monitoring costs, for example, are very likely to be incurred if a patient presents with subclinical damage from asbestos. The psychic costs are even larger. Persons afflicted by such changes live under swords of Damocles that are starting to drop. This is a real and serious psychic burden, as the U.S. Supreme Court notes in *Norfolk & W. Ry. Co. v. Ayers*, 538 U.S. 135, 150 (2003) ("In the course of the 20th century, courts sustained a variety of other 'fear-of' claims. Among them have been claims for fear of cancer. Heightened vulnerability to cancer . . . must necessarily have a most depressing effect upon the injured person. Like the sword of Damocles, he knows it is there, but not whether or when it will fall.") (Internal quotations and citations omitted).

[43] Psychological harm follows not far behind. Impaired psychological capacities wreak similar havoc with normal lives. Child sexual abuse, for instance, often leads to serious harm because it usually damages the capacity to trust other people and so impairs the formation of normal and valuable human relationships. Disfigurement is, intuitively, a core case of harm, but not an easy case to explain. The role of normal human appearance in social relations probably explains the importance of disfigurement as a harm. Erving Goffman, Stigma 41–104 (London: Penguin, 1963).

[44] In *Davis v. Consolidated Rail Corp.*, 788 F.2d 1260 (7th Cir. 1986), Judge Posner remarks that "the loss of a leg is a terrible disfigurement, especially for a young man" even if the victim "is able to walk with the aid of prosthetic devices, to drive, to work, and in short to lead almost a normal life."

then, the gravity of harm is usually a function of the importance to the victim's life of the capacity that the harm impairs and the severity and duration of the impairment.

When harm is conceived of as an impaired condition—and physical impairment is considered the core case—harm delineates a domain of special concern that is much narrower than the domain of cost. Cost is any value given up to obtain some good. It encompasses any disadvantage, anything which diminishes well-being. Ordinary losses—athletic, financial, and romantic—are costs, but not harms.[45] Ordinary losses make their victims worse off than they would otherwise be, but they do not leave their victims physically damaged. The prospect of loss to others does not usually give rise to strong reasons to avoid its infliction. The prospect of harm does give rise to such reasons. It is presumptively wrong to do harm, whereas it is not presumptively wrong to inflict loss. It is not presumptively wrong for one businessman to drive another out of business, fair and square, but it is presumptively wrong for one businessman to break another's finger. Absent some further condition—such as a right to, or a legitimate expectation of, some benefit—losses are not harms.[46]

From an economic perspective, these differences in the treatments of harms, losses, and benefits appear irrational. Harms and losses are both costs, and costs are minuses on a scale on which benefits are pluses. Costs and benefits are symmetrical. These asymmetries make moral sense, however, once we step outside the framework of cost-benefit analysis and adopt a framework that takes our separateness and independence as persons as fundamental and understand ourselves as agents who have a fundamental interest in authoring our own lives. Harm has special significance because harms compromise our powers of agency. Losses do not necessarily do so. Benefits, for their part, enhance our lives only if they are congruent with our commitments. Unsought benefits imposed upon us diminish our autonomy by enlisting us in other people's projects.

Precisely because the idea of harm as impairment is not a part of the economic theory to which Judge Posner subscribes, this appeal to ideas of disability and disfigurement is revealing. *Id.* at 1263.

[45] Influential psychological research by Daniel Kahneman and others has shown that people's ordinary judgments about gains and losses violate the prescriptions of expected utility theory because people treat financial losses and gains differently. See Daniel Kahneman et al., Anomalies: The Endowment Effect, Loss Aversion, and Status Quo Bias, 5 J. Econ. Persp. 193 (1991). There is an obvious resemblance between the asymmetry of harm and benefit in law and morality and the asymmetry of gain and loss in observed human behavior. It is therefore tempting to regard the harm-benefit asymmetry as an instance of a more general psychological aversion to loss. That temptation should be avoided. The two asymmetries are importantly different. Harms generally result in impaired conditions, whereas losses generally do not. Moreover, insofar as the take-home lesson of the psychological research is that people make irrational judgments, that lesson is at odds with the argument developed here. The argument developed here is that people have good reasons—rooted in considerations of autonomy—to treat harms and benefits differently.

[46] See Shiffrin 2012, *supra* note 30, at 372–73, 385–86.

Harm's special, negative significance plays a pervasive role in explaining and justifying tort law as it is. First, it helps to illuminate why it is that tort law—which addresses harms imposed by others—is robust, whereas the law of restitution—which addresses unsought benefits conferred by others—is anemic. Second, harm's special negative significance helps to illuminate why it is that negligence law recognizes a general duty to exercise reasonable care to avoid inflicting physical harm on other people, but only exceptional duties to avoid inflicting economic loss and emotional distress. Third, it helps to explain why it is that harm whose infliction should not have been avoided still has moral significance—thereby helping to explain and justify instances of strict liability. Fourth, the asymmetry of harm and benefit plays an important role in making sense of, and justifying, the stringent standards of "safe" and "feasible" precaution discussed in Chapter Five. These standards normally require actors to take more than cost-justified precaution. From an orthodox economic perspective, they are irrational exercises in making ourselves worse off. From a deontological perspective, they are defensible attempts to respond to the special negative moral significance of harm.

IV. Judgments of Value

One last, pervasive piece of theoretical architecture warrants mention, because it underpins many of the arguments of the book. Value judgments of a particular sort are fundamental to the deontological analysis of risk but frowned upon in economic analysis.

The economic analysis of tort attempts not only to replace the morally freighted idea of reasonableness with a prudential idea of rationality. It also attempts to run judgments of value out of the analysis entirely—except insofar as welfare and efficiency are values—and to convert disagreements over values into disputes about facts. The facts that matter are the prices people would be prepared to pay to effect their preferences.[47] When it comes to risk and precaution, the preferences that matter to rigorous economic analysis are the preferences of the affected parties for imposing and avoiding risks. The proper touchstone in economic analysis, though, is not the preferences that the parties to some risk imposition do have, but the preferences that they would have if they were fully rational and perfectly informed. In cost-benefit analysis, when we ask whether or not some risk-reducing precaution should be taken, we want to know the dollar

---

[47] This is a standing ambition of cost-benefit analysis, conventionally conceived. The blurb for Cass Sunstein's *The Cost-Benefit Revolution* on the MIT Press website explains that "[i]n *The Cost-Benefit Revolution*, Cass Sunstein argues our major disagreements really involve facts, not values." *The Cost-Benefit Revolution*, MIT Press, https://mitpress.mit.edu/books/cost-benefit-revolution.

sum that those exposed to the risk would place on avoiding its imposition if they were fully informed and rational, and we want to compare that dollar sum with the dollar sum that those who wish to impose the risk would place on being able to do so, were they fully informed and rational. As it happens, those facts are exceedingly difficult to ascertain.[48]

A deontological perspective, however, assumes that those who impose and are exposed to risks of harm have diverse preferences and interests and that we must make value judgments of a particular kind to determine whether various risks may be imposed or not. What we owe to other people depends on how urgent the interests at stake are, not on how intensely the parties happen to prefer their own interests. A deontological approach, therefore, adopts objective criteria of urgency, not subjective criteria of preference, as the proper coin of interpersonal comparison.[49] When we consider, say, the standard of care that should be applied to a twelve-year-old piloting a speedboat, the right question to ask is not how intense their preference for joyriding in speedboats is, but how important it is that children of that age be allowed to engage in such a dangerous adult activity. Children have an urgent interest in participating in age-appropriate activities. Doing so is essential to their growth and development. They have no such urgent interest in prematurely participating in adult activities. There is, therefore, a strong case to be made for holding children engaged in age-appropriate activities to a lesser standard of care, and a weak case for holding children engaged in adult activities to a lesser standard of care.[50]

When we think of risk and precaution through a deontological lens, then, we must ask how urgent the ends served by the imposition of the relevant risk are, and how urgent the interests that might be impaired by those risks are. Ordinary ends justify ordinary risks. The interest in getting to the beach early on a hot summer's day, for instance, is an ordinary one, and it justifies imposing only the ordinary risks of careful driving. By contrast, the interest in getting someone who has just suffered a heart attack to the emergency room is an urgent one, and it justifies imposing unusually large risks on others. These judgments of urgency do not track the preferences that matter to cost-benefit analysis. The fact that some people might pay handsomely for the right to speed to get to the beach as fast as possible on a fine summer day does not determine the strength of their claim to do so.

When we take up tort law's treatment of negligence in Chapter Four, we will see that its criteria of interpersonal comparison are objective, and urgency-based.

[48] These matters are discussed in more detail in Chapter Four.
[49] See generally T.M. Scanlon, Preference and Urgency, 72 J. Phil. 655, 668 (1975); Thomas M. Scanlon, The Moral Basis of Interpersonal Comparisons, in Interpersonal Comparisons of Well-Being (Jon Elster & John E. Roemer eds., Cambridge, 1993).
[50] See Chapter Four.

This poses a problem for economic analysis, which regards subjective criteria of interpersonal comparison as the first-best alternative. But it coheres well with a conception of the law of torts as a law concerned with what it is that we owe to each other. When we discuss the competing standards of "safe," "feasible," and "cost-justified" precaution in Chapter Five, we will encounter variations on the same phenomenon. Both the delineation of the proper domains of these competing standards and the applications of the standards to cases require us to make judgments of urgency. Before we turn to these topics, however, we must first dig deeper into influential contemporary theories of tort, to learn the lessons that they teach and the limitations to which they are subject.

2
The Priority of Responsibility over Repair

Throughout the twentieth century, the law of torts was the most dynamic of common-law subjects. Early in the century tort displaced contract as the body of law governing the risks of physical harm created by the sale and use of products. Later in the century that conquest gave birth to modern product liability law, an important legal field in its own right. Less decisively, tort pushed property aside as the body of law governing the obligations of owners and occupiers of real property to entrants onto their premises. New causes of action for invasion of privacy and infliction of emotional distress blossomed, and liability for pure emotional injury and pure economic loss expanded more generally.[1] For most of the twentieth century, as tort took over terrain once held by contract and property, its own criteria for imposing liability grew steadily stricter.[2] And then the march of history reversed. Since the mid-1980s, tort law has been the site of backlash and backtracking. Strict liability has retreated, and negligence has resurged. Tort has stalled, and contract has revived.[3]

This turbulent history was fundamentally a history of shifts in the authority and content of primary responsibilities—shifts in what people owe to one another in the way of obligations not to interfere with or impair each other's persons, property, and projects. When product accidents were taken away from contract and taken over by tort, for example, sellers of products became subject to non-disclaimable—and sometimes strict—obligations running to persons with whom they did not have contractual relations. Prior to that shift, the general rule was that product sellers owed obligations only to those with whom they had contractual relations. That rule left sellers free to disregard entirely the risk of physical harm their products posed to anyone and everyone who was not a customer. Similarly, when the obligations owed to entrants onto land were severed from property law's status categories (invitee, licensee, and trespasser) and reconstructed around the tort idea of reasonable care, landowners found

---

[1] G. Edward White, Tort Law in America: An Intellectual History, Chapter Four 114 (Oxford, 1985, expanded ed. 2003). For a rhetorically brilliant, if not wholly reliable, indictment of tort as the scene of revolutionary developments, see George L. Priest, The Invention of Enterprise Liability: A Critical History of the Intellectual Foundations of Modern Tort Law, 14 J. Legal Stud. 461 (1985).

[2] See Gregory C. Keating, The Theory of Enterprise Liability and Common Law Strict Liability, 54 Vand. L. Rev. 1285 (2001); Priest 1985, *supra* note 1.

[3] White 2003, *supra* note 1, at Chs. 8, 9, pp. 244–338; Ryan Martins, Shannon Price, & John Witt, Contract's Revenge: The Waiver Society and the Death of Tort, Cardozo L. Rev. (forthcoming).

themselves subject to more extensive and less readily disclaimed responsibilities to protect entrants onto their land from physical harm. Under the traditional property regime of status categories, landowners owed obligations of reasonable care only to those whom they invited onto their property in pursuit of economic gain. Under modern tort law's single standard, the trend is for landowners to owe an obligation of reasonable care to everyone except for felony trespassers.[4]

These reworkings of the division of the labor of civil obligation among contract, tort, and property were tectonic shifts in the law's architecture. Relocating a domain of civil obligation from contract or property to tort alters the authority and character of the relevant obligation as well as its content. Obligations rooted in tort attach simply on the basis of personhood and are fixed by the law itself. Obligations based in contract arise through mutual agreement and are generally subject to specification by the contracting parties. Obligations rooted in property arise from and are mediated by the ownership and use of external objects. What one possesses or owns shapes one's rights and duties under property law. The twentieth-century migration of many civil obligations out of contract and property and into tort thus grounded more of civil obligation in equal personhood and less of it in mutual agreement and differential ownership of real property. Concomitantly, that shift rooted more of civil obligation in the law itself and less of it in the wills of the parties.

I. The Academic Turn in Tort Theory

For the most part, these transformations in the landscape of civil liability were the work of great judges reworking the fabric of the common law. Tellingly, Professor White titles one of the four chapters that he devotes to twentieth-century American tort law, "The Twentieth Century Judge as Torts Theorist: Cardozo." He titles another, "The Twentieth Century Judge as Torts Theorist: Traynor." Tort theory was the province of those who made tort law. *Was.* White's last chapter is entitled, "The 1970s: Neoconceptualism and the Future of Tort." In the 1960s, tort law drew the attention of the nascent law and economics movement.[5] The economic understanding of tort was drawn from another academic discipline,

---

[4] See, *e.g.*, Restatement (Third) of Torts: Liability for Physical and Emotional Harm § 4 (2010). §§ 51 & 52. Section 51 "rejects the status-based duty rules and adopts a unitary duty of reasonable care to entrants on the land. At the same time, § 52 reflects a policy-based modification of the duty of land possessors to those on the land whose presence is antithetical to the rights of the land possessor or owner."

[5] See, *e.g.*, Guido Calabresi, Some Thoughts on Risk Distribution and the Law of Torts, 70 Yale L.J. 499 (1961); Guido Calabresi, The Costs of Accidents (Yale, 1970); Richard Posner, A Theory of Negligence, 1 J. Legal Stud. 29 (1972). Ronald Coase, The Problem of Social Cost, 3 J.L. & Econ. 1 (1960), uses tort, nuisance, and accident cases as its primary examples.

and its rise resettled tort theory firmly within the larger Academy. This migration of tort theory from the Halls of Justice to the Halls of The Academy transformed the debates that dominate the field, turning them away from the topic of tort law's primary obligations. In classic dialectical fashion, law and economics gave rise to its own antithesis— corrective justice theory. For more than a generation now, the debate between these two views has preoccupied tort theory.

Law and economics is intensely interested in tort law's liability rules, but it erases obligation from the conversation. Orthodox economic analysis conceives of tort law's liability rules as a market in disguise. The role of tort liability is to shape behavior going forward in a way that minimizes the combined costs of accidents and their prevention—so that wealth is maximized, and welfare is indirectly but optimally promoted. On the economic view, there are no obligations. There are only prices. And the point of those prices is to shape behavior so that the only injuries inflicted are those that are cheaper to inflict than to avoid. Corrective justice theory, for its part, responds to the economic conception by insisting that tort adjudication is just what it seems to be, namely, a backward-looking attempt to assign responsibility for redressing harm wrongly done—not a forward-looking exercise in regulation. Tort instantiates a familiar and intuitive principle of responsibility: those who wrongly harm others should repair the harm they do. This reply to the economic understanding of tort law places tort's secondary responsibilities of repair at its center. Those responsibilities of repair show the economic account of ordinary tort adjudication to be implausible at best. By placing remedial responsibilities at its center, though, corrective justice theory also de-emphasizes tort law's primary obligations. They appear on the scene mostly as the norms whose violation brings tort law's governing principle of corrective justice into play. The ensuing debate between the two camps is not a debate over just what the primary norms of tort do and should prescribe, but a clash between forward- and backward-looking conceptions of the field.

On the economic view, tort defendants who are found liable—and the sunk costs for which they are found responsible—are false targets for cheapest cost-avoiders and preventable future losses. Rational actors recognize that the past is beyond their control. They ignore sunk costs and focus on minimizing future costs—expected costs—because these might still be reduced.[6] The only reason to hold people responsible for past harm is to induce people to avoid future harm, insofar as it is worth avoiding. Therefore, the right people to hold responsible

---

[6] "[C]ost to an economist is a forward-looking concept. 'Sunk' (incurred) costs do not affect a rational actor's decisions. . . . Rational people base their decisions on expectations of the future rather than on regrets about the past. They treat bygones as bygones." Richard A. Posner, Economic Analysis of Law 7 (Aspen, 7th ed., 2007). In both its title and its argument, Cathy Sharkey's critique of civil recourse theory instantiates the forward-looking orientation of the economic analysis of torts. See Catherine M. Sharkey, Preventing Harms, Not Recognizing Wrongs, 134 Harv. L. Rev. 1423 (2021). But by harms, Sharkey really means costs.

are not those who have done past harm wrongly but those who are in the best position to avert future harm efficiently. Properly understood, then, tort is not about responsibility for past harm. Tort is about providing the proper incentives to minimize the combined costs of paying for and preventing *future* accidents.[7] In the same vein, the only reason to recognize plaintiffs' claims to redress for past harm wrongly inflicted is to enlist plaintiffs' participation in minimizing the combined costs of harm and its avoidance going forward. Tort plaintiffs should prevail not when they show that defendants are responsible for wrongly harming them but when plaintiffs show that honoring their claims will promote the social interest in minimizing the combined costs of accidents and their prevention going forward. Plaintiffs are thus private attorneys general deputized to promote the efficient minimization of accident costs. They sue to vindicate the general good, not their own rights.

Corrective justice theorists zero in on this account of tort adjudication and argue that it is strained and unconvincing. Tort adjudication, they say, is just what it seems to be, namely, a backward-looking exercise in attributing responsibility for harm wrongly done (or rights wrongly violated). This criticism of economic analysis hits home, but it also breeds a distinctively remedial conception of tort law. One leading corrective justice scholar, for example, asserts that "tort law is best explained by corrective justice" because "at its core tort law seeks to repair wrongful losses."[8] Other tort theorists, marching under the banner of "civil recourse, not corrective justice," argue that the normative essence of tort law lies not in the defendant's duty to repair the plaintiff's loss but in the plaintiff's right to demand redress from the defendant. The state prohibits people from enforcing their own claims and it is thus obligated to provide a civil mode of redress against wrongdoers.[9] On both views, the essence of tort is to be

---

[7] "I take it as axiomatic that the principal function of accident law is to reduce the sum of the costs of accidents and the costs of avoiding accidents." Guido Calabresi, The Costs of Accidents 26 (Yale, 1970). See also Robert D. Cooter & Thomas Ulen, Law and Economics 359 (Pearson, 5th ed., 2007) (refining the criterion to include administrative costs). The contrast between the forward-looking orientation of economic analysis and the backward-looking orientation of corrective justice and civil recourse theory is nicely epitomized by the title of Cathy Sharkey's review of John Goldberg & Ben Zipursky's Recognizing Wrongs.

[8] Jules L. Coleman, The Practice of Principle: In Defence of a Pragmatist Approach to Legal Theory 9, 36 (Oxford, 2001). The first passage continues: "The central concepts of tort law—harm, cause, repair, fault, and the like—hang together in a set of inferential relations that reflect a principle of corrective justice." The principle of corrective justice "states that individuals who are responsible for the wrongful losses of others have a duty to repair th[os]e losses." *Id.* at 15. Ernest Weinrib advances a similarly influential though not identical thesis that also places corrective justice at the center of tort scholarship. See Ernest J. Weinrib, The Idea of Private Law (Oxford, 1995).

[9] See John C.P. Goldberg, The Constitutional Status of Tort Law: Due Process and the Right to a Law for the Redress of Wrongs, 115 Yale L.J. 524, 601–05 (2005); and Benjamin C. Zipursky, Civil Recourse, Not Corrective Justice, 91 Geo. L.J. 695, 754 (2003). One virtue of the civil-recourse view is that it is more sensitive to the diversity of remedies available in tort than corrective-justice theory is. See Zipursky, *supra*, at 710–14. A second virtue is that civil-recourse theory places much more weight on tort law's primary conduct norms. Nonetheless, the view chooses to emphasize "civil recourse"

found in how it responds to completed wrongs. For corrective justice, reparation is the master value; for civil recourse, accountability is. This preoccupation with redress pushes to the side the questions that Cardozo and Traynor took to be the heart of tort law. The questions that preoccupied Cardozo and Traynor had to do with the nature and scope of our responsibilities not to wrong one another in the first instance.

This chapter argues that the corrective justice critique of economic analysis is compelling, but that the alternative account offered by corrective justice theorists puts the cart before the horse. To be sure, reparation does indeed loom large in tort. Rights require remedies, and reparation for harm wrongly done is the most common tort remedy. Moreover, when we stand back and survey the array of institutions that we bring to bear on wrongful injury in general and accidental harm in particular—an array that includes administrative schemes such as workers' compensation and no-fault automobile insurance, direct regulation of risk, reliance on market mechanisms, and social insurance—tort stands out because of the way it links victims and injurers through the requirement that the tortfeasor repair the injury that she has inflicted on the plaintiff. Nonetheless, the claim that remedial responsibilities are the *core* of tort law is mistaken. Calling corrective justice the heart of tort law makes tort an institution whose raison d'être is repair. Yet in tort law itself, remedial responsibilities arise out of failures to discharge antecedent responsibilities not to inflict injury in the first instance. Tort is a law of wrongs, not just a law of redress for wrongs. In the first instance, it enjoins respect for people's rights. Remedial responsibilities in tort are subordinate, not fundamental.

For their part, law and economics scholars are right to attend to tort law's primary liability rules. They go wrong, however, in recasting those rules as prices. Tort law's primary norms articulate obligations. They spell out the responsibilities that people owe not to interfere with and impair one another's urgent interests as they go about their lives in civil society.

---

as the master feature of tort law and pitches its critique of corrective-justice theory on the claim that corrective-justice theory misconceives tort law's remedial structure. If the argument of this chapter—that substantive obligations to avoid inflicting harm have priority over remedial responsibilities to set matters right—is correct, civil-recourse theory itself suffers from a mistake of emphasis. While civil-recourse theory is correct to say that breaches of primary tort obligations empower plaintiffs to seek redress from those who have wronged them, this power is parasitic on the failure to comply with the primary obligation of harm avoidance in the same way that the duty of repair is. In my view, both of these remedial aspects of tort are among the "successive waves of duty" generated by the right to the physical integrity of one's person. That right underlies and justifies tort's primary obligations. Breach of those primary obligations brings those remedial aspects of tort into play. *See infra* note 61, and accompanying text.

II. Moving Forward

The rest of this chapter develops the argument that we ought to place tort law's primary norms at the center of our understanding. Subsection A explicates "corrective justice" theory, as articulated by one of its preeminent proponents, in detail and argues that corrective justice theory persuasively picks apart the logic of the economic analysis of tort. Subsection B argues that corrective justice is not, as its champions claim, the sovereign principle of tort law. Making corrective justice the sovereign principle of tort law turns the relation between right and remedy upside down. Mistakenly assigning priority to remedial norms over primary ones both misconceives the heart of tort law and obscures its relation to the administrative alternatives which sometimes take tort law's place. Subsection C argues that the structure and content of tort law's primary norms do not conform to the corrective justice account. Corrective justice theory seeks to mold tort law's primary norms in the image of its fundamental remedial principle. It maintains that tort law's primary norms must describe bilateral conduct-based wrongs. The primary wrongs of tort law do not all conform to this prescription. Primary tort duties are omnilateral, not bilateral; important strict liabilities in tort are not conduct-based wrongs as corrective justice theorists use that term; and tort adjudication looks forward to the articulation of general norms as well as backward toward the repair of wrongs.

Subsection D argues that we ought to build on corrective justice theory's claim that tort is a law of wrongs and rights but reorient our thinking to assign pride of place to tort law's primary rights and responsibilities. When we do, we see that tort law has both a role and a core. Its role is to protect people from interference and impairment at each other's hands, and its core consists of primary rights that protect essential personal interests in conditions of effective agency. Subsection E sums up.

A. Corrective Justice

Corrective justice is an ancient concept that has spawned a family of distinct modern conceptions. At its most general, corrective justice is defined in contrast to distributive justice. Distributive justice has to do with the justice of holdings—with the distribution of wealth, income, and property, for example. Persons who participate in the same institutions of distributive justice have their claims against one another mediated by those institutions. Claims in distributive justice are not direct claims on other persons. We may have a claim in distributive justice to a certain share of society's wealth and income, but we do not have a claim in distributive justice against another member of civil society that they personally provide us with that share. Corrective justice, by contrast, involves the relationship between the parties to a civil claim. It has to do with claims that one person has against another—claims to repair a loss to the former for which the latter is accountable. "Corrective justice," Ernest Weinrib tells us, "treats the wrong, and transfer of resources that undoes it, as a single nexus of activity and passivity where actor and victim are defined in relation to each other." "Corrective justice joins the parties directly, through the harm that one of them inflicts on the other." It involves "the correlativity of doing and suffering harm."[10] To be sure, this characterization of corrective justice reflects Weinrib's distinctive emphasis on the "unity of doing and suffering"—with the "doing" being the infliction of the suffering by violating the "abstract equality of free purposive beings under the Kantian conception of right."[11] Other theorists advance different conceptions of the wrong that corrective justice repairs.[12]

1. Sovereign and Subordinate Corrective Justice

Conceptions of corrective justice differ along diverse dimensions. For our purposes, however, the most important division among conceptions is the division between those that take corrective justice to be a subordinate aspect of tort law and those that take it to be tort's paramount or sovereign principle. On the subordinate view, corrective justice is an aspect of tort—perhaps even a necessary and defining feature of the institution—but it does not play a fundamental role in explaining or justifying tort law. Instead, the justifications for tort

---

[10] Weinrib 1995, *supra* note 8, at 56, 71, 77, 142, 213.
[11] *Id.*, at 58.
[12] See, *e.g.*, Richard A. Epstein, A Theory of Strict Liability, 2 J. Legal Stud. 151 (1973) (applying the concept to an essentially causal form of liability). Fault is indispensable in Weinrib's account but is dispensed with by Epstein's. George Fletcher, for his part, applies the label "corrective justice" to a theory of liability for nonreciprocal risk imposition; George P. Fletcher, Fairness and Utility in Tort Theory, 85 Harv. L. Rev. 537 (1972). Catharine Wells takes the term to be concerned essentially with the process through which we should and in fact do determine claims of right between persons in civil society. Catharine Pierce Wells, Tort Law as Corrective Justice: A Pragmatic Justification for Jury Adjudication, 88 Mich. L. Rev. 2348 (1990). Jules Coleman takes corrective justice to require "individuals who are responsible for the wrongful losses of others . . . to repair th[os]e losses." Coleman 2001, *supra* note 8, at 15. See also Stephen R. Perry, The Moral Foundations of Tort Law, 77 Iowa L. Rev. 449, 506–07 (1992) (taking the task of corrective justice theory to specify when the law may legitimately shift losses from one citizen to another); Arthur Ripstein, Equality, Responsibility, and the Law (Cambridge, 1998) (taking the principle of corrective justice to specify when the state may justifiably force the transfer of one person's loss to another by means of compensatory payment); Richard W. Wright, Actual Causation vs. Probabilistic Linkage: The Bane of Economic Analysis, 14 J. Legal Stud. 435, 435 (1985) (positing that corrective justice theories "hold that, as a matter of individual justice between the plaintiff and the defendant, the defendant who has caused an injury to the plaintiff in violation of his rights in his person or property must compensate him for such injury, whether or not imposition of liability will further some collective social goal"); Christopher H. Schroeder, Corrective Justice and Liability for Increasing Risks, 37 UCLA L. Rev. 439, 449–50 (1990) (identifying corrective justice theory with three requirements: "action-based responsibility," "just compensation," and "internal financing of compensation"); and Peter Benson, The Basis of Corrective Justice and Its Relation to Distributive Justice, 77 Iowa L. Rev. 515 (1992).

law—inducing optimal accident prevention, say—call for corrective justice as an aspect of tort law. Accounts that treat corrective justice as the sovereign principle of tort—a principle that grounds and explains the law of torts— work the other way around. Rather than being required by other, more basic, justifications for tort, corrective justice justifies tort law as an institution and shapes its design. Theorists such as Coleman and Weinrib take corrective justice to be the sovereign principle of tort law.

For Coleman, corrective justice is the fundamental principle on which tort law rests and corrective justice requires repairing wrongful losses. The precept that wrongful losses should be repaired by those responsible for them is an independent principle of political morality that governs and justifies the law of torts. This corrective justice principle is important as well as independent because it places a significant constraint on the character of tort's primary norms. For tort to be an institution of corrective justice, tort liability must attach to losses generated by wrongful conduct. The primary norms of tort law must identify *conduct-based wrongs* whose commission results in the infliction of loss. Wrongful losses are losses that issue from wrongful conduct.

For the claim that corrective justice is the sovereign principle of tort to be both important and explanatory, it must meet two conditions. First, it must say something significant. Second, it must explain and justify the institution of tort law instead of being a feature of tort law that is itself explained and justified by some deeper principle—economic efficiency, for instance. To meet the first condition, Coleman's concept of "wrongful losses" must do some work and constrain tort's content to a significant extent. It must identify a class of wrongs to which a duty of repair properly attaches, and familiar torts must be members of that class. For Coleman, the class consists of wrongful losses, harms, or rights violations—all of which result from wrongful conduct.[13] Not all wrongful conduct inflicts losses directly on other people. Cheating on your taxes is wrongful conduct, but it does not inflict a loss on a unique victim. Wrongful conduct disrupts the preexisting distribution of entitlements. It violates rights, inflicts injury, or does harm. Mere disruption, though, does not give rise to liability in *corrective justice*. Wrongful conduct grounds a claim of corrective justice because it is *wrongful*, not just because it is disruptive of a preexisting pattern of entitlement. Innocent disruptions—disruptions that are not wrongful—do not give rise to claims of corrective justice. Corrective justice is thus distinguished from distributive justice, and the criteria of wrongfulness that corrective justice places at the center of tort law do the work of determining when liability in tort is justified.

---

[13] See Jules Coleman, The Practice of Corrective Justice, in Philosophical Foundations of Tort Law 53, 56–57 (David G. Owen ed., Oxford, 1995). Wrongdoing understood as wrongful conduct is also essential to Weinrib's theory of corrective justice in tort. See Weinrib 1995, *supra* note 8, at 140–42, 197–98.

The proposition that corrective justice involves both the infliction of harm (or the violation of a right, or the imposition of loss) *and* conduct that is in some way wrongful establishes the independence of corrective justice from distributive justice, but it does not show that corrective justice explains the law of torts. It doesn't address the second condition. Corrective justice might just be a *description* of what tort adjudication does. If so, it is not an explanation of tort law but a pithy encapsulation of just what it is about tort law that *needs to be explained*. Richard Posner drove this point home in an important paper, arguing that "[o]nce the concept of corrective justice is given its correct Aristotelian meaning, it becomes possible to show that it is not only compatible with, but required by, the economic theory of law."[14] Starting from the premise that corrective justice, in its robust sense, requires wrongful conduct, Posner argued both that economics can supply the requisite standard of conduct and that an economic conception of tort *requires* corrective justice:

> [For an economic theory,] law is a means of bringing about an efficient (in the sense of wealth-maximizing) allocation of resources by correcting externalities and other distortions in the market's allocation of resources. The idea of rectification in the Aristotelian sense is implicit in this theory. If A fails to take precautions that would cost less than their expected benefits in accident avoidance, thus causing an accident in which B is injured, and nothing is done to rectify this wrong, the concept of justice as efficiency will be violated. . . . Since A does not bear the cost (or the full cost) of his careless behavior, he will have no incentive to take precautions in the future, and there will be more accidents than is optimal. Since B receives no compensation for his injury, he may be induced to adopt in the future precautions which by hypothesis . . . are more costly than the precautions that A failed to take.[15]

This passage makes two claims, and they are worth distinguishing. The first is implicit: the identification of tort with wrongful conduct is incomplete. Without a criterion of wrongful conduct, the principle of corrective justice is formal and empty. For Posner, the concept of efficient precaution provides the necessary criterion. The second claim is that unless corrective justice is done, tort law will not provide the incentives necessary to induce appropriate precaution. These points mount a powerful challenge to Coleman's claim (and to any claim) that corrective justice is the sovereign principle of tort. When corrective justice is conceived of as compatible with economics in this way, it is neither sovereign nor

---

[14] Richard A. Posner, The Concept of Corrective Justice in Recent Theories of Tort Law, 10 J. Legal Stud. 187, 201 (1981).
[15] *Id.*, at 201.

justificatory. Corrective justice is a feature of tort law—a constitutive element of the legal subject. As such, it is not a justification but an *aspect of the institution which itself requires justification*. For Posner, economics supplies the justification. When tort law is a society's principal mechanism for addressing accidents—and is otherwise efficient[16]—corrective justice is necessary to ensure that the law of torts induces efficient precaution. Corrective justice, in other words, is an instrument of wealth maximization.

Even though it incorporates the idea that corrective justice involves liability for wrongful conduct, Posner's argument makes corrective justice a subordinate principle of tort liability. Tort law exists to induce rational actors to take those accident-reducing precautions (and only those accident-reducing precautions) that are cost justified, and corrective justice serves this end. Losses inflicted by inefficient conduct must be shifted back onto the parties responsible for them, or else neither injurers nor victims will have the proper incentives to minimize the combined costs of accidents and their prevention. Posner's theory pours the substance of efficiency into the form of corrective justice.

2. Regulating the Future and Rectifying the Past

Clearly something has gone wrong. Corrective justice and the economic theory of tort are rival conceptions. Either the corrective justice theorists or Posner must be mistaken. The leading proponents of corrective justice theory in Posner's time—Coleman and Weinrib—reject Posner's conclusion that corrective justice is merely a feature of tort law to be explained, or even a subordinate principle of tort law. For Coleman and Weinrib, corrective justice is tort law's sovereign principle. "Corrective justice," Coleman writes, "expresses the principle that holds together and makes sense of tort law."[17] The principle that wrongful losses should be repaired is a *morally* authoritative norm. It is sovereign, not subordinate. Tort is a body of law grounded on the principle that wrongful losses should be repaired by those responsible for their infliction.

Posner, Coleman and Weinrib argue, cannot deliver on his claim that doing corrective justice can be reconciled with his economic justification for imposing tort liability. The account of tort adjudication offered by the economic theory of tort cannot, in fact, be squared with doing corrective justice.[18] The economic

---

[16] Without the assumption that tort law is otherwise efficient, this argument does not go through. See John Gardner, Backward and Forward with Tort Law, in Law and Social Justice 255, 269–70 (Joseph Keim Campbell ed., Bradford, 2005).

[17] Coleman 1995, *supra* note 13, at 62.

[18] Weinrib and Coleman converge on tort adjudication as counterevidence to the economic theory of tort, but they interpret that practice differently. For Weinrib, tort adjudication is an autonomous institution whose principles are given by the *form* of tort law, especially the form of tort adjudication; they neither need nor have any further justification. Weinrib 1995, *supra* note 8, at 6, 22–24, 206–08. The next chapter addresses private law formalism.

theory of tort does and must look forward to the reduction of future accident costs. It is, after all, irrational to cry over spilled milk. Tort adjudication, however, looks backward. Consequently, economic instrumentalism cannot adequately explain and justify the law of torts. Abstractly, this counterclaim asserts that the principle of corrective justice and the practice it sustains *can* be explained and justified by reference to more fundamental principles—such as the principle that the costs of malfeasance should be borne by malefactors. Corrective justice must be understood to enforce claims that persons have the standing to assert against one another in their own names, not, say, on behalf of the general good. And it must be understood to look backward because it grounds responsibility for repairing loss on the wrongful infliction of that loss.

Coleman's particular development of this general position asserts that because corrective justice rests on the genuine moral principle that wrongful losses should be repaired, corrective justice is not the goal of tort law.[19] It is instead a justification for holding someone accountable for harm wrongly done. The reason we hold defendants liable in tort is that people who have inflicted wrongful losses on others should make good the losses they have inflicted. The reason is not that holding people who have wronged others liable to those others for the wrongfully inflicted losses will induce cheapest cost-avoiders to minimize future wrongful losses. You are no more justified in recovering from someone in a tort lawsuit by showing only that they are the cheapest cost-avoider with respect to some class of future losses than you are justified in convicting someone of a crime by showing only that their conviction and punishment will deter future crime. Just as putative criminals are punishable only when and because they have committed crimes, putative tortfeasors are liable only when and *because* they have committed tortious wrongs. We are neither justified in hanging the innocent to deter future crimes nor engaging in the practice of criminal punishment if we do so.[20] So, too, we are neither justified in imposing liability merely to deter cheapest cost-avoiders from inflicting future harm, nor engaging in the practice of imposing liability in tort. We are justified in punishing when and because the candidate for punishment committed the kind of serious wrong that warrants criminalization and punishment (and the wrong was, in fact, criminalized). We are justified in demanding corrective justice when we have been

---

[19] To get a well-defined conception on the table, I am therefore taking Coleman's writings as my principal example of a theory of tort that holds that corrective justice is the sovereign principle of the practice. This choice means that not everything I say applies to Weinrib's view, or to other corrective justice accounts.

[20] When John Rawls describes such a forward-looking practice, he calls it "telishment" to underscore that it is not punishment and looks forward to the deterrence of crime, not backward to the righting of a past wrong. John Rawls, Two Concepts of Rules, in Collected Papers 20, 27 (S. Freeman ed., Harvard, 1999).

harmed by the wrongful conduct of the person against whom we are claiming, and when that wrong is serious enough to count as tortious.

In short, the argument is this. First, economic instrumentalism implies a "false-target" view of tort defendants—a view that we hold those who commit tortious wrongs liable because they are surrogates for those who are in the best position to prevent future losses of a similar kind from happening. Second, the false-target view cannot do justice to the fact that the *reason* we hold a defendant liable to a plaintiff in tort is that the defendant has wronged the plaintiff and must therefore repair the harm she has wrongly done. Corrective justice is thus *not* an instrument for the realization of a valuable social objective but the instantiation of a morally authoritative principle of responsibility. It is fair to hold people responsible for repairing the wrongful losses they inflict on others. On the one hand, the practice of holding people responsible for the wrongful losses that they have inflicted on others through their tortious conduct is not an oddly indirect way of inducing other people to behave appropriately in the future. On the other hand, the practice is not simply the fetishistic following of ancient rules. Instead, the principle that people should repair the wrongful losses that they have inflicted on others justifies the practice of tort law, and the practice puts flesh on the bare bones of the principle.

a. *Putting Flesh on the Principle*

Pointing out that, and why, a thoroughly instrumentalist account of tort cannot explain tort law's backward-looking adjudicative practice is a critical exercise, not a constructive one. At most, it prefigures the articulation of an alternative conception. Coleman begins the construction of his alternative corrective justice conception by arguing that *wrongful human agency*, *correlativity*, and *repair* lie at the core of both tort law and corrective justice. That tort law is about *agency* is evident enough to the pre-theoretic eye, but obscured by the theoretical apparatus of economics, with its emphasis on achieving states of the world where value is maximized. The thesis that losses are more easily borne when they are widely dispersed, for example, gives us as much reason to be as concerned with concentrated losses caused by natural disasters as with concentrated losses caused by human malfeasance. Yet tort law denies this equivalence: it is about malfeasance, not misfortune.[21] In this respect, the law of tort taps into deep moral sentiments—sentiments constitutive of the sense of justice itself. We have reason to resent mistreatment by

---

[21] "There is a basic pre-theoretic distinction between misfortunes owing to human agency and those that are attributable to no one's agency. The traditional philosophical distinction between corrective and distributive justice reflects, among other things, this pre-theoretical distinction among kinds of misfortune." Coleman 2001, *supra* note 8, at 44 (footnote omitted).

others, but it is anthropomorphic nonsense to complain of mistreatment by Mother Nature.[22]

That the pertinent agency must be *wrongful* is a proposition that looks to be at once self-evident and overdetermined. Wrongfulness explains why the distinction between malfeasance and misfortune is intuitively basic. By themselves, harmful natural forces—diseases, earthquakes, fires, floods, and the like—are just facts. We might respond well or badly to a disease, generously or selfishly to an earthquake. Diseases and earthquakes themselves, however, are neither wrong nor right, generous nor selfish, fair nor unfair. Moral appraisal applies only to the way in which we act in response to natural misfortune. Human agency, by contrast, is immediately and directly subject to moral appraisal, and to negative moral appraisal when the agency involves the doing of wrong. Wrongfulness gives us a reason to hold people responsible for the losses they inflict on others. Last, but surely not least, wrongful conduct figures very prominently in the law of torts itself. Both intentional and negligent torts involve wrongful conduct. Coleman ties all of this together by concluding that wrongfulness plus agency sums up to a requirement of wrongful conduct. Wrongful conduct, for its part, is wrongful failure to conform one's behavior to a norm of justified behavior. People who fail to conform their conduct to standards required by the rights and interests of others are proper targets of corrective justice when they harm those others or violate their rights.

Correlativity is central to tort, Coleman says, because: "[t]he claims of corrective justice are limited ... to parties who bear some normatively important relationship to one another. A person does not ... have a claim in corrective justice to repair in the air, against no one in particular. It is a claim against someone in particular."[23] Correlativity thus refers to the bilateral (or bipolar) structure of tort adjudication, which itself mirrors the underlying interaction of a tortious wrong. Weinrib explains that "[c]orrective justice joins the parties directly, through the harm that one of them inflicts on the other." It involves "the correlativity of doing and suffering harm."[24] "[T]he direct connection between the particular plaintiff and the particular defendant" is "the master feature characterizing private law."[25] Coleman concurs, calling the bilateral relationship of plaintiff and

---

[22] Isaiah Berlin quotes Jean-Jacques Rousseau's famous remark, "[t]he nature of things does not madden us, only ill-will does." Isaiah Berlin, Two Concepts of Liberty 2 (Oxford, 1958). This appears to be Berlin's own translation of a passage in Rousseau's Emile. See Jean-Jacques Rousseau, Emile, in Oeuvres Complètes 320 (B. Gagnebin & M. Raymond eds., Gallimarde, 1959). Rawls follows Rousseau's lead here in explicating what he calls "the sense of justice." See Rawls 1999, *supra* note 20, at 96–116. See also P.F. Strawson, Freedom and Resentment, in Studies in the Philosophy of Thought and Action 71 (Oxford, 1968) (showing that "reactive attitudes" such as resentment are fundamental to our sensibilities and cannot be accounted for by instrumentalism).
[23] Coleman 2001, *supra* note 8, at 66–67.
[24] See Weinrib 1995, *supra* note 8, at 213.
[25] *Id.* at 10.

defendant, injurer and victim, "the most basic relationship in torts."[26] "Tort law's core is represented by case-by-case adjudication in which particular victims seek redress for certain losses from those whom they claim are responsible."[27]

3. Adjudicative Practice

Because it is only contingently the case that the particular injurers responsible for particular injuries are the cheapest cost-avoiders with respect to the general classes into which those injuries fall, economic theory is hard-pressed to explain why plaintiffs always have rights only against those who have wronged them.[28] To induce efficient precaution going forward, we ought to pin liability on cheapest cost-avoiders. The economic theory of tort can explain tort law's backward-looking focus on past wrongdoers only by saying that we have good reason to think that past wrongdoers are probably the cheapest cost-avoiders going forward. This argument fits tort practice poorly and justifies it only weakly. Tort law's penchant for holding wrongdoers responsible for the wrongs that they commit is deep-seated. There's nothing in the practice itself that suggests that wrongdoers are proxies for some other kind of party. The economic account of adjudication makes tort's practice of holding wrongdoers accountable to their victims for harm wrongly done a mere rule of thumb whose rationale is epistemic. The proposition that society would be better off in the future if some party were held accountable for the costs of accidents they are in the best position to minimize going forward may (or may not) be *a* reason for holding that party liable for harm done in the past, but it is not *the* reason that makes the best sense of tort adjudication. Corrective justice is intrinsically justified. Tortfeasors are responsible for repairing the harm that they have wrongly inflicted on their victims because people who are responsible for wrongly injuring others ought to repair the harm they have wrongly done.[29] The economic analysis of tort cannot acknowledge that simple principle of responsibility.

---

[26] Jules Coleman, Stanford Encyclopedia of Philosophy, Theories of Tort Law § 4 (2003) ("From the normative point of view, the most basic relationship in torts is that between the injurer and the victim whom he has wronged.").

[27] Coleman 2001, *supra* note 8, at 16. *Cf.* Coleman 2003, at § 3 (giving "[t]he bilateral structure of a tort suit—the fact that victims sue those they identify as their injurers and do not instead seek repair from a common pool of resources (as is the case in New Zealand)" as an example of a structural feature of tort law).

[28] Hard-pressed, but not without resources. It may be, as Coleman recognizes, that administrative costs (e.g., search costs) make tort litigation as it now exists a far more competitive institutional mechanism for inducing optimal accident precaution than it appears to be at first glance. See Coleman 2001, *supra* note 8, at 18–20.

[29] Coleman 2001, *supra* note 8, at 14–21, especially at 21. Weinrib likewise argues that extrinsic goals cannot make sense of the bipolar relationship between plaintiff and defendant and that the relationship must be understood in terms of an immanent juridical relationship. See Ernest J. Weinrib, Understanding Tort Law, 23 Val. U.L. Rev. 485 (1989); Weinrib 1995, *supra* note 8, at 37–38, 142, 212–13.

The implausibility of the economic account of tort adjudication is compounded by the weakness of its explanations of the central substantive concepts of tort law—concepts such as duty, "harm, cause, repair, fault and the like."[30] For the law of negligence, breach of duty is a justification for the imposition of liability. Duty specifies an obligatory standard of conduct. In conjunction with the other elements of a negligence claim, failure to conform to that standard is a reason to hold a defendant responsible for harm done to a victim by the breach of that duty. Negligence adjudication looks backward to the past interactions of the parties in order to determine whether the defendant failed to conform their conduct to the standard of care prescribed by the doctrines of duty and breach and should therefore be held responsible for repairing the plaintiff's injury. In this way, the basic concepts of negligence law articulate the *grounds* of liability. For the economic analysis of negligence, however, breach of duty is not a premise but a conclusion. "[S]tandard economic account[s]," Coleman explains, "do not use efficiency to discover an independent class of duties that are analytically prior to our liability practices.... What counts as a 'duty' or a 'wrong' in a standard economic account depends on an assessment of what the consequences are of imposing liability in a given case."[31] Economic analysis fails to do justice to the fact that concepts such as duty and breach are *reasons* for the imposition of liability in tort.

Economic analysis looks forward to the reduction of future accident costs. Legal decisions must, therefore, be justified by good future consequences. They cannot be justified on the ground that they correct past wrongs. Past accident costs are sunk; rationality requires that we disregard them and assign liability to whoever is in the best position to prevent future accidents at the lowest cost. For orthodox economic analysis, liability does not follow from breach of duty when and *because* breach of duty is the actual and proximate cause of harm done. Liability follows from—and because of—a conclusion that the imposition of liability for past harm will induce optimal prevention of accidental harm going forward. The central concepts of tort law—duty, breach, actual and proximate cause, and harm—do no real work.[32] The economic theory of tort does not take an internal point of view on the law of torts; it does not take tort law's principles, concepts, and doctrines seriously as authoritative reasons justifying the

---

[30] Weinrib 1995, *supra* note 8, at 9–10. See also Jules Coleman, The Economic Structure of Tort Law, 97 Yale L.J. 1233 (1988). In conjunction with the basic structural features of tort adjudication, these concepts form what Coleman calls the pre-theoretic core of tort law. Coleman 2001, *supra* note 8, at 15 n.2.

[31] Coleman 2001, *supra* note 8, at 35.

[32] *Id.*, at 34–36. The economic analysis of tort ignores the fundamental insight of H.L.A. Hart, The Concept of Law (Oxford, 1961), namely, that legal rules have an internal aspect insofar as they provide those who accept them with authoritative reasons for action. For law and economics, legal rules are just summaries of independent considerations: they have no authority of their own. "Rule of thumb" or "summary" conceptions of rules are not normative. See generally Rawls 1999, *supra* note 20.

imposition of liability. The economic theory of tort treats the language of the law of torts as a cryptogram. Tort speaks the language of rights, wrongs, and responsibilities, but it embodies a commitment to costs, benefits, and efficient allocation of scarce resources.

For economic analysis, then, the practice of tort adjudication is an exercise in confusion at best, and an instrument of deception at worst. Judges say that they are imposing liability in negligence because duty, breach, actual and proximate cause, and harm, are present, but standard economic analysis takes them to be justified in what they are doing only if they are engaged in a transaction-cost-minimizing search for cheapest cost-avoiders. Duty, breach, actual and proximate cause, and harm are merely evidentiary markers that do a respectable job of identifying cheapest cost-avoiders going forward. Thus, economic analysis cannot take either the adjudicative form of tort adjudication or the substance of tort law at face value. "The relations among the central concepts of tort law—wrong, duty, responsibility, and repair—are best understood as expressing the fundamental normative significance of the victim-injurer relationship as it is expressed in the principle of corrective justice."[33] The normative significance of that relationship, however, entirely eludes economic analysis.

The success of corrective justice as a theory of tort is the flip side of the failure of economic analysis. The basic structural features and main concepts of tort law embody the principle of corrective justice. The bilateral form of the lawsuit tracks the substantive responsibility of a wrongdoer for the wrongful losses she has inflicted. The retrospective character of tort adjudication reflects the fact that tort law is corrective—the fact that its sovereign principle requires wrongdoers to *repair* the wrongful losses they have inflicted. Duty and breach articulate criteria of wrongfulness and thereby ensure that the law of tort honors the principle of corrective justice in its robust form. If tort regularly required the repair of losses inflicted by innocent conduct, it could not be said that the law of tort instituted the principle "that individuals who are responsible for the wrongful losses of others have a duty to repair them."[34] Causation connects the wrongdoer to the loss wrongfully suffered by the victim and so plays an essential role in establishing the special responsibility of the wrongdoer for that loss. Corrective justice thus gives each of the elements of a standard tort suit a straightforward, unforced justification. The institutional practice of tort law puts flesh on the bones of the principle that people who wrongfully harm others ought to repair the harm that they have done.

Corrective justice theory's criticisms of the orthodox economic conception of tort and its own constructive conception form a seamless whole. The two faces

---

[33] Coleman 2001, *supra* note 8, at 23.
[34] *Id.* at 15, 36.

of the conception reinforce one another. Upon close inspection, however, the account that corrective justice theory offers us is implausible its own way. It makes too little of tort law's primary, obligation-imposing norms. The main reason why we have the law of torts is not to repair past wrongs. The economic interpretation of tort is right to say that the law of torts as a whole faces forward and tries to shape the future. The main reason why we have the law of torts is to articulate and enforce obligations that we owe to each other not to interfere with or impair each other's urgent interests. It is better for the wrongs that tort law proscribes not to be committed in the first place than it is to repair them after the fact. Reparation is tort law's second-best solution.

B. The Unity of Right and Reparation

In thinking about the law of torts, it is natural to distinguish between primary (or substantive) responsibilities and secondary (or remedial) ones. Primary responsibilities are responsibilities to avoid harming others in various ways, to avoid violating certain rights even when no harm is thereby done, or to repair harm reasonably inflicted.[35] Secondary, remedial responsibilities are responsibilities of repair—triggered by the breach of various primary obligations. When the distinction between these two kinds of responsibilities is marked, it is likewise natural to think that primary responsibilities are, well, primary—that is, antecedent to and more important than secondary ones. The inference may be too quick, however. The logical priority of primary norms may not make them

---

[35] The second clause of this sentence refers to circumstances where tort law protects autonomy rights. Some batteries, trespasses, and conversions are cases in point. The last clause of the sentence describes the general character of strict liability in tort. For the sake of convenience, I refer to primary duties as "duties of harm avoidance," even though duties of harm avoidance are only the most common kind of primary duty in tort. The distinction between primary or substantive legal norms and remedial ones bears on tort in a particular form, but it is a general distinction. See, *e.g.*, Henry M. Hart Jr. & Albert M. Sacks, The Legal Process: Basic Problems in the Making and Application of Law 122 (William N. Eskridge Jr. & Philip P. Frickey eds., Foundation, 1994) (emphases in original). It explains the general distinction in the following way:

> Every general directive arrangement contemplates something which it expects or hopes to happen when the arrangement works successfully. This is the primary purpose of the arrangement, and the provisions which describe what this purpose is are the *primary provisions*.
> Every arrangement, however, must contemplate also the possibility that on occasion its directions will not be complied with ... The provisions of an arrangement which tell what happens in the event of noncompliance or other deviation may be called the *remedial provisions*.

The distinction appears to be especially prominent in tort theory, in part because corrective-justice conceptions invite the objection I am developing here. See, *e.g.*, Hanoch Sheinman, Tort Law and Corrective Justice, 22 Law & Phil. 21, 32–34 (2003). Its importance is also due to the fact that tort has had to fight off skepticism that it is not a freestanding body of law but a remedial appendage to other bodies of law. See Thomas C. Grey, Accidental Torts, 54 Vand. L. Rev. 1225 (2001); Thomas C. Grey, Holmes on Tort (unpublished manuscript) (on file with author).

normatively more important than secondary ones. Many intentional wrongs, for instance, are both crimes and torts. When we juxtapose, say, wrongful death to murder the most salient difference has to do with remedy, not with primary obligation. Reparation is the remedy for wrongful death (as it generally is for tortious wrongs) whereas punishment is the remedy for murder (as it generally is for crimes). Whether or not rights have priority over repair is therefore something that needs to be examined, not assumed.

1. The Priority of Rights over Reparation

Logically speaking, to be sure, remedial responsibilities arise out of the breach of antecedent primary duties. Logical and normative priority, though, are different and there are reasons to think that tort law's remedial responsibilities are normatively more important than its primary ones. Tort and crime impose many of the same primary obligations. When they do, the salient—and perhaps the normatively important—difference is that crime punishes whereas tort repairs. It is, however, dangerous to infer normative importance from contrastive salience. Were we to juxtapose tort with regulation, the first difference to jump out at us would probably be that tort is ex post whereas regulation is ex ante. Perhaps, then, we should put contrasts to the side, and risk the perils of tunnel vision by focusing squarely on tort itself. When we do, what we see is that the priority of tort law's primary responsibilities over its remedial ones is normative as well as logical.[36] Remedial responsibilities are second-best ways of complying with obligations that are best honored by discharging primary responsibilities. We overlook this fact at our peril.

Just how we should understand the relation between primary and remedial norms depends, first, on how we should understand the relation of rights and duties. Tort duties are best understood as grounded in rights—rights to the physical and psychological integrity of one's person, rights not to be defrauded or defamed, rights to privacy and peace of mind, and so on. Legal rights protect interests of persons urgent enough to justify the imposition of duties on others.[37]

---

[36] For observations along these lines, see Neil MacCormick, The Obligation of Reparation, in Legal Right and Social Democracy 212 (Clarendon, 1982); and Joseph Raz, Personal Practical Conflicts, in Practical Conflicts: New Philosophical Essays 172 (Peter Baumann & Monica Betzler eds., Cambridge, 2004). This line of argument is developed by John Gardner and dubbed "the continuity thesis." John Gardner, What Is Tort Law For? Part I: The Place of Corrective Justice, 30 Law & Phil. 1 (2011) (hereinafter Gardner 2011, What Is Tort Law For?). Sandy Steel, Compensation and Continuity, 26 Legal Theory 250 (2020), distinguishes and analyzes right, duty, and reasons variants of the continuity thesis. See also Sandy Steel & Robert Stevens, The Secondary Legal Duty to Pay Damages, 136 L.Q.R. 284 (2020).

[37] Joseph Raz, The Morality of Freedom 166 (Oxford, 1986); T.M. Scanlon, Rights, Goals, and Fairness, in The Difficulty of Tolerance 26 (Cambridge, 2003). I discuss interests and rights at length in as the separate document completing cross-cites says, there is a cross-cite that should cite to Chapter Three *infra*, pp. 83–93. We also speak of "moral rights," or of "human rights." Following H.L.A. Hart, I think the best way to understand this term is as a measuring stick. When we call something a "moral right" or a "natural right," we are asserting that some interest is weighty enough to warrant legal

Our interest in the physical integrity of our persons is a case in point, and an interest that the law of torts protects in diverse ways. Duties, in turn, govern actions—as the duty of due care in tort law governs the actions of those who put others at risk of physical harm. The actions this highly abstract duty may require are open-ended and diverse, and they depend on the factual circumstances at hand.[38] Due care may require that we drive no faster than twenty-five miles an hour when heavy snow is falling but permit us to drive forty-five miles an hour on the very same stretch of road in sunny, mild, clear weather.

When a tortfeasor breaches a primary obligation and injures a victim, they transform their situation in two ways. First, the tortfeasor makes their own first-best compliance with their primary obligation impossible. Someone who negligently breaks someone else's arm, for example, is no longer able to comply with their obligation of reasonable care in a first-best way by avoiding breaking that arm. Second, in breaching their duty of care and harming their victim, the injurer wrongs their victim, thereby bringing responsibility for repairing the harm that they have done upon themselves. Reparation is now the next-best way of respecting the victim's right to the physical integrity of their person, and responsibility for making that reparation lands on the wrongdoer in virtue of their wrongful infliction of the harm that requires repair. The breach of the primary duty brings it to an end but, in conjunction with the wrong, also gives rise to a new, secondary obligation of reparation.[39]

This secondary obligation of reparation is the joint product of the plaintiff's right, the underlying interest, and the defendant's wrong. The primary duty not to commit the wrong in the first place is extinguished because it can no longer be discharged. The *right*, though, doesn't die with the duty. The right continues, with two effects. First, the existence of the right marks the interest that it protects as urgent enough to justify imposing obligations on others. That interest is normally as urgent as it was before it was impaired, and in now in need of repair.[40] The right and the interest that it protects justify the imposition of secondary duties of repair and secondary powers of recourse when breach of the primary

---

recognition and protection. We might say, for example, that we have a natural right to the integrity of our persons. See H.L.A. Hart, Natural Rights: Bentham and John Stuart Mill, in Essays on Bentham 79 (Oxford, 1982). See also John Stuart Mill, Utilitarianism, 52–53 (Hackett, 1979) (1861).

[38] Here, I agree with Steel 2020, *supra* note 36, at 26–63, and disagree with Gardner 2011, *supra* note 36.

[39] See Steel & Stevens 2020, *supra* note 36, esp. at 284–285 (arguing that the commission of the wrong gives rise to a secondary duty to pay, and not just to a legal liability to be ordered to pay damages by a court). The role of the right in constituting the wrong explains why Stephen Smith is mistaken when he says that the continuity thesis embodies a "model in which wrongs qua wrongs have no significance." See Stephen A. Smith, Duties, Liabilities, and Damages, 125 Harv. L. Rev. 1753 (2012).

[40] Special problems arise when injuries are irreparable as with death. For present purposes, we can set this problem aside.

duty violates the right and impairs the interest.[41] The wrongdoing defendant acquires an obligation of reparation and the wrongly injured victim acquires the power "to invoke the judgment of a tribunal . . . and to secure, if the claim proves well-founded an appropriate official remedy."[42] The protection of the interest now requires the recognition of these further duties. Second, the continuing normative force of the right is the reason why the defendant's wrong matters. Rights are constraints on the conduct of others. Their continuing normative pull is the reason why the responsibility for repairing the wrong lands on the tortfeasor. The tortfeasor's responsibility tumbles out of their breach of a primary obligation—out of *their* wrong. Their wrong is the responsible cause of the injury to the plaintiff which now requires repair. The right fixes the responsibility to repair the harm done by its violation on the party responsible for that violation.

Right and reparation thus form a unity. On the one hand, this unity supports the corrective justice argument that the economic analysis of tort fundamentally misconceives tort adjudication. The economic approach holds that tort adjudication looks forward and toward cheapest-cost-avoiders. In fact, tort adjudication looks backward to wrongs, rights, and the interests that rights protect. It does so because reparation vindicates rights; violation of the right is the reason why the defendant has a duty to repair the injury done to the interest that the right protects. On the other hand, the unity of right and remedy undercuts the corrective justice claim that the obligation to repair harm wrongly done is the sovereign principle of tort. Within the unity of right and remedy, right has priority over reparation. Rights govern remedies; they are the starting point from which deliberation about remedies begins. My right to reasonable care, for instance, is best respected when others take care not to injure me and succeed in doing so—not when they conduct themselves carelessly but patch me back up after they have injured me. Given the choice between a law of torts that effects perfect compliance

---

[41] Jeremy Waldron argues that "rights . . . should be thought of, not as correlative to single duties, but as generating a multiplicity of duties" because that multiplicity is necessary to protect the interest marked out as worthy of protection by the right. Jeremy Waldron, Rights in Conflict, in Liberal Rights: Collected Papers 1981–1991, at 203, 212 (Cambridge, 1993). The way in which secondary duties of repair arise out of the breach of primary responsibilities of harm avoidance illustrates Waldron's thesis. Compare Raz:

> Assertions of rights are typically intermediate conclusions in arguments from ultimate values to duties . . . the implication of a right . . . and the duties it grounds, depend on additional premises and these cannot in principle be wholly determined in advance . . . Because of this rights can be ascribed a dynamic character. They are not merely the grounds of existing duties. With changing circumstances they can generate new duties.

Raz 1986, *supra* note 37, at 181, 185–86.

[42] Hart & Sacks 1994, *supra* note 35, at 137. This is Hart and Sacks's description of the general power which arises in victims of civil wrongs. For an argument that, in the law of torts, violations of primary obligation give rise to a right of recourse on the part of the victim and a duty of reparation on the part of the defendant, see John Gardner, Torts and Other Wrongs, 39 Fla. St. U. L. Rev. 43 (2011). Controversially, Gardner argues that reparation is the only remedy that a tort plaintiff may demand as a matter of legal right.

with its secondary obligations of repair and one that effects perfect compliance with primary responsibilities of wrong avoidance, we should not hesitate a moment before choosing perfect compliance with primary responsibilities of wrong avoidance. When the primary norms of the law of torts are perfectly complied with, there is no work left for its remedial norms.[43]

a. Enforcing Rights

In tort law, as elsewhere, remedies exist to enforce rights and, when they are violated, to repair the harm done to the interests that rights protect.[44] Remedies cure imperfections in compliance with antecedent obligations. To be sure, remedial law has its own distinctive concerns and values, and these too shape the contours of the remedies that courts impose. For instance, administrability matters greatly to remedial law, and for reasons that are not primarily grounded in the rights of the parties before the court. Courts also care about the effects of their remedial determinations on society at large. And remedies are sometimes deflected or defeated by competing reasons or values, as happens in the case of judicial and charitable immunities.[45] All of this qualifies—but none of this defeats—the thesis that rights govern remedies. A freestanding law of remedies makes no sense. It would have no object. A properly ordered body of remedial law has at its center the rights it is responsible for repairing and restoring. This normative sovereignty of remedies over rights has concrete consequences for the law of torts. Because remedies are normatively subordinate to rights, the wrongs with which the law of torts is concerned do not give rise *always and only* to claims that wrongful losses be repaired. Repairing the injury done to an interest protected by a right may, for instance, require not reparation but disgorging an unjust enrichment or enjoining a continuing wrong.[46]

The fact that remedies are the servants of rights and the interests they protect is also shown by the fact that the law of torts shares remedial responsibility with other bodies of law. Tort actions, for instance, often enforce property rights (as trespass, conversion, and nuisance do), yet those rights are also enforced by

---

[43] The position in the text omits one important loss: if there were no tortious wrongs, the common law of torts could not develop, because it develops through adjudication. This collateral benefit of tortious wrongs is not, however, a reason that justifies their commission. It is merely a loss caused by their (hypothetical) disappearance.

[44] See, *e.g.*, Hart & Sacks 1994, *supra* note 35, at 137. On remedial law generally, see Stephen A. Smith, Rights, Wrongs, and Injustices: The Structure of Remedial Law (2019).

[45] See Ori J. Herstein, A Legal Right to Do Wrong, 34 Oxford L.J. 21 (2014) (explaining how immunities confer a "right to do wrong").

[46] "Generally, an injunction will lie to restrain repeated trespasses." Planned Parenthood of Mid-Iowa v. Maki, 478 N.W. 2d 637, 639 (Iowa 1991). See generally Dan B. Dobbs, Law of Remedies: Damages, Equity, Restitution, Chapter 5 (West, 1993) (noting, inter alia, that a plaintiff may be entitled to an injunction prohibiting a recurring trespass). [Edwards v. Lee's Adm'r, 96 S.W.2d 1028, 1029 (Ky. 1936) (disgorging wrongful gain as remedy for trespass)].

property doctrines (e.g., actions to quiet title and to evict) and by public-law doctrines (e.g., the takings clause). Tort's own history includes actions with mixed public and private remedies. The action for "amercement" under medieval trespass included penalties payable to the state among its remedies. Even today, restitution is often matched with criminal punishment, and, in the not too distant past, there was a burgeoning debate over whether and when private (and therefore tort-like) causes of action should be implied from regulatory statutes.[47] Tort law's place in this complex fabric shifts over time, and tort's domain is neither coextensive with the scope of the duty to repair a wrongful loss nor cleanly demarcated from other bodies of law by that principle.

In tort law, and private law more generally, remedies stand in two basic relations to rights: they enforce the right and they repair the injury done the interest that the right protects. The prospect of a remedy in the event that a right is violated helps to assure right-holders that they may confidently rely on their rights. Knowing that you can enforce your rights if need be enables you to count on them. The flip side of this coin is that the prospect of a remedy also gives others reason to respect the right and contributes to the provision of assurance. Rights establish people's security with respect to the interests they protect. Security requires more than the empirical regularity of relatively infrequent interference with an interest. It also requires assurance that respect can be commanded if necessary.[48] The *prospect* of a remedy helps to provide that security. The *enforcement* of a remedy when a right has been violated serves to repair the damage done to the underlying interest.

To be sure, the influence between right and remedy runs in both directions. We look to a right and the interest it protects to determine what a remedy should be, and we look to a remedy to determine what a right is and what interest it serves. Even so—even though remedies are partially constitutive of rights—remedies are fundamentally the servants of rights. The parasitic relation here is practical, not purely logical. Logically speaking, the existence of right requires only a correlative duty—not an effective remedy.[49] Practically speaking, though, rights without remedies do not establish the security that they promise. Rights are constraints on the conduct of others;[50] if they are not backed by effective

---

[47] See, *e.g.*, Cass Sunstein & Richard Stewart, Public Programs and Private Rights, 95 Harv. L. Rev. 1193 (1982). On amercement, see Calvin R. Massey, The Excessive Fines Clause and Punitive Damages: Some Lessons from History, 40 Vand. L. Rev. 1233, 1251–52 (1987); Browning-Ferris Indus. of Vermont, Inc. v. Kelco Disposal, Inc., 492 U.S. 257, 286–92 (1989) (O'Connor, J., dissenting). For a brief but acute explanation of the relation of all of this to the emergence of tort, see Thomas C. Grey, Holmes on Torts 18–22 (unpublished manuscript).

[48] Assurance is a part of security as John Stuart Mill conceives it. See Mill 1979, *supra* note 37, at 53. Scanlon follows Mill in emphasizing its importance. T.M. Scanlon, Rights and Interests, in Arguments for a Better World, Essays in Honor of Amartya Sen, Vol. I, at 68, 75 (Kaushik Basu & Ravi Kanbur eds., Oxford, 2009).

[49] Steel 2020, *supra* note 36, at 264.

[50] Scanlon 2003, *supra* note 37; Raz 1986, *supra* note 37, at 166.

remedies, the constraint promised by the right is at best precarious. The right becomes merely a paper right. For the duties that rights impose on others to serve as effective constraints, they must normally be backed by remedies and those remedies must be reasonably effective at repairing the damage done when the right is violated. In the normal case, then, deliberation about what a right requires in the way of enforcement or repair *centers* on what honoring the right or repairing the interest requires.

b. Repairing Injuries

In tort, the remedy fixed upon by corrective justice theorists—the duty to repair a loss—is preeminent because tort is preoccupied with harm in general and physical harm in particular. Harms—broken arms or legs, for example—leave their victims in conditions which require repair. However, when the underlying right is, say, to exclusive control over—or unimpaired use of—real property, the appropriate remedy is different. For all practical purposes,[51] injunctive relief is available as a matter of right in cases of recurring or ongoing trespass, because injunctive relief is necessary to restore the right to control over who or what enters one's real property.[52] Remedying harmless trespasses by requiring merely that the wrongdoer repair the harm that they have done would not vindicate the interest in exclusive control. It would, indeed, enable those whose trespasses inflict no injury to do so as long as they were prepared to pay nominal damages.[53] Although the appropriate remedies differ, in both the trespass case and the wrongful physical injury case, the primary role of the remedy is to repair the injury done to the interest that the right protects, and to restore the interest to an unimpaired condition.

Moreover, reparation and injunction do not exhaust the list of possible remedies, and rightly so. In order to recognize the existence of a right and its wrongful violation, tort law awards nominal damages in the absence of loss. And it sometimes awards punitive damages. It does so for diverse reasons, which look both backward and forward. Punitive damages may be warranted because the defendant's disregard of the plaintiff's rights was egregious, or because mere compensatory damages provide Holmesian "bad men" with insufficient incentive to respect the relevant right.[54] The forward-looking character of this last

---

[51] Gardner argues that the law of torts is importantly demarcated by the fact that reparation is the only remedy that a tort plaintiff may demand as a matter of legal right. This is a difficult thesis to sustain in the United States, especially given the merger of law and equity. Gardner and 2011, *supra* note 36.

[52] See *Planned Parenthood of Mid-Iowa*, 478 N.W.2d; Dobbs 1993, *supra* note 46, at Chapter 5.

[53] The award of punitive damages in Jacque v. Steenberg Homes, Inc., 563 N.W.2d 154 (Wis. 1997), enforces the right to exclusive control by stripping the one-shot, harmless trespass in that case of the economic advantage that made its commission by the defendant rational. Because its trespass did no harm, defendant was otherwise liable only for nominal damages.

[54] *Id.*; Benjamin C. Zipursky, A Theory of Punitive Damages, 84 Tex. L. Rev. 105 (2005).

reason should not trouble us once we recall that tort remedies exist to enforce rights as well as to repair harm done to the interests they protect. Because remedies are the servants of rights—and because it is better for a right not to be violated in the first place—remedies that deter rights-violations have a place among the panoply of possible remedies.

On the one hand, tortious wrongs give rise to diverse remedies. They do so because the primary rights that tort law protects are not all rights against the infliction of harm and loss. On the other hand, remedies are prominent in tort—as both corrective justice theorists and law and economics scholars think.[55] But their prominence is not the consequence of tort law's adherence to a freestanding principle of corrective justice. Remedies are prominent in tort because rights are fundamental to tort, and right and remedy form a unity. You do not have a practically effective legal right unless you have some remedy for its violation. If I punch you in the nose, I violate your right to the physical integrity of your person. If you have no legal remedy for that violation of your right, your right is legally meaningless. Absent some special institutional arrangement, your claim for redress is naturally directed against me. After all, I am the person who has violated your right, and I have thus opened myself up to the responsibility of repairing my wrong and restoring your right. I stand in a special and unique relation of responsibility to you.

c. Relating and Distinguishing Legal Institutions

Assigning priority to tort's remedial dimension over its primary obligations distorts our understanding of the subject in subtle ways as well. Coleman's identification of tort law as, uniquely, the institutional instantiation of duties of repair misconceives tort law's relation to the rest of private law. Correctly, remedial theories recognize that tort law normally enforces and restores rights in a particular way—namely, by enabling the victims of tortious wrongdoing to obtain redress for the wrongs done to them from those who have done them wrong. This, however, is a distinctive feature of private law in general, not a distinctive feature of the law of torts in particular. We lose sight of the fact that private law in general has a distinctive relation to rights when we identify responsibilities of repair, broadly conceived, with tort and tort alone.[56] Contract, property, and restitution also enforce rights by empowering those whose rights have been

---

[55] Guido Calabresi & Douglas Melamed, Property Rules, Liability Rules and Inalienability: One View of the Cathedral, 85 Harv. L. Rev. 1089 (1972) (identifying tort with liability rules illustrates their importance to the economic understanding of tort law).

[56] Rights present different issues in public law contexts. In private law contexts, if a right cannot generally be enforced by a remedy, the rule of law is usually going unrealized. In public law contexts, the requirements of the rule of law may be very different. Government officials generally owe duties to enforce, say, the commands of the Constitution, but these are not normally relational duties owed to individual citizens akin to the relational duties not to wrong one another that dominate tort law. When public officials engage in conduct that would be tortious if it were engaged in by one private person against another, difficult questions arise as to whether, when, and how public law duties do

violated to seek redress from those who have done the violating. If a duty of *repair* is more characteristic of tort than it is of contract or restitution, that may be because primary tort rights differ from primary contract or restitutionary rights, and those differences are reflected in the corresponding remedies. That is, tort is distinguished from other private-law subjects by the character of the *primary* rights and obligations it enforces. Harm and loss are central to tort, whereas disappointed expectations are central to contract. Reparative damages are therefore central to tort, whereas expectation damages are a salient remedy for breach of contract. The remedies characteristic of the fields are sensitive to the differences in their primary obligations, as they should be.

The three major fields of civil obligation also differ in the sources of the law they enforce. In contract, primary rights and obligations arise from the agreement of the parties. In tort, they are imposed by law. In property, primary rights and obligations arise from a mix of agreement and law. The subject of primary obligation in property is the ownership and use of external objects. The subject of tort is what we owe to one another in the way of obligations not to interfere with or impair interests each of us has that are urgent enough to justify the imposition of coercively enforceable obligations. Tort obligations thus have a particular source and a particular domain. Both of these differences should figure more prominently in our understanding of tort law's distinguishing features than its commitment to reparative damages. That difference is, to a large extent, derivative of tort law's primary rights and obligations.

Putting responsibilities of repair at the center of tort law also obscures tort law's relation to administrative alternatives to tort, such as workers' compensation. Workers' compensation displaces the common law of negligence from the domain of workplace injuries. Kindred administrative schemes for nuclear accidents, vaccine-related harms, and health injuries incident to mining coal, among others, displace tort from other domains. In all of these cases, collective responsibility displaces individual responsibility. Deep differences divide the institutions.[57] Individual fault liability dominates the law of torts; strict enterprise liability dominates administrative plans. Administrative plans are not part of the law of torts proper. Even so, it is wrong to assert that the differences are so great that the two regimes have nothing in common. The history of tort law belies that claim. Administrative alternatives to tort law have exerted a powerful influence over tort law proper ever since workers' compensation first appeared on the scene.[58] One example is the fact that conceptions of responsibility cross

and should alter the obligations that would otherwise attach. See Richard H. Fallon, Bidding Farewell to Constitutional Torts, 107 Cal. L. Rev. 933 (2019).

[57] See Chapter Six.
[58] See Jeremiah Smith, Sequel to Workmen's Compensation Acts, 27 Harv. L. Rev. 235, 244–45 (1914) (arguing that the workmen's compensation acts were organized on the principle of strict

the boundaries between the domains—enterprise liability, for instance, crops up in the law of torts as well as in administrative plans.[59]

More importantly, for present purposes, both the private law of torts and administrative alternatives to it are preoccupied with protecting the physical integrity of our persons. That interest is urgent enough to warrant being called a moral right.[60] In our legal system, the private law of torts and administrative alternatives to it are two different legal institutional forms used to protect our interest in the physical integrity of our persons. When we subscribe to a conception of tort law which holds that it is *exhausted* by duties of repair owed to named victims by named wrongdoers, we must regard workers' compensation and similar administrative plans as entirely discontinuous from the law of torts. They abolish private-law duties of repair and private-law mechanisms for the enforcement of rights. The denial of deep connections between the two institutions impoverishes our understanding of both. We miss both the fact that a common conception of responsibility—namely, enterprise liability—travels back and forth between the two domains, and the fact that the institutions share the common mission of safeguarding our moral right to physical integrity.

Our urgent interest in the physical integrity of our persons generates "successive waves of duty," as Jeremy Waldron says.[61] When the primary duty of reasonable care to avoid causing foreseeable physical harm to others is breached, the interest justifies the duty to repair harm negligently inflicted. For the secondary right to reparation to be effective, the state must be under a duty to provide some forum in which rights of repair can be enforced.[62] The duty of a court properly summoned to assist a tortiously wronged victim is a duty generated by the interest. But the interest does more than just generate waves of duty in the context of a single wrong. Our urgent interest in the physical integrity of our persons also generates diverse primary obligations. Within the law of torts proper, the interest in bodily security is "protected against not only intentional invasion but [also] against negligent invasion or invasion by the mischances inseparable from an

---

liability, which could not be reconciled with the fault liability of the common law, and prophesying that the common law of torts would be reconstructed to be more compatible with the normative logic of workers' compensation).

[59] See generally Keating 2001, *supra* note 2. These issues are discussed at more length in Chapters Three and Seven.
[60] H.L.A. Hart, Natural Rights: Bentham and John Stuart Mill, in Essays on Bentham 79 (Oxford, 1982). Hart argues that the concept of a moral right should be thought of as a kind of measuring stick. When we call an interest a moral right, or a natural right, or a human right, we are saying that it is urgent enough to warrant legal protection.
[61] Waldron 1993, *supra* note 41, at 203, 212.
[62] This last point is emphasized by the "civil recourse theory" of John Goldberg and Ben Zipursky. See Goldberg 2005, *supra* note 9; and Zipursky 2003, *supra* note 9. On the view of "civil recourse" presented in the text, it is essentially complementary to—not competitive with—corrective justice. Both involve secondary responsibilities which support the primary duties of tort law.

abnormally dangerous activity."[63] The interest thus generates primary duties of reasonable care in negligence law; primary duties not to assault or batter other people; and primary duties to conduct abnormally dangerous activities only on the condition that one repair the unavoidable harm that one does. It is only a small extension of this point to say—on the straightforward supposition that the administrative scheme does a better job of protecting the interest—that the interest may also justify displacing tort and adopting an administrative alternative. When a common-law remedy is set aside and replaced by an administrative arrangement, the question that courts most commonly ask is whether the administrative scheme provides an adequate alternative remedy. This makes normative sense. Whether workers' compensation (plus safety regulation) or tort law does a better job of protecting workers' urgent interests in physical safety is, presumably, the most important question to ask about the choice between them.

Within civil society, the private law of tort is the *default* legal institution for the enforcement of the right to the physical integrity of one's person. This is due in part to its temporal priority over its competitors. The law of torts has been with us for a long time; administrative alternatives to it are a recent invention. But tort law's position as the default legal institution for the enforcement of the right to the physical integrity of one's person is also due, as corrective justice theorists think, to tort's instantiation of basic and intuitive ideas of responsibility. When one person violates another person's right, responsibility to repair the harm wrongly done naturally falls on the wrongdoer. But this is *only* the natural default. The private law of tort can be justifiably displaced by administrative alternatives on condition that those alternatives are defensible ways of instituting the underlying right to the security of one's person. And once we see that these institutions share the common mission of protecting our urgent interest in the physical integrity of our persons, we have a starting point for thinking about how and when tort is preferable to its administrative alternatives, and vice versa.

2. Wrongful Losses and Primary Rights

The argument that right and reparation form a unity within which right has priority—and that corrective justice theory therefore puts the cart before the horse—draws on what is now called the "continuity thesis." The nerve of that thesis is the claim that "the way things stood, normatively, between the victim and injurer, pre-wrongful-harm, explains the normative position between them post-wrongful-harm in relation to compensation."[64] Sometimes the essential

---

[63] Restatement (Second) of Torts § 1 cmt. d (1965). The right to bodily security thus grounds diverse tort obligations. I am grateful to Mark Geistfeld for calling my attention to this comment.

[64] Steel 2020, *supra* note 36, at 251. Gardner 2011, *supra* note 36, named the "continuity thesis" and developed it into what Steel helpfully calls "reasons-continuity." Earlier statements of the idea include MacCormick 1982, *supra* note 36; Raz 2004, *supra* note 36. Because the commission of a wrong figures in the explanation of secondary obligations in tort, continuity does not explain all of

continuity is said to be "reasons-continuity"; sometimes it is said to be "duty-continuity"; and sometimes it is said to be "rights-continuity."[65] The argument made in the last section could, I think, be expressed in any of these three vocabularies, but it is most perspicuously presented as a form of rights-continuity. People's rights, grounded in their urgent interests, impose obligations on others. The breach of those primary obligations gives rise to secondary duties of repair and secondary powers to summon the assistance of courts. Corrective justice theory emphasizes the first of these; civil recourse theory emphasizes the second.[66] Reasons figure prominently in this process because—when we are considering what new duty a right gives rise to when an existing duty can no longer be complied with—we turn to the interests that the right protects and the reasons that interest now generates. Casting the matter in terms of rights-continuity asserts that interests urgent enough to warrant protection as legal rights ground the duties, and the continuing reasons to which we appeal when we apply and interpret the rights are the reasons that justify the rights. Normally, what the continuing reasons require is that the party who has violated the right and impaired the interest repair the damage that they have done. Without remedies, legal rights are not coercively enforceable constraints on the conduct of others and the protection that they promise is illusory.

a. Wandering the Law Looking for Wrongs to Repair

By itself, the unity of right and remedy is sufficient reason to reject the corrective justice claim that the repair of wrongful losses is the "overarching ambition or purpose" of tort law.[67] It is, however, well worth observing that no matter how hard we try, we cannot pull the law of torts out of the hat of the principle how matters stand. The commission of the wrong is what singles the wrongdoer out as *responsible* for restoring the right.

---

[65] Steel 2020, *supra* note 36, at 250–51.

[66] Civil recourse theorists Goldberg and Zipursky deny the continuity thesis, as does Steven Smith. See Zipursky 2003, *supra* note 9; John C.P. Goldberg & Benjamin C. Zipursky, Tort Law and Responsibility, in Philosophical Foundations of the Law of Torts 17 (John Oberdiek ed., Oxford, 2014); Smith 2012, *supra* note 39, at 1727. See also Ori J. Herstein, How Tort Law Empowers, 65 U. Toronto L.J. 99 (2014) The basic claim is that the commission of a tortious wrong gives rise only to a legal liability to pay—or to be ordered to pay—damages and not to a duty of reparation. This seems mistaken, both normatively and as a matter of positive law. Persuasive considerations support the view that the duty of reparation arises with the commission of the wrong. The liability is to have that duty enforced. See Sandy Steel & Robert Stevens, The Secondary Legal Duty to Pay Damages, 136 L.Q.R. 283 (2020); John Gardner, Damages without Duty, 69 U. Toronto L.J. 412 (2019).

[67] Jules Coleman, Risks and Wrongs 395 (Oxford, rev. ed., 2002). The general idea of torts as wrongs is Blackstonian. Blackstone described acts that deprived people of rights as "wrongs," 3 Blackstone, Commentaries *116 (1766), and explained that the remedial part of the law provides for the redress of wrongs, 1 Blackstone, Commentaries *54 (1766). Whenever the common law recognized a right or prohibited an injury it also gave a remedy, initiated by filing the appropriate writ. 3 Blackstone, Commentaries *123 (1766).

"wrongful losses should be repaired by those responsible for them." That principle is formal: the word "wrongful" is a placeholder awaiting an infusion of content. It latches onto many torts because we have independent reasons for thinking of torts as wrongs, and many tortious wrongs cause losses. We supply the content that the principle requires without remarking to ourselves that the principle is otherwise empty. This is perfectly natural. We already know that tort is a law of wrongs. When we shed that assumption—and consider the principle of corrective justice on its own terms—we recognize that the law of torts is merely one legal domain to which it might attach. Because the principle's logic is formal, it should wander the law looking for wrongful losses to repair. Turned loose to roam, the principle would surely find wrongful losses in many other departments of the law.

The wrongs to which the principle of corrective justice would attach, moreover, would depend greatly on the content that we used to fill in the principle. Corrective justice can be described both broadly and narrowly. When we interpret corrective justice as having to do with the repair of wrongful *loss*, restitution does not do corrective justice because it undoes wrongful *gain*. On a broader interpretation of corrective justice, the undoing of wrongful gain might be as much a matter of corrective justice as the repair of wrongful loss. Undoing wrongful gain is corrective justice when corrective justice is conceived of as a remedy which repairs the breach of a duty correlative to the right the plaintiff is asserting.[68] Furthermore, if we adopt a conception that does not insist on bilaterality, we are likely to find some wrongful losses in various pockets of public law.[69]

Similar issues arise with respect to contract law. If contract is really about reliance—as Lon Fuller thought—then breach of contract results in wrongful loss and contract damages do corrective justice on a narrow interpretation of the principle. If, however, contract is about expectation damages, then contract damages are about being put in the position that one would have occupied had the contract been performed.[70] That would count as corrective justice only if corrective justice is broadly construed as righting wrongs, not repairing wrongful

---

[68] Weinrib takes this broader view of the matter because he thinks of correlativity of right and duty as the essence of corrective justice. Weinrib 1995, *supra* note 8, at 122–26. Restitution does corrective justice even though it involves wrongful gain, not wrongful loss, because it involves breach of duty correlative to plaintiff's right. *Id.*, at 140–41, 197–98. Weinrib's broad conception of corrective justice also encompasses contract damages. *Id.*, 136–40. See also Tony Honoré, The Morality of Tort Law—Questions and Answers, in Responsibility and Fault 67, 73 (Hart, 1999) ("On a wide view, [corrective justice] requires those who have without justification harmed others by their conduct to put the matter right.").

[69] See generally Lionel Smith, Corrective Justice and Public Law (unpublished, on file with the author).

[70] See L.L. Fuller & William R. Perdue Jr., The Reliance Interest in Contract Damages: I, 46 Yale L.J. 52 (1936). *Cf.* Daniel Friedmann, The Performance Interest in Contract Damages, 111 L.Q.R. 628 (1995); Sheinman 2003, *supra* note 35.

losses. When corrective justice is construed that broadly, however, it can no longer be presented as the paramount principle of liability in tort. It is now at least a principle of private law in general, and it may well be a general principle of law, full stop.

b. Irreparable Injuries and Wrongs without Losses

When our eye is drawn to the full range of cases to which the principle of corrective justice might apply if it is allowed to roam across the law looking for wrongs to repair, we are also drawn to recognize that corrective justice applies in a strikingly imperfect way to the physical harms that preoccupy tort law. Corrective justice seeks to repair. It comes as no surprise, therefore, when a court remarks that "[t]he basic rule of tort compensation is that the plaintiff should be put in the position that he would have been in absent the defendant's negligence."[71] When the wrongful infliction of harm is involved, though, an impediment to the application of this "basic rule" arises almost immediately. When a "tort causes bodily harm or emotional distress, the law cannot restore the injured person to his previous position."[72] Paradoxically, the kind of serious impairments of agency that are the central preoccupation of the law of torts are all but constituted by the property of not being completely repairable.

Both because serious physical harm is often only imperfectly repairable, and because some tortious wrongs do not inflict physical harm, tort damages have expressive, performative, and deterrent aspects.[73] Often, their task is not really to repair wrongful loss; it is to set matters right. When harm cannot be fully repaired, putting matters right cannot require doing the impossible and restoring the plaintiff to the position that she would otherwise have occupied. When wrongful death or egregious intentional wrongs are at issue, the expressive and performative aspects of damages may well dominate their reparative role.[74] A further consequence of the irreparability of serious injury is that instead of being coterminous with the principle that wrongful losses should be repaired by those responsible for their infliction, tort law's primary obligations may, in fact, be inadequately enforced by that remedy. Tort has struggled mightily with the problem of wrongful death, for the simple and straightforward reason that no amount of money can repair the harm of death. Reparation as

---

[71] Keel v. Banach, 624 So.2d 1022, 1029 (Ala. 1993).

[72] Restatement (Second) of Torts § 903 cmt. a (1979). This inability is at the center of Chapter Five.

[73] See Margaret Jane Radin, Compensation and Commensurability, 43 Duke L.J. 56 (1993). Scott Hershovitz emphasizes the performative view of tort's remedial operation. Scott Hershovitz, Harry Potter and the Trouble with Tort Theory, 63 Stan. L. Rev. 67, 95–96 (2010). The civil-recourse point that giving the plaintiff "satisfaction" was once taken to be the purpose of tort damages is also relevant in this context. See John C.P. Goldberg, Two Conceptions of Tort Damages: Fair v. Full Compensation, 55 DePaul L. Rev. 435, 440–45 (2006).

[74] See Radin 1993, supra note 73; Scott Hershovitz, Tort as a Substitute for Revenge, in Philosophical Foundations of the Law of Torts 86 (John Oberdiek ed., Oxford, 2014).

a remedy can be completely inadequate to the enforcement and restoration of the primary rights that tort recognizes. When conduct risks irreparable injury, adequately protecting people's rights to the physical integrity of their persons may require turning away from the private law of torts and to the direct regulation of risk.[75] Less drastically, the irreparability of serious injury may justify supra-compensatory damages which help to deter the infliction of such injury. Generous awards for pain and suffering and even punitive damages may have important roles to play.

Next, recall our earlier discussion of trespass. Sometimes the remedy required to set a wrong right is not reparation but injunctive relief. Sometimes money damages are the correct remedy, but they should be measured not by wrongful loss but by wrongful gain. When my subterranean trespass into the cave below your property allows me to turn a profit selling cave tours, my wrongful gain from my unauthorized use of your property is the proper measure of the damages to which you are entitled.[76] The connection between tort and recovery for wrongful loss is thus contingent, not constitutive, and corrective justice conceptions of the subject overstate that contingent connection.

Most torts protect against harm in one of its manifestations—physical harm to one's person or property; emotional distress sufficient to count as psychological harm; harm to reputation; economic harm in special cases where the relevant economic benefit can be insisted on as a matter of right. Reparation is the natural default remedy for these wrongs because their commission leaves their victims in conditions requiring repair. An important minority of intentional torts, however, guard aspects of our "autonomy" or "sovereignty." "Sovereignty-based" torts proscribe various interferences with zones of control or powers of discretion—control, for example, over one's physical person or one's real property.[77] Some unwelcome physical contact is objectionable and tortious because it impairs physical integrity, but other physical contact is tortious and objectionable because it is profoundly offensive. Unwelcome, but "harmless," sexual contact is a case in point. Sovereignty-based torts thus protect important boundaries against unauthorized crossings.

A salient feature of sovereignty-based torts is that they can be committed without doing harm, and even while benefiting their victims. If, for example, I operate on your ear without your permission and succeed in restoring your

---

[75] This topic, too, is taken up in Chapter Five.
[76] Edwards v. Lee's Adm'r, 96 S.W.2d 1028 (Ky. Ct. App. 1936).
[77] I borrow the term "sovereignty-based" from Arthur Ripstein, Beyond the Harm Principle, 34 Phil. & Pub. Aff. 215 (2006). He is not responsible for my usage. The shorthand distinction between "harm-based" and "sovereignty-based" torts is not meant to imply that the former do not involve rights whereas the latter do. The point, rather, is that some tort rights are grounded in harm, whereas others are grounded in autonomy. To put it in a more cumbersome way, we might call these torts "autonomy-rights-based torts" and distinguish them from "harm-rights-based torts."

hearing, I have not harmed you. Your physical condition has been improved, not impaired. Nonetheless, I have violated your rights and committed the tort of battery because I have operated on you without your consent.[78] In the same vein, I may not enter your real property without your permission, even if I thereby improve that property by trimming your trees and ridding them of bagworms.[79] When primary rights do not protect against harms or losses, the first-best remedy for their violation is not repair of wrongful loss. In the case of trespass, the proper remedy is one that restores the power to exclude. When the trespass is continuing, payment of compensatory damages may merely license a continuing wrong. Punitive damages or injunctive relief may be required to vindicate the right.[80]

Taken together, these diverse examples reveal the corrective justice thesis that tort law is about repairing wrongful losses to be overinclusive, underinclusive, and imperfectly fitted to the diverse injuries that tortious conduct can inflict. The principle is overinclusive because some wrongful losses do not result from torts. It is underinclusive because some torts do not result in wrongful losses. It is imperfectly fitted to tort law because tortious conduct often results in injury which cannot be fully repaired—or inflicts injury which requires damages to serve a performative or expressive or punitive function, not a reparative one. Purely financial losses may be fully repaired by money damages, but physical impairments cannot always be completely corrected. Wrongs to status or dignity may require damages which re-establish equality. The upshot of all this is that it is common for tort law to do corrective justice, but not because the law of torts is a kingdom constituted by the sovereign principle that wrongful losses should be repaired. Tort often does corrective justice because corrective justice is often the best that the private law of torts can do to enforce primary rights and repair damage done to the interests that those rights protect.

The corrective justice theory of tort goes wrong in the way that retributivism goes wrong as a theory of criminal law. Just as we do not have the criminal law primarily to punish the wicked, so, too, we do not have the law of torts primarily to repair wrongful losses.[81] The "overarching aim or purpose" of the law of torts is

---

[78] See Mohr v. Williams, 104 N.W. 12 (Minn. 1905); Kennedy v. Parrott, 90 S.E.2d 754 (N.C. 1956). This prohibition against unconsented invasive medical procedures is a different aspect of the tort of battery.

[79] See, *e.g.*, Longenecker v. Zimmerman, 267 P.2d 543, 545 (Kan. 1954).

[80] See *Planned Parenthood of Mid-Iowa*, 478 N.W.2d; *Jacque*, 563 N.W.2d; Dobbs 1993, *supra* note 46, at Chapter 5.

[81] Coleman anticipates this criticism and argues that retributivism is a defensible explanatory and justificatory theory *of punishment*. Coleman 2001, *supra* note 8, at 32–33. He is quite right about this, but the observation is beside the point. Coleman claims not that corrective justice is a defensible theory of *tort remedies*, but that "tort law is best explained by corrective justice" because "at its core tort law seeks to repair wrongful losses." Just as retributivism is only plausible as a theory of criminal *punishment*, so too corrective justice is only plausible as a theory of tort remedies. *Cf.* Sheinman 2003, *supra* note 35, at 46–47.

not to repair harm wrongly done but to articulate and enforce certain obligations to others—obligations that are grounded in the fundamental interests of persons and which are therefore urgent enough to justify recognizing rights and imposing duties on others. Those primary rights and the duties that they ground are the heart and soul of the subject. To understand tort law, tort theory needs to put those primary norms at its center.

C. The Structure of Primary Norms

The wrongs that tort law recognizes spell out an important part of what we owe to each other in the way of coercively enforceable responsibilities, by virtue of essential interests that we have as persons.[82] In their core, those rights and responsibilities have to do with liberty and security, broadly construed. Primary obligations in tort are obligations not to harm other people in various ways, and to respect powers of theirs that confer on them authority over their persons and possessions. The substance of tort's primary norms may be their most important property, but their form and their role are also important. Corrective justice theorists emphasize the bilaterality of remedial relationships in tort and overlook the fact that its primary duties are omnilateral. By viewing tort through the prism of reparation for wrongful loss, corrective justice theorists stress the backward-looking role of tort adjudication, but tort adjudication in fact looks both forward to the articulation of norms and backward to the rectification of wrongs.

1. The Omnilaterality of Primary Obligation

Tort law's primary obligations have a structure different from its remedial norms. Primary obligations in tort are omnilateral, standing, and unconditional. We are all obligated, for example, not to defame or defraud one another. Everyone owes everyone else those obligations, simply by virtue of being subject to tort law's dominion. Rights and duties run from every person in a jurisdiction to every other person.

When obligations are omnilateral, as tort's primary obligations are, an obligation to one person may be affected by obligations to other people. Much of the time the fact that obligations run from everyone to everyone else has no practical significance. People in France, for instance, have rights that prohibit me from killing them, but their rights do not impose any significant constraint on my conduct in California. A significant amount of the time, though, the omnilaterality

---

[82] The exact content of what we owe to each other in the way of tort obligations depends on the jurisdiction in which we find ourselves, but the basis of our varying obligations is the same, namely, our equal personhood.

of primary obligation does shape the contours of concrete duties. California tort law's incorporation of the traffic code rule "speed limit 25 [in the vicinity of primary and secondary schools] when *children* are present" is a case in point.[83] That norm makes the care owed any one child depend in part on whether that child is in the company of other children. An adult, who happened to be on the grounds of a school when it let out for the day, would also be entitled to the protection of the twenty-five-mile-an-hour speed limit triggered by the presence of children. Because they are omnilateral, primary obligations in negligence are often owed to one person because they are owed to others. Remedial responsibilities, by contrast, are more straightforwardly bilateral. They are owed to named plaintiffs by named defendants because of a wrong done to the former by the latter.

The omnilateral form of primary obligations can thus shape their substance. Moreover, because primary obligations of reasonable care are owed to everyone, they may sometimes conflict.[84] *Lucchese v. San Francisco–Sacramento Railroad, Co.*[85] is an old but still vivid illustration. *Lucchese* involved a train that had two types of brakes. Using one set of brakes was safer for the train's passengers but increased the risk of injury to motorists at crossings. The other set of brakes provided better protection for motorists but increased the risk of harm to passengers. Operating the railroad with reasonable care required reconciling the conflicting claims of these two classes of persons. The care that the railroad owed passengers was thus shaped by its obligations to motorists, and vice versa.

Whereas primary responsibilities in negligence are omnilateral and standing, remedial responsibilities are bilateral and conditional. They come into play only when primary responsibilities are not discharged, only when a wrong has been committed. If I defame or defraud you, you may call me to account in court and require me to repair the harm I have done. That obligation, however, is particular to me, owed to you, and conditioned on my breach of my primary obligation not to wrong you in those ways. Perhaps because they view tort law from the vantage point of its remedial responsibilities, corrective justice theorists are inclined to regard tort law's primary obligations as indefinitely extensible bilateral obligations.[86] Indefinitely extensible bilateral obligations are obligations owed to an indefinite number of people, but the obligation owed to each person is separate and distinct from the obligation owed to each other person. Importing the bilateral logic of remedial rights into our understanding of primary rights thus fosters the misconception that a defendant's obligations to a plaintiff are determined solely by considering the relation of the defendant and the plaintiff.

---

[83] See California Vehicle Code § 22352(a)(2) (2015) (emphasis mine).
[84] See Robert Stevens, Torts and Rights 328 (Oxford, 2007).
[85] Lucchese v. San Francisco–Sacramento R. Co., 289 P. 188 (Cal. 1930).
[86] This possibility was suggested to me by both Martin Stone and Arthur Ripstein.

Primary and secondary norms in tort law embody different forms of relationality. The bilateral structure of the traditional (remedial) tort lawsuit joins a plaintiff and a defendant who have proper names. The obligations are *in personam*. Primary tort norms are also relational, but because they are omnilateral and not bilateral, the duties that they impose do not come with proper names attached to them. They are *in rem*—owed by all of us to each other. Echoing a 130-year-old statute, the California Supreme Court has remarked that "[i]n this state, the general rule is that all persons have a duty to use ordinary care to prevent others from being injured as the result of their conduct."[87] Everyone owes everyone else a duty of reasonable care.

The *in personam* remedial obligations that arise once a tortious wrong is committed prove to be an unreliable guide to the character of tort law's primary norms in another important way. Taking remedial rights as the paradigm case can lead us to think of tort law's primary wrongs as bilateral wrongs committed between named persons. Most intentional wrongs meet this description, but most accidental wrongs do not. In practice, the most prominent primary tort norm—the negligence norm enjoining reasonable care in light of all relevant circumstances—is highly general. When I drive my car carelessly on a busy California street, I act wrongly toward an indefinite plurality of potential victims whose persons and property I unreasonably endanger. The wrong that I commit is relational and directional, but abstract. I risk harm to representative but unknown persons—to other drivers, passengers, and pedestrians who may be in my path. In the same vein, the interest that I jeopardize is fundamental but generic: namely, the fundamental interest that all people have in the physical integrity of their persons. An *in personam* right emerges only when my carelessness ripens into a completed wrong and inflicts injury on an identified passenger or pedestrian.

2. Primary Wrongs

Speaking of tort law as the embodiment of corrective justice suggests that tort law's primary wrongs might themselves be matters of corrective injustice.[88] With the possible exception of an important class of strict liability wrongs—where the primary wrong consists of harming-without-repairing—tortious wrongs

---

[87] Randi W. v. Muroc Joint Unified Sch. Dist., 929 P.2d 582, 588 (Cal. 1997). See also California Civil Code § 1714(a) (West 2002) (enacted 1872) (prescribing that everyone owes to everyone else a duty of ordinary care); Restatement (Third) of Torts: Liability for Physical and Emotional Harm § 7 (2005) (recognizing "a duty to exercise reasonable care" when conduct presents a risk of harm to others).

[88] Weinrib writes: "Corrective justice serves a normative function: a transaction is required, on pain of rectification, to conform to its contours." Weinrib 1995, *supra* note 8, at 76. Corrective justice thus appears to be about the righting of corrective injustices (actions that, say, disturb "the equality between the parties").

themselves are not corrective injustices. Although corrective justice may be characterized by saying that reparation reverses a wrongful interaction—erasing the injury inflicted and returning it to the wrongdoer responsible for its infliction—it does not follow that the commission of the wrong was a corrective injustice. Absent justification or excuse, it is wrong to punch someone else in the face, but it is not a corrective injustice. Committing battery is wrong not because it fails to correct a prior wrongful interaction but because it violates a primary obligation of harm avoidance. That primary obligation is in turn grounded in the victim's right to the physical integrity of their person.[89] Torts—fraud, battery, intentional infliction of emotional distress, negligent infliction of physical injury, and the like—are wrongs that presuppose rights. It is wrong to imprison someone falsely because it violates their right to liberty; it is wrong to defraud someone because deception undoes the sovereignty of their will over their actions as much as coercion does; it is wrong to injure someone negligently because it violates their right to reasonable security; and so on. The question of what rights people have is not a question of corrective justice.

The implication that tortious wrongs are corrective injustices arises out of Weinrib's formulation of corrective justice theory, and it may be unintended. Other corrective justice and civil recourse theorists propose that tort law's primary wrongs are *conduct-based wrongs* and must be so for their commission to give rise to obligations of reparation or rights of recourse.[90] Coleman offers a particular account of the template that tort law's commitment to doing corrective justice imposes on the field's primary wrongs. His account is distinctive in its details, but representative in its insistence that the idea of conduct-based wrongs is not an empty formality, but a template that imposes important constraints on the content of the field's primary norms. Coleman claims that tort's primary wrongs must satisfy the demands of the institution's sovereign principle as his corrective justice theory conceives it—the principle that wrongful losses should be repaired by those responsible for their infliction.[91] The only wrongs whose commission gives rise to claims for corrective justice are wrongs whose commission gives rise to wrongful losses. Tort law's primary wrongs must therefore be conduct-based wrongs which result in the infliction of loss.[92] Wrongful losses, in turn, are losses that issue from wrongful conduct.

---

[89] "The primary objects of the law are the establishment of rights, and the prohibition of wrongs," the former being "necessarily prior" to the latter. 3 William Blackstone, Commentaries *1–*2 (1766). See also Restatement (Second) of Torts § 1 cmt. d (1965).

[90] See, *e.g.*, John C.P. Goldberg & Benjamin C. Zipursky, Recognizing Wrongs 63, 197, 361 (Harvard, 2020).

[91] Coleman 2001, *supra* note 8, at 9, 15, 36.

[92] See Coleman 1995, *supra* note 13, at 56–57. Wrongdoing understood as wrongful conduct is also essential to Weinrib's theory of corrective justice in tort. Weinrib 1995, *supra* note 8, at 140–42, 197–98.

Many tortious wrongs do instantiate the category of "conduct-based wrongs which give rise to wrongful losses." Battering someone, invading their privacy, defrauding them, and failing to exercise due care not to unreasonably endanger them are all wrongs that are committed by conducting oneself in a certain way. Negligent wrongs and most intentional wrongs are wrongs whose commission involves failing to conduct oneself in accordance with a standard of conduct prescribed by the law. Strict liabilities exist in tort law, however, and they pose problems for the thesis that wrongful *conduct* is essential to liability in tort. There is an irony here, because harm-based strict liabilities are the only tortious wrongs that might plausibly be described as corrective. They impose an obligation not to harm-without-repairing.[93]

Two kinds of strict liability are entrenched in the law of torts: one kind includes the infliction of harm among its elements, the other does not. Prominent harm-based strict liabilities do not impose duties not to harm, full stop. They condemn the wrong of harming-without-repairing. More fully stated, the wrong is harming-justifiably-but-unjustifiably-failing-to-repair-the-harm-justifiably-inflicted. These wrongs forbid an injurer who is justified in inflicting harm from loading the costs of that harm off on their victim in circumstances where it would be unjust for the injurer to make the victim bear that burden. The primary obligation is to make reparation for harm fairly attributed to one's *justified or faultless* conduct. The famous conditional privilege case of *Vincent v. Lake Erie Transportation Co.*[94] illustrates the liability. In *Vincent*, it was right and reasonable for the owner of a ship to lash it to another's dock during a storm even though he did not have permission to do so—and even though lashing the ship to the dock saved the ship at the cost of damaging the dock. It was unreasonable and wrong, however, for the shipowner to foist the cost of saving his ship onto the owner of the dock. The shipowner had a duty to repair the harm that he inflicted even though his conduct in inflicting that harm was not itself wrong.

The duty imposed on the shipowner, then, was a duty not to commit the conditional wrong of harming-without-repairing. He committed that wrong when he failed to step forward, in a timely fashion, and repair the damage to the dock. We can fit this wrong into the mold of a conduct-based wrong, but only if we are willing to rework the mold. There is wrongful conduct involved in the commission of this kind of wrong, but the infliction of injury itself is not wrongful. The injury-inflicting conduct—lashing the ship to the dock and damaging the dock—is reasonable and right. The failure to repair the harm reasonably inflicted is unreasonable and wrong. It is wrong for the shipowner to foist the cost of the

---

[93] Strict liabilities are discussed in Chapter Six. The discussion here anticipates positions developed at more length in that chapter.
[94] Vincent v. Lake Erie Transp. Co., 124 N.W. 221 (Minn. 1910).

ship's salvation off on the dock owner. The wrongful conduct is secondary, not primary. For Coleman, this kind of wrong is not conduct-based in the right way, because liability is not predicated on the assertion that the defendant should have acted in a way which would have avoided harming the plaintiff.[95]

Such harm-based strict liability is not peculiar to *Vincent*. It is also embodied by liability for abnormally dangerous activities; by some liability for intentional nuisance; by liability for manufacturing defects in product liability law; and by the liability of employers for the torts committed by their employees within the scope of their employment. The obligation imposed by all of these doctrines is an obligation to undertake an action (e.g., saving your ship from destruction at the hands of a hurricane by bashing the dock to which it is moored), or conduct an activity (e.g., operating a business firm), *only on the condition* that you will repair any physical harm for which your action or activity is judged tortiously responsible. The reciprocal right is a right to have any physical harm done to you repaired by the party responsible for its infliction. Harm-based strict liabilities are important not just because they exist but also because they impose liability on harm that should not have been avoided. Such strict liabilities show very clearly that strict liability in tort is a fundamentally different basis of responsibility from fault liability. Expelling harm-based strict liabilities from the law of torts because their formal structure does not conform to the requirements imposed by tort law's sovereign principle of corrective justice is a case of allowing the tail to wag the dog. Just as tails should be wagged by dogs, so, too, tort theory should generally make sense, not hash, of tort law.

A second form of strict liability is also prominent in our law of torts. "Sovereignty-based" torts such as conversion and trespass, and some batteries, impose a form of strict liability. Here the wrong is the violation of a right that assigns a power of control over some physical object, or in the case of battery, control over one's own self. The law's specification of various powers of control over one's person and physical objects gives rise to a form of strict liability predicted on the voluntary but impermissible crossing of a boundary. If you enter my land or appropriate my pen without my permission, you have violated my right of exclusive control over these objects, even if your entry is entirely reasonable and justified. The wrong consists in the failure to respect the right. Fault

---

[95] The identification of tort with conduct-based wrongs is not particular to Coleman. Weinrib holds the same kind of view, a fact vividly illustrated by his criticisms of strict liability as a norm of conduct that condemns "any penetration of the plaintiff's space." Weinrib 1995, *supra* note 8, at 177. In his recent book, Ripstein also proposes an account of strict liability which assimilates it to negligence. Arthur Ripstein, Private Wrongs 80–158 (Harvard, 2016). Goldberg & Zipursky write that "[a]lthough by convention, strict liability for abnormally dangerous activities clearly is part of what lawyers define as 'tort law,' strictly speaking it does not belong in this department." John C.P. Goldberg & Benjamin C. Zipursky, The Oxford Introductions to U.S. Law: Torts 267 (Oxford, 2010). See also John C.P. Goldberg & Benjamin C. Zipursky, The Strict Liability in Fault and the Fault in Strict Liability, 85 Fordham L. Rev. 743 (2016).

is simply irrelevant. Liability for violation of a right of exclusive control is strict for the simple reason that the right itself would be unacceptably compromised by tolerating all reasonable (or justified) boundary crossings without regard to whether consent was given to those crossings. Powers of control establish sovereignty over the domains they govern. Those who hold such powers are entitled to forbid even reasonable boundary crossings, and they are presumptively wronged whenever the boundaries fixed by the rights are crossed without permission. Their rights thus give rise to stringent "duties to succeed" on the part of others.[96] In this class of cases, the strictness of liability in tort is the consequence of the character of the right being protected. Sovereignty rights would not establish sovereignty if they were not protected by strict liability in tort.

The wrong committed in a sovereignty-based tort is conduct-based *in only the most attenuated sense of the term*. In negligence—the canonical example of a conduct-based wrong—liability is predicated on the wrongfulness of the defendant's injury-inflicting conduct; it is that wrongfulness that does the work and triggers liability. To be liable for negligence a defendant must have acted wrongly. They must be responsible for inflicting on the plaintiff harm whose infliction they should have avoided by conducting themselves more carefully. In "sovereignty torts," it is the violation of the plaintiff's right that does the work and triggers liability. The duty is a duty not to violate the right. Conduct that violates the right is wrongful only because it violates the right. Viewed in isolation from the right, the conduct may be innocent and even commendable. The defendant doctor in *Mohr v. Williams*, for example, benefited the plaintiff by curing her disease.[97]

Thus, the essential features of both forms of strict liability prominent in our tort law are obscured and distorted by calling strict liability torts "conduct-based wrongs." Strict liability wrongs are genuine wrongs—they involve violations of rights. But the conduct necessary to commit them is not wrongful in the sense that corrective justice theorists have in mind with they speak of "conduct-based wrongs." These strict liabilities involve either wrongful failures to repair harm whose infliction was not wrongful, or conduct whose only fault is its failure to respect the plaintiff's power of control over the domain at issue. Neither mold matches the template of conduct-based wrongs as that term is used by corrective justice and civil recourse theorists.

---

[96] The concept of "duties to succeed" is developed in John Gardner, Obligations and Outcomes in the Law of Torts, in Relating to Responsibility: Essays for Tony Honoré on His 80th Birthday 111 (Peter Cane & John Gardner eds., Hart, 2001).
[97] Mohr v. Williams, 104 N.W. 12 (Minn. 1905).

3. Looking Forward and Backward

Placing tort law's adjudicative practice and remedial norms at the center of its account of the field serves the ends of corrective justice theory well. The backward-looking dimension of tort adjudication undermines the plausibility of the economic account. A danger of doing so, though, is to convey the misimpression that tort law's remedial apparatus looks only backward. Tort adjudication does do backward-looking corrective justice, but tort law also puts the *prospect* of reparation to use to *enforce* primary rights and responsibilities, not just to restore them. Tort damages perform, in part, a forward-looking role. Primary tort duties enjoin respect for the rights of others, thereby constraining our freedom and checking the pursuit of our self-interest. People sometimes chafe at these constraints and are tempted to disregard them. Moreover, we may be justifiably wary of discharging our obligations to others if we are not assured that they will discharge their reciprocal responsibilities to us. The prospect of liability in tort serves as a counterweight to our self-interest, as an incentive to discharge our obligations, and as an assurance that others will comply as well. The remedial powers that tort law places in the hands of injured plaintiffs put teeth in tort's primary obligations. Damages may do their most important and effective work when their prospect diminishes the number of occasions on which they must be awarded. Insofar as reparation is a second-best way of safeguarding the interests that primary rights and responsibilities protect, this forward-looking, rights-enforcing aspect of damages should not be dismissed lightly.[98]

Tort adjudication also looks forward in a second way. Tort is a common-law legal institution, and it articulates law through adjudication. Tort cases do not only resolve disputes; they also apply and develop law. On the one hand, a legal decision is a decision made in accordance with preexisting norms. On the other hand, common-law legal decisions do not simply cast their eyes toward the past and govern only the parties before them. They have precedential force. Rulings in individual cases bind prospectively on all who fall within their scope. In their prospective aspect, tort rulings bind very generally. They obligate indefinite classes of potential wrongdoers and protect indefinite classes of potential victims going forward indefinitely.[99] In the general law of negligence, for example, duties are owed by classes of prospective injurers and to classes of potential victims. There are, indeed, few legal duties as general—and few legal norms as abstract—as the general obligation of reasonable care. That obligation is owed

---

[98] This role justifies the award of punitive damages in some circumstances. See, *e.g.*, *Jacque*, 563 N.W.2d. It also justifies inquiring into how much liability is necessary to enforce the rights whose violation is at issue, as proximate-cause cases fixing the outer perimeter of liability often do. Negligence cases involving pure economic loss and pure emotional harm are often acutely sensitive to this concern. See, *e.g.*, Barber Lines v. Donau Maru, 764 F.2d 50 (1st Cir. 1985); Thing v. La Chusa, 771 P.2d 814 (Cal. 1989).

[99] *Cf.* Sheinman 2003, *supra* note 35, at 50–51 (discussing the doctrine of precedent in tort).

both by everyone and to everyone else, and presumptively applies to all actions that create significant risks of physical harm.

Corrective justice theory's insistence that duty and right in tort exhibit a bilateral, *in personam*, structure overlooks the fact that—even in adjudication—tort norms look forward as well as backward. When they look forward, tort norms bind generally and *in rem*. They impose duties on classes of persons—persons conceived abstractly as potential injurers and potential victims; potential landowners and potential entrants onto land; potential drivers and potential pedestrians; and so on. Extending a correct account of the *in personam* structure of tort law's remedial norms to tort law's primary norms thus results in a pervasive misunderstanding of both tort law's form and its substance. For the most part, primary tort obligations are owed to persons simply as persons, because they protect urgent interests that we all possess simply as human beings.[100] Because the first question of tort law is just what it is that we owe to others in the way of respect for their persons, their property, and a diverse set of their economic and "intangible interests," the formal character and structure of tort's primary norms tells us at least as much about tort law as the formal structure and character of its remedial norms does.

In short, corrective justice theory claims that tort is bilateral, backward-looking, and populated by conduct-based wrongs. The subject is molded to match the form of an ostensibly sovereign principle of remedial justice. But the subject does not fit the mold. Tort law's primary obligations are forward-looking and omnilateral. They are owed by everyone to everyone else, and they govern relations among persons prospectively. These primary obligations have a better claim to being the core of tort law than the remedial obligations stressed by corrective justice theorists, because tort's remedial obligations are parasitic on its primary ones. Primary obligations in tort, moreover, do not consist entirely of conduct-based wrongs. Strict liabilities in tort are either conduct-based only in the most attenuated sense—as sovereignty-based strict liabilities are—or condemn as wrongful only the failure to make reparation for harm justifiably done—as important harm-based strict liabilities do. The structure of tort law thus does not bear out the claims of corrective justice theory.

D. Putting Primary Norms First

Theory of the sort under consideration here is an example of the law in quest of itself, the law's quest for self-understanding. We turn to theory because our

---

[100] Affirmative duties are an exception to this. They rest on "special relationships." Dan B. Dobbs, Paul T. Hayden, & Ellen M. Bublick, Hornbook on Torts 1073 (West, 2d ed., 2016).

understanding of some field of law seems inadequate. What we want from theory is orientation—a clear view of the subject at hand which can guide our more particular inquiries. In the case of tort theory, reorientation is in order. The economic account of tort as a law concerned with the costs of accidents is right to care about tort law's impact on the conduct of persons and firms, right to emphasize the centrality of avoiding harm in the first instance, and right to insist that accidental harm is a matter of public concern, not something of concern only to the private parties involved. The *effects* of tort norms on the incidence of accidental injury are important, even if they should not be mistaken for the justification for tort law's primary obligations. But the account of the structure of tort adjudication offered by economic analysis is strained and implausible, as corrective justice theory powerfully argues. It is unconvincing to assert that tort adjudication is a fundamentally regulatory body of law oriented toward pinning the costs of accidents on cheapest-cost-avoiders going forward. It is much more plausible to maintain that tort suits seek to vindicate the rights of those who bring them, usually by requiring wrongdoing defendants to make reparation to those they have wronged for the harm they have wrongly done.

The unconvincing quality of the economic account of adjudication, moreover, is evidence of deeper problems with the view. The economic thesis that the sole value served by tort law is the minimization of the combined costs of accidents and their prevention is difficult to square with the substance of tort law. Sustaining that thesis requires refusing to take basic tort doctrines such as duty, breach, cause, and harm at face value, and recasting them as peculiarly indirect devices through which tort law pursues the ends that economics prizes. There is no reason to reconstruct tort law's deontological language of right and duty as a false front for cunningly concealed instrumental ends. Tort law is what it seems to be—namely, an institution preoccupied with what it is that people owe to one another in the way of coercively enforceable obligations to not impair or interfere with each other's essential interests as members of civil society. Tort law is about rights and wrongs.

For their part, corrective justice theories of tort law have been on the right track in putting wrongs and rights at the center of the institution, but they have missed the mark in asserting that the essence of tort law lies in the rectification of wrongs. Placing primary weight on the reparative aspect of the institution is mistaken in the same way that retributivism in criminal law is mistaken. Just as we do not have the criminal law primarily in order to punish the wicked, so, too, we do not have the law of torts primarily in order to repair wrongful losses. The primary role of tort law is to establish and enforce certain rights that persons have against one another—rights not to be harmed in various ways, and to exercise control over one's person and property in various ways. We need to reorient tort theory in a way which recognizes that tort is a law of rights and wrongs, but which assigns pride of place to its primary rights and responsibilities.

1. Making Sense of Tort Law

Putting primary rights and responsibilities at the center of tort law has the virtue of putting the horse back in front of the cart, but it is not itself free of difficulties. First and foremost, any attempt to put tort law's primary responsibilities at the center of our understanding of the field must confront the claim that tort law's primary rights and duties are heterogeneous, and irreducibly so.[101] On the face of the matter, tort law protects an unruly collection of interests—in physical integrity; in emotional tranquility; in freedom to move about; in dominion over and use of real and moveable property; in reputation and privacy; in not being deceived as we go about our economic lives and enter into agreements; in the legitimate economic expectancies that our agreements create; in not having legal processes used abusively against us; and so on. The law of torts can appear to be a hodgepodge of unrelated wrongs. All the interests that tort protects are taken by the law to be important enough to warrant protection against some kinds of wrongful impairment, but that is all that they have in common.

The question of whether tort is a unified subject and, if so, what gives it its unity, is a difficult one.[102] After all, specific torts come and go. Over the course of the twentieth century, torts protecting privacy and emotional tranquility emerged, while torts treating seduction and champerty as legal wrongs withered and died. Putting tort law's wide-ranging collection of primary rights and responsibilities at the center of our understanding seems likely to awaken deep-seated doubts about the coherence of the institution. We treat tort as a distinct and unified field, yet tort law's primary obligations appear untidy and apparently un-unified.

a. Safeguarding Individual Agency

The interests that tort law safeguards vary over time, but the role of tort law is relatively stable. Tort is our law's default institution for establishing the security of persons with respect to one another as members of civil society. It does so by specifying those interests important enough to warrant the imposition of legally

---

[101] Coleman 2001, *supra* note 8, at 34–35 ("I reject the suggestion that an adequate account of tort practices requires that there be a general theory of primary duties from which we can derive them all systematically. Indeed, I am dubious about the prospects for such a theory. On my view, much of the content of the primary duties that are protected in tort law is created and formed piecemeal in the course of our manifold social and economic interactions."). Goldberg & Zipursky appear similarly inclined. See Goldberg & Zipursky 2010, *supra* note 95, at 27–45. *Cf.* Scott Hershovitz, Two Models of Tort (and Takings), 92 Va. L. Rev. 1147 (2006).

[102] See Grey 2001, *supra* note 35; Grey (unpublished manuscript), *supra* note 35. We will return to this question in Chapter Eight.

enforceable obligations not to interfere with, or impair, each other in diverse ways. It backs those primary obligations with rights of recourse and duties of repair. So conceived, tort law's role still matches Blackstone's conception of the subject as a body of law concerned with protecting people's liberty, property, and security.[103] Tort law is a law of wrongs that hang together in an important way. Most tortious wrongs involve either harm—to persons, to their property, and to their intangible interests[104]—or the violation of powers of control over prized zones of discretionary choice. The rights that these wrongs violate guard important conditions of effective individual agency—important forms of security and freedom of action.

The general law of negligence, for example, stands at the center of modern tort law, and it is primarily concerned with guarding the physical integrity of persons and their property. The exceptional pockets of strict liability that attract the most attention are likewise preoccupied with physical harm. In both cases, harm is an essential element of a claim, and neither pure economic loss nor pure emotional injury generally counts as the kind of harm that gives rise to liability.[105] Intentional torts are more diverse. Many of them protect us against harm, but the harms they protect against are various: battery protects us against physical harm; assault protects us against the fear of *imminent* physical harm; intentional infliction of emotional distress protects us against psychological harm; fraud protects us economic loss effected by deception; defamation protects our reputations; tortious interference with prospective economic advantage protects important economic expectancies from invasion by third parties; and so on. Other intentional torts protect domains of choice or powers of control. To those we have already mentioned—battery in some of its incarnations, trespass, and conversion—we should add false imprisonment, which protects our freedom to move about in the world at large.

Notwithstanding the diversity of intentional torts, tort law has a core which is unified by its concern with establishing important conditions of effective individual agency. Both sovereignty-based and harm-based torts protect our ability

---

[103] See 1 Blackstone, Commentaries *125, *129, *134, *138 (1766) (explaining that the common law is founded on "absolute" rights to liberty, security, and property). By "absolute," Blackstone seems to mean what we would call "natural." For an illuminating discussion, see Grey (unpublished manuscript), *supra* note 35, at 111–27.

[104] The view that tort law is about harm is one of Oliver Wendell Holmes's famous theses, and it has been prominent in the legal academy ever since. See Oliver Wendell Holmes, The Common Law 144 (Sheldon Novick ed., Dover, 1991) ("[T]he general purpose of the law of torts is to secure a man indemnity against certain forms of harm to person, reputation, or estate, at the hands of his neighbors, not because they are wrong, but because they are harms."). Unfortunately, Holmes's distinction between "harms" and "wrongs" sets up a false antithesis between the two. On Holmes and harm, see Grey 2001, *supra* note 35, at 1272–75; Grey (unpublished manuscript), *supra* note 35, at 35–38.

[105] See, *e.g.*, W. Page Keeton et al., Prosser and Keeton on Torts 361 (West, 5th ed., 1984). On pure economic loss, see Robins Dry Dock & Repair Co. v. Flint, 275 U.S. 303 (1927); Barber Lines v. Donau Maru, 764 F.2d 50 (1st Cir. 1985).

to work our wills in the world. They thus protect an important dimension of our efficacy as agents. Sovereignty-based torts protect powers of control over persons and property. Those who hold these powers can use and dispose of the objects governed by the powers as they see fit. These powers are essential aspects of our personal freedom: they go an important distance toward enabling us to do as we please with ourselves and our possessions. The thesis that harm is an assault on agency is less obvious, and more contestable. In fact, it runs contrary to the most influential contemporary account of harm. According to that account, harms are "violations of one of a person's interests, an injury to something in which he has a genuine stake."[106] Setback accounts of harm along these lines conceive of harm in counterfactual or historical terms and locate harm's moral significance in the damage it does to our well-being.[107] Harms are not so very different from costs. They just deliver heavier blows than costs do. Harms set our *vital* interests back, and seriously.

Another account of harm, however, links it more closely to agency. This account conceives of harm as a condition whose badness is not comparative and grounds harm's significance in its impairment of agency. To be harmed is to be put in an impaired condition, a condition in which the normal powers through which one exerts one's will upon the world are diminished.[108] The will, in the general and basic sense relevant here, is simply the capacity we are aware of when we experience our own ability to produce effects in the world. Serious physical injury and agonizing pain impair our powers of agency. They impair and, at the limit, negate, the wills of those they afflict. When we are in agonizing pain, we cannot subject our experience to our agency. In agonizing pain, all that we can do is to suffer and endure.[109] Intense pain may be the most vivid embodiment of the way in which harm overwhelms the will, but all significant physical harm impairs normal powers of agency.

---

[106] Joel Feinberg, Social Philosophy 26 (Pearson, 1973). The interest account of harm is briefly but clearly deployed in Sheinman 2003, *supra* note 35; and in Hershovitz 2006, *supra* note 101, at 1161–68.

[107] For a survey and summary of this and other accounts of harms, including the autonomy account endorsed in this chapter, see Matthew Hanser, The Metaphysics of Harm, 77 Phil. & Phenomenological Res. 421 (2008). It is entirely possible that harm is not a unified concept and covers diverse phenomena.

[108] See Seana Shiffrin, Wrongful Life, Procreative Responsibility, and the Significance of Harm, 5 Legal Theory 117 (1999); Seana Shiffrin, Harm and Its Moral Significance, 18 Legal Theory 357 (2012); Judith Jarvis Thomson, The Realm of Rights 227–71 (Harvard, 1990). Tortious harms, of course, are marked by one more essential property: they are inflicted by some and suffered by others. Tort is concerned with what we may demand from each other as a matter of right, and rights hold only against other agents, not against natural forces.

[109] Raz 1986, *supra* note 37, at 412–20, traces a broader if less intense connection between autonomy and harm: "To harm a person is to diminish his prospects, to affect adversely his possibilities." *Id.* at 414. Raz notes explicitly that he is explicating John Stuart Mill's famous "harm principle." This idea of harm is picked up by John Oberdiek, Imposing Risk: A Normative Framework 86 (Oxford, 2017).

Both the interest and the impaired condition accounts of harm can be mapped onto American law. The "impaired condition" conception of harm, however, fits the core of tort law more precisely because that core is preoccupied with physical harm, and conceives of it as impairment. Tort law distinguishes between a broad conception of tortious wrongdoing as conduct which invades "legally protected interests" (or rights) and a narrower conception of physical harm as the suffering of an impaired condition.[110] The *First Restatement of Torts*, for example, defined bodily harm as "any impairment of the physical condition of another's body or physical pain or illness."[111] The *Second Restatement* refined this definition. "Bodily harm" was defined as "any physical impairment of the condition of another's body" and "an impairment of the physical condition of another's body [exists] if the structure or function of any part of the other's body is altered."[112] The *Third Restatement* now defines "physical harm" as "the physical impairment of the human body ('bodily harm') or of real property or tangible personal property . . . [such impairment] includes physical injury, illness, disease, impairment of bodily function, and death."[113]

Insofar as harms are assaults on agency, harm-based and sovereignty-based torts both protect capacities which are essential to the exercise of individual will. Harm-based torts protect physical faculties and capacities through which we exert our wills, whereas sovereignty-based torts protect normative powers that are essential to the exercise of our freedom in the world. Indeed, the distinction between these two kinds of torts can be collapsed by counting the violation of the victim's power of control over a protected domain as harm. The harm is in the thwarting of agency, even if the agent is not left in an impaired condition.[114] The connection between wrong and the thwarting of agency is different in other torts, but it is often not difficult to draw. The wrong at the heart of fraud, for example, is deception. Deception manipulates the reasons available to its victims, thereby manipulating their wills and making them the unwitting instrument of the wrongdoer's will. Fraud undermines freedom

---

[110] See, *e.g.*, Restatement (Second) of Torts §§ 7, 15 (1965).

[111] Restatement (First) of Torts § 15 (1934).

[112] Restatement (First) of Torts § 15 cmt. a (1965). Section 7 distinguishes "bodily harm" from "injury" with "injury" covering cases in which a "legally protected interest" is invaded, but no harm is done. A harmless trespass would be an injury in this sense. *Id.* at § 7.

[113] Restatement (Third) of Torts: Liability for Physical and Emotional Harm § 4 (2010). The *Third Restatement* extends the idea of harm as an impaired condition to include the impairment of property. The philosophical conception of harm is concerned only with harm to persons. The question of how to account for the importance of property damage to tort is peripheral to the concerns of this chapter. Offhand, the easiest way to make the extension would appear to be to draw upon the fact that we have rights in property. Those rights give rise to claims against others that they not damage our property and make impairment of our property a harm to us.

[114] It is, I think, best to recognize that we can *both* distinguish the two kinds of torts *and* conflate them, but that we can do this only if we understand harm as serious impairment of agency.

every bit as effectively as force does. The latter overpowers bodies; the former subverts minds.

Protection of our sovereignty over our persons and our property as it is found in trespass and battery, and protection against harm as it is found in the general law of negligence, are canonical cases of tort protection. Many torts fit one of these templates because many torts involve harms. The kind of intense fear that the tort of assault protects us against fits the conception of harm as an assault on our persons so severe as to thwart our mastery over our experience. So, too, emotional distress of the acute kind that concerns the law of torts in both its negligent and intentional modes constitutes a brutal assault on agency.[115] Sensibility-based nuisances also fit this account of harm. They are visceral assaults on our senses that prevent us from using and even occupying our property.[116] Other torts stand at greater distance from the core sovereignty- and harm-based torts. Defamation and invasion of privacy are cases in point.

To bring defamation within the ambit of an autonomy account of harm, reputation must be an especially important condition of agency. We have to claim that some capacity to ensure that others' perceptions of us are determined by who we are and what we have done is essential to our capacity to work our will upon the world.[117] To count as an autonomy-based harm, the grounds of defamation must be that reputational harm seriously impairs the efficacy of our agency by making our reputations subject to the false claims of others instead of answering to what we have done in and with our lives. For defamation to meet this description, it would have to have certain features: it could not merely protect the powerful from justified criticism of their conduct or protect the good names of those with high status. It would have to protect everyone from having his or her good name ruined by falsehoods. And one's good name would have to be an important instrument of one's agency. It is at least plausible to think that it might be. Fitting privacy into a framework which takes tort law to be concerned with essential conditions of agency also presents a special challenge. We must show why the opportunity to enter into a social condition where one is

---

[115] See Gregory C. Keating, Is Negligent Infliction of Emotional Distress a Freestanding Tort?, 44 Wake Forest L. Rev. 1131 (2009).

[116] See, e.g., Spur Indus., Inc. v. Del E. Webb Dev. Co., 494 P.2d 700 (Ariz. 1972) (flies and odor from cattle feedlot held to be a nuisance); Berg v. Reaction Motors Div., Thiokol Chem. Corp., 181 A.2d 487 (N.J. 1962) (noise, vibration, and air blasts from test-firing a rocket engine constituted a nuisance); O'Cain v. O'Cain, 473 S.E.2d 460 (S.C. 1996) (presence of hogs in front of plaintiff's residence was a nuisance).

[117] Blackstone counted reputation among the fundamental rights comprising the right of personal security, but the tort may have since become less central in most accounts of the fundamental interests of persons. Blackstone, Commentaries *129 (1766) ("The right of personal security consists in a person's legal and uninterrupted enjoyment of his life, his limbs, his body, health and his reputation.").

immune from unwelcome observation is essential either to the formation of an independent sense of self, or to the exercise of independent selfhood, or to both. With both defamation and privacy, there is a case to be made both for and against the necessary shoehorning.

When we move beyond torts that protect the physical and psychological integrity of the person, the full diversity of tort law becomes vividly apparent. Some torts protect economic interests, others protect property rights, and still others protect rights against harm flowing from the abuse of legal and political processes. The list of tortious mistreatments is long and open-ended. To sort all these torts, it may help to distinguish tort into three domains. At the center of the field are the freestanding torts: these torts protect interests in the physical and psychological integrity of the person. They spell out what we owe to each other simply by virtue of essential interests that we have as persons. This core is the latter-day descendant of Blackstone's "law of security." Tort's freestanding core is flanked on two sides by the protections that it confers on rights originating in other bodies of law, primarily property and contract. In these flanking domains, the role of tort is to help secure the effectiveness of legal rights that are not themselves creatures of the law of torts.

These flanking domains are connected to our powers of agency because the recognition of rights by other bodies of law (e.g., contract) makes those rights secure entitlements and expectancies on which people may justifiably rely as they go about their lives. Tortious interference with contractual expectations protects contract in this way. The formation of a contract converts a fluid economic interest subject to the vagaries of the market into a protected economic expectancy. The security of this expectancy is, then, essential to effective exercises of will. Contract enables planning, and planning requires secure confidence that one can rely on contractual commitments. Planning requires assurance. Tort law's role here is to play handmaiden to contract by putting third parties under binding legal obligations of noninterference. Contracting parties, after all, cannot obligate strangers to their transactions to refrain from interfering with their contractual arrangements, and yet such noninterference may be essential for the parties to a contract to have confidence that their agreements will prove effective in practice. Similarly, parties to property arrangements must bind the whole world to respect their rights but cannot ground that obligation in their own private agreements. The tort of trespass requires everyone to stay off of a piece of real property unless they have the owner's permission to enter—not just those who have contractually agreed not to enter without such authorization. In both cases, tort adds an essential layer of protection by putting third parties under the *obligations* necessary to buttress and secure the effectiveness of rights established by other departments of the law.

E. Summing Up

Corrective justice theory in full flower claims that tort is essentially a matter of repairing losses wrongly inflicted. This claim is unconvincing, both normatively and interpretively. Normatively, duties of repair are parasitic on, and derivative of, primary duties to respect rights and avoid the infliction of injury. Repairing wrongful losses is a next best way of respecting underlying rights against harms and invasions of one's sovereignty. Duties of repair derive from failures to discharge primary obligations in tort in the first instance. Normatively, corrective justice is important but subordinate. Interpretively, corrective justice theory fails (1) because its account of tort law matches only tort's remedial dimension, not its primary obligations; (2) because it is both under- and overinclusive; and (3) because it offers an inadequate account of strict liability in tort. Corrective justice theory's claim that the essence of tort is the repair of wrongful loss excludes some canonical torts from the field and includes some wrongs that are not torts. Its thesis that liability in tort must be a matter of wrongful conduct resulting in wrongful loss is belied by strict liability doctrines that either impose liability on conduct that is justifiable or on conduct that does not cause loss.

We should follow the lead of corrective justice theorists in putting wrongs at the center of our understanding of tort law, but we should reorient tort theory to place primary responsibilities at the subject's core. On the view of those rights and responsibilities that I am suggesting, the law of torts guards essential conditions of agency against harm. Tort law as a whole thus illustrates the Millian proposition that individual liberty ends with the infliction of (unacceptable) harm. In its freestanding core, tort takes the liberty and integrity of the person to be fundamental and guards it against physical and psychological violation. On its flanks, tort guards diverse rights and expectancies. These flanking wrongs are heterogeneous, and the list of such wrongs is in principle an open-ended one. Fundamentally, what ties these wrongs together is simply the determination that the interest at issue is urgent enough to warrant legal protection. But even here we should not overlook the extent to which tort is protecting important aspects of individual agency. The torts that protect our property and contract rights, for example, are safeguarding institutional means through which we extend and exercise our agency.

Putting primary responsibilities at the center of tort theory aligns the preoccupations of theory with the principal concerns of tort practice. Modern tort law has been absorbed with questions of what kinds of harm persons should be protected against, and how stringent those protections should be. The expansion of liability for the infliction of emotional distress, intentional or negligent, implicitly takes the psychological integrity of the person to be an interest important enough to ground coercively enforceable obligations on the part of others. The expansion of tort into the domain of product accidents once governed by contract rests on the assumption that our interest in physical security ought to impose safety obligations on product sellers independent of any contractual relations sellers' have with those who are injured by their products. For its part, the expansion of tort into the domain of landowner liability implies that our common interests as physically vulnerable natural persons trump our differential interests in, and statuses with respect to, the ownership of land.

Questions about whether and when obligations to avoid harm ought to be recognized, and how such obligations ought to be implemented, deserve attention from tort theorists commensurate with their importance to tort law. Giving these questions their due begins with placing them at the center of our understanding of the field.

3
The Importance of Interests

Chapter Two argued that primary norms are the heart and soul of the law of torts, and that the remedial norms assigned pride of place by influential theories of tort law as corrective justice are logically and normatively parasitic on those primary norms. But it is not the case that all the accounts of tort law that we might subsume beneath the labels of corrective justice or civil recourse are essentially remedial. Many theorists who associate themselves with one of those broad orientations have much to say about tort law's primary obligations. The most sophisticated and fully articulated contemporary case in point rallies around the battle cry that tort is "private law." Ernest Weinrib's elegant and influential book, *The Idea of Private Law*,[1] declares its allegiance to that thesis in its title, and the idea figures almost as centrally in Arthur Ripstein's recent and important *Private Wrongs*.[2]

Theorists who rally around the banner of "private law" claim that tort law's governing principles of right and responsibility tumble out of the field's characteristic legal form. Law, as they understand it, is constitutive of just relations among persons, not an instrument for the pursuit of independently valuable ends. For scholars like Weinrib and Ripstein, "private law" is the Kantian "idea of reason" that makes our actual law of torts intelligible.[3] The idea that tort is "private law" enables us to understand it as an institution which establishes rightful relations among independent and equal persons. Tort law spells out what it is that equal and independent persons—pursuing their private purposes in civil society—owe to one another in the way of obligations of mutual noninterference. In Weinrib's articulation of the view, the bipolar form of the traditional tort lawsuit is the master key which unlocks the mysteries of the field.[4] That form relates plaintiff and defendant as opposite poles of the same wrong and instantiates a backward-looking morality of interpersonal responsibility. The plaintiff claims

---

[1] Ernest J. Weinrib, The Idea of Private Law (Oxford, 1995).
[2] Arthur Ripstein, Private Wrongs (Harvard, 2016).
[3] Ernest J. Weinrib, Law as a Kantian Idea of Reason, 87 Colum. L. Rev. 472, 478 (1987) ("For Kant, law is a unity that can be articulated through its doctrines and institutions. Kant calls this unity an idea of reason.").
[4] Weinrib 1995, *supra* note 1. In the literature on this subject, the terms "bipolar" and "bilateral" tend to be used interchangeably. The terms pick out the fact that normal tort suits involve two poles or sides, namely, a plaintiff and a defendant contesting whether or not the defendant has wronged the plaintiff.

to have suffered the very wrong that the defendant committed and demands that the defendant repair the harm that the defendant's wrong has inflicted on the plaintiff. The substantive morality of tort law is the morality that matches that form. In Ripstein's presentation, the spare political principle that *each of us is in charge of ourselves and none of us is in charge of anyone else* holds pride of place.[5] The content of the law of private wrongs lies immanent within that one principle of right.

There is much to be learned from both Ripstein and Weinrib. The idea of tort law as a realm of equal right is a powerful one. Broadly speaking, the most compelling alternative ideal to the economic theory of tort as a waste-minimizing, wealth-maximizing mechanism for managing the costs of accidents is a conception of tort as articulating what it is that we owe to one another in the way of coercively enforceable obligations not to interfere with or impair urgent individual interests. At the core of these interests is our urgent interest in avoiding, and recovering from, physical harm. The physical integrity of our persons—our safety—is a primary good in John Rawls' sense of the term.[6] A decent measure of security against serious physical harm is an essential condition of effective agency. Securing such a measure of security through our civic institutions is one of the things that we owe to one another as a matter of basic justice. Theorists of tort as "private law" are thus right to connect tort both to basic justice and to basic conditions of human agency. They go astray, however, by both *asking and making* too much of form. They *ask too much* of form when they attempt to make sense of the private law of torts solely in terms of its form—eschewing all talk of interests. We cannot understand or justify the law of torts without attending to the interests that it protects. In tort, as elsewhere, rights and the duties they ground protect important individual interests. Our interest in safety is a case in point. It grounds relational obligations in the law of torts, but it also justifies direct regulation of risk and institutions such as insurance.

Theorists of tort as "private law" *make too much* of form when they present the legal category of tort as its own independent kingdom, walled off from surrounding legal fields. For Ripstein and Weinrib, the "private law" of torts is its own self-sufficient domain, sealed off against infection by any legal field whose form identifies it as "public law." This insistence on the autonomy and impermeability of tort is a mistake, and it breeds misunderstanding. Our law of torts is heterogeneous, and best understood as part of a family of institutions—some "private," some "public"—which share responsibility for protecting people's

---

[5] Ripstein 2016, *supra* note 2, at 6, 12, 18, 33, 35, 105, 131, 295.
[6] For Rawls, "primary goods" are goods that we need, whatever else we need, to exercise our powers of agency and pursue our conceptions of the good over the course of our lives. See, *e.g.*, John Rawls, Social Unity and Primary Goods, in Utilitarianism and Beyond (Amartya Sen & Bernard Williams eds., Cambridge University Press, 1982).

urgent interests, especially their interest in safety, from impairment at each other's hands. Legal institutions are instruments for protecting certain interests and realizing certain values. No single legal institution is everywhere and always the institution best suited to protect the interests—and realize the values—that the law of torts protects and seeks to realize. Our law of torts is intimately interwoven with administrative schemes, such as workers' compensation, and with statutory regimes, such as zoning and direct risk regulation. These diverse legal institutions share the labor of establishing an important domain of basic justice.

Moreover, in our law, tort and related institutions embody diverse principles of responsibility. Sometimes, the interests and values at stake, and the circumstances at hand, call for fault liability. Other times, the interests and values at stake, and the circumstances at hand, justify the imposition of strict liability. Sometimes our institutions impose individual responsibility, sometimes they impose collective responsibility. This is as it should be. In our world, unjustified interference with the urgent interests of others as we and they go about our lives in civil society is sometimes best understood and addressed as a matter of individual misconduct. In other circumstances, such interference is best addressed as a social problem. Sometimes these diverse institutions cooperate, and sometimes they compete. This chapter will argue that, taken as a whole, this family of overlapping institutions encompasses and articulates tort law's basic task: to spell out what it is that we owe to one another in the way of mutual responsibilities not to interfere with or impair each other's essential interests.

I. Ideas of "Private Law"

The thesis that the key to understanding tort law is its taxonomic classification as "private law" runs so contrary to the conventional wisdom of the American legal academy that it is often both dismissed out of hand and badly misunderstood. It is dismissed out of hand because—in ordinary American legal usage—references to private and public law merely flag the difference between bodies of law concerned with the relations between citizens and the state (public law) and bodies of law concerned with relations among persons in civil society (private law). The terms slot legal subjects into handy file folders. This thin understanding of the distinction between public and private bodies of law may itself express a substantive claim: namely, that the public-private distinction has been both rightly discredited and badly eroded over the course of the past century.[7] For most contemporary American legal academics, invoking the idea of "private law" brings

---

[7] See, *e.g.*, Duncan Kennedy, The Stages of the Decline of the Public/Private Distinction, 130 U. Pa. L. Rev. 1349 (1982).

to mind the idea of a realm beyond the reach of law. Private realms are sites where some people may exercise unchecked power over others.[8] The very idea that, say, domestic relations are beyond the boundary of public concern is rightly regarded as pernicious, and that perniciousness is thought to attach to any robust version of the public-private distinction. Whether or not present usage is the residue of this particular history, however, the present usage of the term "private law" in the American legal academy yields an anemic concept unsuited to serve as the master key to any legal field.

In contemporary American legal thought, the stigma that attaches to the "public-private" distinction is compounded by a misunderstanding of "private law"—as Weinrib and Ripstein understand it—that arises out of the appropriation of the protean word "private" by a very different philosophical position. Contemporary libertarian political philosophy has rejected the stigmatization of the idea of a "private realm" and appropriated the idea as its own. Libertarianism celebrates the idea of a "private" legal realm in which people are empowered to order the legal relationships in their lives as they choose, fixing the terms on which they interact with others through private contractual agreement.[9] Freedom of contract is the central institution of political ordering as libertarianism conceives it, and "free contract" is to be shielded from diverse state intrusions such as anti-discrimination law, antitrust law, and consumer protection law. Such intrusions constitute impermissible public interferences with interactions whose terms should be specified solely by the parties to those interactions.

This libertarian celebration of "private" legal relations beyond the reach of public scrutiny is rich enough to serve as a rallying cry for a theory. But the libertarian idea of "private law" is radically different from the idea that marches under the banner of tort as "private law." For one thing, the libertarian idea of a realm of private freedom is identified with contract and property, not with tort. Among the three major fields of private law, tort stands out as the domain of collectively imposed obligations. The duties imposed by the law of torts are fixed by law and independent of the will of the parties. For libertarians, free contract—not tort—is the institutional embodiment of a private realm of freedom. Libertarianism asserts that individual freedom is most fully realized when people determine the terms of their own legal relations though actual agreements. Tort should govern

---

[8] Reva Siegel's summary of the legal status of agreements between spouses illustrates the relevant sense of "private" as denoting a realm beyond law's jurisdiction. "Married couples may collaborate, bargain, and bicker over household affairs, but any agreements they arrive at are paradigmatically 'private'—not formalized at law or subject to judicial oversight. Spouses do not look to the courts to interpret or enforce such agreements, and if they did, no aid would be forthcoming." Reva B. Siegel, The Modernization of Marital Status Law: Adjudicating Wives' Rights to Earnings 1860–1930, 82 Geo. L.J. 2127, 2209 (1994).

[9] Robert Nozick, Anarchy, State, and Utopia (Basic, 1974) is the preeminent philosophical exposition of this position.

only when neither contract nor property can take hold of a problem—only when parties who are legal strangers to one another collide in a harmful way.[10] The contemporary champions of "private law," though, are philosophical critics of libertarianism, not allies. Ripstein and Weinrib would almost surely agree with Rawls' pointed remark that "[i]f the so-called private sphere is a space alleged to be exempt from justice, then there is no such thing."[11] Indeed, Ripstein is the preeminent contemporary defender of Kant's view that people can be *coerced* out of the state of nature and compelled to join civil society in the name of equal freedom.[12] Kant's belief that civic freedom must be equal freedom—and that equal freedom can be established only through the creation of a state—is celebrated by Ripstein and repudiated by libertarianism. Freedom, for libertarians, is realized through agreements that are actual and individual, not through agreements that are hypothetical and collective.

A. "Private Law" as Form—And Substance

Perhaps the best way to understand the "idea of private law" championed by Weinrib and Ripstein is to begin with the public law understanding of tort that it challenges. In his early and now classic paper on negligence, Richard Posner presents the private law of torts as public law in disguise. By this he means that the law of torts is public regulation of safety through private means. "We are," he writes, "apt to think of regulation as the action of executive and administrative agencies. But the creation of private rights of action can also be a means of regulation. The rules are made by the judges aided by the parties."[13] For Posner, tort lawsuits are a way of pursuing the socially optimal level of safety. Accidents among strangers are economic externalities. The invisible hand of the market will not work to ensure that accidental injury is inflicted only when the costs of

---

[10] See, *e.g.*, Robert Nozick, Prohibition, Compensation, and Risk, in Nozick, Anarchy, State, and Utopia 54–87 (Basic, 1974); Richard A. Epstein, A Theory of Strict Liability, 2 J. Legal Stud. 151 (1973). Both Nozick and Epstein support strict liability for accidents among strangers because people's natural rights require that they not be made worse off through harms arising out of risks imposed by others unless they have consented to the imposition of the underlying risks. When contract cannot take hold of a problem, however, it is preferable to turn to tort because tort is a form of collectively imposed regulation. See, *e.g.*, Epstein, The Unintended Revolution in Product Liability Law, 10 Cardozo L. Rev. 2193. (1988). Insofar as property is usually acquired through some form of transfer, it has a closer connection to acts of individual will than tort does.

[11] John Rawls, Justice as Fairness: A Restatement 166 (Harvard, 2001).

[12] Arthur Ripstein, Force and Freedom: Kant's Legal and Political Philosophy (Harvard, 2009). See also the criticism and rejection of libertarian accounts of private law in Ripstein 2016, *supra* note 2, at 288–89.

[13] Richard A. Posner, A Theory of Negligence, 1 J. Legal Stud. 29, 31 (1972). See also *id.*, at 73 ("the set of negligence rules constituted not an ambiguous moral imperative but a comprehensive code of safety regulation.").

preventing the accident in question exceed the costs of bearing the injuries that the accident inflicts. Some state intervention is required. Negligence law is well-suited to the task because, economically conceived, negligence consists of failing to take cost-justified precautions against risks of accidental harm. The nominally private form of the normal tort lawsuit is an appropriate procedural mechanism for enforcing the efficient level of safety because tort plaintiffs are private attorneys general in substance if not in name. They seek damage judgments in their own names, but they succeed only when the losses for which they seek redress are the consequence of failures to take cost-justified precautions. Tort lawsuits thus enlist private parties in the production of the cost-justified level of safety, and that level of safety serves the general good.

Contemporary champions of "the idea of private law" have rallied around the phrase in part as a retort to Posner's economic conception of torts as essentially an instrument of public law objectives. That conception dispenses entirely with the idea that tort lawsuits do justice between the parties by redressing a wrong that one of them has done to the other. The "idea of private law" turns toward form to remind us that the private form of the tort lawsuit does not match the public substance that Posner cites as the form's raison d'être. The form of the normal tort lawsuit suggests that such suits are about justice between persons—that they vindicate the rights of plaintiffs and defendants against each other. The economic approach rejects this idea in part because it rejects the larger idea that persons are, as Rawls puts it, "self-originating sources" of moral and legal claims. For economic analysis, welfare is the only thing of intrinsic value, and the role of tort law is to promote states of the world with as much welfare as possible. Persons are merely places where welfare alights. Theories that march under the banner of "private law" reject the regulatory, market-mimicking, account of the law of torts offered by law and economics and find in the form of the normal tort lawsuit a substantive morality of right and responsibility. "Private law" names the form of justice that governs the relations between parties to a bilateral wrong.

The law of torts is fertile ground for this alternative conception. For one thing, tort plaintiffs claim in their own names for harms wrongly inflicted upon them by the parties against whom they proceed. For another, tort law is preoccupied with physical harm to persons (and their property). Physical harm acquires its special moral significance not from any distinctive role it plays in a calculus of social welfare, but because physical impairment deprives persons of normal powers through which they form and exert their wills. In a particularly fundamental way, damage to our physical capacities impairs our ability to lead our lives and pursue our purposes as we see fit.[14] Physical harm is especially bad *for persons* concerned with pursuing their ends as independent agents working their

---

[14] Chapter Two, *supra*, pp. 62–66; Chapter Five, *infra*, pp. 193–198.

wills on the world. And what is true of tort's attention to physical harm looks to be true of tort more generally. It is concerned with relations among persons. Tort articulates and vindicates rights persons have that others not interfere with them in various ways, and it does so by placing people under reciprocal responsibilities to respect those rights.

The theory of tort as "private law" gives the general idea that tort is a law of right and responsibility a very distinct twist by placing the form of the field at the center of its conception. Ernest Weinrib's development of his normative position begins with the structure of a traditional tort law-suit, and moves backward to articulate a system of rights to one's person and property. The bilateral form of the traditional tort lawsuit mirrors the timeless metaphysics of human agency. It is an inescapable feature of our world that, sometimes, one person's doing is another person's suffering. In the crowded conditions under which we live, some people's sharp elbows are bound to collide with other people's ribs. Private law is the legal institution that responds to this "unity of doing and suffering" the same wrong.[15] Its bilateral form institutes bilateral principles of responsibility. Ripstein, too, assigns fundamental importance to bilaterality insofar as he asserts that "the unity of right and remedy is the key to understanding tort law."[16] That unity is realized in and through the normal tort lawsuit, which requires those who commit tortious wrongs to make reparation to those they have wronged. Remedies replace and restore rights when rights are violated. The unity of right and remedy is severed when tort law is displaced by administrative schemes such as workers' compensation or the New Zealand accident scheme.[17] These administrative schemes combine direct regulation of risk with social insurance.

Ripstein's starting point, however, is not the form of the traditional tort lawsuit but an abstract principle of Kantian legal philosophy. He begins with "the moral idea that no person is in charge of another" and develops that idea so that

---

[15] Weinrib 1995, *supra* note 1, at 72–75; Martin Stone, The Significance of Doing and Suffering, in Philosophy and the Law of Torts 131 (Gerald J. Postema ed., Cambridge, 2001). The idea is that the unity of doing and suffering of the same wrong lies at the heart of the Aristotelian idea of corrective justice. See Danielle S. Allen, The World of Prometheus: The Politics of Punishing in Democratic Athens 287–88 (Princeton, 2000).

[16] Ripstein 2016, *supra* note 2, at ix.

[17] The scheme was established in 1972 by Accident Compensation Act 1972 and subsequently refined and adjusted by successor statutes: the Accident Compensation Act 1982, Accident Rehabilitation Compensation and Insurance Act 1992, Accident Insurance Act 1998, and Injury Prevention, Rehabilitation, and Compensation Act 2001 (later renamed the Accident Compensation Act 2001). The most significant feature of the scheme was that it abolished "the right to bring a civil action in tort for damages" when a person suffered "injury by accident" and replaced that right with an entitlement to specified benefits (e.g., medical and rehabilitative expenses, compensation for a percentage of lost earnings, a capped lump-sum payment for non-economic losses) without requiring any proof of fault on the part of someone else for inflicting the accidental injury. The scheme has been revised several times, but its core has endured: victims of personal injury by accident receive entitlements under the scheme and cannot recover compensation from wrongdoers through the civil law. Regulation becomes the primary legal instrument for promoting safety.

it "generate[s] distinctions between the different types of private wrongs, each of which, except for defamation is organized in terms of the use of means."[18] This sequence sounds like an attempt to impose a normative theory on a preexisting and freestanding body of law, but that is not what Ripstein intends. "Rather than importing content from some more general moral or economic theory," Ripstein argues "that the rights enforced by tort law are specific to the form of interaction appropriate to free beings."[19] Tort law "is a system that not only protects but establishes each person's entitlement to use their bodies and property as they see fit," consistent with the equal right of others to do the same.[20] This theory's movement from abstract to concrete mirrors in thought what the law does in time—namely, work its way from general moral principles, which are articulable even in a state of nature, to positive legal rights, which can exist only in civil society and which can be specified only by legal institutions.[21]

Ripstein's theory thus purports to work its way from a single spare moral premise through to the concrete wrongs recognized by the law of torts. It supplements the principle that "no person is in charge of another"[22] with the "simple idea" that "human beings are active beings who are entitled to set and pursue their own purposes, restricted only by the like entitlement of others to do the same."[23] These abstractions make the particular wrongs recognized by the law of torts intelligible, coherent, and justifiable. Importantly, Ripstein tells us that he means for "means" to be understood in a particular way:

> Your means are just those things about which you are entitled to decide the ends for which they will be used. The means that you have, then, are whatever it is that you are entitled to use for setting and pursuing purposes. . . . The means that you have, in the first instance, are just your body—your ability to decide what to do and to manipulate objects in space—and your property, that is, the things outside of your body that you are entitled to use for pursuing purposes.
>
> [T]he law of torts focuses on means in three interrelated ways. First, it protects the means that each person has for setting and pursuing purposes. Second, it restricts the means that each person can use by precluding one

---

[18] Ripstein 2016, *supra* note 2, at 6.
[19] *Id.*, at 8.
[20] *Id.*, at 7–8.
[21] *Id.*, at xii, 4, 13–14, 263, 289.
[22] *Id.*, at 6.
[23] *Id.*, at 8. Further ideas are that "the rights to which this norm of interaction gives rise survive their own violation" and that "no person ever needs to clear his or her own name." *Id.* This political morality is taken directly from Kant, as Ripstein understands him. Compare Ripstein 2009, *supra* note 12, at 33 ("a system of equal freedom is one in which each person is free to use his or her own powers, individually or cooperatively, to set his or her own purposes, and no one is allowed to compel others to use their powers in a way designed to advance or accommodate any other person's purposes.").

person from using means that belong to another without that other's authorization. Third, it restricts the ways in which each person can use his or her own means, to those ways that are consistent with everyone else being able to do the same. The first and third come together in prohibiting interfering with another's means by using yours in dangerous or defective ways; the second generates the prohibitions on trespasses against persons and property.[24]

"Private law" is thus an idea incarnated in an institution. This idea helps to define appropriate terms of interaction for equal, independent persons engaged in pursuing their purposes as members of civil society. The private law of torts specifies what it is that persons owe to one another in the way of coercive obligations of noninterference when everyone is in charge of themselves and no one is in charge of anyone else.

B. Interpretive and Philosophical Challenges

Ripstein's theory of tort as "private law" has both philosophical and interpretive ambitions. Its principal interpretive ambition is to make the law of torts "intelligible"—"to show how the characteristic modes of reasoning, the questions asked, and the inferences permitted or refused fit into an integrated pattern."[25] Its principal philosophical ambition is to spell out the consequences of deeply Kantian ideas for an all too often overlooked but important domain of basic justice.[26] With respect to the account's interpretive ambitions, two questions loom large. One is whether our modern law of torts can really be made sense of as "private law," in gross and in fine. In gross, the claim that tort is "private law" must grapple with the fact that the law of torts in its modern guise is intimately entangled with bodies of law that Ripstein classifies as "public"—with regulatory and administrative schemes—and often displaced by those schemes. Negligence judgments of due care, for example, often track statutory specifications of rights and responsibilities—as they do in the case of the rules of the road. Common law tort liability is sometimes preempted by the prescriptions of statutes and regulations, as is increasingly common in the pharmaceutical context. Indeed, tort sometimes cedes an entire domain of social life—such as workplace accidents or vaccination-related harms—to an administrative scheme. In New Zealand, the bulk of tort law is displaced by a mix of social insurance and direct risk regulation. In all these circumstances, the private law of torts either incorporates or

---

[24] Ripstein 2016, *supra* note 2, at 9.
[25] *Id.*, at xi. See also 19–23.
[26] *Id.*, at 289–92. See also Samuel Scheffler, Distributive Justice, The Basic Structure and the Place of Private Law, 35 Oxford J. Legal Stud. 213 (2015).

yields to bodies of public law. This interweaving of the private law of torts with bodies of public law poses a serious challenge to the claim that tort as we know it is distinctively "private law." On its face, the private law of torts as we know it appears to be one member of a family of institutions. The core of modern tort law is accidental physical harm, and tort shares responsibility for addressing such harm with other institutions. The boundaries that divide these institutions are not hard and fast, but soft and permeable.

In fine, the question raised by Ripstein's theory is whether it can account adequately even for the law of torts proper—for the forms of liability for accidental harm that dominate modern tort law and the diverse intentional torts that still figure prominently in our accident-centric tort law. Here, the fact that Ripstein renounces any appeal to persons' ends or interests is particularly significant. In explaining private law, Ripstein tells us that "[t]he restrictions governing [the interactions of free] beings focus on the ways in which they pursue their purposes, rather than on the content of those purposes."[27] There is, however, good reason to believe that we cannot understand and apply basic torts such as battery, negligence, and nuisance without introducing ideas of interest and urgency. When we do so, we are attending to the uses that people make of their freedom. Our tort law is commonly conceived of as protecting personal interests important enough to warrant mandatory legal recognition and protection.[28] Our interest in the physical and psychological integrity of our persons is one such interest; interests in privacy and reputation are others; interests in dominion over, and use of, our real and moveable property are yet others. In some of these areas, the word "interest" may just be a placeholder which poses no problems for Ripstein's account. In other cases, however, the law of torts may be anchored by judgments about the value and importance of various conditions for the exercise of independent agency, or about the importance of various ends, or about the role that diverse activities play in our lives, generically speaking. These are the very sorts of judgments that Ripstein regards as impermissible.

---

[27] Ripstein 2016, *supra* note 2, at 8.

[28] Francis Bohlen, for instance, thought it best to begin restating the law of torts "from the standpoint of the rights violated." He therefore began his first draft of the First Restatement of Torts with a section on "Rights," and began that section with the sentence, "[a] right is an interest of personality, or property, or of economic or societary condition, which is recognized as of sufficient importance for the state to protect it by imposing upon those who do harm to, or interfere with, such interest, a liability to pay money damages in a common law action." Restatement (First) of Torts, P.D. No. 1, at 3, December 10, 1923 (Francis H. Bohlen, Reporter). The Restatement (Second) of Torts § 7 (1965) adopts Bohlen's formulation ("[i]nsofar as an interest ... is protected against any form of invasion, the interest becomes the subject matter of a 'right' that either all the world or certain persons or classes of its inhabitants shall refrain from the conduct against which the interest is protected, or shall do such things as are required for its protection"). See also Restatement (Second) of Torts § 1 (1965) (defining "interest" and especially comment d, explaining the relation between interests and rights).

The tort of trespass illustrates the circumstance in which talk of an interest does not usually demand an inquiry into the purposes for which property is being used.[29] The "interest" in "dominion" just is an "interest" in "being in charge" of one's property. Trespass is entry without permission, full stop. Normally, no inquiry into how the owner of a piece of property is using their land is required to determine if the defendant entered it without permission. All that is required is an inquiry into whether the defendant acted voluntarily and intentionally entered the plaintiff's property without permission.[30] By contrast, the tort of nuisance illustrates the circumstance in which talk of an interest does call for inquiry into the purposes to which the parties are putting their property. A nuisance is a substantial and unreasonable interference with someone's use and enjoyment of their property.[31] Deciding if an interference is or is not unreasonable usually requires investigating the interests that people are pursuing through the uses that they are making of their property and evaluating the justifiability of those uses. If Ernie likes to read in his backyard next door to Arthur's house, and Arthur likes to blast AC/DC as loudly as possible through his home's open windows, whether Ernie can prevail against Arthur in a nuisance suit will have a great deal to do with whether Arthur's interest in blasting AC/DC as loudly as possible is compelling. To articulate the boundaries of landowners' equal freedom, we must inquire into the purposes that they are pursuing when they put their property to particular uses—and the importance of their doing so.

Philosophically, Ripstein's view defies familiar pigeonholes. On the one hand, he rejects the libertarian ideal of a realm of private ordering beyond the reach of public justice. Tort is, for Ripstein, an important part of public justice. In the Rawlsian terms that he explicitly embraces, tort law is a part of the basic structure of society—but with a caveat.[32] The caveat is that tort answers to principles of justice different from Rawls' first (equal basic liberties) and second (fair equality of opportunity and the difference principle) principles of justice for the basic structure of society.[33] Private law governs the voluntary interactions of persons in civil society, whereas Rawls' principles of justice govern inescapable relations

---

[29] Significantly, though, some trespass cases do explicitly investigate the "interest" protected by the tort. For instance, when courts are trying to determine if some wrong is a trespass and or a nuisance, they often look to the interests protected by those torts—"exclusive possession" and "use and enjoyment," respectively. See *infra* note 68, and accompanying text.

[30] Restatement (Second) of Torts §§ 158, 329 (1965).

[31] O'Cain v. O'Cain, 473 S.E.2d 460, 466 (S.C. Ct. App., 1996).

[32] Ripstein 2016, *supra* note 2, at 290.

[33] The difference principle requires that inequalities in the basic structure of society be to the maximum advantage of the least advantaged representative person. As with all of Rawls' principles of justice, it applies to the operation of institutions, not to individual actions. So if we take the case of income inequality and imagine a society divided between a working and an entrepreneurial class, the difference principle requires that the higher incomes of the entrepreneurial class be more to the advantage of the less advantaged working class than any other distribution. Rawls 2001, *supra* note 11, at 61–66.

between citizens and the state. We are born into the encompassing institutional frameworks of existing states, not into states of nature. Joining or abstaining is not a choice that we are ever in a position to make. We can forgo participation in society only at extraordinary cost. If the terms of our participation are to be fair—and if our interactions are to be reasonably free—the basic structure of society must satisfy appropriate principles of justice.[34]

For Ripstein, tort must exist within a framework of "background justice" if it is to be just, but tort itself is a matter of "foreground justice." "[T]he idea of background justice presupposes what could be called 'foreground justice,' that is, the system in which cooperation is voluntary rather than mandatory, in which the purposes pursued are determined by individuals. . . [T]he foreground justice with which background justice contrasts supposes that individual citizens are in charge of themselves" and free to pursue the purposes they choose to pursue as long as they do so on terms consistent with everyone else's entitlement to do the same. Private law "regulates the relations and interactions among private individuals as they take responsibility for trying to realize their respective conceptions of the good."[35] Ripstein couples this thesis that private law governs the "foreground justice" of voluntary interactions among persons in civil society with the corollary claim that private law and private lawsuits address matters that are of concern only to the parties to the lawsuit at hand. "I will unashamedly maintain that the point of tort litigation is to resolve the specific dispute between the parties currently before the court, based entirely on what transpired between them."[36]

Ripstein's account of the relation of tort law to the basic structure of society and to distributive justice is a bit off the mark. Distributive justice and the principles of responsibility that govern civil wrongs have distinct, but complementary, domains.[37] Both have to do with rights, but they have different things to do with rights. Torts are, as Ripstein and others insist, wrongs, and wrongs are violations of rights.[38] Because it is concerned with wrongs, tort law is concerned with individual and collective accountability for respecting other people's rights. In their core applications, tort law's principles of fault and strict liability are principles of responsibility for avoiding and repairing harm wrongly done. People's rights to the physical integrity of their persons ground those principles, but the

---

[34] Ripstein writes that "[c]reating and sustaining a social world in which no person is in charge of another—in which interpersonal cooperation is voluntary—requires mandatory cooperation in providing the necessary institutions and resources to achieve these public purposes." *Id.*, at 290.

[35] Samuel Scheffler, Distributive Justice, the Basic Structure and the Place of Private Law, 35 Oxford J. Legal Stud. 213, 231 (2015).

[36] Ripstein 2016, *supra* note 2, at 23.

[37] As Erin Kelly has said about criminal justice. Erin I. Kelly, Desert and Fairness in Criminal Justice, 40 Phil. Topics 63 (2012).

[38] See, *e.g.*, John C.P. Goldberg & Benjamin C. Zipursky, Torts as Wrongs, 88 Tex. L. Rev. 917 (2010); Jules Coleman, Risks and Wrongs (Oxford, rev. ed., 2002).

principles govern conduct not distribution. Distributive justice is also concerned with rights, but its concern is with what rights people have. Whether or not we have a right to the physical integrity of our persons is a question of distributive justice. The two domains are thus complementary because the rights that people have as a matter of distributive justice are foundational for the responsibilities that others owe them. We have a right that others exercise reasonable care for our protection when they engage in risky conduct, because we have a right to the physical integrity of our persons, and that right grounds a general, default obligation of due care on the part of others. The two domains remain distinct because the questions of what rights people have—and what those rights require in the way of coercively enforceable reciprocal obligations of respect—are different questions.

The upshot of this is that tort law, done properly, is not, in a direct sense, an instrument of distributive justice. For example, it would be opportunistic and objectionable to use the difference principle to determine the size of damage awards in private lawsuits. The primary role of damage awards is to repair harm wrongly done. Realizing that end should be their basic, if not their only, concern. Converting damage awards in private lawsuits into instruments of society-wide distributive justice would both impair them as instruments of corrective justice and be a haphazard way of pursuing social justice. This, however, does not mean that the law of torts is not a part of basic justice. It is. Tort belongs with institutions and practices as fundamental and diverse as "the legal protection of freedom of thought and liberty of conscience, competitive markets, private property in the means of production, and the monogamous family."[39] Security against various forms of unacceptable interference by others is an essential institutional condition for people to be able to pursue their conceptions of the good as they see fit. Consequently, tort is part of the basic structure, with its own distinctive role and concerns.[40]

In a just society, the answers that tort law may permissibly give to those questions must be constrained by the principles of background justice. Tort law, in this respect, is like any other body of law. Within Rawls' theory, particular legal fields should be governed primarily by principles appropriate to their particular concerns, but these field-specific principles must respect the constraints

---

[39] John Rawls, A Theory of Justice 7 (Harvard, rev. ed., 1999).

[40] Samuel Scheffler, Distributive Justice, the Basic Structure and the Place of Private Law, 35 Oxford J. Legal Stud. 213 (2015); Samuel Freeman, Private Law and Rawls' Principles of Justice, in Liberalism and Distributive Justice 167–202 (Oxford, 2018). In my view, Freeman and Scheffler offer the most persuasive interpretations of the place of private law in Rawls' framework. My approach is generally consistent with theirs. The matter is a subject of dispute. See, *e.g.*, Anthony T. Kronman, Contract Law and Distributive Justice, 89 Yale L.J. 472 (1980); Liam B. Murphy, Institutions and the Demands of Justice, 27 Phil. & Pub. Aff. 251 (1998); Kevin A. Kordana & David H. Blankfein Tabachnick, Rawls and Contract Law, 73 Geo. Wash. L. Rev. 598 (2005); Kordana & Blankfein Tabachnick, The Rawlsian View of Private Ordering, 25 Soc. Phil. & Pol'y 288 (2008).

set by the demands of background justice. Ripstein's thesis that tort law must work "foreground justice" as he conceives it, mostly stands or falls on its own merits, but it does stand in uneasy relation to Rawlsian principles of background justice in several important ways. First, although Ripstein is correct to assert that the domain addressed by the law of torts is one in which people pursue purposes that they set for themselves, his claim that tort pertains to interactions that are "voluntary" is questionable. Many of the interactions governed by the law of torts are woven into the basic fabric of modern life; they are interactions that can be avoided only on pain of forgoing full participation in society. For most people, working, or driving, or using public transportation, or being exposed to the hazards of electrical power or natural gas transmission, or purchasing at least some mass-produced products are not voluntary activities in the strong sense that deciding to, say, take time off after passing the bar to go trekking in Nepal is voluntary. For the most part, the activities with which tort is concerned are the kind of nonoptional activities that are addressed by principles of basic justice.

Second, Ripstein's uncompromising insistence "that the point of tort litigation is to resolve the specific dispute between the parties currently before the court, based entirely on what transpired between them"[41] comes uncomfortably close to suggesting that the realm of private law is autonomous from larger social and political issues and exempt from governance by basic principles of justice. Even in civil society, the relations among persons are entangled with larger questions of justice and injustice. Gender discrimination, past and present, may infect damage awards in tort lawsuits, for example. Reliance on earnings tables to project what a plaintiff would have earned had the defendant not injured her may introduce and reproduce gender- and race-based earnings differentials. Those differentials reflect histories of injustice and discrimination.[42] To simply exclude this fact from consideration because social injustice is not something that "transpired between" the parties is to risk turning tort law into an instrument of systemic injustice.

Third, Ripstein distinguishes sharply between impermissibly interfering with someone else's use of their means by violating their rights, and "failing to provide that person with a favorable context in which to use those means."[43] The former is impermissible, whereas the latter is unobjectionable. This distinction is too crude; it overlooks the fact that private interactions can cumulate in systemic injustice. When tort law is treated as an autonomous realm of voluntary individual interaction, it is likely to prove vulnerable to "the tendency of individual transactions to erode the background conditions necessary for everyone to be a

---

[41] Ripstein 2016, *supra* note 2, at 23.
[42] See Ronen Avraham & Kimberly Yuracko, Torts and Discrimination, 78 Ohio St. L.J. 661 (2017).
[43] Ripstein 2016, *supra* note 2, at 94.

full participant in society."[44] In a social world in which most people need to work to secure a decent living, for example, a rule that permits employees to waive their right to a safe workplace may become a world in which they must waive that right as a condition of employment.

Fourth and last, it is unclear why we should regard the choice for tort—and against regulation or administration—as marking a radical division between a regime of right and responsibility on one hand, and regimes that simply secure people against diverse bad outcomes in the manner of insurance, on the other.[45] Our modern law of torts arose in response to the emergence of accidents as a social problem. The history and structure of the field suggests that the problem of accidental injury may be understood in two basic—but different—ways. One way is to understand accidental wrongs in terms of individual misconduct. The other is to understand accidents as a characteristic feature of activities in an industrial and technological world. The first understanding expresses itself in private law and, for the most part, in individual fault liability. The second understanding expresses itself in the more collective (or enterprise) forms of responsibility found in some tort doctrines and in important administrative alternatives to tort law. Both approaches are extant in our law of torts and in companion legal fields. To cleave the approaches apart by asserting that they occupy watertight independent domains is to tear the fabric of modern tort law in two. When we sever the domains in this way, instead of making the "characteristic modes of reasoning" extant in our law of torts "intelligible," we obscure the conceptions of responsibility at work in our law and the interconnections among them.

These assertions, of course, require arguments. To begin, we shall develop the claim that Ripstein's theory of tort as private law goes awry when it insists on doing without any account of the interests that the law of torts protects. Next, we shall take up the thesis that the architecture of modern tort law confounds the idea of "private law" in important ways. Last, we shall examine why the freedom and equality of persons in civil society may be secured against unjustified interference by a diversity of institutions, not just by "private law" as Ripstein conceives it.

II. Torts without Interests

Ripstein's claim that "[t]he restrictions governing [the interactions of free] beings focus on the ways in which they pursue their purposes, rather than on the content of those purposes"[46] is not only basic to his theory, but it also differentiates

---

[44] *Id.*, at 291 (citing to Rawls, Political Liberalism 267 (Columbia, 1993)).
[45] *Id.*, at 292–95 draws this contrast.
[46] *Id.*, at 8.

his view (and Weinrib's similar view) from the views of philosophers like Rawls and Scanlon, with whom Ripstein otherwise has much in common. In making this claim, Ripstein is asserting that tort law cannot and should not inquire into people's "interests." Negligence law, for example, should not ask whether one person's interest in imposing some risk is urgent enough to justify imperiling someone else's security. According to Ripstein, the law of negligence does not protect "an interest that can be characterized apart from your entitlement that you, rather than others, determine the purposes for which your means will be used."[47] Ripstein's claim contradicts both the *Restatement* view and deeply embedded ways of thinking about the subject.[48] When discussing the rights and duties recognized by tort law, we speak routinely about people's interests in the physical and psychological integrity of their persons, in not being defrauded, in not being subjected to severe emotional distress, and so on. Indeed, the link between rights and interests is often so tight that "[r]ights often take their names from the interests they protect."[49] The right to privacy, for example, takes its name from our interest in being free of unwelcome observation.

To be sure, rights are not simply reducible to interests. If they were, they would be superfluous. Legal rights, and the duties that they ground, are institutional instruments. They confer special protection on some interests. When we protect an interest with a right, we are asserting that the interest is important enough to warrant imposing coercively enforceable duties on other people.[50] In the case of tort law, the protection secured through the imposition of duties is protection against various forms of interference by others. The law of negligence, for example, protects our urgent interest in the physical integrity of our persons against harm at the hand of others by imposing duties of reasonable care upon them. When we justify rights by reference to interests, we are assuming, contra Ripstein, that these interests are antecedent to and independent of the legal rights and duties that they justify. Legal rights put flesh on the bones of the interests that they serve by specifying constraints on others, but the interests themselves can be described independent of the rights.

---

[47] *Id.*, at 83.
[48] See *supra* note 29, and accompanying text.
[49] T.M. Scanlon, Rights and Interests, in Arguments for a Better World, Essays in Honor of Amartya Sen 68, 75 (Kaushik Basu & Ravi Kanbur eds., Oxford, 2009). Tort law commonly links rights and interests in just this tight way. See, *e.g.*, Restatement (Second) of Torts § 652B cmt. a (1965) (explaining the privacy tort of "intrusion upon seclusion": "the form of invasion of privacy covered by this Section ... consists solely of an intentional interference with [a person's] interest in solicitude or seclusion.").
[50] Joseph Raz, The Morality of Freedom 166 (Oxford, 1986). See also H.L.A. Hart, Natural Rights: Bentham and John Stuart Mill, in Essays on Bentham: Jurisprudence and Political Theory 79 (1982) (arguing that a claim of moral right is a claim that some interest is important enough to warrant legal protection); John Stuart Mill, On the Connection between Justice and Utility, in Utilitarianism 41 (Hackett, 1979) (1861).

The flip side of the coin that interests are partially independent of the rights that protect them is that rights are also partially independent of the interests from which they spring.[51] Once we protect an interest with a right, we give the right a significant degree of autonomy from the interest. If there were no daylight between rights and the interests that they serve, it would be, at best, superfluous to talk about rights. We would be thinking and speaking more clearly if we spoke only in terms of underlying interests. The property right of exclusive control, for example, may be justified by reference to the way that ownership of property enables people to exercise their agency, pursue valuable projects, and cooperate with others in ways that they could not if they were unable to exercise secure control over external objects. In a particular case, however, a landowner may exercise their right of exclusive control in a way that does not serve a worthy interest. Suppose that, in cold winter weather, one neighbor trespasses across another's snow-covered property to shorten their walk to the nearest grocery store. The trespass does no damage to the property, and does not interfere with the owner's use of their land in any significant way. Even so, the entry falls within the core of the right of exclusive control, and the landowner whose property is crossed may forbid the trespass simply because they have the authority to do so. On an interest view of rights, then, three conditions obtain:

(1) a claim of moral right asserts that some interest is important enough to warrant legal protection;
(2) legal recognition of a right imposes constraints on others in service of that interest; and
(3) the protection that legal rights confer on interests creates some gap between the interest and the right.

We should not, however, make *too much* of the gap between legal rights and the interests that they serve. Interests are independent of rights in the sense that they are antecedent to the rights that confer legal protection upon them and are the reasons for recognizing the rights. Legal rights are independent of interests in that they specify constraints on others and confer correlative powers and protections on those who hold the rights. Normally, we can apply the right without inquiring into the interest that it protects. The tort of trespass, for instance, protects the interest in dominion over real property by prescribing that others may not enter onto property without the owner's permission. The requirement of consent is a constraint that can normally be applied without invoking the interests. Less happily, in some cases the constraints imposed by rights may be used to further

---

[51] See generally, Scanlon 2009, *supra* note 49.

ends that do not further worthy interests.[52] In most cases, however, the relation of rights and interests is more harmonious. Normally, when we apply rights without appealing to the interests that justify them, the rights do, in fact, serve the underlying interests. In hard cases—novel, borderline, or otherwise difficult cases in which the proper application of the right is unclear—we appeal to the interests that justify the right and rely on the interest to articulate the right. When the implication of a right in some circumstance is unclear, the right should be articulated in the way that best serves the underlying interests. Unlike ladders and scaffolding, then, interests do not depart the scene once rights are constructed. They anchor the rights that they justify, providing the basis for their articulation and interpretation. When Jeremy Waldron argues that rights ground "waves of duty," he is implicitly appealing not only to the rights in question but also to the interests which ground those rights.[53] Those interests play a central role in determining the duties that the rights require for their realization.

Because rights are grounded in interests, the norms of tort law cannot be understood fully by attending only to the *form* of the relations among the parties to a tort lawsuit. We need to attend to the substance of people's interests as well. Tort law is preoccupied with the problem of physical harm, in part, because people have an urgent interest in avoiding it. Avoiding pure economic loss is less urgent. Physical harm impairs basic powers of human agency whereas pure economic loss does not.[54] Property damage is an intermediate case. Personal property rights put external objects under our dominion and will, and damage to property impairs the powers at our disposal. Tort law, therefore, has reason to sweep it within its conception of physical harm. In short, unlike pure economic loss, physical harm impairs basic powers of human agency. The fact that persons are physically embodied rational agents who effect their purposes through their bodies and minds, makes the integrity of their persons an essential interest. Indeed, Ripstein once spoke this way himself, opening a paper on self-defense with the declaration, "[t]he prohibition against murder protects a vital interest."[55] He now takes inquiries into interests to be impermissible. This commitment is central to

---

[52] *Cf.* Jeremy Waldron, A Right to Do Wrong, in Liberal Rights: Collected Papers 63 (Cambridge, 1993) ("It seems unavoidable that, if we take the idea of moral rights seriously, we have to countenance the possibility that an individual may have a moral right to do something that is, from the moral point of view, wrong.").

[53] Jeremy Waldron, Rights in Conflict, in Liberal Rights: Collected Papers 203 (Cambridge, 1993). For example, the right to the physical integrity of one's person generates a duty not to batter. When a battery has been committed, the right generates remedial duties of reparation on the part of the batterer, and duties on the part of courts to assist the victim in holding the batterer liable when the assistance of courts is properly summoned. For rights to do the work that Waldron is describing, they must be the kinds of rights Hart describes in Hart 1982. T.M. Scanlon has suggested to me that we think of this as "Mill's conception of rights without the appeal to utility."

[54] See Chapter Three, *infra*, pp. 144-50; and Chapter Five, *infra*, *passim*.

[55] Arthur Ripstein, Self-Defense and Equal Protection, 57 U. Pitt. L. Rev. 685, 685 (1996).

his anti-instrumentalism, to the anti-instrumentalism of the "private law" position, and to the claim that the canonical tortious wrong consists of impermissibly taking charge of someone else.

On occasion at least, Weinrib is more receptive to the thought that rights protect interests. In an important paper, he quotes approvingly Judge Cardozo's remark that "[n]egligence is not actionable unless it involves the invasion of a legally protected interest, the violation of a right."[56] But the concept of an interest does not play an important role in Weinrib's ensuing discussion of how rights and duties should be articulated casuistically. He simply observes that negligence law generally recognizes a right to the physical integrity of one's person, whereas it does not recognize a general right against the negligent infliction of emotional loss or emotional injury. But he is silent both on the fact that negligence law recognizes a significant number of exceptions to these general rules and on how it is that negligence law determines what counts as physical harm. Hard cases force courts to say what interest the physical integrity of the person protects, and exactly when that interest is invaded. Long before it results in impairment of its victims' powers of physical agency, exposure to asbestos manifests itself in physical changes that a pathologist would count as an injury. Subclinical cellular changes are "physical injuries" to pathologists.[57] The law of torts, though, requires "functional impairment due to asbestos exposure . . . In other words, the mere presence of asbestos fibers, pleural thickening or pleural plaques in the lung unaccompanied by an objectively verifiable functional impairment is not enough."[58] For the law of torts, physical injury is clinically discernible physical detriment. The right to the physical integrity of our person is grounded in, and governed by, our interest in having intact powers of agency. The law of torts has good reasons to regard the physical integrity as an especially urgent interest, and those reasons guide its judgments of what does and does not count as physical harm.

Most economic losses and most episodes of emotional distress do not impair our agency in the way that physical harm does. Emotional distress and economic loss usually leave our powers of agency intact. But some economic losses and some emotional injuries *do* impair our agency in enduring and serious ways. When they do, the reasons we have for recognizing a right to the physical integrity of our persons call for recognizing exceptions to the general rules that we do not have a right not to suffer negligently inflicted economic losses or emotional

---

[56] Ernest Weinrib, The Disintegration of Duty, 38 Corrective Justice 50 (2012) (quoting Palsgraf v. Long Island Railroad Co., 162 N.E. 99, 99 [N.Y. 1928]).

[57] "As a pathologist, I define an 'injury' to be the alteration of structure and/or function of a cell, tissue, or organ. An 'injury' also would include physical or chemical damage to the body which may be detectable only on a microscopic or subclinical level." Owens-Illinois, Inc. v. Armstrong, 604 A. 2d 47, 54 (Md. 1992).

[58] In re Hawaii Federal Asbestos Cases, 734 F. Supp. 1563, 1567 (D. Haw. 1990).

harm. For example, a mother who witnesses the death of her child at the hands of a careless driver may never be the same.[59] Her trauma may leave her physically intact but psychologically shattered. Like physical integrity, psychological integrity is an essential condition of effective agency. Just as some forms of physical injury do not impair our powers of agency, so, too, some instances of pure emotional distress and some cases of pure economic loss do. Both the rules and the exceptions are justified by our interest in having intact powers of agency. In hard cases, reasons rooted in the interests that justify legal rights guide the application and articulation of the rights that they justify. Interests matter even after they come to be protected by legal rights.

A. Wrongly Taking Charge of Another

Ripstein, however, steers clear of appeals to interests. He argues that the principle that "everyone is in charge of themselves and no one is in charge of anyone else" justifies all of tort law. Some sovereignty-based strict liabilities certainly seem to vindicate the claim. The tort of trespass, in its core incarnations, seems to express the principle hand and glove. A trespass is the wrongful assertion of control over real property which is, in fact, legally subject to the will of someone else. It is an attempt to "take charge" of something that is not, in fact, properly subject to your powers of choice. So, too, the wrong of false imprisonment consists of exerting unauthorized control over the movement of someone else's body.[60] Some batteries instantiate Ripstein's thesis equally well.[61] A surgeon who, without the patient's consent, opportunistically removes a postmenopausal female patient's ovaries on the ground that doing so is in her best interest, is taking charge of someone else in just the way that Ripstein's principle forbids.[62] A surgeon who operates on someone's ear without their permission commits a battery, even if the surgery succeeds in curing a diseased condition.[63] These wrongs incarnate

---

[59] Dillon v. Legg, 441 P.2d 912 (Cal. 1968). See generally, Gregory C. Keating, When Is Emotional Distress Harm?, in Tort Law: Challenging Orthodoxy (Stephen G.A. Pitel et al. eds., Hart, 2013). The core circumstance in which an economic loss may count as a harmful impairment of agency may be the circumstance in which an economic expectancy has crystallized into a legal right.

[60] "In the case of false imprisonment, I treat you as subject to my choice; your legal right to freedom of movement is just your entitlement that others not be in charge of your body." Ripstein 2016, *supra* note 2, at 48.

[61] Ripstein writes: "[I]f I run my fingers through your hair without your authorization . . . I am using something of which you are in charge." *Id.*, at 46. Compare Ripstein 2009, *supra* note 12, at 15 ("The person who uses your body or a part of it for a purpose you have not authorized makes you dependent on his or her choice; your person, in the form of your body, is used to accomplish somebody else's purpose, and so your independence is violated. This is true even if that person does not harm you, and indeed, even if he benefits you.").

[62] Kennedy v. Parrot, 90 S.E.2d 754 (N.C. 1956).

[63] Mohr v. Williams, 104 N.W. 12 (Minn. 1905).

both the idea of specifying tortious conduct without inquiring into the use that the victim was making of their body or their land, and the idea of a wrong that consists of taking charge of someone else. But these wrongs are neither the only kind of tortious wrong, nor the most common kind. In many cases, the presence or absence of tortious conduct turns on whether the conduct invades an interest, not on whether it constitutes an unauthorized crossing of a boundary in a way which, ipso facto, "takes charge" of someone else. In many cases, tortuousness turns on whether an interest in privacy, or reputation, or peace of mind, or in enjoying one's contractual rights is wrongly impaired. The diversity of interests that the law of torts protects, moreover, confounds Ripstein's effort to wrestle all tortious wrongs into the Procrustean bed of his two types.

Even battery can require an overt inquiry into interests.[64] The tort of battery prohibits two kinds of unconsented-to contacts: harmful ones and "offensive" ones.[65] Sometimes, one person's touching of another constitutes a battery simply because it is unauthorized. We take it to be axiomatic that invasive medical procedures require permission. If we dug a bit deeper, we might conclude that we regard the matter this way because we share a reasonably clear understanding of just how important it is not to operate on competent adults without their consent. Tacitly, we are appealing to interests and making judgments of urgency. It is one thing to tap me on the shoulder without asking my permission to point out to me that I've dropped my pen on the floor of a restaurant. It is another thing entirely to pull out my appendix without my permission. I may not need it, and I may be no worse off without it, but that does not mean that someone else may take it if they are so inclined. In some other cases, however, whether conduct constitutes a battery requires an explicit inquiry into whether the contact is "offensive." Gently relying on the bodies of other passengers to stabilize yourself in a crowded New York City subway car where you cannot avoid the contact is not a battery; the uninvited physical contact and use are not offensive. Rubbing up against someone in a sexual way on the subway is a battery; unconsented *sexual* contact *is* offensive. Explaining the difference between these two contacts requires recognizing the role that sexuality plays in people's lives and why that role makes control over who touches you in a sexual way a matter of special importance. Our interest in exercising control over sexual contacts with our physical persons is far stronger than our interest in exercising control over *all* contacts. A judgment about our interests—about the special importance of control over sexually charged contact—is what makes a sexually charged touching on a subway a battery, whereas an intentional, nonsexual touching is not. The

---

[64] *Cf.* Scott Hershovitz, The Search for a Grand Unified Theory of Tort Law, 130 Harv. L. Rev. 942, 949–52 (2017). See also Andrea Sangiovanni, Rights and Interests in Ripstein's Kant, in Freedom and Force: Essays on Kant's Legal Philosophy 77–90 (Sari Kisilevsky & Martin J. Stone eds., Hart, 2017).
[65] Restatement (Second) of Torts § 13 (1965).

absence of authorization is common to both cases. The lesson here is plain: authorization is important to battery, but it is not *the* master key to the wrong.

What is true of battery is true more generally. "Peeping Tom" cases require us to distinguish the interests protected by the privacy tort of "intrusion upon seclusion" from the interest protected by trespass. When a Peeping Tom alters the door of someone's hotel room so that they may film the occupant of the room,[66] they commit the wrong of trespass against the owner of the room. By altering the keyhole, they "take charge" of the owner's property without the owner's permission. But they do not commit a trespass against the occupant of the room whom they observe. The wrong to the occupant of the room is "intrusion upon seclusion"—a violation of the occupant's interest in privacy. In a loose, popular sense, the Peeping Tom is using their victim's body for their own sexual enjoyment. That sense of using someone else for your own benefit and without their consent resonates with Ripstein's classification of intentional wrongs as wrongs that involve using other people's means without their permission. The wrong made tortious by "intrusion upon seclusion" though, is not the wrong of using someone else's body for purposes of sexual fantasy without their permission. If the very same Peeping Tom were to post a video of Erin Andrews strolling the sidelines of a football game fully clothed, it might well be that the point of doing so was to enable others to use her body for purposes of sexual fantasy. Even so, that use would not implicate the interest protected by the tort of intrusion upon seclusion. From the point of view of tort law, no wrong at all would be committed against Ms. Andrews.

The tort of "intrusion upon seclusion" protects the privacy interest in being free from unwelcome observation. In the presumed privacy of your hotel room, you may reasonably expect that others will not be observing you. When you stroll the sidelines of a football game as a sportscaster, you may not reasonably expect the same privacy. In the eyes of the law, the observation to which you are exposed is not objectionable. The distinctive nature of the interest that the tort of intrusion upon seclusion protects is obscured, not illuminated, if the tort is assimilated to the idea of wrongfully taking charge of someone else. So, too, it is odd and baffling to describe privacy as part of a person's "means" in the way that their property is. Privacy is a social condition, not an instrument. It receives the protection that it does from the law of torts not because invasions of privacy are wrongful interferences with people's means, or impermissible uses of other people's bodies. Privacy receives the protection that it does because our interest in being free of unwelcome observation is taken to be an urgent one. We regard

---

[66] Erin Andrews, the ESPN reporter, was the victim of this wrong. The wrongful conduct included posting the videos on the internet. See Adam Tamburin & Stacey Barchenger, Erin Andrews Awarded $55 Million in Civil Case over Nude Video, The Tennessean (Mar. 7, 2016). My discussion here follows Scott Hershovitz's use of this example in Hershovitz 2017, *supra* note 64, at 953.

access to spaces within which we are not subject to the scrutiny of others as an important good. *Some* privacy may well be a necessary condition of a certain kind of personhood. Or so Warren and Brandeis thought.[67]

In fact, even the tort which fits Ripstein's theory best—namely, trespass—rests on an interest. In *Amphitheaters, Inc. v. Portland Meadows*,[68] the Oregon Supreme Court decided that rays of light could constitute a nuisance but not a trespass. This ruling does not rest on implausible conclusion about the metaphysics of entry. Surely, I can enter your property by firing my laser ray gun across your land and burning a hole in the side of your house. Still, I do not commit trespass merely by casting light on your land, any more than I commit trespass by opening my window and letting the murmur of ordinary conversation waft onto your property. These entries do not impair your exclusive control over your property any more than the first rays of sunlight to touch your land in the morning do. In the right circumstances, however, casting light on your land can interfere with your reasonable use of your property. If you use your property as a drive-in outdoor movie theater, my shining of light upon it may interfere with your projection of movies. The interest in reasonable use protected by the tort of nuisance may be invaded, whereas interest in exclusive control protected by the tort of trespass is not. The trespass cases that fit Ripstein's account hand in glove are easy cases in which we can apply the right without recourse to the interest that grounds and justifies the right. When a hard case arises, the interest comes into play.

The reliance of tort law on judgments about persons' interests becomes even more pervasive when we turn to torts whose elements include harm in some form. Negligence liability for accidental harm is generally regarded as the heart of modern tort law, and it presents serious difficulties for Ripstein. Physical harm is an element of a negligence claim. The defendant must violate the plaintiff's legally protected interest in physical security by inflicting an injury that impairs the plaintiff's powers of physical agency. *Restatement* renderings of the elements of the wrong absorb general negligence claims into a broad conception of tortious wrongdoing as conduct which invades "legally protected interests"—or rights. The particular interest protected by the general tort of negligence is an interest in the physical integrity of one's person. To bring a negligence claim, a plaintiff must therefore prove physical harm caused by the carelessness of the defendant.[69] Negligently injuring someone violates a right; the right is grounded in an interest; and that interest is an interest in the physical integrity of one's person.

---

[67] Samuel D. Warren & Louis D. Brandeis, The Right to Privacy, 4 Harv. L. Rev. 193, 213 (1890).
[68] Amphitheaters, Inc. v. Portland Meadows, 198 P.2d 847, 851 (Or. 1948). The plaintiff alleged that light from the defendant's property impaired the plaintiff's use of its cinema screen.
[69] See, *e.g.*, Restatement (Second) of Torts § 7 (1965).

The precise interest at stake here is easy to mischaracterize. In one influential philosophical usage, a harm is a "violation of one of a person's interests, an injury to something in which he has a genuine stake."[70] So understood, an interest is an especially important aspect of individual well-being.[71] Harm takes diverse forms, both within and beyond the law of torts. Some of those forms may be aptly characterized as setbacks to important aspects of well-being. In the context of negligence, though, emphasizing well-being as the value implicated by harm can lead to misunderstanding. As understood by the law of torts, harm is not related so much to well-being as it is to agency. The *First Restatement of Torts* defined bodily harm as "any impairment of the physical condition of another's body or physical pain or illness."[72] The *Second Restatement* refined this conception: "Bodily harm" was defined as "any physical impairment of the condition of another's body" and "an impairment of the physical condition of another's body [exists] if the structure or function of any part of the other's body is altered."[73] The *Third Restatement* now defines "physical harm" as "the physical impairment of the human body ('bodily harm') or of real property or tangible personal property ... [such impairment] includes physical injury, illness, disease, impairment of bodily function, and death."[74] What these definitions track is the damaging of powers through which we exert our wills.

There is, then, an important connection between the conception of harm deployed in negligence law and Ripstein's overarching concerns. A social world where "everyone is in charge of themselves and no one is in charge of anyone else" is a world where an important condition of independent agency is satisfied. Harm, as conceived in negligence law, is also concerned with a condition of effective human agency. Broken bones, severed limbs, disabilities of sight and hearing, diseased organs, disfigured body parts, and persistent pain all compromise normal capacities through which we exert our wills. Harm so understood connects to autonomy as a value.[75] We are not fully in charge of ourselves when

---

[70] Joel Feinberg, Social Philosophy 26 (Pearson, 1973).
[71] Joel Feinberg, Wrongful Life and the Counterfactual Element in Harming, in Freedom and Fulfilment 3, 4 (Princeton, 1992); Raz 1986, *supra* note 50, at 166. For an adept deployment of this conception of "harm" and "interest" in a tort context, see Scott Hershovitz, Two Models of Tort (and Takings), 92 Va. L. Rev. 1147 (2006).
[72] Restatement (First) of Torts § 15 (1934).
[73] Restatement (Second) of Torts § 15 cmt. a (1965). Section 7 distinguishes "bodily harm" from "injury," with "injury" covering cases in which a "legally protected interest" is invaded but no harm is done. A harmless trespass would be an injury in this sense. *Id.*, at § 7.
[74] Restatement (Third) of Torts: Phys. & Emot. Harm § 4 (2010). The Third Restatement extends the idea of harm as an impaired condition to include the impairment of property. The philosophical conception of harm is concerned only with harm to persons. The question of how to account for the importance of property damage to tort is peripheral to the concerns of this paper. Offhand, the easiest way to make the extension would appear to be to draw upon the fact that we have rights in property. Those rights give rise to claims against others that they not damage our property, and make impairment of our property a harm to us.
[75] See Chapters One and Five" to "See Chapter One, *supra*, pp. 9-13; and Chapter Five, *infra*, p. 198.

we are seriously harmed, and we are, therefore, unable to act as independent agents. Even so, negligence liability does not fit well with Ripstein's account. Negligently harming someone is not a way of impermissibly taking charge of them in the way that making use of their property or their body without their permission is. The core of negligence as a wrong is not domination but disregard. In the law of torts, negligence is the failure to take precautions required by the right that others have to the physical (and, sometimes, the psychological) integrity of their persons.[76] If, at two in the morning, I whip my car around a corner too quickly to stop for a pedestrian who might be crossing the street, my conduct reflects insufficient appreciation of the fact that I might seriously injure and even kill someone. My disregard for the safety of someone who might be in my path is not an indirect and inept way of going about imposing my will on them. It is a failure to show sufficient respect for an important condition of their purposive agency—namely, their physical integrity. They have a legal right to their physical integrity, and it grounds a duty of care on my part (and on everyone else's part).

B. Damaging Means

To be sure, Ripstein has an account of negligent wrongs. That account begins by distinguishing between two kinds of torts. "[U]se-based wrongs" such as trespass and battery involve someone "using what is yours without your authorization"—someone taking charge of another's person or property without their permission. "[D]amage-based torts involve using [one's] own means in a way that is inconsistent with the [equal] entitlement of others to use theirs."[77] The two are linked by the fact that damaging someone else's means impairs their ability to pursue the purposes that they set for themselves.[78] Because people need intact bodies (and property) to pursue their ends, negligence law requires that each person "conduct himself or herself in a way that is consistent with other people's secure possession of their bodies and property."[79] The problem is that

---

[76] See, *e.g.*, Altman v. Aronson, 121 N.E. 505 (Mass. 1919) (distinguishing among ordinary negligence, gross negligence, and recklessness, in terms of the degree of disregard shown for the rights of others); Sinram v. Pennsylvania Railroad Co., 61 F.2d 767, 770 (1932) ("it is an element of imposed liability that the wrongdoer shall in some degree disregard the sufferer's interest"); W. Page Keeton et al., Prosser and Keeton on Torts 169–70 (West, 5th ed., 1984). Seana Shiffrin, The Moral Neglect of Negligence, in 3 Oxford Studies in Political Philosophy 197 (Steven Wall et al. eds., Oxford, 2017).

[77] Ripstein 2016, *supra* note 2, at 48. See also *id.*, at 123 ("Each is entitled to use his or her body in ways consistent with the continuing ability of others to use theirs.").

[78] *Id.*, at 103 ("The wrongfulness of injuring others through excessive risk is that it is using your means in ways that compromise the ability of others to use theirs.").

[79] *Id.*, at 83.

the equal right not to have one's means interfered with cannot be an absolute one. "Anything you might do with your means has some potential side effects. Your entitlement to use your means to set and pursue your own purposes cannot be limited by the mere potential effects of your doing so on the security and bodies of others."[80] *Some* risk of physically harming others is a byproduct of acting in what Lord Reid called the "crowded conditions of modern life."[81] Requiring people to refrain from activities that carry trivial or remote risks would effectively disable them from "using their means at all and so would be inconsistent with their independence."[82]

For Ripstein, the solution to this predicament is to base liability for damage-based wrongs on a principle of increased risk imposition. "The ordinary activities of careful people are just part of the context in which you have whatever it is that you have," whereas "[i]f you injure another by doing something that carries a greater than background risk of injury to the person or property of others, you are liable because you have wronged that person by interfering with what he or she already has."[83] The most immediate implication of this principle is that the two basic forms of liability for accidental harm—negligence and strict liability—are expressions of the same underlying wrong of injuring someone else through a harm which arises out of the imposition of an excessive risk. The imposition of excessive risk *is* fault in negligence law, and strict liability is a special form of fault liability. The canonical strict liability case of "*Rylands* [*v. Fletcher*] is a case of a wrong involving fault, as all damage-based torts must be."[84] The standard understanding of negligence is that it is a failure to exercise sufficient care for the protection of others from harm at your hands. Failing to exercise sufficient care for the protection of others against harm at your hands is legal fault. The standard understanding of strict liability is that it is liability *without fault*. For Ripstein, fault in negligence law is not a failure to exercise sufficient care, and strict liability is not liability without fault. In explaining the imposition of liability in *Rylands*, Ripstein writes:

> Landowners have the liberty to use their land in ways that will affect their neighbors, but only up to a point. If they exceed the rightful use of their means, they are answerable for the damage that ensues. The scope of the defendant's liberty is measured by *the increased likelihood of damage to others*, not by the ease or difficulty of moderating that danger.[85]

[80] *Id.*, at 49.
[81] *Id.*, at 103.
[82] *Id.*, at 103.
[83] *Id.*, at 102, 144–45.
[84] *Id.*, at 136.
[85] *Id.*, at 140 (emphasis mine).

The thought, apparently, is that the construction of a reservoir on one's own property is itself wrong because that reservoir exposes your neighbor's mine to excessive risk.

Because Ripstein's one principle of liability for damage-based wrongs does not rest liability on any failure to exercise due care, many American tort scholars might be inclined to call his principle a principle of strict liability. Ripstein calls it fault because he regards fault as a defect in conduct and treats the imposition of excessive risk as defective conduct. Whichever classification one chooses, the most salient feature of Ripstein's principle of increased risk is that, in an effort to avoid addressing the competing *interests* that people have in both imposing risks and avoiding harm, it awkwardly denies the existence of *any difference at all* between two principles of responsibility that are commonly understood to be defined by their differences from each other.

C. Assimilating Disregard to Domination

Ripstein's distinction between "use-based" and "damage-based" wrongs is a step in the direction of distinguishing domination from disregard. He touches on something important when he emphasizes the significance of increasing risk beyond the level that cannot be avoided in the crowded conditions of modern life. Freedom of action (liberty) and freedom from harm (security) do conflict in our social world. *Some* threat to the physical integrity of our persons from the ordinary activities of others is an unavoidable feature of social life. And his argument that the surface complexity of tort law conceals a simple skeleton consisting of just two kinds of wrongs—which themselves derive from only one value—is elegant and provocative. Still, the account misses the mark in important ways. Because he eschews all explicit talk of interests and claims that the value of independence is the only value at stake, Ripstein cannot really capture the distinction between domination and disregard. Negligence is *not* a matter of wrongly taking charge of someone else; it is failing to act in a way that shows sufficient respect for the security of someone else's person and property.

At times, Ripstein frames the basic question posed by negligence cases in terms of adequate regard for other' people's safety. He approvingly cites John Gardner's remark that the reasonable person test in negligence directs the finder of fact's attention to whether the defendant was "being careful enough in the light of the potential interference with the plaintiff's safety."[86] "Safety," however, is the kind of good that "can be characterized apart from your entitlement that you, rather than others, determine the purposes for which your means will be used."[87]

---

[86] Ripstein 2016, *supra* note 2, at 106, n.60.
[87] *Id.*, at 83.

A hurricane, or an earthquake, or a fire can imperil my safety, even though they are incapable of taking charge of my person or my property. Natural forces are just that—forces, not purposive beings that can subject others to their wills. Speaking about "safety" is therefore inconsistent with Ripstein's framework. Unsurprisingly, Ripstein usually shuns talks of safety and attempts to wedge negligence into the overarching category of impermissibly taking charge of someone else. Interests must be excluded from the analysis, and negligence must be explained entirely in terms of the relation between plaintiff and defendant. And that relation must be one of mutual independence.

It helps to take a step back. In general, relational theories take tort obligations to be concerned with what people owe to one another. Consequentialist theories, by contrast, take tort to be concerned with producing states of the world in which some value (e.g., wealth or welfare) is maximized. A natural and attractive way to explain the law of negligence is to say that it is concerned with what persons owe to each other in the way of precaution when they undertake risky actions. Negligence liability therefore lends itself to relational articulation. Ripstein's own account of relationality, however, is especially austere. It holds that tortious wrongs and rights can be understood only in relation to each other. A "plaintiff's right is to be identified, not with his or her interest, but with the constraint on the defendant's conduct."[88] Ripstein's framework allows him to explain negligence up to a point, but his refusal to recognize interests causes the account to fall silent at the very point where the rubber meets the road. Negligence, as Ripstein explains it, is a careless increase in the level of risk that people impose on one another. There is a baseline level of risk arising out of ordinary activities, carefully conducted. "The ordinary activities of careful people are just part of the context in which you have whatever it is that you have. . . . A departure from the ordinary risks that careful people impose on each other is negligence."[89] The most obvious way to interpret this identification of acceptable risk with ordinary risk is to identify due care with customary care. The care that people are required to exercise is the care that people in general usually do exercise.

A different idea is expressed by the standard of care that Baron Alderson endorses in *Blyth v. Birmingham*: "Negligence is the omission to do something which a reasonable man, guided upon those considerations which ordinarily regulate the conduct of human affairs, would do, or doing something which a prudent and reasonable man would not do."[90] Here, the care due is identified by reference to an idealization; it is the care that people *would exercise* if they were

---

[88] *Id.*, at 88.
[89] *Id.*, at 102. The increase must be understood not just relationally, but personally. "The question always concerns how careful the defendant was in relation to the plaintiff." *Id.*
[90] Blyth v. Birmingham, 11 Ex. Welsh. H. & G. 781, at 783 (1856) (quoted approvingly in Ripstein 2016, at 105).

to act reasonably. In fact, people do often act in unreasonably dangerous ways. Ripstein is well aware of that fact:

> A social world in which people regularly drove while impaired or blindfolded, discharged weapons in public places, and discarded explosives without any precautions, would not be acceptable just because everyone did those things. The law works with a very different idea of reasonable risk imposition: You are entitled to impose risks on others only to the extent that those are the inevitable concomitant of people using their means.[91]

Ripstein is no doubt right about the unacceptability of the social world he describes, but this tells us only that reasonable care cannot be identified with actual care, whatever that happens to be. So what is reasonable care, and how do we go about specifying it?

It might help to put several different standards of care on the table.[92] In the United States, the common law of negligence speaks mostly of reasonable care, full stop, though it sometimes says that custom or statutory prescription fixes just what it is that reasonable care requires. In the American law of risk-regulation more generally, distinctions are drawn between "safety," "feasibility," and "cost-justification" standards. These diverse standards differ in the amount of risk that they tolerate. The "safety" or "safe level" standard requires reducing risks to the point where a reasonable person would regard the remaining risks as insignificant. The "safety" standard tolerates only those risks that are the price of activity—the background risks of life that Ripstein thinks Cardozo is pointing to when he speaks of a "busy world." The "feasibility" standard tolerates significant risk when the price of reducing some risk to insignificance would be the elimination of the activity responsible for the risk, and the activity is one we are not prepared to forgo. The "cost-justified" level of precaution is the level where the costs of further precaution would exceed the benefits. Normally, though not always, the standard of cost-justification demands the least in the way of precaution, and the safety standard demands the most. The feasibility standard falls in between. Customary care occupies a different space. It defines due care by what some people do. Customary care is the care that some community of risk imposition takes.

It is hard to know where Ripstein's conception of reasonable care falls with respect to any of these standards. The assertion that people "are entitled to impose risks on others only to the extent that those are the inevitable concomitant of people using their means" sounds like the safety standard. By contrast,

---

[91] Ripstein 2016, *supra* note 2, at 103.
[92] See Chapter Five.

the assertion that a "departure from the ordinary risks that careful people impose on each other is negligence"[93] appears to identify reasonable care with customary care. Except, of course, for the fact that people may conduct themselves unreasonably as they do when they drive while blindfolded, set off explosives without taking any precautions, and discharge weapons in public. No matter how common it might be for people to conduct themselves in these ways, their conduct would never become reasonable. The immediate problem here is that Ripstein's account of reasonable care is vague. The deeper problem is that Ripstein's refusal to take interests into account makes it all but impossible to avoid being vague. We normally think that the probability and gravity of a risk, the strength of the reasons for imposing the risk, and the burden of avoiding it play fundamental roles in determining whether a risk may be imposed and how much care must be exercised if it is imposed. That, after all, is what the Hand Formula—understood as a maxim of ordinary morality and a useful rule of thumb—proposes.[94] We need to balance the burden to us of reducing some risk to others against the magnitude and probability of the harm that we risk inflicting on those others. The value of Hand's "formula" is not that it enables quantification and the avoidance of evaluative moral judgment, but that it focuses our attention on the factors that are central to the normative judgment that we must make. But from Ripstein's point of view, this inquiry is unacceptable; it violates his prohibition on the consideration of just how urgent the interests at stake are.

In eschewing all talk of interests, Ripstein breaks with negligence law as it actually exists. In our law of negligence, right and interest are not opposed but complementary. Rights are fairly represented as relational constraints on conduct, but they are constraints imposed in the name of urgent interests. Our law of negligence treats our interest in the physical integrity of our persons as urgent enough to ground a general duty of due care in others. By contrast, our law of negligence does not regard our interests in being free from emotional distress and economic loss as sufficient to justify imposing *general* duties to avoid their careless infliction.[95] The reasons that might justify this differential treatment are, no doubt, complex and debatable. We might think, for example, that no matter how urgent our interest in freedom from emotional distress is, providing general legal protection for that interest is infeasible. For present purposes, however, the

---

[93] Ripstein 2016, *supra* note 2, at 102.

[94] The Hand Formula is now the most common encapsulation of negligence in our law. See, *e.g.*, Restatement (Third) of Torts: Phys. & Emot. Harm § 3 (2010). "Negligence" lists "the foreseeable likelihood that [a] person's conduct will result in harm, the foreseeable severity of any harm that may ensue, and the burden of precautions to eliminate or reduce the risk of harm" as "[p]rimary factors to consider in ascertaining whether the person's conduct lacks reasonable care." See Chapter Four" to "See Chapter Four, *infra*, pp. 130-34."

[95] Compare Restatement (Third) of Torts: Phys. & Emot. Harm § 6 cmt. b (2010) ("Ordinarily, an actor whose conduct creates risks of physical harm to others has a duty to exercise reasonable care.") with § 47 cmt. a, stating the duty to take reasonable care to avoid inflicting emotional harm on others ("This section limits a negligent actor's liability for emotional harm to two situations.").

point is that our law of negligence does treat the interest in physical integrity as urgent enough to ground a general duty of reasonable care. Moreover, physical harm, as negligence law conceives it, is independent of rights recognized and constraints imposed by the law of negligence. A natural disaster, an illness, or one's own carelessness can all inflict the kind of physical impairment that counts as harm in negligence law. What negligence law attempts to do is to secure our interest in physical integrity against harm that has, as its source, the insufficiently careful conduct of others.

D. Balancing Security and Liberty

Ripstein rightly recognizes that the only way to achieve perfect security is by preventing people from engaging in activities that create any risk at all to others. Doing so would effectively disable people from "using their means at all and so would be inconsistent with their independence."[96] Conversely, unfettered freedom to do as we please would unacceptably jeopardize the ability of others to use their means as they see fit. We must, therefore, balance the competing claims of liberty and security particular to the case at hand. Negligence law does so by taking interests into account. Perverse purposes may be incapable of justifying any risk imposition at all whereas urgent ends may justify especially great risk impositions. Unsurprisingly, the normal activities of equal persons going about their daily lives fall between these two poles. Thus, we regard it as unacceptable for people to drive blindfolded because—whatever thrill-seeking interest so doing might serve—that interest is insufficiently important to justify imposing significant risk on other people. Conversely, we regard it as permissible for a driver to impose abnormally great risks on others when they are rushing a person who has just suffered a heart attack to a hospital emergency room. The interest that this risk imposition furthers is especially urgent. Unsurprisingly, normal activities fall between these extremes. They justify the imposition of roughly equal risks at the level that Ripstein has in mind when he speaks of the background level of risk created by the ordinary activities of careful people.[97]

---

[96] Ripstein 2016, *supra* note 2, at 103.
[97] See Restatement (Second) of Torts § 291 cmt. e (1965):
> The law attaches utility to general types or classes of acts as appropriate to the advancement of certain interests rather than to the purpose for which a particular act is done, except in the case in which the purpose itself is of such public utility as to justify an otherwise impermissible risk. Thus, the law regards the free use of the highway for travel as of sufficient utility to outweigh the risk of carefully conducted traffic, and does not ordinarily concern itself with the good, bad, or indifferent purpose of a particular journey. It may, however, permit a particular method of travel which is normally not permitted if it is necessary to protect some

Other examples of the operation of interests in negligence law may also be mustered. Negligence law holds children to a lesser, age-appropriate standard of care when they engage in age-appropriate activities. It does so, in part, because the interest that children have in engaging in age-appropriate activities is an important one. However, negligence law holds children to the same standard of care as adults when they engage in adult activities—when they, say, operate powerboats—in part because their interest in engaging in adult activities is weak.[98] Participation in age-appropriate activities plays an important role in the lives, the growth, and the development of children. Participation in adult activities does not. The doctrine of primary assumption of the risk provides yet another illustration.[99] In the context of various sports, that doctrine suspends the normal duty of reasonable care owed by participants to one another. Requiring reasonable care might impair the pursuit of the values that the sport seeks to realize. Making ski slopes "safe," for instance, might require eliminating icy, challenging conditions even from ostensibly expert ski runs. Doing so would deprive expert skiers of slopes difficult enough to challenge their skills. Implicit in the doctrine's decision to exempt diverse sporting activities from the ordinary duty of reasonable care is the judgment that the interest that participants have in realizing the distinctive goods pursued by those sports is strong enough to warrant bearing abnormally great risks.

Evaluations of the urgency of the interests at stake are thus a basic ingredient in judgments of negligence. Their central role is not hard to explain. Articulating the care owed in some context requires balancing the plaintiff's interest in avoiding physical harm against the defendant's interest in imposing risk.[100] In its attention to underlying interests, negligence law is of a piece with tort law more generally. Almost any tort can be described in terms of some interest that it protects—nuisance protects an interest in the use of property; trespass protects an interest in dominion over property; privacy torts protect our interest in

---

interest to which the law attaches a pre-eminent value, as where the legal rate of speed is exceeded in the pursuit of a felon or conveying a desperately wounded patient to a hospital.

[98] For the rule, see Restatement (Third) Torts: Phys. & Emot. Harm § 10 (2010). Charbonneau v. MacRury, 153 A. 457, 462 (N.H. 1931) explains the interest:

Unless [children] are to be denied the environment and association of their elders until they have acquired maturity, there must be a living relationship between them on terms which permit the child to act as a child in his stage of development.... For the law to hold children to the exercise of the care of adults "would be to shut its eyes, ostrich-like, to the facts of life and to burden unduly the child's growth to majority."

(quoting Harry Shulman, The Standard of Care Required of Children, 37 Yale L.J. 618, 618 (1928).

[99] See, e.g., Scott v. Pacific West Mountain Resort, 834 P.2d 6 (Wash. 1992).

[100] Because judgments of due care in negligence law involve balancing competing claims of liberty and security, negligence law may be more a matter of fairness than of right, even if the ground of the duty of due care is the right to the physical integrity of our persons. This is discussed in Chapter Four, infra, pp. 150–153.

freedom from unwelcome observation; defamation guards our interest in reputation; fraud secures our interest in not having our wills manipulated to our detriment through the provision of false information. In all of these cases, an interest underlies the right and governs the articulation and application of the tort. In all of these cases, the interest extends beyond the boundaries of tort. Our interest in not having our wills manipulated to our detriment through the provision of false information, for instance, is also protected by laws against false advertising.

E. Strict Liability

Ernest Weinrib shares Arthur Ripstein's conviction that our law of torts incarnates something approaching universal fault liability. For Weinrib, "fault" is a kind of golden mean between the extremes of no liability and strict liability. For Weinrib, fault liability's intermediate position simply falls out of his particular framing of the tripartite architecture of the possibilities. No liability allows the terms on which potential injurers and potential victims interact to be fixed unilaterally by the wills of potential injurers. No liability allows potential injurers to impose any risks that they choose to impose. Strict liability (as Weinrib understands it) errs in the opposite direction. Under strict liability, the claims of potential victims to security unilaterally fix the terms of interaction. Strict liability condemns any imposition of risk by potential injurers because it imposes liability on all risks that result in injury.[101] Fault liability then is the equilibrium which reconciles the wills of potential injurers and potential victims in a way that is properly mutual. No inquiry is necessary into the burdens that negligence and strict liability ask prospective injurers and victims to bear in various circumstances is necessary. We need not ponder how devastating the collapse of Rylands's reservoir was for Fletcher, nor consider whether the absence of mutuality of risk imposition between Rylands's reservoir and Fletcher's mine bore on the choice between negligence and strict liability. The antecedent fairness of the distribution of risk between Rylands and Fletcher is as irrelevant as the urgency of their respective interests in freedom of action and security.[102] Neither burdens to interests in liberty and security nor relational moral reasons (such as reciprocity or nonreciprocity of risk imposition) matter. The choice of the correct liability rule is settled by fault liability's formal position as a midpoint between no liability and absolute liability.

[101] This represents strict liability as a kind of absolute liability. I believe that this view is mistaken. "Damage-based" strict liabilities are better understood as conditional wrongs, where the wrong is "harming-without-repairing," not imposing any risk at all. See Chapter Six.
[102] Ripstein 2016, *supra* note 2, at 156–58.

Ripstein, for his part, asserts that all "[d]amage-based torts ... include a fault requirement: the defendant's act must not only damage the plaintiff's body or property; it must also be defective because it is the kind of thing that is excessively likely to interfere with the usability of the object of the right."[103] He denies that there is any such thing as strict liability for a damage-based wrong:

> [I]n damage-based torts, *fault is a defect in the defendant's conduct*, namely, acting in a way that is too dangerous with respect to the type of injury suffered. If you injure another by doing something that carries a greater than background risk of injury to the person or property of others, you are liable because you have wronged that person by interfering with what he or she already has.[104]

Ripstein also asserts that his account of tort law makes the law of torts as we know it "intelligible." It is, therefore, fair to test his account against extant examples of "damage-based" strict liability in American tort law. The problem is straightforward. Ripstein's assertion of sameness simply denies the law's assertion of difference.

Tort law's actual application of strict liability, however, shows that strict liability is not a form of fault liability but its opposite—liability *without* fault. Whereas negligence liability imposes responsibility for physically harming someone else *because the defendant should have taken care to avoid inflicting that harm*, harm-based strict liability imposes responsibility *on the ground that it was wrong to harm-without-repairing*. Distinctively, the harm that strict liability doctrines hold defendants responsible for repairing is not harm that they should have avoided inflicting by conducting themselves more carefully. The most prominent instances of this type of strict liability include the conditional privilege of private necessity; nuisance liability in its most distinctive modern form; strict liability for manufacturing defects; *respondeat superior* in its modern form; and strict liability for abnormally dangerous activities.[105] Liability in these cases is strict because it is imposed on primary conduct that is free of any defect. Liability for harm caused to others by engaging in an abnormally dangerous activity attaches, even if all possible care was exercised in conducting the activity.[106] Fault, as Ripstein says, is a defect in (primary) conduct. Proving defective primary conduct is not part of any harm-based strict liability. When we impose strict liability on the abnormally dangerous activity of blasting, we

---

[103] *Id.*, at 123.
[104] *Id.*, at 144 (emphasis mine).
[105] See Chapter Six, *infra*, pp. 247–60.
[106] Restatement (Second) of Torts § 519(1) (1965) ("One who carries on an abnormally dangerous activity is subject to liability ... although he has exercised the utmost care to prevent the harm."); Restatement (Third) of Torts: Phys. & Emot. Harm § 20 cmt. b (2010).

do not claim either that it was wrong for the defendant to have undertaken that dangerous activity or that the defendant should have conducted its activity more carefully. We hold that those who engage in abnormally dangerous activities are responsible for repairing harms to others that arise out of the aspects of their activities that make them abnormally dangerous, regardless of how much care they exercise. "[S]trict liability signifies liability without fault."[107] The name itself makes the point.

Ripstein, and Weinrib too, are not blind to the problem that our law of torts presents for them insofar as they embrace a kind of universal fault liability. In their work, they go to considerable trouble either to deny that forms of tort liability commonly conceived of as strict really are strict, or to expel those forms of liability from tort law proper. Weinrib, for example, acknowledges that nuisance liability, *respondeat superior* doctrine, and the conditional privilege of private necessity are all strict. But he dispatches all of these as special cases. Nuisance liability is an expression of property law conceptions—not tort ones. *Respondeat superior* is an expression of agency law conceptions—not tort ones. And conditional privilege is an expression of restitutionary conceptions—not tort ones.[108] Ripstein, for his part, takes a similar view of *respondeat superior* liability; he absorbs *Rylands* into nuisance liability—even though the leading opinions in the case are careful to point out that the accident cannot be squeezed into that pigeonhole—and he calls strict liability for nuisance and abnormally dangerous activities negligence by another name.[109]

These maneuvers to recast tort so that it is not riven by competing principles of fault and strict liability may "work" in a limited way. They reconstruct the law of torts so that it corresponds to the template prescribed by Ripstein's and Weinrib's normative conceptions of tort as "private law." They do so, however, by purifying the law of torts of those forms of "damage-based" liability that fail to square with a preexisting commitment to universal fault liability. Each of these purifications is individually problematic; cumulatively, they are untenable. The cost of purifying and recharacterizing tort law in this way is that Ripstein's and Weinrib's theories do not so much make our law of torts intelligible as reconfigure it so that it conforms to their own ideal conceptions of tort as "private law." A theory that makes our law of torts intelligible needs to elucidate strict liability instead of

---

[107] Restatement (Third) of Torts: Phys. & Emot. Harm 4 Scope Note (2010).
[108] Ernest J. Weinrib, The Idea of Private Law 171–203 (Oxford, rev. ed., 2012).
[109] Ripstein 2016, *supra* note 2, at 167. It is, I think, a mistake to classify *Rylands* as a nuisance case because building a reservoir on your own land is not itself a nuisance. When a reservoir collapses and floods a neighboring mine, what has transpired is an accident. A standing risk has exploded into harm. See Gregory C. Keating, Recovering Rylands: An Essay for Robert Rabin, 61 DePaul L. Rev. 543, 551–54, 558–62 (2012); Warren A. Seavey, Nuisance: Contributory Negligence and Other Mysteries, 65 Harv. L. Rev. 984, 986 (1952). English courts, however, have recently taken a revisionary view and classified it as a nuisance. Ripstein 2016, *supra* note 2, at 127–28. This misrepresents the decision in order to cabin it.

obliterating it, and to explain why it is that strict liability doctrines have a place in our law.

Negligence and strict liability leave the burdens of accidents that should not be avoided on different parties. Negligence leaves those burdens on victims; strict liability shifts them back on to injurers. It happens that we have good reasons to think that sometimes the burdens of accidents that should not be prevented ought to be borne by those responsible for the accidents, and sometimes those burdens should be allowed to lie on the victims on whom they fall. On one account, negligence liability is appropriate when the underlying risks are reciprocally imposed, and strict liability is appropriate when they are not.[110] Tracking reciprocity and nonreciprocity of risk imposition in this way fairly allocates the burdens of accidents that should not be avoided. On another, economically oriented, account we should impose strict liability when we want to induce potential injurers to take into account the level of risk at which they conduct their activities, not just the care with which they conduct each action—for example, the number of trains that a railroad company runs every day, not just how carefully it operates each train.[111] The existence of different, circumstance-based reasons that speak to who should bear losses that should not be prevented is one basic cause for the divided state of our law of "damage-based" torts between competing principles of fault and strict liability. A theory of tort law that simply excludes such reasons from consideration begs the questions it claims to answer.

III. The Permeability of Modern Tort to "Public Law"

Modern, accident-centric, tort law developed hand in hand with two other institutions—namely, direct risk regulation by statute or administrative edict, and administrative schemes such as workers' compensation. These schemes compensate victims of accidental harm upon a showing that their injury was suffered in the course of the activity to which the scheme applies. In New Zealand, these two institutional instruments displace the private law of torts almost entirely when it comes to accidental harm.[112] The orthodox view of these schemes takes

---

[110] George P. Fletcher, Fairness and Utility in Tort Theory, 85 Harv. L. Rev. 537 (1972).
[111] Steven Shavell, Strict Liability Versus Negligence, 9 J. Legal Stud. 1 (1980); Steven Shavell, The Mistaken Restriction of Strict Liability to Uncommon Activities, 10 J. Legal Analysis 1 (2018).
[112] "Almost" is an important qualifier here. Importantly, under the New Zealand scheme, "a victim is *not* precluded from bringing a civil tort action for damages with respect to injuries not covered by the scheme; therefore, a rule or court decision of no coverage opens the door to a possible claim for damages under the common law of torts." Richard S. Miller, An Analysis and Critique of the 1992 Changes to New Zealand's Accident Compensation Scheme, 52 Md. L. Rev. 1070, 1072 (1990). The fact that tort law steps up to address gaps in, and limits of, the New Zealand scheme nicely illustrates the point that administrative schemes are part of the same larger whole as the law of torts. Even the most extensive such scheme is a carveout from the law of torts.

them to be part of the same family of institutions as the private law of torts because they respond to the same pressing social problem, namely, the emergence of accidental harm as a basic feature of industrial and technological activities. Sometimes these institutions compete and sometimes they cooperate. Workers' compensation schemes, for instance, both displace the common law of torts and serve as a source of modern strict liabilities within tort law.[113] Theorists of tort as "private law," however, insist that direct risk regulation and administrative compensation schemes have nothing to do with the law of torts. Recall Ripstein's declaration on the first page of the Preface to *Private Wrongs*: "The central claim of this book will be that the unity of right and remedy is the key to understanding tort law."[114] That unity is severed by administrative schemes. Claimants recover from funds, not from the individual wrongdoers responsible for their harms.

The distinction that Ripstein draws between the "private law" of torts and the "public law" of administrative alternatives to it is pithy and correct, but the implication of radical discontinuity is misleading. In fact, severing the two seriously impedes an adequate understanding of tort law. It is impossible, for instance, to recount the history of assumption of the risk in American law without discussing workers' compensation. When it was imposed at the turn of the twentieth century, workers' compensation directly repudiated the principles of responsibility—namely, fault on the employer's side and assumed risk on the employee's—that the common law of torts brought to bear on workplace accidents. Strict liability replaced fault on the employer's side, and assumption of the risk on the employee's side was banished entirely.[115] Reduced damages were the gain on the employer's side of the ledger. By displacing tort law from the domain of workplace accidents, workers' compensation schemes deprived an important, well-articulated doctrine of its principal domain of application. After "assumption of the risk" was deprived of its principal domain of workplace application, it was eventually reconstructed as a less important—and dramatically different—doctrine centered on recreational activities.[116] Some risks are assumed in the context of some recreational activities because they

---

[113] Gregory Keating, The Theory of Enterprise Liability and Common Law Strict Liability, 54 Vand. L. Rev. 1285, 1303–17, 1323–29 (2001).

[114] Ripstein 2016, *supra* note 2, at ix.

[115] Jeremiah Smith, Sequel to Workmen's Compensation Acts, 27 Harv. L. Rev. 235, 344 (1914). See also Jeremiah Smith, Tort and Absolute Liability—Suggested Changes in Classification, 30 Harv. L. Rev. 241, 319, 409 (1917).

[116] Farwell v. Boston & Worcester Rail Road Corp., 45 Mass. 49 (1842) (Shaw, C.J.) and Lamson v. American Ax & Tool Co., 177 Mass 144 (1900) (Holmes, C.J.), illustrate the way in which the doctrine worked to deprive workers of their rights to safe workplaces in the nineteenth century. Scott v. Pacific West Mountain Resort, 834 P.2d 6 (Wash. 1992), is a representative modern application of the doctrine in a recreational context. For a judicial discussion of the nineteenth-century doctrine which characterizes the consent that it invokes as fictional and the result as a stripping of the right to a safe workplace, see Tiller v. Atlantic Coast Line Railroad Co., 318 U.S. 54 (1943) (Black, J.).

are essential to the enjoyment of those activities. The risks that were assumed in the nineteenth-century workplace, by contrast, were to be regretted, not welcomed. They were assumed by workers because employers insisted that workers bear them.

Workers' compensation did more than utterly upend the doctrine of assumption of risk. It also effected a seismic shift in the landscape of tort law more generally. Writing in 1914, Jeremiah Smith argued that, by repudiating the fault liability around which the common law of torts had been constructed in the latter half of the eighteenth century and embracing strict liability, the Workers' Compensation Acts made the law of accidents a house divided against itself. The Acts were therefore bound, in Smith's view, to initiate a revolution in the common law of torts.[117] Smith's predictions were eerily prescient. Just as he foretold, strict liabilities expanded within the common law of torts, and forms of fault liability were rebuilt in ways that narrowed the gap between strict and fault liability.[118] To this day, interpretations of the scope of employment under the doctrine of *respondeat superior* show the explicit influence of the enterprise conception of responsibility embodied in workers' compensation law.[119] In both cases, legal doctrines attempt to articulate the zone of harm for which *firms* are responsible. A non-fault conception of enterprise responsibility transcends the boundary between the "private law" of torts and a "public law" administrative scheme, and binds them through a common principle of responsibility.

It helps here to recall that our modern law of torts arose in the second half of the nineteenth century, when the writ system was cast aside and substantive law ceased to be subservient to the procedural pigeonholes of the forms of action. Once liberated, the law of torts underwent a profound transformation. It ceased to be a collection of discrete and heterogeneous wrongs sorted into separate boxes, and became a field ruled by general principles of responsibility. The tort law that emerged from this reconstruction was preoccupied with the accidental infliction of physical harm and dominated by the fault principle.[120] This reconfiguration of the field was so sweeping and successful that we tend to experience the architecture that it imposed more as fact than as construct. That architecture is part of our pre-theoretical sense of what tort law is. We assume that tort has a core of accidental wrongs governed by negligence liability. That core is flanked by the competing, but subordinate, principle of strict liability on one side, and by the still heterogeneous intentional torts on the other. The standard first-year torts class instantiates this configuration. After a few classes on selected intentional torts—assault, battery, and trespass, perhaps—the course

---

[117] Smith 1914, *supra* note 115; Smith 1917, *supra* note 115.
[118] Keating 2001, *supra* note 113, at 1292–1303.
[119] *Id.*, at 1323–29.
[120] Tom Grey, Accidental Torts, 54 Vand. L. Rev. 1225, 1260–75 (2001).

turns to accidental harms and to intense immersion in the structure of fault liability. Sections on strict, and perhaps product, liabilities follow. But accidents are where the action is.

This organization of the field is not, of course, pre-theoretic fact. It is a construct, and one that obscures as well as illuminates. Whatever its faults, this construct has the considerable virtue of placing two fundamental features of modern tort law front and center: it is preoccupied with accidental physical harm and dominated by a general principle of negligence liability. Modern tort law was born out of the emergence of accidental physical harm as a pressing *social* problem. It is "a body of law created when the industrial revolution and industrial accidents began to wreak havoc on the bodies of workers and passengers."[121] Oliver Wendell Holmes's famous aphorism that "[o]ur law of torts comes from the old days of isolated, ungeneralized wrongs, assaults, slanders, and the like," whereas "the torts with which our courts are kept busy today are mainly the incidents of certain well-known businesses . . . railroads, factories, and the like"[122] epitomizes the point. Premodern tort law was a law of nominate, mostly intentional, wrongs, whereas modern tort law is mostly a law of accidents that are recurring byproducts of basic activities in an industrial and technological society. The twin preoccupations that gave birth to modern tort law—with accidental wrongs instead of intentional ones, and with a social problem instead of with individual wrongs—had, and continue to have, large implications for torts as a legal field. Because the accidents with which it is preoccupied are characteristically associated with activities, responsibility for those accidents may be lodged *either* with individuals or with activities. Administrative schemes instantiate the activity alternative. For its part, our common law of torts contains both individual and enterprise forms of responsibility. These alternatives are competitive, but not wholly independent of one another.

The origins of our tort law help to explain why the contemporary revival of the idea that tort is "private law" goes too far. "Private law," as Ripstein and Weinrib articulate it, is insufficiently attentive to the way in which the modern law of torts is entangled with bodies of law that the theorists of "private law" count as public—with statutory and administrative risk regulation and with administrative compensation schemes. The relations among these diverse legal institutions are complex, but tort's location within a web of institutions is a basic fact about modern tort law. Negligence works hand in hand with statutes regulating risky

---

[121] Sarah A. Seo & John Fabian Witt, The Metaphysics of Mind and the Practical Science of Law, 26 Law & Hist. Rev. 161, 164 (2008) (Modern tort law is "a body of law created when the industrial revolution and industrial accidents began to wreak havoc on the bodies of workers and passengers."). See generally John Witt, The Accidental Republic (Harvard, 2006).

[122] Oliver Wendell Holmes, The Path of the Law, in Collected Legal Papers 167, 183 (1920) (originally delivered 1897).

activities; nuisance works hand in hand with zoning; product liability sometimes defers to, and sometimes does battle with, pharmaceutical regulation. The negligence and nuisance examples are particularly instructive. Proponents of tort as "private law" take the bipolar relation of the plaintiff and the defendant as the most important relationship in the law of torts. Primary obligations, however, are omnilateral, not bilateral. As far as negligence law is concerned, the standard modern rule is that everyone owes everyone else a duty of reasonable care.[123] The adjudicative practice of the common law of torts, though, is not well-suited to the task of prescribing comprehensive schemes of coordinate precaution. Tort turns to the traffic code to help determine the duties of care that people owe to one another as owners and operators of vehicles, and as drivers and pedestrians on roads, because it lacks the institutional competence to spell those duties out by itself. So, too, the law of nuisance is not well tailored to coordinating a diversity of incompatible uses of property across a neighborhood. The "private law" of torts needs to draw on the "public law" of traffic regulation and zoning to articulate primary rights and responsibilities.

More broadly, health and safety regulations are often needed because the law of torts is not up to the task of addressing some emerging forms of harm. It is, for example, perfectly intelligible to say that we need environmental law only because the private laws of tort and property are incomplete. If the private law of property could specify and institute entitlements to external objects completely and perfectly—and if the law of torts could specify and redress impermissible interferences with property and physical health with equal completeness—we would not need environmental law. As it happens, a phenomenon like pollution eludes the grasp of tort law. Pollution in its most characteristic form is a critical mass phenomenon, and it therefore presents tort law with intractable causal problems. Regulation must be brought to bear. New technologies, too, can burst the seams of existing law. The impending arrival of driverless cars may require a revision of our tort law as sweeping as the one brought about by the emergence of industrial accidents and the subsequent creation of workers' compensation schemes at the turn of the twentieth century.[124]

Overemphasizing tort law's "private law" status also obscures the fact that accidental harm is a basic and systemic feature of a technologically advanced

---

[123] "In this state, the general rule is that all persons have a duty to use ordinary care to prevent others from being injured as the result of their conduct." Randi W. v. Muroc Joint Unified Sch. Dist., 929 P.2d 582, 588 (Cal. 1997). See also California Civil Code § 1714(a) (West 2002) (enacted 1872) (prescribing that everyone owes to everyone else a duty of ordinary care); Restatement (Third) of Torts: Liability for Physical and Emotional Harm, *supra* note 71, § 7 (recognizing "a duty to exercise reasonable care" when conduct presents a risk of harm to others). On the omnilaterality of primary duties, see Chapter Two, supra, pp. 51–53.

[124] See Kenneth S. Abraham & Robert L. Rabin, Automated Vehicles and Manufacturer Responsibility for Accidents: A New Legal Regime for a New Era, 105 Va. L. Rev. 127 (2019)

society. The private law of torts is one—but only one—institutional instrument available to address this basic fact of our social life. How we respond to accidents is a matter of public concern. Accidental harm is a pervasive feature of our social life; it is the byproduct of basic productive activities. Because we have diverse institutional devices at our disposal, we have choices to make. Preferring the "private law" of torts to some combination of direct risk regulation and social insurance expresses a collective judgment about how to institute responsibility for avoiding and repairing harm in some sphere of social life. To choose one of these approaches over the other, is to choose to emphasize one set of relations among persons over others. Private law adjudication puts the relation of the parties as doer and sufferer of the same wrong at its center. Administrative regimes pick out diverse communities of risk and responsibility—workplaces, industries (e.g., nuclear power), activities (e.g., vaccination or driving)—as the locus of the important relations. Of course, when we choose among these diverse institutional instruments, our choice of instrument implicates value judgments as well as an interest in efficacy. Workers' compensation, for instance, differs from the common law of torts in several significant ways. For one thing, it makes workplace accidents more a matter of collective responsibility and less one of individual responsibility. Implicitly, workers' compensation asserts that the relations among participants in a particular enterprise are the relations that matter for determining rights and responsibilities. The private law of torts, by contrast, implicitly asserts that the relations that matter are the relations among individual wrongdoers and their victims. This is a disagreement over the relevant relations of responsibility.

Workers' compensation differs from the private law of torts not only in lodging responsibility at an enterprise level instead of an individual one, but also in trading powers of recourse for assured protection. Workers relinquish the private right to call their employers to account through civil lawsuits in exchange for greater assurance of recovery for harm suffered. The value implications of preferring private law to direct regulation of risk, or an administrative scheme to private law, are real and important. Even so, it makes sense to see tort and workers' compensation as alternatives on the same institutional menu, battling for dominion over the same legal domain. That is how our law characteristically sees them, as applications of "remedy clauses" in state constitutions to statutory reforms of common law tort doctrine show.[125] Private law is a central feature of the domain of our law that addresses responsibility for avoiding and repairing

---

[125] See, e.g., Horton v. Oregon Health and Science University, 373 P.3d 1158 (Or. 2016) (interpreting, inter alia, Oregon's constitutional requirement that every person has a right to "remedy by due course of law for injury done him in his person, property, or reputation"). See generally John C.P. Goldberg, The Constitutional Status of Tort Law: Due Process and the Right to a Law for the Redress of Wrongs, 115 Yale L.J. 524 (2005).

accidental physical harm, but it is not the whole of the field. And the law of torts itself is one member of a larger family of institutions. The choice between tort and workers' compensation should not be made simply by classifying one as private and the other as public—and then declaring an allegiance to private law. Doing so short-circuits the normative analysis that ought to precede any choice. The right question to ask and to answer is, "In the circumstances at hand, which institution is more appropriate, in light of the relations among those who impose risk and those on whom it is imposed?"

Stepping back even further from the various corners of the subject and turning our eyes toward the whole reminds us that it is a singular, and striking, feature of tort law that—alone among the major fields of law—it is vulnerable to near total eclipse. The tort law of accidents can be all but eliminated by direct risk regulation and "social insurance"—as it has been in New Zealand. We would think differently about the criminal law if we knew, through existing institutional proof, that it could be replaced entirely by a regime of therapeutic treatment. We would think differently about property if some modern legal system had reconfigured it as an institution composed only of use-rights, and differently about contract if it we had to grapple with an instance of it being wholly displaced by a scheme consisting only of unilaterally imposed private obligations. Yet modern tort law is vulnerable to just this sort of eclipse. Partial eclipse by regulatory preemption and by administrative schemes such as workers' compensation, no fault liability for vaccination-related injuries, occupational diseases such as black lung, and nuclear accidents is familiar and commonplace. Near total eclipse is New Zealand.

The vulnerability of our law of torts to such eclipse casts doubt on the thought that tort law is an autonomous realm of "private law," governed by its own *sui generis* internal principles. When it comes to grappling with accidental injury, tort is one institutional contender among several. Other, alternative institutions might—and do—take its place. Our institutions do not have to lodge responsibility for accidental harm primarily with individuals. They might lodge primary responsibility with activities, as both administrative schemes and forms of enterprise liability within tort law proper do. Lodging responsibility primarily with enterprises, not individuals, responds to the distinctive characteristic of modern risk as the byproduct of basic productive activities. The form of private law is not forced upon us as the only institution capable of constituting right relations among equal and independent persons.

Relatedly, the contemporary conception of tort as pure "private law" appears to underrate the extent to which modern tort law is an aspect of the "background justice" that governs interactions which can be avoided only on pain of forgoing a normal life. For Ripstein, the private law of torts both is and is not a matter of what John Rawls called "background justice."[126] It is a matter of "background justice"

---

[126] Rawls 2001, *supra* note 11, at 10.

insofar as background justice encompasses the justice of society's main political, social, and legal institutions. Tort is a basic legal institution, whose rights and responsibilities are backed by the coercive power of the state. Moreover, tort law's distinctive domain is not coextensive with the "foreground justice" of Holmes's "isolated, ungeneralized wrongs." It also addresses harms inflicted by basic social activities. For Ripstein, tort law governs interactions among individual persons in civil society whose paths happen to run afoul of one another as they go about their separate lives and pursue their distinct ends. Persons, in this picture, are independent agents pursuing their own distinctive, private purposes. When these persons and their pursuits collide, the question is whether their collision is a case of one person wronging the other through faulty conduct. Modern tort law, however, is centered on interactions that are woven into the basic fabric of modern life and which can be avoided only on pain of forgoing a normal life.

Tort may have moved on from its nineteenth-century preoccupations such as mining, milling, and railroading, but driving, flying, consuming mass-produced products, and using natural gas and electrical power are equally basic productive activities. Indeed, even when accidental injuries attributable to basic productive activities are not at issue, the law of torts seems to be a full member of the family institutions which fall under the purview of background justice. Tort obligations protect persons against various forms of impairment and interference by others as they go about their lives as members of civil society. The responsibilities that tort imposes, and the rights that it recognizes, play central roles in establishing the security necessary for people to shape their own lives; those rights and responsibilities are enforced through the coercive powers of the state. Critical scrutiny of Ripstein's argument that tort governs a distinctive domain of "foreground justice" whose subject is the voluntary interactions of persons in civil society is therefore warranted.

IV. Tort and the Domains of Justice

Philosophically speaking, Ripstein's theory is proudly and distinctively liberal. It is therefore unsurprising that he has taken pains to situate his theory within and against the most famous liberal theory of justice of modern times—namely, John Rawls's theory of "justice as fairness." In his 2004 engagement with Rawls, Ripstein zeroes in on the fact that justice as fairness takes the basic structure of society as its subject.[127] The "basic structure of society," as Rawls conceives it, consists of a society's "main political and social institutions and how they

---

[127] Arthur Ripstein, The Division of Responsibility and the Law of Tort, 72 Fordham L. Rev. 1811 (2004). Ripstein revisits the matter in Ripstein 2016, *supra* note 2, at 288–95. Other scholars concerned with the application of Rawls's theory to private law have also focused on private law's relation to the "basic structure." See Freeman 2018, *supra* note 40; Kronman 1980; Kordana & Blankfein

fit together into one unified system of social cooperation."[128] It encompasses institutions and practices as fundamental and diverse as "the legal protection of freedom of thought and liberty of conscience, competitive markets, private property in the means of production, and the monogamous family."[129] For Ripstein, tort law is a part of the basic structure, but Rawls's principles of justice for the basic structure are not suited to govern the law of torts. Tort is a part of the basic structure because protection against various forms of interference is necessary for individuals to freely form and pursue their conceptions of the good. "If what is mine is not subject to my choice, but to yours . . . then it is not mine to use in setting and pursuing my own conception of the good."[130] Securing my means against interference by others requires not only a system of criminal law but also a body of tort law. Rawls's principles are not, however, suited to govern the law of torts because Rawls's arguments from the original position are consequentialist and, therefore, preclude recognition of the deontological principles of duty and right that govern private law. "The parties to the original position," Ripstein writes, "attach value only to states of affairs."[131] They cannot, therefore, make sense of a body of law preoccupied with who did what to whom—with rights, wrongs, and responsibilities. The deontological structure of tort law "will always be invisible from the point of view of the contract argument."[132]

Ripstein's location of the law of torts within the basic structure of society appears to distinguish his view from Weinrib's. In Weinrib's hands, the "idea of private law" might be read to suggest that tort law is an essentially autonomous realm of social life, answering only to its own internal ideals. "[P]rivate law," Weinrib remarks, is "just like love" in that it needs no independent justification.[133] Ripstein has the better view. Tort obligations specify the extent to which our essential interests—in physical and psychological integrity, in privacy, in reputation, in economic expectancies—are protected against interference by each other, and what kinds of interference they are protected against. The questions that tort law is concerned with are questions of basic justice because some institution must secure people against diverse forms of interference and

---

Tabachanik 2005; Kordana & Blankfein Tabachanik 2008; Murphy 1998; and Scheffler 2015, *supra* note 40.

[128] Rawls 2001, *supra* note 11, at 39–40.
[129] Rawls 1999, *supra* note 39, at 7.
[130] Arthur Ripstein, Tort, The Division of Responsibility and the Law of Tort, 72 Fordham L. Rev. 1811, 1839 (2004).
[131] *Id.*, at 1822–23.
[132] *Id.*, at 1824. Both this and the preceding quotation from Ripstein are quoted in Freeman 2018, *supra* note 40, at 185.
[133] Weinrib 2012, *supra* note 108, at 6 ("Explaining love in terms of extrinsic ends is necessarily a mistake, because love does not shine in our lives with the borrowed light of an extrinsic end. Love is its own end. My contention is that, in this respect, private law is just like love.").

impairment in order for them to be able to pursue their ends and purposes as equal and independent members of civil society. Tort's domain is a domain of private justice, not public justice, simply because tort is concerned with what we owe *to one another* and not with our relations to the state. Part of what we owe to each other in the way of justice, however, is to devise and uphold institutions that protect our essential interests against unwarranted interference as we go about our lives in civil society.[134]

Ripstein's Reduce the space assertion that Rawls cannot recognize deontological principles of duty and right hinges on his agreement with Thomas Pogge's argument that the methodology of the original position is "unavoidably consequentialist and aggregative . . . [because] it focuses only on outcomes. The self-interest of the parties leads them to compare alternative principles and the states of affairs they result in, and to choose the one that best guarantees a maximum share of primary goods and conditions that enable them to most effectively pursue their conceptions of the good."[135] No attention is paid, Pogge believes, to how these states of affairs are brought about. Consequently, there is no room in Rawls's apparatus for the kinds of principles that govern tort law. Those principles are concerned with what people owe—and do—to each other. Tort law distinguishes between affirmative duties to aid and negative duties not to harm, between bringing harm upon ourselves and inflicting harm on others, between violating other people's rights and merely inflicting losses upon them, and so on. Because the parties' reasoning in the original position is (Ripstein thinks) consequentialist and concerned only with end states of affairs, Rawlsian justice cannot recognize these distinctions and principles.

Whatever the best characterization of the reasoning of the parties to the original position may be, Ripstein is mistaken to maintain that Rawls's framework prevents the recognition of deontological principles of justice and morality. The first principle of justice is a principle of equal freedom, and the difference principle itself is a principle of reciprocity among equal, independent persons. It does not prescribe an end state of affairs but, instead, governs ongoing social cooperation. The natural duties that the parties to the original position recognize—duties to uphold justice, of mutual respect, to not injure others or harm the innocent, and so on, are all deontological.[136] To be sure, Rawls's principles of justice do not speak directly to the problems with which the law of torts grapples. Rawls's principles are fundamentally concerned with questions of distributive justice, and torts are, as Ripstein thinks, wrongs. However, the two domains are

---

[134] Compare Scheffler 2015, *supra* note 40, at 19.
[135] Freeman 2018, *supra* note 40, at 185–86, discussing Ripstein 2004, *supra* note 130, and Thomas Pogge, Three Problems with Contractarian-Consequentialist Ways of Assessing Social Institutions, 12 Soc. Phil. & Pol'y 221, 258 (1995).
[136] Freeman 2018, *supra* note 40, at 184–85 (citing Rawls 1999, *supra* note 39, at 97).

complementary, in a way that Ripstein resists. The rights that people have as a matter of distributive justice are fundamental to the responsibilities imposed by the law of torts. The right to the physical and psychological integrity of one's person grounds obligations on the parts of others to exercise reasonable care, not to touch others in harmful or offensive ways, to avoid inflicting emotional distress by outrageous conduct, and so on. The right brings reciprocal principles of responsibility into play. Tort is like crime in this respect. Both bodies of law embody principles requiring people not to mistreat one another in various ways, and both bodies of law ground their core responsibilities in the rights that people have.

In *Private Wrongs*, Ripstein frames the distinction that interests him as the distinction between "background justice" and "foreground justice," which he explicates in terms of a distinction between vertical and horizontal relations. The basic role of the state is to provide "the background conditions for a social world in which everyone is a full member.... To be entitled to act on behalf of everyone, [the state] must stand in the right relation to each citizen over whom it exercises power. This vertical relationship is different in kind from the horizontal relations between private persons that are governed by the principle that no person is in charge of another."[137] Horizontal relations between private persons are the domain of "foreground justice" and private law. Ripstein's discussion in *Private Wrongs* is a further articulation of his earlier discussion of the division of responsibility between the foreground justice of the law of torts and background justice continues:

> Creating and sustaining a social world in which no person is in charge of another—in which interpersonal cooperation is voluntary—requires mandatory cooperation in providing the necessary institutions and resources to achieve these public purposes.
>
> Providing people with the conditions of full membership in society is a matter of what John Rawls once described as "background justice," that is providing conditions for free persons to set and pursue their own purposes.
>
> [T]he idea of background justice presupposes what could be called "foreground justice," that is, a system in which cooperation is voluntary rather than mandatory, in which the purposes pursued are determined by individuals... the foreground justice with which background justice contrasts supposes that individual citizens are in charge of themselves.

To be sure, justice writ large does not require that accidental injuries must be handled by foreground justice and "private law." A state may choose to make accidental injury a matter of "mandatory social insurance" and thereby absorb

---

[137] Ripstein 2016, *supra* note 2, at 289.

the institutional mechanisms that handle such injury into the domain of "background justice."[138] In the common law world, though, the default institution managing accidental injury is the private law and it is governed by principles of foreground justice.

V. Background and Foreground Justice

The background principles of justice for the basic structure of society establish a framework that constrains the law of torts, just as those principles constrain other legal institutions. Nothing in those principles, though, requires "foreground justice" in the form of private law as Ripstein conceives it. For Ripstein, private law must have as its master principle that everyone is in charge of himself or herself, and no one is in charge of anyone else. That principle, in turn, must yield a tort law divided between strict liability for use-based intentional wrongs and universal fault liability for accidental injuries. Interpretively, this account of tort is unattractive because its division of wrongs renders basic features of our law unintelligible. Philosophically, this severing of tort from background justice goes too far, for a number of reasons. First, Ripstein's characterization of private law as "foreground justice" implies that tort law's domain consists of essentially voluntary interactions. This is unpersuasive. In our world, the principal preoccupations of the law of torts are basic social activities avoidable only on pain of forgoing a normal life—activities like driving, or taking public transportation, or walking, or bicycling, or consuming electric power or natural gas, or being vaccinated, or purchasing and using pharmaceutical products. Participation in these activities is not voluntary in the strong sense that deciding to, say, spend your summer vacation trekking in Nepal is voluntary. Participation in these activities is part of ordinary life, not easily escaped. The law of torts and related institutions, therefore, play important roles in establishing (or failing to establish) the background justice necessary for persons to pursue independent lives as equal members of society. They are a basic part of basic justice.

Second, Ripstein's uncompromising insistence that "the point of tort litigation is to resolve the specific dispute between the parties currently before the court, based entirely on what transpired between them,"[139] is also cause for concern. Putting the matter this way suggests that tort law is not just private in the sense of involving relations among persons in civil society in contrast to relations between persons and the state, but private in the sense of dealing with matters that are not of public concern, full stop. Matters that are private in this second sense

---

[138] *Id.*, at 294.
[139] *Id.*, at 23.

are autonomous from larger social and political questions, and therefore exempt from governance by basic principles of justice. Yet even in civil society, the relations among persons are always entangled with larger questions of justice and injustice. Damage awards in tort lawsuits, for example, may be infected by gender and racial discrimination, past and present.[140] To simply exclude this fact from consideration because those social injustices are not actions that "transpired between" the parties is to risk injustice. Whatever one ultimately makes of the contamination of the tables that courts use to compute tort damages by past and present injustice, it is a mistake to claim that the existence of such contamination is irrelevant to how tort law should proceed. Justice between the parties to a civil wrong cannot be unquestionably entitled to reinforce larger injustices.

Third, Ripstein distinguishes sharply between interfering with someone else's use of their means by violating their rights, and "failing to provide that person with a favorable context in which to use those means."[141] The former is an impermissible wrong; the latter is unobjectionable. This distinction is too crude; it overlooks the fact that private interactions can cumulate in systemic injustice. When tort law is treated as an autonomous realm of voluntary individual interaction, it is vulnerable to "the tendency of individual transactions to erode the background conditions necessary for everyone to be a full participant in society."[142] That is one of the lessons of the struggles over assumption of risk and workplace safety in the latter half of the nineteenth century. In a world in which employers require employees to waive their rights to safe workplaces as a condition of employment, the cumulative effect of each worker "choosing" to waive her right to a safe workplace may be to strip all workers of the right to a safe workplace. In such a world, no single worker has the bargaining power to insist that their right to a safe workplace be honored. Only a critical mass of workers (a union) would have that power. Individual workers must choose between not working and waiving the right. For anyone who is not independently wealthy, that choice is no choice at all. Holding a paying job is necessary, not optional.

To be put to a choice between having a job and having a right to a safe workplace is to be deprived of one's right to a safe workplace. Yet that right is itself one of the conditions of effective agency as an equal, independent, and fully participating member of society. Moreover, the problem of individual contractual choices cumulating in systemic injustices that undermine the "background conditions necessary for everyone to be a full participant in society" is not peculiar to the workplace. The history of product liability law in the first half of the twentieth century is another case in point. Contractual disclaimers of warranty

---

[140] Ronen Avraham & Kimberly Yuracko, Torts and Discrimination, 78 Ohio St. L.J. 661, 661–731 (2017).
[141] Ripstein 2016, *supra* note 2, at 94.
[142] *Id.*, at 291 (citing to Rawls 1999, *supra* note 39, at 267).

protection in contracts of adhesion left product users with little or no legal assurance of protection against harm at the hands of defective products.[143] Economic analyses of how free contractual choice can lead to "races to the bottom" in terms of product quality and safety show why the threat of contractual agreement cumulating in injustice is a standing and pervasive one.[144] History and theory teach the same lesson: contractual waivers of rights to safety can cumulate into systematically unjust institutional arrangements. Systems of voluntary cooperation must be policed by principles of background justice to avoid these pitfalls.

Next, it is unclear why we should regard the choice for tort—and against regulation or administration—as marking a radical division between the domains of background and foreground justice. Here, we need to recall that modern tort law took shape as a response to the rise of accidental injury as a pressing *social* problem. The forms of liability that Ripstein rejects are misunderstood whey they are represented purely as forms of social insurance. These schemes characteristically combine social insurance in some form with direct regulation of risk in order to construct communities of collective *responsibility*. They respond to the fact that "the torts with which our courts are kept busy today are mainly the incidents of certain well-known businesses . . . railroads, factories, and the like"[145] by lodging responsibility at the activity or enterprise level. The insight captured by Jeremy Waldron's tale of "Fate" and "Fortune" at the outset of his defense of the New Zealand accident compensation scheme in Rawlsian fairness terms is fundamental to these forms of responsibility:

> Two drivers, named Fate and Fortune, were on a city street one morning in their automobiles. Both were driving at or near the speed limit, Fortune a little ahead of Fate. As they passed through a shopping district, each took his eyes off the road, turning his head for a moment to look at the bargains advertised in a storefront window. (The last day of a sale was proclaimed, with 25 percent off the price of a pair of men's shoes.) In Fortune's case, this momentary distraction passed without event. The road was straight, the traffic in front of him was proceeding smoothly, and after a few seconds he returned his eyes to his driving and completed his journey without incident. Fate, however, was not so fortunate. Distracted by the bargain advertised in the shoe store, he failed to notice that the traffic ahead of him had slowed down. His car ploughed into

---

[143] See Henningsen v. Bloomfield Motors, Inc., 161 A.2d 69 (N.J. 1960); Escola v. Coca Cola Bottling Co. of Fresno, 250 P.2d 436 (Cal. 1944) (Traynor, J., concurring).

[144] See George A. Akerlof, The Market for "Lemons": Quality Uncertainty and the Market Mechanism, 48 Q. J. Econ. 488 (1970). For a brief, incisive discussion of the phenomenon in the context of product safety, see Duncan Kennedy, Distributive and Paternalist Motives in Contract and Tort Law, with Special Reference to Compulsory Terms and Unequal Bargaining Power, 41 Md. L. Rev. 563, 597–603 (1982).

[145] Holmes 1920, *supra* note 122, at 183.

a motorcycle ridden by a Mr. Hurt. Hurt was flung from the motorcycle and gravely injured. His back was broken so badly that he would spend the rest of his life in a wheelchair. Fate stopped immediately of course to summon help, and when the police arrived he readily admitted that he had been driving carelessly. When Hurt recovered consciousness in [the] hospital, the first thing he did was instruct his lawyers to sue Fate for negligence. Considering the extent of his injury, the sum he sought was quite modest—$5 million. . . . But modest or not, it was sufficient to bankrupt Mr. Fate.[146]

For Waldron, the injury that Fate inflicted on Hurt is characteristic of the activity of driving. We are all prone to lapses. In any individual instance, it is merely a matter of luck whether a lapse results in devastating injury—or not. It misses the point to pin individual responsibility on Fate just because he inflicted the injury in question—and it is unfair to boot. Fate did not *do* anything different from Fortune, he was just unlucky. Ripstein's view is that Fate and Fortune *did* two very different things. Fortune committed "negligence in the air," whereas Fate negligently wronged Hurt.

Both Ripstein's and Waldron's *descriptions* of Fate and Fortune's respective actions are plausible. The choice between their positions cannot be made merely as a matter of act description. For our present purposes, though, no choice between them needs to be made. The important point is that—because accidents in our social world are mostly the incidents of organized activities—accidents can be described *either* in terms of individual responsibility or in terms of collective responsibility at the activity or enterprise level. Descriptions like Ripstein's very strongly dispose us to see the matter in terms of individual responsibility. Descriptions like Waldron's very strongly dispose us to see the matter in terms of collective responsibility. Both descriptions, and both forms of responsibility, are present in our law. Individual fault liability is the heart of private law as Ripstein conceives it and is the dominant principle of responsibility in our own common law of torts. Collective responsibility is evident in forms of enterprise liability within and outside the law of torts. Within the law of torts, enterprise responsibility manifests itself in aspects of vicarious liability, products liability, abnormally dangerous activity liability, and nuisance liability. Beyond the law of torts, enterprise responsibility manifests itself in workers' compensation schemes, in no-fault automobile insurance, and in statutory schemes for vaccination injuries,

---

[146] Waldron, Moments of Carelessness and Massive Loss, in Philosophical Foundations of Tort Law 387, 387 (David G. Owen ed., Oxford, 1995). Waldron's example is fiction, but not fantasy. A 1970 U.S. Department of Transportation Study reported: "In Washington, D.C., a 'good' driver viz., one without an accident within the preceding five years, commits on average, in five minutes of driving, at least nine errors of different kinds." U.S. Department of Transportation: Automobile Insurance and Compensation Study 177–78 (1970) (quoted in Tony Honoré, Responsibility and Fault 36–37 (Hart, 1999)).

black lung disease, and nuclear accidents. Most grandly, it expresses itself in the New Zealand Accident Compensation scheme, which takes the relevant community of responsibility to be society at large.[147]

Ripstein's presentation of enterprise responsibility alternatives to tort casts them as purely a matter of (social) insurance. They are not. Insurance is normally one piece of the package—with some form of risk-regulation being the other major piece. As this combination of institutional instruments suggests, these schemes govern forms of human agency. They are concerned with the harmful effects of activities. Broadly speaking, they are relational. They are concerned with responsibilities among persons as participants in dangerous but beneficial activities, and toward those whom the activities injure. Social insurance, as Ripstein conceives it, characteristically addresses harms qua harms—injury and illness, whatever their origins. Harms inflicted by natural forces (famines, floods, earthquakes, and epidemics) are as much the province of social insurance as are harms arising out of human agency. Yet, enterprise responsibility only governs harmful human agency.

Finally, Rawls's theory of justice is compatible with either enterprise responsibility schemes or the individual responsibility of "private law" as Ripstein conceives it. Rawls's theory no more chooses between these alternative forms of responsibility for human agency which is harmful, wrongful, or both, than it settles the choice between capitalism and socialism as an economic matter. Waldron, pithily, makes the basic Rawlsian case for the New Zealand approach:

> Both schemes [individual fault liability and a New Zealand–style accident scheme] treat equals equally, and in that sense both of them satisfy principles of fairness. So how are we to choose between them? The question seems to be one for the drivers, since the victims should receive exactly the same (full) compensation, provided each scheme is perfectly administered (on its own terms). Which scheme would the drivers choose—particularly if they did not know in advance (how could they?) whether their negligence was actually likely to cause injury or not?
>
> The answer seems to me to be obvious: if there was ever a case for maximin, this is it. If people opt for the liability lottery, drivers face a non-trivial chance of complete ruin if they lose—all for the hope of a gain which consists simply of not losing anything if they win.[148]

We do not need to come to a settled conclusion on the ultimate, respective merits of New Zealand's accident compensation scheme and fault liability in tort as

---

[147] See Chapter Seven, *infra*, pp. 291–97.
[148] Waldron 1995, *supra* note 146, at 406–07.

regimes for governing automobile accidents. To form such a judgment, we would need to know not just what these schemes aspire to as a matter of normative theory but also how they work in practice. For our purposes, it is sufficient to note that both sides of the debate can draw on Rawlsian ideas to support their positions. Ripstein, for his part, makes the case that a "foreground justice" of "private law" can be integrated with a Rawlsian (or other liberal) account of "background justice." With the caveat that "private law" must be properly constrained by principles of background justice so that it does not, for instance, permit individual actions to cumulate in social injustice or allow reparation in private law to do gender or racial injustice, Ripstein is right. The mistake would be to think that Rawls's framework—or some other liberal theory of justice—mandates either "private law" or a New Zealand scheme, or some intermediate arrangement, as a matter of first principles of justice. It does not. To choose between these institutional alternatives, we need to supplement basic principles of justice with additional considerations and information.

VI. Form and Substance

Theorists of tort as "private law" are right to reject Posner's purely public law conception of the field as a "comprehensive code of safety regulation" pursuing the end of optimal accident deterrence through private rights of action.[149] The bilateral form of the traditional tort lawsuit does in fact teach us something important about its substance. Tort plaintiffs are not mere conduits through which social costs and benefits pass. They claim in their own names. They assert their own rights against defendants who they say have wronged them. And they seek to hold these defendants responsible for repairing the harm that they have done. More generally, the law of torts is a law of right and responsibility, governing the relations among persons in civil society. Tort as "private law" is right about all of this. Ripstein's version of the theory is also right to insist that the law of torts is an institution which governs an important domain of basic justice. The kind of security from diverse forms of unjustifiable interference and impairment that the law of torts seeks to establish is one of the background conditions necessary for people to be able to pursue their ends and purposes as free and equal members of civil society.

The insistence on the autonomy and impermeability of tort, however, is a mistake, and it breeds misunderstanding. "Private law" is not a category constitutive of a highly autonomous activity constructed around institution-specific concepts such as bilateral wrongs. "Private law" and "public law" are legal categories that

---

[149] Posner 1972, *supra* note 13, at 31, 73.

precede the emergence of the administrative state. In our legal world, they do a poor job of sorting out our diverse legal institutions.[150]

Law, like games and sports, is a practice.[151] Our understandings play a role in its formation. Legal theory, for its part, is the law in quest of itself, the law's quest for self-understanding. In torts, the self-understanding that we need is an understanding that accepts and builds upon private law theory's claim that the law of torts embodies a deontological political morality, concerned with what it is that people owe to one another in the way of coercively enforceable obligations of noninterference. But the theory we need will depart from the theory of tort as "private law" by recognizing interests and the central role they play in our law. Establishing rightful relations among free and equal persons in civil society requires that institutions secure protection for persons' urgent interests, not just institutions that express our formal independence from one another. Next, making perspicuous the political morality of right and responsibility embodied in our private law of torts requires acknowledging and accounting for the presence of both fault and strict liabilities. Harm that either cannot be—or should not be—avoided is a basic feature of our social life; our law of torts is divided over the question of who should shoulder the burdens of unavoidable harm. Theories of tort law should help us to understand and evaluate that division, not deny its existence. Last, we need to recognize that the private law of torts is one member of a family of institutions that address accidental harm. We misunderstand even the private law of torts itself if we sever it entirely from forms of collective responsibility for avoiding and repairing accidental harm with which it competes and cooperates.

---

[150] The classic discussion of private law, public law, and the law of nations is found in Charles de Secondat, Baron de Montesquieu, The Spirit of Laws 40–42, 189–96 (Thomas Nugent trans., Batoche, 2001) (1748).

[151] In Rawls's sense. John Rawls, Two Concepts of Rules (1955), 64 Phil. Rev. 3 (1955).

4
Fairness and Fault

When modern tort law took shape in the latter half of the nineteenth century, accidental physical harm was its principal concern, and fault was its dominant principle of responsibility. Then, as now, fault's dominance was challenged by the competing principle of strict liability. Over time, both principles of responsibility have ebbed and flowed, and over time the preoccupations of tort law have changed. Today, tort law is less concerned with the toll that railroads inflict on human lives and more concerned with the looming hazards of self-driving cars. Modern tort law's preoccupation with accidental physical harm—and its domination by fault liability—have, however, endured. There is, then, no making sense of tort law without making sense of negligence law. The most basic feature of fault (or negligence) liability is the feature that sets it apart from strict liability: it is concerned with avoidable harm. Negligence liability holds those who inflict harms on others responsible to those they have harmed for the harm that they have done when—and only when—they should have conducted themselves more carefully and thereby have avoided inflicting those harms. In the language preferred by the law itself, negligence liability holds injurers responsible for those accidental harms that issue from their *unreasonable* risk impositions.

When are risk impositions unreasonable? Various answers to this question proposed in case rhetoric—when a reasonable person would not have imposed the risk, when reasonable care would have averted the harm—can seem question-begging and circular. Upon reflection, though, these complaints seem too harsh. Personification has its uses. Most of us, including jurors, have ideas about who a reasonable person is and how they act. The figure of the reasonable person stimulates useful tacit understandings and orients us in a helpful way. Moving from tacit understandings to explicit articulation, though, has proven difficult. Sometimes, the idea of reasonable care seems to direct us toward what philosophers call "justification." The reasonable person imposes only risks which should be imposed. They figure out which risks are worth imposing and what precautions should be taken to minimize the harm threatened by those risks, and act accordingly.[1] The idea of justification comes to the fore when we consider cases where an actor is responsible for an activity that imposes recurring

---

[1] See, *e.g.*, John Gardner, The Mysterious Case of the Reasonable Person, in Torts and Other Wrongs 226 (Oxford, 2019).

risks, and the basic question posed by their conduct is what precautions should be taken to reduce the risks imposed by the activity.

Davis v. Consolidated Rail nicely illustrates the circumstance where justification comes to the fore.[2] Davis was injured when a train that he had crawled underneath (to inspect its undercarriage for cracks) moved suddenly and without warning. As Davis tried to scramble to safety, his legs were pinned beneath the wheels of the car. One leg was severed below the knee; most of the foot on his other leg was also sliced off. The basic questions that arose, about both Davis's and Conrail's conduct, were questions about proper precaution. What steps should Conrail take before moving its trains in rail yards? What should an inspector of trains do to alert those in charge of operating trains to their presence beneath a train? Conrail's engineers might, for instance, sound their train's horns before starting. Inspectors might post "blue flags" at both ends of the train to signal their presence beneath its cars. Should either of those precautions be taken? Should they both be taken? These are questions about the justified level of care, primary and contributory.[3]

In other cases, though, the question of reasonable conduct seems to have less to do with what precaution to take, and more to do with whether we can reasonably expect a given defendant to take the correct precaution. Some feature of the defendant's capacities—or something about the circumstances in which they acted—makes us think that we would be demanding too much from them if we expected them to take the correct precaution. We are asking a question of this kind when we ask what we may reasonably expect of people in the way of competent responses to emergency circumstances.[4] When someone pulls their car out of a shopping center, mistakenly turns the wrong way, and drives into oncoming traffic, what can we expect in the way of competent accident avoidance from a driver whose life they have suddenly jeopardized? We know what the correct precaution is—swerve to avoid the oncoming car without hitting someone else. The difficult question is whether it is fair to expect a normal person to execute that precaution correctly, or if we should cut them some slack given the unfavorable conditions in which they are forced to act. The issue here has to do with what philosophers' call "excuse."[5] Both types of questions arise in negligence law, but the question of justification dominates. Excuse comes to the fore in cases in we know what justified conduct requires and are asking if we may demand it from

---

[2] Davis v. Consolidated Rail Corp., 788 F.2d 1260 (7th Cir. 1986).
[3] Primary negligence refers to the conduct of the party imposing the risk; contributory negligence refers to the conduct of the person upon whom the risk is imposed.
[4] See, *e.g.*, Myhaver v. Knutson, 942 P.2d 445 (1997).
[5] See, *e.g.*, John Gardner, The Negligence Standard: Political Not Metaphysical, in Torts and Other Wrongs 196, 215 (Oxford, 2017).

the actor involved, or in the circumstances in question. Justification is the prior, deeper, more basic question.

I. Reasonableness and Rationality in Negligence Theory

In the United States, the leading scholarly account of justified care is economic: reasonable care is cost-justified care.[6] On an economic view, the role of tort liability is to minimize the combined costs of accidents and their prevention.[7] So doing helps to maximize the resources—the wealth—at society's disposal. Lives, limbs, and the resources we spend guarding and repairing them must be put to prudent use, not wasted. Responsibility for preventing and paying for accidental injuries should therefore be assigned in a way that reduces their combined costs to as low a level as possible. We should impose a risk when the cost of avoiding the expected harms likely to flow from that risk exceeds the cost of bearing those expected harms. Conversely, we should avoid imposing a risk if the present costs of avoiding it are less than the expected harms likely to be caused by its imposition. Reasonable precaution, then, is efficient precaution—cost-justified precaution. Taking either more or less than cost-justified precaution is irrational. Inefficient precaution prefers less value to more value.

The overarching argument of this chapter is that we understand reasonable care better by situating it within a deontological moral framework. Duties of care are concerned with what people owe to one another when they engage in acts and activities that create reasonably foreseeable risks of physical harm to others. Indeed, negligence law gives its deontological affinities away through its pervasive use of the word "reasonable." Economic analysis models reasonable care as socially *rational* care—as the care that society should take, imagining society to be a single actor who bears all the costs and all the benefits of risk impositions and who seeks to make itself as well off as possible. Reasonableness and rationality, however, are distinct concepts.[8] When we act rationally, we pursue our

---

[6] The case for negligence as cost-justified precaution, economically speaking, is first made in Richard Posner's classic, A Theory of Negligence, 1 J. Legal Stud. 29 (1972).

[7] "The normative efficiency goal of tort law most widely accepted in law and economics is that first proposed by Dean Calabresi: that the rules of tort law should be structured so as to minimize the sum of precaution, accident, and administration costs." Robert D. Cooter & Thomas Ulen, Law and Economics 347 (Harper Collins, 1988) (italics omitted).

[8] John Rawls, Political Liberalism 48 (Columbia, rev ed., 2005). Rawls traces the philosophical recognition of the distinction to Kant. See also W.M. Sibley, The Rational Versus the Reasonable, 62 Phil. Rev. 554, 554 (1953) (discussing the distinction and the affinity between reasonableness and Kant's categorical imperative); T.M. Scanlon, What We Owe to Each Other 32–33 (Harvard, 1998). Arthur Ripstein, Equality, Responsibility, and the Law (Cambridge, 1998), emphasizes the concept of reasonableness in negligence law. The philosophical literature theorizes the distinction between rationality and reasonableness, but the distinction is present in ordinary usage of the words. Recent empirical work in psychology has shown that people do not equate reasonableness with economic rationality. See Igor Grossman et al., Folk Standards of Sound Judgment: Rationality Versus

self-interest in an instrumentally intelligent way. When we act reasonably, we take the rights and interests of those others that our actions affect into account, and act in ways that are justifiable to them. Reasonable risk impositions fairly reconcile the liberty of potential injurers with the security of potential victims.

One test of reasonableness is whether those who are affected by the conduct in question would regard it as acceptable if they were to change places—if, say, those who imposed some risk were to step into the shoes of those whom they were exposing to risk.[9] When someone acts rationally, but unreasonably, they pursue their self-interest intelligently but fail to conduct themselves in a way that accords appropriate weight to the equally legitimate interests of others. Suppose, for instance, that you are managing a restaurant. You have figured out that some employee is stealing money from the restaurant, but your efforts to identify the thief have failed. To flush them out, you decide to line the staff up and fire them in alphabetical order.[10] Shame, fear, or peer pressure may out the thief, or at least deter further theft. There's nothing obviously irrational about your choice of tactic; its expected benefits may well exceed its costs, especially from your point of view. Even if the tactic is rational, however, it is deeply unreasonable. Firing someone because their name comes first in the alphabet treats them as responsible for a wrong that you have no reason to think they committed. Firing someone because their name comes first in the alphabet treats their job security as a resource available for you to dispose of as you wish. It shatters their security simply because it is expedient for you to do so. None of us would shatter our own security and sacrifice our own well-being in this way.

This way of distinguishing between reasonableness and rationality suggests that when the law of negligence speaks in terms of *reasonable* conduct and *reasonable* persons, not in terms of *rational* conduct and *rational* persons, its choice of word is telling. Reasonableness is a morally inflected term and a moral virtue. Rationality is a prudential virtue. Duties of care are owed to others. They are a matter of interpersonal obligation, not individual prudence. It is therefore correct to articulate duties of care in terms of reasonableness and mistaken to reduce them to rational self-interest, even if the self-interest is conceived collectively. Because reasonableness and rationality are not synonymous—and because

---

Reasonableness, 6(2) Sci. Adv. (2020) ("It appears that laypeople systematically differentiate rationality and reasonableness along the lines outlined in . . . legal scholarship." [citations omitted]). See also Christopher Jaeger, The Empirical Reasonable Person, 72 Ala. L. Rev. 887 (2021). These findings are discussed in Kevin P. Tobia, "Experimental Jurisprudence" (Aug. 24, 2021), https://papers.ssrn.com/sol3/papers.cfm?abstract_id=3680107.

[9] See T.M. Scanlon, Contractualism and Utilitarianism, in Utilitarianism and Beyond 103, 117 (Amartya Sen & Bernard Williams eds., Cambridge, 1982) (noting that the "connection between the Idea of 'changing places' and the motivation which underlies morality explains the frequent occurrence of 'Golden Rule' arguments within different systems of morality").

[10] These are the facts of Agis v. Howard Johnson, 355 N.E.2d 315, 318 (Mass. 1976).

reasonableness is a morally freighted concept, whereas rationality is not—it is tempting to dismiss the economic account of reasonable care as socially rational care as a nonstarter. It cannot be squared with the language of the law itself.

Brisk dismissal of the economic conception of due care as linguistically untenable is, however, both too quick and uncharitable. Too quick, because an idea that has dominated its corner of academic discourse for decades cannot be dislodged so easily. Uncharitable, because a better way of understanding the economic substitution of "socially rational" for "reasonable" is as an implicit rejection of the adequacy of the law's preferred terminology. Skepticism about tort law's morally inflected rhetoric runs deep in American legal scholarship. Oliver Wendell Holmes, the founding father of tort theory in the United States, regarded all such terminology as ripe for reduction to something allegedly clearer and less morally saturated.[11] Guido Calabresi, a law and economics scholar of unusual moral sensitivity, once referred to the word "right" as a "weasel word"—as a vague and elusive term deployed to disguise the fact that we do not really know how to articulate the ground of some judgment.[12] Implicitly, the economic analysis of tort takes this skeptical view of the word "reasonable"—that it eludes clear and satisfactory explication and should be replaced by the concept of rationality, with the twist that individual rationality should be recast as social rationality. The question to ask is what an actor who bore both the costs and the benefits of some risk imposition—and who wished to make themselves as well off as possible—would have reason to do. Interpersonal obligation should be reduced to intelligent self-interest.

Reducing reasonableness to rationality economically conceived integrates the central concept of negligence law with a ready-made framework fashioned for conceptualizing trade-offs. The importance of this is hard to overstate. For more than fifty years, the dominant understanding of negligence has characterized reasonable care as care that correctly balances competing considerations. The black-letter text of the *Third Restatement*, for example, announces that the "[p]rimary factors to consider in ascertaining whether [a] person's conduct lacks reasonable care are the foreseeable likelihood that the person's conduct will result in harm, the foreseeable severity of any harm that may ensue, and the burden of precautions to eliminate or reduce the risk of harm."[13] This is "Hand Formula" negligence.[14] Hand's statement of his formula was a watershed moment in

---

[11] Oliver Wendell Holmes, The Common Law 6-8, 41-42, 55-61, 111-12 (Sheldon Novick ed., Dover, 1991). For discussion and criticism, see John C.P. Goldberg & Benjamin C. Zipursky, Recognizing Wrongs 61-65, 83-86 (Harvard, 2020).

[12] Guido Calabresi, Concerning Cause and the Law of Torts, 43 U. Chi. L. Rev. 69, 96 n.39 (1975).

[13] Restatement (Third) of Torts: Liability for Physical and Emotional Harm § 3 (2010). *The Second Restatement* also embraced a balancing conception of negligence, though its presentation has something of a laundry list quality. See Restatement (Second) of Torts §§ 292-93 (1965).

[14] Judge Learned Hand stated the "formula" in *United States v. Carroll Towing Co.*, 159 F.2d 169 (2d Cir. 1947).

American tort law. When he framed his famous formula, Judge Learned Hand crystallized negligence law's pivot away from the nineteenth-century idea that due care is *customary* care—the care that people *do, in fact*, exercise—and toward the modern idea that due care is *reasonable* or justified care—the care that people *should* exercise.[15] To figure out how much care people should exercise, we must balance the burdens and benefits of doing so. Risk impositions are not categorically wrong; they are regrettable byproducts of legitimate actions. We must therefore balance what we stand to gain from an action against the harm that it threatens. Trade-offs are thus the bread and butter of negligence analysis. Consequently, economic analysis appears to have something very attractive to offer negligence law: a rigorous and comprehensive framework for making trade-offs. Indeed, many legal scholars have thought that Hand Formula negligence just *is* economic analysis by another name. Richard Posner's remark that Judge "Hand was adumbrating, perhaps unwittingly, an economic meaning of negligence" has struck both friend and foe as irresistibly true.[16]

Theorists of torts who resist the economic account of the field have also tended to resist the balancing character of modern American negligence law. Corrective justice and civil recourse scholars are inclined to embrace nonbalancing conceptions of negligence which hark back to the older idea that reasonable care is the care that reasonable people do, in general, exercise.[17] Arthur Ripstein's position is representative. "The ordinary activities of careful people," he writes, "are just part of the context in which you have whatever it is that you have," whereas "[i]f you injure another by doing something that carries a greater than background risk of injury to the person or property of others, you are liable because

---

[15] Gregory C. Keating, Must the Hand Formula Not Be Named?, 163 U. Pa. L. Rev. 367, 370 (2015). Nonbalancing conceptions of negligence were dominant until well into the twentieth century. For example, Oliver Wendell Holmes had a nonbalancing conception of negligence. See Thomas C. Grey, Accidental Torts, 54 Vand. L. Rev. 1225, n.168 (2001). Balancing conceptions of negligence did not become prevalent until at least a generation after Holmes wrote. See Michael D. Green, Negligence = Economic Efficiency: Doubts, 75 Tex. L. Rev. 1605 (1997).

[16] Posner 1972, *supra* note 6, at 29, 32 (1972) (footnote omitted); see Cooter & Ulen 1988, *supra* note 7, at 360 ("[Judge Learned Hand] set the legal standard of care by explicitly balancing the benefits and costs of precaution, just as an economist would have done."). The conviction that the Hand Formula is frankly economic is hardly confined to economists. See, *e.g.*, Jules L. Coleman, Markets, Morals and the Law 131 (Oxford, 1988) ("Following Learned Hand [a judge] might . . . provide an economic analysis of fault or negligence."); Ronald Dworkin, Hard Cases, in Taking Rights Seriously 98 (London, 1977) ("Learned Hand's theory of negligence is the most familiar example of [an] explicit reference to economics."); Gary T. Schwartz, Contributory and Comparative Negligence: A Reappraisal, 87 Yale L.J. 697, 700–01 (1978) ("[The Hand Formula] suggests nothing more than an ordinary cost-benefit analysis . . . as a technique for achieving the economic goal of efficiency.") (footnote omitted). On the allure of the "too irresistible," see Zoë Hitzig, "Objectivity as Blanket," The New Yorker (Mar. 17 2017).

[17] See, *e.g.*, Arthur Ripstein, Private Wrongs 40–41, 97–98 (Harvard, 2016); Ernest J. Weinrib, The Idea of Private Law 147–52 (Oxford, 2012); Benjamin C. Zipursky, Reasonableness In and Out of Negligence Law, 163 U. Pa. L. Rev. 2131 (2015); Stephen R. Perry, The Impossibility of General Strict Liability, 1 Can. J.L. & Jurisprudence 147, 169–71 (1988).

you have wronged that person by interfering with what he or she already has."[18] The threshold picked out by this conception of negligence is elusive, but the description of the threshold comes close to asserting that customary care is reasonable care. In theory, Ripstein's idea of negligence is distinct from customary conduct. The conduct of *reasonable* people—not the conduct of people, full stop—constitutes due care. But Ripstein never says what makes conduct reasonable. In the abstract, Ripstein's conception of reasonable care is elusive. In practice, his idea that due care is the care that reasonable people exercise tends to make the care that actual people do exercise an attractive measure of the care that people should exercise.

The fact that Ripstein's account is categorical is as important as the fact that it tends to identify reasonable care with ordinary care. For Ripstein, risks fall into two domains, depending on how great they are. Risks that are irreducible byproducts of living are *not* negligent and *are* relatively modest. Risks that exceed this level are negligent. This kind of categorical approach has its attractions and some support in case law.[19] But it risks legitimating unacceptably large risk impositions that happen to be common, and it is out of step with the dominant contemporary understanding of negligence in the United States, which regards judgments of reasonable care as judgments that balance the burdens of reducing risk against the benefits of doing so. Noneconomic theorists of tort seem to be in the unattractive position of trying to resuscitate a superseded and inadequate conception of care. What we need is a way of coming to grips with the fact that negligence does involve balancing, without having to swallow the objectionable aspects of the economic account of negligence. Such an alternative, in fact, lies ready to hand. Balancing negligence can also be understood as an attempt to reconcile liberty and security on fair terms. Before we explore that alternative, though, we must first sort out what balancing negligence involves and what the economic interpretation of negligence claims.

A. Reasonableness as Social Rationality

The economic conception of reasonable care as rational care revolves around the Hand Formula, which it takes to be cost-benefit analysis incarnate. Indeed, the economic conception has become so closely identified with the Hand Formula that the distinction between the formula and its economic interpretation can no longer be taken for granted. Identifying the formula with its economic

---

[18] Ripstein 2016, *supra* note 17, at 102, 144–45.
[19] Lord Reid's opinion in *Bolton v. Stone*, A.C. 850 (1951), is the standard citation for a categorical conception of negligence. It is roughly contemporaneous with Hand's statement of his formula.

interpretation, though, is a mistake. Hand's own understanding of his formula differs significantly from its standard economic interpretation. The contribution that he imagined it making to negligence analysis was more conceptual and less normative than the economic interpretation supposes. Our first task, then, is to distinguish the Hand Formula from its economic interpretation.

1. The Hand Formula

Doctrinally, the Hand Formula is usually deployed to help determine whether a defendant has breached its duty of care, though it can also be used to determine whether a duty of care should be imposed in the first instance. The formula tells us that the care owed in any given context is "a function of three variables: (1) the probability [that the harm will materialize]; (2) the gravity of the resulting injury [if the harm does materialize]; [and] (3) the burden of adequate precautions."[20] This simple formulation is helpful in two distinct ways.[21] First, it identifies the variables relevant to determinations of due care and specifies the basic trade-offs that must be made among them. Precautions reduce the probability (and/or the magnitude) of accidents, and their (present) costs must be traded off against the (expected) costs of the accidents that they prevent. The formula thus lends coherence and analytical precision to the concept of due care. Without its molding influence, the law of duty and breach threatens to dissolve into a formless laundry list of the factors that define due care and the qualities that characterize the careful person.[22]

Second, the Hand Formula directs our attention to the precaution necessary to prevent the accident at issue and asks us to compare its costs with the *set of*

---

[20] *Carroll Towing Co.*, 159 F.2d at 173.

[21] See James A. Henderson, Richard N. Pearson, & John A. Siliciano, The Torts Process 204–05 (Wolters Kluwer, 4th ed., 1994) (calling the "balancing of costs and benefits suggested by" the Hand Formula "the core question in determining whether an action has been negligent"); W. Page Keeton et al., Prosser and Keeton on the Law of Torts 173 (West, 5th ed., 1984) ("It thus is fundamental that the standard of conduct which is the basis of the law of negligence is usually determined upon a risk-benefit form of analysis."); Robert E. Keeton et al., Tort and Accident Law 14 (West, 4th ed., 2004) (introducing the Hand Formula as "[t]he best known formulation of the idea of reasonable care"); Marshall S. Shapo, Tort and Injury Law 187 (Carolina Academic Press, 1990) (describing the Hand formula as "[a] modem statement of the negligence formula that many courts cite and that forms a basis for much scholarly discussion"). But see Richard A. Epstein & Catherine M. Sharkey, Cases and Materials on Torts 167 (Wolters Kluwer, 12th ed., 2020) (distinguishing between "the common-sense, intuitive meaning of negligence as it applies to ordinary individuals" and "the judicial effort to impart a more precise economic meaning to the terms, adopting the language of costs and benefits" and noting that "[b]oth approaches have uneasily coexisted throughout the history of the common law").

[22] The multifactor tests of the Restatement (Second) of Torts have a laundry list flavor. See Restatement (Second) of Torts §§ 292–93 (1965) (listing the factors to be considered in determining the utility of an actor's conduct and the magnitude of risk for purposes of determining whether an actor was negligent).

expected accident costs that precaution would have avoided.[23] As Judge Posner has noted:

> [I]n determining the benefits of a precaution—and PL, the expected accident costs that the precaution would avert, is a measure of the benefits of the precaution—the trier of fact must consider not only the expected cost of this accident but also the expected cost of any other, similar accidents that the precaution would have prevented.[24]

In the *Davis* case, for example, blowing the train's horn before moving the train "would have saved not only an inspector who had crawled under the care (low P), but also an inspector leaning on a car, a railroad employee doing repairs on the top of a car, a brakeman straddling two cars, and anyone else who might have business in or on (as well as under a car ... [t]he train was three-quarters of a mile long."[25] The benefits of the precaution are thus measured by the accidents that it might avert, drawing on our powers of reasonable foresight to imagine the kinds of people who might be endangered by a train that starts without warning in a rail yard.

Judge Posner's populating of the scene of Davis's injury with imaginary potential victims is important. Negligence lawsuits are brought after the fact by particular people who have been harmed, but judgments of risk and precaution for purposes of duty and breach are made ex ante. Most tortious accidental harms take place among parties who are strangers to one another. In most cases, therefore, judgments about the care owed are made not by considering risks to named persons but by contemplating risks to "representative" people—the kinds of people that we can envision being endangered when we think about the situation in the abstract. In the *Palsgraf* case, for instance, at the duty and breach phase we must imagine the representative people who might be endangered when a train pulls out of a station with its doors still open and prospective passengers still trying to climb aboard. Categories of those who might be harmed come to mind: passengers boarding and exiting the train; passengers on the platform; perhaps passengers on the train if some mishap caused by boarding a moving train requires slamming on the brakes; property of those who might be harmed personally, or personal property in the vicinity of the train. Lists like this are

---

[23] See Mark F. Grady, Untaken Precautions, 18 J. Legal Stud. 139, 146 (1989) (arguing that any foreseeable risk can be included in the calculations of due care as long as it would be reduced by the untaken precaution).

[24] *Davis*, 788 F.2d at 1264. By "PL" Judge Posner means the magnitude of the loss discounted by its probability.

[25] *Id.*

open-ended and a bit vague because the future is open-ended and only dimly foreseen.

The lesson here is that negligence norms articulate obligations that run to and from named persons, but their content is filled out by contemplating representative persons who might be endangered by some risk imposition. We cannot foresee the future precisely enough to realize that we might harm Mrs. Palsgraf. But we can foresee that we might harm someone, and we can be expected to identify representative examples of those we might harm. When we take to the road, for instance, we may foresee that careless driving will endanger passengers in our own cars, other drivers, passengers in other cars, pedestrians, and so on. The possibilities are at once finite and indefinite. The point is that we must orient ourselves with such *possibilities* in mind.

Economic interpretations of the Hand Formula often represent it in terms of calculus, implying that it does not just orient us but prescribes a formidably precise decision procedure.[26] Doing so is of a piece with much of the rhetoric of law and economics, which aspires to "scientific policymaking"[27] and "rigorous cost-benefit judgments."[28] Juries are chastised for their inability to weigh the relevant criteria as a regulatory agency might.[29] In taking the Hand Formula to provide a precise technique for the determination of duties, the economic conception departs from Hand's own understanding. Hand thought his formula fell well short of technical precision because our foresight is subject to unavoidable epistemic limitations. Practically speaking, the kind of precision that law and economics yearns for is unattainable:

> [O]f [the factors in the Hand Formula,] care is the only one ever susceptible of quantitative estimate, and often that is not. The injuries are always a variable

---

[26] See, *e.g.*, Cooter & Ulen 1988, *supra* note 7, at 348–50.

[27] The term is Bruce Ackerman's. See Bruce A. Ackerman, Private Property and the Constitution 10–20 (Yale, 1977) (contrasting the "Ordinary Observer," whose legal discourse is rooted in the common practices and language of laymen, with the "Scientific Policymaker," who understands legal rules as instruments to the end of achieving certain policy goals.) Through the work of Michael Wells, the term has entered the negligence literature to describe the economic interpretation of the Hand Formula. See Michael Wells, Scientific Policymaking and the Torts Revolution: The Revenge of the Ordinary Observer, 26 Ga. L. Rev. 725, 727–28 (1992) (arguing that traditional tort law better fits the realm of the Ordinary Observer, while contemporary tort law is driven by Scientific Policymaking); see also Gary T. Schwartz, The Vitality of Negligence and the Ethics of Strict Liability, 15 Ga. L. Rev. 963, 991 (1981) (using the term "ordinary observing" to describe the tort theory of Richard Epstein).

[28] George L. Priest, Products Liability Law and the Accident Rate in Liability: Perspectives and Policy 184, 198, 201 (Robert E. Litan & Clifford Winston eds., Brookings Institute, 1988).

[29] The American Law Institute, Enterprise Responsibility for Personal Injury 46–47 (The Institute, 1991) (stating that the use of juries to evaluate the safety of complex products and processes is less desirable than establishing regulatory standards); Alan Schwartz, The Case Against Strict Liability, 60 Fordham L. Rev. 819, 824 (1992) (noting that much of the criticism of products liability law centers on the belief that juries do a poorer job of reviewing products than administrative agencies do); see also Cotton v. Buckeye Gas Prod. Co., 840 F.2d 935, 937–39 (D.C. Cir. 1988) (criticizing juries for their inability to weigh the costs of information overload in failure-to-warn cases).

within limits, which do not admit of even approximate ascertainment; and, although probability might theoretically be estimated, if any statistics were available, they never are; and, besides, probability varies with the severity of the injuries. It follows that all such attempts are illusory, and, *if serviceable at all, are so only to center attention upon which one of the factors may be determinative in any given situation.*[30]

For Hand, then, the value of his formula was *conceptual*: it isolates the elements of due care and the relations among them.

A strong normative claim is also embedded in the economic interpretation of the Hand Formula. The normative claim is that Hand Formula negligence commits us to economic valuation of the costs of accidents and their avoidance. Hand's own understanding of his formula, however, was firmly opposed to the theory of value that underpins this normative thesis. The economic conception of due care models social choice on individual choice. Just as an economically rational individual seeks to maximize the satisfaction of her preferences, an economically rational society seeks to maximize the satisfaction of its members' preferences. It therefore combines the preferences of distinct persons into a single calculus of risk and tallies them. Precautions should be taken, or risks imposed, when doing so will produce the greatest total satisfaction of preferences. Following the practice of actual markets, which measure the intensity of preferences through the medium of dollars, the economic conception urges that we cash out preferences into dollars: rational precautions are ones whose benefits exceed their costs.

This procedure treats all interests as "commensurable"—as fungible at some ratio of exchange. All relevant considerations can be assigned dollar values and traded off against one another. Figuring out what to do—figuring out whether to take a precaution and, if so, what precaution to take—is a matter of math. No evaluative judgment or normative decision ever needs to be made. There is only one value, namely, welfare. Everything else matters only insofar as it promotes or detracts from welfare.[31] When the Hand Formula is embedded in this economic framework, the implication is that it can be applied without exercising normative judgment. Costs and benefits can simply be computed. Judge Hand subscribed

---

[30] Moisan v. Loftus, 178 F.2d 148, 149 (2d Cir. 1949) (emphasis added); see also Stephen G. Gilles, The Invisible Hand Formula, 80 Va. L. Rev. 1015, 1028 (1994) (the Hand Formula is, in practice, an "intuitive" version of cost-benefit analysis which cannot support a "rigorous quantitative inquiry"). Judge Posner agrees, at least some of the time. See Villanova v. Abrams, 972 F.2d 792, 796 (7th Cir. 1992) ("In practice, the application of standards that can be expressed in algebraic terms still requires the exercise of judgment, implying elements of inescapable subjectivity and intuition in the decisional calculus."); United States Fid. & Guar. Co. v. Jadranska Slobodna Plovidba, 683 F.2d 1022, 1026 (7th Cir. 1982) ("[The Hand] [F]ormula is a valuable aid to clear thinking about the factors that are relevant to a judgment of negligence and about the relationship among those factors.").

[31] Louis Kaplow & Steven Shavell, Fairness Versus Welfare (Harvard, 2002).

to an opposite view. He thought that "a solution [to a problem framed by his formula] always involves some preference, or choice between incommensurables, and it is consigned to a jury because their decision is thought most likely to accord with commonly accepted standards, real or fancied."[32] To speak colloquially, for Judge Hand, the question is always whether the "game is worth the candle." Does the end being pursued justify the risk being imposed? Does the burden of taking some risk-reducing precaution diminish unacceptably the value we realize through imposing the risk? For Learned Hand, these are irreducibly normative questions that can only be answered through the exercise of evaluative judgment.

When we separate the Hand Formula from its economic interpretation, we see that it only identifies the basic variables of negligence and their relation to one another. It is a conceptual tool, not an algorithmic decision procedure that converts inputs in the form of preferences expressed in dollars into welfare-maximizing outputs. The formula permits, but does not require, economic valuation of the variables that it identifies. It also (and equally) permits noneconomic valuation of those variables. And it does not displace evaluative judgment. On the contrary, it requires that we exercise evaluative judgment. The orthodox economic interpretation of the Hand Formula is a different beast. It departs from the formula itself by endowing it with a distinctive theory of value and embedding it in a larger normative apparatus. When it does so, the economic interpretation does more than fill in some blank spaces in a plausible way; it remakes negligence law in the image of economics. On its face, the law of negligence is relational. It articulates obligations owed by people whose actions impose reasonably foreseeable risks of physical harm on others to those on whom they impose those risks. And it insists that the interests at stake in those risk impositions be evaluated objectively. The economic interpretation of the Hand Formula, by contrast, holds that obligations of reasonable care are concerned with producing states of the world in which wealth is maximized, and it understands wealth to be the metric for measuring persons' subjective preferences for their own well-being.

2. Reasonableness as Rationality—The Economic Interpretation

The economic interpretation of the Hand Formula brings the criterion of "Kaldor Hicks efficiency"—or "potential Pareto superiority"—to bear on the choice between taking a precaution and allowing preventable accidents to occur. One state

---

[32] Conway v. O'Brien, 111 F.2d 611, 612 (2d Cir. 1940), rev'd, 312 U.S. 492 (1941). Stephen Gilles identifies this opinion as Judge Hand's first intimation of the formula. Gilles 1994, *supra* note 30, at 1029 n.36. For Judge Hand's general assertion of this view, see Learned Hand, Address at the National Conference on the Continuing Education of the Bar, in Continuing Legal Education for Professional Competence and Responsibility: The Report on the Arden House Conference (Dec. 16, 1958); 1959 Joint Committee on Continuing Legal Education of the A.L.I. and the A.B.A. 116, 119. Reprinted in The Spirit of Liberty: Papers and Addresses of Learned Hand 302, 307 (Knopf, 3d ed., 1974).

of the world is potentially Pareto superior to another if, and only if, those whose welfare increases from the move to the potentially Pareto superior state could fully compensate those whose welfare diminishes and still be better off than they would be without the change.[33] Changes whose marginal benefits exceed their marginal costs are thus potentially Pareto superior. Because efficiency criteria evaluate the effects in terms of their impacts on the welfare of human beings, the use of such criteria requires a conception of welfare and some way of measuring the amount of welfare in different states of the world. Following mainstream neoclassical economics, law and economics deploys subjective criteria of value. It evaluates costs and benefits to people "solely from the point of view of that person's tastes and interests."[34] To measure people's preferences for their own well-being, the economic interpretation of the Hand Formula adopts the standard approach in cost-benefit analysis and compares preferences by asking what people are "willing to pay" to have their preferences honored. Taken together, these three commitments remake reasonable care in the image of economic efficiency.[35]

The most important commitments of this framework are to a subjective conception of well-being and to measuring subjective satisfaction in the metric of money. Subjective criteria of well-being pose a problem for interpersonal comparison. The subjective value of the same good, or social condition, may be

[33] For a clear explanation of the conceptions, see Coleman 1988, *supra* note 16, at 97–105; see also E.J. Mishan, Introduction to Normative Economics 301–14 (New York, 1981) (discussing the development of Kaldor-Hicks efficiency and its implications for allocation theory); A. Mitchell Polinsky, An Introduction to Law and Economics 7, n.4 (Little, Brown, and Co., 2d. ed., 1989) (relating Pareto criteria to the basic intuitive idea behind the concept of efficiency—the idea of maximizing "the size of the pie"); Robert D. Cooter, The Best Right Laws: Value Foundations of the Economic Analysis of Law, 64 Notre Dame L. Rev. 817, 827–29 (1989) (identifying cost-benefit analysis as a technique for applying Pareto efficiency criteria).

[34] T. M. Scanlon, Preference and Urgency, 72 J. Phil. 655, 668 (1975). Representative statements of the commitment to subjective valuation within neoclassical economics include Paul A. Samuelson, Foundations of Economic Analysis 90 (Harvard, Enlarged ed., 1983) ("If one were looking for a single criterion by which to distinguish modem economic theory from its classical precursors, he would probably decide that this is to be found in the introduction of the so-called subjective theory of value into economic theory."); Robert Cooter & Peter Rappoport, Were the Ordinalists Wrong about Welfare Economics?, 22 J. Econ. Literature 507, 522 (1984) (explaining how the ordinalist revolution in economics involved the replacement of an "objective definition of utility (socially useful) [with] a subjective definition (satisfaction of desire)."). For representative statements within law and economics, see Cooter & Ulen 1988, *supra* note 7, at 23 ("It is important to remember that the preferences of the consumer are purely *subjective*. That is, they are his or her preferences, to be discovered by finding out what he or she likes, not by telling him or her what to like."); Richard Craswell, Passing on the Costs of Legal Rules: Efficiency and Distribution in Buyer-Seller Relationships, 43 Stan. L. Rev. 361, 368–69 (1991) ("I adopt the consumer sovereignty position that consumer welfare is to be judged solely by reference to consumers' own tastes and preferences.").

[35] The economic interpretation of the Hand Formula is identified with the academic writings and judicial opinions of Judge Richard Posner. In developing the three aspects of the interpretation that I have highlighted, however, I shall, for the most part, draw on Robert Cooter and Thomas Ulen's presentation of the position. See Cooter & Ulen 1988, *supra* note 7, at 340–62. *Cf.* Richard A. Posner, The Problems of Jurisprudence Ch. 12, esp. at 356–58 (Harvard, 1990).

very different for different people. Orthodox neoclassical economics responds to this problem by distinguishing ordinal utility from cardinal utility. Cardinal utility, the absolute pleasure that a person derives from the consumption of some good or from enjoying some state of the world, is now largely abandoned by economists because quantifying the subjective pleasure of different persons proved exceedingly difficult.[36] Orthodox neoclassical economics seeks to avoid these problems by taking individual persons' ordinal preferences rankings as its starting point.

> Consumers are assumed to know the things that they like and dislike and to be able to rank the available alternative combinations of goods and services according to their ability to satisfy the consumer's preferences. This involves no more than ranking the alternatives as being better than, worse than, or equally as good as one another.[37]

When they are used to represent the phenomenon of consumer choice, ordinal preference rankings do not involve any explicit interpersonal comparisons of welfare. They simply represent individual consumers' preferences among various goods and services.

The application of the potential Pareto efficiency criterion to the problem of due care, however, requires *interpersonal* comparisons of welfare because present precaution costs borne by injurers must be compared with expected accident costs that will fall on victims. To compare these interpersonal costs for purposes of applying Pareto criteria, the concept of full compensation must be specified. The potential Pareto superiority of a particular risk imposition depends on the possibility of those who will benefit from the imposition (injurers) fully compensating those who will lose some measure of security (prospective victims). The relevant ordinal preferences—the orders in which injurers and victims each rank the state of the world in which the risk is imposed and the state in which it is not imposed—do not permit us to compare the relative intensity of victim and injurer preferences. We need to measure something suspiciously like cardinal utility so that we can compare the intensity of injurer and victim preferences.

---

[36] Steven T. Call & William L. Holahan, Microeconomics 29–30 (Pearson, 2d ed., 1983); see also Jack Hirshleifer, Price Theory and Applications 61–69 (Cambridge, 3d ed., 1984) (defining the properties of cardinal utility); Cooter 1989, *supra* note 33, at 818–20 (distinguishing between cardinal utility, with its roots in Bentham's theory of utility, and ordinal utility, which can be observed and quantified).

[37] Cooter & Ulen 1988, *supra* note 7, at 22. "For example, the consumer might be a shopper deciding how much beef and chicken to buy. If x denotes beef and y denotes chicken, then a function $u = u(x,y)$ can be used to describe the consumer's ranking of alternative combinations of beef and chicken." *Id.* at 22. Cooter and Ulen call this concept of utility as preference ranking or ordering the "simplest meaning" of the "slippery" concept of utility. *Id.* at 23.

This is where "willingness-to-pay" comes in.[38] "Willingness-to-pay" measures the intensity of different persons' preferences in the common coin of money. The Hand Formula compares expected accident costs with present precautions, thereby framing the relevant preferences as the injurer's preference for forgoing the precaution in question and the victim's preference for the reduction in risk effected by that precaution. To measure the intensity of these preferences, the economic interpretation of the Hand Formula asks how much injurers would pay to be relieved of the obligation to take a particular precaution and how much victims would pay to have that precaution taken. By translating preferences into dollars, "willingness-to-pay" establishes money as the metric of interpersonal comparison.[39] By virtue of this translation, the economic interpretation of the Hand Formula (again, like cost-benefit analysis generally) becomes wealth-maximizing, not (except coincidentally) utility-maximizing.[40]

[38] The use of willingness to pay as a criterion for measuring welfare gains and losses is characteristic of cost-benefit analysis in general, and of law and economics in particular. See, *e.g.*, W. Kip Viscusi, Risk by Choice: Regulating Health and Safety in the Workplace 94–96 (Harvard, 1983) (conceptualizing a willingness to pay standard for use in evaluating risk-reduction policies); Cooter 1989, *supra* note 33, at 828 ("cost benefit analysis equates the value of things with the amount that people are willing to pay for them."); Craswell 1991, *supra* note 34, at 369 ("I . . . assume that [consumer] tastes and preferences can be meaningfully translated into a dollar amount and that the appropriate amount is whatever each consumer is willing to pay to satisfy those preferences."). The idea of using willingness to pay to measure the value of life and limb originated in T.C. Schelling, The Life You Save May Be Your Own, in Problems in Public Expenditure Analysis 127 (Samuel B. Chase Jr. ed., Brookings, 1968). While most of the relevant literature speaks of willingness to *pay*, it is not clear that this measure should be preferred to willingness to *accept*. Willingness to pay measures what one would be willing to spend to acquire an entitlement that one does not possess; willingness to accept measures what one would accept to relinquish an entitlement that one does possess. To my knowledge, the economic interpretation of the Hand Formula has not settled on either of the measures.

[39] Armen A. Alchian, Cost, in Encyclopedia of the Social Sciences 404, 405 (David L. Sills ed., New York, 1968). The application of the potential Pareto superiority criterion requires some metric of comparison to make sense of the requirement of full compensation, but neither that criterion nor the commitment to subjective criteria for the evaluation of personal welfare entail selecting money (or wealth) as the metric. Money is an appealing metric (or unit of account) for economists because it is the medium of exchange and therefore is the convenient denominator for comparing interpersonal exchange values of events or options. Nevertheless, other metrics are, in principle, equally satisfactory. We might, for example, measure preferences in number of kiwi fruit that persons would pay to see them honored. *Id.*

[40] The economic interpretation of the Hand Formula would only be invariably utility maximizing (invoking the slippery concept of utility here in a quasi-cardinal sense) "if a dollar were equally valuable to everyone," and in all circumstances. Cooter & Rappoport 1984, *supra* note 34, at 526. This is an implausible assumption. It is more plausible to assume that additional dollars have diminishing marginal utility. The fact that the tort system does not maximize utility by maximizing wealth does not mean that wealth maximization should not be the goal of the tort system if our ultimate aim is to maximize utility. Legal economists argue that it is cheaper (either generally or invariably) to redistribute wealth through the tax system than through the legal system. Maximizing wealth in the tort system is therefore one element of the most promising strategy for maximizing utility, because increases in wealth can be redistributed through the tax system in a manner that maximizes utility. See, *e.g.*, Louis Kaplow & Steven Shavell, Why the Legal System Is Less Efficient than the Income Tax System in Redistributing Income, 23 J. Legal Stud. 667, 669 (1994) ("[G]iven any regime with an inefficient legal rule (notably, one intended to help achieve a redistributive goal), there exists an alternative regime with an efficient legal rule and a modified income tax system in which all individuals are better off."); Kaplow & Shavell 2002, *supra* note 31.

The Hand Formula was devised to help triers of fact determine whether a defendant was negligent in failing to take some accident-averting precaution. The comparison that the economic interpretation of the formula prescribes, though, is not easy to make. No market exists to measure either what injurers are prepared to pay to forgo taking certain precautions, or what victims are prepared to pay to have injurers take those precautions. To apply the economic interpretation, juries would have to guess at these matters, and appellate courts supervising their verdicts would, at best, seem to have two courses available to them. Following the approach intimated by Landes and Posner, appellate courts could rely on average estimates (or guesses) of what injurers and victims are prepared to pay.[41] Or, following the approach intimated by Schelling, Viscusi, and Schwartz, they could extrapolate such estimates from data indicating the market value that persons place on their lives.[42]

Both approaches are likely to leave considerable leeway for judges to exercise their own normative judgment in the guise of finding facts. The more important point, though, is that the economic deference to subjective preferences require us to figure out which preferences count. Are the relevant preferences those that persons presently have, or those that they would have if they were perfectly informed? As a matter of economic theory, perfectly informed preferences are superior to imperfectly informed ones. Perfectly informed preferences express our best true judgments about our own welfare; imperfectly informed preferences are unlikely to do so.[43] This means that the ostensibly empirical inquiry required by the economic conception of due care in fact asks us to answer a counterfactual question and an unanswerable one at that. The question is counterfactual because it directs our attention *not* to actual preferences but to perfectly informed ones. It is unanswerable because, if we suppose—as economics does—that

---

[41] See William M. Landes & Richard A. Posner, The Economic Structure of Tort Law 34–38 (Harvard, 1987).

[42] Viscusi 1983, *supra* note 38, at 98–102 (discussing empirical studies of the values people place on life); Schelling 1968, *supra* note 38, at 134–35, 144 (discussing methods and problems in valuing a person's life); Gary T. Schwartz, The Myth of the Ford Pinto Case, 43 Rutgers L. Rev. 1013, 1026 n.46 (1991) (citing work by Viscusi and Moore dating from 1990 which placed a value of $6.2 million on a life); W. Kip Viscusi, The Value of Life, 2 New Palgrave Dictionary of Economics and the Law (2005) (placing a value of $7 million on an American life).

[43] Economic analyses usually take informed preferences as their touchstone. See, *e.g.*, Craswell 1991, *supra* note 34, at 369 ("I . . . assume consumers have perfect information about the presence or absence of the warranty and about its value to them."); Alan Schwartz, Products Liability Reform: A Theoretical Synthesis, 97 Yale L.J. 353, 355 ("[The] consumer sovereignty . . . norm holds that the law should reflect the preferences of competent, informed consumers regarding risk allocation."). For a philosophical discussion of the justifications for, and problems with, this move, see John C. Harsanyi, Morality and the Theory of Rational Behavior, in Utilitarianism and Beyond 103 (Amartya Sen & Bernard Williams eds., Cambridge, 1982), at 39, 55 (formulating the principle of Preference Autonomy, which holds that a person's informed preferences for her own welfare are the only legitimate criteria for deciding what is best for that individual), and T.M. Scanlon, The Moral Basis of Interpersonal Comparisons, in Interpersonal Comparisons of Well-Being 17 (Jon Elster & John E. Roemer eds., Cambridge, 1993).

preferences are subjective, it is simply impossible to know what preferences perfectly informed persons would have. In practice, the requirement that we defer to the preferences persons have and not impose our preferences on them turns to be almost empty.[44] In practice, the application of the economic interpretation of the Hand Formula must make less use of *individual* preferences with respect to costs and benefits of diverse precautions and accidents than it does in theory; must draw on guesswork and incomplete, imperfect empirical data; and must answer a question that is essentially unanswerable. Combined, these limitations undermine any argument that the economic interpretation of the Hand Formula replaces the vague, morally inflected language of the law with something clearer, more precise, and more easily applied.

Unlike economics, negligence law is firmly committed to the objective valuation of the urgency of claims and the importance of interests. This commitment to objectivity is most vividly articulated in average reasonable person (ARP) doctrine. ARP doctrine plays as important a role as the Hand Formula in articulating the general concept of due care, though the domains of the doctrines differ. Whereas the Hand Formula's natural habitat is the realm of planning and considered precaution—the sort of thing that institutions undertake most fully—the natural habitat of ARP doctrine is the conduct of natural persons. ARP doctrine is therefore concerned with questions of excuse (questions of what we may reasonably demand of people in the way of competence) as much as with questions of justification (questions of what a competent person should do). Part of what ARP doctrine prescribes is that the evaluative judgments of the reasonable person are objective in two respects. First, the reasonable person gives "an impartial consideration to the harm likely to be done the interests of the other as compared with the advantages likely to accrue to his own interests, free from the natural tendency of the actor, as a party concerned, to prefer his own interests to those of others."[45] Let us call this "the impartiality of equal consideration." Second, the reasonable person also "give[s] to the respective interests concerned *the value which the law attaches to them.*"[46] Let us call this "the impartiality of objective valuation."

The economic interpretation of due care proposes a plausible interpretation of negligence law's commitment to the impartiality of equal consideration.

---

[44] See Duncan Kennedy, Distributive and Paternalist Motives in Contract and Tort Law, with Special Reference to Compulsory Terms and Unequal Bargaining Power, 41 Md. L. Rev. 563, 597–604 (1982) (arguing that economic analysis disguises normative judgments as questions of fact); Scanlon 1993, *supra* note 43, at 42 (discussing problems with estimating "fully informed and ideally rational" preferences). It is important to distinguish asking an unanswerable question from simply leaving plenty of room for empirical and normative disagreement. All credible approaches to the problems of due care thrust some difficult questions on juries and leave plenty of room for disagreement. Not all approaches ask unanswerable questions, however.

[45] Restatement (Second) of Torts § 283 cmt. E (1965).

[46] *Id.* (emphasis added).

A reasonable person, economically conceived, thinks and acts as a single, rationally self-interested person would if they bore both the costs and the benefits of the risks that they impose. An unreasonable person, by contrast, gives more weight to his or her benefits than to the costs they impose on others.[47] "This interpretation of reasonableness in effect requires the decisionmaker to act as if all costs and benefits were internalized, as required for efficiency."[48] The economic idea of reasonable conduct as cost-internalizing conduct articulates a plausible conception of reasonableness as impartiality. But the economic commitment to subjective valuation stands "the impartiality of objective valuation" on its head. The law of negligence asserts that the valuations of the parties should track the objective valuations of the law. The economic interpretation of reasonable care asserts that the valuations of the law should follow the subjective valuations of the parties.

To be sure, economic analysis has ways of explaining why negligence law's average reasonable person is standardized, not particularized. Steven Shavell, for example, observes that attaining the socially optimal level of care requires determining each individual's actual costs of care, but that it may in practice be hard (or impossible) for courts to obtain individualized cost information.[49] For this reason, courts may have no choice but to use average costs of care.[50] Landes and Posner make essentially the same argument.[51] There is an important point here, but it goes only so far. The cost of tailoring care to the idiosyncrasies of individual actors may explain why negligence law has reason to use an empirical average, but the word "average" in ARP doctrine identifies a *normative* standard that people are expected to meet—not an empirical regularity. That standard is objective in the sense that it identifies conduct that people may reasonably demand of each other, even though not everyone will be up to doing so.[52] As Holmes

---

[47] Cooter & Ulen 1988, *supra* note 7, at 360. The metaphor of the single actor appears early on in cases explicating the idea of reasonable care. See The Nitro-glycerin Case (Parrott v. Wells, Fargo, & Co., 82 U.S. (15 Wall.) 524, 538 (1872)) ("[T]he measure of care against accident, which one must take to avoid responsibility, is that which a person of ordinary prudence and caution would use if his own interests were to be affected, and the whole risk were his own."). Torts scholars have often emphasized the metaphor, for both moral and efficiency reasons. See, *e.g.*, Ward Farnsworth, The Single Owner, in The Legal Analysist: A Toolkit for Thinking about the Law, 37–46 (University of Chicago, 2007) (noting that the single owner principle links economic talk about costs and benefits to the Golden Rule); Samson Vermont, The Golden Hand Formula, 11 Green Bag 2d 203 (2008). Green 1997, *supra* note 15, at 1614 ("[T]he Learned Hand formula can also be understood noninstrumentally to reflect the Golden Rule.").

[48] *Id.* Other scholars have also used the single person metaphor to explain the economic conception of due care. See, *e.g.*, Gilles 1994, *supra* note 30, at 1032–35.

[49] Steven Shavell, Economic Analysis of Accident Law § 4.1 (Harvard, 1987).

[50] *Id.*

[51] Landes & Posner 1987, *supra* note 41, at 125–31; see also Richard A. Posner, Economic Analysis of Law 167 (Little, Brown and Co., 4th ed., 1992) (noting that the court's failure to measure the actual costs of accidents to the parties can only be justified by the high cost of individuated measurement).

[52] See Prosser & Keeton 1984, *supra* note 21, at 175 (observing that the reasonable person is "a personification of a community ideal of reasonable behavior, determined by the jury's social judgment");

famously observed: "[The awkward person's] slips are no less troublesome to his neighbors than if they sprang from guilty neglect."[53] Because they are no less troublesome, the law demands compliance with a normative standard of competence that defines due care. The economic idea of an empirically average person is not the law's idea of an acceptably competent person.

For orthodox economics, objective criteria are a second-best solution to the problem of interpersonal comparison. Indeed, for orthodox economics the subjectivity of value makes tort law a second-best alternative to contract. "Because individual preferences are subjective and are truly known only by an individual himself, economics generally encourages reliance on voluntary transactions to reallocate resources in a way that promotes individual (and thus social) welfare."[54] The conflict between economics preference for subjective criteria of interpersonal comparison and tort law's preference for objective ones is stark enough to undercut the thesis that the law of negligence is immanently economic. Objective standards are endemic in tort law, and the cases generally insist on their superiority to subjective standards.[55] From a deontological perspective, tort doctrine's embrace of objectivity is not a second-best concession to the formidable difficulties of ferreting out people's subjective preferences. In a world where people have diverse values, aspirations, and conceptions of the good, objective criteria of interpersonal comparison are preferable to subjective ones. They are the best criteria for reconciling the competing claims of liberty and security on fair terms.

---

cf. Jules Coleman, Risks and Wrongs, 280, 471 n.11 (Oxford, rev. ed., 2002) (distinguishing between "normative" and "epistemic" expectations, and arguing that tort duties to repair are grounded in normative expectations).

[53] Holmes 1991, *supra* note 11, at 108.
[54] Jennifer H. Arlen, Reconsidering Efficient Tort Rules for Personal Injury: The Case of Single Activity Accidents, 32 Wm. & Mary L. Rev. 41, 52 (1990).
[55] Some examples of courts applying objective standards in intentional torts include: the manifestation of consent, O'Brien v. Cunard Steamship Co., 28 N.E. 266 (Mass. 1891); intending the natural consequences of one's actions, Garratt v. Dailey, 279 P.2d 1091 (Wash. 1955); the *mens rea* of trespass, Cleveland Park Club v. Perry, 165 A.2d 485 (D.C. 1960); the apprehension element of assault, State v. Ingram, 74 S.E.2d 532 (N.C. 1953); and the objective component of self-defense, Nelson v. State, 181 N.E. 448 (Ohio Ct. App. 1932). In negligence law, examples besides ARP doctrine include nuisance law, Rogers v. Elliot, 15 N.E. 768 (Mass. 1888), and assumption of risk, Knight v. Jewett, 834 P.2d 696 (Cal. 1992). There are, of course, counterexamples in which courts use subjective standards, such as: the abused spouse defense, State v. Leidholm, 334 N.W.2d 811 (N.D. 1983); the "actual malice" subjective recklessness standard for defamation, New York Times Co. v. Sullivan, 376 U.S. 254 (1964); and intentional infliction of emotional distress, Hustler Magazine v. Falwell, 485 U.S. 46 (1988).

B. Reasonable Care as Fair Precaution

The metaphor of the single actor captures something important about the idea of reasonable care—namely, that it requires treating the rights and interests of those one might endanger as equal in importance to your own. Reasonable care requires impartiality. When, however, the metaphor of the single actor is spelled out to call for balancing the preferences of distinct persons against one another as though they were the preferences of a single person, it leads us badly astray. The fundamental question of negligence law is whether it is reasonable to impose some risk of physical harm on *other* people. The metaphor of the single actor recasts that question as the question of what risks it is rational for us to take upon ourselves. Reasonable risk imposition becomes rational risk assumption. We may reasonably impose risks on others whenever it would be rational for us to take such risks upon ourselves. Yet we rightly regard the circumstance where we take risks upon ourselves in pursuit of our own ends as very different from the circumstance where others impose risks on us in pursuit of their ends. In the first circumstance, we both bear any harm that arises out of the risk and reap the benefits of taking the risk upon ourselves. In the second circumstance, we are exposed to the harm, but the benefits accrue to others. And because the compensation required by Kaldor-Hicks efficiency is potential, not actual, the criterion licenses the imposition of risks that in fact leave their victims worse off.

The fault here is the one John Rawls identified in classical utilitarianism. By modeling social choice on individual choice in the way that it does, the economic interpretation of the Hand Formula "does not take seriously the distinction between persons."[56] We have distinct lives to lead, and diverse ends and aspirations to pursue. Our lives are not fungible at some ratio of exchange, like goods in a market. Nor are the values and ends that we seek to realize interchangeable. The values are realized in our lives, projects, and activities and are not usually detachable from them. Living the life of a monk and living the life of a rock star are not just two ways of realizing the same level of preference satisfaction. The goods that those lives realize are inseparable from the lives that realize them. Given the separateness of our lives, and the diversity of the values and ends that we pursue, the justification for accepting risk impositions by others is not common allegiance to the shared end of wealth- or welfare-maximization or social welfare, but *reciprocity*. Others may impose reasonable risks on us because we may impose reasonable risks on them. Reasonable care doctrine is a matter of mutuality.

The fundamental problem that negligence law faces is the one that Ripstein identifies when he quotes Lord Reid's remark that we live "in a crowded world."[57]

---

[56] John Rawls, A Theory of Justice, 27 (Harvard, rev. ed., 1999).
[57] Ripstein 2016, *supra* note 17, at 103. Weinrib and Stone are making the same kind of point, in more metaphysical way, when they describe the circumstance where one person acts and another

In the world as we know it, some risk is the unavoidable byproduct of activity. We cannot lead our own lives—and pursue our own ends— without imposing risks on others. In turn, they cannot lead their lives without imposing risks on us. The law of negligence, and the law governing accidental harm more generally, reconciles two essential conditions of human agency: freedom of action (or liberty) and security (or safety). Fairly reconciling freedom of action and security is necessary for people to have favorable conditions for pursuing their conceptions of the good over the course of their lives as equal and independent persons. The terms of reasonable risk imposition must be terms of equal freedom and mutual benefit, so far as possible.

Liberty and security are both important interests, but between them security has priority. In Rawlsian terms, safety is a kind of "primary good." Safety is something we need no matter what our aims and aspirations are. The value of various goods that enable us to realize our ends, by contrast, is much more contingent on what our ends happen to be. Physical integrity is an essential condition of agency for both a monk and an entrepreneur. Great wealth, by contrast, impedes the monk's, but enables the entrepreneur's, pursuit of value. This difference is reflected in the asymmetry of harm and benefit, found in both morality and law.[58] Our reasons not to harm other people are generally stronger than our reasons to benefit them, and our legal obligations are too. Avoiding harm has priority over conferring benefit. In our legal system, for instance, the government is under a constitutional obligation to compensate those from whom it takes property to promote the general good. Those who receive special benefits from the government (when, say, it locates a new highway near their businesses) are not under a parallel obligation to compensate the government for the benefits it has bestowed upon them. Private law embodies the same asymmetry. "[T]he legal remedies available to victims of harms are far superior to those enjoyed by analogous providers of non-bargained benefits."[59] Torts is a major legal field; restitution is a minor one.

For economically inclined scholars, like Saul Levmore, the harm-benefit asymmetry is an "anomaly." From an economic point of view, harms and benefits are pluses and minuses on the same scale. Torts addresses negative externalities; restitution addresses positive ones. The two fields should be similar in size and significance. But they are not: the avoidance of harm has priority over the

---

suffers as inherent in the structure of human action. Weinrib 2012, *supra* note 17, at 72–75; Martin Stone, The Significance of Doing and Suffering, in Philosophy and the Law of Torts 131 (Gerald J. Postema ed., Cambridge, 2001).

[58] This asymmetry figures even more strongly in the justification of regulatory standards that prescribe more than cost-justified precaution. See Chapter Five, *infra*, pp. 193–199.

[59] Saul Levmore, Explaining Restitution, 71 Va. L. Rev. 65, 71 (1985). Levmore explicitly calls this the "harms-benefits asymmetry" and describes it as an "anomaly." *Id.* at 71.

conferral of benefit. Harm's special and negative moral significance is intelligible only when we put the distinctness of our separate lives, and our interest in leading those lives in accordance with our own aspirations for them, at the center of our thinking. Costs and benefits may be symmetrically important from an economic perspective, but harms and benefits are not symmetrically important from a deontological perspective.[60] Harm—*especially* physical harm—impairs our basic powers of agency, the capacities through which we work our wills on the world. Serious physical harms impair the pursuit of a wide range of human ends and aspirations and deny normal human lives to those whose powers are impaired. Very few benefits, by contrast, are comparably essential conditions of effective agency. Benefit, like happiness, is mostly for each of us to pursue as best as we can.

The priority of avoiding harm has a pervasive influence on our law of torts. Insofar as the law of negligence distinguishes physical harm from pure economic loss and pure emotional injury—and confers general protection against physical harm but not against pure emotional injury or pure economic loss—the delineation of the domain of negligence law reflects the priority of avoiding harm. Harm's priority is manifested more subtly in average reasonable person doctrine and in cases that conceive of negligence in broad Hand Formula terms. Average reasonable person doctrine's famously harsh refusal to recognize morally compelling claims of excuse assigns priority to the avoidance of unjustifiable harm. And the Hand Formula can be understood as a heuristic that helps us to determine when a risk imposition is fair—when the terms on which a risk is imposed reconcile the liberty of potential injurers and the security of potential victims on terms that both should regard as acceptable.

1. The Priority of Physical Harm and the Domain of Negligence Law

Conceptualizing the problem of accidental harm in terms of liberty and security resonates with readily accessible moral intuitions[61] and fits with much of tort law. "Tort actions," one court has written, "are created to protect the interest in freedom from various kinds of harm."[62] For its part, the delineation of the domain of negligence law embodies an immanently deontological understanding of harm's special negative significance. In general, establishing a prima facie case of negligence requires proving that the wrongful conduct of the defendant harmed either one's physical person or one's property. In general, someone who

---

[60] We shall say a bit more about this in the next chapter. See Chapter Five, *infra*, pp. 193-94, 197–98.

[61] Judith Jarvis Thomson, Remarks on Causation and Liability, in Rights, Restitution, & Risk: Essays in Moral Theory 192, 199 (William Parent ed., Harvard, 1986) (arguing that tort compensation for accidental injury protects our "moral space, in which to assess possible ends, make choices, and then work for the means to reach those ends").

[62] Victorson v. Bock Laundry Mach. Co., 335 N.E.2d 275, 277 (N.Y. 1975) (quoting William L. Prosser, Handbook of the Law of Torts § 92, at 613 (West, 4th ed. 1971)).

suffers either pure economic loss or pure emotional distress cannot normally sue for negligence, even if their suffering was carelessly inflicted.[63] This recognition that we have an urgent and generic interest in avoiding physical harm is reinforced by the inalienability of tort protections against accidental injury. Contract is a live alternative to tort in the product liability context, but tort protections are imposed as a matter of law and are not easily disclaimed.[64]

To make out a prima facie case of negligence, a plaintiff must normally prove harm in the form of physical impairment.[65] What physical harm to our person impairs is the principal instrument through which we work our wills in the world. Broken limbs, disabilities, serious illness, and disfigurement are conditions in which people are unable to exercise normal powers of agency. By contrast, losses—economic and otherwise—do not normally leave their victims in impaired conditions. It may be devastating to lose a race and to have to settle for a silver medal, but it does not leave you with a broken body. Physical harm to our property falls between our bodies and our bank accounts. In our social world, personal property is both an essential social condition for the development of personhood and an especially valuable instrument for the efficacious pursuit of most conceptions of the good. Rawls's first principle of justice, for example, includes among the "basic liberties of the person . . . the right to hold and to have the exclusive use of personal property."[66] It does so because this liberty is necessary to "allow a sufficient material basis for a sense of personal independence and self-respect."[67] There is thus a case to be made for

---

[63] The majority rule denies recovery for economic losses caused by negligence unless the victim's property or physical security also suffers harm. See, *e.g.*, Robins Dry Dock & Repair Co. v. Flint, 275 U.S. 303, 309 (1927); Stevenson v. East Ohio Gas Co., 73 N.E.2d 200, 203, 204 (Ohio Ct. App. 1946). Similarly, one cannot recover in a products liability action for damage to the defective product itself. See, *e.g.*, East River S.S. Corp. v. Transamerica Delaval, Inc., 476 U.S. 858, 871 (1986) ("The tort concern with safety is reduced when an injury is only to the product itself."); Moorman Mfg. Co. v. Nat'l Tank Co., 435 N.E.2d 443, 450 (Ill. 1982). Recovery for pure emotional injury is likewise exceptional. See Keeton et al., 2004, *supra* note 21, at 664–76; Dan B. Dobbs, Paul T. Hayden, & Ellen M. Bublick, Hornbook on Torts 189 (West, 2d ed., 2016).

[64] The imposition of non-disclaimable duties of care with respect to product accidents that result in physical injury and property damage was a major element of the progression of product liability law from *MacPherson*, through *Henningsen*, and on to the adoption of § 402A of the Restatement (Second) of Torts. See MacPherson v. Buick Motor Co., 111 N.E. 1050 (N.Y. 1916) (extending the duty owed by defendant manufacturers to foreseeable users other than the immediate purchasers); Henningsen v. Bloomfield Motors, Inc., 161 A.2d 69 (N.J. 1960) (recognizing a non-disclaimable warranty of merchantability); Restatement (Second) of Torts § 402A (1965) (making the seller of a product strictly liable to either the consumer or the user of a defective product).

[65] See, *e.g.*, Restatement (Third) of Torts: Liability For Physical & Emotional Harm § 4 (2010) (defining "physical harm" as "the physical impairment of the human body ('bodily harm') or of real property or tangible personal property . . . [such impairment] includes physical injury, illness, disease, impairment of bodily function, and death.").

[66] Rawls 2005, *supra* note 8, at 298.

[67] *Id.* Rawls objects to including property "rights of acquisition and bequest" and the "right to own means of production and natural resources" within the equal basic liberties, as libertarians might. Rawls also objects to including the right to equal ownership of natural resources and means of

grouping property damage with physical harm to persons instead of with pure economic loss.[68]

The exclusion of pure emotional distress—emotional injury unaccompanied by physical harm—is a more difficult problem for a view that puts the urgent interests and integrity of persons at its center. Some distress is miserable to suffer, but fleeting; it does not leave its victims in states of enduring impairment. Such distress is legitimately excluded, just as economic loss is. Other distress, intentionally inflicted, may be enduringly damaging but must be borne because its infliction involves the exercise of important liberties. One spouse telling another, "I don't love you anymore and I want a divorce," and "shunning" by a religious group with which one had previously been associated, are cases in point.[69] Some negligently inflicted psychological harm, however, *is* devastating. Psychological integrity is as important as physical integrity, and some psychological harms impair powers of agency in an enduring way.[70] Witnessing the death of one's child at the hands of a negligent driver is a sad example.[71] Because negligently inflicted harm is unjustified harm, negligently inflicted emotional harms cannot be said to be warranted by the important interests of those who inflict them.

Nonetheless, general liability for negligent infliction of emotional distress is neither feasible nor desirable. Some emotional distress must simply be suffered as a condition of life in this world. More importantly, general liability for negligent infliction of emotional distress would be unmanageably large, and predicating liability on the suffering of emotional distress would put us at the mercy of the emotionally hypersensitive. Negligence law favors objective standards for a reason. Using the sensibilities of the hypersensitive as the benchmark for the imposition of liability would create a standard

---

production within those liberties, as a socialist might, on the ground that these "wider conceptions are not ... necessary for the development and exercise of the moral powers." *Id.* On the connections between property and personhood, see generally Margaret Jane Radin, Property and Personhood, 34 Stan. L. Rev. 957 (1982).

[68] The extent to which tort law protects property interests probably exceeds the protection contemplated by Rawls. Whether this is a relatively harmless overgeneralization of protections centered on personhood, or the hijacking of those protections to protect private property instead of personhood, is too large a question to address here.

[69] See Whelan v. Whelan, 588 A.2d 251 (1991); Paul v. Watchtower Bible and Tract Society, 819 F.2d 875 (9th Cir. 1987).

[70] See Gregory C. Keating, When Is Emotional Distress Harm?, in Tort Law: Challenging Orthodoxy (Stephen G.A. Pitel, Jason W. Neyers, & Erika Chamberlain eds., Hart, 2013).

[71] This is the circumstance that occasioned the suit in *Dillon v. Legg*, 441 P.2d 912 (1968) (permitting mother who witnessed the death of her child at the hands of a negligent driver to recover, even though she was not herself in danger of being physically harmed by the driver's negligence). Suffering the death of a child under any circumstances is to suffer a harm that inflicts enduring impairment.

so uncertain and fluctuating as to paralyze industrial enterprises.... The character of [a use] might change from legal to illegal, or illegal to legal, with every change of tenants of an adjacent estate, or with an arrival or departure of a guest or boarder at a house near by; or even with the wakefulness or the tranquil repose of an invalid neighbor on a particular night.[72]

Recovery for emotional injury in negligence law is the exception, not the rule, and for good, if regrettable, reason. Emotional distress is not, in general, as serious a harm as physical injury, and general protection against emotional distress is not practicable.

Negligence law's delineation of its domain shapes the way that courts make judgments of due care. Because courts generally restrict the protection of negligence law to physical injury and property damage, determinations of due care of the sort called for by the Hand Formula compare the magnitude of threats to the physical integrity and personal property of victims with the cost to injurers of reducing those threats. The very procedure of negligence adjudication thus singles out the liberty and integrity of natural persons for special protection, and so reflects the priority of avoiding harm. Because the avoidance of harm has special priority, James Henderson's complaint that the application of negligence criteria to product design is fatally flawed by negligence law's narrow focus on safety concerns is mistaken. Henderson is right to observe that good product design must "consider such factors as market price, functional utility, and aesthetics, as well as safety, and achieve the proper balance among them."[73] But he is wrong to suppose that all these features are equally important. Safety has *relative priority* over these other goods.[74] Considerations of safety are more urgent than

---

[72] Rogers v. Elliott, 15 N.E. 768, 772 (Mass. 1888) (holding that ringing a church bell every day was not a nuisance even though it caused convulsions in the plaintiff, who was recovering from sunstroke, and stating the rule that what constitutes a nuisance must be determined by the standard "of ordinary people, as it is in determining [questions of] negligence"). The very same problems would arise if actors were exposed to negligence liability whenever someone experienced emotional distress because of their activity. The rule that victims may recover damages for emotional injury only when accompanied by physical injury is subject to various subtleties and some recent erosion. See Guido Calabresi, Ideals, Beliefs, Attitudes, and the Law: Private Law Perspectives on a Public Law Problem 69–71 (Syracuse, 1985) ("There are exceptions . . . and they have been growing. . . . The exceptions, however, remain just that, and emotional damages . . . are treated with great suspicion in torts."); Prosser & Keeton 1984, *supra* note 21, at 359–66 (discussing tort protections for "mental disturbances"); Dobbs 2016, *supra* note 63, at 189.

[73] James A. Henderson Jr., Judicial Review of Manufacturers' Conscious Design Choices: The Limits of Adjudication, 73 Colum. L. Rev. 1531, 1540 (1973). Henderson directs his critique against judicial review of conscious design choices, but it seems equally applicable to all complex questions of negligence.

[74] Negligence law does not exclude these factors from consideration, but it assigns priority to safety in its calculations. As Henderson's frequent coauthor, Aaron Twerski, put it, "[t]o the extent that factors such as cost, aesthetics and functional utility are examined, they are examined not in isolation but in relation to safety." A.D. Twerski, A.S. Weinstein, V.A. Donaher, & H.R. Piehler, The Use and Abuse of Warnings in Product Liability-Design Defect Litigation Comes of Age, 61 Cornell L. Rev. 495, 526 (1976).

considerations of price, utility, and aesthetics because physical integrity is an essential condition of effective agency.

The *inalienability* of tort protections against accidental physical harm likewise reflects the special urgency of safety. Because physical integrity is one of the preconditions of effective agency, disclaiming the protections of tort law puts basic powers of agency at risk. It is one thing to assume risks in pursuit of an end that you value highly—free soloing El Capitan, for instance. It is another to put your safety in the hands of sellers of cars and toasters and at the same time relieve them of responsibility to sell you a safe product. We have strong reasons not to alienate our basic political rights,[75] and we have similar reasons not to put our safety at the mercy of market forces. A mass market is not an institutional framework that can be counted on to deliver contractual terms that accord appropriate priority to product safety. Firms have reasons of self-interest to disclaim responsibility for accidents caused by product defects. Whether or not the free play of market forces will compel them to accept terms properly protective of safety depends on how well or how poorly informed consumers are; on whether consumers have the time and skill to evaluate contract terms; on whether well-informed consumers constitute a critical mass; on whether consumers discount risks of future harm excessively; and so on. Whatever their merits for registering consumer preferences, mass markets are not attractive mechanisms for recognizing our mutual obligations to safeguard each other's physical integrity.[76]

Negligence law's preoccupation with physical harm, and the inalienability of the protections of product liability law, fit well with the proposition that safety is a kind of primary good whose provision is a matter of special urgency and justice. Reconciling these commitments with an economic understanding of negligence is more difficult. Insofar as legal economists take wealth as a surrogate for welfare, the exclusion of purely economic damages is difficult to explain. Losses of wealth or income clearly affect people's welfare as economists understand it. The effort to reconcile economic theory with the restricted domain of accident law therefore leads economists to hypothesize that the overall effect of the victim's economic losses on *social* utility may be too small, or too uncertain, to justify awarding damages for purely economic losses.[77] Excluding

---

[75] *Cf.* Jean-Jacques Rousseau, The Social Contract 12–13 (Lester G. Crocker trans., Pocket Books, 1967) (1761) ("To renounce one's liberty is to renounce one's quality as a man, the rights and also the duties of humanity. For him who renounces everything there is no possible compensation. Such a renunciation is incompatible with man's nature, for to take away all freedom from his will is to take away all morality from his actions.").

[76] See Chapter Five, *infra*, pp. 220–23.

[77] For example, economists sometimes argue that victims suffering only economic loss are not entitled to recovery because their economic loss is likely to be recouped by other parties so that there will be no social loss. See, *e.g.*, Shavell 1987, *supra* note 49, at 137–39 (suggesting that the "no recovery for purely economic loss" rule is appropriate where other actors in the same market experience corresponding economic gains. A bridge collapse caused by a negligent automobile accident may harm one

purely emotional harm as a general matter also presents a problem. Orthodox economics conceives of value as subjective—as the satisfaction of subjective preference. Emotional distress is subjective harm incarnate, and suffering emotional distress is surely a cost. For tort law, though, the very subjectivity of pure emotional harm is a reason not to impose liability for inflicting such harms, as *Rogers v. Elliot* says.

Inalienability is equally problematic from an economic perspective. Preferences are subjective, difficult to know, best known by those whose preferences they are, and, in principle, infinitely variable.[78] Other things equal, legal economists typically prefer freedom of contract over immutable liability standards because contract permits the tailoring of legal terms to the tastes of the parties.[79] The inalienability of product liability protections prevents buyers and sellers from tailoring the terms of their transactions to their (subjective) tastes for levels of product risk. From an economic perspective, inalienability raises the specter of unjustified paternalism.[80] Absent information problems— or some other market failure—tort protections should be disclaimable. From an

---

set of actors (those who operate gas stops and restaurants on that highway) but simultaneously help another set of actors (those who offer the same services on the detour). See W. Bishop, Economic Loss in Tort, 2 Oxford J. Legal Stud. 1, 4–7 (1982). Courts have, however, rejected claims for pure economic loss, even in cases where the loss was not captured as a gain by someone else. In *Amoco Transport Co. v. SIS Mason Lykes*, 768 F.2d 659, 661–62 (5th Cir. 1985), for example, a shipper was forced to pay twice to ship his goods. The first attempt failed when the cargo ship crashed into another boat. No offsetting or net social gain resulted from the accident because the shipper just paid the same shipping company to re-ship the cargo on a different boat. For a summary of doctrine and policy relating to the rule, see then Judge Breyer's opinion in *Barber Lines NS v. MN Donau Maru*, 764 F.2d 50 (1st Cir. 1985).

[78] The assumption that consumer tastes for both product safety and insurance coverage are heterogeneous is attractive partly because consumers differ greatly in their wealth. Economists tend to suppose that even if the taste for safety does not vary with wealth, poorer consumers are not likely to pay as much for product safety and insurance against product accidents because they have less to spend and more urgent things to spend it on (such as food). See, *e.g.*, James M. Buchanan, In Defense of Caveat Emptor, 38 U. Chi. L. Rev. 64, 66 (1970) ("For the most part, but not exclusively, demanders of ... low quality product[s] will be poor people who can ill afford to purchase a high degree of risk avoidance."); Craswell 1991, *supra* note 34, at 379 ("[T]he correlation between a low willingness to pay for [a] product and a low willingness to pay for the warranty [may be] due to a lack of resources.").

[79] See, *e.g.*, Anthony T. Kronman, Specific Performance, 45 U. Chi. L. Rev. 351, 370 (1978) ("[A] legal system that denies private parties the right to [contract around its rules] will tend to be less efficient than a system that adopts the same rules but permits contractual variation."). This point is essential to Alan Schwartz's and James Buchanan's cases against strict liability and for contract in product liability law. See Schwartz 1991, *supra* note 42, at 836–40 (equating consumer sovereignty with free markets and freedom of contract, and criticizing strict liability for its rejection of the market); Alan Schwartz, Products Liability Reform: A Theoretical Synthesis, 97 Yale L.J. 353, 372 (1988) (arguing for a contract regime and against strict liability for product liability); Buchanan 1970, *supra* note 78, at 72–73 (lamenting the shift toward strict liability because it pushes toward a uniform level of product safety).

[80] See, *e.g.*, Ian Ayres & Robert Gertner, Filling Gaps in Incomplete Contracts: An Economic Theory of Default Rules, 99 Yale L.J. 87, 88 (1989) ("Immutability is justified only if unregulated contracting would be socially deleterious because parties internal or external to the contract cannot adequately protect themselves.").

economic point of view, then, both the restricted domain of accident law and the inalienability of tort protections are problematic.

The differences between the economics and deontological views sketched here revolve around their different understandings of a very slippery idea—autonomy. Economics equates autonomy with consumer sovereignty, holding that we respect people's freedom when we respect their preferences. Because individual preferences for risk vary widely, in the absence of serious market imperfections economics favors the flexible and individuated protections of contract over the uniform and inalienable safeguards of tort. The deontological view deployed here, by contrast, interprets autonomy as the freedom to pursue one's conception of the good and favorable conditions for doing so. We respect people's freedom when we respect their rights to the physical integrity of their persons. Everyone has the *same* fundamental interest in the physical integrity of their person. Physical harm is an assault on our powers of agency. It impairs the capacities through which we act and exert our wills on the world.

2. Precaution and Proportionality: Revisiting the Hand Formula

When we think about taking a risk upon ourselves, bearing a risk imposed by someone else, or imposing a risk on others, we are naturally drawn to think about the factors identified by the Hand Formula—the probability and magnitude of the harm and what we would have to give up to reduce or eliminate the risk.[81] Nonetheless, the Hand Formula came along relatively late in the development of modern negligence law, and to this day corrective justice and civil recourse theorists of tort are wary of the Hand Formula's balancing commitments.[82] Ripstein's categorical view of reasonable care, with its tendency to collapse reasonable care into customary care, is representative. On its face, though, a categorical view of negligence is implausible. Intuitively, we think of risk as a matter of balancing danger and advantage. To grasp the attractions of a categorical view, we need to step back and consider how and why it is that the intentional torts are both fruitfully viewed as grounded in natural (or moral) rights *and* as taking legal form as categorical prohibitions on conduct. Our legal right not to be battered reflects a balancing of underlying interests, but when we apply it, we take the balance among underlying interests to have been settled by the way that the law articulates the wrong. In easy cases, tortious wrongs can be determined

---

[81] Judith Jarvis Thomson, The Realm of Rights 243–46 (Harvard, 1990), nicely illustrates this point in discussing the permissibility of imposing risks of harm. Without ever citing the Hand Formula by name, Thomson shows that the probability and the gravity of the harm risked, and the strength of the reasons for risking harm, play fundamental roles in our thinking about permissible risk imposition.

[82] On the prehistory and emergence of the Hand Formula, see Green 1997, *supra* note 15. For corrective justice and civil recourse unease with the Hand Formula, see Ripstein 2016, *supra* note 17, at 102, 144–45; Weinrib 2012, *supra* note 17, at 147–52; Zipursky 2015, *supra* note 17, at 2153–61; Perry 1988, *supra* note 17, at 169–71.

without reference to the interests that justify their recognition and without regard to what a fresh balancing of the interests on the facts of the case might conclude. Normally, we can identify a trespass to land without inquiring into the subtleties of the underlying interest in dominion. Intentional entry without consent just is a prima facie trespass.

The same is true of the tort of battery. Our interest in the physical integrity of our persons is urgent enough to justify the recognition of a legal right that others not intentionally touch us in harmful or offensive ways.[83] That legal right is categorical: it condemns harm or offensive intentional touchings as presumptively wrong. When we litigate a battery claim, we do not balance the plaintiff's interest in, say, not being punched in the face, against the defendant's interest in doing so. A prima facie case of battery can be made out simply by establishing an intentional, unconsented to, harmful or offensive touching. Justificatory or exculpatory reasons for committing a battery must be raised as defenses or privileges. If every claim of battery triggered an "all things considered" balancing of the plaintiff's interest in not being punched in the face and the defendant's interest in doing so, we would not really have a legal right not to be battered. For us to have a robust, well-realized legal right, the law must strike a balance between various competing interests (or values) and confer an according special protection on an interest.[84] Standard conceptions of legal rights thus take them to have a categorical character.

Because the Hand Formula prescribes balancing, theorists who regard torts as fundamentally a matter of wrongs and rights regard it with suspicion. Orthodox understandings of legal rights incline them toward accounts of reasonable care that state the doctrine's demands in categorical terms. This inclination is reinforced by the identification of the Hand Formula with economics. Theorists of torts as wrongs rightly insist that negligence norms are relational: they articulate obligations that run between those who impose risk and those on whom the risks are imposed. When negligence is conceived in economic terms, it is not relational. It is about producing states of the world in which wealth is maximized. Persons are merely conduits for social costs and benefits.

Nonetheless, it is a mistake to reject the Hand Formula's balancing account of negligence. Negligence liability governs the imposition of risks of physical harm. Unlike punching someone in the face unprovoked, imposing risk is not categorically wrong. Risk impositions are only wrong insofar as they fail to reconcile the

---

[83] I am following H.L.A. Hart's understanding of a natural or moral right. See H.L.A. Hart, Natural Rights: Bentham and John Stuart Mill, in Essays on Bentham 79 (Oxford, 1982).

[84] This is true on Scanlon's or Raz's conceptions of rights, for instance. See Joseph Raz, The Morality of Freedom 166 (Oxford, 1986); T.M. Scanlon, Rights and Interests, in Arguments for a Better World, Essays in Honor of Amartya Sen, Vol. I, at 68 (Kaushik Basu & Ravi Kanbur eds., Oxford, 2009). These matters are discussed more fully in Chapter Three, supra, pp. 83–87.

competing claims of liberty and security appropriately. We have urgent interests in both freedom of action and security. Each is an essential condition for pursuing our aims, aspirations, and projects. We must therefore reconcile liberty and security on terms that give each of the interests its due—on terms that are both *favorable* and *fair*. We need to strike a favorable balance between liberty and security in order to provide people with advantageous circumstances for leading their lives. We need to reconcile their competing claims fairly for people to interact with each other on terms that are mutually acceptable. Risks must be imposed on terms that are justifiable even to those whom they endanger. Because a balancing conception of negligence can be understood in terms of fairness, it is a mistake to identify the Hand Formula with an economic conception of negligence. Hand's Formula can be used to help us determine whether some risk imposition reconciles the liberty of potential injurers with the security of potential victims in a way that is justifiable to both parties.

From a deontological perspective, then, reasonable care is a matter of interpersonal fairness. Exercising reasonable care requires giving due weight to one's own claims to act in ways that endanger others and the claims of those others to security from suffering harm at your hands.[85] Obligations of reasonable care are both relational and abstract. They are relational because they run to and from representative persons, as Posner's peopling of the rail yard in the *Conrail* case shows. When Conrail ponders what precautions to take before moving its trains in a rail yard, it must contemplate the kinds of persons who might be endangered and the kinds of things they might be doing. Judgments of duty and breach do not depend on "factors specific to an individual case" but instead must be "applicable to a general class of cases" involving "categories of actors or patterns of conduct."[86] Obligations of reasonable care are abstract because the relevant relations are relations between and among representative persons, with respect to the kinds of dangers that we might reasonably foresee happening. Negligence law frames its duties in terms of abstract classes of persons and bases them on generic judgments about the urgency of the interests at stake.

The abstractness of normal duties of care is worth underscoring. When Ripstein remarks that "the point of tort litigation is to resolve the specific dispute between the parties currently before the court, based entirely on what transpired between them,"[87] he might be read to imply that duty and breach in negligence are more personal than they really are. It is true, as Cardozo famously says in

---

[85] On the nature of fairness, see John Broome, Fairness, 91 Proc. Aristotelian Soc'y 87 (1990–1991). Fairness requires, as Broome says, that claims "be satisfied in proportion to their strength." (96).
[86] Restatement (Third) of Torts: Liability for Physical and Emotional Harm § 7 cmt. A (2010).
[87] Ripstein 2016, *supra* note 17, at 23. For an argument that duty in negligence law is very much personal, see John Oberdiek, It's Something Personal: On the Relationality of Duty and Civil Wrongs, in Civil Wrongs and Justice in Private Law 301 (John Oberdiek & Paul B. Miller eds., Oxford, 2020).

Palsgraf, that to prevail on a negligence claim "the plaintiff must show 'a wrong' to herself, i.e., a violation of her own right, and not merely a wrong to some one else."[88] *Complete* negligence wrongs (wrongs where the elements of duty, breach, actual and proximate causation, and injury are all satisfied) *are personal* to those wronged. The individual injuries suffered by wronged victims, for instance, are unique to them. It is a mistake, however, to infer that negligence law's judgments of *duty and breach* are also personal. The Long Island Railroad could not reasonably have been expected to foresee that *Mrs. Palsgraf* would be waiting on the platform on that fateful day. It could, though, have been expected to foresee that *some* prospective passengers might be waiting on the platform. So, too, Conrail could *not* have been expected to foresee *Lonny Davis's* presence beneath the train, but it could have been expected to foresee that *someone* might be under the train inspecting for cracks. Judgments of duty and breach work with representative persons for both epistemic and normative reasons. People can only be asked to take account of risks that they can foresee, and reasonable foresight is limited. Precognition is the stuff of science fiction.[89] In the world as it is, when we see someone standing on a railway platform or crossing a street, their individuating characteristics may still elude us. All that we can do is to treat them as generic persons.[90] Moreover, we have normative reasons—as well as epistemic ones—to deliberate in terms of representative persons who have generic interests. We can only live with each other on fair terms if we step back from the particularities of our situations and think of our interests in more representative ways. We must accept, as negligence law does, that children have strong interests in engaging in age-appropriate activities but weak interests in engaging in adult activities; that getting to the hospital after a heart attack is more important than getting to the beach on a hot summer Saturday; and so on.[91]

The *Second Restatement of Torts* points us in the direction of grasping the way in which negligence is a matter both of abstract fairness and interpersonal responsibility when it remarks that our interest in bodily security is "protected against not only intentional invasion but [also] against negligent invasion or invasion by the mischances inseparable from an abnormally dangerous activity."[92]

---

[88] Palsgraf v. Long Island Railroad, 161 N.E. 99, 100 (1928).
[89] *Minority Report,* directed by Stephen Spielberg (20th Century Fox, 2002).
[90] "So far as the driver of the bus was concerned, I think that he was thoroughly competent . . . driving his best in a perfectly normal way. He saw plaintiff at a time when he could have averted this accident. Of course, he did not know whether the woman he saw was young and quick or rather elderly and slow. If the woman had been young, there would not have been an accident. If the woman had been elderly—as in fact she was—there was a very grave chance of an accident." Daly v. Liverpool Corporation [1939] 2 All ER 142, 144.
[91] See *infra,* § C, pp. 173–74 for discussion of negligence law's use of normalizing assumptions. For the importance of representative persons and generic interests to contractualism, see Raul Kumar, Contractualism and the Roots of Responsibility, in New Essays on Moral Responsibility 251, 275, 277 (Randolph Clarke, Michael McKenna, and Angela M. Smith eds., Oxford, 2015).
[92] Restatement (Second) of Torts § 1 cmt. D (1965).

In H.L.A. Hart's terms, our interest in bodily security is a moral or natural right; it is urgent enough to justify the creation of legal rights and duties. Not all the legal protections that the interest grounds, however, have the categorical character that our rights against battery and trespass have. It does not follow from this that the contours of those legal protections can only be determined by reference to efficiency or social utility. The alternative to both categorical legal right and efficiency is fairness. Reasonable care might be understood as the level of care that reconciles the conflicting liberties of injurers and victims on terms that treat both parties fairly. The advantages that accrue to injurers from being free to impose risks must be balanced against the threat those risks pose to the security of those they endanger. Precautions should be proportional to the risks imposed. This way of describing reasonable care arises naturally within a deontological framework. And the general idea of reasonable care as proportionate precaution is easy to find in commentary, case law, and pattern jury instructions.[93]

The overwhelming majority of American jurisdictions describe negligence as the "failure to exercise ordinary care" and then define ordinary care as "the conduct of the reasonably careful or reasonably prudent person."[94] No more than five jurisdictions use jury instructions that might be read to enjoin cost-benefit analysis, economically conceived.[95] However the instruction is worded, though, empirical research indicates that neither judges nor juries apply the norm of reasonable care in the manner contemplated by economics. Judges and juries alike treat the prospect of serious physical harm to persons as a matter of special and negative moral significance.[96] Moreover, American negligence law and practice suppose that determinations of due care require the exercise of evaluative judgment—not just the computing of costs and benefits. Even when the facts are

---

[93] See, e.g., Prosser & Keeton 1984, supra note 21, at 208 ("The amount of care demanded by the standard of reasonable conduct must be in proportion to the apparent risk. As the danger becomes greater, the actor is required to exercise caution commensurate with it."); Gilles 1994, supra note 30, at 1018 n.6 (quoting Galligan v. Blais, 364 A.2d 164, 166 (Conn. 1976) ("Reasonable care is care proportionate to the dangers existing in light of the surrounding circumstances"), and Forcier v. Grand Union Stores, Inc., 264 A.2d 796, 799 (Vt. 1970) ("The duty of care increases proportionately with foreseeable risks of the operations involved.").

[94] Patrick J. Kelley & Laurel A. Wendt, What Judges Tell Juries about Negligence: A Review of Pattern Jury Instructions, 77 Chi.-Kent L. Rev. 587, 622 (2002).

[95] Id. at 618–20.

[96] Studies by Kip Viscusi, a prominent proponent of an economic approach to risk and precaution, have shown the following. First, a survey of eighty-nine judges found that most of them applied the negligence standard in a more demanding way when the risk imposed threatened serious physical injury to persons instead of property damage. See W. Kip Viscusi, How Do Judges Think about Risk?, 1 Am. Law Econ. Rev. 26, 40–46 (1999). A study of laypeople and jurors found that they placed even more weight on the importance of safety in cases involving the imposition of risks of serious physical harm to persons who were strangers to the risk-imposing enterprise. See W. Kip Viscusi, Jurors, Judges, and the Mistreatment of Risk by the Courts, 30 J. Legal Stud. 107, 130–34 (2001). By Viscusi's lights, these are "mistreatments" because they are inefficient. Viscusi's findings are better understood as evidence that participants in the legal system do not see reasonable care as a matter of efficiency.

undisputed, negligence is for the jury to decide if reasonable people could disagree over how to evaluate the significance of those undisputed facts.[97]

From an economic perspective, the facts fully spelled out should settle the matter. If the cost of the precaution necessary to prevent an accident is less than the discounted value of the harm it prevents, then the precaution should be taken. If the cost is greater, then the precaution should not be taken. In principle, efficient care is entirely a matter of fact. Negligence doctrine disagrees. It does so because it supposes that the weight (or importance, or urgency) of the interests at stake must be evaluated to determine if due care has been exercised. As Mark Geistfeld says, negligence is a "normative conception of the type conveyed by maxims like 'the punishment must fit the crime.'"[98] The idea of proportionality embodied by due care doctrine is normative all the way down.

3. Ineliminable Risks and Inefficient Precautions

The first question for a deontological conception of reasonable care is whether it can help us to interpret the Hand Formula in a way that registers the priority of avoiding harm. The second question is whether case law is receptive to that interpretation. In case rhetoric, the alternative to the economic interpretation of the Hand Formula is the proposition that due care enjoins proportionate precaution. Proportionate precaution is a relation between harm risked and care taken; it is also a relation between persons. It spells out the content of what injurers owe to victims, with both parties conceived of in representative terms. The idea of proportionality, though, needs to have content poured into it. Offhand, we might think that proportional relations between risks and precautions would be smooth and continuous: very small risks should require very small precautions, modest risks should require modest precautions, great risks should require great precautions, and so on. Case law, however, appears to embrace two distinct discontinuities. First, when the risk of significant injury is exceedingly low, negligence law does not demand that the actor take any precaution. Second, when the magnitude of harm is substantial, but the probability of that harm is low, negligence law may require the actor to take "disproportionate" precaution.

The first discontinuity involves cases where the magnitude of the accidental harm threatened by an act is nontrivial, but the probability of that harm materializing is very, very low. Modern English law may hold explicitly that actors have

---

[97] See Restatement (Third of Torts): Liability for Physical and Emotional Harm § 8(b) (2010) ("When, in light of all the facts relating to the actor's conduct, reasonable minds can differ as to whether the conduct lacks reasonable care, it is the function of the jury to make that determination."); Mark P. Gergen, The Jury's Role in Deciding Normative Issues in the American Common Law, 68 Fordham L. Rev. 407, 430, 434 (1999).

[98] Mark A. Geistfeld, The Principle of Misalignment: Duty, Damages, and the Nature of Tort Liability, 121 Yale L.J. 142, 152 (2011).

no duty to take precautions against the materialization of such risks.[99] Modern American law may reach the same result implicitly. *Van Skike v. Zussman*[100] illustrates the category. In *Van Skike*, a child set himself on fire after he won a toy lighter as a prize in a gumball machine and tried to fill the toy with lighter fluid that he purchased from the store on whose premises the machine was located. He and his mother sued Zussman, the operator of the gumball machine, and the store that sold the child the lighter fluid. The claim against Zussman was predicated on the argument that "[Zussman] knew of or should have known that he had placed his cigarette lighter dispensing machines in a store that sold flammable fluids."[101] Placing the machines in the store created a risk of harm. Precautions should therefore have been taken to reduce that risk. Or so the plaintiff argued. The court disagreed, concluding that these allegations failed to state a claim against Zussman on the ground that the "creation of a legal duty requires more than a mere possibility of occurrence."[102]

The point, I take it, is that every activity creates *some* risk of accidental injury, however small in probability, and trying to reduce that risk below the rough level characteristic of ordinary activities is likely to be a game not worth the candle. A certain level of risk is, as Ripstein says, an unavoidable feature of life in a "crowded world." More important, it seems likely that risks of this kind can only be eliminated by shutting down the activity responsible for the risks. The only effective precaution against the possibility that toy lighters will inspire children old enough to get their hands on lighter fluid to start fires is to withdraw the toy lighters from sale. This is hardly the end of the world, but if generalized to all activities that create similar risks, it would be burdensome indeed. All kinds of activities can inspire children to play with fire: matches, real lighters, forest fires seen on TV, and gas grills among them. A regime of "no duty" is therefore the right regime for very, very low probability risks. Some risk is simply the price of freedom to act. With certain variations, ordinary activities, ordinarily conducted, produce a mutually imposed and mutually beneficial level of background risk.[103] We need the activities and must therefore accept the risks.

The second discontinuity involves cases where the probability of the relevant risks is low, but not very, very low, and where the magnitude of those risks is significant. The risks created by having inspectors crawl underneath temporarily

---

[99] See Weinrib 2012, *supra* note 17, at 149–50.
[100] 318 N.E.2d 244 (Ill. App. Ct. 1974).
[101] *Id.* at 246.
[102] *Id.* at 247.
[103] Charles Fried, An Anatomy of Values 193 (Harvard, 1970). Some variation in the risks ordinarily created by different activities seems inevitable. A severe heart attack while driving endangers bystanders more than an equally severe heart attack while skateboarding, if only because cars are larger and faster than people on skateboards.

parked trains to inspect their undercarriages for cracks are typical of the risks involved in such cases, as are the costs (slower operation of the trains, more disruptive inspections, reduced income) of the precautions that would reduce or eliminate those risks (blowing a whistle or visually inspecting trains before moving them, discontinuing the practice of crawling beneath temporarily parked trains). In cases like these, Judge Posner argues that trade-offs between precaution and accident costs should be made along a razor's edge. A penny's difference between present precaution costs and expected accident costs should tip the balance one way or another.[104] However highly we value life, once we have assigned it an appropriately high dollar value, we should trade life off against everything else at the margin in a wealth-maximizing way.

As a way of registering the asymmetry of harm and benefit—and the concomitant priority of avoiding harm—placing a high dollar value on life is inadequate. Life is still traded off against anything and everything else at some ratio of exchange within a welfarist framework. Safety, however, has special importance because it is an essential condition of effective agency. Safety's priority is justified by its importance to our powers of agency, not by its special importance to our welfare. Registering safety's special priority requires something like the "disproportion test" of modern English negligence law. Modern English negligence law generally identifies the considerations relevant to determinations of due care in the same terms as the Hand Formula. For instance, one English judge identifies the elements of due care the following way:

> [In] considering whether some precaution should be taken against a foreseeable risk, [it is the duty of the injurer] to weigh, on the one hand, the magnitude of the risk, the likelihood of an accident happening and the possible seriousness of the consequences if an accident does happen, and, on the other hand, the difficulty and expense and any other disadvantage of taking the precaution.[105]

An important strand of English law goes further than the Hand Formula, however, because it *specifies the relative weights that must be given to precaution and accident costs*. "[I]n order for the cost of precautions to excuse an actor who

---

[104] Duckworth v. Franzen, 780 F.2d 645, 652 (7th Cir. 1985), cert. denied, 479 U.S. 816 (1986) (Posner, J.). On the one hand, actors are negligent if they fail to take precautions whose costs are "less, even if just a hair's breadth less, than the expected cost of the accident that would be averted." On the other hand, they are not negligent if they fail to take precautions which cost more, even just a hair's breadth more, than the expected costs of the accidents they would avert.

[105] Morris v. West Hartlepool Steam Navigation Co., 1956 App. Cas. 552, 574 (appeal taken from C.A.) (Reid, L.). See also Latimer v. A.E.C. Ltd., [1952] 2 Q.B. 70 I, 711 (Denning, L.) ("In every case of foreseeable risk, it is a matter of balancing the risk against the measures necessary to eliminate it.").

has caused foreseeable harm to others, the cost must be 'disproportionately' greater... than the benefit."[106]

The clearest circumstance where the presumption of disproportionality is rebutted is the circumstance where the costs of precaution are crushing. *Marshall v Gotham Co.*,[107] a leading English disproportion case involving a mining accident, is an example. The miner plaintiffs in *Marshall* were injured when the mine collapsed from "slickenside," a rare geological condition leading to sudden collapses of large slabs of rock from the roofs of mines. Because slickenside was undetectable, the only precaution capable of preventing it was to timber the entire ceiling of the mine (this in a mine where the ceiling is mined). The cost of timbering the ceiling was disproportionate to its benefits because it "would have been so great as to make the carrying on of the mine impossible."[108] In this application, the disproportion test matches the feasibility test found in American health and safety regulation and discussed in the next chapter. Feasible precaution requires going beyond the point of cost-justification and to the point where further precaution would jeopardize the long-run flourishing of the activity whose risks are at issue. The reason to draw the line at feasibility is that further precaution would deprive the miners of their jobs. For anyone who is not independently wealthy—and gypsum miners surely are not—having a job is itself a condition of effective agency. Having a job is essential to leading a decent life. It is an interest as urgent as safety.

As Hand himself emphasized,[109] his "formula" does not make the evaluative judgments required to determine whether a precaution should be taken. In the United Sates, judgments of reasonable care are generally for juries[110]—and rightly so, according to Hand. Juries have a special authority to settle disagreements of value. Because American practice assigns determinations of breach to juries, however, the common law of negligence in the United States has not articulated well-formed standards of precaution such as the "safety," "feasibility," and "cost-justification" standards discussed in the next chapter.[111] Similarly, American negligence law has not explicitly embraced the "disproportion test" developed by English judges. Some leading American cases do, however, balance the burdens of precaution against the benefits of harm avoidance in a way which prioritizes

---

[106] Gilles 1994, *supra* note 30, at 34–35. Gilles argues that the "disproportion test" has a second element in that it implicitly employs a "sliding scale" "in which the 'disproportion' necessary to escape liability increases as the risk increases in seriousness." *Id.*

[107] [1954] App. Cas. 360 (appeal taken from N.I.) (Reid, L.).

[108] *Id.* at 362.

[109] The determination of due care always "involves some preference, or choice between incommensurables, and it is consigned to a jury because their decision is thought most likely to accord with commonly accepted standards, real or fancied." Conway v. O'Brien 111 F.2d 611, 612 (2d Cir. 1940), rev'd 312 U.S. 492 (1941).

[110] See *supra* note 97.

[111] See Chapter Five, *infra*, pp. 199–211.

the avoidance of harm. *Helling v. Carey*[112] is one such case. The plaintiff in *Helling* brought a malpractice suit against her ophthalmologists, alleging that she suffered permanent damage to her vision because they failed to diagnose and treat her glaucoma.[113] Consistent with the custom of the profession, the defendants had not routinely tested the plaintiff for glaucoma because she was under forty, and the incidence of glaucoma for persons under forty was believed to be 1 in 25,000.[114]

Setting aside the normal rule that in medicine, customary care is due care,[115] the *Helling* court ruled as matter of law that the "standard that should have been followed under the undisputed facts of this case was the timely giving of this simple, harmless pressure test to this plaintiff and that, in failing to do so, the defendants were negligent."[116] In support of its ruling, the court stated:

> The incidence of glaucoma . . . may appear quite minimal. However, that one person, the plaintiff in this instance, is entitled to the same protection, as afforded persons over 40, essential for timely detection of the evidence of glaucoma where it can be arrested to avoid the grave and devastating result of this disease. The test is a simple pressure test, relatively inexpensive. There is no judgment factor involved, and there is no doubt that by giving the test the evidence of glaucoma can be detected. The giving of the test is harmless if the physical condition of the eye permits.[117]

In Hand Formula terms, the high magnitude of the harm, the low cost of the precaution, and the high efficacy of the precaution offset the low probability of the harm and require the precaution to be taken.[118]

The fact that the *Helling* court found the administration of the glaucoma pressure required *as a matter of law* is difficult to square with an economic interpretation of reasonable care. The court's conclusion condemned what it took to be the customary practice of the medical profession as a practice that *no* reasonable person could regard as justified.[119] From an economic point of view, it is hard to

---

[112] 519 P.2d 981 (Wash. 1974).
[113] *Id.* at 982.
[114] *Id.* at 982–83.
[115] *Id.* at 983. The rule that, with respect to medicine and other true professions, the care that is customary in the profession *is* due care is an exception to the general rule that custom is normally merely evidence of the level of care due. See Dobbs 2016, *supra* note 63, at 507.
[116] *Helling*, 519 P.2d at 983 (emphasis added).
[117] *Id.*
[118] There may be reasons other than those offered in the text of the opinion that support the outcome in *Helling*. Landes and Posner note that medical texts had recommended for years that the test be given to anyone old enough to cooperate. Landes & Posner 1987, *supra* note 41, at 138; see also Jerry Wiley, The Impact of Judicial Decisions on Professional Conduct: An Empirical Study, 55 S. Cal. L. Rev. 345, 383 (1981) (stating that even before the *Helling* decision over half of opticians quite often or always tested for glaucoma).
[119] *Helling*, 519 P.2d at 983.

see how the matter could be so clear. The cost of the precaution is the increased time and expense borne by 25,000 patients; the harm that precaution prevents is one otherwise undetected case of glaucoma. Failing to detect that case will result in failing to mitigate the effects of the disease in that one patient. From an economic point of view, it seems entirely possible for the quantified, monetary costs of administering 25,000 tests to exceed the quantified, monetary benefits of doing so by a "hair's breadth"—or more. For failing to administer the test to be unreasonable as a matter of law, avoiding "the grave and devastating result of this disease"[120] must be accorded special weight. It is far easier to argue that no reasonable ophthalmologist would fail to administer the test from within a deontological framework that puts persons and the relations among them at its center.

Within a deontological framework, harm to persons is a matter of special concern, and its avoidance rightly has the priority that the harm-benefit asymmetry treats it as having. The case for requiring the pressure test is far stronger when the avoidance of harm to persons has special priority. Forgoing the test imposes a small but significant risk of delayed detection and treatment of a devastating disease, a disease whose disabling effects can be avoided if the disease is detected early. Administering the test, by contrast, imposes minor inconvenience and modest expense on everyone. The costs of the precaution are eminently reasonable. This is so both because the magnitude of the harm that the precaution averts is great and because the precaution costs are modest. Whatever the *total* dollar cost of the pressure test, the costs borne *by each patient* are quite modest. Those precaution costs are dispersed across all those at risk from the disease, and the impact on any single person's liberty is minimal. No one's life is seriously disrupted. For the person on whom it falls, the harm that the test averts is, by contrast, devastating. When the matter is framed in these terms, the case for administering the test is compelling.

4. The Specter of Paternalism

From an economic point of view, there are reasons to think that treating the administration of the pressure test as a matter of collective choice—as a decision that the courts or the medical profession ought to make for patients—is paternalistic. *Helling* is not an accident among strangers. It does not arise out of the involuntary exposure of some to risks imposed by others. The harm in *Helling*

Under the facts of this case reasonable prudence required the timely giving of the pressure test to this plaintiff. The precaution of giving this test to detect the incidence of glaucoma to patients under forty years of age is so imperative that irrespective of its disregard by the standards of the ophthalmology profession, it is the duty of the courts to say what is required to protect patients under forty from the damaging results of glaucoma.

Questions of special medical expertise dropped out because the court took the choice of the pertinent precaution and its efficacy to be beyond dispute. *Id.* at 982.

[120] *Id.*

arises among participants in a joint enterprise. In a deep sense, the victims and injurers are the same people. Doctors are the fiduciaries of patients, professionally devoted to serving their patients' best interests. They act on behalf of patients. Patients thus expose *themselves*—not others—to burdens and to risks by taking and forgoing precautions. *Patients* suffer the permanent blindness of glaucoma when it occurs, and they bear the financial costs and the inconvenience of the pressure test.[121] These circumstances make contract a live alternative to tort. Instead of deciding what is best for patients, we might educate them about glaucoma and its prevention and let them decide whether to have the test administered. Why, then, should courts impose a "one size fits all" requirement that the pressure test always be administered?

When we take interpersonal fairness as the test of justified precaution, the case for insisting on the administration of the pressure test—rather than educating patients and letting them choose whether to take the test—depends on whether the choice is worth having. Not every choice is. Choices bring their own burdens. Whether a burden is worth bearing depends on whether it serves a valuable enough end. The precaution at stake in *Helling* places a very modest burden on people's freedom of action and confers a significant protection on their security. People who care about obtaining favorable conditions for the exercise of their independent agency over the course of their lives have strong reason to insist that the pressure test be administered. Permanent blindness at a relatively early age profoundly alters the lives that they may live and impairs the pursuit of many aims and aspirations. Reasonable people would, if fully informed, opt for the pressure test. Why not inform everyone anyway and let them choose whether to take the test? Because the burden that a regime of full disclosure places on patients, in terms of time, education, and concentration, is substantial. Nothing of real value is gained.

Insisting that pressure tests be given—instead of leaving the choice of whether to take the test in the hands of patients—is not, then, necessarily paternalistic. And this is so even if it is true that some patients would prefer to forgo the test and pocket the savings. Practices are not paternalistic simply because they fail to satisfy every idiosyncratic whim, or every eccentric taste. The market fails to satisfy every taste, and that hardly makes it a paternalistic institution.[122] Both a

---

[121] It is virtually impossible to know whether *all* of the financial costs of the pressure test were passed through to the patients, though the patients necessarily shouldered the time and inconvenience of those tests. See generally Craswell 1991, *supra* note 34. And even if the costs were passed through, they may have been covered by insurance, in at least some cases.

[122] See Alan Schwartz, Products Liability Reform: A Theoretical Synthesis, 97 Yale L.J. 353, 372 (1988) ("Some consumers probably want planes with couches and amphibious cars, and are the victims of unequal bargaining power in the sense that too few such consumers exist to make serving them in these ways profitable. But unless one believes that every commercial preference should be satisfied, regardless of its cost" this is not an objection to the market's failure to satisfy these tastes.).

warning regime and a regime of mandatory precaution impose burdens, and the burdens of mandatory precaution are less than those of a warning regime. A regime of mandatory precaution burdens those who would prefer to forgo the test as part of a standard ophthalmological exam by denying them the opportunity to do so. A warning regime burdens those who see no advantage in being given the choice of whether to take the test and who are nonetheless burdened by being required to make that decision. The dispositive judgment is not that some people's irrational preferences for their own welfare should be overridden in the name of their own good, but that the burden of education and decision imposed by the warning regime is not worth the benefits of the choice it enables.

The case for a regime of mandatory precaution over a warning regime thus rests on a judgment about how the two possible regimes reconcile the competing claims of liberty and security for a plurality of persons. The case for a warning regime would be more compelling if the interests served by forgoing pressure tests were more urgent. As matters stand, it is unreasonable for the few who would prefer the freedom to decline the test to ask the many who would take it happily to bear the burdens of a warning regime. There are ways of taking foolish risks with one's eyesight that impose lesser burdens on others. Skipping eye exams entirely should be at least as effective as taking such exams while declining sensible tests. The marginal disadvantage of this strategy—that it denies the opportunity to take eye exams and still forgo pressure tests—is slight. It is paternalistic to tell people that they cannot gamble with their own eyesight, but it is not paternalistic to tell people that they cannot insist on a regime of ophthalmological precaution tailored to their foolish tastes, when such a regime imposes unreasonable burdens on others. The issue at hand is the choice of a practice, and it is fair to choose the less burdensome practice.

5. Jury Adjudication

In American law, questions of reasonable care are mostly for juries to decide. Even when reasonable people cannot disagree what the relevant facts are, if reasonable people can disagree over the conclusions to be drawn from those facts, judgments of whether a party exercised reasonable care are for the jury to make.[123] In the vast majority of jurisdictions, juries are instructed to measure the injurer's conduct against the yardstick of a reasonable person's conduct, not by the Hand Formula.[124] The Hand Formula is used mostly by appellate courts evaluating the reasonableness of jury verdicts on appeal. Nothing in the black-letter law made by those appellate decisions requires either other judges or juries to weight the Formula's variables in accordance with the dictates of efficiency,

---

[123] See *supra* note 97.
[124] Kelley & Wendt 2002, *supra* note 94, at 622.

feasibility, or any other normative standard. Assigning the authority to determine what due care requires to juries whenever reasonable persons might disagree undercuts the thesis that reasonable precaution is efficient precaution in a subtle but significant way. This assignment of authority expresses the judgment that we must often exercise evaluative judgment to determine whether due care has or has not been exercised. From an economic perspective, only facts should be needed to determine if due care has been exercised.[125]

As practiced by both judges and juries, negligence adjudication undercuts the thesis that reasonable care is efficient care. Celebrated cases like *Helling* fit poorly with an economic conception of care, and they are part of a larger pattern of judges regarding safety as a matter of special moral importance.[126] Jury decision-making undercuts the thesis that due care is efficient care. Empirical evidence indicates that juries, too, regard the safety of persons as as an especially urgent interest. Indeed, there is substantial evidence that juries are, in fact, outraged by the use of cost-benefit analysis when life and limb are at stake. Years ago, in a perceptive analysis of product liability law, Gary Schwartz summarized the folklore on that hostility.[127] According to Schwartz, defense lawyers should never argue that a firm "deliberately included a dangerous feature in the product's design because of the high monetary cost that the manufacturer would have incurred in choosing another design." This argument leads to almost certain defeat on liability and exposes the defendant to the risk of punitive "damages as well."[128] Schwartz's observations are paralleled by the belief, shared by many torts professors (including myself), that when first introduced to the cost-benefit conception of the Hand Formula, most torts students find it morally objectionable.[129] Empirical studies have since confirmed these perceptions.[130] Legal doctrine, legal practice, and social scientific studies all support the proposition that judges and juries reject the economic understanding of reasonable care and

---

[125] See *supra* note 95, and accompanying text.
[126] Viscusi 1999, *supra* note 96, at 40–46; Viscusi 2001, *supra* note 96, at 130–34.
[127] Schwartz 1991, *supra* note 42, at 43.
[128] Schwartz 1991, *supra* note 42, at 1038. Schwartz's remarks are a "composite of the observations" of "several lawyers who defend manufacturers at trial in design defect cases." *Id.* Most of the evidence in this area is anecdotal, and the aversion to cost-benefit reasoning is most pronounced in product liability cases, the one area in which Hand Formula instructions are commonly given. See Gilles 1994, *supra* note 30, at 1022–23; Benjamin C. Zipursky, Sleight of Hand, 48 Wm. & Mary. L. Rev. 1999, 2013–17 (2007).
Revulsion against explicit cost-benefit analysis of risk impositions is hardly confined to juries; law students and the public at large seem to share it. Schwartz 1991, *supra* note 42, at 1035–37 & nn.94–95.
[129] Kenneth W. Simons, Rethinking Mental States, 72 B.U. L. Rev. 463, 513 (1992).
[130] W. Kip Viscusi, Corporate Risk Analysis: A Reckless Act?, 52 stan L. Rev. 547 (2000) (discussing cases in which real juries or mock jurors found that corporate decisions—based on cost-benefit analysis and concerning the imposition of risks of serious physical harm to persons—constituted negligence).

suggest that the judgments made by judges and juries cohere better with a deontological conception of due care that assigns priority to the avoidance of serious physical harm.

C. Reasonable Persons

The general concept of reasonable care in negligence law is constructed not only by the Hand Formula but also by Average Reasonable Person ("ARP") doctrine. When we juxtapose the two doctrines, two differences are cast into relief. First, the principal domain of ARP doctrine is the conduct of natural persons, whereas planned precaution is the natural habitat of the Hand Formula. Second, the Hand Formula is more preoccupied with questions of justification, whereas ARP doctrine attends more to excuses.[131] Notwithstanding its interest in questions of excuse, though, ARP doctrine plays an important role in determining justified standards of care. It performs three relevant tasks: (1) it holds that some precautions are required as a matter of law;[132] (2) it articulates substantive duties of care for certain classes of persons (the awkward, the insane, experts, children) and the activities that parallel them; and (3) it specifies the qualities of the reasonable person. In general, ARP doctrine's articulation of duties places great relative weight on victim security. Where injurers claim that they should owe a reduced standard of care because of their diminished capacities, the security of potential victims conflicts starkly with the liberty of potential injurers. The flip side of this coin is that affording adequate protection to the security of prospective victims conflicts with the precept that it is unfair to hold actors liable for conduct they could not have helped. ARP doctrine comes down overwhelmingly on the side of security at the expense of both freedom of action and claims of diminished injurer capacity,[133] thereby assigning high relative value to security.

---

[131] See the discussion in the text accompanying notes 1 & 5, *supra*.

[132] One instructive case rules that automobile drivers must know the condition of their tires and must be held accountable for the hazards posed by worn tires. Delair v. McAdoo, 188 A. 181, 184 (Pa. 1936) (holding defendant negligent as a matter of law for driving a car whose tires were worn through to the fabric); see also Theisen v. Milwaukee Auto. Mut. Ins. Co., 118 N.W.2d 140, 144 (Wis. 1962) (holding that falling asleep while driving is negligent as a matter of law).

[133] As the Florida Court of Appeals has observed:

> So liability without subjective fault, under some circumstances, is one price men pay for membership in society. The sane and the insane, the awkward and the coordinated are equally liable for their acts or omissions. In such cases we do not decide fault, rather we determine upon whom our society imposes the burden of redress for a given injury. As Holmes implied in his "awkward man" parable, a principle at least co-equal with that of the fault principle in the law of torts is that the innocent victim should have redress.

Jolley v. Powell, 299 So. 2d 647, 648 (Fla. Dist. Ct. App. 1974).

Persons with poor judgment are held to the same standard of care as those with good judgment, regardless of their ability to conform to that standard.[134] Children engaged in adult activities and adults with permanent mental disabilities are held to the same standard as adults with normal capacities.[135] Finally, those who are inexperienced with a dangerous activity are held to the same standard as persons competent to engage in the activity.[136] These rules place a heavy burden on the pertinent classes of injurers: they must either measure up to a standard of care that exceeds their abilities or forgo the relevant activities. Justifying these rules is a difficult matter. The assumption that most actors, with enough training and preparation, can exercise the same level of care as a normally competent person may justify holding people in general to an objective standard of care. But that assumption seems unrealistic in the case of children and the permanently disabled. Another justification comes to mind. Society is lodging its judgments of negligence deeper than it usually does, by finding children and disabled persons who engage in activities beyond their competence negligent in their choice of activity, rather than in their method of carrying out the activity. This seems partly correct. The cases seem to be pinning implicit responsibility on parents for the conduct of their children and on guardians for the conduct of insane persons.[137]

The question remains, however, why responsibility should be driven so deep. The answer seems to be that avoiding harm is an asymmetrically important interest. Adjusting duty downward in these cases to make it commensurate with capacity is inconsistent with the priority of avoiding harm. Precisely because of their diminished capacities, children and the disabled impose great and nonreciprocal risks: children driving cars and powerboats are far more dangerous than adults engaging in the same activities. Moreover, the absence of effective victim precautions compounds the threat to security created by diminished capacity.

---

[134] Prosser & Keeton 1984, *supra* note 21, at 176–77 ("The fact that the individual is a congenital fool, cursed with in-built bad judgment . . . obviously cannot be allowed to protect him from liability.").

[135] *Jolley*, 299 So. 2d at 649 (holding insane defendant to the same standard of care as an ordinary adult); Miller v. State, 306 N.W.2d 554 (Minn. 1981) (holding minors to the adult standard of care when they are driving an automobile); Dellwo v. Pearson, 107 N.W.2d 859, 863 (Minn. 1961) ("[I]n the operation of an automobile, airplane, or powerboat, a minor is to be held to the same standard of care as an adult."); Prosser & Keeton 1984, *supra* note 21, at 177 ("[A mentally] deranged or insane defendant [is] accountable for his negligence as if the person were a normal, prudent person.").

[136] *E.g.*, Hughey v. Lennox, 219 S.W. 323, 325 (Ark. 1920) (holding that an inexperienced driver is liable for injuries caused by his inexperience).

[137] See *Jolley*, 299 So. 2d at 649 (noting that guardians of insane persons should bear the burden of injury caused by their charges, because they have the power to prevent such injury); McGuire v. Almy, 8 N.E.2d 760, 762 (Mass. 1937) ("Thus it is said that a rule imposing liability tends to make more watchful those persons who have charge of the defendant and who may be supposed to have some interest in preserving his property."); Breunig v. American Family Ins. Co., 173 N.W.2d 619, 624 (Wis. 1970) ("The policy basis of holding a permanently insane person liable for his tort [includes] to induce those interested in the estate of the insane person (if he has one) to restrain and control him.").

Our ability to identify those cars on the road that are driven by children (or uncontrolled epileptics), and to steer clear of them, is poor. Relaxing the standard of care for such persons would debilitate security even further by undermining our capacity to estimate the risks of undertaking various activities. It would impair our ability to base our risk exposures on relatively reliable expectations about other people's conduct.

Exceptions to the general rule that all actors will be held to the standard of the "average reasonable person" also assign significant priority to avoiding harm. For example, children engaged in age-appropriate activities are held to a lower standard of care—a standard suitable to their age and maturity.[138] As a class, age-appropriate activities, such as riding bicycles and peddling paddleboats, are inherently less risky to others than adult activities such as driving cars and operating powerboats.[139] Moreover, because children engaged in childlike activities are often readily identifiable or exposed to view (in fact, the activities themselves often identify their participants as children), prospective victims can often take additional precautions to guard against any increased risks associated with the children's diminished capacities.[140] Lowering the standard of care for children engaged in age-appropriate activities is thus compatible with the assignment of priority to security: responsibility is relaxed as risk is reduced. Conversely, ARP doctrine holds experts to a *higher* standard of care.[141] Experts tend to impose greater risk because they tend to engage in more dangerous activities. Moreover, by virtue of their greater knowledge and skill, experts can usually exercise greater care for the protection of prospective victims.[142] Responsibility increases as risk imposition and capacity for care increase. Beginners, by contrast, do not impose less risk by virtue of their lesser skill; if anything, they impose more. Thus, by holding experts to a higher standard of care, and beginners to the same standard of care as persons of normal competence, tort law favors security over freedom of action.

---

[138] See Prosser & Keeton 1984, *supra* note 21, at 179–80.

[139] See, *e.g.*, Daniels v. Evans, 224 A.2d 63, 64 (N.H. 1966) (holding nineteen-year-old motorcyclist to standard of an adult and contrasting the activity with less risky activities); *Dellwo*, 107 N.W.2d at 863 (holding minor operating powerboat to adult standard of care and contrasting activity with less risky ones).

[140] As the court in *Dellwo* remarked: "A person observing children at play ... may anticipate conduct that does not reach an adult standard of care or prudence. However, one cannot know whether the operator of an approaching automobile ... is a minor or an adult, and usually cannot protect himself against youthful imprudence even if warned." *Dellwo*, 107 N.W.2d at 863 (citations omitted).

[141] Brillhart v. Edison Light & Power Co., 82 A.2d 44, 47 (Pa. 1951) (holding supplier of electric current to the "very highest duty of care practicable"). The public at large is under no such duty. "[T]he general public is not bound to the high degree of foresight in respect of danger from electric wires as is the company maintaining them." *Id.* at 48. See Public Serv. Co. v. Elliot, 123 F.2d 2, 6 (1st Cir. 1941) (holding that expert's conduct must be judged in light of his superior knowledge).

[142] See Prosser & Keeton 1984, *supra* note 21, at 185 & nn.14–20.

In setting the standards of care for experts, children, and beginners, ARP doctrine treats the level of risk created by an activity as a "two-way ratchet," and the capacity for care as a "one-way ratchet." When both the level of risk and the capacity for care increases, duty increases; when both the level of risk and the capacity for care diminish, duty decreases. But when capacity diminishes without a corresponding decrease in risk creation, duty remains constant. This pattern, too, is evidence that ARP doctrine assigns special weight to security. Because experts are capable of more competent care, our demand that they do so is less onerous and thus more reasonable. Yet, although those with lesser capacities may be unable to meet a standard of ordinary competence, we are justified in demanding more of them because those lesser capacities put others at greater—not lesser—risk. Finally, the exculpation of actors in "those exceptional cases of loss of consciousness resulting from injury inflicted by an outside force, or fainting, or heart attack, or epileptic seizure, or other illness which suddenly incapacitates the driver of an automobile when the occurrence of such disability is not attended with sufficient warning or should not have been reasonably foreseen"[143] is also consistent with the substantial value of security. No effective precautions can be taken against sudden, unforeseeable disabilities. Holding actors liable for them would debilitate freedom of action without securing any corresponding gain to security.

The upshot of this is that, even though American negligence doctrine does not explicitly embrace a more stringent standard of precaution than efficient care, the argument that it does in fact demand more stringent precaution is stronger than it seems. The Hand Formula is open to a mode of valuation that assigns priority to the avoidance of harm; jury practice appears to reject cost-benefit analysis; and ARP doctrine regularly prioritizes security over liberty.

1. The Irrelevance of Subjective Valuation
Economic approaches to negligence embrace a subjective conception of value as the satisfaction of subjective preferences and favor flexible, tailored, legal norms as the best way for legal institutions to register such preferences. These commitments collide head-on with ARP doctrine, which is famously and aggressively "objective." Negligence law's reasonable persons are both standardized and idealized. So far as capacities and competencies are concerned, they possess sufficient skill to take the precautions that reasonable care requires. They are not inattentive, maladroit, or afflicted by any physical impairment. Their powers of evaluation and judgment are sufficient for them to reach "objectively" correct conclusions about the importance of the interests at stake in various risk

---

[143] Breunig v. American Family Ins. Co., 173 N.W.2d 619, 623 (Wis. 1970) (excusing driver from liability for accident when it was caused by unforeseeable mental delusions).

impositions, and their powers of cognition and calculation are such that their assessments of the probabilities of various risks, and the efficacy of various precautions, are accurate.

Faced with these firm commitments to objectivity, economic approaches to negligence have recast ARP doctrine's normative commitment to an ideal of adequate competence as an embrace of an empirical average. That embrace, in turn, is justified by the administrative and information costs of tailoring judgments of negligence to individual costs and benefits.[144] Epistemic concerns and administrative costs do matter, and legal economists are right to argue that they favor using standardized persons. Automobile drivers, for instance, are normally able to foresee possible harm only to representative persons—to other drivers and their passengers, to pedestrians on sidewalks and in crosswalks, to people who might be sitting outside at cafes, and so on. ARP doctrine's thoroughgoing rejection of subjective valuation, though, also has a deep normative justification. Subjective valuation undermines—whereas objective valuation underwrites—the fair reconciliation of liberty and security.

"Subjective" criteria of interpersonal comparison evaluate "the level of well-being enjoyed by a person in given material circumstances or the importance for that person of a given benefit or sacrifice . . . solely from the point of view of that person's tastes and interests."[145] "Objective" criteria appraise burdens and benefits in terms that are "the best available standard of justification that is mutually acceptable to people whose [aims, aspirations, and] preferences diverge."[146] Objective criteria make "substantive claims about what goods, conditions, and opportunities make life better," but the claims that they make are meant to be ones that people whose aims and aspirations diverge can accept.[147] ARP doctrine is firmly committed to objective criteria: it makes its calculations of reasonableness *not* by investigating the values that the persons involved in risk impositions subjectively place on the interests at stake, but by insisting that injurers assign those interests "the value which the law attaches to them."[148] It rejects the use of individualized costs of care, even when individualized information seems readily available. For example, it would be relatively easy to tailor costs of care figures

---

[144] See *supra* notes 50–52, and accompanying text.
[145] Scanlon 1975, *supra* note 34, at 656.
[146] *Id.*, at 668; see also Scanlon 1993, *supra* note 43, at 39 (describing the aim of the "objective" approach as being to "construct a more concrete conception of welfare in terms of particular goods and conditions that are recognized as important to a good life even by people with divergent values"). Scanlon expresses some misgivings about using the label "objective" on the ground that "its name may seem to imply a controversial claim to objectivity" that need not be made. The claim being made is that reasonable people can agree on the acceptability of the criteria. T.M. Scanlon, Value, Desire, and Quality of Life, in The Quality of Life 185, 188–89 (Martha Nussbaum & Amartya Sen eds., Oxford, 1993). ARP doctrine is also objective in this sense.
[147] Scanlon 1993, *supra* note 43, at 189.
[148] Restatement (Second) of Torts § 283 cmt. E (1964).

to children and persons with diverse disabilities as classes. Claims of childhood status and physical disability, unlike claims of subpar judgment, are reliably verifiable, and thus less susceptible to self-serving manipulation.[149] Moreover, the economic case for tailoring is strong: children and the disabled surely find it far more difficult to exercise the care expected of normal adults. Nevertheless, ARP doctrine places more weight on the activities in which people engage, than it does on their characteristics. Children are only given the benefit of a lesser, age-appropriate standard of care when they engage in less risky, age-appropriate activities.[150]

In fact, ARP doctrine rejects subjective valuations of the interests at stake in risk impositions as *irrelevant in principle*. Consider the circumstance of teenagers who linger on railroad bridges in the path of onrushing trains, and then leap into the water below at the last possible moment. Surely, they place enormous value on the thrill of "cheating death."[151] Taking subjective valuation seriously requires taking the satisfaction of these tastes seriously. This is both counterintuitive and unconvincing. It implies that the operation of trains (the speed at which they run, the risks to which they expose their passengers) should be affected by the tastes that such teenagers have for cheating death. Taking subjective valuation seriously might require train engineers to barrel down the tracks recklessly in order to endanger such teenagers, and then slam on their brakes at the last minute to avoid killing them. Few, if any, of us think that the safety of the train's passengers and crew should be at the mercy of a foolish teenage taste for cheating death.

The law of negligence lines up with our considered convictions. Lingering too long on a railroad bridge in order to experience the thrill of being nearly killed by an oncoming train evidences an utterly foolish disregard for the value of one's own life. Any duty that the operator of the train might have to take precautions to protect such teenagers from their own foolishness would not be justified by the *subjectively* high value that they place on putting their lives at risk. Any such duty would be justified by the *objectively* high value of human life and would exist *despite* the failure of those whose lives were in danger to respect that value. Settled negligence doctrine holds that extraordinary risks can be imposed only in the name of objectively important ends. Leaping in front of an onrushing train

---

[149] A claim of subpar judgment was the original occasion for the decision not to consider subpar capacities in fixing the standard of care. See Vaughan v. Menlove, 132 Eng. Rep. 490, 492–94 (C.P. 1837) (holding that the conduct of the prudent man is the metric for measuring negligence).

[150] See *infra* note 165, and accompanying text.

[151] John M. Glionna, Trestle-Jumping Fad Puts Youths in Path of Danger, L.A. Times, A1 (Aug. 10, 1992) (quoting one trestle-jumping youth as saying, "at the peak of danger, you bail out. You cheat death. It's a feeling nothing else can beat"). In explicating the flaws in subjective valuation, I shall focus on the problems presented by injurers who have unusually intense preferences of a sort that incline them to impose great risks *on* others or themselves. But, with appropriate modifications, these difficulties might also be illustrated by focusing on victims who have unusually intense preferences for avoiding risk impositions *by* others.

to rescue a child in imminent danger of death is not negligent, despite the high magnitude and probability of the risk involved.[152] So, too, it is not negligent for police officers and firefighters to speed when they are saving life and limb from grave and imminent danger.[153] But it is negligent for me to speed simply to get a good spot at the beach on a hot summer's day.[154] Speeding in hot pursuit of a good spot on the beach is a canonical instance of unreasonableness. The end being pursued is mundane, whereas the risk being imposed is great. It simply does not matter how intensely I care about getting a choice spot on the beach, or how indifferent my prospective victims might be to the risk that I impose. The intensity of my preference for getting to the beach early has no weight at all within the framework of negligence analysis.[155] What counts is the *objective* importance of my end. Life and limb are fundamental interests. They are the very center of the security and integrity of persons. Getting to the beach early is an ordinary interest, akin to countless other interests. Ordinary interests justify imposing only ordinary risks.

The objection to subjective valuation at work here is *not that it is irrational to risk one's neck for the thrill of "cheating death" but that it is unreasonable to ask others to bear substantial risks so that you may do so.* These are markedly different objections. The rationality of "playing chicken" with trains is largely irrelevant to tort law, whereas the reasonableness of imposing such risks on others is centrally important to negligence law. Negligence law is only secondarily concerned with the risks that we *should take upon on ourselves*, whereas the risks that we *should be permitted to impose on others* are its primary preoccupation. It is unreasonable to expose others to substantial risks for the thrill of cheating death both because physical integrity is an urgent human interest and because the burden of forgoing activities that expose others to significant risks so that one may oneself experience the thrill of cheating death is modest at best. However important the thrill of cheating death may be to a given person, there are ways of experiencing it that do not require imposing substantial risks on other people. You can free solo El Capitan, deep sea dive into the wreck of the *Andrea Doria*, or open your

---

[152] As the New York Court of Appeals explained:

The law has so high a regard for human life that it will not impute negligence to an effort to preserve it, unless made under such circumstances as to constitute rashness in the judgment of prudent persons. *For a person engaged in his ordinary affairs. Or in the mere protection of property. Knowingly and voluntarily to place himself in a position where he is liable to receive a serious injury. Is negligence, . . . but when the exposure is for the purpose of saving life. It is not wrongful. And therefore not negligent unless such as to be regarded either rash or reckless.*

Eckert v. Long Island R. Co., 43 N.Y. 502, 506 (N.Y. 1871) (emphasis added).
[153] See, *e.g., Delair*, 188 A.; Dobbs 2016, *supra* note 63, at 574–75.
[154] A person who knowingly and willingly puts others in danger when "engaged in his ordinary affairs, or in the mere protection of property" is negligent. *Eckert*, 43 N.Y. at 506.
[155] See *supra* note 47, and accompanying text.

parachute at the last possible moment during a skydive.[156] Reasonable people do not have an extravagant sense of the importance of their own preferences in comparison with the preferences of others. They do not believe that it is uniquely important that *they* get to the beach early on a sunny summer day. And they do not make great demands on others in the name of ends that are either unimportant or idiosyncratic.

To a striking extent, the contours of ARP doctrine track the nuances of reasonableness in their treatment of individual idiosyncrasy. Whatever our capacities, we are expected to exercise reasonable care when we impose risks on others, but we are allowed our weaknesses and idiosyncrasies when we are protecting ourselves from the carelessness of others. For example, children below a certain age are often held to be incapable of contributory negligence,[157] whereas children engaged in adult activities are held to an adult standard of care;[158] those with subpar mental capacities are held to the standards of those with normal capacities when their primary negligence is at issue,[159] but their limitations are generally considered when secondary (contributory or comparative) negligence is at stake.[160] Finally, we excuse victims from the duty to mitigate damages when mitigation would require them to act inconsistently with their moral or religious convictions, even if most of us would regard the convictions as odd at best and evidently wrong at worst.[161] On the one hand, we may not ask innocent strangers to bear the costs of our particular religious convictions. On the other hand,

---

[156] *Free Solo*, directed by Elizabeth Chai Vasarhelyi & Jimmy Chin (National Geographic, 2018); Peter Holley, The Mysterious Shipwreck that Swallows deep-sea divers who try to find it, Washington Post, May 19, 2016 (noting that sixteen people have lost their lives diving into the wreck and calling it the "Mount Everest of underwater exploration").

[157] See, *e.g.*, Cusick v. Clark, 360 N.E.2d 160, 163 (111 App. Ct. 1977) (stating that three-year-old children cannot be charged with contributory negligence).

[158] See *supra* notes 139–40, and accompanying text.

[159] Restatement (Third) of Torts: Physical and Emotional Harm § 11(e) (2010).

[160] See, *e.g.*, De Martini v. Alexander Sanitarium, Inc., 13 Cal. Rptr. 564, 567 (Cal. Dist. Ct. App. 1961) (noting that those who are completely devoid of reason are incapable of contributory negligence). For a general discussion of tort law's treatment of victims and injurers who are not "average," see Calabresi 1985, *supra* note 72, at 20–26.

[161] Three much noted cases make this point. Lange v. Hoyt, 159 A. 575, 577–78 (Conn. 1932) (refusing to hold as a matter of law that mother's refusal to seek medical treatment on religious grounds unreasonably aggravated the plaintiff daughter's fractured arm and pelvis); Troppi v. Scarf, 187 N.W.2d 511, 520 (Mich. Ct. App. 1971) (holding that the jury could not consider plaintiff's refusal to have an abortion as an unreasonable failure to mitigate damages from her accidental pregnancy after defendant pharmacist negligently sold plaintiff tranquilizers, rather than oral contraceptives); Friedman v. State, 282 N.Y.S.2d 858, 865–66 (N.Y. Ct. Cl. 1967) (holding that it was reasonable for the plaintiff, a Jewish woman, to leap from the chairlift on which she was stranded with a male friend, because she had been taught that it was a violation of Jewish law for an unmarried woman to be in the company of a man after dark in a place not easily accessible by a third party). It is, of course, critical that in all three of these cases, the person made to bear the cost of idiosyncrasy is the person who wronged the victim in the first place. Guido Calabresi, argues, I think convincingly, that the cases would come out differently if the injurers had held the idiosyncratic beliefs. Calabresi 1985, *supra* note 72, at 64–65, 116.

those who have wronged us may not ask us to ease their burden by acting against beliefs which play a central role in our lives.

Subjective criteria of valuation thus suffer from three serious drawbacks. First, subjective valuation licenses *deeply nonreciprocal risk impositions and puts the reasonable at the mercy of the unreasonable*. The reasonable—those who moderate their preferences for beating everyone else to the beach and who cultivate a modest sense of the importance of their own ends—will be denied by their modesty the right to inflict great risks on others. By contrast, the unreasonable— those who do not moderate their self-interested preferences and who have an immodest sense of the importance of their own ends—will endow themselves with the right to impose great risks on others. The asymmetry means that those engaged in identical activities (driving, for example) for identical reasons (to get to the beach) will be authorized to impose very different risks on each other. Those who moderate their self-interest and rein in their egos will confer the benefits of their restraint *on* others. In return for their restraint, they will be made to bear the extravagant demands *of* others. The reasonable will impose lesser risks and bear greater ones, whereas the unreasonable will impose greater risks and bear lesser ones. Subjective valuation upsets reciprocity of risk and undermines the fair reconciliation of liberty and security.

Second, subjective valuation further debilitates security by legitimating haphazard and unpredictable risk impositions. If actors were permitted to impose risks that were justified solely by their own subjective valuations of the importance of the ends that the risk impositions serve, we could not reliably predict the risks to which we might legitimately be exposed in pursuing any particular course of action. Drivers, for example, could no longer estimate the legitimate risks of freeway driving by assuming reasonable compliance with the rules of the road. The risks of freeway driving would turn on the subjective valuations that different drivers attached to their activities. If the subjective benefits that persons derive from driving vary greatly, the legitimate risks of highway driving would also vary enormously and unpredictably.[162]

Third, the uncertainty created by subjective valuation tends to erode trust and cooperation. Trust and cooperation depend heavily on terms of interaction being both fair and *perceived to be fair*. Subjective valuation tends to frustrate social cooperation. It makes the legitimacy of particular risk impositions turn on information that is rarely, if ever, publicly accessible—namely, the valuations that actors really do place on the ends that they are pursuing. Under a regime of

---

[162] The flip side of this coin is the problem of the emotionally hypersensitive plaintiff. If prospective victims could set up a duty of care whenever injurers disturbed their emotional tranquility, the ensuing uncertainty would debilitate freedom of action.

subjective valuation, those who are prepared to honor given terms of interaction on condition that others do so as well will have difficulty telling if their good faith is being reciprocated. For this reason, their confidence in the fairness of the scheme will diminish, as will their willingness to do their part. Even worse, the principle of subjectively rational risk imposition creates powerful incentives to misrepresent, ex post, one's subjective valuation of the ends that justify risk impositions. In the absence of some credible way of distinguishing the sincere from the insincere, this is no small defect. When cheating is easy, profitable, and difficult to detect, both the incentives to cheat and the incentives to defect are great. Those who abide by the terms of social cooperation only so long as others do so will have reason to suspect that their good faith is not being reciprocated. They will thus have reason to defect.

To be sure, the problems created by subjective valuation for the economic analysis of negligence may loom larger in theory than in practice. In practice, economists tend to make use of objective assumptions (say, of uniform risk neutrality), in part because they perceive substantial information and administration problems with subjective valuation.[163] As a defense of the economic approach to negligence, this observation has the facts of economic practice right, but the implications of those facts wrong. "Objective" valuation is a second-best solution for economics, and something is clearly wrong with a theory whose second-best solution to a problem is superior to its first-best solution.

2. The Role of Normalizing Assumptions

There is one more piece to the puzzle: ARP doctrine draws tacitly on "normalizing assumptions." Such assumptions abound in our ordinary moral discourse.

> [F]or example, we take it as given for purposes of moral argument that it is very important that what one wears and whom one lives with be dependent on one's choices and much less important that one be able to choose what other people wear, what they eat, and how they live. And we do this despite the fact that there may be some who would not agree with this assignment of values.[164]

---

[163] See *supra* note 49, and accompanying text.
[164] T.M. Scanlon Jr., The Significance of Choice, in 8 The Tanner Lectures on Human Values 149, 183 (Sterling M. McMurrin ed., Utah, 1988). As the examples in the text show, normalizing assumptions are thoroughly evaluative, but they are not exclusively evaluative. They are also partly a matter of descriptive generalization. Their thoroughly evaluative character should not trouble us. Interpersonal comparisons must be evaluative all the way down, so to speak. We should be troubled only if the evaluations strike us as wrong or objectionable in some way. *Cf.* Robert Nozick, Anarchy, State, and Utopia 54–87 (Basic Books, 1974) (advocating use of a baseline of normal risk imposition to determine when persons must be compensated if they are forbidden to impose particular risks); Jules Coleman & Arthur Ripstein, Mischief and Misfortune, 41 McGill L.J. 91, at 109–13 (1995) (describing and embracing use of normalizing conceptions, rather than subjective assessments to make judgments of reasonable care).

The doctrines delineating the duties of children demonstrate clearly the role of normalizing assumptions. From a subjective viewpoint, the cost of holding children engaged in adult activities to an adult standard of care is sure to be great most of the time. Children are not competent to engage in adult activities. The cost of achieving competence exceeds their powers of payment. If, however, we subscribe to the normalizing assumption that engaging in adult activities does not usually have a place in the healthy development and maturation of children, the objective cost of care is very low. By contrast, the normalized benefits of holding children to lesser, age-appropriate standards of care when they participate in age-appropriate activities is very high. Participating in age-appropriate activities is an important part of healthy development and an urgent interest.[165] The doctrines delineating the duties of children are thus anomalous if we take subjective, individualized costs as our touchstone, but sound if we make normalizing assumptions and assess burdens and benefits objectively.

These examples are representative. ARP doctrine is normalizing through and through. In order to fix the boundaries of our freedoms and responsibilities, ARP doctrine rejects the use of subjective costs of care for the simple but powerful reason given in *Vaughan*: a rule measuring the adequacy of care by individual capacities to take care "would leave so vague a line as to afford no rule at all."[166] The doctrine, therefore, requires "in all cases a regard to caution such as a man of ordinary prudence would observe."[167] In order to interact fairly with one another, we must use objective standards of conduct and we must make judgments about the interests that people normally and legitimately have.

---

[165] As the Supreme Court of New Hampshire stated in *Charbonneau v. MacRury*:

Unless [children] are to be denied the environment and association of their elders until they have acquired maturity, there must be a living relationship between them on terms which permit the child to act as a child in his stage of development.... For the law to hold children to the exercise of the care of adults "would be to shut its eyes, ostrich-like, to the facts of life and to burden unduly the child's growth to majority."

153 A. 457, 462 (N.H. 1931) (quoting Harry Shulman, The Standard of Care Required of Children, 37 Yale L.J. 618, 618 (1928)), overruled on other grounds, Daniels v. Evans, 224 A.2d 63 (N.H. 1966). The relaxation of duty for children engaged in age-appropriate activities relies on normalizing assumptions in another, more descriptive, way. The doctrine supposes that age-appropriate activities impose less risk than adult ones and enable more victim precautions. See *supra* notes 139–40, and accompanying text. Insofar as the rules governing the duties of children both reflect the priority of avoiding harm and enable their pursuit of age-appropriate activities, they are natural focal points for fair interaction.

[166] *Vaughan*, 132 Eng. Rep.
[167] *Id.*

D. The Template of Reasonableness

Earlier in this chapter we distinguished reasonableness from rationality. Rationality, we said, has to do with the pursuit of a given end or objective; the intelligence that it identifies is instrumental. Reasonableness is morally inflected; it is concerned with interacting with others on mutually acceptable terms. ARP doctrine bears this distinction out and brings it to bear on matters of risk and precaution. Reasonable people approach questions of risk and precaution with distinctive dispositions and convictions. They assign substantial weight to security; they do not prefer their interests to those of others; they restrain the intensity of their preferences so that they do not make demands upon others that they would not be prepared to honor themselves; and they are willing to interact on fair terms with others who are prepared to reciprocate their cooperation. These commitments and dispositions structure negligence law's approach to questions of appropriate precaution in a fertile way, but they are abstract. Negligence law makes them concrete through a set of less fundamental doctrines that help to articulate the demands of reasonable care.

1. Reasonable Expectations and Salient Precautions

Most accidents arise within ongoing social activities. Driving is an example. For the most part, automobile accidents take place among parties who are strangers to one another, legally and socially. Driving itself, though, is an ongoing social activity. Drivers who observe the rules of the road impose roughly reciprocal risks on one another.[168] When reasonable people are engaged in ongoing interaction, particular precautions often prove to be "natural focal points"[169] for fair interaction. Given the background facts of the risky situation, the disposition to reasonableness, and the fundamental interests of reasonable persons, particular precautions become salient. As Thomas Schelling once observed, "[m]ost situations... provide some clue for coordinating behavior, some focal point for each person's expectation of what the other expects him to expect to be expected to do."[170] It is common for precautions that ARP doctrine identifies as required as a matter of law to be salient in just this kind of way.

---

[168] A point noted long ago by Lord Blackburn in *Fletcher v. Rylands*, I L.R.-Ex. 265 (Ex. Ch. 1866) (Blackburn, J.).

[169] See John Rawls, Justice as Fairness: A Restatement 123 (Harvard, 2001) (describing the difference principle as "a natural focal point between the claims of efficiency and equality". Rawls is following Thomas Schelling. See Thomas C. Schelling, The Strategy of Conflict 57 (Harvard, 1980). See also Conrad D. Johnson, On Deciding and Setting Precedent for the Reasonable Man, 62 Archiv Rechts & Sozialphil. 161 (1976) (bringing Schelling's work, and David Lewis's work on convention, to bear on the phenomenon of judicial precedent, and developing his theses in the context of tort).

[170] Schelling 1980, *supra* note 169, at 57. The salience of certain solutions is a highly contextual matter. "A prime characteristic of most of these 'solutions' to the problems, that is, of the clues or coordinators or focal points, is some kind of prominence or conspicuousness. But it is a prominence that depends on time and place and who the people are." *Id.* at 57-58. This is why judgments

Consider the circumstance addressed by *Delair v. McAdoo*.[171] *Delair* holds that, as a matter of law, all drivers must be held to be aware of the hazards of tires which are "worn through to the fabric" and must therefore be found negligent for accidents caused by using tires in such condition.[172] Drivers are participating in a complex and mutually beneficial activity. That activity enables its participants to pursue their own separate ends and requires each of them to take precautions for each other's benefit—observing the rules of the road, maintaining the brakes on their vehicles, tempering their intake of alcohol, and so on. The choice confronting the court is a restricted one; it must choose between an "objective" rule requiring persons to know the dangers of worn-out tires, and a "subjective" rule exculpating people who are, in good faith, ignorant of those dangers. Once the choice is framed by the context of driving, and by the alternative rulings available to the court, it is an easy choice for reasonable people concerned with interacting on fair terms to make. The subjective rule suffers from the vices that we have reviewed: it puts the security of other drivers at considerable risk; it increases the uncertainty surrounding the risks of the road; and it undermines fair interaction. The objective rule has the converse virtues: it protects the security of other drivers; it makes the risks of the road more predictable; and it underwrites interaction on fair terms. Moreover, it makes comparatively modest demands—the burden of examining *one's own* tires to determine if they are "worn through to the fabric" and of recognizing the hazards posed by such tires to oneself and others. Making drivers bear the risks of accidents caused by other vehicle owner' tires worn through to the fabric, by contrast, asks the impossible. The rule chosen by the court is clearly the superior one.

Many exceptions to the general rule that all actors are held to the standard of the average reasonable person also lend themselves to interpretation and defense as natural focal points for fair interaction. It is reasonable, as discussed earlier, to permit police and firefighters to impose greater than average risks when responding to emergencies.[173] The importance of preserving life and limb

---

of reasonable precaution are deeply affected by the circumstances in which they arise. Because salience is contextual in this way, it "lends itself poorly to fruitful idealization" and so escapes formal modeling. Allan Gibbard, Constructing Justice, 20 Phil. & Pub. Aff. 264, 273 (1991) (reviewing Brian Barry, Theories of Justice (University of California, 1989)).

[171] 188 A. 181 (Pa. 1936).
[172] *Id.* at 184.
[173] See, *e.g.*, Baltimore Transit Co. v. Young, 56 A.2d 140, 142 (Md. 1947) (holding that an emergency vehicle responding to an emergency call is not held to the same standard of care as an ordinary driver); Magee v. West-End St. Ry., 23 N.E. 1102, 1102 (Mass. 1890) (holding that a firefighter responding to a call cannot be held to an ordinary standard of care); Warren v. Mendenhall, 79 N.W. 661, 663 (Minn. 1899) (holding that a city fire truck driver may take risks that would be negligent if taken in the pursuit of ordinary business); Mansfield v. City of Philadelphia, 42 A.2d 549, 549 (Pa. 1945) (holding that a municipality is only liable for the actions of a fire truck driver responding to an alarm if the actions were reckless); La Marra v. Adam, 63 A.2d 497, 500 (Pa. 1949) (holding that a

from grave and imminent harm is evident to all reasonable people. Moreover, by driving specially marked vehicles, using flashing lights, and sounding sirens, police and firefighters can alert potential victims to the increased risks they impose, thereby permitting potential victims to take additional precautions for their own safety. And because the conditions that permit greater risk imposition are objectively defined and publicly known,[174] courts are in a good position to determine whether the power to impose increased risk is being properly exercised. These considerations show not only that the exception is easy to justify but also how it is that appropriate solutions "depend on time and place and who the people are."[175] The facts these considerations point out are distinctive to the circumstances of police work and firefighting. Similar justifications can be offered for ARP doctrine's articulation of the duties of children and its treatment of statutes.

In establishing norms of reasonableness, ARP doctrine can be either *legislative* or *adjudicative*. The doctrine is legislative if it prescribes canonical norms of reasonableness and requires persons to honor those norms. It is adjudicative if it acknowledges and enforces preexisting norms recognized by reasonable persons and so *describe* the norms that reasonable persons engaged in the practices should arrive at by themselves.[176] This is a distinction that matters. If ARP doctrine merely articulates the judgments that reasonable persons would reach when confronted with the matter at hand, the doctrine respects preexisting rights instead of creating rights retroactively. It therefore realizes the rule of law and secures freedom from retroactive penalties.[177] When reasonable precautions are salient and courts are competent, persons who act reasonably will find that the reach of their responsibilities is clear even in the absence of judicial precedent, customary practice, or statutory prescription. Reasonable people will not find their freedom violated by the judicial creation of retroactive duties and liabilities.

Two statutory negligence cases—*Martin v. Herzog*[178] and *Tedla v. Ellman*[179]— illustrate both the difference between the legislative and adjudicative roles of

municipality is liable for injury caused by a police officer or ambulance only if the injury was caused by recklessness).

[174] There are usually statutory or administrative specifications of the circumstances under which police and fire personnel are permitted to impose greater risks. See Dobbs 2016, *supra* note 63, at 574–75; Gerrit De Geest, Who Should Be Immune from Tort Liability?, 41 J. Legal Stud. 292–93 (2012).
[175] Schelling 1980, *supra* note 169, at 58.
[176] See Johnson 1976, *supra* note 169, at 172–77.
[177] This involves two aspects of the rule of law-prospectivity and publicity. See Gregory C. Keating, Fidelity to Preexisting Law and the Legitimacy of Legal Decision, 69 Notre Dame L. Rev. 1, 16–21, 27–29, 35–36 (1999).
[178] 126 N.E. 814 (N.Y. 1920).
[179] 19 N.E.2d 987 (N.Y. 1939).

reasonableness and the priority of the adjudicative role. *Martin* lays down the rule that the unexcused violation of a statutory prohibition is negligence per se.[180] *Tedla* carves out an exception to that rule. The plaintiffs in *Tedla* were wheeling a baby carriage full of junk along the right side of the road one Sunday evening after dark. "[V]ery heavy Sunday night traffic" was headed in the opposite direction, so the plaintiffs chose to walk with the lighter traffic on the other side of the road.[181] The plaintiffs' conduct appeared to be contributory negligence per se because, although it was consistent with customary practice, it was contrary to a recently enacted statute.[182] Yet the court came down on the side of customary practice, creating an exception to the statute for the circumstances of the case.[183] The court's decision rested not on divining unexpressed legislative intent but on the evidently superior safety of the preexisting customary practice. Walking with the traffic was clearly safer than walking into it.[184]

Tedla is thus an example of a decision which announces norms of reasonable behavior. It implies that when actors hit upon reasonable precautions and legislatures do not, both legislation and judicial precedent enshrining statutes as authoritative specifications of reasonable behavior must yield. This is a defensible position, not a flat-out denial or evasion of legislative supremacy. The duties of care that people owe to one another are *natural duties*.[185] We all have duties not to harm one another. Legislation ratifies and specifies those duties; it does not create them. To be sure, ARP doctrine is not purely adjudicative; at the very least, it instructs people to act reasonably. This requirement may seem legislative even if the norm of reasonableness itself derives from beliefs to which our practices and moral judgments, properly reconstructed, commit us. This fact, however, does not undermine the adjudicative character of *judgments* of reasonableness: such judgments follow the template of reasonable behavior, they do not form that template. Insofar as they do, the canons of reasonableness ensure that liability is not imposed retroactively, thereby realizing one of the liberties associated with the rule of law.

The normalizing assumptions inherent in ARP doctrine also help to make judgments about the merits and demerits of particular precautions salient.

---

[180] *Martin*, 126 N.E. at 815.
[181] *Tedla*, 19 N.E.2d at 989.
[182] *Id.* The statute required pedestrians to walk *against* the traffic.
[183] *Id.* at 991.
[184] *Id.* ("We cannot assume reasonably that the Legislature intended that a statute enacted for the preservation of life and limb of pedestrians must be observed when observance would subject them to more imminent danger.").
[185] See Rawls 1999, *supra* note 56, at 97 (discussing, inter alia, the natural duty not to injure others). Natural duties do not depend on the presence of institutions for their very existence, while artificial duties do. For an explication of the distinction between artificial and natural duties in a related context, see generally Thomas Scanlon, Promises and Practices, 19 Phil. & Pub. Aff. 199 (1990).

Delair,[186] for example, relies implicitly on the normalizing assumption that the benefits that accrue to drivers from continuing to use worn tires are not urgent. Some of those benefits, in fact, are not even legitimately counted as benefits. Not having to attend to the safety your car's tires enables you to be lazy, to be inexcusably ignorant, and to show insufficient regard for the well-being of others. These are vices, not virtues; it is wrong to indulge them.

2. Subordinate Doctrines of Due Care

In a wide range of cases, the template of reasonableness fashioned by ARP doctrine will not pick out a single precaution as uniquely reasonable and therefore required as a matter of law. When the Hand Formula and ARP doctrine are considered jointly, they structure and guide our thinking in helpful ways, and with significant detail. Nonetheless, in many cases these doctrines do not identify a single precaution as uniquely reasonable. They leave room for reasonable people to disagree. And reasonable people do disagree. Reasonable people might well, for instance, disagree over whether forty-five miles per hour is a reasonable speed limit for a major surface street, especially when they consider the bearing of different weather conditions, different levels of traffic, the visibility at diverse times of day, the condition of the road at different times of year, and so on. Faced with such reasonable disagreement, it would be arbitrary and wrong for ARP doctrine to declare some precise precaution required and reasonable as a matter of law—and it is not inclined to do so.

Negligence law responds to the indeterminacy of the general canons of reasonableness through subordinate doctrines that specify concrete duties of care. Custom, jury adjudication, and statutes all perform this role. Consider, for example, a victim who, hurrying to get out of the rain, injures herself by running into a plate-glass door, which shatters when she collides with it. If the door is one-half inch thick and could be made thicker in one-twentieth-of-an-inch increments, modest and incremental safety improvements can be made almost indefinitely. We might hazard the guess that those improvements would all yield modest and incremental reductions in accident costs. Under these circumstances, it is difficult to squeeze some unique thickness out of the general canons of reasonable care and to call that thickness the correct level of precaution. There is no uniquely salient and correct increment of precaution.

In the case from which this example was drawn, the court permitted industry custom with respect to thickness to fix the appropriate standard of care.[187] ARP

---

[186] *Delair*, 188 A. at 184 (holding defendant negligent for driving car with tires worn through to the fabric).
[187] Raim v. Ventura, 113 N.W.2d 827, 830 (Wis. 1962) ("[T]here was evidence that more than two thousand doors like the respondent's have been installed in the Kenosha area during the past eight years; 98% of all the glass doors in such area are like the one in question in that they employ ¼-inch plate glass.").

doctrine's concern with salience surely helps to explain why negligence law shows the regard for custom that it does. Precisely because they are customary, customary precautions are salient, and this makes them natural focal points of precaution. So, too, ARP doctrine's concern with normalization—with setting normal levels of risk and precaution—supports assigning some weight to custom. Customary conduct *is* normal conduct, and what is normal is plainly relevant to, though not dispositive of, the question of what *should be* normal. Deferring to custom also helps to dispel uncertainty, especially in cases where general canons of negligence do not prescribe a unique precaution. Injurers have good reason to want the boundaries of their responsibilities to be clear: uncertainty frustrates planning, impairs the coordination of activities, and debilitates freedom of action. Less obviously, in many circumstances, victims also have reason to favor clear specification of injurers' responsibilities. Knowledge of the precautions that injurers can be expected to take enables victims to adjust their own conduct and to coordinate their own precautions. Establishing a uniform level of precaution is therefore desirable, and reliance on such a level is justified and reasonable, if that level falls within the boundaries of reasonableness fixed by the Hand Formula and ARP doctrine. The practice of assigning *some* weight to custom thus draws support from diverse sources—from due care doctrine's quest for salient precautions, from the parties' joint interest in settling on a precaution that the can coordinate around, and from the principle that reasonable reliance should not be disappointed.

Jury adjudication also serves to identify superior precautions in circumstances where the general canons of due care are indeterminate. Jury adjudication gathers its support partly from its identification of salient precautions and partly from independent moral principles. Salience is contextual. It "depends on time and place and who the people are."[188] Insofar as juries presumably embody the culture and conventions of their communities, they are well-suited to selecting contextually salient precautions. Salience is not the end of the matter, however. The practice of jury adjudication also has independent moral support. Jury adjudication is intended to bring the moral sense of the community to bear on controversial disputes. Thus, it draws authority from its claim to articulate some community's shared sense of justice.[189] By virtue of this claim, jury adjudication legitimizes controversial outcomes even in the face of persistent disagreement. It is presumptively implausible for any single person to insist that their sense of the care that should be exercised in cases where the correct precaution is unclear should trump the sense of eleven or twelve of their peers. Last, negligence law

---

[188] Schelling 1980, *supra* note 169, at 58.
[189] See Catharine Pierce Wells, Tort Law as Corrective Justice: A Pragmatic Justification for Jury Adjudication, 88 Mich. L. Rev. 2348, 2408-10 (1990) (arguing that jury adjudication of tort disputes produces "local objectivity" in jury decisions).

determines concrete standards of due care by deference to statutes. Legislative specification of precautions as mandatory surely makes those precautions salient. So too the principle of legislative supremacy and the duty to comply with just institutions[190] provide further—and independent—grounds for deferring to statutes.

These observations do no more than situate the roles of custom, statutes, and jury adjudication within the larger framework that we have explored. But even brief discussion brings into view a fundamental difference between instrumental and deontological approaches to the construction of due care doctrine. Economics is instrumental in its thinking. Doctrines of due care are all means to the same end of balancing accident and precaution costs in a wealth-maximizing way. There are no differences of kind, role, or legitimate authority among the Hand Formula, ARP doctrine, statutes, custom, and jury adjudication. Economics uses the doctrines to address the same question in the same way and evaluates the duties specified by these doctrines according to the same criteria of optimality.[191] By contrast, the deontological approach developed here envisions the enterprise as a sequential one, which "work[s] from a general framework for the whole to sharper and sharper determination of its parts."[192] Subordinate principles of institutional legitimacy play an important role in that sequence.

A deontological approach takes due care doctrine to work from general canons of reasonableness through to the specification of concrete duties through a sequence of doctrines. The Hand Formula and ARP doctrine specify general substantive and methodological criteria of reasonableness; jury adjudication, custom, and statutes specify precise duties of care. The more basic doctrines frame and limit the more particular ones, and the more particular ones draw their authority both from general notions of reasonableness and from their own distinctive principles.[193] Juries, customs, and statutes may set duties of care only insofar as they respect the boundaries set by the general canons of reasonable precaution. When they transgress against those boundaries, they forfeit their authority. Within those boundaries, distinctive institutional principles such as legislative supremacy reinforce the authority of these subordinate doctrines.

---

[190] For a discussion of this duty, see Rawls 1999, *supra* note 56, at 350–55.

[191] See, *e.g.*, Posner 1992, *supra* note 51, at 168–69 (arguing that custom will represent optimal care only when existing contractual relationships between buyers and sellers fix industry custom at the optimal level and making no attempt to fit this with the treatment of custom by tort doctrine); Posner 1972, *supra* note 6, at 38–39 (noting that statutes probably did not reflect optimal care levels). In his analysis of custom and statutes, Posner does not suppose that there are independent principles (such as legislative supremacy or reasonable reliance) that require respect for statutes or customs.

[192] Rawls 1999, *supra* note 56, at 566.

[193] See Rawls 2005, *supra* note 8, at 262.

E. Taking Negligence Law Seriously

Following in the footsteps of Oliver Wendell Holmes, the economic analysis of negligence is skeptical and reductionist.[194] It is suspicious of negligence law's rhetoric of rights, wrongs, reasonableness, and even its emphasis on harm. It finds all these morally freighted terms to be vague and hortatory at best, and mere blather at worst. Its solution is to replace them with an ostensibly clearer and more analytically powerful framework. In doing so, economic analysis ends up leaving behind the law that it sets out to explain and clarify. That end point puts the authority of economic analysis in question. It is, after all, the law that claims authority over us, not some independent normative system. This chapter has argued against this kind of dismissal of the language, doctrines, and decisions of the law of negligence. Reasonableness is not, in fact, reducible to rationality. Reasonableness is a morally freighted term; rationality is not. The moral commitments to interpersonal fairness that are constitutive of reasonableness are lost, not clarified, when reasonableness is reduced to social rationality. Sympathetically read, the morally freighted language of negligence law is not vague or empty. It is abstract. The doctrines and decisions of negligence law make its overarching abstractions concrete enough to guide conduct and govern disputes.

The Hand Formula clarifies the basic trade-off that we face when we balance risk and precaution. Case law and doctrine show us how we might make that trade-off in ways that reflect the priority of avoiding harm, and reconcile liberty and security not efficiently, but fairly. For its part, ARP doctrine's commitment to objectivity is better seen not as a second-best way of approximating subjective value, but as the best way of making interpersonal comparisons of burdens and benefits for people whose aspirations, projects, and preferences diverge. ARP doctrine's search for precautions that are natural focal points for fair interaction and its use of normalizing conceptions are of a piece with its commitment to objectivity, and likewise help to make its commitment to fair terms of risk imposition concrete. Custom, statutes, and jury adjudication all enable negligence law to pour even more precise content into its abstract norm of reasonable care.

Our tort law of negligence thus articulates a defensible—and admirably adaptable—regime of responsibility for avoiding and repairing harm. It is not, however, the body of law best suited to govern every kind of risk imposition. In some cases, the very severity of the harm that we must address disempowers the law of torts. Tort law enforces its primary norms of harm avoidance through

---

[194] On Holmes, see the acute observations in Goldberg & Zipursky 2020, *supra* note 11, esp. at 83–85.

secondary powers of recourse and rights of reparation. Irreparable injury therefore presents special problems for the law of torts. In other cases, negligence law's exclusive concern with avoidable harm is troubling. Unavoidable harm often looms large in our world. Unlike negligence, strict liability is responsive to the significance of unavoidable harm. These are the topics to which we must now turn.

5
From Reparation to Regulation

I. Harm beyond Repair

"Reparative damages," John Gardner writes, "have pride of place as a remedy for tortious wrongdoing."[1] On reflection, this preeminence seems both unavoidable and unsatisfying. It seems unavoidable because reparative damages awarded ex post and injunctive relief granted ex ante appear to be the only options available, and injunctive relief is generally infeasible. In part, injunctive relief is infeasible because accidental harm is at the center of modern tort law. Individual accidents happen when and because people lose control—either over themselves or over instrumentalities under their command. The fact that individual accidents happen when and because someone's agency misfires puts them beyond the reach of prevention by injunction. Furthermore, because there is no law of attempts in tort—because suffering harm or having one's rights violated is an element of most intentional wrongs—opportunities to enjoin even intentional wrongs are exceptional. Usually, there is no wrong to enjoin until harm has been done and the time for injunctive relief has passed. Consequently, even when the wrongful conduct at issue is intentional—and hence the kind of conduct that we might in principle prohibit—in practice injunctive relief is common only when some course of conduct constitutes an ongoing wrong. Recurring trespasses and some nuisances fit this description, but these nuisances and trespasses are the exception not the norm.

If money damages appear inevitable because injunctive relief is generally impossible, impractical, or unjustifiable, at first glance, money damages themselves appear both easy to award and appropriate. Tortious wrongs normally *do* inflict impairment and loss—disability, disfigurement, physical injury, and the economic costs and emotional stresses that accompany being subjected to serious harm, wrongly inflicted. Tortious wrongs generally do leave their victims in need

---

[1] John Gardner, Torts and Other Wrongs, in Torts and Other Wrongs 1, 10 (2019). Pride of place is not sole and despotic dominion; other remedies are sometimes available. Importantly, injunctive relief is exceptional. Injunctions are sometimes available in cases involving property torts, dignitary torts, and constitutional torts. See Dan B. Dobbs, Paul T. Hayden, & Ellen M. Bublick, Hornbook on Torts 851 (West, 2d ed., 2016). Nonetheless even theorists who are not strongly attracted to reparative damages accept Gardner's claim. See, *e.g.*, John C.P. Goldberg & Benjamin C. Zipursky, Recognizing Wrongs 164 (Harvard, 2020) ("The question arises as to why courts have settled on money damages as pretty much the only kind of demand a victim is entitled to receive judicial assistance in making (and having heeded) as a matter of right.").

of repair. Normally, therefore, tort remedies must shoulder the task of erasing the effects of wrongful harm. And that is what reparative damages are designed to do. On closer inspection, however, reparative damages appear chronically incapable of discharging the responsibility that tort law assigns to them. The "basic rule of tort compensation is that the plaintiff should be put in the position that [they] would have been in absent the defendant's [wrong]."[2] By enabling victims to replace the diverse goods that wrongfully inflicted harm takes from them— emotional tranquility, good health, and intact bodies, as well as wealth and income—reparative damages attempt to restore to victims the powers of agency and levels of well-being that they once enjoyed. Yet "[m]oney," as one leading remedies scholar explains, "is an adequate remedy if, and only if, it can be used to replace the specific thing that was lost."[3] When the specific thing lost is physical intactness, this test of adequacy is not easy to satisfy. "[B]roken legs," one tort scholar observes, "don't zero out. No sum of money returns someone who has been injured to the position they would have been in had the tort not been committed, unless their injury is monetary."[4] The standard test of remedial adequacy thus seems to condemn the books of account that the law of torts keeps to perpetual imbalance.

Harm to real or tangible personal property, moreover, is not always so very different from physical harm to persons. Some damaged property is either fully restorable or fully replaceable. A battered and beaten commercial dock can be rebuilt or replaced.[5] Moreover, because a commercial dock is an instrument for producing wealth and income, its value can be converted into cash with little or no loss. Personal property, however, is not so readily restored or replaced. In part, we live our lives by and through the objects that we acquire and use. Our ownership and use of things incorporates them into our personhood and our projects.[6] If you lose your home and all your earthly possessions to a negligently started fire, money damages will enable you to purchase a new dwelling and new possessions, but your purchases will go toward building a new, and different, life. Money does not have the power to summon either your previous home—or the life that you lived in it—back to life. Serious physical harm to property invested with personality thus has much in common with serious physical harm to persons. It is normally the case that the damage done is not fully repairable, and that

---

[2] See, *e.g.*, Keel v. Banach, 624 So.2d 1022, 1029 (Ala. 1993). Compare Porter v. City of Manchester, 849 A.2d 103, 118–19 (N.H. 2004) ("The usual rule of compensatory damages in tort cases requires that the person wronged receive a sum of money that will restore the person as nearly as possible to the position he or she would have been in if the wrong had not been committed.").

[3] Douglas Laycock, The Death of the Irreparable Injury Rule, 103 Harv. L. Rev. 687, 703 (1990).

[4] Scott Hershovitz, Corrective Justice for Civil Recourse Theorists, 39 Fla. St. U. L. Rev. 107, 110 (2011).

[5] This was the damage done in the celebrated case of *Vincent v. Lake Erie Transportation Co.*, 124 N.W. 221 (Minn. 1910).

[6] See generally Margaret Jane Radin, Property and Personhood, 34 Stan. L. Rev. 934 (1982).

the goods damaged are not readily replaced. "Reparative damages" thus seem to be both a necessary response to the harm wrought by most torts, and an inadequate one.

A. Possibilities, Limits, and Lessons

Perhaps the problem here is that the law's rhetoric of repair asks too much. We must accept the fact that repair is second-best. Even so, money damages perform invaluable roles and realize important ends. If parts of both of your legs are severed by someone else's negligence, money damages will enable you to purchase artificial replacements.[7] Prosthetic limbs are second-best substitutes for real ones, but terribly important if the limbs that you were born with have been damaged beyond repair. On the one hand, severed limbs are not snapped walking sticks, and money damages do not enable you to replace a lost leg with a new and even better one. To acquire a prosthetic limb is to alter one's physical self and to suffer a rupture in the course of one's life.[8] On the other hand, even though artificial replacements do not put you in the same position that you would have been in had your natural limbs not been sliced off, they do restore a considerable part of the capacity that has been wrongly taken from you. Moreover, because money is an all-purpose resource, putting it in the hands of victims enables them to rebuild their lives as they see fit. Because money can purchase diverse goods, and can itself be put to various uses, putting money in the hands of victims allows them to be the authors of their own narratives of recovery and renewal.[9] This responds to the impairment of agency by stimulating the exercise of agency. It is intrinsically fitting. The goods that money damages can deliver are thus real and important, even if they do not restore people to the position that they would have been in had they not been harmed.

Yet, even when we give money damages their due, it remains the case that tort law's powers of repair fall short of the aspiration that they set for themselves. The fact that money damages cannot wholly erase the effects of disability, disfigurement, chronic pain, and other harms to persons and to property, has not escaped the attention of either courts or commentators. The *Second Restatement*, for instance, acknowledges that when a "tort causes bodily harm or emotional distress, the law cannot restore the injured person to [their] previous position."[10]

---

[7] As in *Davis v. Consolidated Rail Corp.*, 788 F.2d 1260 (7th Cir. 1986).

[8] See generally Sean Williams, Self-Altering Injury: The Hidden Harms of Hedonic Adaption, 96 Cornell L. Rev. 535 (2011).

[9] This is part of what John Gardner is driving at in his chapter, "It's Not About the Money." John Gardner, It's Not About the Money, in From Personal Life to Private Law 88–124 (Oxford, 2018).

[10] Restatement (Second) of Torts § 903 cmt. a, (1979). See also Zibell v. S. Pac. Co., 160 Cal. 237, 255 (Cal. 1911) (quoting Heddles v. Chi & Nw. Ry., 42 N.W. 237 (Wis. 1889)) ("No rational being would change places with the injured man for an amount of gold that will fill the room of the court.") The

Recognizing the problem, however, is one thing; resolving it is another. Confronted with the pervasive inability of money damages to repair the most serious of tortiously inflicted harms, courts and commentators have often assigned a second role to money damages. Money damages can serve the expressive end of marking the moral significance of harms and wrongs, even when they cannot erase those harms or undo those wrongs.[11] And courts have sometimes deployed punitive damages to condemn and discourage wrongful conduct that risks and inflicts injury beyond repair.[12] These agile and inventive uses of damages are often justified and desirable, but their very existence underscores the fact that reparation in tort cannot undo the devastating effects of those tortiously inflicted harms that we have most reason to fear.

Traditional remedies doctrine has it that, when money damages are unable to erase a wrong, injunctive relief should step in to prevent the wrong. Perhaps we were too quick to dismiss this possibility. The fact that accidents commonly arise out of the malfunction of agency does not close all doors. We might still enjoin the activities within which accidents arise. Railroading accidents cannot be enjoined, but railroading can be. And the same is true of manufacturing, milling, driving, flying, building, blasting, and an indefinitely long list of other risky activities. Enjoining such activities, however, is a cure worse than the disease it treats. None of these activities are wrong in themselves. Basic productive activities make everyone better off. They are valuable—worth having even if their price is a certain amount of accidental harm that cannot, in fact, be eliminated. Tort law must therefore make do with money damages as its default and normal remedy, notwithstanding the fact that money damages will often be unable to restore wrongly injured victims to the positions that they would otherwise have occupied.

---

incommensurability of money damages and harm is most vivid when death is the harm. "The death of a family member, particularly a child, involves inconsolable grief for which no amount of money damages can compensate. Counsel's suggestion that the Roberts [family] would not have traded Michael's life for $10,000,000 is entirely accurate—but they would also not have traded Michael's life for $100,000,000 or even a $1,000,000,000." Roberts v. Stevens Clinic Hosp., Inc. 176 W.Va. 492, 499 (1986). For perceptive discussion, see Mark Geistfeld, The Principle of Misalignment: Duty, Damages, and the Nature of Tort Liability, 121 Yale L.J. 142, 161–64 (2011). Geistfeld draws heavily on Laycock 1990, *supra* note 3.

[11] See Margaret Jane Radin, Compensation and Commensurability, 45 Duke L.J. 36 (1993); Hershovitz 2011. See also Restatement (Second) of Torts § 903 cmt. a (1979) (damages for pain, humiliation, harm, "give to the injured person some pecuniary return for what he has suffered or is likely to suffer").

[12] See Grimshaw v. Ford Motor Co., 174 Cal. Rptr. 348, 388–89 (Cal. App. 1981) (concluding that punitive award of $3.5 million was not excessive in light of Ford's "conscious and callous disregard of public safety" and "tortious conduct endanger[ing] the lives of thousands of Pinto purchasers"). See also Geistfeld 2011, *supra* note 10, at 165–69, discussing how punitive damages can provide potential tortfeasors with incentives to discharge their duties of care with great diligence.

The very real limits of reparative damages undercut both corrective justice and economic theories of tort. The traditional corrective justice view "that damages really do make it as if a wrong had never happened"[13] cannot be squared with the fact that the more serious the harm the less reparative damages can do to restore "to the wronged party the means he or she is entitled to."[14] Most starkly, reparative damages cannot restore to those who suffer the most serious harm of all—premature death—the life that was wrongly taken from them. The limits of reparative damages also cut the legs out from underneath the economic conception of tort as a price system. "For the [tort] system to bring about an efficient level of accidents and safety the damage awards must be equal to the costs of accidents resulting from negligent conduct."[15] Because compensatory damages cannot take the full measure of irreparable injuries, "the secondary obligation to pay compensatory damages is not fully interchangeable with the primary obligation to exercise reasonable care."[16] A would-be tortfeasor "cannot unilaterally choose to pay compensatory damages in exchange for acting unreasonably."[17] From an economic perspective, the fact that compliance with a secondary duty of harm repair is not a perfect substitute for compliance with a primary duty of harm avoidance shows that tort damages are not well-calibrated prices coughed up by an efficient market. Tort damages do not price serious physical harms properly for the simple reason that no amount of compensation can fully repair such harms. Tort law is therefore a flawed price system, and its forward-looking powers of deterrence are most impaired when our interest in deterrence is most intense—when avoiding harm is the only way of escaping serious impairment.

B. Damages for Wrongful Death

The problem here does not disappear if we reject standard economic and corrective justice accounts of tort law. It haunts the law of torts itself. From its birth in the middle of the nineteenth century down to the present day, the law of damages for wrongful death has wrestled with the most acute incarnation of the limits of reparative damages. The lesson of that history is that tort damages can be towed away from their reparative anchor only so far, and that the creative powers of the common law simply fail when the harm at issue is death. Because the harm of death is total and beyond any repair, wrongful death puts a body of law wedded

---

[13] Arthur Ripstein, Private Wrongs 233 (Harvard, 2016). Ripstein understands himself to be defending the orthodox view of the work done by reparative damages.
[14] Ripstein 2016, *supra* note 13, at 234.
[15] Richard A. Posner, A Theory of Negligence, 1 J. Legal Stud. 29, 92 (1972).
[16] Geistfeld 2011, *supra* note 10, at 145. As we shall see, wrongful death damages do not try to compensate the dead victim for the value to them of the life that they have lost.
[17] *Id.*

to the remedy of reparation under severe strain. The common law of torts has been under no illusions on this score. "The effect to be given the death of a person connected with a tort rests almost entirely upon statutory foundations."[18] Even today, after a hundred and seventy-five years of statutory and judicial expansion of liability for wrongful death, a defendant whose tortious conduct fatally injures someone else is not liable for damages compensating the victim for the value *to them* of the life that they have lost.[19] The core harm done by death goes uncompensated because it is beyond compensation. Nothing will restore a dead victim to the position that they occupied prior to their death.

The original common law rule—dating to medieval England—was that tort actions were "personal" and therefore died "with the person of either the plaintiff or the defendant."[20] For the most part, that rule has been reversed by widespread enactment of two kinds of statutes: Survival Statutes and Death Statutes. If the defendant has injured but not killed someone—and either the injured victim or the defendant has died before trial—only the Survival Statute comes into play. If, however, the defendant's tortious conduct results in the death of the victim, two distinct statutory rights of action come into play. One of these rights is held by the estate of the deceased and includes elements of damage for which the deceased could have recovered had they not died; this is the cause of action under the Survival Statute. The other cause of action is created by the Death Statute. The first Death Statute (commonly known as Lord Campbell's Act) was enacted in England in 1846.[21] It provided damages for near relatives who were dependents of the person killed, damages being given in accordance with pecuniary benefits they probably would have received but for the death.[22] Lord Campbell's Act has

---

[18] Wex Malone, The Genesis of Wrongful Death, 17 Stan. L. Rev. 1043, 1044 (1965).

[19] See, *e.g.*, Andrew J. McClurg, Dead Sorrow: A Story About Loss and a New Theory of Wrongful Death Damages, 85 B.U. L. Rev. 1, 6–7, 20–22 (2005) (the decedent's loss of enjoyment of life is not compensable in the vast majority of jurisdictions). Courts are well aware of this fact and its significance. See, *e.g.*, Acosta v. Honda Motor Co., 717 F.2d 828, 837 (3d Cir. 1983) ("[C]ompensatory damages may prove an inadequate deterrent even when victims do bring suit. Current doctrine does not for example, allow the estate of a decedent killed by a defective product to recover the value of the life to the decedent himself, recovery is instead limited to the pecuniary loss to those immediately surrounding the decedent."). Quiroz v. Seventh Ave. Center, 45 Cal. Rptr. 3d 222, 226 (Cal. Ct. App. 2006) (citations omitted), observed: "At common law, personal tort claims expired when either the victim or the tortfeasor died. Today, a cause of action for wrongful death exists only by virtue of legislative grace. The statutorily created 'wrongful death' cause of action does not effect a survival of the decedent's cause of action. [Instead,] it gives to the representative a totally new right of action, on different principles."

[20] Malone 1965, *supra* note 18, at 1044.

[21] The history of wrongful death is recounted in Malone 1965 and John F. Witt, From Loss of Service to Loss of Support: The Wrongful Death Statutes, the Origins of Modern Tort Law, and the Making of the Nineteenth Century Family, 25 Law & Soc. Inquiry 717, 733–37 (2000).

[22] Dobbs 2016, *supra* note 1 at 686. "Survival statutes provide for the survival of whatever tort cause of action the deceased herself would have had if she had been able to sue at the moment of her death." (Defining survival statutes). "Wrongful death statutes, by contrast, create a new action in favor of certain beneficiaries who suffer from another's death." (Defining wrongful death statutes and contrasting them with survival statutes).

been widely copied in the United States, with variations as to the amount of recovery and the persons who may be beneficiaries.[23]

The present-day legacy of Lord Campbell's Act is thus the standard practice of awarding wrongful death damages for "relational harm." Diverse persons related to the victim, who have suffered losses because of the victim's wrongful death, now have their losses recognized and compensated as best the law can.[24] Damages for relational harm, though, do not redress the greatest harm inflicted by wrongful death—the harm suffered by the victim whose life has been cut short. At first glance, it may seem that the long evolution of damages law away from its strictly reparative role has produced an appropriate adaption. The victims of wrongful death have lost lives that they would otherwise have enjoyed, and damages for lost enjoyment of life are now available in many jurisdictions. But reparative damages can be stretched only so far. Before damages can be awarded for *any* loss, there must be someone around who suffers the loss. "Loss of enjoyment of life," one court explains, "must... be experienced in life before it can become the basis for an award of damages."[25] The dead, however, do not experience the lost enjoyment of the lives that have wrongly been taken from them.

In refusing to award damages for the value to the victim of the life they have lost, the law of wrongful death damages is true to its own inexorable logic. But this perfection of tort law's own internal logic also clarifies the imperfections of tort as an institution. Because the law of torts relies on reparation both to enforce its primary obligations and to erase the effects of tortious wrongs, its powers depend on the possibility of adequate reparation. On the one hand, the harm of death disables the doing of corrective justice. There is no repairing the most severe loss that tortious wrongs can inflict upon us. On the other hand, death diminishes tort law's powers of deterrence. For good reason, courts and commentators alike grimly quote "the old adage that it is cheaper to kill your victim than to leave him maimed."[26] Empirical evidence bears them out: "[T]he average jury verdict in New York City between 1984 and 1993 in case of wrongful death was over $1 million, whereas verdicts in cases of damage averaged over

---

[23] *Id.* "In the latter half of the 19th century, following the lead of... Lord Campbell's Act, the American states addressed the problem by legislation which remains the source of almost all rights arising out of a person's death."

[24] Dobbs 2016, *supra* note 1, at 686.

[25] Otani v. Broudy, 59 P.3d 126, 129 (Wash. Ct. App. 2002). See also Keene v. Brigham & Women's Hosp., Inc., 775 N.E.2d 725, 739 (Mass. App. Ct. 2002) (concluding that there should be no award of damages for loss of enjoyment of life when the "plaintiff lacks the cognitive awareness of his loss"), modified on other grounds, 786 N.E.2d 824 (Mass. 2003); Dan B. Dobbs, Law of Remedies: Damages, Equity, Restitution 678 (3d ed. 2018) (noting that "[c]ourts have rejected a pain and suffering claim when the plaintiff is not aware of pain, as where he is comatose" (citing *Leiker v. Gafford*, 778 P.2d 823 (Kan. 1989)).

[26] Mattyasovszky v. West Towns Bus Co., 61 Ill.2d 31, 38 (1975). The remark is made in a dissenting opinion which would have upheld the award of punitive damages that the majority overturned.

$3 million."[27] Insofar as the right to repair is the mechanism through which our rights not to be wrongly harmed in the first instance are enforced, the more serious and irreparable the harm done, the weaker the protections against that harm conferred upon us by the law of torts.

The larger lesson of wrongful death damages, then, is that the law of torts is fundamentally incomplete. Its remedy of reparation for harm done does not protect us against irreparable injury. Because they are primarily targeted at conduct that is seriously wrongful, punitive damages and criminal sanctions can remedy this incompleteness only to a limited extent.[28] Some seriously harmful conduct is also seriously wrongful, but only some. Irreparable injury can be caused by a momentary lapse of the most ordinary and least blameworthy sort. Taking one's eyes off the road for just a split second while driving can maim or kill another human being, but doing so is ordinary human carelessness, not appallingly callous disregard for the safety of others. Injunctive relief, for its part, is a remedy tailored to the different problem of activities that do so much harm that they should not be allowed to continue. Direct regulation of risk is the institutional response best tailored to cure the problem of harms too severe to remedy ex post. Legislatures and administrative agencies can impose, ex ante, mandatory standards of precaution keyed to the fact that the risks at issue threaten severe and irreparable injury. Direct regulation of risk cannot bring the dead back to life, but it can enact and enforce a level of precaution commensurate with the irreparable injury being risked.

Stringent standards of precaution against irreparable injury are, in fact, prominent features of federal statutes addressing environmental and workplace harms. They are overlooked by philosophically inclined theorists of torts, however, and sharply criticized by economically inclined scholars. The prevailing economic view of these standards is that they are irrational exercises in preferring states of the world with less wealth—and therefore less in the way of possible welfare—to states of the world with more wealth and more possible welfare. These stringent standards of precaution deserve both more attention and more respect. When we take the distinctions among persons seriously—and put the conditions of effective agency at the center of our view—we recognize that harm has a special, negative moral significance and that harm's avoidance has special priority. Part of what gives harm avoidance its special priority is the fact that serious harm is generally not fully repairable, but other features of harm also give us especially

---

[27] See Geistfeld 2011, *supra* note 10, at 159–60. Richard Pierce, Jr., Encouraging Safety: The Limits of Tort Law and Government Regulation, 33 Vand. L. Rev. 1281, 1290–95 (1980), perceptively discusses how the tort law of wrongful death is constructed in such a way that it grievously undercompensates in cases of child victims.

[28] Geistfeld 2011, *supra* note 10, at 165–69. Erik Encarnacion, Resilience, Retribution, and Punitive Damages, 100 Tex. L. Rev. 1025, 30–31 (2021).

strong reasons to prioritize its avoidance. Safety is a kind of Rawlsian primary good; it is an essential condition of effective agency. Unlike financial "losses" and ordinary "costs," physical harms impair our basic powers of agency. Physical harm diminishes our power to work our wills on the world. Devastating, irreparable injury permanently and profoundly diminishes that power and may even extinguish it entirely. Legal standards that require more than cost-justified precaution respond appropriately—not irrationally—to significant risks of severe and irreversible injury.

Tort law's primary norms can and do obligate people to take care not to inflict irreparable injury on each other. They do not extend only to fully repairable injuries. But tort law's remedial apparatus is not up to the task of backing up these primary obligations in a fully satisfactory fashion. When the reparative powers of tort damages are diminished, so too is their power to enforce tort law's primary norms. Holmesian "bad men" really do have less reason to avoid accidentally killing people than they do to avoid badly impairing the earning capacities of those with high incomes. Regulation must come to the rescue of tort. And so we too must turn from tort to regulation. Turning to regulation both brings us face to face with the argument that efficient precaution is the only rational standard of precaution and puts us in contact with well-defined alternatives to efficient precaution. In the contexts to which they apply, those standards are illuminating and credible attempts to implement the proposition that the avoidance of harm has special priority. We must now join the debate over harm's significance more fully than we have so far.

II. Safety as a Primary Good

In one of his *New York Times* columns, the economist Paul Krugman remarks that "liberals don't need to claim that their policies will produce spectacular growth. All they need to claim is feasibility: that we can do things like, say, guaranteeing health insurance to everyone without killing the economy."[29] Krugman's belief that providing everyone with health insurance is desirable unless doing so would "kill the economy" expresses a common conviction. *Some* goods should be provided to everyone, even if their provision comes at a cost in economic efficiency. The goods in question are the kinds of goods that Rawls calls "primary." They are essential to leading decent, independent lives, and their provision therefore has a special priority. Physical safety is, like health, a strong candidate for inclusion on a list of the essential conditions of a decent and independent life. Accidental injury can impair people just as much as bad health can. Unsurprisingly, assertions

---

[29] Paul Krugman, Mornings in Blue America, New York Times (Mar. 27, 2015).

that safety has priority over ordinary "needs and interests" are commonplace in popular discourse. In commenting on the desirability of self-driving cars, for instance, the editors of *Consumer Reports* remark that they "support any new technology that advances the needs and interests of consumers, but at CR, we're always going to make safety our priority."[30]

Because safety has a claim to be an essential condition of effective agency, one might expect to find a vigorous debate in the legal literature on risk and precaution over whether safety should be prioritized over efficiency. Prominent federal statutes take this very position, enjoining either that activities be made "safe" or requiring that the risks of certain activities be reduced as far as it is "feasible" to do so. By "feasible," they mean exactly what Krugman means. The risks in question should be reduced as far as possible without "killing the activity" in question.[31] A chorus of contemporary commentators insists, however, that there is no debate to be had. Safety- and feasibility-based risk regulations are simply irrational. Jonathan Masur and Eric Posner, for example, write that feasibility analysis "does not reflect deontological thinking . . . , [does not] reflect welfarism in any straightforward sense," and "no attempt to reverse engineer a theory of well-being that justifies feasibility analysis has been successful."[32] This criticism of feasibility analysis is a particular manifestation of the general thesis that efficiency is the only plausible standard of precaution, and its handmaiden cost-benefit analysis is "the only game in town for determining appropriate standards of conduct for socially useful but risky acts."[33]

Professors Masur and Posner's skepticism that feasibility analysis is a serious alternative to cost-benefit analysis—and Professor Fried's assertion that cost-benefit analysis is the only game in town when it comes to legal standards governing the appropriate level of precaution—are hardly outlier opinions. Cass Sunstein, easily the most influential American legal academic now writing on risk and precaution, asserts that "[u]ncontroversial" considerations "suggest" that "[i]t is not possible to do evidence-based, data-driven regulation without assessing both costs and benefits, and without being as quantitative as possible."[34]

---

[30] Consumer Reports, How Safe Is Safe Enough? 15 (Apr. 2017) (discussing autonomous vehicles).

[31] See *infra*, § III.B, pp. 202–209.

[32] Jonathan S. Masur & Eric A. Posner, Against Feasibility Analysis, 77 U. Chi. L. Rev. 657, 707, 709 (2010).

[33] Barbara Fried, The Limits of a Nonconsequentialist Approach to Torts, 18 Legal Theory 231, 231 (2012).

[34] Cass R. Sunstein, Humanizing Cost-Benefit Analysis, Remarks Prepared for American University's Washington College of Law Administrative Law Review Conference, 13, 20 (Feb. 17, 2010) ("[I]t would be premature to say that CBA has received the kind of social consensus now commanded by economic incentives and deregulation of airlines, trucking and railroads. I believe that CBA should command such a consensus, at least as a presumption, and that the presumption in favor of CBA should operate regardless of political commitments."). See also Cass R. Sunstein, The Cost-Benefit State, at ix, 19 (ABA, 2003); Cass R. Sunstein, The Real World of Cost-Benefit Analysis: Thirty-Six Questions (And Almost as Many Answers), 114 Colum. L. Rev. 167 (2014); Cass R. Sunstein, Thanks, Justice Scalia, for the Cost-Benefit State, Bloomberg Opinion, 19 (July 7, 2015)

In Sunstein's view, cost-benefit analysis is indispensable to thinking rationally about risk and regulation.[35] Unless and until we embrace cost-benefit analysis, he believes, our thinking about risk and precaution will be ruled by rank sentimentality and cognitive error. The most recent Supreme Court decision on point asserts that—absent specific statutory instruction to the contrary—regulatory agencies must engage in cost-benefit analysis the moment they contemplate regulating a harmful substance. According to this worldview, it is irrational even to *think about* reducing harm without considering costs.[36]

Over time, American legal scholars have become ever more strident in their assertions that the only way to think about risk and precaution is through the lenses of cost-benefit analysis. Early in the history of law and economics, Guido Calabresi argued for a capacious approach that sought to incorporate a whole range of values. We should, he wrote, assign special weight to "justice constraints."[37] For all Calabresi's influence and importance, however, in this respect law and economics has not followed in his lead. By the time Louis Kaplow and Steven Shavell published their influential *Fairness versus Welfare*,[38] the law and economics community had largely coalesced around the idea that welfare is the master value and efficiency is its legal expression. Within economics, this consensus is understandable. But there is no reason to think that either economics or some variant of utilitarian consequentialism—the parent philosophy of economic analysis—has a monopoly when it comes to understanding the morality of risk imposition. Nonconsequentialist approaches to risk both provide the best framework for making sense of the legal standards that we shall soon examine and are alive and well in philosophical discourse.[39]

Cost-benefit analysis, conventionally conceived, is efficiency embodied. Cost-justified precaution is efficient precaution. Risks to health and safety should be managed by minimizing the combined costs of avoiding and suffering the illnesses and injuries in question, thereby maximizing the net benefit that we extract from the activities responsible for the illnesses and injuries at issue. In lay language, inefficiency is wastefulness. In economic terms, waste avoidance is articulated more precisely as wealth-maximization. Within contemporary law and economics, wealth-maximization is the proper end for most legal institutions to

(praising the Supreme Court's decision in *Michigan v. EPA* "as a ringing endorsement of cost-benefit analysis by government agencies").

[35] See Cass R. Sunstein, Risk and Reason: Safety, Law, and the Environment 7 (Cambridge, 2002).
[36] See Michigan v. EPA, 135 S. Ct. 2699, 2707–08 (2015).
[37] Guido Calabresi, The Costs of Accidents, esp. at 24–26 (Yale, 1970). See also Guido Calabresi, An Exchange: About Law and Economics: A Letter to Ronald Dworkin, 8 Hofstra L. Rev. 553 (1980), and Ronald Dworkin, Why Efficiency?—A Response to Professors Calabresi and Posner, 8 Hofstra L. Rev. 563 (1980).
[38] Louis Kaplow & Steven Shavell, Fairness Versus Welfare (Harvard, 2002).
[39] See especially John Oberdiek, Imposing Risk: A Normative Framework (Oxford, 2017).

pursue, but the value which justifies making efficiency the master criterion for evaluating most legal regimes is welfare.[40] Welfare, for its part, is taken to be not only *a* value, but *the* value. Other things are good only insofar as they promote welfare.

Champions of cost-benefit analysis are correct on their own terms. Within the closed framework of cost-benefit analysis, taking more than cost-justified precaution is flatly irrational. However high a price we set on avoiding serious physical injury, illness, and premature death, we should still trade the benefits of averting those harms off against the costs of obtaining them in a way that maximizes benefit and minimizes costs. When we press beyond the point of cost-justified precaution, the cost of avoiding harm is greater than the benefit of doing so. Taking more than efficient precaution makes us less wealthy. That squandering of wealth diminishes the pool of resources available to us to pursue social welfare. However, the terms according to which inefficient precaution is *unreasonable* precaution are themselves suspect. Cost-benefit analysis insists that all good and bad things are fungible at some ratio of exchange. This assertion depends on the deeper claim that welfare is the only value, and that welfare can and should be measured in the metric of money. Our law and our morality contradict these claims.

Philosophical and political liberalism have long denied that welfare is a master value and have long asserted that values are irreducibly plural.[41] The basic role of the state, on a liberal view, is to establish the institutional and material conditions of effective agency so that people may pursue happiness as they conceive it. Securing the conditions of effective agency is a matter of justice, and the claims of justice have priority over the claims of efficiency. This is hardly a novel thought. Indeed, this claim is asserted by the most prominent liberal theory of justice of the past century. Safety is a natural candidate for special priority. We don't need to invoke efficiency to explain why we want our cars, our schools, our air, and our drinking water to be safe. Safety secures the physical and psychological integrity that is a precondition of effective agency. It therefore has a claim to

---

[40] Kaplow & Shavell 2002, *supra* note 38, assumes both that welfare is the touchstone of economic analysis and that welfare is the only ultimate value. Most proponents of cost-benefit analysis identify it as welfarist. See, *e.g.*, Cass R. Sunstein, The Cost-Benefit Revolution 24 (2018) ("the cost-benefit revolution is welfarist"); Michael A. Livermore & Richard L. Revesz, Rethinking Health-Based Environmental Standards and Cost-Benefit Analysis, 46 Envtl. L. Rep. 10674, 10675 (2016). ("Cost-benefit analysis . . . places both costs and benefits along a common metric and supports the standard that maximizes net benefits (the difference between benefits and cost). As practiced in the United States . . . cost-benefit analysis is grounded on a welfare economic conception of social good."); Peter Schuck, Why Government Fails So Often: And How It Can Do Better 45 (Princeton, 2014) ("CBA is a welfarist decision-making tool, focusing on the actual consequences of policies for human well-being.").

[41] For discussion of the diversity of valuable things and criticism of the idea that welfare is a master value, see T.M. Scanlon, What We Owe to Each Other 79–143 (Harvard, 1998).

being especially important, and its special importance presumably means that it is worth securing at some cost in economic efficiency.

Acting efficiently is, to be sure, presumptively desirable. Efficiency is a value—something whose realization is presumptively good—but efficiency is one value among many. Other values also bear on the desirability of various risk-reducing measures, particularly in the realm of our personal safety where the balance of harm and benefit are asymmetric. Precautions may be fair or unfair as well as efficient or inefficient; they may respect or disrespect people's rights; they may enable or disable desirable forms of choice; they may be sensitive or insensitive to the distinctive values realized by some activity (some sport or line of work, for instance); and so on. Moreover, standards of precaution other than cost-benefit analysis are common in our law. We should not be quick to presume that these standards are unjustifiable.

Justifying standards of precaution more stringent than cost-justification begins with recalling that the asymmetry of harm and benefit is a firmly entrenched feature of both law and morality. Common sense moral conviction holds that the avoidance of harm does and should have special priority.[42] Liberal deontology explains why this entrenchment is not irrational but justifiable. The supposition "at the heart of deontological (or non-consequentialist)" moral theory is that the "subject matter of morality is not what we should bring about, but how we should relate to one another."[43] On a deontological view, both the distinction between persons and the relations among persons are central. The fundamental moral questions posed by issues of risk and precaution are questions about what people owe to each other. This question is a coin with two sides. One side of the coin is what people owe to one another in the way of freedom to impose risks of harm on each other so that we may each have the freedom we need to pursue the ends we regard as worth pursuing. The other side of the coin is what people owe to one another in the way of precaution to reduce risks of harm at each other's hands. To lead valuable lives, we need both the freedom to impose risks of harm on others and security from harm at each other's hands. Questions about risk and precaution are questions about the terms of just interaction among equal and independent persons. Cost-benefit analysis places end states of the world in which costs are minimized, wealth is maximized, and the good of welfare is most effectively pursued at the center of its consciousness. Deontology puts the claims of persons—abstractly conceived as representative members of classes of potential injurers and victims—at the center of its thinking.

---

[42] Seana Shiffrin, Harm and Its Moral Significance, 18 Legal Theory 357 (2012).
[43] Rahul Kumar, Contractualism on the Shoal of Aggregation, in Reasons and Recognition: Essays on the Philosophy of T.M. Scanlon 129, 150 (R. Jay Wallace, Rahul Kumar, & Samuel Freeman eds., Oxford, 2011) (quoting Christine Korsgaard, The Reasons We Can Share: An Attack on the Distinction Between Agent-Relative and Agent-Neutral Values, 10 Soc. Phil. & Pol'y 24 (1993)).

Putting persons and their essential interests as agents in the moral foreground casts the harm-benefit asymmetry in a favorable light. When we focus on the essential conditions of effective agency, harms and benefits are not symmetrically important. Physical harms—death, disability, disease, and the like—rob us of normal and foundational powers of action. They are bad for us no matter what our ends. Few benefits, by contrast, comparably augment our basic powers of agency. The value of a benefit turns on whether it does or does not further the ends of the person upon whom it is conferred. Whereas physical harm is usually bad for people because it impairs basic powers of agency that enable us to pursue a wide variety of ends, the value of any given benefit is usually contingent on the aims and aspirations of the person on whom the benefit is conferred. Extraordinary hand-eye coordination is indispensable for an elite tennis player but largely wasted on a law professor. A talent for abstract mathematical thinking is immensely valuable to a physicist but of little value to a woodworker. Unsought benefits, moreover, usually diminish our autonomy by imposing upon us. Benefits thrust upon us in the name of our own welfare can be positively disempowering.

Because serious physical harm severely impairs basic powers of human agency—whereas most benefits do not comparably enhance our powers of agency—we have reason to assign special priority to the avoidance of harm. Because deontology takes persons and their claims against one another to be the fundamental concern of morality, a deontological framework brings the special badness of harm into focus. Because we persons are physically embodied agents, bodily harm is presumptively—and especially—bad for us. It cripples capacities and powers on which the pursuit of all our ends depend. The welfarist underpinnings of cost-benefit analysis, by contrast, obscure harm's special significance. From a welfarist perspective, harm is just another cost in a social calculus of costs and benefits. That social calculus, moreover, models social choice on individual choice. It swallows our separate lives within a single computation of costs and benefits accruing to society. When some people have their lives devastated by harms inflicted by risks imposed by others—while those others profit from imposing the risks—it is a mistake to model social choice on individual choice. We must take the distinction between persons seriously and adopt principles which are justifiable from the standpoints of both those who might be harmed by the imposition of some risk and those who, in the pursuit of their own ends, wish to impose the risk.

Our law is torn between standards of cost-justified precaution and norms of safe and feasible precaution because our law is torn between two moral outlooks. So, too, is our moral consciousness. That deep division cannot be made to go away by asserting falsely that a broadly welfarist outlook is the only one available, and that this one available outlook condemns taking more than cost-justified precaution as flatly irrational. The putative irrationality of standards of precaution that insist on more than cost-justified precaution vanishes once we recognize that the reasons that support those standards are deontological ones. To develop that point, though, we must first explain the competing standards. The next section takes up that task. Section IV confronts the skeptical challenge that the differences among the standards are a matter of meaningless words and argues that the three standards do, in fact, identify different levels of care. Section V returns to the judgments of value that inform the safety and feasibility standards, elaborating on the points made in the last few paragraphs.

III. Three Standards of Precaution

In legal discourse, the claim that cost-benefit analysis is the only plausible way to think about risk and precaution is often deployed as a criticism of two other standards of precaution—namely, the "safe-level" and "feasibility" standards.[44] Federal statutory standards governing health, environmental, and safety regulation often insist that some activity be made "safe," or that some risk be reduced to the point where further reduction would be "infeasible." The regulation of air, food, and water quality is the principal habitat of the "safe-level" standard, and the regulation of occupational health and safety is the principal habitat of the "feasibility" standard. The three standards identify distinct levels of permissible risk imposition. Normally, they stand in linear, vertical relation to one another, with the safety standard tolerating the least risk and the cost-justification standard tolerating the most.[45]

The two standards of most interest to us—the safety and feasibility standards—deploy a relatively well-integrated set of concepts. The concepts of "safe level," "feasible risk reduction," and "significant" risk that form the core of both statutory standards are terms of art. The feasibility standard, for its part, is further broken down into technological and economic prongs. The legal regimes that the standards establish need to be understood in terms of these concepts; in relation

---

[44] Michael A. Livermore & Richard L. Revesz, Rethinking Health-Based Environmental Standards and Cost-Benefit Analysis, 89 N.Y.U. L. Rev. 1184 (2014), refers to what I call "safe-level" analysis as "health-based analysis." I shall sometimes refer to the "safe-level" standard as the "safety" standard.

[45] It is debatable whether this relation is necessary. Arguably, there are circumstances where it is not cost-justified to engage in an activity in the first place and where the activity is also governed by feasibility analysis. In this circumstance, feasible precaution will be less protective of safety than cost-justified precaution. None of the circumstances discussed in this chapter fit this template. Examples that might fit the template involve freely chosen but very risky activities. Some people might argue that it is foolish to engage in some such activity (e.g., in "free solo" rock climbing). At the same time, it will be true that the risks of such activities cannot be reduced to insignificance because that would destroy the value of the activity. See, e.g., Coomer v. Kan. City Royals Baseball Corp., 437 S.W.3d 184 (Mo. 2014) (illustrating this point in the context of baseball).

to one another; in relation to the idea of cost-justified risk reduction; and in light of their usual domains of application.

A. The Safe-Level Standard

The safe-level standard is adopted in some aspects of clean air, clean water, and pure food legislation, particularly regulation of toxic substances that may endanger public health. The Food Quality Protection Act of 1996 is one case in point.[46] Clean air statutes also incorporate safety-based regulation.[47] A provision of the Clean Air Act,[48] for example, focuses on cancer risks remaining after technology-based regulations for hazardous pollutants have been in effect for six years.[49] If a numerically defined level of cancer risk has not been achieved at that point, the EPA is directed to issue additional regulations that will "provide an ample margin of safety to protect public health."[50] The regulatory aim behind these provisions is to "reduce lifetime excess cancer risks to the individual most exposed to emissions . . . to less than one in one million."[51] Some residual risk thus survives safe-level regulation. Requiring that "lifetime excess cancer risks to the individual most exposed to emissions" be reduced "to less than one in one million" expresses a judgment of significance. A lifetime risk of cancer (from a regulated emission) that crosses the "one in one million" threshold crosses from the domain of insignificant risk into the domain of significant risk.[52]

1. The Significance of a Risk: Quantity and Quality

"Significance" is an underspecified term of art. We can begin to clarify it by noting that some risk of accidental harm is the price of activity itself.[53] We

---

[46] Food Quality Protection Act of 1996, Pub. L. No. 104-170, sec. 405, § 408(b)(2)(A)(ii), 110 Stat. 1489, 1516 (codified as amended at 21 U.S.C. § 346a (2012)) (requiring reduction of pesticide residue on foods to a "safe" level, where "safe" means there is "reasonable certainty that no harm will result").
[47] See Union Elec. Co. v. EPA, 427 U.S. 246, 258 (1976) (stating that the Clean Air Act's three-year deadline purposely "leaves no room for claims of technological or economic infeasibility").
[48] Act to Amend the Clean Air Act, Pub. L. No. 101-549, 104 Stat. 2399 (codified as amended at 42 U.S.C. §§ 7401-7671).
[49] 42 U.S.C. § 7412(f)(1).
[50] *Id.* § 7412(f)(2)(A).
[51] *Id.*
[52] See §7412(f)(2)(A). In their important 2014 paper, Michael Livermore and Richard Revesz argue that this kind of regulation (which they call "health-based") is fatally afflicted by a "stopping-point problem." "[W]hen costs cannot be considered, it is difficult to justify any stopping point other than zero." Michael A. Livermore & Richard L. Revesz, Rethinking Health-Based Environmental Standards and Cost-Benefit Analysis, 89 N.Y.U. L. Rev. 1184, 1187 (2014). The significance requirement is the law's answer to Livermore and Revesz. Safety-based regulation stops when the remaining risk is insignificant.
[53] The impossibility of preventing *all* accidental injury is a fundamental fact that any approach to accident law must acknowledge. James Buchanan, for example, begins his defense of caveat emptor in products liability law with the following comment:

cannot farm, build, drive, or fly without taking and imposing risks of devastating injury. We cannot help but eat and drink—but eating and drinking expose us to risks of death and disease. We cannot help but travel—but traveling by whatever means we can devise puts both us and others in physical peril. Some risk is therefore unavoidable in two senses of the word. Some risk *cannot* be avoided without bringing all activity to a halt, and some risk *should* not be avoided because it is better to bear the risks than to forgo the activities that give rise to them. Risks that cannot be eliminated without ceasing the activity that engenders them are both endemic, if slight, and the background against which all other risks arise. The fact that a low-level risk of devastating injury—the background level of risk—is an inescapable price of activity explains why a significance requirement must be introduced, implicitly or explicitly, into even the most stringent standards of risk regulation. Before we attempt to reduce some risk, we must first conclude that it crosses the threshold that separates risks that we might eliminate from those that we must accept.

A "significant" risk, then, is one whose long-run incidence is noticeably increased by the presence of the activity in the world. Exposure to asbestos dust significantly increases the risk of contracting mesothelioma; exposure to benzene in refining petroleum increases significantly the risk of being struck by leukemia.[54] "Significance" thus has a quantitative aspect. It is a matter of the correlation between some form of harm and an activity. The flip side of this coin is that the elimination of "significant" risk is a matter of reducing the incidence of some harm. The 1990 amendments to the Clean Air Act, for example, aim to "reduce lifetime excess cancer risks to the individual most exposed to emissions . . . to less than one in one million."[55] Judgments of significance are not, however, purely quantitative because they entail evaluation. To be significant, a risk must ripen into serious harm—the kind of harm that severely compromises normal powers of agency. For example, occupational exposure to cotton dust can lead to byssinosis (commonly known as brown lung disease), a chronic, permanent disability resulting in reduced breathing capacity and premature death.[56] The relation of significance to serious harm builds qualitative evaluation into the concept of significance. Judgments that some harm is severe measure

> It is useful to note at the outset that *accidents cannot be prevented*, in the sense that the probability of occurrence cannot be reduced to zero. We live in an uncertain world, whether we like it or not, and the working properties of either human or material agents cannot be completely specified. Any discussion of products liability, therefore, involves only the possible modification in the probability distribution of accidents.
>
> James M. Buchanan, In Defense of Caveat Emptor, 38 U. Chi. L. Rev. 64, 64 (1970).

[54] See Daniel A. Farber, Toxic Causation, 71 Minn. L. Rev. 1219, 1252, 1229–31, n.55 (1987).
[55] 42 U.S.C. § 7412(f)(2)(A) (2012).
[56] See Am. Textile Mfrs. Inst. v. Donovan, 452 U.S. 490, 495–96, n.8 (1981).

the seriousness of the harm against the baseline of normal life. The diseases and disabilities that the norms of safe and feasible precaution address deprive their victims of normal lifespans and normal capacities in ways that cannot be repaired.

Moreover, significant risks are salient ones, and salience is a matter of prominence. Salient phenomena stand out in some *context*—here, in the setting of the activity subject to regulatory scrutiny.[57] *Probability* of harm can be expressed by a purely quantitative measure, but the salience of some risk of harm depends on the background against which that probability is framed. Even the purely quantitative criterion of significance employed by the 1990 amendments to the Clean Air Act operates against a background that fixes the acceptable level of risk. The salience of the risk of cancer addressed by those amendments depends on the background risk of cancer. Discussion of "excess cancer risks" presumes a preexisting risk of cancer—a risk independent of exposure to the emission being evaluated. The Clean Air Act's one-in-a-million threshold for "excess risk" thus assumes a preexisting level of risk and defines an acceptable level of increased risk—for a harm whose gravity we can largely agree upon.

Among the three standards, the safe-level standard tolerates the least risk. Safety-based regulations require risk to be reduced to a point where no "significant risk" of devastating injury remains. This may well require moving *beyond* the point of cost-justified precaution (and beyond the point of feasible precaution, too). If efficient precaution is taken and significant risk remains, the safe-level standard requires further reduction.[58] The standard may therefore require plowing past the point of maximum net benefit, economically conceived.

B. The Feasibility Standard

The feasibility standard is at least as salient in federal risk regulation as the "safe-level" standard. The Clean Air Act, for example, provides that standards for hazardous air pollutants "shall require the maximum degree of reduction in emissions" that the EPA, "taking into consideration the cost of achieving such emission reduction," determines to be "achievable."[59] Feasible risk reduction

---

[57] As Lewis Sargentich puts it, "[t]he risk to be averted must be ... noteworthy in comparison with other risks of the same activity that might also be reduced further by costly measures." Robert E. Keeton et al., Teacher's Manual to Accompany Tort and Accident Law: Cases and Materials, 23-7 to 23-8 (West, 1998).

[58] Efficient precaution is taken when the marginal benefit of the next increment of precaution would exceed its marginal cost (i.e., when a dollar more in precaution would yield more than a dollar's worth of harm avoided).

[59] 42 U.S.C. § 7412(d)(2). This requirement is part of the 1990 Amendments to the Clean Air Act. Feasible risk reduction is a statutory standard in the Occupational Health and Safety Act of 1970, and it is in this context that it has received its most extensive application and articulation.

does not require the elimination of all significant risk. It is, in general, less stringent than the safety standard but more stringent than cost-justified precaution. Feasible precaution calls for reducing an activity's risks as far as it is possible to do so without jeopardizing the long-term flourishing of the activity. Feasible risk regulation, too, may thus require pressing precaution beyond the point where a dollar more spent on the prevention of harm yields more than a dollar's worth of harm prevented. The feasibility standard requires that significant risks be reduced until further reduction would jeopardize the long-run survival of the activity responsible for imposing the risks at issue. Feasibility analysis thus rests on the judgment that the activity at issue is one that we need—one that we cannot do without even if, regrettably, it inflicts significant injury. Tellingly, feasibility analysis is applied most prominently in the context of occupational health and safety. In an industrial, technological society, we regard many basic productive activities as activities that we cannot forgo even when they inflict a significant level of irreparable harm.

The determination of whether it is feasible to reduce a risk without crippling the activity that imposes it has two aspects—a "technological" one and an "economic" one. Technological feasibility analysis asks how much we could reduce this risk if we single-mindedly set out to reduce it as much as possible.[60] Economic feasibility analysis asks what is the lowest level of risk that the risk-imposing activity can afford to achieve.[61] The aim of feasibility analysis is to protect "worker health and safety within the limits of economic possibility."[62] "Congress itself defined the basic relationship between costs and benefits [when it enacted the Occupational Safety and Health Act of 1970 with its feasibility standard], by placing the 'benefit' of worker health above all other considerations save those making attainment of this 'benefit' unachievable."[63] In the workplace, feasibility analysis looks to achieve the lowest level of occupational risk that can be attained without eliminating the workplace.

1. Technological Feasibility

The technological side of feasibility analysis investigates engineering possibility. Any limit set on risk—a "permissible exposure limit" (PEL) for a toxic substance, for example—must be technologically attainable.[64] Technological achievability, however, is not fixed by the outer limit of technological possibility

---

[60] See Robert E. Keeton et al., Tort and Accident Law, 1238–39, 1252–53 (West, 4th ed., 2004) (discussing the technological feasibility prong of feasibility analysis).
[61] See *id.* at 1253–55 (discussing the economic feasibility prong).
[62] United Steelworkers of Am., AFL-CIO-CLC v. Marshall, 647 F.2d 1189, 1263 n.102 (D.C. Cir. 1980).
[63] Am. Textile Mfrs. Inst. v. Donovan, 452 U.S. 490, 509 (1981). *American Textile* involved occupational exposure to cotton dust, which causes brown lung disease. *Id.* at 490–91.
[64] *Id.* at 500, 503.

at a given moment in time because the most advanced techniques of risk control in place at a given moment in time may fall short of the frontier of what might be achieved. The frontier of technological feasibility is fixed by the engineering practice that might be realized through a dogged commitment to feasible risk reduction. A regulatory agency promulgating a feasibility-based risk regulation may therefore specify an acceptable level of risk that is lower than the level attainable through the application of existing techniques, if the agency can reasonably predict that technical capability will advance sufficiently to make a lower level of risk imposition attainable within the time frame of the regulation.

In *American Iron & Steel Institute v. Occupational Safety & Health Administration,* for example, OSHA's standard for coke oven emissions was upheld as technologically feasible even though "the most modern and clean coke oven battery operating" met the standard only one-third of the time.[65] Evidence of one-third compliance using less than all suitable technology—plus dramatic progress toward compliance at another plant after new engineering controls were implemented—showed sufficiently that the standard was not "impossible of attainment."[66] The question was not what could be done at the moment, but "what the industry could achieve in an effort to best protect its ... employees," given a determination to exploit "technological potentialities."[67] The court therefore approved OSHA's reliance on "innovative technology currently in the experimental stage"[68] and its faith in new techniques "looming over the horizon."[69]

In *United Steelworkers of America, AFL-CIO-CLC v. Marshall,* Judge J. Skelly Wright gave the following summary of the concept of "technological feasibility":

> The oft-stated view of technological feasibility under the [Occupational Safety and Health] Act is that Congress meant the statute to be "technology-forcing." This view means, at the very least, that OSHA can impose a standard which only the most technologically advanced plants in an industry have been able to achieve even if only in some of their operations some of the time. But under this view OSHA can also force industry to develop and diffuse new technology. At least where the agency gives industry a reasonable time to develop new technology, OSHA is not bound to the technological status quo. So long as it presents substantial evidence that companies acting vigorously and in good faith can develop the technology, OSHA can require industry to meet [Permissible Exposure Levels] never attained anywhere....

---

[65] Am. Iron & Steel Inst. v. Occupational Safety & Health Admin., 577 F.2d 825, 832 (3d Cir. 1978).
[66] *Id.* at 834 (quoting *Soc'y of Plastics Indus. v. Occupational Safety & Health Admin.,* 509 F.2d 1301, 1309 (2d Cir. 1975)).
[67] *Id.* at 833–34.
[68] *Id.* at 835.
[69] *Id.* at 833.

As for [proof of] technological feasibility, we know that we cannot require of OSHA anything like certainty. Since "technology-forcing" assumes the agency will make highly speculative projections about future technology, a standard is obviously not infeasible solely because OSHA has no hard evidence to show that the standard has been met. . . . OSHA's duty is to show that modern technology has at least conceived some industrial strategies or devices which are likely to be capable of meeting the PEL and which the industries are generally capable of adopting.

Our view finds support in the statutory requirement that OSHA act according to the "best *available* evidence." OSHA cannot let workers suffer while it awaits the Godot of scientific certainty.[70]

The technological side of feasibility analysis thus determines the presumptively appropriate level of precaution by reference to the best that *might* be done, given an unstinting commitment to the goal of feasible risk reduction—not by reference to what is customarily done, or even by reference to the best that is now done.

2. Economic Feasibility

In *Portland Cement Association v. Ruckelshaus*, the court interpreted language in the Clean Air Act of 1970 requiring "a standard for emissions of air pollutants which reflects the degree of emission limitation achievable . . . taking into account the cost of achieving such reduction."[71] It held that this language did *not* direct the EPA to undertake "a quantified cost-benefit analysis" in order to justify its air pollution standard for new or modified cement plants.[72] The EPA's conclusion that the cement industry could absorb the cost of control devices without detriment to competition between cement and substitute products, even though some plants might have to close, sufficed to answer the "essential question" under the Act: "whether the mandated standards can be met by a particular industry for which they are set."[73] Judgments of economic feasibility require "tak[ing] into account the costs," but they do not require "cost-benefit analysis."[74]

Provisions of the Clean Water Act that mandate pollution control to the extent "technologically and economically achievable" also shed light on the economic prong of feasibility-based regulation.[75] The Clean Water Act subjects

---

[70] United Steelworkers of Am., AFL-CIO-CLC v. Marshall, 647 F.2d 1189, 1264–66 (D.C. Cir. 1980) (emphasis added) (citations omitted).
[71] Portland Cement Ass'n v. Ruckelshaus, 486 F.2d 375, 378 (D.C. Cir. 1973) (citation omitted).
[72] *Id.* at 387.
[73] *Id.* at 389.
[74] *Id.* at 387.
[75] 33 U.S.C. §§ 1311(b)(2)(A), 1314(b)(2)(B), 1317(a)(2) (2012).

water pollution sources to two different sorts of effluent limitations: those based on "the best practicable control technology currently available" (BPT)[76] and those based on "the best available technology economically achievable" (BAT).[77] The BPT standard generalizes "the best existing performance" in an industry—control practices in "exemplary plants"—despite an expectation of "economic hardship, including the closing of some plants."[78] The BAT standards are more stringent. They require "a commitment of the maximum resources economically possible to the ultimate goal of eliminating all polluting discharges."[79] Setting BPT standards involves "cost-benefit analysis," but cost-benefit analysis is not part of BAT determinations.[80] To determine economic achievability, "the EPA must consider the cost of meeting BAT limitations, but need not compare such cost with the benefits of effluent reduction."[81]

For "economic feasibility" analyses, then, the ultimate question is not whether costs are outweighed by benefits but whether the industry is able to bear the cost.[82] Economic feasibility regulation by OSHA means "protecting worker health and safety within the limits of economic possibility."[83] Again, Judge Wright explains:

> The most useful general judicial criteria for economic feasibility comes from Judge McGowan's opinion in *Industrial Union Dep't, AFL-CIO v. Hodgson*. . . . A standard is not infeasible simply because it is financially burdensome, or even because it threatens the survival of some companies within an industry:
>
>> Nor does the concept of economic feasibility necessarily guarantee the continued existence of individual employers. It would appear to be consistent with the purposes of the Act to envisage the economic demise of an employer who has lagged behind the rest of the industry in protecting the health and safety of employees and is consequently financially unable to comply with new standards as quickly as other employers.
>
> A standard is feasible if it does not threaten "massive dislocation" to, or imperil the existence of, the industry. No matter how initially frightening the projected

---

[76] *Id.* § 1311(b)(1)(A).
[77] *Id.* § 1311(b)(2)(A).
[78] EPA v. Nat'l Crushed Stone Ass'n, 449 U.S. 64, 76 n.15, 79 (1980).
[79] *Id.* at 74.
[80] *Id.* at 71 n.10 (citation omitted).
[81] Rybachek v. EPA, 904 F.2d 1276, 1290–91 (9th Cir. 1990) (internal quotation marks omitted).
[82] United Steelworkers of Am., AFL-CIO-CLC v. Marshall, 647 F.2d 1189, 1272 (D.C. Cir. 1980).
[83] *Id.* at 1263 n.102.

total or annual costs of compliance appear, a court must examine those costs in relation to the financial health and profitability of the industry and the likely effect of such costs on unit consumer prices.... [T]he practical question is whether the standard threatens the industry's competitive stability, or whether any intra-industry or inter-industry discrimination in the standard might wreck such stability or lead to undue concentration....[84]

[A]s for [proof of] economic feasibility, OSHA must construct a reasonable estimate of compliance costs and demonstrate a reasonable likelihood that these costs will not threaten the existence or competitive structure of an industry, even if it does portend disaster for some marginal firms.[85]

In the consolidated *American Textile* cases, litigating cotton dust standards, both the District of Columbia Circuit and the Supreme Court upheld OSHA's assessment of economic feasibility.[86] OSHA had concluded that "compliance with the standard [was] well within the financial capability" of the cotton industry.[87] The agency noted that "although some marginal employers may shut down rather than comply, the industry as a whole will not be threatened."[88] Both courts agreed that OSHA had shown that the industry would be able to absorb the projected costs.[89] According to the court of appeals, regulatory requirements remain economically feasible even though they "impose substantial costs on an industry ... or ... force some employers out of business," as long as they are not "prohibitively expensive" and do not make "financial viability generally impossible."[90] Controls on cotton dust fit "the plain meaning of the word 'feasible,'" the Supreme Court wrote, given OSHA's conclusion "that the industry will maintain long-term profitability and competitiveness."[91]

OSHA makes the standards articulated by the courts more concrete in the course of applying them. Its assessment procedures approach the question of whether a particular standard of precaution will threaten the competitive stability of an industry by conducting an industry-by-industry analysis. The aim of that analysis is to determine the percentage of the industry's revenues and profits

---

[84] *Id.* at 1265 (citations omitted) (quoting *Indus. Union Dep't, AFL-CIO v. Hodgson*, 499 F.2d 467, 478 (D.C. Cir. 1974)).
[85] *Id.* at 1272.
[86] See *AFL-CIO v. Marshall*, 617 F.2d 636, 662 (D.C. Cir. 1979), *aff'd in part, vacated in part sub nom. Am. Textile Mfrs. Inst. v. Donovan*, 452 U.S. 490, 536, 540–41 (1981).
[87] *Am. Textile*, 452 U.S. at 531 (citation omitted).
[88] *Id.*
[89] *Id.* at 530–36.
[90] *AFL-CIO*, 617 F.2d at 655, 661 (citations omitted).
[91] *Am. Textile*, 452 U.S. at 530 n.55 (citations omitted).

that compliance will consume. One OSHA report explains the agency's practice as follows:

> [W]hile there is no hard and fast rule, in the absence of evidence to the contrary OSHA generally considers a standard economically feasible when the costs of compliance are less than one percent of revenues.... [P]otential impacts of such a small magnitude are unlikely to eliminate an industry or significantly alter its competitive structure particularly since most industries have at least some ability to raise prices to reflect increased costs.... There is an enormous variety of year-to-year events that could cause a one percent increase in a business's costs, e.g., increasing fuel costs, an unusual one-time expense, changes in costs of materials, increased rents, increased taxes, etc.[92]

Thus, in a case where the costs of complying with a particular standard came to less than both 1 percent of an industry's revenues and 10 percent of its profits, implementation of the standard did not threaten the competitive stability of the industry.[93] The logic here is instructive.[94] OSHA's approach assumes that revenue and profits normally fluctuate within certain limits. If an industry can absorb fluctuations within certain limits without seeing its competitive stability undermined, then a regulatory standard that has an impact in the same range will not threaten an industry's competitive stability.

Of course, not every standard necessary to eliminate significant risk falls into this sweet spot of acceptable impact. Where an industry's compliance costs considerably exceed these thresholds, OSHA makes industry-by-industry determinations of whether complying with a given standard will threaten the industry's competitive stability. In these cases, the inquiry is centered on continued profitability. In analyzing the economic feasibility of a PEL of 1 µg/m³ and whether it would affect the electroplating industry, OSHA concluded that "the costs associated with such a PEL could alter the competitive structure of the industry."[95] The cost of the standard came to 65 percent of profits, though only 2.7 percent of revenue.[96] After considering demand elasticity for electroplating,

---

[92] Occupational Exposure to Hexavalent Chromium, 71 Fed. Reg. 10, 100, 10, 299–300 (Feb. 28, 2006) (to be codified at 29 C.F.R. pts. 1910, 1915, 1917–18, 1926). "OSHA's obligation is not to determine whether any plants will close, or whether some marginal plants may close earlier than they otherwise might have, but whether the regulation will eliminate or alter the competitive structure of an industry." *Id.* at 10, 281. I am grateful to Dov Waisman for calling this report to my attention. My discussion follows his. See Dov A. Waisman, Reasonable Precaution for the Individual, 88 St. John's L. Rev. 653, 659–61 (2014).

[93] Occupational Exposure to Hexavalent Chromium, 71 Fed. Reg. at 10, 300. The standard at issue determines a permissible exposure limit for a particular toxic substance.

[94] Waisman 2014, *supra* note 92, at 675.

[95] Occupational Exposure to Hexavalent Chromium, 71 Fed. Reg. at 10, 301.

[96] *Id.*

OSHA concluded that "a price increase that would assure continued profitability for the entire industry would require almost tripling the annual nominal price increase. . . . That would represent a significant real price increase that might not be passed forward, particularly by older and less profitable segments of the industry."[97] Requiring a PEL of 1 μg/m³ might therefore make the activity of electroplating unprofitable. Making an industry unprofitable is, for OSHA, an unacceptable threat to its "competitive stability."[98]

Under OSHA practice, then, the "economic feasibility" prong of feasibility analysis requires the reduction of significant risk up until the point where the long-term flourishing of the industry would be imperiled by further risk-reduction.

C. The Cost-Benefit Standard and Its Claims

The basic idea of cost-justified risk imposition is easy to state, perhaps deceptively so. Cost-justified precaution requires risks to be reduced to the point where the costs of further precautions exceed their benefits. Cost and benefit, for their part, are all-encompassing concepts. In a lucid and accessible defense of cost-benefit analysis, the economist Robert Solow explained that "the cost of the good thing to be obtained is precisely the good thing that must or will be given up to obtain it."[99] "Cost," then, is anything given up to obtain something else. "Benefit" is the flip side of the coin—anything worth attaining. An ideal cost-benefit analysis takes all costs and all benefits into account and identifies the point at which costs and benefits are balanced so that net benefit is maximized. In practice, almost all cost-benefit analyses take more restricted sets of costs and benefits into account. In the context of accidental injury, for example, the criterion of cost-justification is usually said to require minimizing the "sum of precaution, accidental harm, and administration costs."[100] For present purposes, it will do to say that cost-justified precaution holds that risk should be reduced to the point of maximum net benefit, economically conceived. That point is the point at which a dollar more spent avoiding harm yields less than a dollar's worth of harm avoided. In general, cost-justified precaution is the least stringent of the three standards of precaution.

---

[97] *Id.* at 10, 301–02.
[98] Occupational Exposure to Hexavalent Chromium, 71 Fed. Reg. at 10, 102 (quoting Indus. Union Dep't, AFL-CIO v. Hodgson, 499 F.2d 467, 478 (D.C. Cir. 1974)).
[99] Robert M. Solow, Defending Cost-Benefit Analysis, 5 Regulation 40, 40 (1981). This basic idea of cost is often called "opportunity cost."
[100] Robert D. Cooter & Thomas Ulen, Law and Economics 237 (Pearson, 6th ed., 2012).

IV. Myth or Reality: Three Applications

The safety and feasibility standards were born in the 1960s and 70s, in the last great flowering of liberal legal reform. They were, and are, championed by political liberals. They have their roots in the founding of the Environmental Protection Agency in 1970 and the Occupational Health and Safety Administration in 1971. They dominated the regulatory landscape into the 1980s, and they received important legislative reaffirmation during the 1990s—as the Food Quality Protection Act of 1996 itself shows.[101] Early in the 1980s, however, the political right began championing cost-benefit analysis and cost-justified precaution as its preferred alternative to safe and feasible risk-reduction. In 1982, the Reagan administration put into place an executive order requiring cost-benefit analysis for all "significant" federal regulations unless conducting such analysis was prohibited by law—if, for example, the authorizing statute itself forbade consideration of cost.[102] Since the early 1980s, the two approaches have been engaged in a prolonged struggle.

This struggle is worth continuing only if the standards really do identify different levels of required precaution. It is plain from what has been said so far that the standards purport to express different normative judgments, but that does not show that they *in fact* imply different levels of precaution. Guido Calabresi has long and famously argued that stringent precaution is myth, not reality. We pay lip service to the idea that lives have infinite value, but in practice we balance lives against other goods in a manner that would be made more rational if it were explicitly recognized as cost-benefit balancing.[103] The truth in this claim is that all standards of precaution against risks of physical harm make trade-offs. The mistake is to think that those "trade-offs" must be made in the manner prescribed by cost-benefit analysis. The following examples show, I hope, that

---

[101] Only two of "ten major regulatory statutes enacted in the 1960's, 1970's and 1980's ... expressly authorize the balancing of benefits and costs for core agency actions." Jonathan Cannon, The Sounds of Silence: Cost-Benefit Canons in Entergy Corp. v. Riverkeeper, Inc., 34 Harv. Envtl. L. Rev. 425, 426 (2010).

[102] Exec. Order No. 12, 291, 3 C.F.R. 127 (1982) (repealed 1993). The courts have long held that the major environmental and occupational safety statutes forbid consideration of cost. In 2001, a unanimous Supreme Court held that the EPA "may not consider implementation costs" in setting ambient air quality standards under the Clean Air Act. Whitman v. American Trucking Associations, 531 U.S. 457 (2001). Writing for the court, Justice Scalia observed: "Were it not for the hundreds of pages of briefing respondents have submitted on the issue, one would have thought it fairly clear that this text does not permit the EPA to consider costs in setting standards.... The EPA ... is to identify the maximum airborne concentration of a pollutant that the public health can tolerate, decrease the concentration to provide an 'adequate' margin of safety, and set the standard at that level." *Id.* at 465. Entergy Corp v. Riverkeeper, Inc., 556 U.S. 208 (2009), may represent a slight retreat from this position. See Cannon 2010, *supra* note 101.

[103] See, *e.g.*, Calabresi 1970, *supra* note 37, at 17 (listing the preservation of life "at all costs" as the first of four "myths" that "will make our analysis difficult if not cleared up"); Guido Calabresi & Philip Bobbitt, Tragic Choices 187–89 (1978).

these three standards prescribe fundamentally different levels of precaution and that those different levels reflect judgments of value. These examples have been chosen both to cast the differences among the standards into sharp relief and to suggest that the standards are intuitive, robust, and pervasive. Even when they have not been formally promulgated, the three standards of precaution are discernible in diverse domains and call for different results. Their persistence across diverse contexts suggests that the normative convictions they express have a firm grip on us and that the levels of precaution they require are different in practice as well as in theory.

A. The Safety Standard: Consumer Expectations

In the United States, the two most common tests of product design defectiveness are the risk-utility test and the consumer expectation test. Modern product liability law has roots in both tort and contract. These two tests reflect those different roots and the different orientations of those two bodies of law. The risk-utility test reflects product liability law's negligence origins and adopts the perspective of a product engineer. It evaluates the design of a product by asking if the product is, on balance, reasonably safe in light of alternative design possibilities. It asks if the design's advantages outweigh its disadvantages. The consumer expectation test reflects product liability law's warranty law origins. It looks at the challenged design from the standpoint of a product user. It asks: Do the risks of the design meet the expectations of a normal consumer? Or do they disappoint expectations about safety? Law and economics scholars usually take the risk-utility test to be an application of cost-benefit analysis to product design.[104] By contrast, in some applications, the consumer expectation test works as a "safe-level" standard. Sometimes people expect products to be safe—not perfect, but safe. And sometimes a product design whose advantages outweigh its disadvantages is not safe. And sometimes a product design whose advantages outweigh its disadvantages is not safe.[105]

The doctrine of *Barker v. Lull Engineering* formulates the basics of California's design defect law.[106] *Barker*'s regime is an attempt to flesh out the "defective

---

[104] See, *e.g.*, Alan Schwartz, Products Liability Reform: A Theoretical Synthesis, 97 Yale L.J. 353 (1988); see also Alan Schwartz, The Case Against Strict Liability, 60 Fordham L. Rev. 819 (1992); W. Kip Viscusi, Corporate Risk Analysis a Reckless Act?, 52 Stan. L. Rev. 547, 566 (2000).

[105] Denny v. Ford Motor Co., 87 N.E.2d 730 (N.Y. 1995), is a case in point. The design of an SUV failed to pass muster under the expectation test imposed by New York's implied warranty law even though the advantages of the design outweighed its disadvantages under the risk-utility test. The design feature at issue was the vehicle's high, narrow wheelbase. That feature was justified overall because it enabled off-road use, but it disappointed reasonable consumer expectations because it made the vehicle more dangerous than expected on slick pavement.

[106] See, *e.g.*, Barker v. Lull Engineering, 573 P.2d 443 (Cal. 1978).

condition, unreasonably dangerous" standard of Section 402A of *Restatement of Torts, Second* (1965). To make the norms of design defect liability more stringent than ordinary negligence liability, *Barker* made three moves. First, it adopted a two-test regime in which the two tests—consumer expectation and risk-utility— were independently sufficient. Failing either test would result in liability. Second, *Barker* endorsed hindsight balancing, not foresight balancing; it held that the risk-utility test should be applied using the knowledge available at the time of trial, not the knowledge available at the time of sale. Third, it loosened the burden of proof borne by the plaintiff so that the burden under the risk-utility test is easier to meet than the normal negligence burden of proving a superior alternative design and so that the burden of justifying the safety of the challenged design shifts quickly to the defendant.

Both the particulars of the *Barker* regime and the consumer expectation test itself have proven enduringly controversial. The *Restatement (Third) of Torts: Product Liability* Section 2(b) (1998) adopts a foresight balancing version of the risk-utility test as its only test of defective design.[107] That formulation makes the test for design defect a matter of Hand Formula negligence applied to products, not conduct. At the time the *Third Restatement*'s promulgated its test, critics accused the Reporters of misstating, not restating, the existing law.[108] Controversy over whether the consumer expectation test is an independently adequate test of design defectiveness persists to this day. By the count of one of the Reporters for the *Third Restatement*—who is himself an ardent proponent of an exclusive risk-utility test for design defects—seventeen jurisdictions continue to use the consumer expectation test in some form.[109] The apparent robustness of the test, though, has not settled even the dispute over its existence, much less the dispute over its merits. Professor Twerski regards the test itself as defective and takes a dim view of its official persistence. In application, he thinks, the test collapses into risk-utility analysis.

---

[107] "A product is defective when, at the time of sale or distribution, it . . . is defective in design. . . . A product: . . . (b) is defective in design when the foreseeable risks of harm posed by the product could have been reduced or avoided by the adoption of a reasonable alternative design by the seller . . . and the omission of the alternative design renders the product not reasonably safe." Comment (d) says: "[s]ubsection (b) adopts a reasonableness ('risk-utility balancing') test as the standard for judging the defectiveness of product designs."

[108] See, *e.g.*, Frank Vandall, The Restatement (Third) of Torts, Products Liability, Section 2(b): Design Defect, 68 Temple L. Rev. 167 (1995). According to Professor Vandall, the following propositions (italicized in the original) were true at the time that the *Third Restatement* was drafted and adopted: "a majority of jurisdictions do not support the [exclusive] use of risk-utility balancing in design defect cases"; "a majority of the jurisdictions do not support the reasonable-alternative-design requirement"; "the jurisdictions are split evenly on whether a seller should be charged with knowledge at the time of sale or the time of trial."

[109] Aaron D. Twerski, An Essay on the Quieting of Products Liability Law, 105 Cornell L. Rev. 101 (2020).

Prominent cases contradict Twerski's position, asserting that they are applying the consumer expectation test and reaching results that diverge from those that the risk-utility test appears to require. *Denny v. Ford Motor Co.* is one example. *Green v. Smith & Nephew AHP, Inc.* is another.[110] In *Green*, the expectation test's application has much more in common with the safety standard than it does with the standard of cost-justified precaution that law and economics scholars take the risk-utility test to enact. Plaintiff Green worked as a medical technologist in a hospital.

Her job required her to wear protective gloves while attending patients, up to 40 pairs of gloves per shift. She wore powdered latex gloves manufactured by [the defendant. After a period of prolonged use] Green experienced increasingly severe health problems—cold-like symptoms, wide-spread rash, acute shortness of breath. She was hospitalized four times. In 1991 Green was diagnosed with latex allergy. Given her allergy, Green must avoid contact with latex. So she had to change jobs and must limit the items she buys, things she eats, and activities she pursues. On account of the allergy, Green developed asthma.[111]

Exposure to latex proteins "sensitizes" some people to latex. Subsequent exposure of a sensitized person to latex may produce progressively worse allergic reactions including irreversible asthma and life-threatening anaphylactic shock (which Green suffered). Since latex allergy is caused mainly by use of latex gloves, it disproportionately afflicts healthcare workers. According to the evidence that Green put on at trial, the frequency of latex allergy among healthcare workers in the United States is 5 to 17 percent. At the time Green became sensitized to latex, the medical community was unaware of the possibility of latex allergy. Because latex allergy was unknown prior to the widespread use of latex gloves, if Green's claim were judged by the risk-utility test, it would most likely have failed.[112] The cost of discovering the defectiveness of latex gloves years before that defect manifested itself in health injuries to regular users was surely very high. Indeed, it might have been impossible to discover the hazardous effects of long-term use

---

[110] Green v. Smith & Nephew AHP, Inc., 629 N.W.2d 727 (Wis. 2001). Denny v. Ford Motor Co., 87 N.E.2d 730 (N.Y. 1995) is another case where a court, using an implied warranty framework, determines that a product passes muster under the risk-utility test but not under the expectation test imposed by implied warranty law.

[111] Robert E. Keeton, Lewis D. Sargentich, & Gregory C. Keating, Tort and Accident Law 975–76 (West, 4th ed., 2004). See also *Green*, 629 N.W.2d at 732 (summarizing the facts of Ms. Green's case).

[112] The outcome under the risk-utility test depends greatly on whether that test is applied with foresight or hindsight. The trend is to apply the test with foresight. For an example of a case with virtually identical facts where the court refused to apply the expectation case and refused to impose liability under the risk-utility test, see *Morson v. Superior Court*, 109 Cal. Rptr. 2d 343 (Cal. Ct. App. 2001).

of latex gloves in any way other than by using such gloves for a prolonged period of time.

When Wisconsin evaluated the gloves under the consumer expectation test, however, the plaintiff's claim prevailed. The consumer expectation test measures product defectiveness by asking if a product is "dangerous to an extent beyond that which would be contemplated by the ordinary consumer."[113] That the defendant's latex gloves were defective under the expectation test seemed self-evident to the court. The users of the defendant's gloves reasonably expected that they would not suffer injury from normal use of the product. Consequently, the court did not bother to state the relevant expectation precisely.[114] It does not seem difficult, however, to do so. All of us reasonably expect that wearing ordinary clothing will not put us at significant risk of serious physical harm. So, too, healthcare workers reasonably expect that wearing *protective* gear will not put them at significant risk of disabling physical harm.

Generalizing, we may say that clothing is a simple and familiar example of a product that we normally expect to be safe. In saying that, we mean that we believe that the clothes we ordinarily wear do not put us at significant risk of physical harm. The question of whether this expectation is cost-justified never arises. When the clothing is presented specifically as protective gear, the expectation that it will not put us at significant risk of serious harm seems even more reasonable.

B. The Feasibility Standard: Rescues

The literature on "statistical lives" is haunted by the apparent irrationality of many rescues.[115] Money seems to be no object when miners are trapped in a

---

[113] *Green*, 629 N.W.2d at 735.

[114] The *Green* opinion would have been better if the court had discussed just what kind of expectation was disappointed by the product failure. Not every consumer expectation articulates a defensible standard of safety. On the one hand, some expectations are mere wishful thinking. It would, for example, be wishful thinking to expect that no user would ever have an allergic reaction to a product. Idiosyncratic reactions exist. A one-in-a-billion susceptibility to illness does not impugn a product's safety under the expectation test. We take the one-in-a-billion reaction to reflect a rare sensitivity on the part of the victim. What's surprising and disappointing about latex gloves is that *so many* users (5 to 17 percent) suffer severe harm. On the other hand, it asks too much to expect consumers to form expectations about underlying mechanisms of possible product malfunction. The *Green* court agreed with the defendant that "most consumers... generally do not have expectations about... technical or mechanical design aspects of the product." It disagreed that such expectations are necessary. What it found necessary was a secure and reasonable expectation about product performance.

[115] The term "statistical lives" was coined by Thomas Schelling, The Life You Save May Be Your Own, in Problems in Public Expenditure Analysis 127 (Samuel B. Chase, Jr. ed., Brookings, 1968). Schelling distinguished statistical lives from "identified" ones. Identified lives are actual persons who will live if certain steps are taken and die if they are not. Statistical lives are abstract lives; they are the lives that will be saved down the road if some precaution is taken, or some safety program is implemented. Statistical lives are not identifiable at the time a precaution is taken. Indeed, they may

mine, or when children are trapped in a flooded cave.[116] From an economic perspective, though, our conduct seems foolish and extravagant. The rational way to budget our "rescue money" is to spend it in a way that maximizes the number of lives saved with the least sacrifice of other objectives. Lives are lives, and the extra money spent rescuing identified persons might be better spent on safety measures that would save more lives. This, of course, is simply an application of the standard argument for cost-justified precaution to the special case of rescues.[117] When actual lives are endangered, however, we think it would be unseemly, and probably morally wrong, to undertake a cost-benefit analysis of the value of the lives at stake and what it would take to save them. We rescue the victims if we can, and rescuers often take great risks upon themselves to do so. By ruling that taking such risks is neither contributory negligence, nor a superseding cause relieving an original wrongdoer of responsibility, tort doctrine implicitly applies a feasibility standard to rescues.[118] Admiralty law does the same, requiring that the master of a vessel "use every reasonable means to save [a] seaman's life if he goes overboard."[119] In both law and life, our rescue practices appear to be governed by a norm of feasibility, not by a norm of efficiency.

remain unidentifiable even after a precaution has been implemented and has saved lives. Dogs that don't bark are not always easy to spot. The term was coined by Schelling, but the phenomenon had been recognized before it was named. See Guido Calabresi, The Decision for Accidents: An Approach to Nonfault Allocation of Costs, 78 Harv. L. Rev. 713 (1965).

[116] Helier Chung & Tessa Wong, The Full Story of Thailand's Extraordinary Cave Rescue, BBC News (July 14, 2018).

[117] The questions raised by the distinction between "statistical" and "identified" lives in the rescue context are multiple and difficult. For one thing, if we suppose that even the best of precautions will not prevent all accidents, it may be eminently rational in even a cost-benefit sense to commit ourselves in advance to rescue practices which look extravagant at the time we undertake them. For another, contra Schelling, the distinction between identified and statistical lives may make a major moral difference. Obligations may be owed to actual persons, but not to theoretical constructs. These complexities are beyond the scope of this chapter.

[118] In tort law, the question of appropriate precaution framed by rescue efforts arises as a question of reasonable risk assumption not reasonable risk imposition. The question is what risks—including risks of their own death—rescuers may reasonably take upon themselves to save the lives of others. Doctrinally, this raises questions of contributory negligence and superseding cause. In *Eckert v. Long Island RR*, the deceased plaintiff's claim presented a question of contributory negligence. The plaintiff had died in the course of successfully rescuing a small child from the path of an oncoming train. The court held that the plaintiff's rescue attempt, though fatal, was not imprudent because the plaintiff might have succeeded both in saving the child and avoiding his own death. The court's test of prudence seems to have been, in substance, a test of possibility or feasibility. Eckert v. Long Island R.R. Co., 57 Barb. 555 (N.Y. 1870). Rescue efforts sometimes present a question of superseding cause: Did the rescuer's attempt cut off the liability of the original wrongdoer and make the rescuer responsible for their own injury or death? Tellingly, the rule here—that "danger invites rescue"—holds that rescue efforts which might have succeeded are not superseding causes. See Wagner v. Int'l Ry., 133 N.E. 437 (1921) (Cardozo, J.) ("Danger invites rescue."). The economic approach erases the distinction between risk assumption and risk imposition, subsuming both within an inquiry into how society should deploy its scarce resources.

[119] Gardner v. National Bulk Carriers, Inc., 310 F.2d 284, 286 (1962).

Nothing illustrates more vividly the importance to us of rescuing if we can than the military tradition of undertaking rescues to recover the *corpses* of slain soldiers. In the introduction to his sad and moving memoir of the American war in Vietnam, Philip Caputo observed:

> Two friends of mine died trying to save the corpses of their men from the battlefield. Such devotion, simple and selfless, the sentiment of belonging to each other, was the one decent thing in a conflict noted for its monstrosities.[120]

It is hard to believe that the actions Caputo so admires were cost-justified. Losing a life to save a corpse seems like a bad trade. But it also seems correct to say that the economic mindset of cost-benefit analysis is out of place here. There is something morally grotesque about trying to figure out if losing one's life trying to rescue a corpse is a potential Pareto improvement or not. Rescuing the bodies of one's fallen comrades is about solidarity and sacrifice, not about improving one's own welfare. It is about the realization of values taken to be of paramount importance. Members of a military unit are a "band of brothers," and a band of brothers does not fix the terms of its members' relations to one another in accordance with the morality of the market. A band of brothers is held together by an ethic of mutual sacrifice. Rescuing the corpses of fallen comrades from the field of battle is an eloquent embodiment of the "devotion, simple and selfless" that makes a battalion a band of brothers. Therein lies its justification.

The rescue of corpses on the battlefield is, of course, an extreme example, but it teaches important lessons about less extreme cases. For one thing, all rescues involve the affirmation of a common value. Solidarity is the word—and the value—that comes to mind. The plight of a teenage soccer team trapped in a flooded cave differs from the plight of fallen soldiers, but it too implicates solidarity. We are all vulnerable to accidents and premature death. That vulnerability is part of our shared fate as human beings. Honoring the value of solidarity does not deny the value of efficiency; it merely asserts that solidarity matters more in the context of rescues. In the very special context of the military, solidarity is even more important. The goods intrinsic to military excellence can only be realized if solidarity is valued very highly. There is nothing irrational about this. It is eminently rational to believe that some very valuable

---

[120] Phillip Caputo, A Rumor of War, at vii (Holt, Rinehart and Winston, 1977). A more recent example can be found in *Black Hawk Down* (book written by Mark Bowden in 1999, film released in 2001). During the Battle of Mogadishu in 1993, the United States sent soldiers to rescue the crews of downed Black Hawk helicopters, notwithstanding the enormous risk involved. A number of soldiers were posthumously awarded the Medal of Honor for sacrificing their own lives in the course of such rescue attempts. Mark Bowden, Black Hawk Down 10–12 (Grove Press, 1993).

human goods cannot be realized unless we recognize that "no man is an island," and when the bell tolls for one of us, it tolls for all of us.

It is, no doubt, romantic to extend the ideal of solidarity from the battlefield to the ordinary workplace, but it is also a mistake not to recognize that even military rescues are governed by a standard of feasibility. Some chance of success is essential to the morality. It is heroic to attempt to recover the bodies of your fallen comrades only if there is some chance of succeeding. Without that possibility, an attempted rescue may be foolish or tragic (or both), but it is not noble or heroic. Rescue is ruled by a norm of possibility.

C. Cost-Justification and Commensurability: Private Necessity

The flip side of the coin that cost-justified precaution is *not* the proper principle for regulating serious harms to persons is that the criterion of cost-justification *is* a proper criterion for regulating harm to goods which are fungible and replaceable. The doctrine of private necessity, articulated in the famous case of *Vincent v. Lake Erie*, illustrates this point nicely.[121] There are two issues in *Vincent*. The first is whether the owner of the ship should be privileged to tie up at the plaintiff's dock in order to avoid the ship's near-certain destruction at the hands of a sudden and fierce winter storm. The second is whether any such privilege should be conditional. If the privilege is absolute, the shipowner may damage the dock in order to save its ship and owe no reparation to the dock owner for the damage done. If the privilege is conditional, the defendant must make good any harm that it does to the plaintiff's dock in the course of saving its ship. The court both affirms the existence of the privilege and holds that it is conditional.

Vincent is a case where efficient precaution is the proper standard of precaution. The dock and the ship are both fungible pieces of property. Their value is their use or consumption value, and it can be fully cashed out in dollars. The metric of money is well-suited to measuring both the damage done by bashing the dock and the damage avoided by keeping the ship out of the storm. The rational course of action in *Vincent* is to minimize combined harm and maximize combined benefit. The question of who should bear the cost of the ship's salvation—the owner of the ship or the owner of the dock—can be addressed after the harm has been done. Efficient precaution is thus compatible with the fair distribution of the burden of unavoidable harm; fair distribution can be

---

[121] Vincent v. Lake Erie Transp. Co., 124 N.W. 221 (Minn. 1910). In *Vincent*, a ship was lashed to a dock to avoid being cast out to sea in a storm. The ship's otherwise trespassory entry onto the plaintiff's property was held to be privileged under the doctrine of necessity, but the privilege was held to be conditional. The defendant was thus authorized by the law to dock without the owner's permission but had to repair the damage it did to the dock.

accomplished after the dock is damaged, simply by requiring the defendant to pay appropriate money damages to the plaintiff. Matters are different when serious, irreparable injury to persons is involved. Fairness must be done ex ante or not at all. Precautions commensurate with the harm risked must be taken before the risk is imposed. Reparation can neither undo the harm nor make up for, say, the unfairness of imposing a grave risk for a trivial end.

The standards applied in these examples thus differ in their stringency. The safety standard insists on the lowest level of risk; the cost-justification standard accepts the highest level; and the feasibility standard falls in the middle. None of the standards insists on absolute safety. All three standards specify permissible trade-offs. They vary significantly, however, in the trade-offs that they license. Their differences are responsive to the harms and interests at issue. As the application of the consumer expectation test to latex gloves in *Green* shows, the "safety" standard is the most stringent of the standards. *Significant* risk of harm to normal users is unacceptable. Latex gloves are defective because they precipitate severe allergic reactions in a nontrivial number of users. By contrast, the basic commitment of the feasibility standard is to reduce risk if it is possible to do so without endangering the long-run flourishing of the activity responsible for the risk. The value of the activity whose risks are at issue justifies the imposition of more risk than the safety standard permits. "Significant" risk is permitted when reducing risk to the point of "insignificance" would jeopardize the activity. The norm of cost-justification, implicit in *Vincent*, assigns no priority to avoiding harm. It trades harm off against other goods in a way that maximizes net benefit. The injury in *Vincent*, however, is not severe and irreparable impairment, but fully compensable loss of economic value. Cost-justified precaution responds appropriately to the kind of injury inflicted and taking cost-justified precaution is compatible with fairly distributing the burden of the damage done.

V. Judgments of Value

In the context of irreparable harms, the fundamental issue is not exactly how cost-benefit analysis is practiced but why its proponents claim that cost-benefit analysis is the "only game in town"—the only justifiable way of evaluating risks of harm and the precautions that might prevent them. The argument is usually made in economic terms, and in economic terms the argument is simple. When we minimize the combined costs of preventing accidental harms (precaution costs) and paying for those harms that we do not prevent (accident costs), we maximize net benefit (benefit minus cost). We diminish net benefit if we take either more precaution or less precaution. If we take more precaution, the increased marginal spending on precaution costs exceeds the increased marginal savings in accident costs. If we take less precaution, the marginal savings in precaution costs are exceeded by the marginal increases in accident costs. This is why law and economics scholars like Masur and Posner conceive of the cost-justified level of precaution as *the* rational level of precaution. In their view, the stricter safety and feasibility norms are fundamentally irrational because they prescribe inefficient levels of precaution. Life may be precious, but safeguarding life comes at a cost, and its value is not infinite. The benefits of achieving some level of safety must therefore be traded off against the costs of doing so. The rational way to trade costs off against benefits is to balance them so that we maximize net value and thereby make ourselves as well-off as we can be.[122] Pressing precaution beyond the point of cost-justification yields less value and preferring less value to more value is simply illogical.[123]

Sometimes, this claim is presented as a matter of mere common sense,[124] but it is in fact the child of a theory of "value." That theory is deeply intuitive in some contexts (e.g., when harms are fully repairable by money) and a profound affront to our considered convictions in others (when harm is irreparable). Cost-benefit analysis of risks to health and safety is an attempt to extend a market mode of valuation and choice to areas where actual markets fail—where actual markets either do not exist or are incomplete and imperfect.[125] If this theory is, in fact, the "only game in town," the safety and feasibility standards are wrongheaded, even if they can be coherently applied. This chapter argues, of course, that the safety and feasibility standards make sense only against the backdrop of conceptions of value and justification different from those found in economic analysis. The natural habitat of the safety and feasibility standards is a moral outlook which recognizes the intrinsic value of persons; which takes the distinctions between persons and the relations among them as fundamental; and which denies the fungibility of lives both with each other and with an indefinite list of other goods. From one angle, this denial of fungibility rests on a claim about people's interests. People have an especially urgent interest in safety, because the physical integrity of one's person is an essential precondition of effective agency and a decent life.

---

[122] Orthodox cost-benefit analysis embodies the Kaldor-Hicks or potential Pareto-superiority criterion of efficiency. That criterion maximizes net benefit. See Matthew D. Adler, Cost-Benefit Analysis, Encyclopedia of Law and Society: American and Global Perspectives 304 (David S. Clark ed., Sage Publications, Inc., 2007).

[123] The proposition that it is irrational to act in ways which do not maximize net benefit is a piece of the thesis of Kaplow & Shavell 2002, *supra* note 38, at xviii. They write, "[u]nder any method of evaluating social policy that accords positive weight to a notion of fairness, there must exist situations in which all individuals will be made worse off." Maximizing net benefit makes it possible for everyone to be better off than they would be in a world with less net value. There is more value to go around.

[124] See, *e.g.*, Schuck 2014, *supra* note 40. Robert H. Frank, Why Is Cost-Benefit Analysis So Controversial?, 29 J. Legal Stud. 913, 913 (2000) (noting that many find it "hard to imagine" that anyone could disagree with the "commonsensical" principle that we should take only those actions whose benefits exceed their costs).

[125] As has long been recognized. See Calabresi 1970, *supra* note 37, at 205–08.

That urgent interest is not fungible with lesser ones. Therein lies an important justification for the safety and feasibility standards.

From another, perhaps more illuminating, angle, the safety and feasibility standards rest on assertions about value. The conception of value has more in common with Kant's famous claim that rational beings have dignity—and that beings which have dignity are "above all price, and therefore [admit] of *no equivalent*"[126]—than it does with the conception of value implicit in cost-benefit analysis. And the intuitive justifications for the safety and feasibility standards find philosophical expression in contractualism philosophy. To clarify these ideas of value and justification, we need to attend first to the value framework embedded in regarding risks of death and irreparable injury through the prism of consumer choice as it is understood by contemporary economic analysis.

A. Consumer Choice: Valuing Other People's Lives

Even though markets for other people's lives do not exist by name, we might think about risks to life, in market terms. Indeed, Thomas Schelling founded the modern economic approach to the valuation of human life by observing that we can view the question of "what it is worth to reduce the risk of death" as a "consumer choice."[127] "We nearly all want our lives extended and are probably willing to pay for it."[128] Schelling was quite right to point out both that we can think of about whether or not to reduce some risk of death as a consumer choice and that doing so seems quite natural and appropriate in many contexts. In the context of purchasing a new car, for example, it seems eminently sensible to ask if some new safety device is worth its cost, or if our money would be better spent elsewhere.

When we think of risk and precaution as "consumer choices," we compare costs and benefits and seek to maximize net benefits. Pricing various costs and benefits makes our thinking more rigorous and precise, as long as it can be done credibly. Moreover, we can proceed this way not only when we are making individual decisions but also when we are making collective ones. In deciding whether or not some automobile safety improvement—automatically engaging backup cameras which avert a certain number of deaths per year, say—is worth installing, we can place a value on each life saved (e.g., $5 million) and then estimate how

---

[126] Immanuel Kant, Groundwork for the Metaphysic of Morals 33 (Jonathan Bennett ed., 2017) (1785). In *The Basic Liberties and Their Priority*, Rawls explains that the priority of the basic liberties rests in part on the premise that not all interests are fungible at some ratio of exchange. John Rawls, Justice as Fairness: A Restatement 105 (Harvard, 2001).

[127] Thomas C. Schelling, The Life You Save May Be Your Own, in Choice and Consequence 113, at 113–15 (Harvard, 1984). See also Gary Schwartz, The Myth of the Ford Pinto Case, 43 Rutgers L. Rev. 1013 (1991).

[128] *Id.*

many lives the safety device would save.[129] That benefit—the monetary value of the lives saved—can then be compared to the cost of the safety device to see if the installation of the safety device is net beneficial or not. Conceptually, the lives of potential victims (ideally, as valued by the victims themselves) are commodities, legitimate objects of use and consumption. Lives are goods whose value is determined by what people (including those people whose lives they are) are willing to pay for them; they are properly exchanged for other goods at appropriate rates of exchange; and they are rightly sacrificed when the cost of saving a life exceeds the benefit doing so. "[E]conomics . . . envisages rational man as seeking many goals, all substitutable at the margin. On the margin, economic man is prepared to trade off some freedom for some security, some privacy for some wealth, some freedom for some paternalism, and vice versa."[130] There is always some rate of exchange at which a rational person is willing to accept less of some good in exchange for more of another.

The extension of the consumer choice model from individual to social decision, however, is immensely problematic—and not only because it collapses the distinctions among our separate lives. A market conception of value assumes that everything has a price—explicitly or implicitly[131]—and that the *value of everything is its price*. On a market conception of value, prices are not an attempt to track the inherent value of the goods priced. On the contrary, value is *conferred* by the preferences for which prices are proxies. Prices reflect the value that would-be purchasers place on goods. Would-be purchasers value goods by determining how much they would gain from consuming, using, and enjoying them. This is a perfectly good way to think about ordinary consumer goods, but it is a moral mistake to regard other people's lives as goods available for our use and consumption. Other people's lives are not resources available for us to consume. Other people have moral standing equal to our own and equal authority over their own lives. Their standing, authority, and interests set boundaries to our permissible pursuit of our ends just as our standing, authority, and interests set boundaries to their permissible pursuit of their ends. We are all required to act on terms that are mutually justifiable. The terms on which risks of serious physical harm are imposed must accord proper weight to the claims and interests

---

[129] See W. Kip Viscusi & Ted Gayer, Rational Benefit Assessment for an Irrational World: Toward a Behavioral Transfer Test, J. Benefit-Cost Analysis 1 (2016).

[130] Harold Demsetz, Professor Michelman's Unnecessary and Futile Search for the Philosopher's Touchstone, in Nomos XXIV: Ethics, Economics, and the Law 41, 44 (J. Roland Pennock & John W. Chapman eds., New York University, 1982).

[131] In the context of health and safety regulation, orthodox cost-benefit analysis recommends monetizing all of the costs and all of the benefits of a regulation in order to compute net benefit. Heterodox forms of cost-benefit analysis make various allowances and adjustments. See, *e.g.*, Matthew D. Adler & Eric Posner, New Foundations of Cost-Benefit Analysis (Harvard, 2006).

of those on whom the risks are imposed—and to the claims and interests of those doing the imposing. Market metrics do not measure the right kind of value.

Stepping back and observing that discrepancies among diverse modes of valuation are not confined to circumstances where harm to human beings is at issue may help us shake the sense that economics embodies the uniquely correct mode of rational valuation. In 2005, a prominent dealer in rare books was caught cutting maps out of manuscripts in Yale's Beinecke library.[132] From an economic point of view, if rare books attract their highest prices when they are sold page by page—and not when they are sold intact—dismembering rare books and maps is a step toward putting them to their highest use. From a cultural point of view, though, dismembering rare books destroys the value that the larger, intact whole has. The economic argument for dismembering Gutenberg Bibles and selling them off page by page may well be correct empirically and on its own terms. But it misses the entire point of why we gather such books in libraries in the first place. Thinking of Gutenberg Bibles in purely economic terms fails to register their significance as cultural artifacts. Rare books and ancient maps have special meaning for us as cultural and technological achievements and as constitutive elements of our collective history. They also have special importance as resources for historical understanding. Storing and exhibiting them in museums and libraries is the best way to register and preserve their value—and the best way to use them, too. Carving up rare books and scattering their separate pages across private collections may well put them to their highest economic use, but it destroys the cultural value and historical usefulness they have as intact objects. Unsurprisingly, what is true of precious cultural artifacts is even more true of human lives. The value that we place on our own lives, and on human life more generally, is not exhausted by the prices that our lives can command in any marketplace.

Practitioners of cost-benefit analysis are often quick to acknowledge that the conceptual and practical problems of pricing lives and other nonmarket goods are substantial. The normative implausibility of assuming that human lives are goods whose value is properly fixed by a price mechanism is less frequently noted. Yet it is surely counterintuitive normatively to assert that people's lives have no intrinsic value, and that the only value persons have is the value conferred by expressed demand to use and consume their lives. The market's assumption that the goods traded on it are fungible is equally out of place when our separate and unique lives are the goods at issue. From an economic point of view, the claim that rational beings are "above all price" is a senseless statement.[133]

---

[132] William Finnegan, A Theft in the Library, The New Yorker (Oct. 17, 2005). The thief turned out to have stolen nearly one hundred maps in all, worth approximately $3 million. See Michael Blanding, The Map Thief (Gotham, 2014).

[133] See, e.g., Calabresi 1970, supra note 37, at 17; Calabresi & Bobbitt 1978, supra note 103, at 187–89.

Kant's point, though, is not that life has infinite value *within* an economic framework but that we should not understand the value of rational agency in economic terms. The Kantian objection to the economic mode of valuation is that human lives have intrinsic value by virtue of their rational nature and that we must treat each other accordingly. Persons are ends in themselves, not objects of consumption for others. Their lives command respect. Unlike commodities, human lives are neither available for consumption by others, nor interchangeable at an appropriate rate of exchange. They are not fungible because each of us has only one life to live. They are not commodities because they are ours to live, not resources for others to consume. It is, therefore, a mistake to govern risks to human life by the metric of the market. Respecting the distinctive value of human lives is a desideratum that acceptable principles of risk imposition must meet.

One way of articulating the demands imposed by the intrinsic value of human lives is to say that it requires treating people "only in ways that would be allowed by principles that they could not reasonably reject insofar as they, too, were seeking principles of mutual governance which other rational creatures could not reasonably reject."[134] This is a demanding standard of justice, and it may be that none of our non-ideal norms of risk regulation can meet this standard. Even so, it provides a backdrop against which we can understand the safety and feasibility standards as plausible attempts to articulate reasonable terms of risk imposition.

B. From Efficiency to Fairness and Equal Right

Implicit in both Thomas Schelling's observation that we can view the question of "what it is worth to reduce the risk of death" as a "consumer choice" and in his general thesis that "the life you save may be your own" is an invitation to think about matters of risk and precaution not only in the mode of market valuation but also as individual choices.[135] When we are taking risks upon ourselves, this seems unobjectionable. In other cases, however, treating safety decisions as wholly self-regarding should strike us as wildly inappropriate. Imagine, for example, a peculiar person who is attracted to the idea of exposing himself to the level of risk involved in climbing K2 but utterly averse to the pain, suffering, and intense exertion of Himalayan mountaineering. To tailor his life to his special taste for both risk and indolence, he hits on the idea of rigging up his car with an external gas tank so that even a minor fender bender might prove fatal. Because this way of pursuing his preferences for his own life seriously endangers others, it

---

[134] T.M. Scanlon 1998, *supra* note 41, at 106.
[135] See Schelling 1984, *supra* note 127.

is implausible to think that the matter should be settled solely by reference to this person's peculiar preferences for risk and exertion.

The cost-benefit analysis of risk of death is far from indifferent to the distinction between risk assumption and risk imposition. It is keenly aware that risk imposition involves a major negative externality, whereas risk assumption does not. But it responds to the difference between the two circumstances in a problematic way. Cost-benefit analysis instructs us to think about situations where some individuals' actions negatively impact the lives of others by incorporating the benefits to some and the costs to others into a single calculus of risk and benefit. In doing so, cost-benefit analysis models social decision on an intuitively appealing conception of individual rationality. In many circumstances, the prudent thing for each of us to do is to balance the costs and benefits of alternative courses of action and choose the action that is most net-beneficial. The extension of this conception to the circumstances of social choice, where costs and benefits fall on different people, is much less attractive. It replicates the fault that Rawls found in classical utilitarianism. By combining all costs and all benefits into a single calculus of risk, cost-benefit analysis eclipses "the distinction between persons."[136]

When we take the distinction between persons seriously, the proper test of principles of risk imposition becomes not whether they maximize net benefit but whether they are justifiable to those whose lives they govern. More particularly, taking the distinction between persons seriously in the context of accidental risk imposition brings interpersonal fairness to the fore. Risk impositions are irreducibly social. In our highly industrial and technological society, risks of physical harm are endemic. They are the inevitable byproducts of basic productive activities, and therefore part of the basic structure of society. Like it or not, to lead a normal life in our world is to be exposed to risks of physical injury and death imposed by others and to in turn impose risks on those others. Risk impositions must, therefore, be imposed terms that are justifiable both to those who impose them and to those upon whom they are imposed, when each of these is understood as representative persons. Principles of risk imposition must be justified from the basic "standpoints" of those affected, with potential injurers and potential victims being the basic points of view.[137]

When we take the distinctions among persons seriously and think about risk within a deontological framework, we ask about the reasonableness of risk impositions, not about their rationality. We ask, that is, if risk impositions are

---

[136] This, of course, is a longstanding criticism of utilitarianism, the parent philosophy of cost-benefit analysis. See John Rawls, Theory of Justice (Harvard, 1999).

[137] See, *e.g.*, Kumar 2011, *supra* note 43 at 134–35. Contractualist philosophy develops the idea of justification to diverse standpoints in rich and complex ways. See, *e.g.*, Rawls 1999, *supra* note 136 at 15–19, 102–67 (discussing the Original Position); Scanlon 1998, *supra* note 41; Thomas Nagel, Equality and Partiality (Oxford, 1991).

fair, not if they are efficient. Fairness is a distinct domain of political morality, different from both the domain of rights and the domain of efficiency. Efficiency is primarily concerned with overall welfare; rights are primarily concerned with the claims of individual persons. Fairness is concerned with the distribution of burdens and benefits—"with how well each person's claim is satisfied compared with how well other people's [claims] are satisfied."[138] Fairness looms large when the imposition of risk is at issue because risk impositions pit the claims of those who impose the risks and stand to benefit from them against those who are exposed to and endangered by those risks. We must reconcile those claims in ways that are acceptable to persons in both positions.

In thinking about the fair distribution of risk, precaution, and harm, we must distinguish between harms that are repairable and those that are not. When harms are fully repairable, as they are in *Vincent v. Lake Erie*, we can achieve efficiency ex ante and fairness ex post. Damaging the dock to save the ship is efficient; it minimizes the total property damage done by the storm. Requiring reparation after the fact is fair; the shipowner who benefits from saving the ship also bears the cost of its salvation. Matters are different when the harms suffered by one individual are serious and irreparable impairments of normal agency, and even death. Fairness cannot be achieved after these risks have ripened into injury. It must be done ex ante, by ensuring that the terms on which the risks in question are imposed are justifiable to those on whom they are imposed. When the burdens of risk imposition are borne by some people in the form of serious, irreparable harm and the benefits of imposing those risks are reaped by others, the distinction between persons looms especially large. A single person may rationally choose to bear some burden to achieve an end she values. It is eminently rational for a single person to settle on a level of precaution that maximizes their net benefit, ex ante. A plurality of distinct persons, however, lacks the unity necessary to make the imposition of significant harm on one person straightforwardly offset by the conferral of benefits on other people.

When risk imposition is interpersonal, risks of severe, irreparable injury ripen into harms that devastate the lives of some, while the activities responsible for those injuries redound to the benefit of others. This inequity cannot be justified by treating benefits to some and devastating harms to others as if they were benefits and harms being borne by the same individual and maximizing overall benefit to this fictive single person. The gains to some may be insufficient to justify the harms to others. Reasonable principles of risk imposition must be justifiable both to those who stand to gain and to those who stand to lose. Reasonable

---

[138] John Broome, Fairness, 91 Proc. of the Aristotelian Soc'y 87, 94–95 (1990–91). See also Waisman 2014, *supra* note 92; Kenneth W. Simons, Tort Negligence, Cost-Benefit Analysis, and Tradeoffs: A Closer Look at the Controversy, 41 Loy. L.A. L. Rev. 1171 (2008).

principles of risk imposition seek to safeguard the essential conditions of rational agency for every person, so far as possible. Securing such protection may well conflict with promoting overall welfare. The claims of those whose lives are at risk of accidental destruction and devastation at the hands of valuable activities may require those who reap the benefits of the risky activities at issue to accept standards of safety that require more than efficient precaution. The justification for the safety and feasibility standards lies in the strength of the claims that those who stand to suffer such injuries have by dint of the separateness of our lives and the priority we reasonably place on the avoidance of harm.

C. Tying the Threads Together

Taking the distinction between persons and the priority of avoiding harm seriously—and situating them within the larger philosophical framework where they are at home—puts us in a position to understand the logic at work in the safety and feasibility norms. Health and physical integrity are kinds of primary goods. Safety secures the physical integrity of the person against harm. Values, for their part, are plural and incommensurable. The point of protecting the essential conditions of agency for each person is to enable people to shape their own lives in accordance with their aspirations. Within a framework that prioritizes the protection of each person's essential interests, the attraction of the "safety" norm is evident enough. Just as efficient precaution is the first-best standard of precaution from the point of view of economic theory, "safety" is the first-best standard of precaution from the point of view of a deontological political morality that seeks to establish the terms of fair interaction for equal, independent persons with separate lives to lead and diverse ends to pursue. Safety, like health, is a precondition of effective agency, and the best social world is a social world that is safe for everyone.

We might, of course, think that the first-best social world is a world of "no risk," not a world in which "significant" risks have been eliminated but "insignificant" ones live on. On plausible assumptions about the nature of our world, however, a world of "no risk" is not a world worth having. So far as risk is concerned, our predicament is that liberty and security conflict.[139] Perfect safety is unattainable. Risk of physical harm—diminished security—is the byproduct of action. Without a "significance" requirement, one essential condition for leading a worthwhile life—the freedom to act in the world—would be destroyed in the name of another essential condition, namely, safety. We cannot farm, build,

---

[139] For these purposes, liberty is the freedom to impose risk *on others* and security freedom from harm arising out of risk imposed *on us* by others.

drive, fly, eat and drink, or mill cotton and refine benzene without taking and imposing some risks of devastating injury. We must therefore bear a certain low level of ineliminable risk. Call it the background level of risk. Some risk of devastating injury is the price of activity, and activity is worth having.

If this broad account of our predicament is correct, the safety norm with its "significance" requirement identifies the best attainable standard of precaution given the constraints of the world as we know it. The feasibility norm presents a more difficult case. It sacrifices safety to secure some other good. In principle, health and safety should only be sacrificed to promote some even more urgent interest. Trading health or safety off against other goods requires making judgments of urgency (or need), not judgments about what people want or prefer. Safety should be sacrificed only when its sacrifice furthers a more urgent need. The basic prescription of feasibility analysis—that risks should be reduced only to the point where further reduction would jeopardize the long-run survival of the activity that generates those risks—makes the implicit claim that the long-run survival of the activity at issue is more important than reducing the activity's risks to the "safe" level. When this claim is well founded, forgoing the more stringent standard of "safe" precaution and accepting the standard of "feasible" precaution is justified.

In the domain of its original formulation, the feasibility norm addressed basic industrial activities (milling cotton, refining petroleum) that were taken to be so deeply embedded in the economy that their elimination was unthinkable. Now, we may come to very different conclusions about the indispensability of refining petroleum. Changing judgments of whether we can live without some basic economic activity underscore the fact that the plausibility of the feasibility standard depends on the persuasiveness of the judgment that the value secured by the long-run flourishing of the activity in question is greater than the value secured by reducing risk to the "safe" level. Whether or not a given activity is important enough to justify moving from safety to feasibility lies beyond the scope of this chapter. Here, we can say only that the measure of the feasibility norm's success is whether, in some domain of its application, it registers the priority of avoiding harm properly and retreats from the "safe level" of risk only in pursuit of some greater value. From the point of this chapter, the feasibility standard is important even if its application is often flawed. Flawed or not, the standard prescribes the eliminate risk of devastating, irreparable injury insofar as it seems possible to do so. In conjunction with the "safe-level" norm the "feasibility" norm shows that the priority of avoiding harm is, in fact, a value instantiated by well-established legal norms.

Last, we need to recall where we began this chapter. Because reparative damages are its default remedy, the private law of torts struggles in the face of risks of death and severe, irreparable injury. These are the harms that we have most reason to fear and to avoid. Direct regulation of risk is the best available response to the limitations of the law of torts, and the regulation required must be responsive to the gravity of the harm at issue. Seen in this light, standards of safe and feasible precaution are not sentimental exercises in economic irrationality. They are important and credible attempts to establish one of the conditions necessary for equal and independent persons to exercise their agency effectively, and to pursue the ends, aspirations, and values that give meaning to their lives.

Irreparable injury undoes the tort law of negligence because tort is a system of reparation. Negligence liability is also problematic when harm that should not or cannot be avoided looms large. Negligence law is concerned only with avoidable harm. Strict liability, the subject of the next two chapters, is the form of responsibility that takes unavoidable harm seriously.

6
Strict Responsibilities

Ever since modern tort law took shape in the latter half of the nineteenth century, fault has been its dominant principle of responsibility. Even so, fault liability has never established sole and despotic dominion over the law of torts. Our common law of torts is—and long has been—split between fault and strict liabilities.[1] Fault liability imposes responsibility on actors for harms which should have been avoided through the exercise of due care *because* those harms should have been avoided. It is the injurer's failure to avoid inflicting those harms—when they should have done so—that makes the harms wrongful. Strict liability is, as the name says, liability without fault. It imposes responsibility on actors for harms (and harmless wrongs) which flow from the purposeful agency of the actors who inflict them, even when those harms either should not, or could not, have been avoided. Both fault and strict liability have powerful intuitive appeal. Fault liability appeals to the intuition that people are responsible for the harm that they inflict on others when they ought to have avoided inflicting that harm—but not when they have acted carefully and justifiably. Strict liability appeals to the competing intuition that people who undertake purposeful activity for their own benefit should not be allowed to foist the burdens of their actions, activities, and choices, onto others simply because they have proceeded carefully. Strict liability appeals to the intuition that I should bear the burdens of my activities and you should bear the burdens of yours.

Perhaps because both principles have strong intuitive appeal, strict and fault liability have long histories in the law of torts. Early English incarnations of trespass and nuisance are usually taken to embody strict liability, whereas early forms of liability for accidentally inflicted injury are usually taken to embody an embryonic form of fault liability.[2] In the latter half of the nineteenth century—when the law of torts broke free from the fetters of the forms of action and was reconstructed around substantive principles of responsibility—negligence and

---

[1] This division is well known, though the best way to understand the division is highly contested. For one influential older account, see Charles Gregory, Trespass to Negligence to Absolute Liability, 37 Va. L. Rev. 359 (1951). It is less often observed that the landscape of tort law is also constituted by the size and location of domains of "no liability"—realms where tort yields to contract, or to property, or to simply to "no duty." For a perceptive and elegant account, see Robert L. Rabin, The Historical Development of the Fault Principle: A Reinterpretation, 15 Ga. L. Rev. 925 (1981).

[2] W. Page Keeton et al., Prosser and Keeton on the Law of Torts § 6 at 30 (West, 5th ed., 1984).

strict liability were recast as competing general principles of responsibility.[3] Ever since, fault liability has had the upper hand, but the extent of its dominance has ebbed and flowed. At the outset of the twentieth century, fault liability's dominance was so extensive that strict liability was confined to a few corners of tort law. By the middle of the 1980s, fault had ceded so much of tort law's dominion to strict liability that the eminent law and economics scholar George Priest could claim that the entire law of torts was on track to being swallowed by strict enterprise liability.[4] In the thirty-five years since Priest penned his jeremiad, fault liability has experienced a renaissance and strict liability has waned.[5] At present, fault is tort law's default principle of responsibility for accidentally inflicted harm, but abnormally dangerous activity liability, nuisance liability in its most important modern incarnation, the vicarious liability of firms for the torts of their employees committed within the scope of their employments, and some dimensions of product defect liability are strict.[6]

Strict liability is, moreover, more pervasive than the standard sorting of tort liabilities between negligence and strict liability suggests. For one thing, doctrines formally classified as fault-based sometimes embody liabilities that are in fact strict. Roger Traynor's assertion that the doctrine of *res ipsa loquitur*—officially classified as a rule of evidence for establishing the existence of negligence—had come to be construed so liberally that it was "in reality liability without negligence" is a famous case in point.[7] Moreover, it is a commonplace of torts scholarship that—because fault liability in tort is objective—from a moral point of view, fault liability is strict liability. Objective fault liability divorces judgments of wrongful conduct from judgments of moral blameworthiness. Actors who are blameless because—through no fault of their own—they lack the capacities of objectively reasonable persons may be held liable when they fail to take the precautions that a reasonable person would take.[8] This covert embedding

---

[3] See Gregory C. Keating, Recovering Rylands: An Essay for Robert Rabin, 61 DePaul L. Rev. 543 (2012).

[4] George L. Priest, The Invention of Enterprise Liability: A Critical History of the Intellectual Foundations of Modern Tort Law, 14 J. Legal Stud. 461 (1985). Priest's paper was a Jeremiad decrying the triumph of enterprise liability and a clarion call for a counterrevolution.

[5] For a fine general overview of the arc of American tort law, see G. Edward White, Tort Law in America: An Intellectual History (Oxford, 1985, expanded ed. 2003).

[6] Restatement (Second) of Torts § 519 (1977); Restatement (Second) of Torts § 821D (1979); Restatement (Third) of Agency § 7.07 (2006); Restatement (Third) of Torts: Products Liability § 1 cmt. a (1998).

[7] Escola v. Coca-Cola Bottling Co., 150 P.2d 436, 463 (Cal. 1944) (Traynor, J., concurring). Jeremiah Smith, Sequel to Workmen's Compensation Acts, 27 Harv. L. Rev. 235, 344, 367 (1914), presciently describes how negligence liability might come to approach strict liability through the reconstruction of a handful of key doctrines, including *res ipsa loquitur*. Many of the changes Smith foresaw came to pass. See Gregory C. Keating, The Theory of Enterprise Liability and Common Law Strict Liability, 54 Vand. L. Rev. 1285, 1292–1303 (2001).

[8] See Richard A. Epstein, A Theory of Strict Liability, 2 J. Legal Stud. 151, 153 (1973) ("[T]he law of negligence never did conform in full to the requisites of the 'moral' system of personal responsibility invoked in its behalf. In particular, the standard of the reasonable man, developed in order

of strict liability within fault liability ensures that strict liability is anything but a curiosity confined to a few corners of the law, but it gives rise to a new puzzle: If strict liability is embedded within fault liability, how is it that the two principles are also opposed principles of responsibility? What do we mean by strict liability?

The basic principle of fault liability is easy to state. Negligence liability is liability imposed because the party inflicting the harm *should have avoided doing so*. Negligent injurers are responsible for repairing the harm that they have done because they have failed to conduct themselves as carefully as they should have. Had they been appropriately careful, they would not have inflicted the injury at issue. Even though we may summarize the basic difference between negligence and strict liability by saying that strict liability is liability for unavoidable harm, that summary harbors ambiguities. Strict liability comes in two basic forms. In one case, the term "strict liability" identifies a kind of tort liability which imposes responsibility for repairing harm on a party responsible for the infliction of that harm, even though that party cannot be faulted for failing to prevent the harm. Using dynamite to excavate the site of a dam, for example, is subject to strict liability. That liability attaches to accidental, wayward, explosions of the dynamite, even if all reasonable precautions have been taken to avoid the accidental explosion. Liability is strict because it is imposed on inflictions of injury that the law does not think the defendant should have avoided. The remark "strict liability is liability for unavoidable harm whereas fault liability is liability for avoidable harm" is spot on as a characterization of this form of strict liability. In a second case, strict liability means liability without moral culpability, responsibility without blame. This is the sense of strict liability that scholars who point out that objective fault liability is strict liability for people with subpar competencies are invoking. Liability that is strict in this sense is strict because it is imposed on people who should not be blamed for having acted as they did. What these negligent actors did was *not* justified—because they did not do what a reasonable person would have done—but, from a moral point of view, they should not be blamed (or "faulted") for having acted as they did. Limitations of capacity prevent them from exercising the care of the reasonably competent.

This second sense of strict liability as moral blamelessness is instantiated by an important class of strict liabilities that govern impermissible crossings of normative boundaries—impermissible interferences with what are often called "autonomy rights." Autonomy rights articulate powers of control over some prized zone of discretion. The most prominent incarnations of this form of strict liability involve rights which confer control over one's own person and one's real

---

to insure injured plaintiffs a fair measure of protection against their fellow citizens, could require a given person to make recompense even where no amount of effort could have enabled *him* to act in accordance with the standard of conduct imposed by the law.") (emphasis in original); Kenneth S. Abraham, Strict Liability in Negligence, 61 DePaul L. Rev. 271 (2012).

and moveable property. Innocent violations of these rights are common enough to be a staple of cases and casebooks. Sometimes, for example, people trespass because they are unaware that they are on someone else's property. Their unawareness may well be reasonable. Through no fault of their own, they may be mistaken about the boundary between their property and the property of a neighbor. Their presence on the plaintiff's property is not legally *justified*; they do not have the owner's permission to be on the property, and they are therefore trespassing. But their presence is, morally speaking, *excusable*. Their violation of the owner's property right is unwitting. They were ignorant of the owner's right, and reasonably so. Thus, unlike the first form of strict liability—which attaches to inflictions of harm that are justified in the eyes of the law—this form of strict liability attaches to conduct which is not legally justified but which is morally *innocent*. The relevant moral category here is *excuse*: an innocent trespasser is committing a wrong, but, from a moral point of view, they should not be held responsible for committing the wrong. Through no fault of their own, they did not realize that they were committing a wrong. This form of strict liability rests on the same idea of strictness as the criticism of objective fault liability as "strict liability for those with subpar capacities." The three usages of "strict liability" that we have canvassed thus identify only two different forms of liability. One form is liability imposed for inflicting a harm whose infliction should *not* have been avoided; the other is liability imposed for crossing a normative boundary established by a right. Liability attaches even if that crossing is wholly innocent and therefore morally excusable.

It is somewhat unfortunate that the term "strict liability" is used to express criticism of the subset of cases where fault liability is imposed in the absence of moral blameworthiness. The point being made is sound, but the way in which the point is made is a source of confusion. The point is sound because modern tort law measures fault by reference to the care that an objective reasonable person would take. Substandard capacities rarely relieve people of their legal responsibility to conduct themselves in accordance with the requirements of reasonable care objectively construed. The application of the objective standard therefore licenses the imposition of liability on actors who are, morally speaking, free of fault. Someone whose capacities are inescapably inferior to the capacities of the objective reasonable person will be unable to exercise objectively reasonable care in some cases. Morally speaking, we ought to excuse their failure. "Ought implies can," and they cannot. Morally, they should be neither blamed nor held responsible, but legally they may be held liable. From a moral point of view, insofar as it fails to recognize excusing conditions necessary to align legal fault with moral blame, objective fault liability is liability imposed on actors who are *blameless*. Expressing this point by saying that objective fault liability is strict liability morally speaking has its rhetorical advantages, but it also has the disadvantage of muddying the waters when it comes to distinguishing fault and strict liability doctrines from one another.

As a matter of tort doctrine, then, the term "strict liability" identifies two different kinds of liability. Simplifying, I shall call the first kind of strict liability "harm-based." Borrowing a term of Arthur Ripstein's, I shall call the second kind "sovereignty-based."[9] Rights are involved in both forms of strict liability, but the interests that ground the relevant rights are different. Harm-based strict liabilities safeguard our interests in the physical integrity of our persons and the external objects that we are entitled to count as our own whereas sovereignty-based strict liabilities safeguard our interests in being able to subject our physical persons and various external objects to the control of our wills. Harm-based strict liabilities embody liability for the conditional wrong of harming-without-repairing.[10] They differ from negligence liability in that—under a regime of harm-based strict liability—the imposition of liability is not predicated on the judgment that the harm inflicted should have been avoided. Instead, harm-based strict liabilities assert that the harms to which they apply are justifiably inflicted, but only on condition that the cost of repairing those harms is borne by the party responsible for their infliction.

The leading nuisance case of *Boomer v. Atlantic Cement* illustrates nicely what it means to say that harm-based strict liability is a type of conditional wrong.[11] The *Boomer* court refused to enjoin the defendant from operating its cement plant, even though that plant's operation interfered with the plaintiffs' reasonable use and enjoyment of their property in a way which could be cured completely only by shutting down the plant. Injunctive relief would have been the right remedy if the defendant's interference with the plaintiffs' use and enjoyment of their property should have been avoided altogether (because it was entirely unjustified). Instead, the court required the defendant to make reparation to the plaintiffs for the harm that the operation of its plant inflicted upon them. The wrong righted by this remedy was the wrong of harming-without-repairing. In the court's eyes, injunctive relief was inappropriate because the harm to the plaintiff was the unavoidable (if regrettable) consequence of the plaintiff's justified activity. The defendant "took every available and possible precaution to protect the plaintiffs from dust" but "nevertheless . . . created a nuisance insofar as the lands of the plaintiffs [were] concerned."[12] Once it took all possible precautions to reduce the plant's pollution it was *not* wrong for the defendant to operate its cement plant, even though the operation of that plant interfered with the plaintiffs' reasonable use and enjoyment of their property. But it *was* wrong for the defendant

---

[9] Arthur Ripstein, Beyond the Harm Principle, 34 Phil. & Pub. Aff. 215 (2006).
[10] See the text accompanying notes 48–52, *infra*.
[11] Boomer v. Atlantic Cement Co., 257 N.E.2d 870 (N.Y. 1970).
[12] Boomer v. Atlantic Cement Co., 287 N.Y.S.2d 112, 113–14 (N.Y. Sup. Ct. 1967).

not to compensate the plaintiff for the harm done by the defendant's interference with the plaintiff's reasonable use and enjoyment of its property.

Sovereignty torts, by contrast, involve crossing normative boundaries that define domains subject to the control of those who hold the relevant autonomy rights. Sovereignty-based strict liabilities do not include the infliction of physical injury among their elements. The intangible harm of intruding into a zone subject as a matter of legal right to the dominion of another replaces the tangible harm of inflicting physical injury. Trespass is an instance of sovereignty-based strict liability. Real property rights confer on those who hold them the authority to determine who enters and under what conditions. People trespass by crossing the boundary of someone else's real property and entering that property without the owner's permission. Therefore, you do not need to damage someone's property to commit the tort of trespass; all that you need to do is to enter without their consent. Paradoxically, perhaps, some important intentional torts are strict in the sense that they can be committed without being "at fault" according to the standard of fault applied by the tort law of negligence. For an entry onto a piece of real property to be a trespass, it does not have to be the case that a reasonable person would not have entered the property as the defendant did. The tort of conversion is strict in the same way, as is battery in some of its incarnations.[13]

To be liable for common law trespass, you do not need either to know that you are entering without permission or to be at fault for failing to know that you are entering without permission.[14] You simply need to enter without, in fact, having permission. The torts of conversion and battery can be committed in similarly innocent ways. I may convert your umbrella by mistaking it for mine, retrieving it (or so I think) from its place in a restaurant umbrella stand, and taking it home with me. Similarly, I may commit a battery when, as a doctor, I mistakenly believe that I have your consent to a blood transfusion that you have forbidden because such transfusions violate your religious beliefs. Despite my belief that I'm helping you—and despite my intent to do so—I batter you when I transfuse a pint of blood into your body. And I batter you even if that transfusion improves your health. Sovereignty-based strict liability is imposed on conduct which is legally wrong because it violates the plaintiff's right. But the conduct need not be legally wrong in the sense that a reasonable person would have avoided the boundary crossing at issue.

The two dominant contemporary approaches to tort law treat these strict liabilities very differently. Economic analysis makes a place for harm-based strict liability, whereas corrective justice and civil recourse theory generally do not. The economic analysis of tort assimilates strict liability for harm accidentally

---

[13] See note 46, *infra*, and accompanying text.
[14] See the discussion in the text accompanying note 42, *infra*.

done into its conception of tort as a kind of market. Because economic theories model tort law on the market, they conceive of liability rules as prices, of harms and rights violations as costs, and they conceive of tort law itself as an institution which addresses a pervasive form of market failure. The wrongs at the heart of tort law involve accidents between parties who are strangers to one another.[15] In economic terms, tortiously inflicted injuries normally arise between parties who do not have bargaining or market relationships with one another. The costs that torts inflict are therefore externalities. The role of liability rules is to correct these externalities by forcing injurers to take the costs of the accidents that they inflict on strangers into account and adjust their behavior accordingly.

Strict liability has an obvious attraction within the economic framework. It requires injurers to internalize accident-related externalities by pinning the costs of *all* accidents—not just those accidents that should have been prevented through the exercise of cost-justified care—on the injurers responsible for those accidents. Whereas negligence liability taxes only accidental harms that should have been avoided, strict liability prices the costs of all accidents and requires those responsible for them to pay up. To be sure, strict liability is not self-evidently superior to negligence from an economic point of view. The economic understanding of negligence takes the Hand Formula to be the center of the field and understands the Hand Formula to call for cost-benefit analysis as economics understands it.[16] So understood, the calculus of care in negligence law incarnates economic analysis. But strict liability's claim to make tort liability into a version of the price system by building the costs of *all* accidents into liability rules, and inducing actors to adjust their actions accordingly, is equally attractive from an economic point of view. Whereas negligence liability economically understood replicates in judicial and jury decision-making the cost-benefit thinking that is the hallmark of economic rationality, strict liability replicates the price system itself. Economic analysis thus makes a home for both major forms of tort liability.[17]

Recent work within the corrective justice and civil recourse paradigms has been much less hospitable to strict liability. Indeed, earlier in this book I argued that Jules Coleman's, Arthur Ripstein's, and Ernest Weinrib's theories of tort all shared the fault of failing to acknowledge and justify the presence in tort law of significant strict liabilities.[18] The overarching suspicion that prominent

---

[15] There are exceptions to this generalization, the most important of which at present is product liability law. Product accidents normally arise between parties who are sellers and buyers. The problem they present is not an externality problem but an information problem. See Steven Shavell, Economic Analysis of Accident Law 51–56 (Harvard, 1987).

[16] Richard A. Posner, A Theory of Negligence, 1 J. Legal Stud. 29 (1972). See the discussion in Chapter Four, *supra*, pp. 129–41.

[17] Steven Shavell, Strict Liability versus Negligence, 9 J. Legal Stud. 1 (1980). Economic analysis has more difficulty with autonomy sovereignty-based strict liabilities. Autonomy rights carve out zones where those who hold the rights are free to act as they please. They may act efficiently—or not.

[18] See Chapter Two, *supra*, pp. 51–53; Chapter Three, *supra*, pp. 101–104.

contemporary corrective justice and civil recourse theorists share is that strict liability is not a wrongs-based form of liability. This is a mistake. Harms-based strict liabilities are conditional wrongs. The wrong that they condemn is the wrong of "harming-without-repairing." Harm-based strict liabilities are justified by values and considerations fundamental to the law of torts. For one thing, serious physical harm does not cease to be especially bad for those who suffer it when its infliction should not have been avoided.[19] Even when we are not prepared to forgo an activity—and even when the risks that the activity imposes have been reduced as far as feasible—the activity can still devastate human lives. Consider the facts of *Siegler v. Kuhlman*:

> Seventeen-year-old Carol J. House died in the flames of a gasoline explosion when her car encountered a pool of thousands of gallons of spilled gasoline. She was driving home from her after-school job in the early evening of November 22, 1967, along Capitol Lake Drive in Olympia; it was dark but dry; her car's headlamps were burning. There was a slight impact with some object, a muffled explosion, and then searing flames from gasoline pouring out of an overturned trailer tank engulfed her car. The result of the explosion is clear, but the real causes of what happened will remain something of an eternal mystery.[20]

The facts of *Siegler* show, moreover, that even when harm inflicted by human agency is unavoidable, it is not simply a matter of misfortune, as Jules Coleman and Arthur Ripstein suggest.[21] Natural misfortune—being struck by lightning while standing on a street corner, say—is not something for which anyone is accountable. Non-negligent agency, by contrast, is still agency; it is subject to moral appraisal and to judgments of accountability. Even when serious physical injury arises out of risks which cannot or should not be avoided, that injury can destroy people's lives. Physical harm impairs and sometimes destroys an essential condition of effective agency, and it inflicts a great deal of pain and suffering. We have reason to reduce even unavoidable harm as much as possible; reason to repair unavoidable harm when it is inflicted; and reason to care about the justice of the terms on which it is inflicted. The failure to repair harm reasonably inflicted may itself be unreasonable—and a wrong to those harmed.

The moral significance of harm whose infliction is not wrongful is an important justification for tort law's strict liabilities, but it is not the only justification. Sometimes, tort law adopts strict liability because it is required by respect for people's powers of control over their persons and their property. Other times,

---

[19] Seana Shiffrin, Harm and Its Moral Significance, 18 Legal Theory 357 (2012).
[20] Siegler v. Kuhlman, 502 P.2d 1181, 1182 (Wash. 1972).
[21] Jules Coleman & Arthur Ripstein, Mischief and Misfortune, 41 McGill L.J. 91 (1996).

considerations of interpersonal fairness play a role. The benefits of inflicting harms that should not be avoided tend to accrue primarily to those who inflict the harms, whereas the burdens of the harms fall on those who suffer them. *Boomer* illustrates this point well. Strict liability mitigates that unfairness by requiring injurers to repair the unavoidable harms that they inflict. And, in many cases where strict liability is imposed, the law is also influenced by the fact that the harm that persists once all reasonable precaution has been taken is not only significant but also primarily under the control of the party responsible for its infliction. There is very little that victims like Carol House can do to control the risk of being killed by the practice of transporting vast quantities of gasoline by tanker trailer. Strict liability induces the defendant to do as much as it can to reduce the incidence of the harms that it inflicts. *Boomer* nicely illustrates these considerations, too.

But we are getting a bit ahead of ourselves. We must first explore the reasons why civil recourse and corrective justice scholars disfavor strict liability. Arthur Ripstein's objections are a good place to start. For Ripstein, the only alternative to his own view that strict and fault liability are one and the same is an essentially economic description of strict liability as a "'pay-as-you-go' scheme designed to see to it that costs are internalized."[22] "Paying as you go" is not a matter of making reparation for harm wrongly done; it is merely a matter of mimicking the market and thereby putting resources—including, here, other people's lives and property—to their highest use. So conceived, strict liability is the price system in liability form, and the price system is not a matter of duty, breach, right, wrong, and responsibility. If torts is a law of wrongs, strict liability so conceived is not a form of tort liability. Agents who inflict efficient injury on others—who pay the proper price for the injuries they inflict and walk away richer—do no wrong. On the contrary, *they do the right thing*. That characterization cannot be reconciled with the most basic fact about tort liability—the fact that torts are "wrongs." To say that torts are wrongs is to say that *there are no justified torts*.[23] When we label conduct tortious, we are asserting that the conduct is wrong in the sense that the injury inflicted on the plaintiff was unjustifiable. Conversely, when we model liability in tort on the price system, we are denying that tortious conduct is unjustified. When you pay the price of something and thereby purchase it, you are not wronging anyone.

Strict liability is a familiar form of liability in tort. You might, therefore, expect corrective justice and civil recourse theorists to resist the economic assimilation of strict liability to the price system on the ground that it treats tortious

---

[22] Arthur Ripstein, Private Wrongs 126 (Harvard, 2016).
[23] A point rightly emphasized by both John Gardner and Goldberg & Zipursky. See John Gardner, Torts and Other Wrongs, 39 Fla. St. U. L. Rev. 43 (2011); John C.P. Goldberg & Benjamin C. Zipursky, Recognizing Wrongs (Harvard, 2020).

conduct as justified conduct; you might expect corrective justice and civil recourse theorists to offer an alternative account. Instead, contemporary corrective justice theorists have tended to embrace the idea that strict liability does not involve wronging and have sought to expel it from the law of torts.[24] John Goldberg and Ben Zipursky, the leading proponents of a civil recourse conception of tort, also adopt this view:

> We must acknowledge that our insistence that tort law is a law of wrongs puts us in a difficult spot when it comes to explaining the presence of common law strict liability for abnormally dangerous activities. After all ... the rationale that seems to prevail in this domain is that liability should attach to activities that are not wrongful in and of themselves, and without regard to whether they are undertaken in a wrongful (i.e., careless) manner. How does liability imposed in these terms fit within a law that is supposed to be all about defining wrongs and providing victims of wrongs with recourse?
>
> The short answer is that it does not.[25]

This admirably candid answer encapsulates the predicament of most contemporary noneconomic theorists of tort. Strict liability is an embarrassment to their theories.

There is reason to wince. Corrective justice and civil recourse theorists have charged economic analysis with being unable to explain the law of torts from the internal point of view of either the lawyer concerned with bringing the law of torts to bear on the appraisal of injurious conduct or the citizen concerned with conducting herself in accordance with other people's rights. From the internal point of view the law of torts is a law of obligations. Tort law shares much of its vocabulary with morals. Concepts such as duty, breach, right, wrong, obligation, responsibility, and fairness figure prominently in tort discourse. Interpretive inconsistencies need not trouble law and economic scholars all that much. Their view treats basic tort concepts as so much window dressing obscuring the forward-looking calculus of cost and benefit that actually drives the law of torts.[26] Corrective justice and civil recourse theorists, though, claim that their views can recognize the main concepts of tort for what they are—namely, mandatory reasons governing the conduct of persons in civil society. When it comes to strict liability, however, leading corrective justice and civil recourse theorists find themselves either confessing that they cannot make sense of it as a form

---

[24] See Chapter Two, *supra*, pp. 51–53; Chapter Three, *supra*, pp. 101–104.
[25] John C.P. Goldberg & Benjamin C. Zipursky, The Oxford Introductions to U.S. Law: Torts 267 (Oxford, 2010). See also John C.P. Goldberg & Benjamin C. Zipursky, The Strict Liability in Fault and the Fault in Strict Liability, 85 Fordham L. Rev. 743 (2016).
[26] See Chapter Two, *supra*, pp. 32–34..

of tortious wrong or shoehorning strict liability into the mold of negligence liability.[27] Any account of tort law that specifies the constitutive features of tortious wrongs in such a way that the account cannot acknowledge—or properly characterize—strict liability in tort is, for that reason alone, less than wholly satisfactory. Strict liability exists, and it has long and deep roots in the law of torts.

Both harm-based and sovereignty-based strict liabilities are embedded in our law. Over time, strict liability in tort waxes and wanes, but it never vanishes. Sovereignty-based strict liabilities are surprisingly common among intentional torts, and harm-based strict liabilities are entrenched in corners of accident law and in nuisance law. Their presence shows both that tortious wrongs are not all based on fault and that we need to revise the claim made by corrective justice and civil recourse theorists that tort is a law composed exclusively of "conduct-based wrongs."[28] Negligence liability fits the template of a "conduct-based wrong" very smoothly. Negligence *is* faulty conduct—the failure to conform one's conduct to the standard of care required by the law for the protection of others. In negligence, the wrongdoer's conduct is the focus of our inquiry. Negligence is conduct which is defective in failing to take the precaution(s) necessary to avoid inflicting injury on others. We determine if someone is negligent by examining their conduct. By contrast, when liability is strict and sovereignty-based, the wrong committed is "conduct-based" in only the most attenuated sense of the term. The core of the wrong is the violation of the plaintiff's right. The duty breached by the defendant is a duty not to violate the right; conduct that violates the right is wrongful because—and merely because—it violates the right. The plaintiff's right, not the defendant's conduct, does the work. Viewed in isolation from the right, the conduct may be innocent and even justified. The defendant doctor in *Mohr v. Williams*, for example, benefited the plaintiff by curing her disease.[29] He also wronged the plaintiff—because he operated on her ear without her permission. If you operate on someone without their permission, you violate their right to determine who may touch their body and for what purpose. You commit a wrong because you violate a right. And this is true even if your conduct, considered without reference to the right, is commendable. The fact that your conduct cures the plaintiff's diseased condition, though, makes describing it as a conduct-based wrong less than perspicuous. Instead of inflicting harm, the conduct confers benefit. It's not the conduct that makes the wrong, it's the violation of the right. Harm-based strict liabilities are likewise conduct-based only in an extended sense. The wrong that these strict liabilities instantiate is the conditional wrong of "harming-without-repairing." Unlike negligence, that wrong is

---

[27] See *infra* note 82, and Chapter Three, *supra*, pp. 101–104.
[28] See Chapter Two, *supra*, pp. 26 & 54.
[29] Mohr v. Williams, 104 N.W. 12 (Minn. 1905).

not committed when the tortfeasor's conduct inflicts injury. The legal wrong is committed when the injurer fails to repair the harm that they have done.

Theories of tort need to illuminate both fault and strict liability, and both forms of strict liability, too. The fact that the economic analysis of tort accommodates both fault and non-fault liability is a point in its favor. Any theory of tort true to the subject must do so. To distinguish their views from the economic view—and to register the fact that torts *always* involve unjustified conduct—theorists of tort as a law of wrongs need to explain why strict liability torts are *wrongs*—why they involve either violations of rights or conduct that is unjustified in some way.

I. Sovereignty and Strict Liability: Harms to Autonomy Rights

As we have seen, important intentional torts incarnate a form of strict liability, a fact that tends to come as a surprise to first-year law students. Entering law students usually know very little about tort law, but they soon discover that, whatever torts are, they seem to come in three forms: intentional, negligent, and strict. This tripartite division of wrongs appears to track the state of mind with which the wrongs are committed, and therefore to track the relative culpability involved in their commission. Intentional torts appear to involve the most serious wrongdoing; negligent ones involve less serious wrongdoing; and strict liability torts involve the least serious wrongdoing. This understanding of tort law's tripartite division of wrongs in terms of relative culpability is roughly accurate in an important way. The intentional tort cases that tend to come to mind as core examples of the domain generally *do* involve heightened culpability. Their commission expresses ill will or malice, whereas core examples of negligent wrongdoing involve conduct which expresses only indifference or inadvertence. Core assaults and batteries, for example, involve the intent to inflict injury. When you hurl a hatchet at an innkeeper's face you intend either to harm her or to put her in fear for her life.[30]

Moreover, in committing intentional wrongs tortfeasors sometimes act in ways which express "contempt for [the victim], often more unbearable than the harm itself."[31] Because "actions speak louder than words," intentionally tortious conduct can be an especially powerful way of expressing scorn for someone else. The foul spit in the face that was the subject of *Alcorn v. Mitchell* is a vivid

---

[30] I. de S. and Wife v. W. de S., At the Assizes, coram Thorpe, C.J., 1348 or 1349 Year Book, Liber Assisarum, folio 99, placitum 60.
[31] Jean-Jacques Rousseau, The Social Contract and the Discourses 82 (G.D.H. Cole trans., Dutton, 1979). The quotation is from the Discourse on the Origin of Inequality. I have altered the translation slightly.

example.³² The act was a battery, but the injury it inflicted was not primarily physical. Alcorn "could have hurled insults at [Mitchell], but his spit showed a contempt that words could hardly communicate."³³ But even when intentional wrongs do not aim primarily at expressive ends, their core instances commonly involve conduct which aims at inflicting harm on the victim in violation of her rights. Most batteries, for example, are committed with the intent to inflict physical harm and the pain that the infliction of such harm normally involves. This kind of intentional wrongdoing is worse than ordinary negligent wrongdoing. Ordinary negligent wrongdoing involves only insufficient attention to the rights or the safety of the victim. As a matter of empirical fact, then, most intentional wrongs express a more intense and objectionable disregard for the rights of their victims than most negligent wrongs do.

The surprise for first-year law students is that this contrast between intentional and careless wrongdoing is instantiated in the law of torts as a matter of general empirical truth, but it is repudiated in the legal basis of important intentional tort liabilities. Important tort liabilities are strict in the sense that they may be committed by intentional acts that are innocent, morally speaking. Core intentional torts (batteries, trespasses, and conversions) can be committed without intending *either the wrongs or the harms* being committed. The intent required to commit them need reach only as far as the act that impermissibly crosses a protected boundary and no further. To commit the tort of trespass, you need to intend to enter property that, in fact, belongs to someone else, but you do not need to intend either the wrong of entering without permission or any harm to the property. To commit the tort of battery, you need to intend to touch someone else in a way that is either harmful or offensive—and not to have permission to do so—but you do not need either to intend to touch without permission or to do any harm.

This divergence between general empirical truth and legal basis of liability is the source of pervasive misunderstanding of both important intentional torts and of tort law more generally. The assumption that the familiar tripartite division of torts into intentional, negligent, and strict domains tracks distinctive bases of responsibility leads to the misunderstanding that there are three grounds of tort liability: intention, fault, and strict liability. There are not: the division between fault and strict liability cuts across the intentional torts. Some intentional torts require mental states more culpable than ordinary negligence, whereas others require mental states less culpable than ordinary negligence.³⁴

---

³² Alcorn v. Mitchell, 63 Ill. 553 (1872). The case is the centerpiece of Scott Hershovitz, Tort as a Substitute for Revenge, in Philosophical Foundations of the Law of Torts 86 (John Oberdiek ed., Oxford, 2014).
³³ Hershovitz 2014, *supra* note 32, at 96.
³⁴ Examples of intentional torts whose commission requires heightened culpability include the "actual malice" standard required to defame a public official and the standard of intent applied by

There is no distinctive "intentional" form of tort culpability. The instructive contrast is between kinds of actions, not bases of responsibility. Accidents happen when people lose control over their physical conduct or over an instrumentality subject to their agency. Accidental wrongs involve the realization of *risk* and the misfire of agency. Intentional wrongs involve neither risk nor misfire of agency; either they are committed on purpose, or they are the certain results of conduct under the full control of the wrongdoer.[35]

Unsurprisingly, the mistaken assumption that tort law is partitioned among three bases of liability—intentional, negligent, and strict—impairs recognition of just how strict important intentional torts are. The reason why these intentional tort liabilities are strict is that they protect autonomy rights—powers of control over persons and property, real and moveable. These powers would be seriously compromised by tolerating all unconsented to boundary crossings that were free of fault or innocent in intent.[36] The right at issue is a power to determine who and what does and does not cross the boundary that the power protects. The wrong is the violation of that power of control over some external object, or in the case of battery, control over some subject. People who hold the rights in question are entitled to forbid even reasonable and innocent boundary crossings, and they are presumptively wronged whenever their boundaries are crossed without permission. If reasonable but unconsented to boundary crossings did not give rise to liability, the rights would not be rights to forbid boundary crossings, full stop. They would be rights to forbid only unreasonable boundary crossings, or rights to forbid only boundary crossings committed on purpose, or only intended boundary crossings motivated by ill will. These would be very different—and diminished—rights. The strictness of the liability imposed by these torts is a consequence of the robustness of the rights of control on which they rest.

The term "sovereignty torts" nicely epitomizes this form of tort liability because the wrong proscribed is interference with the right-holder's dominion

---

the tort of intentional infliction of emotional distress. See New York Times Co. v. Sullivan, 376 U.S. 254 (1964); Hustler Magazine v. Falwell, 485 U.S. 46 (1988) (holding that the First and Fourteenth Amendments require plaintiffs bringing claims for intentional infliction of emotional distress to prove "actual malice" in addition to the normal elements of the tort, at least in the context of parody).

[35] For a clear example of how the tort of battery can be committed by an actor whose mental state is properly described as with "substantial certainty" (and not, say, "on purpose"), see Garratt v. Dailey, 279 P.2d 1091 (Wash. 1955).

[36] "[S]trict liability for trespass—to the person or to property—is morally demanded. With respect to battery, for instance, we surely cannot adopt the view that people are at liberty to touch each other without consent, as long as that touching be not angry, hostile, unordinary or even unreasonable. Why should one have to put up with being intentionally touched just because that form of touching is . . . thought reasonable . . . ? As Cardozo . . . said, 'Every human being of adult years and sound mind has a right to determine what shall be done with his own body.'" Allan Beever, The Form of Liability in the Torts of Trespass, 40 Common L. World Rev. 378, 392 (2011) (citing *Schloendorff v. Society of New York Hospital*, 105 N.E. 92, 130 (N.Y. 1914)).

over the object or subject in question. "Stated generally," the California Supreme Court tells us, "'[c]onversion is any act of dominion wrongfully exerted over another person's personal property in denial of or inconsistent with his rights therein.'"[37] If you enter my land or appropriate my pen without my permission, you have violated my right of exclusive control over these objects. You violate my right even if you believe that the land or the pen belong to you, and reasonably so. The wrong consists in the failure to respect the right. Fault is simply irrelevant. If you enter my property under an entirely reasonable and innocent misapprehension of just where the boundary between my property and yours lies, you trespass. You need not even know that you have entered my property without my permission, much less intend *the wrong* of entering my property without permission. You need intend no wrong, and you need do no *harm*.

Indeed, you may trespass on my property even if you are benefiting me. If you trim, top, and clean my trees of bagworms without my permission, you still wrong me by trespassing on my property.[38] So, too, you may trespass if you are innocently and reasonably mistaken about which building you have permission to use as a set for your movie,[39] or if you are simply mistaken about the scope of the permission that I have given you.[40] Similarly, liability for battery may be predicated on innocent intentional touchings,[41] and even on touchings that benefit those who are touched without their consent. If you have permission to operate on my left ear, but instead operate on my right ear, you batter me even if you succeed in curing the diseased condition that was the reason for the operation. And you batter me even if your decision to operate on my other ear was eminently reasonable—if, say, you made the decision after putting me under anesthesia and undertaking exploratory surgery, thereby determining that the disease in fact afflicted my other ear, not the ear on which I had given you permission to operate.[42]

Even with this explanation and justification in hand, we may still find sovereignty-based strict liabilities hard to swallow. They impose extraordinarily stringent duties. To borrow, a vivid turn of phrase of John Gardner's, sovereignty-based strict liabilities put us under "duties to succeed"—duties to respect the relevant right of control or be held liable. They impose duties to do, not duties to try.[43] Duties to succeed—not to try as best one can, or to make a reasonable

---

[37] Zaslow v. Kroenert, 176 P.2d 1, 6 (Cal. 1946) (quoting *Gruber v. Pacific States Savings & Loan Co.*, 88 P.2d 137, 139 (Cal. 1939)).

[38] Longenecker v. Zimmerman, 267 P.2d 543 (Kan. 1954).

[39] Bigelow v. RKO Radio Pictures, 327 U.S. 251 (1946).

[40] Cleveland Park Club v. Perry, 165 A.2d 485, 488 (D.C. 1960).

[41] See, *e.g.*, Vosburg v. Putney, 50 N.W. 403 (Wis. 1891); White v. University of Idaho, 797 P.2d 108 (Idaho 1990).

[42] See, *e.g.*, Mohr v. Williams, 104 N.W. 12 (Minn. 1905). The touching exceeded the scope of the consent given.

[43] The concept of "duties to succeed" is developed in John Gardner, Obligations and Outcomes in the Law of Torts, in Relating to Responsibility: Essays for Tony Honoré on His 80th Birthday 111

effort—seem to violate important and justifiable conditions for holding people responsible. They appear to violate the precept that "ought implies can" and to call for imposing liability on people even when they may rightly claim that they could not reasonably have been expected to succeed in discharging the duties in question. Derek Parfit's distinctions among *belief-relative*, *evidence-relative*, and *fact-relative* standpoints help to frame the issues here a bit more sharply.[44] Innocent batteries, trespasses, and conversions are *wrongs relative to the facts*—relative to the rights that people actually have. If I own a piece of land, or an umbrella, I have the right that others refrain from exercising dominion over those objects without my authorization. Someone who enters my property—or takes my umbrella—without my permission, violates a right that I have. However, if that person does not know that I own the land or the umbrella, the wrong they commit is not a wrong *relative to their beliefs*. They believe themselves to be acting with due regard for everyone's rights. If the person who enters my land or seizes my umbrella could not reasonably determine, from the facts available to them, that I owned those objects, the wrongs they commit are not wrongs relative to the *evidence*. They reasonably believed that they had consent, or that they were on their own property, or that they owned the chattel in question.

The paradox of strict liability intentional wrongs thus surprises us by showing us that a class of wrongs that we thought consisted exclusively of belief-relative wrongs—and thus of wrongs involving the highest degree of culpability in Parfit's pecking order—in fact includes prominent examples of wrongs which are merely fact-relative wrongs. This returns us to the question of whether liability this strict is justifiable and, if so, why. Strict legal liability seems to extend further than fault-based moral responsibility does. It is axiomatic that we are most at fault (most blameworthy) when we commit wrongs that we believe to be wrong, and least at fault when we commit wrongs that in fact are wrongs, even though we did not believe them to be and—on the evidence available to us—should not have determined were wrong. On its face, liability without fault in the standard negligence sense—that is, liability in circumstances where the wrongdoer's conduct is not wrong relative to the reasonable appraisal of the relevant evidence—raises difficult questions of responsibility. Corrective justice and civil recourse theorists, for whom responsibility has a central place, may have particular reason to be uneasy with liability this strict. But we all have reason to pause. Holding people responsible for committing wrongs when they believed their conduct to

---

(Peter Cane & John Gardner eds., Hart, 2001). My colleague, Bob Rasmussen, explains similar contractual duties to students by reminding them of Yoda's reprimand of Luke: "Do or do not. There is no try."

[44] Derek Parfit, Moral Concepts, in On What Matters, Vol. 1, at 150 (Oxford, 2011).

be rightful—and could not determine that it was wrong by reasonable appraisal of the evidence available to them—is troubling.

Nonetheless, tort law has good reason to hold people strictly accountable for violating other people's rights, even when they could not reasonably have been expected to avoid committing those wrongs. First, the rights are worth having. Powers of control over our persons and our property are central both to our independence as persons and to our abilities to work our wills in the world. For these powers to be realized, they must impose correlative duties of respect on others. Doing away with the duties would diminish the rights and thereby diminish the powers that the law puts at our disposal to pursue our ends and purposes. Because the rights are relational, reshaping the wrongs so that innocent intention or reasonable ignorance defeated liability also would shift the burden of bearing "in-fact rights-violations" from those who commit the violations to those whose suffer them.[45] Tort law's preference for imposing responsibility on those who violate other people's rights, however unknowingly or unavoidably, is justified by the ancient maxim that "where one of two persons must suffer a loss, it should be borne by the one who occasioned it."[46] The maxim may be ancient, but it is neither morally primitive nor obsolete. Requiring someone whose rights were violated through neither fault nor action on their part to suffer the unrepaired consequences of that wrong is surely more unjust than holding the party who innocently wronged them responsible for having done so.

When we consider the consequences of imposing liability on instances of, say, innocent trespass, it becomes clear that there is no general cause for alarm. Consider the innocent trespass in *Longenecker v. Zimmerman*—the topping, trimming, and cleaning of the plaintiff's trees without permission. Failing to award nominal damages would be tantamount to denying that the plaintiff, in fact, owned the property. But the plaintiff did own the property, and nominal damages should therefore have been awarded—as they were. Conversely, requiring Longenecker to pay for the benefit that Zimmerman mistakenly conferred on him would be to allow the defendant to put the plaintiff under an obligation to the defendant to pay for value received when that value was thrust

---

[45] Strict liability crimes give rise to substantial rule of law concerns because they raise the prospect of being punished for committing a wrong that no amount of care could have avoided. Whatever the merits of these worries in the criminal context, they have little force in the tort context. Tort law normally addresses a circumstance where a "bad" will land on the plaintiff unless it is shifted to the defendant. Negligence liability leaves unavoidable "bads" on plaintiffs. Strict liability returns them to defendants. There is, therefore, little reason to worry more about strict liability than about negligence. See John Gardner, Some Rule-of-Law Anxieties about Strict Liability in Private Law, in Torts and Other Wrongs, 173–95 (2020).

[46] Jolley v. Powell, 299 So.2d 647, 649 (Fla. Dist. App. 1974). *Cf.* Kremen v. Cohen, 337 F.3d 1024, 1035 (9th Cir. 2003) (Kozinski, J.) (observing, in the context of upholding a claim for conversion, that "there is nothing unfair about holding a company responsible for giving away someone else's property even if it was not at fault").

upon the plaintiff in violation of his rights. Next, imagine different facts. Suppose that Zimmerman—innocently and mistakenly thinking that he owned the trees—had them cut down for sale as lumber. Surely someone who was prepared to cut down trees that they thought they owned—someone who was prepared to damage their own property—cannot complain about paying for that damage when they turn out to have inflicted that damage on someone else. Pursuing this line of thought further, it is equally clear that when someone profits from selling property that they mistakenly think they own, the profits that ought to accrue to the party who does, in fact, own the property. In all these cases, the strictness of sovereignty-based liability leads to correct results.

An additional reason why the strict liability of sovereignty torts is not as harsh as it seems is that the assumed contrast to fault liability is overstated. It is true that negligent wrongs are wrongs relative to the available evidence. Those who commit them should therefore have known that they were not exercising reasonable care. Tort liability for negligence, though, is objective, and famously so. As we have already seen, objective fault liability is itself faulted (sometimes by proponents of "true" strict liability such as Richard Epstein) for holding substandard actors liable notwithstanding the fact that they lack the capacity to appraise the relevant evidence accurately and act accordingly.[47] Liability which is strict relative to the capacities of the persons on whom it is imposed, is imposed on the ground that the defendants acted wrongly by failing to appraise the relevant evidence reasonably. The basic justification for this de facto strictness is the same as the basic justification for the strictness of sovereignty torts. It is unfair to impose the burdens of people's incompetence on those they happen to harm. Even if the incompetent are not to blame for being incompetent, it is more unfair to ask others to bear the burdens of their incompetence than it is to ask the incompetent themselves to bear those burdens. The incompetence, after all, is theirs.

The presence of sovereignty-based wrongs in our law of torts is an important counterexample both to the claim that tort is a law of fault-based wrongs and to the claim that tort is a law of conduct-based wrongs. These wrongs are not mere curiosities, or vestiges of now discredited forms of liability. They are wrongs we can do without only if we are prepared to compromise the reciprocal rights of control over our physical persons and property that they defend. We are deeply attached to having the power to determine who may exert control over our persons and our property. The powers are important components of our legal autonomy. The wrongs that these powers ground are ancient and deeply entrenched because we are committed to the values that they embody.

---

[47] See, *e.g.*, Epstein 1973, *supra* note 8, at 153.

II. Harm-Based Strict Liabilities: Responsibility without Fault

Harm-based strict liabilities are found in intentional nuisance law, in abnormally dangerous activity law, in the conditional privilege of private necessity, and in some parts of product liability law. The modern American law of intentional nuisance may illustrate this form of strict liability most clearly. Contemporary American nuisance law distinguishes between unreasonable conduct and unreasonable harm. The liability that contemporary nuisance law imposes on the infliction of unreasonable harm is strict liability.[48] Negligent conduct, or faulty conduct, is unreasonable conduct: it exposes others to a risk of harm which ought to have been avoided. By contrast, unreasonable harm is harm which should not go unrepaired by the party responsible for its infliction, even though that harm issued from justified (or reasonable) conduct. Unreasonable harm is harm that we cannot justifiably ask the victim to bear. Unreasonable harm should be *repaired* by the party responsible for inflicting it, even though they should not be *faulted* for inflicting the harm in the first place. When we impose liability on the infliction of unreasonable harm, we are imposing a form of liability without fault. Nuisance law imposes liability for the infliction of unreasonable harm when, as in the famous case of *Boomer v. Atlantic Cement Co.*,[49] it holds that damages should be paid for an unreasonable interference with plaintiffs' rights to the reasonable use of their property, even though the conduct responsible for that interference is justified and ought to be continued.

Corrective justice and civil recourse theories favor fault liability, and their conception of a conduct-based wrong is inhospitable to the formal structure of harm-based strict liabilities. When harm issues from an abnormally dangerous activity—and strict liability is imposed on the party engaging in that activity—neither the activity in which the injurer is engaged nor their conduct in going about that activity are declared to be wrong.[50] Consequently, contemporary corrective justice and civil recourse theorists tend either to expel harm-based strict liabilities from the law of torts proper or to recast them as forms of negligence liability. Goldberg and Zipursky pursue the first approach, asserting that it is merely a matter of convention that we house strict liability within the law of torts. Harm-based strict liabilities, they argue, do not involve wrongs and therefore are not really torts. For his part, Jules Coleman assimilates harm-based strict

---

[48] The distinction is drawn, though not quite labeled, in Restatement (Second) of Torts § 826 (1979). Compare subsections (a) and (b). For general discussion of modern intentional nuisance liability as a canonical instance of harm-based strict liability, see Gregory C. Keating, Nuisance as a Strict Liability Wrong, 4(3) J. Tort L. [ii] (2012).

[49] *Boomer*, 257 N.E.2d 870.

[50] Goldberg & Zipursky 2010, *supra* note 25; Goldberg & Zipursky 2016, *supra* note 25.

liabilities to the general form of negligence by asserting that the duty involved is a duty to do no harm, full stop.[51] Ripstein and Weinrib deploy mixes of these two strategies of expulsion and absorption to recast the branch of tort law that covers accidents as wholly fault-based.

Neither the expulsion of harm-based strict liabilities from the law of torts proper nor the reconceptualization of such liabilities as forms of fault liability do justice to harm-based strict liabilities. Formally, the wrong committed in these liabilities is the conditional wrong of harming-without-repairing. Recasting harm-based strict liabilities as negligence ones obliterates this formal difference. Substantively, harm-based strict liabilities are characteristically justified by reasons distinct from those that are characteristically used to justify the imposition of liability for negligence. First, harm-based strict liabilities invoke the support of both commutative and corrective justice. They do corrective justice because they repair harm done and restore plaintiffs to the positions that they would have occupied had they not been harmed. They do commutative justice because they align the burdens and benefits of mutually beneficial but harmful activities fairly. Second, in contrast to negligence liability with its focus on wrongful conduct, strict liabilities focus on the control that the party subject to strict liability has over the harm that they inflict. Whereas negligence imposes responsibility for avoidable harm on the party that should have avoided it, strict liability imposes responsibility for harm which should *not* have been avoided on the party responsible for its imposition.

Boomer is again instructive. The decision in the case revised the normal remedy for the wrong of nuisance in New York, overturning the traditional rule that proof of a substantial nuisance entitled a plaintiff to injunctive relief as a matter of right. *Boomer*'s new rule provided that proof of a nuisance entitled a plaintiff only to damages as a matter of right. Injunctive relief would now be available only on a showing of unreasonable conduct on the part of the defendant. By revising the remedy available as a matter of right in this way, *Boomer* also revised the underlying right. Reasonable conduct resulting in unreasonable interference with another's use and enjoyment of land is wrong only if the party inflicting the interference fails to make reparation for the harm that they do. Reparation transforms unreasonable harm into reasonable harm, and fairly reconciles competing, equal, rights to the use and enjoyment of land. *Boomer* is thus a canonical instance of strict liability for unreasonable harm, as is the distinctive modern

---

[51] Jules Coleman, Facts, Fictions, and the Grounds of Law, in Law and Social Justice 327, 329 (Joseph Keim Campbell et al. eds., MIT, 2005). See also Jules Coleman, The Practice of Principle: In Defence of a Pragmatist Approach to Legal Theory 35 n.19 (Oxford, 2001) ("The concept of a duty in tort law is central both to strict and fault liability. In strict liability, the generic form of the duty is a 'duty not to harm someone,' while in fault, the generic form of a duty is a 'duty not to harm someone negligently or carelessly.'").

American form of liability for intentional nuisance more generally.[52] Other entrenched instantiations include private necessity cases such as *Vincent v. Lake Erie*;[53] liability for abnormally dangerous activities;[54] liability for manufacturing defects in product liability law;[55] and the liability of employers for the torts committed by their employees within the scope of their employment.[56]

When we dig into the details of different harm-based strict liabilities, we find that their grounds are diverse. For instance, the fact that abnormally dangerous activities impose risks that are not reciprocal often plays an important role in justifying the imposition of strict liability on such activities.[57] On other occasions, strict liability for abnormally dangerous activities is justified by appealing to the three core justifications for enterprise liability—fairness in the distribution of burden and benefit, loss-dispersion, and placing responsibility in the hands of the party best able to control the risks of the activity.[58] The vicarious liability of employers for the torts of their employees committed in the course of their employment originated in agency law, but its best contemporary justification may be, as Judge Henry Friendly said, the enterprise liability idea that "a business enterprise cannot justly disclaim responsibility for accidents which may fairly be said to be characteristic of its activities."[59] Strict liability for manufacturing defects in product liability law originated in the warranty idea that products with such defects disappoint reasonable consumer expectations, but when that liability is incorporated into the tort law of products liability, it attracts the justification that manufacturing defects are characteristic of the product manufacturer's activity because the incidence of such defects is determined by manufacturing and quality-control procedures under the manufacturer's control.[60]

For our purposes, the first important point is the common character of the obligation imposed by all these doctrines. That obligation is to undertake an action (e.g., saving your ship from destruction at the hands of a hurricane by bashing

---

[52] Restatement (Second) of Torts § 826(b) (1979).
[53] Vincent v. Lake Erie Transp. Co., 124 N.W. 221 (Minn. 1910).
[54] Restatement (Second) of Torts § 519 (1977); Restatement (Third) of Torts: Physical & Emotional Harm § 20 (2010).
[55] Restatement (Third) of Torts: Products Liability § 2(a) cmt. a (1998).
[56] Restatement (Third) of Agency § 7.07 (2006).
[57] See Rylands v. Fletcher, L.R. 3 H.L. 330 (1868); Francis H. Bohlen, The Rule in Rylands v. Fletcher: Part I, 59 U. Pa. L. Rev. 298 (1911); George P. Fletcher, Fairness and Utility in Tort Theory, 85 Harv. L. Rev. 537 (1972).
[58] See, *e.g.*, *Siegler*, 502 P.2d at 1188 (Rosellini J., concurring). For discussion of enterprise liability's basic rationales, see Chapter Seven, *infra*, pp. 278–82.
[59] Ira S. Bushey & Sons, Inc. v. United States, 398 F.2d 167, 171 (2d Cir. 1968).
[60] For the first point, see Barker v. Lull Engineering Co., 573 P.2d 443, 454 (Cal. 1978) (explaining that "a product may be found defective in design if the plaintiff demonstrates that the product failed to perform as safely as an ordinary consumer would expect when used in an intended or reasonably foreseeable manner. This initial standard, somewhat analogous to the Uniform Commercial Code's warranty of fitness and merchantability . . . reflects the warranty heritage upon which California product liability doctrine in part rests.").

the dock to which it is moored), or conduct an activity (e.g., operating a business firm), only on the condition that you will repair any physical harm for which your action or activity is responsible, even though there is no fault in your infliction of the harm itself. The reciprocal right is a right to have any physical harm inflicted upon you repaired by the party responsible for its infliction. All these harm-based liabilities are strict in that they impose liability on conduct which is not wrongful. Harm-based strict liability imposes liability on conduct which is justified on inflictions of harm which are reasonable. Negligence liability, by contrast, predicates liability on conduct which is unjustified—on conduct which is unreasonable because it does not show due regard for the property and physical integrity of those that it harms. A second important point is closely connected to this first one. Negligence liability imposes responsibility when and because it determines that the harm inflicted should have been avoided. Harm-based strict liabilities tend to impose responsibility when and because the party who inflicts the harm is in the best position to minimize the harm that they inflict.

Like sovereignty-based strict liabilities, harm-based ones also put pressure on the corrective justice and civil recourse claim that tort is a law solely of conduct-based wrongs, but the pressure they place is different. With sovereignty-based strict liabilities, the requirements of the right determine when conduct is tortious. Conduct figures more centrally in harm-based strict liabilities, but the conduct that counts as tortious does not match the concept of a conduct-based wrong as corrective justice and civil recourse theorists articulate that concept. To understand why, we need to distinguish between criticizing an actor's primary, risk-imposing conduct and their secondary conduct. Secondary conduct has to do not with whether an actor imposes or avoids inflicting an injury but with responding to harm whose infliction should not be avoided.[61] Conduct-based wrongs as corrective justice and civil recourse theorists understand them involve wrongful primary conduct—conduct which is wrongful because it inflicted injury that should not have been inflicted. The defendant should not have conducted themselves as they did, and the injury that they inflicted should never have been suffered.[62] Harm-based strict liability, by contrast, predicates responsibility on the judgment that the defendant's injury-inflicting conduct was reasonable, but their failure to repair the injury inflicted was unreasonable. The conduct criticized is *secondary, not primary*. The law lodges its criticism against harming justifiably-without-repairing. The wrong in harm-based strict liability

---

[61] I owe this term to Lewis Sargentich. Robert Keeton's contrast between "fault" and "conditional fault" also describes the distinction drawn in the text. See Robert E. Keeton, Conditional Fault in the Law of Torts, 72 Harv. L. Rev. 401 (1959).

[62] The fundamental question in negligence law is whether conduct falls below "a standard established by the law for the protection of others against unreasonable harm." Negligence law fixes that standard by the *conduct* of a "reasonable [person] under like circumstances." Restatement (Second) of Torts §§ 282, 283 (1965).

is a conditional one. It governs a domain within which the infliction of harm is not wrong as long as the conduct inflicting injury is justified or reasonable and reparation is made for the harm done.

Conditional privilege in the law of private necessity—the doctrine of *Vincent v. Lake Erie*[63]—clearly illustrates the distinction between primary and secondary criticisms of conduct. The defendant shipowner's conduct in lashing his ship to, and damaging, the plaintiff's dock was reasonable not unreasonable, right not wrong. The shipowner was justified in lashing his ship to the dock to save his ship from destruction at the hands of the storm, even if using the dock involved damaging the dock. The defendant's privilege[64] to trespass was *not* conditioned on doing no harm to the dock, a requirement which would have been impossible to meet in the circumstances. The defendant's privilege *was* conditioned on making reparation for any harm done to the dock—even though that harm was done rightly and not wrongly. The wrong in *Vincent* lay not in the defendant's doing damage to the dock but in the defendant's failure to step forward in the aftermath of the storm and make good the damage he had done to the dock in order to save his ship. The defendant's conduct was wrongful (or unreasonable) only insofar as the defendant failed to step forward and volunteer to repair the damage done by his (reasonable) conduct. *Vincent*'s strict liability is thus liability for unreasonable harm, not liability for unreasonable conduct. It is unfair for the shipowner to save his ship by damaging the dock and then refusing to repair the damage to the dock. The benefit of doing that damage is borne by the shipowner, and the burden is borne by the dock owner. Fairness prescribes proportionality of benefit and burden. Making reparation for the harm done prevents the injustice of shifting the cost of the ship's salvation from the shipowner who profits from it onto the dock owner who suffers from it. At trial, the imposition of liability on the shipowner for failing to make such reparation rights the wrong of shifting the

---

[63] *Vincent*, 124 N.W. 221.

[64] Taxonomically, the characterization of this privilege is something of tempest in a teapot, at least for those attracted to Hohfeld's typology of rights. In Hohfeldian terms, the ship's privilege to enter is a right: the ship is entitled to enter, and the dock owner is under a duty not to resist. See Francis H. Bohlen, Incomplete Privilege to Inflict Intentional Invasions of Interests of Property and Personality, 39 Harv. L. Rev. 307 (1926). This privilege is also a power in Hohfeld's terms, because it enables the shipowner to alter his relations with the dock owner without the dock owner's permission, as long as the ship enters the dock owner's property for certain purposes (to save his own property), and conducts himself in certain ways (only does what is necessary to save his own property). Along with Keeton 1959, *supra* note 61, Bohlen's article is a classic statement of the idea of strict liability I am developing in this chapter. Similar positions have also been reached by others. See, *e.g.*, Howard Klepper, Torts of Necessity: A Moral Theory of Compensation, 9 Law & Phil. 223, 239 (1990) ("The need to compensate in the necessity cases is best explained by the wrongfulness of knowingly benefitting oneself by transferring a loss or risk of loss to another, however reasonably, and then letting the loss like with one's unwitting benefactor. Such a transfer of the loss or risk is wrongful in that it does not allow the innocent party to freely choose the risks she is willing to undertake.").

cost of the ship's salvation onto the dock owner whose property is the instrument of that salvation.[65]

Structurally, strict liability in tort resembles eminent domain in public law. Eminent domain doctrine holds that it is permissible for the government to take property for public use only if the government pays just compensation to those whose property it takes. This is a two-part criterion. First, the taking must be justified—it must, that is, be for a public use. Second, compensation must be paid for the property taken. Harm-based strict liability in tort has a parallel structure.[66] In practice, no doubt, many harms covered by harm-based strict liabilities are negligently inflicted, but the distinctiveness of strict liability lies in its extension of liability to harm which is justifiably inflicted. Strict liability presumes that the harms that are its special focus result from reasonable conduct. Harm-based strict liability in tort also parallels eminent domain doctrine in prescribing that the costs of necessary or justified harms should be borne by those who benefit from their infliction, and not by those whose misfortune it is to find themselves in the path of someone else's pursuit of their own benefit, however reasonable that pursuit may be.

Harm-based strict liability thus involves both fairness and rights. To say that it is unfair for an injurer to thrust the cost of its activities onto a victim is not the same as saying that imposing that cost violates the victim's rights. Suppose, for example, that you and I own neighboring hotels in some sunny southern location and that I decide to increase the height of my hotel. During the winter tourist season—when tourists flock to both of our hotels in search of sunshine and warm weather—from two in the afternoon onward, the addition to my hotel will cast a shadow over the previously sunny pool of your hotel. Increasing the height of my hotel will therefore injure you; you will suffer economic losses. It may be unfair of me to inflict these losses on you. Perhaps the economic gains to me from a taller hotel will be less than the economic losses to you. Perhaps you had come to rely on the sunniness of your pool in marketing your hotel to guests. With some justification, you expected your pool's present, sunny, situation to persist, even though not enough time had passed to give you a legal right (by prescription) to the sunlight in which the pool basks. I am well aware of the situation—and of your expectation—and go ahead and increase the height of my hotel anyway. The cost that I am imposing on you is a cost of my activity, of the

---

[65] *Vincent* is thus a clear counterexample to the claims of some prominent tort scholars that strict liability involves a duty not to do harm. Coleman and Gardner hold views of this kind. See Coleman 2001, *supra* note 51; Gardner 2001, *supra* note 43.

[66] This "private eminent domain" conception of strict liability may make its first appearance in American tort theory in the writings (some famous and some obscure) of Oliver Wendell Holmes. These writings are cited and discussed in Thomas C. Grey, Accidental Torts, 54 Vand. L. Rev. 1225 (2001), and at greater length in his unpublished manuscript, Holmes on Torts (on file with author). Two other classic statements are Bohlen 1926, *supra* note 64, and Keeton 1959, *supra* note 61.

expansion of my hotel. Because, however, you have "no legal right to the free flow of light and air from the adjoining land," the injury that you suffer is *damnum absque injuria*—a loss that does not violate a legal right.[67] Legally, I have done you no wrong.[68]

The facts of the *Fontainebleau* hotel case differ from those of *Vincent* in an essential way. The injured party in *Vincent* (the dock owner) has a claim of legal right. In *Vincent*, it is not only unfair for the shipowner to shift the cost of saving its ship onto the dock owner, this action also violates the dock owner's property rights. In *Vincent*, the shipowner's right to preserve its property conflicts both with the dock owner's right to exclude others from occupying and using its property without its permission and with the dock owner's right that others do not damage its property. We must reconcile competing claims of right, and that brings fairness into play. Fairness requires that competing claims "be satisfied in proportion to their strength."[69] In the circumstances of *Vincent*, the dock owner's right to exclude the ship must yield to the dire emergency—the "necessity"—in which the ship found itself.[70] But there is no reason why the dock owner's right to the integrity of its property should give way once and for all. It must yield to the necessity of saving the ship, but it need not yield any further than that necessity requires. Saving the ship requires damaging the dock, but it does not require that the cost of saving the ship be shifted onto the owner of the dock instead of being borne by the shipowner who profits from inflicting the damage. The fair reconciliation of these competing rights requires that burden follow benefit and that property rights yield no more than necessity requires. The shipowner should therefore make reparation for the damage it inflicts on the dock in order to save its ship.

Strict liability is thus justified both by a principle of fairness—that those who benefit from inflicting harm on others should shoulder the cost of that harm—*and* by the further claim that the harm done is the invasion of a right so that failure to make reparation for harm done would be a wrong. Harm-based strict liability asserts that injurers subject to its strictures do wrong when they fail to step forward and repair harm rightly inflicted, and it makes this assertion because leaving the cost of the harm on the victim who suffers it shows insufficient respect for the victim's rights. In the case of both nuisance and conditional privilege to trespass, the relevant rights are property rights. In other cases,—including

---

[67] These are the facts, and the ruling, of Fontainebleau Hotel Corp. v. Forty-Five Twenty-Five, Inc., 114 So.2d 357, 359 (Fla. 3d Dist. App. 1959). Bryant v. Lefever, 4 C.P.D. 172 (1878–79), reaches the same conclusion about Lefever obstructing the free passage of air through the chimney of his neighbor's house. The obstruction was the result of Lefever's rebuilding of his house.
[68] *Id.*
[69] John Broome, Fairness, 91 Proc. Aristotelian Soc'y 87, 96 (1990–1991) (emphasis omitted).
[70] "The situation was one in which the ordinary rules regulating property rights were suspended by forces beyond human control." *Vincent*, 124 N.W. at 221.

many accidental harms arising out of abnormally dangerous activities and the use of defective products—the relevant rights are rights to the physical integrity of one's person.

The appeal to rights in this account of harm-based strict liabilities may seem to beg the question that it claims to answer. Saying that the plaintiff in *Vincent* has a right that the defendant violated—whereas the plaintiff in *Fontainebleau* did not— may describe the difference between the two cases, but it does not justify the difference that it describes. Why is it that the hotel in *Fontainebleau* did not have a right to unobstructed sunlight, whereas the plaintiff in *Vincent* did have a right that its dock not be damaged? The answer sufficient to settle the cases that come before courts is that this just is what the relevant law provides. For our purposes, the deeper and more important answer is the point that we have been developing throughout this book. Physical harms have special negative moral significance because serious physical harms impair basic powers of agency. We are therefore subject to stringent obligations to avoid inflicting harm and to repair harm when its infliction cannot be avoided. Losses do not have this special negative moral significance, because losses do not generally leave their victims in conditions where their powers of agency are impaired.[71] The right at work in *Vincent* is a right that obligates others not to inflict physical harm on your property, whereas the injury whose infliction the *Fontainebleau* court licenses is an economic loss. Because the law classifies the damage to the dock in *Vincent* as physical harm, that damage brings legal rights into play. Because the law classifies the injury suffered in *Fontainebleau* as economic loss, that injury does not bring legal rights into play. Tort law generally regards economic losses as *damnum absque injuria*.

Even though rights violations are a necessary element of harm-based strict liabilities, the important role that fairness plays in the justification of these liabilities is a source of unease for some tort scholars. Theorists of wrongs, in both crime and tort, often believe that ideas of fairness cannot capture the moral force of wrongs. This belief is correct with respect to some wrongs, but it is mistaken when it is directed against the account just presented of the moral basis of harm-based strict liability. The argument that unfairness does not capture the force of canonical wrongs is more prominent in criminal than tort scholarship, but it is deployed in both domains. Modern instances of the argument are particularly prominent in responses to theories asserting that the obligation to obey the law is rooted in a principle of fairness or fair play.[72] John Rawls explained the "main idea" of the "fair play" view as follows:

---

[71] See Chapter Five.
[72] The original and most important statements of the view are H.L.A. Hart, Are There Any Natural Rights?, 64 Phil. Rev. 175 (1955); and John Rawls, Legal Obligation and the Duty of Fair Play, in Law and Philosophy 3 (Sidney Hook ed., NYU, 1964) (reprinted in John Rawls, Collected Papers 117–29

Suppose there is a mutually beneficial and just scheme of cooperation, and that the advantages it yields can only be obtained if everyone, or nearly everyone, cooperates. Suppose further that cooperation requires a certain sacrifice from each person, or at least involves a restriction of his liberty. Suppose finally that the benefits produced by cooperation are, up to a certain point, free: that is, the scheme of cooperation is unstable in the sense that if any one person knows that all (or nearly all) of the others will continue to do their part, he will still be able to share a gain from the scheme even if he does not do his part. Under these conditions a person who has accepted the benefits of the scheme is bound by a duty of fair play to do his part and not to take advantage of the free benefit by not cooperating. The reason one must abstain from this attempt is that the existence of the benefit is the result of everyone's effort, and prior to some understanding as to how it is to be shared, if it can be shared at all, it belongs in fairness to no one.[73]

In an influential application of this kind of view to criminal punishment, Herbert Morris argued that criminal wrongdoers were free riders. When people commit crimes, they are failing to abide by moral constraints that others accept. Criminals enjoy the benefits that come from other people's acceptance of the constraints imposed by the criminal law while shirking the burdens imposed by those constraints. By inflicting pain on criminals equal to the benefits they wrongly appropriate to themselves, retributive punishment, Morris argued, is a way of evening the score. Retributive punishment deprives criminals of the benefits they wrongly appropriate through their free-riding.[74]

Critics of this account of the moral wrongness of criminal conduct object that it "essentially makes retributive justice a species of distributive justice." Doing so gets the basis of retributive justice very wrong, because it misrepresents the moral significance of core criminal wrongs:

> [The] basic difficulty with this theory is its assumption that the fundamental reason why we censure and punish *all* wrongdoers is because they are free riders. This assumption makes sense only if we believe that constraining ourselves so that we do not rape or murder or steal imposes a *cost* upon us. Yet that idea makes sense only if raping, murdering, and stealing are viewed by us as desirable and attractive (either intrinsically, or in view of the ends such actions achieve), and therefore individually rational but collectively irrational actions

---

(Samuel Freeman ed., Harvard, 1999)). See also Richard J. Arneson, The Principle of Fairness and Free-Rider Problems, 92 Ethics 616 (1982).

[73] Rawls 1999, *supra* note 72, at 122.
[74] Herbert Morris, Persons and Punishment, 52 Monist 475 (1968).

(for example, because such behavior destabilizes the community or damages the economy). However, surely this is exactly what most of us *do not* think about crime. Very few of us understand our refusal to murder or assault our fellows as imposing a cost upon ourselves, and very few of us resent murderers, muggers, or rapists because they have unfairly enjoyed benefits coveted by the rest of us. To make retributive justice a species of distributive justice is to claim that the wrongfulness of criminals' behavior consists in the fact that they have behaved *unfairly*. Although there are a few wrongs that we might be prepared to analyze in this way (for example, when people park for free in "no parking zones" while the rest of us pay a fortune to park in the local garage), it seems absurd to say that this is what is wrong with wrongdoers who murder, assault, or abuse others. (Indeed, it seems particularly indecent to analyze child abuse or rape along these lines.)[75]

The objection is well taken. However attractive or unattractive one finds retribution, it is properly understood as a response to the perceived wrongfulness of the actions to which it responds, not to their unfairness. The circumstance where the unfairness of the action is what makes it a wrong is a special one.

Theories of tort law that put the idea that torts are wrongs at their center implicitly accept a parallel point. In general, the civil wrongs that concern tort law are no more distributive injustices, or unfair actions, than criminal wrongs are. Tortious wrongs are violations of rights. Just as the intrinsic wrongness of crimes requires the response of retribution so, too, the intrinsic wrongness of torts requires that we do corrective justice. From this perspective, the dependence of harm-based strict liabilities on a principle of fairness is further evidence that harm-based strict liabilities are not really a form of tortious wrong in good standing. This objection gets most wrongs right; but it gets harm-based strict liability wrongs wrong. Most wrongs are not, in fact, distributive injustices, though some are. Parking illegally, evading taxes, cheating in sports and games, and using more than your fair share of water during a drought are all wrongs that can be described as distributive injustices. Harm-based strict liability wrongs are members of this exceptional subclass of wrongs because their distinctiveness lies in their imposition of liability on unavoidable harm. They impose liability on harm whose infliction is regrettable but justifiable. The infliction of such harm is not intrinsically wrong in the way that murder or rape are.

Recall *Boomer*. The *Boomer* court refused to enjoin Atlantic Cement from operating its cement plant, even though the plant's operation interfered with the plaintiffs' reasonable use and enjoyment of their property in a way which could

---

[75] Jean Hampton, Correcting Harms versus Righting Wrongs: The Goal of Retribution, 39 UCLA L. Rev. 1659, 1660–61 (1992) (emphasis in original).

only be averted by shutting down the plant. The court refused the injunction because Atlantic Cement was justified in operating its plant notwithstanding the pollution, and even though that pollution interfered with plaintiffs' use and enjoyment of their land (and probably their health, too). The harm inflicted on the plaintiffs was regrettable, but unavoidable. Atlantic Cement had taken "every available and possible precaution to protect the plaintiffs from dust" but "nevertheless . . . created a nuisance insofar as the lands of the plaintiffs are concerned."[76] Once it took all possible precautions to reduce the plant's pollution, it was not wrong for the defendant to operate its cement plant; the productive value of the plant is something we are not prepared to forgo even though it does serious harm. We are not collectively prepared to live without cement, and we must therefore live with the unavoidable harms involved in its manufacture.

The wrong involved in *Boomer* is, therefore, in Hampton's terms, a "distributive" one. The wrong is not "harming unjustifiably" but "harming-justifiably-but-not-repairing-harm-justifiably-inflicted." That wrong is a matter of unfairness. The infliction of the harm is bad for those on whom it is inflicted; it is to be regretted even when it is not to be avoided. Even so, the infliction of the harm is not a wrong. But it is wrong—not just regrettable—for those who inflict the harm to appropriate the benefits of doing so to themselves, while leaving those harmed to cope with the harm as best they can. It is wrong because it is unfair, and this kind of unfairness is exploitative. It sacrifices some to the private good of others. Harm-based strict liability therefore rectifies a wrong that can be described as a distributive injustice. When that unfair distribution goes unrectified, those who inflict the harm exploit those on whom they inflict it. Exploitation is surely a wrong to those who are exploited.

III. Correcting Corrective Justice Theory

Harm-based strict liabilities have a significant place in our law of torts. This is so even though strict liability has ebbed—and negligence liability has flowed—over the course of the past thirty-five years. Moreover, strict liability has always had a place in our law of torts; the ebb and flow of tort's two competing principles of responsibility is an enduring and important part of the history of the field. Consequently, we may reasonably ask that theories of tort law be able to explain and justify the existence of both strict liability and negligence. Contemporary corrective justice and civil recourse theories of tort are now flunking this test. In a variety of ways, they cast strict liabilities out of the law of torts. For one thing, their apparently innocuous conception of torts as conduct-based wrongs implies

---

[76] *Boomer*, 287 N.Y.S.2d at 114.

that strict liability wrongs are not really tortious wrongs.[77] Corrective justice and civil recourse theories favor a relatively narrow construction of conduct-based wrongs, and that narrow construction is inhospitable to harm-based strict liabilities. Both views prefer fault to strict liability, and both views take negligence to be a representative conduct-based wrong. Someone is negligent when their *primary* conduct is insufficiently careful, when they impose more risk than they should impose.

Harm-based strict liability criticizes conduct, but in a different way. The conduct that it criticizes as wrongful is *secondary*, not primary. The primary conduct in *Vincent*—lashing the ship to the dock and damaging the dock—was not wrongful. The wrongful conduct was the failure to repair the damage done. Harm-based strict liability is not predicated on the assertion that the defendant should have conducted themselves differently and avoided harming the plaintiff. It asserts that defendants should not harm-without-repairing. If the concept of a conduct-based wrong were understood broadly enough, it would encompass harm-based strict liabilities. Such liabilities attach to forms of conduct—to creating a nuisance; to engaging in an abnormally dangerous activity; to selling a product; and to increasing the incidence of various kinds of tortious wrongs committed by employees. This broad sense of wrongful conduct is not what corrective justice and civil recourse theorists have in mind when they speak of conduct-based wrongs.[78]

There are variations among the views of leading corrective justice and civil recourse theorists, but they all tend to disfavor strict liability and to push it either to the margins of the field or out of the field entirely. Goldberg and Zipursky, for example, think that abnormally dangerous activity liability does not belong in the law of torts.[79] Jules Coleman marginalizes and minimizes strict liability in several ways. First, Coleman conceives of substantial portions of strict liability as lying outside the core of tort that corrective justice succeeds in explaining. He notes that corrective-justice theory "does not explain" various features of tort law, "for example, vicarious liability or perhaps product liability."[80] Coleman excludes product liability from the core of tort and tentatively suggests that it should be understood not in terms of corrective justice but in terms of rational bargaining.[81] Both the concession and the exclusion are troubling. A theory of

---

[77] See, *e.g.*, Jules Coleman, The Practice of Corrective Justice, in Philosophical Foundations of Tort Law 53, 56–57 (David G. Owen ed., Oxford, 1995); Goldberg & Zipursky 2016, *supra* note 25.

[78] The identification of tort with conduct-based wrongs is not exclusive to Coleman or Goldberg & Zipursky. Ernest Weinrib holds the same kind of view, a fact vividly illustrated by his criticisms of strict liability as a norm of conduct that condemns "any penetration of the plaintiff's space." Ernest J. Weinrib, The Idea of Private Law 177 (Oxford, 1995).

[79] See Goldberg & Zipursky 2010, *supra* note 25; Goldberg & Zipursky 2016, *supra* note 25.

[80] Coleman 2001, *supra* note 51, at 36.

[81] Jules Coleman, Risks and Wrongs 417–29 (Oxford, rev. ed., 2002).

tort that succeeds in explaining its domains of strict liability is interpretively superior to a theory that cannot. Coleman cannot. The absorption of product liability into tort, moreover, is the most important development in twentieth-century tort law. An adequate theory of tort ought to be able to recognize and explain the most important development in the field over the course of the past hundred years.

Coleman's views on the nature of strict liability have changed over time as he has struggled to shoehorn the liability into his template of conduct-based wrongs. His most recent discussion, though, advances the argument that strict liability involves a "duty not to harm." In contradistinction to what he calls "the standard view," Coleman's view models strict liability on negligence liability. On the standard view, negligence liability is—and strict liability is not—based on the failure to conform one's conduct to a norm of obligatory conduct. On Coleman's contrary view, both strict liability and negligence are conduct-based norms: both involve breaches of duty. The only difference is the content of the duty. Whereas negligence liability imposes a duty to exercise reasonable care to avoid inflicting physical harm on others, strict liability imposes a duty not to harm others, full stop.

> [T]he relevant concept in the law of torts is *wrong*.... A wrong is a breach of a duty. Strict and fault liability are different ways of articulating the content of one's duty to others....
>
> In torts, blasting is governed by strict liability and motoring by fault liability. The way to understand the difference is as follows. In the case of motoring, my duty of care is a duty to exercise reasonable care; it is a duty not to harm you through carelessness, recklessness or intention.... In the case of blasting, however, the law imposes on me the duty-not-to-harm-you. The way I am to take your interests into account is to make sure that I don't harm you by blasting.[82]

When strict liability is understood to impose a "duty-not-to-harm," it conforms to Coleman's conception of torts as conduct-based wrongs. Whereas Goldberg and Zipursky want to expel strict liability for abnormally dangerous activities such as blasting from tort—on the ground that such liability is not liability for a conduct-based wrong—Coleman wants to rehabilitate such harm-based strict liabilities by recasting them in the mold of negligence liability.

Unfortunately, this recasting fundamentally distorts harm-based strict liability. Recall what we have just seen. Structurally speaking, harm-based strict

---

[82] Jules Coleman, Facts, Fictions, and the Grounds of Law, in Law and Social Justice 327, 329 (Joseph Keim Campbell et al. eds., MIT, 2005); Coleman 2001, *supra* note 51, at 35 n.19; see also the discussion in the text accompanying note 51, *supra*.

liability in tort resembles the public law of eminent domain, not negligence liability.[83] Indeed, strict liability *competes* with fault liability because it imposes liability on *reasonable* conduct. Eminent domain law holds that it is permissible for the government to take property for public use only if the government pays just compensation to those whose property it takes. Strict liability makes a parallel assertion that the costs of the justified harms to which it applies should be borne by those who benefit from their infliction, not by those whose misfortune it is to find themselves in the path of the justified infliction of harm. Supposing that harm-based strict liabilities impose a duty not to harm also impairs our understanding of negligence liability. The stringency of negligence obligations of care increases with—and is calibrated to—the seriousness of the risk at issue. Courts often decline to impose strict liability precisely because they perceive the law's default norm of negligence liability as an adequate alternative.[84] The availability of negligence liability—and its capacity to calibrate the care owed to the seriousness of the harm threatened—make an *independent strict duty not to harm* superfluous. Negligence enables courts to adjust the care due so that it is commensurate with the harm threatened. The ground of strict liability is simply different from the ground of fault liability. Strict liability asserts that when harm is done even though all reasonable precautions have been taken, it is unfair to leave the cost of that harm on the plaintiff. The injurer ought to take the bitter with the sweet.

The distinguishing features of strict liability wrongs are thus obscured and distorted by Coleman's reconstructions of them. Such wrongs are not based on wrongful primary conduct of the sort contemplated by Coleman. Tort law's strict liabilities are predicated either on violations of autonomy rights, or on secondary failings of conduct—on conditional, not primary, fault.[85]

IV. Indeterminacy and Morality in Harm-Based Strict Liability

This chapter has argued that harm-based strict liabilities differ from negligence-based ones in that strict liability wrongs involve justified conduct inflicting harm, whereas negligence-based wrongs involve conduct that is objectively unjustified. And it has argued that harm-based strict liability wrongs involve both

---

[83] See *supra* note 66 and accompanying text.
[84] See, *e.g.*, Foster v. City of Keyser, 501 S.E.2d 165, 175 (W. Va. 1997). In *Foster*, the West Virginia Supreme Court of Appeals reversed the circuit court's imposition of strict liability on a natural gas company for an explosion caused by the escape of gas from one of its transmission lines because "other principles of law—a high standard of care and *res ipsa loquitur*—can sufficiently address the concerns that argue for strict liability in gas transmission line leak/explosion cases."
[85] See Keeton 1959, *supra* note 61.

a wrong—that is, the violation of a right—and unfairness in failing to bear the cost of repairing harm reasonably inflicted. But the chapter has not explained just when a harm-based strict liability wrong is committed. There is a special problem here, arising from the fact that the obligation to repair the harm is part of the primary norm governing the conduct in question. Harm-based strict liabilities are the only primary obligations in tort that are, in part, corrective. The wrong that they condemn bears a close resemblance to the wrong committed in cases of unjust enrichment. In unjust enrichment, the wrong is the retention of a benefit whose retention will unfairly enrich the party retaining it at the expense of the party to whom the benefit should be returned. Disgorging the benefit rights the wrong. In harm-based strict liabilities, the wrong lies in reasonably inflicting harm on another but unreasonably failing to make reparation for the harm inflicted. The wrong occurs when an actor—having inflicted harm—fails to discharge its primary obligation to make reparation for that harm. A lawsuit based on a strict liability harm therefore enforces a preexisting duty of repair just as a negligence suit does, albeit a different preexisting duty of repair.

On this account, harm-based strict liabilities suffer from a distinctive indeterminacy: it is difficult to say exactly when they are committed.[86] When, exactly, should Lake Erie Transportation Co. have compensated Vincent for the damage done to its dock? A legislature codifying the rule of the case could answer that question by adopting a precise time requirement; the common law implicitly invokes the somewhat vague idea that compensation should be made "within a reasonable time." This indeterminacy is an imperfection in the law, but not a fatal one. Comparable flaws appear elsewhere in tort law. Negligence law, for instance, has great difficulty specifying coordinate precautions. In the context of automobile accidents, negligence law can draw on statutes and customs to do that work. When there are no statutes or customs to fall back on, negligence law must muddle through as best it can. In the case of tortious harm caused by a toxin, it is usually impossible to say just when the harm was inflicted. Lung cancer, for instance, cannot be traced to the smoking of any one cigarette, and mesothelioma cannot be traced to a decisive episode of exposure to asbestos. The law must accept that indeterminacy and identify harm and causation as best it can. The moment when compensation must be paid to prevent committing the conditional wrong of harming-without-repairing is similarly uncertain, and here, too, tort law must muddle through.

This indeterminacy may not be a significant impediment to the self-application of harm-based strict liabilities. Ordinarily, it is clear enough when a harm has occurred. The principal obstacle to making reparation for that harm may not be indeterminacy as to when, exactly, the obligation to make such

---

[86] John Goldberg has expressed this worry to me on several occasions.

reparation ripens but the fact that the obligation can only be performed through the cooperative efforts of both the injurer and the victim. They must agree on the reparation required. Neither inflicting a serious harm on someone else nor suffering a harm at someone else's hands are promising conditions for stimulating subsequent cooperation between those involved. It is not, therefore, terribly surprising that the parties to strict liability wrongs (and other tortious wrongs, too) cannot always manage to settle matters by themselves. When such settlement is not forthcoming, adjudication is required for the defendant to perform its obligation.[87] Notwithstanding the possibility that either indeterminacy concerning just when the obligation of reparation ripens—or a breakdown in the cooperation required for the defendant to discharge that obligation—will prevent the defendant from discharging its obligation of reparation, it is a mistake to say that a court order requiring the payment of damages in a case of harm-based strict liability prevents the commission of what would *otherwise be* a wrong.[88] A court's imposition of liability and its award of damages to the plaintiff rectify a wrong which has already been committed. The ruling in *Vincent*, for instance, implies that—at some prior moment in time—Lake Erie Transportation Co. should have owned up to its responsibility for the damage that it inflicted on the dock to save its ship and compensated Vincent appropriately for that damage. Prompt payment by the party inflicting the harm is what prevents commission of the wrong, because it constitutes compliance with the primary norm of responsibility.

This account of the morality of harm-based strict liability wrongs makes strict liability corrective in a fundamental way: it undoes interactions in which one person profits through reasonably harming someone else. Ironically, given the general inhospitality of corrective justice theorists to strict liability, then, harm-based strict liability is the only form of liability in tort that requires corrective primary conduct. Corrective justice is transaction centered; it is, as Aristotle said, "justice as rectification." Corrective justice is justice between parties to a wrong. The morality of harm-based strict liabilities is, however, not fully captured by conceiving of them in terms of corrective justice. The liability imposed by harm-based strict liabilities is also justified in part by an idea of fairness that goes beyond corrective justice. One way to understand this additional dimension is in terms of distributive justice. Harm-based strict liabilities rectify injustices in the distribution of harm. There is nothing wrong with this way of explaining

---

[87] See Sandy Steel & Robert Stevens, The Secondary Legal Duty to Pay Damages, 136 L.Q.R. 283, 287 (2020) (discussing the necessity of cooperation in the case of the secondary duty to pay damages that arises, say, upon the commission of a negligent wrong).

[88] The law of unjust enrichment has a structure similar to harm-based strict liabilities except that it is concerned with gains not losses. Gardner can be read to say that the remedy of disgorgement ordered by a court *prevents* the commission of the wrong of unjust enrichment rather than rectifying a wrong (of unjust enrichment) which has already been committed. Gardner 2011, *supra* note 23, at 46. I am not so sure that Gardner is right about this, but my concern here is with strict liability in tort.

the matter, but distributive justice is often understood to have properties which are missing from the circumstance addressed by harm-based strict liabilities. Distributive justice is often thought to be, in its core incarnation, society-wide. And it is thought to be something done by the state, not a matter of obligations running among persons in civil society. Tort obligations are relational in the sense that they are owed by some people directly to other people. Even when distributive justice is not society-wide, duties to do distributive justice are usually duties to uphold some institution which institutes such justice—to abide by the restrictions on water usage imposed by a locality in the face of a drought, for instance, so as not to consume more than one's fair share of a scarce resource. The further dimension of harm-based strict liability may therefore be captured better by invoking the ancient but little-used concept "commutative justice."

Harm-based strict liabilities are corrective insofar as they undo wrongs whose essence lies in benefiting through harming a particular person and thereby *benefiting at that person's expense*. But harm-based strict liabilities are also commutative; they involve the proportional alignment of burden and benefit across a plurality of persons. Commutative justice is, for Aristotle, distinct both from corrective justice and distributive justice.[89] Commutative justice distributes burden in accordance with benefit. Like corrective justice—and unlike distributive justice as Aristotle understands it—commutative justice is concerned with conduct, with what has been done, with who has suffered, and with who has benefited. Unlike corrective justice, however, commutative justice does not just seek solely to right a wrong. It seeks to bring into existence a state of the world in which burdens and benefits are properly aligned.

The commutative aspect of harm-based strict liabilities is most vividly present in enterprise liability, the subject of the next chapter.

---

[89] Aristotle, Nicomachean Ethics, Book V, Ch. 5 (David Ross trans., Oxford, 1980). The appropriation of the term "commutative justice" to defend forms of non-fault liability is illustrated by Joel Feinberg, Doing & Deserving: Essays in the Theory of Responsibility 221 (Princeton, 1970). It is a fair question whether this use of the term is faithful to Aristotle's usage.

7
Enterprise Liability: Collective Responsibility and Commutative Justice

Harm-based strict liabilities prescribe that actors who inflict harm on others must repair the harm that they inflict, in order to align burden and benefit fairly. Harm-based strict liabilities thus do both corrective and commutative justice. They do corrective justice by righting the wrong of "harming-without-repairing." They do "commutative justice" by aligning the burden of harm reasonably inflicted with the benefit reaped from its infliction. The scope of the commutative justice done by tort's common law strict liabilities, though, is generally modest. In *Vincent v. Lake Erie*, for instance, the imposition of strict liability aligns burden and benefit between the parties to an "isolated, ungeneralized wrong." The commutative dimension of harm-based strict liabilities flowers, however, when strict liability is brought to bear on the "the torts with which our courts are kept busy today"—torts that "are mainly the incidents of certain well-known businesses... railroads, factories, and the like."[1] When harm-based strict liability is brought to bear on activities instead of acts, it blossoms into "enterprise liability." In a nutshell, enterprise liability asserts that the costs of accidents should (1) be imposed on the enterprises responsible for their infliction, and (2) be dispersed among all those within the enterprise—that is, all those who benefit from risk impositions which result in enterprise related harm. Enterprise liability is fundamentally commutative because it holds that accidental losses should be borne in accordance with the benefit that people derive from the enterprise or activity in question.

Writing in 1985, George Priest described the theory of enterprise liability as the force behind a revolution in private law "[t]he dimensions... [of which] are comparable only with those of Realism and *Brown v. Board of Education*."[2] Priest

---

[1] The language and the contrast are from Oliver Wendell Holmes, The Path of the Law, in Collected Legal Papers 167, 183 (1920) (originally delivered 1897). I have rearranged the punctuation.
[2] George L. Priest, The Invention of Enterprise Liability: A Critical History of the Intellectual Foundations of Modern Tort Law, 14 J. Legal Stud. 461, 461 (1985). Priest's claim is really about products liability law. He is correct about the significance of products liability as a common law phenomenon. See also G. Edward White, Tort Law in America: An Intellectual History 180–210 (Oxford, 1985, expanded ed. 2003). I discuss Priest's claim and the role of enterprise liability in products liability more generally in Gregory C. Keating, Products Liability as Enterprise Liability, 10 J. Tort L. 41 (2017).

had products liability law in mind when he made his observation, but, over the course of the twentieth century, enterprise liability shaped new forms of liability both within and beyond the law of torts. It shaped products liability law within tort and workers' compensation beyond tort.[3] Enterprise liability logic also seeped into established forms of strict liability such as vicarious liability, nuisance, and abnormally dangerous activity liability, remaking them in ways which expanded responsibility for unavoidable harm.[4] Even negligence liability—the natural habitat of individual, fault-based responsibility—has been pushed toward greater strictness and more collective forms of responsibility by enterprise liability.[5]

When enterprise liability takes hold of a field, its logic pushes both toward collective responsibility and toward strict liability. Enterprise liability is liability for the harms distinctive to a firm, to an institution, or to an activity. For example, when enterprise liability ideas get a grip on vicarious liability law, they tend to expand the scope of a firm's responsibility for the tortious wrongs committed by its employees. Enterprise liability ideas direct courts' attention away from traditional questions about employee intention and employer authorization, and lead courts to ask whether a firm's activities significantly increased the risk of the kind of tortious wrongdoing committed by the employee in the case at hand.[6] In exceptional circumstances, enterprise liability logic even leads courts to kick doctrine to the curb and to impose strict liability simply because the normative arguments that the enterprise should be held responsible for harms it should not have avoided inflicting are so compelling.[7]

---

[3] See generally Gregory C. Keating, The Theory of Enterprise Liability and Common Law Strict Liability, 54 Vand. L. Rev. 1285 (2001). On products liability as enterprise liability, see Priest 1985, *supra* note 2; Keating 2017, *supra* note 2. Virginia E. Nolan & Edmund Ursin, Understanding Enterprise Liability: Rethinking Tort Reform for the Twenty-first Century (Temple, 1995), rightly criticizes Priest's narrow focus. Correctly, they identify workers' compensation as the original manifestation of enterprise liability and no-fault auto insurance as an important incarnation.

[4] Examples of enterprise liability logic reshaping vicarious liability include *Ira S. Bushey & Sons, Inc. v. United States*, 398 F.2d 167 (2d Cir. 1968) (Friendly, J.) (hereinafter *Bushey*); *Taber v. Maine*, 45 F.3d 598 (2d Cir. 1995) (Calabresi, J.). Paula Giliker, A Revolution in Vicarious Liability: Lister, the Catholic Child Welfare Society Case and Beyond, in Revolution and Evolution in Private Law 121 (Sarah Worthington et al. eds., Hart Publishing, 2017), traces how the adoption of an enterprise liability conception of vicarious liability in England expanded liability for intentional wrongs, especially sexual assault. In nuisance liability, enterprise liability is embodied by the shift by *Boomer v. Atlantic Cement Co.*, 257 N.E.2d 870 (N.Y. 1970), away from injunctive relief as the traditional remedy and to damages. That shift recognizes that productive industrial enterprises may inflict harm that it is infeasible for them to avoid, but which it would be wrong for the enterprise simply to foist off on its neighbors. See Gregory C. Keating, Nuisance as a Strict Liability Wrong, 4(3) J. Tort L. [ii] (2012). *Siegler v. Kuhlman*, 502 P.2d 1181 (Wash. 1972), reflects the influence of enterprise liability on abnormally dangerous activity liability.

[5] Robert L. Rabin, Some Thoughts on the Ideology of Enterprise Liability, 55 Md. L. Rev. 1190 (1996); Keating 2001, *supra* note 3.

[6] See, *e.g.*, *Bushey*, 398 F.2d 167; *Taber*, 45 F.3d 598; Giliker 2017, *supra* note 4.

[7] See, *e.g.*, Lubin v. Iowa City, 131 N.W.2d 765 (Iowa, 1964) (imposing strict liability on a waterworks for a cost-justified decision to leave water pipes in place until they ruptured). The *Lubin* court tossed trespass, nuisance, and abnormally dangerous activity doctrines aside on the ground that it

I. The Significance of Enterprise Liability

The significance of enterprise liability lies both in its embrace of collective responsibility and in the way that its inner logic presses toward strict liability. Enterprise liability's commitment to collective responsibility is an appropriate answer to the fact that—in a highly organized industrial and technological society—accidental injury is a social problem. Modern tort law is "a body of law created when the industrial revolution and industrial accidents began to wreak havoc on the bodies of workers and passengers."[8] Enterprise liability is tort law's response to Oliver Wendell Holmes' insight that organized activities and firms—not isolated actions and individual actors—are responsible for the lion's share of risk in the modern world.[9] Tellingly, enterprise liability finds even more powerful expression in administrative alternatives to tort law proper than it does in the common law of torts. Untethered by the constraints of preexisting common law forms, enterprise liability's commitment to collective responsibility blossoms in administrative schemes as diverse as workers' compensation; no-fault automobile insurance; the Price-Anderson Act covering nuclear accidents; the Black Lung Benefits Act; the National Childhood Vaccination Act; and the New Zealand Accident Compensation Scheme. All of these impose collective responsibility on some identifiable form of activity—the activity of a particular firm, or of a particular industry, or of a particular widespread social practice—for harms that the activity introduces into social life.

Enterprise liability's tendency to strictness is an appropriate answer to the significance of unavoidable harm in modern social life and the fact that distinctively significant unavoidable risks tend to arise from large activities and institutional actors. The basic activities of an industrial and technological society inflict a significant amount of regular, predictable—and, practically speaking, unavoidable—harm. Some of this unavoidable harm is harm that should—in each individual instance—be prevented but which persists in the aggregate because human beings are lapse-prone and erratic. Automobile accidents are a case in point. Automobile accidents injure around two and a half million people every year. Nearly 40,000 people are killed.[10] More than 90 percent of these

was manifestly unfair to make particular persons whose pipes happened to rupture bear the costs of a practice whose cost savings benefited all participants in the enterprise.

---

[8] Sarah A. Seo & John Fabian Witt, The Metaphysics of Mind and the Practical Science of Law, 26 Law & Hist. Rev. 161, 164 (2008). See also John Fabian Witt, The Accidental Republic (Harvard, 2006); Thomas C. Grey, Accidental Torts, 54 Vand. L. Rev. 1225, 1275 (2001).

[9] Oliver Wendell Holmes, The Path of the Law, in Collected Legal Papers 167, 183 (Peter Smith 1952) (1920) (the talk was originally presented 1897).

[10] National Highway Traffic Safety Administration (NHTSA), Traffic Safety Facts Annual Report Tables (2018).

accidents may be attributable to driver error.[11] Each of those errors was avoidable and should have been avoided—or so negligence liability asserts. Yet until perfected automated vehicles rule the road, we cannot reasonably expect all of these accidents to disappear, and reductions in the incidence of accidents will be hard won.

Other unavoidable harm is harm that we shoulder because we cannot avoid it without shutting down the activity responsible for the harm, and we are not prepared to do so. The activity is too valuable to forgo, and we therefore allow it to inflict significant harm. Pollution is a case in point. In *Boomer v. Atlantic Cement*, the court found that "[t]he company installed at great expense the most efficient devices available to prevent the discharge of dust and polluted air into the atmosphere . . . [T]he evidence in this case establishes that Atlantic took every available and possible precaution to protect the plaintiffs from dust" but "nevertheless . . . created a nuisance insofar as the lands of the plaintiffs are concerned."[12] The unavoidability of much harm, however, does not make that harm insignificant. Harm is a matter of moral significance even when its infliction is unavoidable.[13] Tort law correctly concludes that failing to repair harm reasonably inflicted is sometimes unreasonable, and a wrong to those harmed. Enterprise liability extends this insight, claiming that, in the circumstances to which it applies, it is unfair of an enterprise to foist the costs of the harms that it should not or cannot avoid on those whose misfortune it is to get in the way of the enterprise.

II. The Justice of Enterprise Liability

When Professor Priest commented on the significance of enterprise liability in 1985, its prominence in our law was at its peak. Products liability law's enterprise liability moment had yet to pass, and the National Childhood Vaccine Injury Act would soon be enacted.[14] The long, rising wave of enterprise liability—which had begun with the enactment of the Workmen's Compensation Acts—was, however, cresting. Products liability law would soon retreat from its commitment to enterprise liability; no-fault automobile insurance would wane; and new forms of enterprise liability would appear only as sporadic responses to mass accidents or

---

[11] The NHTSA estimates that 94% of auto crashes can be related to "human choice or error." NHTSA, Federal Automated Vehicles Policy 5 (2016).

[12] Boomer v. Atlantic Cement Co., 287 N.Y.S.2d 112, 113–14 (Sup. Ct. 1967). Restatement (Second) of Torts § 826(b) (1979), encapsulates *Boomer* as a general regime of liability for nuisance. The regime is an enterprise liability one. For discussion, see Keating 2012, *supra* note 4, at 32–38.

[13] See Chapter Six, *supra*, pp.231, 236, 256–57

[14] Keating 2017, *supra* note 2, at 45–53. The National Childhood Vaccine Injury Act was enacted in 1986 and is now codified in 42 U.S.C. §§ 300aa-10 to 300aa-34 (2000).

disasters.¹⁵ This turning of the tide was partly the result of a political movement external to the law's own internal logic. The tort reform movement opposed enterprise liability and helped to arrest its progress.¹⁶ But the waning of enterprise liability was also accelerated by an academic literature arguing that enterprise liability was itself a deeply defective product. That literature presented enterprise liability as an ersatz insurance scheme which pursued the socially desirable end of loss-spreading and sought to fuse the provision of insurance with the pursuit of optimal accident avoidance.¹⁷ Enterprise liability's academic defenders struck back by claiming that it was indeed a *defensible* scheme of deterrence and insurance.¹⁸ The contending parties, though, implicitly agreed on at least one thing. Enterprise liability was *not* a regime of right and responsibility.

---

[15] On products liability, see Keating 2017, *supra* note 2. On no-fault automobile insurance, see Nora Freeman Engstrom, An Alternative Explanation for No-Fault's "Demise," 61 DePaul L. Rev. 303 (2012). The victim compensation fund set up to handle the claims of those killed and injured in the terrorist attacks of September 11, 2001, is an example of an enterprise liability scheme being set up to respond to a mass disaster. For discussion, see Robert L. Rabin, The September 11th Victim Compensation Fund: A Circumscribed Response or an Auspicious Model?, 53 DePaul L. Rev. 769 (2003).

[16] For example, three California Supreme Court Justices, including the Chief Justice, were popularly recalled in 1986. The movement to recall those judges made its popular case in terms of their death penalty jurisprudence, but the objective of ending the pro-enterprise liability jurisprudence of the Court was at least as important to the recall movement. Stephen D. Sugarman, Judges as Tort Law Un-Makers: Recent California Experience with "New" Torts, 49 DePaul L. Rev. 455, 455–72 (1999). See also Rose Bird Deserved to Be Removed, Chicago Tribune, Nov. 9, 1986.

[17] See, *e.g.*, Priest 1985, *supra* note 2; Richard A. Epstein, Products Liability as an Insurance Market, 14 J. Legal Stud. 645, 648–53 (1985) (arguing that modern products liability law frustrates the tripartite insurance ideals of limiting moral hazard, ameliorating adverse selection, and diversifying risk); George L. Priest, The Current Insurance Crisis and Modern Tort Law, 96 Yale L.J. 1521, 1553 (1987) (hereinafter Priest, Current Insurance Crisis) (arguing that first-party insurance is preferable to third-party insurance through tort liability because the former can incorporate copayments, whereas the latter cannot); George L. Priest, Modern Tort Law and Its Reform, 22 Val. U. L. Rev. 1, 17, 22 (1987) (hereinafter Priest, Modern Tort Law) (arguing that product manufacturers are in a poor position to acquire adequate information about the riskiness of insureds and cannot charge higher product prices to higher risk purchasers and users); Alan Schwartz, The Case Against Strict Liability, 60 Fordham L. Rev. 819, 820, 832–40 (1992) (arguing that product defects should be subject to a "market" regime of "free contract" with compulsory disclosure, because strict liability forces consumers to purchase excessive amounts of insurance and inefficiently depresses demand by forcing manufacturers to insure for nonpecuniary harm). For a perceptive assessment of this position, see Jane Stapleton, Tort, Insurance and Ideology, 58 Mod. L. Rev. 820, 820–21 (1995) ("Once this 'tort as insurance' construction of liability is embraced, the normative agenda for the future of tort inexorably points to retrenchment: an agenda, it can then be claimed, which arises from the mere logic of what tort is and not from any ulterior ideological motive.").

[18] See, *e.g.*, Jon D. Hanson & Kyle D. Logue, The First-Party Insurance Externality: An Economic Justification for Enterprise Liability, 76 Cornell L. Rev. 129, 137 (1990) (arguing that first-party insurers fail to adjust premiums according to consumption choices and that a negligence regime therefore induces manufacturers to make suboptimal investments in product safety, whereas enterprise liability optimizes manufacturer care and activity levels); Steven P. Croley & Jon D. Hanson, What Liability Crisis? An Alternative Explanation for Recent Events in Products Liability, 8 Yale J. Reg. 1, 109–10 (1991) (arguing that enterprise liability is stimulating the rise of mutual insurance companies, which are constructing more homogeneous and thus more efficient risk pools). For a more sophisticated discussion of insurance markets and insurability than is found in the tort literature, see Tom Baker, Uncertainty > Risk: Lessons for Legal Thought from the Insurance Run-Off Market, 62 B.C. L. Rev. 59 (2021).

This tacit agreement utterly ignored enterprise liability's foundational moral commitments. To overlook these moral commitments, however, is to misunderstand enterprise liability badly. Those moral commitments are responsible for enterprise liability's internal coherence, for its moral intelligibility, and for its moral urgency. Enterprise liability is a response to the intrinsic moral significance of unavoidable harm, and it embodies a collective conception of responsibility fitted to the collective character of risk in our world and That conception of responsibility embodies commutative justice by constructing communities of risk and responsibility within which the burdens and benefits of organized risk imposition are shared fairly. And, in distributing burden and benefit fairly, enterprise liability also does corrective justice.[19] For an enterprise to fail to repair harm that it unavoidably inflicts on others wrongly sacrifices victims to the good of the enterprise. Reparation rights that wrong.

Subsection A proposes an account of what enterprise liability is. It explains that enterprise liability finds expression within both negligent and strict liabilities, but that enterprise liability finds its fullest realization in strict liability because it seeks to impose liability on the characteristic risks of an activity. Subsection A also addresses influential objections which assert that enterprise liability simply does not amount to a coherent alternative to negligence liability. Subsection B discusses the three justifications usually offered for enterprise liability—accident avoidance, risk-distribution, and fairness—and argues that the fairness justification is underappreciated and underdeveloped in the scholarly literature. The principle of fairness justifies enterprise liability as a form of *responsibility* for harm inflicted without legal fault. When enterprise liability is justified only by forward-looking policies of accident prevention and loss-dispersion, it ceases to be a regime of responsibility. Enterprise liability becomes simply a price mechanism that pursues the socially optimal level of accidental harm.

Subsections C, D, and E develop the fairness justification. Subsection C explains how the enterprise liability idea of fairness is a principle of commutative justice which directs our attention to communities of risk and responsibility; this redirection of our attention responds appropriately to the increasingly institutionalized risks of modern society. Subsection D advances normative arguments that—when risks are the byproduct of organized activities—enterprise liability is fairer than negligence liability. Subsection E explains why enterprise liability cannot consume the whole of tort law, even in a world where risk is highly organized. Enduring practical problems and competing normative considerations often call for fault, or even no, liability.

---

[19] See Chapter Two, *supra*, pp. 53–55

A. What Is Enterprise Liability?

Enterprise liability lends itself to explanation in short slogans: "activities should bear the costs of those accidents that result from their characteristic risk impositions"; "it is only fair that an industry should pay for the injuries it causes"; "losses should be borne by the doer, the enterprise, rather than distributed on the basis of fault." These slogans suggest, though, a shared understanding and acceptance that do not exist. Enterprise liability is enduringly controversial. Prominent critics claim that it should be purged from the law of torts as a defective form of liability. Some objections are unqualifiedly normative: corrective justice and civil recourse theorists reject enterprise liability on the ground that it does not belong in a law of wrongs as they understand it.[20] Other critics, though, claim that enterprise liability's own internal logic is fatally flawed. For example, George Priest identifies enterprise liability with three "presuppositions"—manufacturer power, manufacturer insurance, and cost-internalization.[21] The "unavoidable implication of the three presuppositions," Priest writes, "is absolute liability. The presuppositions themselves do not incorporate any conceptual limit to manufacturer liability."[22] Absolute liability is, of course, untenable. Liability must end somewhere. Practice, Priest argued, confirmed the flaws of theory. The liability crisis of the late 1980s was the consequence of the rise of enterprise liability over the course of the twentieth century and real-world proof that enterprise liability is itself defective.[23] *The Problem of Social Cost*—the founding text of modern law and economics—can be read to make an even more sweeping claim. In Ronald Coase's telling, sparks from railroads do not damage adjacent farms when they set fire to fields of crops, and pigs do not disrupt the harmony of parlors. Farming and railroading, pigs and polite society, *interact* to create social costs. If all harms should be conceived of as joint costs arising out of the clash of

---

[20] See John C.P. Goldberg & Benjamin C. Zipursky, The Oxford Introductions to U.S. Law: Torts 267 (Oxford, 2010) (discussed in Chapter Six, *supra*, p.238.); Jules Coleman, The Practice of Principle: In Defence of a Pragmatist Approach to Legal Theory 36 (Oxford, 2001). Jules Coleman, Facts, Fictions, and the Grounds of Law, in Law and Social Justice 327, 329 (Joseph Keim Campbell et al. eds., MIT, 2005) (discussed in Chapter Six, *supra*, pp. 247–49.); Arthur Ripstein, Private Wrongs 102, 103, 136, 244–45 (Harvard, 2016) (discussed in Chapter Three, *supra*, pp. 101–104.); Ernest J. Weinrib, The Idea of Private Law 171–203 (Oxford, rev. ed., 2012) (discussed in Chapter Three, *supra*, pp. 103–104.).

[21] Priest 1985, *supra* note 2, at 527. Priest argues that the twin policies of preventing accidents whose costs outweigh their benefits and dispersing the costs of those accidents that are not worth preventing coalesced into these three propositions because they were linked to three empirical assumptions about the characteristics of modern consumer markets. First, manufacturers had "vastly greater power" with respect to "all relevant aspects of the product defect problem." Second, manufacturers had commensurately superior ability to spread risks. Third, forcing manufacturers to internalize the costs of all accidents attributable to their products would provide appropriate incentives for them to take cost-justified precautions; to modulate the level of their activities correctly; and to engage in desirable levels of safety research, development, and innovation. *Id.* at 520.

[22] *Id.* at 527.

[23] *Id.*

incompatible activities, then the very business of attributing accidents to activities is impossible.[24] The quest to make activities "bear the costs of those accidents that result from their characteristic risk impositions" is doomed to fail because all accidents are the joint costs of multiple activities.

1. Features of the Form

Our first task, then, is to explain what enterprise liability is and why it is minimally coherent. The terse slogans quoted earlier are too compact to serve as satisfactory explications. Elaborating them begins with saying that enterprise liability is constituted by the three following commitments:

(1) The costs of those accidents that are characteristic of an enterprise should be absorbed by the enterprise as an operating expense, not left on those whose bad luck it is to get in the enterprise's way;

(2) The costs of enterprise-related accidents should not be concentrated either on the victim who originally suffered the injury or on the particular agent who inflicted the injury; and

(3) The costs of such accidents should instead be distributed among those who benefit from the imposition of the enterprise's risks.

When these commitments are brought to bear on private firms large enough to impose recurring, statistically predictable risks, they prescribe that the costs of enterprise-related harms should be distributed among customers, employees, suppliers, and shareholders, rather than concentrated either on the victim or on the particular agent responsible for the harm at issue.

Enterprise liability's prescriptive theses that characteristic accident costs should be internalized by the enterprise responsible for their infliction and then distributed across the beneficiaries of the enterprise are tied together by a factual assumption. The assumption is that when an enterprise is made liable for its characteristic toll in life, limb, and property damage, it will usually insure (or self-insure) against that liability and will factor the cost of such insurance into the cost of its products, the prices that it pays to its suppliers, the wages of its employees, and so on. The enterprise liability principle of fairness thus depends on the fact that enterprises meet basic conditions of insurability. Fairness requires distributing the costs of enterprise related harms across those who benefit from their infliction. The capacity of enterprises either to self-insure or to purchase insurance against the accidents characteristic of their activities enables fairness to be done.

---

[24] Ronald Coase, The Problem of Social Cost, 3 J.L. & Econ. 1, 12–13 (1960).

Enterprise liability's commitment to the internalization of the costs of accidental harms characteristic of a firm's activity also supposes that requiring an enterprise to bear the costs of those accidents that are characteristic of its activities will have desirable consequences for the incidence of accidental harm as well as for its distribution. As a form of strict liability, enterprise liability differs most saliently from negligence liability in imposing responsibility for non-negligently inflicted harm in addition to imposing liability for the negligent infliction of injury. On the one hand, then, enterprise liability assumes that the activity it addresses is worthwhile and ought to continue—provided it repairs the harm that it inflicts. On the other hand, enterprise liability also presumes that the imposition of strict liability on enterprises for the characteristic risks of their activities will induce them to reduce risk as much as they feasibly can.[25] Being held strictly liable should induce enterprises to comb through their activities for ways to reduce the risks of their activities as far as possible and to adjust the intensity with which they conduct their activities as well as the care with which they do so.[26] Incentive and obligation will align.

2. Why Enterprise Liability Is Most Fully Realized through Strict Liability
Enterprise liability justifications are sometimes married to negligence liability doctrine. The California Supreme Court's famous *Tarasoff* decision is an example. *Tarasoff* imposes an affirmative duty on psychotherapists to warn third persons of credible threats to their safety made by the therapist's patients.[27] The fact that psychotherapists are in the business of treating people with mental health issues—some of whom pose threats of violent harm to others—figures in the justification of the duty. Their training puts psychotherapists in an unusually good position to distinguish patient threats that are credible from those that are not, and their relationship with their patients gives them special access to the facts necessary to make good predictions. In other words, their enterprise makes them especially well positioned to minimize a distinctive kind of harm to others—so well positioned in fact that, in certain circumstances, their failure to avert the possible infliction of harm on some third person by their patients may be regarded as form of professional incompetence giving rise to negligence liability in tort. The expertise and unique position characteristic of psychotherapy

---

[25] See, *e.g.*, Boomer, 257 N.E.2d 870. For discussion, see the text accompanying *supra* note 11, and Keating 2012, *supra* note 4, at 32–38.

[26] See Guido Calabresi & Jon T. Hirschoff, Toward a Test for Strict Liability in Torts, 81 Yale L.J. 1055, 1060 (1972) (strict liability puts the decision about which accidents to avoid in the hands of those best positioned to make that decision); Steven Shavell, Strict Liability versus Negligence, 9 J. Legal Stud. 1 (1980) (strict liability will induce more precaution than negligence by inducing injurers to adjust the level at which they conduct their activities as well as the care that they exercise when engaging in those activities); Steven Shavell, Economic Analysis of Accident Law 21–31 (Harvard, 1987).

[27] Tarasoff v. Regents of the University of California, 529 P.2d 553 (Cal. 1974).

as an enterprise was an essential ingredient in the California Supreme Court's decision to impose a duty to warn on psychotherapists, as Robert Rabin argues.[28] *Tarasoff* is not an exceptional example. Enterprise liability's influence on negligence doctrine is also evident in the "movement to a more robust principle of fault in medical malpractice cases, such as abandonment of the same locality rule, more expansive use of *res ipsa loquitur*, less restrictive standards for qualifying experts and establishing informed consent claims," and also in the liability of accountants and auditors for negligent misrepresentations.[29]

Enterprise liability's appearance within negligence liability shows that its commitment to an institutional conception of responsibility has influenced the law of torts quite widely. Even so, enterprise liability does not flower fully when it is married to fault as the criterion of liability. As one of the standard slogans has it, enterprise liability is liability for the characteristic risks of an activity. When it is tied to a fault criterion for determining which accidents some activity is responsible for, enterprise liability cannot fully realize its ambition to impose liability for the "characteristic risks" of the activity at hand. Liability for "characteristic risk" is liability for *all* harms flowing from risks for whose creation an agent is responsible, whether or not those risks should have been eliminated through the exercise of due care. Consequently, strict liability is required for the full realization of enterprise liability's aspirations. Indeed, as discussed in Chapter Six, harm-based strict liability *is* liability for characteristic risk.[30] Consequently, even though enterprise liability ideas infuse some instances of fault liability, the logic of enterprise liability pushes toward strict liability.

The law of vicarious liability provides a fine example of how enterprise liability conceptions can take hold of and reshape preexisting law. *Respondeat superior* liability is an ancient doctrine whose roots lie in agency law and run back to the Middle Ages.[31] Those agency roots, in turn, manifest themselves in traditional tests for the scope of liability. Those tests make the intention of the "servant" and the authorization of the "master" the basic touchstones for determining whether a tort was committed in the course of an employee's employment. In the *Restatement of Agency*'s influential formulation of the traditional test, for example, the actions of an employee may fall within the scope of the employee's employment only if the action "is actuated, at least in part by a purpose to serve the master."[32] An enterprise liability approach to vicarious liability

---

[28] Rabin 1996, *supra* note 5, at 1200.

[29] *Id.*, at 1200–03. See also Keating 2001, *supra* note 3, at 1329–32.

[30] See Restatement (Third) of Torts: Liability for Physical and Emotional Harm § 18 cmt. G (Am. Law Inst., Council Draft No. 2, 2000) (characterizing strict liability as liability for "characteristic risk").

[31] Giliker 2017, *supra* note 4, at 121 (citing to John G. Fleming, The Law of Torts 433 (LBC Information Services, 9th ed., 1998)).

[32] Restatement (Second) of Agency § 228 (1) (1958); see also Rabin 1996, *supra* note 5, at 1198–99.

reinterprets the scope of employment test" so that it serves as an instrument for holding firms accountable for "accidents which may fairly be said to be characteristic of [their activities]."[33] "Characteristic" accidents, in turn, are those "that flow from [an enterprise's] long-run activity in spite of all reasonable precautions on [the enterprise's] part."[34] The Coast Guard, for instance, inevitably increases the incidence of drunk sailors in and around its ships when they are docked for shore leave.[35]

Cooping up sailors in confined spaces under strict hierarchical authority for long periods of time—and then turning them loose on shore for short, intense bursts of recreation—may well be a justified practice. Even so, the practice increases the incidence of drunken mischief around docked Coast Guard vessels and subjects the Coast Guard to responsibility for that mischief when it takes the form of tortious harm to others. The enterprise liability interpretation of *respondeat superior* doctrine thus takes the doctrine to express "the desire to include in the costs of [a firm's] operation inevitable losses to third persons incident to carrying on an enterprise, and thus distribute the burden among those benefitted by the enterprise."[36] This enterprise liability justification implies that the scope of vicarious liability should hinge not on the intentions of the servant whose tort is at issue—or on the instructions of their master—but upon whether the activity of the firm involved tends to expose third parties to the kind of risk that materialized in injury in the case at hand. The right question to ask is whether the institutional characteristics of the defendant's enterprise contribute to or trigger commission of the individual wrong at issue sufficiently for us to say that we may fairly charge the enterprise with responsibility for the wrong.

3. Objections

Academic critics of enterprise liability often take it to be based exclusively on policies of optimal accident prevention and optimal loss-dispersion. They then assert that enterprise liability fails because its internal logic calls for unlimited liability and leads to unworkable forms of insurance.[37] Enterprise liability's merits as an insurance mechanism are debatable,[38] but the flaws in this critique of enterprise liability run deeper than a debatable preference for first-party loss insurance over third-party liability insurance. Because enterprise liability is liability *for the characteristic risks of an activity*, it has a clear conceptual limit.

---

[33] *Bushey*, 398 F.2d at 171.
[34] *Id.*
[35] *Id.*
[36] Young B. Smith, Frolic and Detour, 23 Colum. L. Rev. 444 & 716, 718 (1923).
[37] See, *e.g.*, Priest 1985, *supra* note 2; Priest, Current Insurance Crisis 1987, *supra* note 17; Richard A. Epstein, Products Liability as an Insurance Market, 14 J. Legal Stud. 645, (1985).
[38] See, *e.g.*, Hanson & Logue 1990, *supra* note 18; Croley & Hanson 1991, *supra* note 18.

Enterprise liability ends when " 'the activities of the enterprise' do not . . . create risks different from those attendant on activities of the community in general."[39] Enterprise liability is as preoccupied with identifying the characteristic risks of the activities that it governs as negligence liability is with determining whether or not the actions that it governs evidence reasonable care. Enterprise liability's particular difficulties matching accidents to activities have to do not with a logic which leads to unlimited liability but with the often formidable conceptual and practical problems of determining which accidents should be attributed to which activities.[40] But the normative logic of enterprise liability asserts that responsibility ends when the risks of the enterprise cease to be distinctive and merge into the general risks of social life.

Professor Priest's representative account of enterprise liability, for example, leaves out one of the form's defining features—it overlooks entirely the criterion of "characteristic risk." Moreover, Priest's failure to notice the importance of the "characteristic risk" criterion evidences a flaw in his account of enterprise liability's normative presuppositions. Enterprise liability rests not only on policies of accident avoidance and loss-dispersion but also on an overarching principle of fairness. That principle of fairness has normative priority over the policies that Professor Priest cites. It justifies the "characteristic risk" criterion as the fair boundary of enterprise responsibility. What fairness requires is that enterprises bear both the benefits and the burdens of their distinctive risk impositions. They should neither harvest the benefits while dumping the burdens of their distinctive risks nor bear the burdens of harms that are not properly charged to their activities.

For enterprise liability to embody an idea of fairness, however, it must be possible to identify the "characteristic risks" of activities. Following Coase, a prominent line of criticism denies the very possibility of accurately attributing harms to activities without the use of a fault criterion. Stephen Perry, for example, has argued that "general strict liability" is impossible, a thesis he develops largely by criticizing the theories of strict liability propounded by Richard Epstein and Robert Nozick.[41] Perry's criticisms of Epstein and Nozick have considerable merit, in my view, but they miss the mark when they are directed against tort law's strict liability doctrines. For one thing, if what Perry means by "general strict liability" is "universal strict liability," he is attacking a position that no one really holds. Even strict enterprise liability in full flower does not imply "universal strict liability." Enterprise liability contemplates a world in which there is strict liability for activities or enterprises and fault liability for individual

---

[39] *Bushey*, 398 F.2d at 172.
[40] These difficulties loom particularly large in products liability law. See Keating 2017, *supra* note 2.
[41] Stephen R. Perry, The Impossibility of General Strict Liability, 1 Can. J.L. & Juris. 147 (1988).

actors.⁴² For another, when Perry generalizes his arguments against Epstein and Nozick, the nerve of the argument is that a purely causal criterion of liability is unworkable because all accidents arise at the intersection of two or more activities and are thus jointly caused.⁴³ This is Coase's famous argument. Coase regards it as a mistake to attribute accidental harm to any one activity. When sparks from a railroad engine set fire to crops in an adjacent field, for example, Coase regards the ensuing fire as caused *both* by the activity of railroading *and* by the activity of farming, and equally so.⁴⁴

If we think, with Coase, that all harms are jointly caused, then enterprise liability is a hopelessly misconceived enterprise. But Coase's view is not so much a credible claim about causation as it is a point about the implications of his own normative framework. From an economic point of view, the right question to ask when productive economic activities interfere with one another is how to arrange the activities so that we extract as much value as we can out of them. In other words, the only question that we should ask is how to minimize the joint costs and maximize the joint benefits of the activities that are colliding in costly ways. The question "who did what to whom" is both obliterated by the framework and entirely irrelevant. The tort law of strict liability, however, neither incarnates this economic idea of value nor embraces a purely causal conception of responsibility.

Our law of torts is a law of right and responsibility. The particular concern of enterprise liability is with what we owe to each other when basic activities impose recurring risks of harm, and inevitably so. The characteristic risk criterion is a plank in this normative framework; it is not purely causal. It is a normative, non-fault criterion for attributing harms to activities. It fuses factual and evaluative judgment in the way that reasonable person judgments do, but without appealing to fault. When Judge Friendly rules that a reasonable jury could find that the practice of shore leave, as conducted by the Coast Guard, increases the risk of drunken accidents in the vicinity of berthed Coast Guard ships, he is making both a factual conjecture and an evaluative claim.⁴⁵ The factual conjecture is that sailors on shore leave are more likely than most people are to imbibe alcohol to the point of being drunk. The evaluative judgment is that the activities of the Coast Guard are responsible for promoting more than the normal amount of drinking to excess. Cooping up people in confined physical spaces under strict

---

⁴² See James A. Henderson Jr., The Boundary Problems of Enterprise Liability, 41 Md. L. Rev. 659, 659–60 (1982) ("For the enterprises singled out for the imposition of enterprise liability, strict liability will replace fault-based liability; .... [T]raditional negligence principles will continue to govern the tort liabilities of what might be termed 'non-enterprises'—that is, the noncommercial, nonprofessional, nongovernmental activities of individuals and groups of individuals in our society.").

⁴³ Perry 1988, *supra* note 41, at 157 (citing Coase 1960, *supra* note 24, at 12–13).

⁴⁴ Coase 1960, *supra* note 24.

⁴⁵ See *Bushey*, 398 F.2d 167.

authority—and then turning them loose for short bursts of rest and recreation—tends to induce drinking to excess.

In the same vein, when Coke bottles explode in the course of normal use, courts have no trouble saying that they are defective, because they disappoint reasonable consumer expectations about product performance.[46] We justifiably expect Coke bottles not to function like hand grenades. Vessels prone to explode are ill-suited to their purpose of enabling the safe consumption of the soda they contain. When Coke bottles explode, we have reason to say that the ensuing physical harm is caused by their malfunction, not by the fact that we happen to be physically put together in a way that makes us vulnerable to injury by sharp slivers of glass projected in our direction by exploding bottles. In context, the explosion of the Coke bottle is salient in a way which allows us to pick out the bottle as the responsible cause of harm. This kind of normative, non-fault judgment—not a purely causal judgment—is the kind of judgment that the attribution of wrongs or injuries to activities requires in a strict liability regime.

To be sure, there are times when it is impossible to attribute harms to activities. We shall return to this problem at the end of the chapter, in the course of examining why it is that enterprise liability cannot swallow the entire law of torts. For present purposes, it will do to observe that a problem we might call "the boundary problem in enterprise liability" is sometimes easy to manage and sometimes impossible to solve. When the attribution of accidents to activities is infeasible, enterprise liability is not a live alternative to negligence liability. Whether or not satisfactory non-fault attribution rules can be devised for some domain can only be determined by trying to devise them.

B. Policy, Principle, and Responsibility

1. The Policies of Accident Avoidance and Loss-Spreading

As a form of responsibility for harm done, enterprise liability is summarized by the proposition that the costs of accidents that are characteristic of an enterprise should be absorbed by the enterprise and distributed across all those who benefit from its activities. So conceived, enterprise liability rests on an intuitive notion of fairness widely articulated in case rhetoric. In the legal academy, however, defenses of enterprise liability often appeal to two other distinct justifications. The first such justification is that cost-internalization will induce an appropriate level of accident prevention. The second is that the dispersion of accident costs is desirable because it is easier for many people to bear a small fraction of a large cost than it is for any one of them to shoulder the large cost by

---

[46] Escola v. Coca Cola Bottling Co., 150 P.2d 436 (Cal. 1944).

themselves. Although the loss-spreading and accident-prevention justifications often converge with the fairness justification in support of enterprise liability, the justifications have different sources and divergent implications.

The first rationale—accident avoidance—identifies a way in which enterprise liability embraces an idea different from the negligence liability idea of how accident prevention is to be effected. Where negligence law asks "What precaution should have been taken to guard against this risk?," enterprise liability asks "Who is in the best position to take precautions against this kind of risk?" Where negligence seeks to induce appropriate accident prevention by determining whether some untaken precaution should have been taken, enterprise liability seeks to induce appropriate accident prevention by determining who should make the choice between preventing an accident and letting it happen. It institutes that commitment by holding the party that is in the best position to determine whether to avoid accidents in a given domain liable for the accidents that ensue, including those that it does not prevent because it judges them not worth preventing.[47]

The second rationale—loss-spreading—has its roots in insurance ideas and does not have any counterpart in the reasoning or rhetoric of negligence liability. Theorists of negligence generally suppose that—if it is desirable to spread the costs of accidents that should not be avoided—loss-spreading can and should be accomplished by the purchase of first-party loss insurance by prospective victims. The theory of enterprise liability supposes, on the contrary, that the dispersion of accident costs is plainly desirable and should be realized by loss-spreading within the liability system. Loss-spreading is desirable for the same reason that insurance is desirable. Most people prefer bearing a small, certain cost to a large but uncertain and potentially devastating individual loss. When this is the case, insurance is an important instrument of security: it protects us against fortuities that would otherwise devastate us and keeps us from retreating in existential dread from the unavoidable background risks of everyday life. Insofar as it secures persons and property against serious harm, the institution of insurance is an institution which shares a mission with strict liability in tort law. Enterprise liability is infused with this insurance logic, and it therefore seeks to supply insurance-like redress to victims. It obligates enterprises to pay reparative damages to victims of enterprise-related harm even when that harm could not have been avoided by the exercise of reasonable care. It asserts that this "insurance" against unavoidable harm should be supplied by the enterprises responsible for inflicting that harm on the supposition that enterprises are generally the best insurers of the risks that characterize their activities.

---

[47] Calabresi & Hirschoff 1972, *supra* note 26.

The loss-spreading and accident-avoidance justifications for enterprise liability are, in standard legal parlance, policies. They identify objectives worth pursuing. Because policies face forward toward the realization of future ends, they are not well-suited to serve as the sole justifications for the imposition of enterprise liability. The law of torts faces both forward toward the avoidance of future wrongs and harms and backward toward the repair of past ones. Tort law's forward-facing dimension makes it hospitable to forward-looking policy arguments. The fact that tort is also a law of responsibility for harm (wrongly) done, however, places limits on the work that policy arguments may permissibly do. The facts that some actor (natural or artificial) is in an excellent position to avoid the infliction of future harm, and to disperse such harm should it happen, are good reasons for imposing on that actor responsibility for doing so going forward. But they are not good reasons for holding actors responsible for past harm. In order to be held responsible for the infliction of harms, people must act in ways which make the attribution of those harms to their agency justifiable.[48] In legal doctrine, this is the role played by the "scope of employment" rule in vicarious liability law; by defect rules in product liability law; and by the scope of the risk rule for abnormally dangerous activities liability—the rule that an actor engaged in an abnormally dangerous activity is liable for harms arising out of the characteristics of the activity that make it abnormally dangerous. Product defect rules, for example, determine when a product accident should, prima facie, be attributed to the activity of the product manufacturer because the product is flawed in some way.

It is unjust to hold someone responsible for a harm that has already been inflicted simply because doing so will have desirable deterrence and insurance effects.[49] Simply by virtue of his immense wealth, Jeff Bezos may be able to disperse the costs of all accidents implicating the self-driving capacities of Tesla's automobiles. That, however, is not a good reason to attribute responsibility to him for accidents implicating the self-driving capacities of Tesla's cars to him. Bezos has nothing to do with the design, manufacturing, distribution, or sale of Teslas. He has done nothing that makes it fair to charge him with responsibility for any flaws in Tesla's automobiles. By itself, then, the fact that an actor is in a good position to disperse the costs of some accident is not a good reason to attribute responsibility for that accident to the actor. Moreover, while the loss-spreading justification has often appeared in the rhetoric of enterprise liability, the claim that an enterprise—say, a product manufacturer—is almost always the best insurer of accidents implicating the enterprise has proven to be, at

---

[48] See, e.g., T.M. Scanlon, What We Owe to Each Other, 282–90 (1998); Gary Watson, Two Faces of Responsibility, in Agency and Answerability: Selected Essays 260–88 (2004).
[49] See Chapter Two, supra, pp. 28–30

best, debatable. Sometimes victims are the best insurers of product accidents and sometimes loss insurance is superior to liability insurance as a mechanism for dispersing the costs of product accidents.[50]

2. The Principle of Fairness

The fairness rationale—that the burdens and benefits of enterprise-related accidents should be proportionally distributed—is a principle not a policy. It expresses an idea of responsibility based on doing, and it is deontological, not consequentialist. It makes an assertion about the just distribution of the burdens and benefits of mutually, if locally, valuable cooperative activity and about the wrong done when an enterprise foists the costs of the unavoidable harms that it inflicts onto those who happen to get in its way. The fairness rationale asserts that when an enterprise imposes the costs of unavoidable harms characteristic of its activities upon those that it happens to harm, the enterprise wrongly exploits those victims for its own gain. Repairing harm so inflicted erases that exploitation. The wrong, then, lies not in the infliction of injury. The infliction of injury is the unavoidable, if regrettable, consequence of an activity worth having. The wrong lies in foisting the cost of a harm that is an unavoidable byproduct of the activity onto the victim instead of taking responsibility for the harm and repairing the injury inflicted. When reparation is volunteered promptly, it prevents the wrong of making the victim the involuntary instrument of the enterprise's self-enrichment. When reparation is not forthcoming, the enterprise commits the wrong of harming-without-repairing. Unfairness is the moral nerve of the wrong. Leaving the harm unrepaired foists the costs of the enterprise's unavoidable harms onto the victims of its activities, whereas repairing the harm fairly distributes the burdens and benefits of its activities. All those who benefit from the enterprise share the burden of the unavoidable injuries that it inflicts.

In contrast to the loss-spreading rationale—which nestles nicely within the embrace of economic theory—the fairness rationale has been relatively underplayed in the academic literature. It is not, for example, one of the justifications for enterprise liability that Priest considers important.[51] Stripped of the fairness justification—and the "characteristic risk" boundary that it places on enterprise responsibility—enterprise liability ceases to be a form of responsibility for harm wrongly done and transforms into a haphazard, and therefore defective, form of insurance. In fact, the principle of fairness is what links enterprise liability to tort law proper. The principle of fairness roots responsibility

---

[50] Epstein 1985, *supra* note 37; Priest, Current Insurance Crisis, 1987, *supra* note 17; Priest, Modern Tort Law, 1987, *supra* note 17; Schwartz 1992, *supra* note 17. *Cf.* Hanson & Logue 1990, *supra* note 18; Croley & Hanson 1991, *supra* note 18.
[51] See Priest 1985, *supra* note 2.

to repair harm in antecedent responsibility for having inflicted that harm.[52] The policy of loss-spreading that it resembles is not a ground of responsibility. As Judge Friendly says:

> It is true, of course, that in many cases the plaintiff will not be in a position to insure, and so expansion of liability will, at the very least, serve *respondeat superior*'s loss spreading function. But the fact that the defendant is better able to afford damages is not alone sufficient to justify legal responsibility, and this overarching principle must be taken into account in deciding whether to expand the reach of *respondeat superior*.[53]

By contrast, the principle that those who impose risks on others in pursuit of their own benefit should also bear the harms to others that are the unavoidable consequence of that pursuit, articulates a ground of responsibility. Fairness thus has a strong claim to be—as Judge Friendly says—the "overarching principle" of enterprise liability. It trumps the claims of efficiency when the policies of efficient accident prevention and loss-dispersion call for the imposition of a liability that goes beyond the boundary of fair responsibility.[54]

C. Fairness in the World of Organized Risk

When, in the latter half of the nineteenth century, modern tort law freed itself from the fetters of the forms of action, it recognized both fault and strict liability as competing principles of responsibility. *Rylands v. Fletcher* and other cases put strict liability on the table as an alternative to fault liability, but cast strict liability as the exceptional principle, confined to nonreciprocal risks.[55] *Rylands*' division

---

[52] See Chapter Two, *supra*, pp. 24–41
[53] *Bushey*, 398 F.2d at 171 (citations omitted). Friendly's choice of the word "responsibility" as the phenomenon that loss-spreading cannot justify could not be more on point. He goes on to remark that *respondeat superior* rests "not so much" on policies of accident avoidance and loss-spreading as on "a deeply rooted sentiment that a business enterprise cannot justly disclaim responsibility for accidents which may be said to be characteristic of its activities." *Id.* See also Robert E. Keeton, Conditional Fault in the Law of Torts, 72 Harv. L. Rev. 401 (1959) (arguing that loss-spreading concerns almost never account for the imposition of tort liability and distinguishing such concerns from the fair apportionment of burdens and benefits).
[54] Within the boundaries fixed by an overarching principle of fairness, there is room for the policies of efficient accident avoidance and efficient loss-spreading to operate. For example, the capacity to insure against—and therefore distribute—the costs of enterprise-related accidental harms is an ingredient in the judgment that it is fair to impose the costs of their unavoidable harms on enterprises. Similarly, when efficient accident avoidance or the taking of efficient precautions does not transgress the boundaries of fair responsibility, fairness and efficiency can interact cooperatively, for instance, when harm can be fully repaired after it is done by the payment of money damages.
[55] See generally Gregory C. Keating, Recovering Rylands: An Essay for Robert Rabin, 61 DePaul L. Rev. 543 (2012).

of labor between fault and strict liability rested on an eminently plausible perception of the nature of tortious wrongs and the effects of liability rules. In the late nineteenth century, tortious wrongs were mostly a matter of discrete, individual acts—of one actor building a reservoir to power its mill and flooding a neighbor's mine, of one man picking up a stick to separate fighting dogs and putting out another man's eye. When tortious wrongs arise out of one-off actions, liability rules do not disperse and distribute the costs of accidental injury; they shift the concentrated burdens of accidental harm. It therefore makes sense for *Rylands* to alight on the distribution of risk as the essential matter and to call for the imposition of strict liability on those risks that are not reciprocally imposed. The implicit supposition is that risk is distributed fairly when risks are reciprocal, and the implicit inference is that negligence is therefore the appropriate principle of responsibility for harm accidentally inflicted. Negligent action upsets the equilibrium of reciprocal risk by imposing increased risk. Imposing liability on negligent acts that inflict injury does corrective justice by restoring the equilibrium that negligence disrupts. When risks are nonreciprocal to begin with, some actors are already imposing increased risks on others. Strict liability rectifies that unfairness by holding those who impose the risks responsible for all of the harms that they inflict.

George Fletcher's influential presentation of the link between fairness as the master principle of tort and reciprocity as the master criterion of liability in tort spells out the logic latent in *Rylands v. Fletcher*.[56] Negligence liability fairly apportions the burdens and benefits of risky activities within a community of reciprocal reasonable risk imposition, whereas strict liability does so when risks are imposed by one community on another.[57] Subjecting reasonable—that is, non-negligent—reciprocal risks to strict liability affects only the distribution of non-negligent accident costs. It does not improve the fairness of the distribution of the burdens and benefits of risk imposition; it simply "substitute[s] one form of risk for another—the risk of liability for the risk of personal loss."[58] Put differently, when risks are reasonable and reciprocal, negligence and strict liability allocate the costs of accidents that should not be prevented in ways which are equally fair, though different. Because strict liability is more expensive to operate, negligence is the more attractive liability regime within a community of reciprocal risk.

Matters are different when risks are not reciprocal—when the exercise of reasonable care does not reduce risk to roughly the same, normal level. This is the

---

[56] George P. Fletcher, Fairness and Utility in Tort Theory, 85 Harv. L. Rev. 537, 541–49 (1972) (reciprocity of risk criterion both explains and justifies tort law's division of labor between negligence and strict liability).
[57] *Id.* at 550–51.
[58] *Id.* at 547.

circumstance that catches Arthur Ripstein's eye when he describes strict liability as applying to activities which impose excessive risk.[59] Ripstein's thought is that normal activities, carefully conducted, impose roughly the same level of residual (or background) risk. That residual level is acceptable; it is the price of living in a "crowded world." We may, and do, let the harms and losses that issue from the residual risks of normal activities lie where they fall. Some activities, however, impose greater than normal levels of risk even when they are conducted carefully. Fletcher describes Ripstein's excessive risks as nonreciprocal risks, emphasizing that the imposition of nonreciprocal risk is not mutually beneficial in the way that the imposition of reasonable reciprocal is. The greater-than-normal risks imposed by transporting thousands of gallons of gasoline in tanker trucks[60] are illustrative. Gasoline-dependent modes of transportation are so woven into the fabric of our social life that we may all benefit from the transport of thousands of gallons of gasoline over the roads in tanker trailers, even though this method of transporting gasoline creates risks of massive explosion, and even though most of us never expect to make use of the legal right to transport vast quantities of gasoline in this manner.

We may all benefit to some extent from the risks of transporting gasoline by tanker trailer, but we do not all benefit as much as we would if we all routinely drove such vehicles ourselves. If we all routinely transported thousands of gallons of gas by tanker trailer, we would be compensated in kind for having the risks of such transportation imposed on us by a valuable equal right to impose identical risks on others. In fact, the right to impose the greater-than-normal risks of transporting gasoline by tanker trailer is not worth much to most of us. The victims of the nonreciprocal risks imposed by gasoline tanker trailers are not fully compensated ex ante for bearing these risks by the right to impose equal risks in turn. The imposition of such nonreciprocal risks is not part of a normal life, and the value of the right to impose such risks does not offset the disvalue of being exposed to them. For Fletcher, the imposition of strict liability is the answer to this unfairness. Strict liability restores mutuality of benefit, as far as it can be restored. Risk is unfairly distributed ex ante, but the costs of harms resulting from those risks are distributed fairly ex post. Those who reap the lion's share of the benefit from imposing the risks also bear the costs of the harms that result from their imposition.

Fletcher's argument is elegant and powerful. The theory's emphasis on risk imposition as the most important aspect of tortious wronging, though, seems misplaced. In the law of torts, the significance of risk is largely parasitic on the significance of harm. Risk matters mostly because it ripens into harm. When

---

[59] Ripstein 2016, *supra* note 20, at 102, 136, 244–45. See Chapter Two, *supra*, pp. 93–95
[60] See *Siegler*, 502 P.2d at 1185.

risk imposition does not result in harm, tort law generally does recognize a completed wrong and does not confer on the victims of the risk imposition a right of action. There are exceptions to this rule, but, for the most part, it governs cases where a wrongful action imposes what we might call a "balloon of risk." When harm does not materialize out of the blossoming of ordinary background risk into a balloon of significant risk, the air quickly goes out of the balloon, and we return to the normal level of background risk. Strikingly, tort law is reluctant to recognize recovery even when this paradigm case is not instantiated and risk of future harm lingers long after risk imposition has ended.[61] The merits of tort law's resistance to recovery for the imposition of risk which does not immediately ripen into physical harm are open to debate, but the logic at work is evident enough. Harm impairs, whereas risk that does not result in harm alone usually does not. In the implicit paradigm case, the fright we may feel at almost being seriously injured and the accompanying fury we may feel toward the actor who endangered us fade quickly once we realize that we have escaped unscathed. We are intact, if briefly traumatized. Because harm matters more than risk, we might well think that tort theory should treat harm as more important than risk and adjust its sights accordingly. Enterprise liability tracks this supposition. Harm is what the enterprise liability principle of fairness focuses on, and persuasively so. Distributing the costs of accidents across an activity both disperses the concentrated impact of suffering serious physical injury—thereby mitigating the blow that harm inflicts on its victims—and fairly aligns the burdens and benefits of valuable but risky activity. Putting risk, not harm, at the center of our theorizing about accidental injury seems to put the emphasis in the wrong place.

1. The World of Acts and the World of Activities

The puzzle here disappears once we recognize that theory of fairness as reciprocity of risk and the theory of enterprise liability assume different social worlds. Reciprocity of risk theory was given its most influential formulation by George Fletcher in the 1970s, but the view itself is framed with the shape that modern tort law took when it first emerged late in the nineteenth century, and the social world that late nineteenth-century tort law addressed, in mind. Turn-of-the-twentieth-century tort law was dominated by fault liability but punctuated by exceptional domains of strict liability. Enterprise liability had just begun to emerge; its ability to explain or justify the contours of tort law was slight. By

---

[61] Exposure to carcinogenic toxins and radiation, for instance, can result in risks of harm that persist long after the exposure ends. Genetic damage may be inflicted before any normal bodily power is impaired. Subclinical injury is usually insufficient to ground a cause of action. See, *e.g.*, Anderson v. W.R. Grace & Co., 628 F. Supp. 1219 (D. Mass. 1986); Schweitzer v. Consolidated Rail Corp., 758 F.2d 936, 942 (3d Cir. 1985). Recovery for enhanced risk of injury is also usually insufficient to support an award of money damages but has been held to warrant imposing the remedy of medical monitoring. See Ayers v. Township of Jackson, 525 A.2d 287 (N.J. 1987).

contrast, the presence or absence of reciprocity of risk went a considerable distance toward explaining and justifying the division of labor between the two principles.[62] More importantly, for our purposes, the reciprocity of risk principle is tailored to the social world of the late nineteenth century, whereas enterprise liability is tailored to the social world that has since emerged. The difference is captured, albeit cryptically, in Holmes' distinction between the world of "isolated, ungeneralized wrongs" and the world in which "torts . . . are mainly the incidents of certain well known businesses . . . railroads, factories, and the like."[63] Implicit in Holmes' remark is a distinction not just between two kinds of accidents but between two kinds of social worlds. Stylizing and simplifying, we can call these two worlds the "world of acts" and the "world of activities," respectively.

In the "world of acts," risks are discrete. The typical actor is an individual or a small firm which creates risk so infrequently that harm is not likely to materialize from any single actor's conduct. The typical accident materializes out of the activity of isolated, unrelated actors acting independently (i.e., natural persons or small firms separately engaging in activities on an occasional basis). Taken as a whole, the activities of these individual actors are diffuse and disorganized and quite possibly actuarially small. The dogfight that is the subject of the seminal nineteenth-century negligence case *Brown v. Kendall*[64] is a representative tort in this world. The plaintiff's accidental injury arose out of a chance encounter between unrelated parties, neither of whose activities were large enough to make such misfortunes commonplace and expected. One person who owns a dog is not likely to become involved in dogfight which results in putting out someone's eye. But they also cannot count on *not* becoming entangled in such a fight. The risk that they will be is low, but, in insurance terms, it is also highly uncertain.[65] There are too few "exposures" for anyone to predict with confidence whether the risk will materialize into injury. In the "world of acts," risks are isolated, "one-shot" events. Harm materializes sporadically and unpredictably. Because actors

---

[62] *Ayers*, 525 A.2d at 543–49.
[63] Holmes 1920, *supra* note 9, at 183.
[64] Brown v. Kendall, 60 Mass. 292 (1850).
[65] Insurance is all about mitigating the impact of risk, but it does not do so by reducing the *chance* that a loss will be suffered. It does so by diminishing *uncertainty* as to whether a loss will be suffered. For insurance purposes *risk is uncertainty concerning loss*—not *chance of loss happening*. Uncertainty as to whether a loss will happen is a function of the number of "units" (e.g., dog owners) exposed to the same risks—e.g., the number of dog owners exposed to the risk of dogfights. The greater the number of exposures, the more actual loss will track expected loss. If a house has a 1 in 1,000 chance of being struck by lightning, whether a single house will be struck is highly uncertain. If a thousand houses are exposed to a 1 in 1,000 chance of being struck by lightning, the prediction "one will be struck by lightning" is less uncertain. If 10,000 houses are exposed to that risk, the prediction is that ten will be struck by lightning is more certain still. And, if 100,000 houses are exposed to the risk, actual loss and predicted loss will converge even more. See Robert E. Keeton et al., Tort and Accident Law 724–31 (West, 4th ed., 2004) (excerpting Robert I. Mehr et al., Principles of Insurance (Irwin, 8th ed., 1985)).

are small—and because risks are independent and uncorrelated—liability rules shift, but do not spread, losses. In this world, as Fletcher says, the imposition of strict liability on reciprocal risks simply "substitute[s] one form of risk for another—the risk of liability for the risk of personal loss."[66] A fair distribution of the costs of accidental harm is beyond the reach of liability rules. We can only distribute the costs of accidents across activities if the activities are large enough to satisfy basic criteria of insurability. Foremost among these criteria is the law of large numbers.[67] When numbers are large, accidental injuries become statistically predictable. But, in the purest form of the "world of acts," both actors and activities are small.

In the "world of activities," risks are generalized and systemic. The typical injury arises not out of the diffuse and disorganized acts of unrelated individuals or small firms but out of the organized activities of firms that are either large themselves or are component parts of relatively well-organized enterprises. The defendant in *Lubin v. Iowa City*[68] (a case where a waterworks left water mains uninspected until they broke) is large in the first sense: a single entity is responsible for the piping of water through underground pipes throughout a city; for laying and maintaining those pipes; for charging consumers for the water so transported; and so on. The transportation of large quantities of gasoline in tanker trucks on highways is large in the second sense: the firms that do the transporting may (or may not) be small and specialized, but they are enmeshed in contractual relationships with those who manufacture and refine the gasoline, those who operate gasoline stations, those who manufacture tractor trailers, and so on.[69] When an activity is actuarially large, "accidental" harm is statistically certain to result from the risks that it routinely creates. If you make enough Coke bottles, some are sure to rupture;[70] if you transport enough gasoline, some tankers are sure to explode;[71] if you leave water mains uninspected in the ground long enough, some are sure to break;[72] if you turn loose enough sailors on shore leave, some of them are bound to get drunk and wreak havoc.[73] In the "world of activities," both actors and activities are large. The cost of accidents can therefore be dispersed and distributed.

[66] Fletcher 1972, *supra* note 56, at 547.
[67] See Keeton et al., 2004, *supra* note 65, at 724–31 (excerpting Mehr et al., 1985, *supra* note 65).
[68] *Lubin*, 131 N.W.2d 765.
[69] The perception that the separate actors form a connected enterprise is clear in *Siegler*, 502 P.2d at 1181.
[70] See *Escola*, 150 P.2d 436.
[71] See *Siegler*, 502 P.2d 1181.
[72] See *Lubin*, 131 N.W.2d 765. The waterworks chose not to replace pipes until they broke because it was inefficient to inspect the mains for signs of incipient breakage and replace them before they broke.
[73] *Bushey*, 398 F.2d at 171.

The move from the "world of acts" to the "world of activities" thus changes the way in which liability rules operate. In the "world of acts," the imposition of liability on an accidental injury shifts concentrated harm from the victim to the injurer. When strict liability is imposed on risks that are both reasonable and reciprocal, it yields a different, but no fairer, distribution of the financial burdens and benefits of accidental harm. In the "world of activities," however, accidental harms can be spread across the enterprises that engender those harms. When activities are actuarially large, the accidents that they engender will likewise be predictable and regular, and the costs of those accidents can be factored into the costs of conducting the enterprise. The costs of manufacturing and distributing Coke can include the costs of injuries from exploding Coke bottles; the costs of supplying water to households and businesses can include the costs of the damage caused by broken water mains. Under enterprise liability, those who benefit from the imposition of the characteristic risks of a large activity will also bear the financial burdens of the accidents that issue from these risks. Strict enterprise liability will *both disperse concentrated loss and distribute it* across the enterprise responsible for its infliction, thereby aligning the benefits and the burdens of risk imposition.

Enterprise liability is thus both a response to the emergence of risk as a social problem created by the emergence of industrial and technological activities and enabled by the world of activities to which it responds. Only in the world of activities can the costs of accidental harm be fairly distributed across the activities responsible for them.

D. Fate, Fortune, and the Facets of Fairness

The enterprise liability conception of fairness has three dimensions: fairness toward injurers as a class; fairness toward victims as a class; and fairness toward both actual and potential injurers as classes. Taken together, these three facets of enterprise liability fairness combine to relax the fairly stiff requirement of causation characteristic of negligence liability; they also help to explain why enterprise liability flourishes in administrative plans, where it does not have to struggle against the fetters of causation as it is traditionally understood in tort law.

1. Three Facets of Fairness

First, enterprise liability is *fair to victims*. It is unfair to concentrate the costs of characteristic enterprise risk on those who, without fault, simply happen to suffer injury at the hands of such risk, when those costs might be absorbed by those who impose the characteristic risk, and who are in a position to control its imposition. It is unfair to concentrate the costs of the harms that arise out of characteristic risks even if the imposition of those risks is justified and free of fault. Fairness prescribes proportionality of burden and benefit. Victims who are strangers to an enterprise derive little or no benefit from it, and it is therefore unfair to ask them to bear individually a substantial loss when that loss might be dispersed across those who participate in the enterprise and therefore do benefit from the imposition of the risk that inevitably results in such harms. Victims who are themselves participants in an enterprise share in its benefits, but not in proportion to the detriment they suffer when they are physically harmed by the enterprise. Here, too, enterprise liability is fairer than negligence. It disperses the costs of enterprise-related accidents and distributes them within the enterprise, so that each member of the enterprise bears a share.

Second, enterprise liability is *fair to injurers* because it simply asks them (without the blame of fault) to absorb the costs of their choices. Those who create characteristic risks do so for their own advantage, fully expecting to reap the benefits that accrue from imposing those risks. If those who impose characteristic risks choose wisely—if they put others at risk only when they stand to gain more than those they put in peril stand to lose—even under enterprise liability they will normally benefit from the characteristic risks that they impose. If they do not, they have only their poor judgment to blame, and society as a whole has reason to penalize their choices. The Coast Guard lets its sailors loose on shore leave for its own benefit (as well as for the sailors'), and it reaps the rewards of their shore leave. If the costs of shore leave are greater than the benefits, the Coast Guard has reason to reconsider the practice, and society has reason to discourage it. The conception of responsibility invoked in the last paragraph is a familiar and widely accepted one. We take it for granted, for example, that:

> [T]he person to whom the income of property or a business will accrue if it does well has normally also to bear the risk of loss if it does badly. In the law of sales, when the right to income or fruits normally passes to the buyer, the risk of deterioration or destruction normally passes to him as well.[74]

The same point might be made about the purchase of stocks, or even lottery tickets. It is fair to ask agents who choose to act in pursuit of their own interests and stand to profit if things go well to bear the losses that accrue when things go badly.

Third, enterprise liability is fair to both *actual and potential injurers*. Enterprise liability distributes the non-fault luck of various risk lotteries more fairly than negligence does. Put differently, enterprise liability treats those who impose the same characteristic risks in a more even-handed way than negligence does.

---

[74] Tony Honoré, Responsibility and Fault 79 (Hart, 1999).

Jeremy Waldron's well-known contrast between "Fate" and "Fortune", recounted in Chapter Two, makes this point.[75] For Waldron, it misses the point to pin individual responsibility on Fate, because he inflicted the injury in question—and it is unfair to boot. Fate and Fortune are separated by luck, not by culpability. Singling out Fate for crushing financial responsibility and sparing Fortune any responsibility is not just arbitrary, it is unjust.

Negligence liability does not require that the costs of accidents—even negligent accidents arising from essentially identical risk impositions—be spread among those who create similar risks of harm, whereas enterprise liability does. Whereas enterprise liability asserts that accident costs should be internalized by the enterprise whose costs they are and be dispersed and distributed among those who constitute the enterprise, negligence liability holds that injurers have a duty to make reparation when they injure others through their own carelessness. Negligence liability justifies *shifting* concentrated losses, whereas enterprise liability justifies *dispersing and distributing* concentrated losses.

To be sure, nothing in negligence liability forbids injurers from insuring against potential liability, but nothing in negligence liability requires it either. Insurance is not integral to negligence liability, even though insuring against negligence liability is standard modern practice. Moreover, using insurance to disperse the non-negligent accident costs characteristic of an activity across pools of victims who are bound together only by their actuarial similarity is likewise less reasonable than dispersing them across the injurers who create similar risks and benefit from doing so. People who do not benefit from an activity may reasonably object to bearing its costs when those who do benefit might be made to bear its costs with equal ease. Fairness thus favors dispersing the costs of non-negligent accidents among all those who create similar risks of such accidents, just as much as it favors dispersing the costs of accidents precipitated by wrongdoing among lucky and unlucky wrongdoers. Pooling the risks of negligent accidents, but not the risks of non-negligent accidents, is presumptively less fair than pooling both sets of risks.

2. Relaxing Causation

The argument that enterprise liability treats actual and potential enterprise injurers more fairly than negligence liability does de-emphasize the importance of linking responsibility for harm to stringent proof of actual causation. It casts doubt on the moral desirability of the traditional tort insistence on a relatively

---

[75] See Chapter Three, *supra*, pp. 117–20. Waldron's example is fiction, but not fantasy. A 1970 US Department of Transportation Study reported: "In Washington, D.C., a 'good' driver viz., one without an accident within the preceding five years, commits on average, in five minutes of driving, at least nine errors of different kinds." US Department of Transportation, Automobile Insurance and Compensation Study 177–78 (1970), quoted in Honoré 1999, *supra* note 74, at 36–37.

strict conception of actual causation when the harm at hand arises from the organized activities and systemic risks to which enterprise liability applies. When cause and cause alone distinguishes those who injure from those who do not, luck and luck alone distinguishes those who bear liability from those who escape it. Insisting on actual causation of harm as a necessary condition of responsibility when luck and luck alone determines who among equally culpable parties caused harm is arbitrary and unjustifiable.[76] There is no good reason why a person unfortunate enough to have her carelessness issue in massive injury should bear massive loss, while many others who have been identically culpable are spared all responsibility.

Within the law of torts proper, the attenuation of causation in enterprise liability is most visible in the market share liability devised to respond to the DES[77] mass accident. Market share liability seeks to align financial responsibility with tortious risk imposed, not with actual causation of harm traditionally conceived.[78] Even in more ordinary cases, where enterprise liability reconfigures a preexisting form of liability in tort, it attenuates causation by seeking to hold activities responsible for those tortious wrongs that are increased above their background level by the presence in the world of the activity at issue. In a doctrine such as vicarious liability, for example, the underlying tort whose imputation to the enterprise is at issue is governed by traditional criteria of causation. But the imputation of that underlying wrong to the enterprise is determined by asking if the underlying tort is *characteristic of*—rather than *caused by*—the firm's activity. By relaxing tort law's rigid causation requirements, enterprise liability in many cases can offer a fairer way to assign responsibility for the redress of harms arising within our modern, interrelated world of activities.

This relaxation of causation is, as we shall see, at least as pronounced in administrative plans that embody enterprise liability principles beyond the law of torts.

E. Enterprise Liability beyond Tort

For diverse reasons, administrative alternatives to the law of torts—workers' compensation schemes, no-fault automobile insurance, statutory schemes for the compensation of certain kinds of injuries (e.g., ones inflicted by vaccination)—deserve our attention. First, these administrative schemes are themselves

---

[76] With small numbers, this is the lesson of *Summers v. Tice*, 199 P.2d 1 (Cal. 1948).

[77] During 1938–1971 millions of pregnant women were prescribed DES, a synthetic estrogen. It has been linked to increased rates of breast cancer for the women who were prescribed DES and to increased rates of vaginal cancer, infertility, and pregnancy complications for daughters born to women who were prescribed DES. Center for Disease Control, About DES, https://stacks.cdc.gov/view/cdc/11784.

[78] See, *e.g.*, Sindell v. Abbot Laboratories, 607 P.2d 924 (Cal. 1980).

versions of enterprise liability. In light of contemporary claims of radical discontinuity, their continuity with the law of torts is worth establishing. Second, administrative schemes are important because they can institute the idea of *fairness* that animates enterprise liability in circumstances where tort law cannot do so. This contradicts the common belief that these schemes embody only loss-spreading or insurance ideas which have little or nothing in common with the law of torts.[79] Third, administrative schemes illuminate vividly important elements of enterprise liability logic. Not only do they highlight the attenuation of causation that characterizes enterprise liability as a whole, they also underscore the elasticity of the idea of an "enterprise." Indeed, the idea of enterprise liability found its first full expression not in the law of torts, but in one of these schemes—namely, workers' compensation law.[80]

1. Advantages of Administrative Alternatives

In the course of examining the common law of negligence, we saw that direct, statutory regulation of risk sometimes steps in to help negligence law articulate duties of care, and sometimes takes over the task of articulating and enforcing such duties. The doctrine of statutory negligence, for instance, enables the common law of negligence to incorporate precise statutory specifications of rights and responsibilities. Traffic codes spell out comprehensive systems of coordinate precaution in a way that the common law cannot. In Chapter Five, we saw that, because tort is a law of reparation, direct regulation of risk can respond more effectively than the law of torts to risks that threaten serious and irreparable injury. The ex post remedy of reparation falters in the face of irreparable injury, whereas legislatures and administrative agencies have the power to require appropriately stringent precautions against such harm ex ante. Enterprise liability within tort stands in a similar relation to administrative schemes such as workers' compensation. Administrative schemes can sometimes institute enterprise liability better than the common law of torts because legislatures and administrative agencies have institutional powers of law articulation that common law courts lack.

No-fault automobile insurance is one of the more familiar administrative alternatives to tort, and a particularly illuminating example of the capacity of an administrative scheme to effect enterprise liability in a circumstance where the common law of torts cannot do so. It may seem surprising to characterize

---

[79] See, *e.g.*, Jules Coleman, Risks and Wrongs 395–406 (Oxford, rev. ed., 2002); Weinrib 2012, *supra* note 20, at 38–42; Ripstein 2016, *supra* note 20, at 294.

[80] See, *e.g.*, Jeremiah Smith, Sequel to Workmen's Compensation Acts, 27 Harv. L. Rev. 235, 344 (1914); Young B. Smith 1923, *supra* note 36, at 456 (addressing the idea that accident costs should be distributed among those who benefit from the enterprise that creates them as a distinctive conception of strict liability, and tracing that idea to the Workmen's Compensation Acts adopted around the turn of the twentieth century). For discussion, see Keating 2001, *supra* note 3.

an insurance scheme as a form of enterprise liability, but when potential victims are equally potential injurers, mandatory loss insurance can be used to institute a kind of enterprise liability. In the common law of torts, enterprise liability takes the form of strict injurer liability, and it is linked to liability insurance. No-fault automobile insurance, by contrast, is a form of loss insurance which displaces negligence liability in tort. And loss insurance itself is usually thought of as an alternative to tort liability. Moreover, within the boundaries of traditional tort law, the availability of loss insurance has long been conceived as a reason to restrict tort liability. If the victim is in a better position to insure against a loss than the injurer is, that superior loss-bearing capacity is a reason to restrict the scope of a negligent tortfeasor's responsibility more than we otherwise might.[81] Loss insurance disperses costs that would otherwise be concentrated on the victim, thereby diminishing the need for tort liability. Where enterprise liability tends to expand tort liability, loss insurance tends to contract it.

Loss insurance seems like an unlikely instrument for instituting enterprise liability for another reason as well. In traditional tort cases, loss insurance is unlikely to disperse injury costs across those who benefit from the creation of the relevant risk. When victims and injurers are strangers to one another, strict liability coupled with liability insurance will tend to disperse the costs of characteristic risks across those who benefit from their creation because efficient risk-pooling requires pooling injurers who impose similar risks of injury. This tends to disperse the costs of any given type of non-negligent accident across those who create similar risks of such accidents. Loss insurance does not have an equally strong tendency to disperse losses across those who benefit from the risks that cause those losses, because efficient loss insurance only requires dispersing accident costs across some pool of actuarially similar victims. Loss insurance pools victims who suffer similar injuries, not injurers who impose similar risks.

When injurers and victims are members of the same closed community of risk, however, loss insurance can distribute the costs of that community's characteristic risks as fairly as liability insurance does. It can do so for reasons illustrated by theorists of tort as a law of reciprocity of risk correct assertion that the practice of driving is a canonical instance of a "community of risk." Under compulsory loss insurance, each member of such a community of risk bears his

---

[81] See, e.g., Ryan v. N.Y. Central Railroad Co., 35 N.Y. 210, 217 (1866) (holding that negligence liability for starting a fire should not extend beyond the house immediately set afire by the defendant's negligence, in part because "each man" is "enabled to obtain a reasonable security" by insuring against loss). For modern opinions adjusting the scope of liability in light of the availability of first-party loss insurance, see *Barber Lines v. Donau Maru*, 764 F.2d 50 (1st Cir. 1985) (Breyer, J.); *Weinberg v. Dinger*, 524 A.2d 366 (N.J. 1987). In the same vein, modern critics of enterprise liability in tort have often favored (victim) loss insurance as an alternative to (injurer) enterprise liability. See Epstein 1985, *supra* note 37; Priest, Current Insurance Crisis, 1987, *supra* note 17; Priest, Modern Tort Law, 1987, *supra* note 17.

or her fair share of its characteristic accident costs in the form of a loss insurance premium. Under liability insurance, they bear their fair share in the form of a liability insurance premium. Within a community of risk, then, it may be possible to use either compulsory loss insurance or strict liability to institute enterprise liability and thereby distribute the costs of characteristic risk fairly—across those who benefit from its creation. When compulsory loss insurance or strict liability can both distribute accident costs fairly, the choice between them turns on considerations of administrability, cost, and risk reduction. In the automobile accident context, for instance, no-fault insurance appears cheaper and easier to administer. Cheaper, because it does not require transferring the costs of non-negligent accidents from victims to injurers. Easier to administer, because in the absence of fault, it is hard to attribute automobile related accidents to one party as the "injurer." This attribution problem is, in fact, so acute that strict liability in its usual form—holding injurers liable for all the physical harms that issue from the characteristic risks of their activity—is not a live alternative to negligence.[82] By contrast, it is easy to identify an injury inflicted by the activity of driving, and therefore easy to implement no-fault automobile insurance.

No-fault automobile insurance illustrates two general advantages that non-tort administrative schemes have over enterprise liability in tort. First, such schemes are often able to solve attribution problems that common law incarnations of enterprise liability cannot. "Causal" problems—the inability to distinguish injurer from victim in the absence of some fault criterion—prevent the law of torts from imposing strict liability in tort on automobile accidents. No-fault insurance circumvents this problem. By requiring victims to insure against non-negligent losses (as well as negligent ones), no-fault insurance is able to attribute the non-negligent accident costs of driving to the activity. Compulsory loss insurance attributes the costs of automobile accidents to the activity of driving without requiring us to sort injurers from victims in cases of non-negligent injury. Other administrative schemes also solve attribution problems which would bedevil, if not defeat, the common law of torts, by specifying in detail which injuries are to be attributed to a particular activity. The National Childhood Vaccine Injury Act, for example, incorporates a "Vaccine Injury Table," listing illnesses associated with various vaccines and time periods following the administration of a vaccination within which the first symptom or manifestation of an illness may occur. Proof that an illness occurred within a specific time period creates a rebuttable presumption that the vaccination was its cause. Aggregate statistical connections between exposure and illness establish causation.

---

[82] See Fletcher v. Rylands, 159 Eng. Rep. 737, 744 (Ex. 1866), quoted *infra* note 88. See also Hammontree v. Jenner, 97 Cal. Rptr. 739, 741–42 (Ct. App. 1971) (declining to apply strict liability to automobile accidents in part because only legislation is capable of articulating a comprehensive non-fault system for attributing accidents to actors).

The second advantage of administrative schemes is that they often can effect enterprise liability in circumstances where the common law cannot, because administrative schemes can exert more control over the mechanisms and institutions of insurance. Enterprise liability in tort must, for the most part, hope that the imposition of strict liability will stimulate the provision of appropriate self or third-party insurance against liability. Administrative schemes, by contrast, can compel the purchase of insurance,[83] which both stimulates the demand for insurance and facilitates risk-spreading by expanding the pool of the insured and preventing adverse selection.[84] Indeed, administrative schemes can foster the provision of insurance even more directly. Legislatures and administrative agencies can create appropriate insurance mechanisms and require the provision of insurance to parties who are either unable to self-insure or unable to purchase private insurance in the marketplace. State-sponsored insurance funds are a familiar part of workers' compensation law, for example, as is the practice of providing for assignment of rejected risks.[85]

Moreover, as no-fault automobile insurance itself shows, administrative schemes are capable of conceptualizing the relevant enterprise more broadly than it is normally conceptualized in the law of torts. Vicarious liability and product liability conceive of the relevant "activity" largely as the activity of a particular firm—the activity of a particular employer or product manufacturer. Workers' compensation shares this focus on the particular firms as the relevant unit of enterprise responsibility, but other administrative schemes do not. Other enterprise liability schemes attribute harms and wrongs to activities that cross the boundaries of firms, to entire industries, and even to society at large. No-fault automobile insurance governs the activity of driving, and the National Childhood Vaccination Act governs the society-wide practice of vaccination. The Price-Anderson Act covering nuclear accidents and the Black Lung Benefits Act are schemes of industry-wide liability. And the New Zealand Accident Compensation Scheme is society-wide. All of these schemes impose collective responsibility on some identifiable form of activity—the activity of an industry, or of a widespread social practice, or of society at large—for harms

---

[83] Compelled insurance is a universal feature of workers' compensation schemes, for example. See 14 Larson's Workers' Compensation Law § 150.01 (2019) ("All states require that compensation liability be secured.").

[84] See Mehr et al., 1985, *supra* note 65, at 35 (listing "a large group of homogeneous exposure units" as the first of seven criteria that "need to be considered before attempting to operate a successful insurance plan"). Note that a pool of insureds that is larger but less homogenous is not necessarily easier to insure. It depends on whether size dominates homogeneity in the context at hand.

[85] See 14 Larson's Workers' Compensation Law § 150.01 (2019) ("Six states require insurance in an exclusive state fund. Fourteen states have competitive state funds."); see also *id.* at § 150.05 (discussing Assigned Risk Practice). In a similar vein, the National Childhood Vaccine Injury Act of 1986, 42 U.S.C. §§ 300aa-10 to 300aa-34 (2000), creates a trust fund to pay compensation to those eligible to recover under the Act.

and wrongs that the activity introduces into social life. They construct communities of risk and responsibility larger than those constructed by the law of torts, and thereby write the idea of enterprise responsibility larger than the law of torts does.

Administrative alternatives to tort raise a host of important questions, particularly when they are compared with tort law itself. Some of those questions probe the logic of the fair distribution of accident costs. What, for example, are we to make of the reduced damages typically found in such schemes?[86] Is it fair to trade size of recovery for certainty of recovery and to key damages solely to the category of the injury and not to the particular loss suffered by the victim, as workers' compensation schemes typically do? Or is fairness better served by pegging damages at the level necessary to restore the particular victim to the condition that she was in before she was injured, as tort liability tries to do? Other questions raise important issues about the role of enterprise liability in reducing risk to a reasonable level. What effect does reducing damages, but making their payment more certain, have on the level of risk-reduction?[87] What effect does instituting enterprise liability by victim insurance—instead of by injurer strict liability—have on the level of avoidable or unavoidable risk associated with an activity? Still other questions have to do with the consequences of conceiving the relevant enterprise ever more broadly. Does the construction of ever larger communities of risk diminish the ability of these schemes to claim the mantle of enterprise responsibility? Do the activities that the schemes cover become too heterogeneous for us to speak meaningfully about shared participation in common activities and shared responsibility for the risks, harms, and wrongs characteristic of those activities? Is an alternative, instrumentalist, account of these schemes as institutions that leave responsibility out of the mix—and merely institute policies of deterrence and insurance—more convincing?

For anyone concerned with the inner logic, the extent, and the limits of enterprise liability, these are important questions, but they are beyond the scope of this chapter. For the purposes of this chapter, it suffices to show that these administrative schemes are linked to the law of torts through the idea of enterprise liability and the principle of fairness that informs it. How best to understand and evaluate particular schemes, and whether and when administrative schemes transcend enterprise liability and become something different altogether, are topics for another day.

---

[86] See Keeton et al., 2004, *supra* note 65, at 1159–64, 1203–06.

[87] For an attempt to investigate an aspect of this problem, see Yu-Ping Liao & Michelle J. White, No-fault for Motor Vehicles: An Economic Analysis, 4 Am. L. & Econ. Rev. 258 (2002).

2. Limits and Exceptions: The Resilience of Negligence Liability

The coin that we have been examining has a flip side. Even if the greater fairness of enterprise liability were widely accepted—and even if considerations of fairness were widely agreed to be decisive—enterprise liability would not expand to consume the whole of tort law. Priest's nightmare of ever expanding and endless enterprise liability is a dark fantasy, not a lucid reading of the logic of the liability form and its place in the larger law of torts. Within tort law, the prominent place of negligence liability would prove remarkably resilient, for at least three reasons.

First, it may often be impossible in practice for the common law to attribute accidents to activities without the benefit of fault criteria. Enterprise liability is liability for "characteristic risk," meaning reasonable risks of a particular kind of injury which *exceed* the *background level* of risk and flow from the long-run activity of an enterprise. The idea of an occupation's or a firm's "characteristic risks" is a comprehensible one, relatively well developed in case law. Even so, hard cases stemming from everyday facts are easy to conjure up. In many circumstances, we may have no way of attributing responsibility for harm to a specific activity without falling back on fault criteria. Baron Bramwell was pointing to this kind of problem when he observed in his opinion in *Rylands* that "[w]here two carriages come in collision, if there is no negligence in either it is as much the act of the one driver as of the other that they meet."[88] The rules of the road—rights of way, speed limits, and so on—fix the contours of reasonable care and allow us to attribute responsibility when vehicles collide. Without those rules, it is impossible for the law of torts to attribute responsibility for automobile accidents to any of the actors involved.

Second, risks may sometimes be idiosyncratic and therefore uninsurable from an actuarial perspective. When that is the case, we are back in Holmes' world of "isolated, ungeneralized wrongs." We are back in the world of individual acts. Enterprise liability presupposes the world of organized activities—the social world in which accidents are the actuarially predictable byproducts of large and enduring enterprises. In the world of acts, enterprise liability is unable to realize its aspiration to distribute unavoidable harm fairly across an activity and therefore across all those who benefit from the activity. When we are cast back into the world of acts, strict liability shifts the costs of accidents that should not be avoided from victims to injurers, but it does not distribute those costs across all those who benefit from the imposition of the risk in question. It simply "substitute[s] one form of risk for another—the risk of liability for the risk of personal loss."[89]

---

[88] *Fletcher*, 159 Eng. Rep. at 744. (Bramwell J. dissenting).
[89] Fletcher 1972, *supra* note 56, at 547.

Third, competing normative considerations may overcome the presumption that the principle of fairness generates in favor of enterprise liability. On a deontological conception, right relations among persons are the paramount concern of tort law. This chapter argues that the enterprise liability principle of fairness expresses a compelling conception of the proper relations among persons in the distinctively modern "world of activities." The general conception of enterprise liability, however, works with a spare notion of the relevant relations among persons, taking persons to be legal equals pursuing diverse ends and activities, and both imposing and bearing risks of accidental physical harm. In many circumstances, however, the relevant relations among persons are more complex than this, and those complexities bring other rights and responsibilities into play. The list of possible circumstances is open-ended; the march of time inevitably tosses up new cases. However, property rights and activities whose internal goods require assuming unusually great risks are two useful illustrations of the general truth.

a. Property Rights
When property rights circumscribe zones where people are free to do as they choose so long as they do not transgress the boundaries of those zones and harm others, the presence of those rights increases the attractiveness of enterprise liability and facilitates its administration.[90] Real property rights increase the attractiveness of enterprise liability when accidents arise from the overflow of one landowner's activities onto another's because ownership of real property confers special freedom of action within the property's borders and sharpens the boundaries between zones of activity. Within the borders of their properties, owners and occupiers are free to build reservoirs and keep wild boars, even if these activities impose abnormally great risks of injury. The special freedom conferred by property rights includes the freedom to use one's own property in an unusually risky way. When boars run beyond the boundaries of their owners' properties and reservoirs burst, however, owners and occupiers are justly subject to enterprise liability.[91] Overstepping the boundaries of one's property—and imposing the cost of one's activities on one's neighbors—is a paradigm case of unfairness.[92]

---

[90] See William K. Jones, Strict Liability for Hazardous Enterprise, 92 Colum. L. Rev. 1705, 1729, 1757, 1779 (1992) (emphasizing how strict liability can protect various zones of activity, including ones defined by property rights, from intrusion).

[91] See Marshall v. Ranne, 511 S.W.2d 255 (Tex. 1974) (holding a defendant strictly liable for injuries inflicted by his vicious hog when it escaped from his property and injured his neighbor); Rylands v. Fletcher, L.R. 3 H.L. 330 (1868).

[92] As is shown by *Rylands*, but also by the imposition of strict liability in *Shipley v. Fifty Associates*, 106 Mass. 194, 199 (1870) (addressing a claim brought by a plaintiff who walked on a public sidewalk and was struck by falling ice and snow that had accumulated on the defendant's peaked roof); and *Tuchkashinsky v. Lehigh & W. Coal Co.*, 49 A. 308 (Pa. 1901) (addressing claim brought by a plaintiff who was standing in the doorway of her father's house, 700 feet from the defendant's mine, and was harmed by the concussion from a blast caused when lightning ignited explosives stored at the mine).

When property rights circumscribe zones where people are free to do as they choose so long as they do not transgress the boundaries of those zones and harm others, the presence of those rights enables enterprise liability both normatively and practically. Normatively, the property rights increase the appeal of enterprise liability by constructing sharply differentiated zones. Within one zone, people are especially free to do as they please. When that zone ends, it is met by someone else's zone of discretionary choice and especially stringent obligations of non-interference take hold. Strict liability for escaping things—be those things cattle, water, or noxious fumes—becomes especially attractive.[93] Practically, property rights can enable enterprise liability by constructing crisp boundaries between activities, between what is mine and what is yours. Harms can be attributed to one party or another without recourse to fault criteria.

b. When Risk Is Essential to an Activity
By contrast, when risk is essential to the achievement of the goods that certain activities seek to realize, strict liability is particularly unattractive. Strict liability pushes toward the lowest level of risk that might be achieved. When risk is essential to the goods realized by an activity, however, reducing the risk destroys the value of the activity. Sports are the preeminent example here. Expert ski runs are more dangerous than novice ones because their dangers are inseparable from the challenges that make them worth skiing. To impose even ordinary negligence liability on the "inherent risks" of many risky recreational activities would often defeat the point of those activities. The risks are constitutive of the goods the activities pursue. When distinctive—and greater than normal—risks are essential to the realization of the good that an activity pursues, it is necessary to retreat from our normal conceptions of responsibility to prevent and rectify harm done. In tort doctrine, this is the domain of "primary assumption of the risk" and "relaxed duty."[94]

Enterprise liability's limitations need to be noted if we are to apply it well. For present purposes, however, we need not dig deep into the details of when and how to construct enterprise liability regimes. Our concern is with the larger lesson to be learned from these limitations. That larger lesson is that enterprise liability cannot, should not be, and is not irresistibly bent on swallowing the whole

---

[93] Fletcher v. Rylands, I L.R. Exch. 265, 279 (Ex. Ch. 1866) (Blackburn, J.) ("[T]he person who for his own purposes brings on his lands and collects and keeps anything likely to do mischief if it escapes, must keep it in at his peril.").

[94] See, *e.g.*, Crawn v. Campo, 643 A.2d 600 (N.J. 1994) (suspending duty of ordinary care in the recreational sports context, and adopting a recklessness standard); Scott v. Pacific West Mountain Resort, 834 P.2d 6, 13 (Wash. 1992) (applying the doctrine of "primary assumption of risk," which relieves prospective injurers of their duty of ordinary care, to skiing); Summer J. v. United States Baseball Federation, 258 Cal. Rptr. 3d 615, 621–24 (Ct. App. 2020) (discussing assumption of the risk in the context of baseball spectators).

of tort law or dealing with every domain of accidental injury in the very same way. The flip side of this coin is a lesson about why enterprise liability is important, namely, because it is a collective and strict framework of responsibility and a genuine overarching alternative to individual fault liability. We live in a world of organized enterprises and systemic risks. Unlike individual fault liability, enterprise liability arose in response to the emergence of the social world in which we now live. Unsurprisingly, it often responds to the distinctive features of risk in the modern world better than individual fault liability does. For one thing, unavoidable harm looms large in our world. The imposition of enterprise liability will often minimize its imposition, mitigate its impact, and distribute its costs fairly. Negligence liability, by contrast, sacrifices those whose misfortune it is to get in the way of the reasonably imposed risks of valuable activities to whatever good it is that the activity realizes. Negligence liability leaves the victims of these risks to cope with often devastating physical harm as best they can, while others profit from the infliction of that harm. This difference alone makes enterprise liability a powerful competitor to fault liability.

8
The Heterogeneity of Tort

This book began by remarking on the fact that the law of torts is both fundamental and elusive. In part, the subject's elusiveness is evidenced by the vastly different conceptions of tort proposed by contending contemporary theories. For economically inclined scholars, the law of torts is a law of accidents. Its primary role is to deter those—and only those—accidents which should be avoided because it costs less to avoid them than to allow them. For more traditionally inclined scholars, the law of torts is a law of wrongs, and its distinctive character is revealed more by its backward-looking remedial apparatus than by any forward-facing role it plays in discouraging the commission of wrongs or encouraging the avoidance of harm. For those less taken by theory, the heterogeneity of the wrongs recognized by the law of torts stokes the fear that the field is simply a grab bag of unrelated wrongs. Writing in 2021, Kenneth Abraham and G. Edward White concluded a learned study of attempts to impose order on the unruliness of modern tort law by declaring that tort law is "fundamentally... inherently fragmented [so that] the only fully accurate characterization of tort law [is that it] consist[s] of (some) civil wrongs not arising out of contract."[1] This nightmare that torts is merely a motley collection of heterogeneous wrongs meets and matches the theorists' Noble Dream that a spare and stark unity is latent beneath the field's turbulent surface.[2]

Ever since law and economics first colonized the field—and sought to show that tort law is a price system in fact if not in name—"unified grand theor[ies]" of tort law have proliferated in North American legal scholarship.[3] In contemporary American tort scholarship, the proposition that "it takes a theory to beat a theory" has an almost axiomatic quality, and what theories of tort tend to pursue is unification of the subject around a single, bold idea.[4] Arthur Ripstein's *Private Wrongs*—with its thesis that all torts reflect a single, spare principle of political morality—is

---

[1] Kenneth S. Abraham & G. Edward White, Conceptualizing Tort Law: The Continuous (and Continuing) Struggle, 80 Md. L. Rev. 293, 342 (2021).
[2] Tort scholarship echoes a larger oscillation in American legal thought. See H.L.A. Hart, American Jurisprudence Through English Eyes: The Nightmare and the Noble Dream, 11 Ga. L. Rev. 969, 972, 978 (1977) (arguing that American jurisprudence has been preoccupied with legal decision and oscillated between a nightmare of no constraint and a noble dream of complete determinacy).
[3] Scott Hershovitz, The Search for a Grand Unified Theory of Tort Law, 130 Harv. L. Rev. 942 (2017).
[4] John Gardner, Tort Law and Its Theory, in The Cambridge Companion to the Philosophy of Law 352–70, at 352 (John Tasioulas ed., Harvard, 2020). Gardner attributes the slogan to Richard A. Epstein, Common Law, Labor Law, and Reality: A Rejoinder to Professors Getman and Kohler, 92

a powerful case in point. As we have seen, for Ripstein, all of tort law instantiates the principle that "everyone is in charge of themselves and no one is in charge of anyone else."[5] In the same vein, Jules Coleman claims that corrective justice is the sovereign principle of tort; Ernest Weinrib asserts that the bipolar form of the traditional tort lawsuit is the master key to the morality of the field; and John Goldberg and Ben Zipursky propose that the power of civil recourse that tort confers on the victims of tortious wrongs is the defining feature of the legal subject.[6]

Grand unifying theories have provided the foil and the inspiration for this book's own perspective. The belief that grand unifying theories of tort tend to resist both the incompleteness and the conflict that characterize the field informs many of the book's more particular discussions. Grand, unifying theories are disposed to insist that the law of torts can be construed in such a way that it is fundamentally coherent and that the theory on offer reveals this coherence. Ernest Weinrib, for instance, asserts that once we recognize that the distinctive morality of "private law" is immanent in the law torts, we also recognize "the character of private law as a distinctive and coherent mode of ordering."[7] To vindicate this claim, however, Weinrib must recharacterize and reclassify forms of tort liability that do conform to his conception. For Weinrib, fault is the principle of responsibility that falls out of the equality of the parties to a tortious wrong and all strict liabilities are anomalous. He therefore recharacterizes the strict liability doctrine of abnormally dangerous activity liability as a stringent form of fault liability; he reclassifies the strict liability doctrine of *respondeat superior* as a body of agency law operating within tort; he explains the strict liability of nuisance doctrine as resting fundamentally on property conceptions; and he recasts the strict liability of the conditional privilege of private necessity as an instance of restitutionary liability.[8] In the same spirit, Arthur Ripstein eliminates the conflict between fault and strict liability by arguing that these competing principles of responsibility are both instances of the same wrong—two names for damaging someone else's person or property through the imposition of "excessive risk."[9] And both Weinrib and Ripstein tend to wall the "private law" of torts off from the "public law" of direct risk regulation and administrative alternatives to tort.[10]

Yale L.J. 1435, 1435 (1983). Gardner observes immediately that in England "theories are disposed of a lot more easily."

[5] See Chapter Three, *supra*, pp. 88-93
[6] For discussion of Coleman's view, see Chapter Two, *supra*, pp. 25–30. For discussion of Weinrib's view, see Chapter Three, *supra*, pp. 69–75. For Goldberg & Zipursky's view, see generally John C.P. Goldberg & Benjamin Zipursky, Recognizing Wrongs (2020), and the comments in Chapter Two, *supra*, pp. 22–23.
[7] Ernest J. Weinrib, The Idea of Private Law 50 (Oxford, rev. ed., 2012).
[8] *Id.* at 184–203.
[9] See Chapter Three, *supra*, pp. 93–95
[10] See Chapter Three, *supra*, pp. 104–111.

This book has tried to chart a course between the Scylla of intellectual incoherence and the Charybdis of seamless, but untenable, intellectual unity. Chapter Two engaged corrective justice theory as developed by Jules Coleman and others and—through the lens of those writings—the economic analysis with which corrective justice theory itself wrestled. On the one hand, Chapter Two argued that corrective justice theorists were right to argue that orthodox economic analysis offers an implausible account of tort adjudication as a forward-looking search for cheapest cost-avoiders—not the backward-looking search for tortious wrongdoers that it presents itself as being. On the other hand, Chapter Two argued that corrective justice theory goes wrong in casting corrective justice as the sovereign principle of tort. This puts the cart before the horse. First and foremost, the law of torts is a law that imposes mutual obligations not to impair or interfere with each other's urgent interests. Its duties of repair and powers of recourse come into play only when some actor fails to comply with its primary norms. Chapter Three engaged the most elegant and important "unified grand theory" of tort law's primary obligations now in circulation, namely, the view that marches under the banner of "tort as private law." Chapter Three argued that neither the "idea of private law" nor the principle "that everyone is in charge of themselves and no one in charge of anyone else" is a master concept that makes the basic structure and content of tort clear, coherent, and convincing. We cannot understand the law of torts without attending to the diverse interests that tort law protects, and we go astray when we regard tort as an autonomous body of "private wrongs," walled off from the "public law" of the administrative state.

Chapter Three therefore concluded by taking a position that some might characterize as a unifying theory of its own. Once we give interests their due, and situate tort within the structure of basic justice, we see that tort is an internally complex institution and one member of a family of institutions that seek to rule an important domain of basic justice. Basic justice requires that *some* institution secure people against diverse forms of interference and impairment so that persons may pursue their ends and purposes as equal and independent members of civil society. The law of torts proper is private in form because it is concerned with what we owe *to one another* and not with our relations to the state, but the private law of torts has public concerns. It does justice, and justice is a matter that affects all of us. Part of what we owe to each other in the way of basic justice is to devise and uphold institutions that protect our essential interests against unwarranted interference by each other as we go about our lives in civil society. In our legal system, tort law shares responsibility for addressing those matters with legal institutions that are part of the administrative state—with direct regulation of risk and administrative schemes addressing diverse domains of accidental harms and health injuries.

Direct risk regulation and administrative schemes addressing domains of accidental harm are both cooperative with, and alternative to, the private law of torts. Direct risk regulation completes the law of torts because reparation is the default and dominant tort remedy. Tort is therefore undone by injuries which are severe and irreparable. Indeed, it concedes defeat by refusing to award damages for the value to the victims of wrongful death of the lives that those victims have lost. Responding adequately to severe, irreparable injury requires resources that the law of torts does not have. Especially stringent precautions are the proper response to the prospect of irreparable injury; its harmful effects cannot be erased after the fact. Ex ante regulation of risk thus steps in to plug the hole in the law of torts. Administrative schemes are related to the common law of torts through the idea of enterprise liability. Enterprise liability asserts that major social activities, not isolated individual actions, are the chief sources of serious accidental harm in modern social life and should be made to bear responsibility for the harms that are the price of their presence in the world. Enterprise liability is found both in modern American tort law and in administrative alternatives to tort. Because legislatures and administrative agencies have superior capacities to construct communities of responsibilities, they can institute enterprise liability in ways that the common law cannot. Courts cannot construct workers' compensation schemes or vaccination injury schemes piecemeal through case-by-case adjudication. Administrative alternatives can thus perfect forms of enterprise liability whose full realization is beyond the institutional powers of the common law of torts.

Direct regulation of risk and administrative schemes frequently displace as well as complete the common law of torts because they vie with the private law of torts for dominion over the same domains of social life. The New Zealand Accident Compensation Scheme, for instance, displaces the private law of tort in a wholesale way. It takes accidental injury away from tort law. The schemes we are familiar with in the United States—for workplace accidents, nuclear accidents, automobile accidents, black lung disease, and vaccination-related harms—effect less drastic displacements. They displace tort from diverse activities (e.g., vaccination, automobile accidents), domains (e.g., workplace injuries), or industries (e.g., coal mining). Tort remains the default institution governing our rights and responsibilities with respect to accidental wrongs. Direct risk regulation, for its part, displaces the law of torts by fixing standards of precaution for diverse kinds of risk imposition—occupational and environmental, especially. Direct risks regulation thus takes away the default common law power of courts to fix standards of reasonable precaution.

The overarching structure of tort law that emerges from these chapters approximately tracks the structure that Tom Grey attributes to the mature thought of Oliver Wendell Holmes.[11] Our modern law of torts—the law that emerged

---

[11] Thomas C. Grey, Holmes on Torts (unpublished manuscript) (on file with author). See also Thomas C. Grey, Accidental Torts, 54 Vand. L. Rev. 1225, 1256–81 (2001).

when tort was freed from the forms of action and reorganized around substantive principles of responsibility—is centered on accidental harm and dominated by the fault principle. Domination, however, is not absolute dominion. Modern tort law makes room for significant strict liabilities and for an open-ended list of intentional wrongs. On the one hand, tort law's internal divisions and conflicts reflect the diversity of the ways in which we may wrong one another. On the other hand, tort's heterogeneity and internal conflict embody debate over just what kind of rights we should confer on one another and what kind of reciprocal responsibilities we should demand of each other. The collective responsibility articulated by enterprise liability differs fundamentally from the individual responsibility articulated by average reasonable person doctrine in negligence law.

The persistence of sharp disagreement within tort law may well frustrate attempts to unify tort around a *single principle* of right and responsibility, but the problem here may lie with our theoretical ambitions not with our law. Our law of torts is heterogeneous for good reasons. Its diversity and its internal disagreements reflect reasonable responses to the wrongs and harms that it addresses. The diversity and transience of various intentional torts teaches this lesson. Over the course of the past century, torts protecting privacy and emotional tranquility have blossomed while torts treating seduction and champerty as legal wrongs have withered and died. At any given moment, the list of intentional torts is diverse and open-ended. We can create new intentional torts, legislatively or judicially, whenever we conclude that there is an interest serious enough to warrant legal recognition as a right, and deliberate interferences with that interest serious enough to protect that right against. We can adopt and abandon torts identifying wrongs as diverse as alienation of affection; malicious prosecution; spoliation of evidence; abuse of legal process; criminal conversation; wrongful interference with expectancy of inheritance; and internet harassment.[12] The list of intentional torts changes over time, and even individual torts ebb and flow. Scholars who think torts is a disorganized, fragmented mess see in this heterogeneity compelling evidence that the law of torts is just a laundry list of "civil wrongs not arising out of contract."[13]

Unless we are gripped by the urge to reduce all of tort to a single principle of political morality, though, the threat posed by the diversity of the intentional torts—and by their transformations over time—is difficult to discern. Why should we presume that the coercively enforceable obligations we owe not

---

[12] Dan B. Dobbs et al., Hornbook on Torts (West, 2d ed., 2016), includes all these wrongs, besides internet harassment, as examples of torts. The Ontario Court of Justice in Canada recently recognized internet harassment as a tort. See Caplan v. Atas, 2021 ONSC 670 (Ont. Super. Ct. Mar. 20, 2021).

[13] Kenneth S. Abraham & G. Edward White, Conceptualizing Tort Law: The Continuous (and Continuing) Struggle, 80 Md. L. Rev. 293, 303 (2021).

to interfere with or impair each other's essential interests should not be diverse and should not change over time? The interests that we have that are urgent enough to warrant legal protection—and the ways in which we can wrong one another—are diverse. We have good reason to regard our privacy, our property, our psychological integrity, and our contractual relations as important, and we can wrongly interfere with each of these in diverse ways. Furthermore, social conditions change. There can be no tort of internet harassment until there is an internet. Our judgments of which interests are urgent enough to warrant protection by legal rights also change over time. The slow, halting expansion of recovery for emotional suffering reflects a judgment that psychological integrity can be as urgent an interest as physical integrity.[14] The relative decline of defamation evidences a devaluation of the importance of a certain kind of status.[15] The recognition of privacy as a distinct interest not reducible to property reflects the judgment that the existence of social spaces where one may be free from unwelcome observation is essential to the formation of a particular kind of personal identity.[16] There is no reason to be worried by the fact that particular torts ebb and flow over time. Whatever objections we have should be directed against the adoption, articulation, abandonment, or absence of specific intentional wrongs. Debate over which interests are urgent enough to warrant the protections of the law of torts *ought* to be a part of the larger discourse of tort law.

Moreover, the heterogeneity of the intentional torts does not entail that the legal subject is simply a laundry list of civil wrongs. The *role* of tort law is stable. By specifying interests important enough to warrant the law's protection, tort law establishes an essential part of our security as members of civil society—an important part of what John Stuart Mill called "the groundwork of our existence." Furthermore, the core concerns of modern tort law have been quite stable. The wrongs that we count important enough to teach in our first-year classes involve either physical harm to persons and their property, or the violation of powers of control over valuable zones of discretionary choice. Tort is thus a law of wrongs that hang together in an important way. Both sovereignty-based and harm-based torts protect basic powers of agency. Sovereignty-based torts protect powers of control over our persons and our property. These powers are essential aspects of our personal freedom: they enable us to work our wills on the world. Physical harm to our persons, for its part, is an assault on the basic instrument we use to work our wills in the world. In Rawlsian terms, the security from physical harm

---

[14] See Gregory C. Keating, The Ambiguous Standing of Suffering in Negligence Law, in Knowing the Suffering of Others 78, 78–121 (Austin Sarat ed., 2014).

[15] *Cf.* David S. Ardia, Reputation in a Networked World: Revisiting the Social Foundations of Defamation Law, 45 Harv. C.R.-C.L. L. Rev. 261, 304–05 (2010); David A. Anderson, Is Libel Law Worth Reforming?, 140 U. Pa. L. Rev. 487, 489 (1991).

[16] Samuel D. Warren & Louis D. Brandeis, The Right to Privacy, 4 Harv. L. Rev. 193, 205 (1890).

that is tort law's chief concern is a kind of primary good. The physical integrity of our persons is an essential condition of effective agency. To be harmed is to be put in an impaired condition, a condition in which the normal powers through which one exerts one's will upon the world are diminished. The core concerns of tort law today thus fit Blackstone's conception of the subject as a body of law concerned with protecting people's liberty, property, and security.[17]

The stability of tort law's role and the persistence of its core concerns over time coexist, however, with internal turbulence and incompleteness. Tort is incomplete because it is our default institution for addressing risks of physical harm, and it cannot adequately address severe and irreparable harms. And its power to construct complex systems of coordinate rights and responsibilities is limited. Tort law is turbulent because it is torn between competing principles of fault and strict liability, and between individualistic and collective conceptions of responsibility. Within the overarching envelope fixed by its role and its enduring concerns, then, tort law encompasses a diversity of institutional forms and a plurality of principles and conceptions of right and responsibility.

The inclination to insist on a single grand unifying principle which eradicates all conflicts from the law is, therefore, a mistake. Insofar as the ambition of grand theories is to unify tort law by denying the conflicts that characterize our law, grand theory has set itself the wrong task. Tort law is split between fault and strict liabilities because we have good reasons to care about both harm that should be avoided and harm that should not be avoided. Tort and its alternatives are split between individual and collective conceptions of responsibility because accidental harm is both a matter of individual wrongdoing and the inevitable byproduct of basic, social activities. Norms of safe, feasible, and cost-justified precaution contend with one another in our law in part because we ourselves are deeply divided between consequentialist and deontological moral conceptions, and our law reflects our divisions. Safe and feasible precaution reflects the priority of avoiding harm, a priority that is justified from a deontological perspective but wrongheaded from an economic perspective. Cost-justified precaution reflects a broadly consequentialist outlook, cashed out in economic terms. For their part, tort's entrenched conflicts between fault and strict liability and individual and collective responsibility cannot be purged from our law by any theory. We misunderstand the law of torts when we recast negligence and strict liability as the same wrong, and we deform the law when we cast non-fault-based forms of liability out of tort on the ground that tort liability is fault-based.

---

[17] See 1 Blackstone, Commentaries ∗125, ∗129, ∗134, ∗138 (1766) (explaining that the common law is founded on "absolute" rights to liberty, security, and property). By "absolute," Blackstone seems to mean what we would call "natural." For an illuminating discussion, see Grey 2001, *supra* note 11, at 1247–55.

The fault here is with the theories, not with the law. The point of these efforts to recharacterize and rearrange tort law's strict liabilities is to make the law fit the Procrustean bed that the theory itself is determined to impose. We do better to conceive of tort theory in a broadly interpretive way. The basic task of tort theory is to make the best sense it can of the law that we have. Our law has developed in response to ever-changing social conditions and social problems; the fact that it does not conform to the prescriptions of a single theory is usually not a compelling reason to toss it out. We do better to pursue the interpretive enterprise of attempting to fit and to justify the law that has developed as best we can.[18] The basic task is thus twofold: to make sense of the law we have and to make it the best law that we can reasonably hope it to be. Because our law of torts contains competing principles and conceptions of responsibility, an interpretively adequate theory of tort law needs to make *some* place for those competing principles and conceptions. This is what the dimension of "fit" requires. The dimension of "justification" seeks to shape and present our law of torts in its best incarnation, subject to the constraint of fit.

Pursuing these two ambitions, this book advances and argues for its own contestable interpretations of negligence and strict liability, and advances arguments in favor of standards of precaution that other normative conceptions criticize. But it has also sought to domesticate the conflicts embedded in tort law by making *some* place for the diverse standards of precaution, principles of responsibility, and conceptions of agency embedded in the law. Fault liability, strict liability, direct regulation of risk, and administrative schemes all have their places. The book also argues for recognizing an appropriate scope of application for more particular doctrines which tend to conflict and compete with one another if they are treated as universally applicable. Chapter Five, for example, argues that safe, feasible, and cost-justified precautions all have places in our law because they are fitting responses to different circumstances. Safe precaution is the first-best norm for the physical integrity of persons; feasible precaution is the best we can do when we cannot make activities "safe" but cannot forego them either; and cost-justified precaution is appropriate when the injury inflicted is repairable and the interests at stake are fungible. That argument is the offspring of an ambition to accept and make sense of tort law's heterogeneity.

Equally important, the book supposes that two competing views of accidental harm are compelling. One view sees accidental harm as primarily the side effect of wrongful individual agency. The other sees accidental harm as primarily the byproduct of basic, productive social activities. The first view sees tort as a part of the "world of acts," whereas the second view sees tort as part of the

---

[18] Broadly speaking, the view here is Dworkinian. See, *e.g.*, Ronald Dworkin, Law's Empire (Belknap Press, 1986).

"world of activities."[19] Both views fix on relations among persons, but the first view conceives of the normal tort lawsuit as arising out of a one-off collision between two parties going about their lives as members of civil society. The first view conceives of tort as institution that governs Holmes' world of "isolated, ungeneralized wrongs." The second view, by contrast, focuses on our participation in diverse activities, which make us members of diverse communities of risk and responsibility. The second view conceives of tort as an institution that governs Holmes' world of "organized activities." Traditional fault liability is the regime of right and responsibility presumptively fitted to the "world of acts," whereas strict enterprise liability is the regime fitted to the "world of activities." This way of thinking is first and foremost a heuristic for making sense of the factual assumptions and normative commitments of two competing tort conceptions, but it does suggest a starting point for dividing the labor of tort law between the two regimes. Individual fault liability is, presumptively, the regime better suited to governing the one-off collisions of natural persons going about their lives in civil society, whereas enterprise liability is, presumptively, the regime better suited to governing the activities of public agencies and private firms. To be sure, that starting point is only a presumption and leaves much hard work to be done. The two categories do not themselves tell us when it is that some form of accidental harm should be understood as the byproduct of an organized, enduring activity and when accidental harms should instead be understood to arise out of the isolated acts of individuals going about their lives idiosyncratically. Theory can orient us, but it cannot construct complete legal regimes for us. And competing normative considerations may call for departing from this presumptive division of labor.

Interpretive theories have a prescriptive side. The arguments of this book therefore go well beyond attempting to make sense of tort law's diverse and often conflicting commitments. The accounts of tort law's basic principles of responsibility, conceptions of agency, and institutional forms advanced in this book embody normative commitments and make normative claims. Most importantly, the primary normative framework of the book is deontological. It takes tort law to be concerned not with the production of states of the world containing as much wealth or welfare as possible but with what it is that we owe to one another with respect to a basic domain of justice. Tort law seeks to secure basic conditions of effective agency for equal and independent persons by spelling out what we owe to each other in the way of mutual rights not to be interfered with and impaired in various ways—and reciprocal responsibilities not to do so. The view that tort law is fundamentally about the relations among persons is both extracted from tort law and rhetoric and shapes the book's account of tort. Tort

---

[19] See Chapter Seven, *supra*, pp. 285–288

law's embrace of reasonableness as its central concept, for instance, invites us to theorize tort in a deontological way, because reasonableness is an intrinsically moral concept. We act reasonably when we take the rights and interests of those others that our actions affect into account and act in ways that are justifiable to them. Conversely, tort law's embrace of reasonableness has something to teach us about the moral concept. Legal doctrine develops the norms of reasonable risk imposition in detailed ways, and these deepen our understanding of what reasonableness requires.

This deontological conception of tort law as an institution which seeks to establish basic conditions of effective agency for persons with their own distinct lives to lead also shapes the book's treatment of diverse standards of precaution. The book defends the common-sense conviction that harm and benefit are asymmetrically important and that harm has a special, negative moral significance. Serious physical harm compromises basic powers of agency and even ends agency itself; its avoidance therefore has special priority. The priority of avoiding harm helps to justify negligence law's placement of physical harm at its center, and it also helps to justify stringent standards of safe and feasible precaution as sound in principle and plausible in practice. Last, the special, negative significance of harm also provides important support for strict liability. Distinctively, strict liability holds actors responsible for inflicting harms that should not have been avoided. Harm is bad for those who suffer it even when the infliction of that harm could not or should not have been averted. Part of the case for strict liability, as Judge Traynor saw long ago, is that even unavoidable harm has moral significance. It is an "overwhelming misfortune to the person injured." When it can "be insured by the [defendant] and distributed among the public as a cost of doing business," strict enterprise liability is preferable to negligence.[20]

Normative theory generally underdetermines legal norms and institutions.[21] No morality of right and responsibility, deontological or otherwise, is so fully specified that it can settle the details of doctrine. Were this not the case, we would not need to construct law. The details of doctrine put flesh on the bones of abstract principles and values. This fleshing out, in turn, reshapes our understanding of the values themselves. When we interpret law, the extant law that we interpret helps to shape our understanding of the values that we take that law to embody. Tort doctrine thus stands both in an instrumental relation *and* in a constitutive relation to the values that it institutes. On the one hand, diverse tort doctrines and institutions are instruments for realizing values and interests that can be stated independently of the law. "Safety" nicely illustrates this point. We

---

[20] Escola v. Coca Cola Bottling Co., 150 P.2d 436, 440 (Cal. 1944) (Traynor, J., concurring).
[21] See Richard Craswell, Contract Law, Default Rules, and the Philosophy of Promising, 88 Mich. L. Rev. 489 (1989) (observing that the morality of promising underdetermines contract doctrine). Craswell's point holds more generally.

can speak of safety and its significance without talking about tort doctrines that are animated by the pursuit of safety.[22] On the other hand, the law articulates these interests and values in ways which illuminate the values themselves. Standards of safe and feasible precaution show us that the inchoate and abstract conviction that "life has a value beyond all price" can, in fact, be cashed out in norms which reflect the asymmetrical badness of harm and define a set of legal commitments different from those that express the value of efficiency. The safety and feasibility standards show that the normative commitment to the pricelessness of life need not be soft-minded sentimentalism.

This book's normative and interpretive arguments might lead readers to see this book, too, as an exercise in grand unifying theory. And perhaps it is— a theory that articulates a pluralistic account of tort law's basic institutions, conceptions of legal right and wrongful agency, and principles of responsibility. There is, I think, no reason to resist this characterization. What we have reason to insist on, or at least aspire to, is that interpretive tort theory both help us to understand tort law's commitments as they are and offer a vision of how tort law might be the best version of itself. That vision will, no doubt, be partial, imperfect, and tentative. But once we think of tort theory as an interpretive enterprise, we should also think of it as an essentially contestable enterprise. In tort theory, progress may be marked not by the perfection of agreement or the imposition of a Procrustean unity on tort law but by the deepening and refining of debate.[23] That debate never ends, and it never should. Its persistence is both a sign and an aspect of tort law's vitality.

---

[22] In calling safety an interest, we are asserting that people generally do regard it as urgent. In calling safety a value, we are asserting that people are right to regard safety as an urgent interest.

[23] Cf. Clifford Geertz, Thick Description: Toward an Interpretive Theory of Culture, in The Interpretation of Cultures 3, 29 (1973) ("Anthropology, or at least interpretive anthropology, is a science whose progress is marked less by a perfection of consensus than by a refinement of debate.").

Bibliography

Books

Ackerman, Bruce A., Private Property and the Constitution (Yale, 1977).
Adler, Matthew D., Cost-Benefit Analysis, Encyclopedia of Law and Society: American and Global Perspectives 304 (David S. Clark ed., Sage Publications, Inc., 2007).
Adler, Matthew D. & Posner, Eric, New Foundations of Cost-Benefit Analysis (Harvard, 2006).
Alchian, Armen A., Cost, in Encyclopedia of the Social Sciences 404 (David L. Sills ed., New York, 1968).
Allen, Danielle S., The World of Prometheus: The Politics of Punishing in Democratic Athens (Princeton, 2000).
The American Law Institute, Enterprise Responsibility for Personal Injury (The Institute, 1991).
Aristotle, Nicomachean Ethics (David Ross trans., Oxford, 1980).
Augustine, The Confessions (Michael P. Foley ed., Hackett, 2006).
Berlin, Isaiah, Two Concepts of Liberty (Oxford, 1958).
Blanding, Michael, The Map Thief (Gotham, 2014).
Bowden, Mark, Black Hawk Down (Grove Press, 1993).
Calabresi, Guido & Bobbitt, Philip, Tragic Choices (W.W. Norton, 1978).
Calabresi, Guido, Ideals, Beliefs, Attitudes, and the Law: Private Law Perspectives on a Public Law Problem (Syracuse, 1985).
Calabresi, Guido, The Costs of Accidents (Yale, 1970).
Call, Steven T. & Holahan, William L., Microeconomics (Pearson, 2d ed., 1983).
Caputo, Phillip, A Rumor of War (Holt, Rinehart and Winston, 1977).
Charles de Secondat, Baron De Montesquieu, The Spirit of Laws (Thomas Nugent trans., Batoche Books, 2001) (1748).
Coleman, Jules, Facts, Fictions, and the Grounds of Law, in Law and Social Justice 327 (Joseph Keim Campbell et al. eds., MIT, 2005).
Coleman, Jules, Risks and Wrongs (Oxford, rev. ed., 2002).
Coleman, Jules, Stanford Encyclopedia of Philosophy, Theories of Tort Law (Stanford, 2003).
Coleman, Jules, The Practice of Corrective Justice, in Philosophical Foundations of Tort Law 53 (David G. Owen ed., Oxford, 1995).
Coleman, Jules, The Practice of Principle: In Defence of a Pragmatist Approach to Legal Theory (Oxford, 2001).
Coleman, Jules L., Markets, Morals and the Law 131 (Oxford, 1988).
Cooter, Robert D. & Ulen, Thomas, Law and Economics (Harper Collins, 1988).
Cooter, Robert D. & Ulen, Thomas, Law and Economics (Pearson, 1st ed., 1988).
Cooter, Robert D. & Ulen, Thomas, Law and Economics (Pearson, 5th ed., 2007).
Cooter, Robert D. & Ulen, Thomas, Law and Economics (Pearson, 6th ed., 2012).

Demsetz, Harold, Professor Michelman's Unnecessary and Futile Search for the Philosopher's Touchstone, in Nomos XXIV: Ethics, Economics, and the Law 41 (J. Roland Pennock & John W. Chapman eds., New York University, 1982).
Dobbs, Dan B. et al., Hornbook on Torts §§ 1.3, 1.5, 1.6, 38.1 (West, 2000).
Dobbs, Dan B., Hayden, Paul T., & Bublick, Ellen M., Hornbook on Torts (West, 2d ed., 2016).
Dobbs, Dan B., Law of Remedies: Damages, Equity, Restitution (West, 1993).
Dobbs, Dan B., Law of Remedies: Damages, Equity, Restitution (West, 3d ed., 2018).
Dworkin, Ronald, Hard Cases, in Taking Rights Seriously 98 (London, 1977).
Dworkin, Ronald, Law's Empire (Belknap Press, 1986).
Epstein, Richard A. & Sharkey, Catherine M., Cases and Materials on Torts (Wolters Kluwer, 12th ed., 2020).
Farnsworth, Ward, The Single Owner, in The Legal Analyst: A Toolkit for Thinking about the Law 37 (University of Chicago, 2007).
Feinberg, Joel, Doing & Deserving: Essays in the Theory of Responsibility (Princeton, 1970).
Feinberg, Joel, Social Philosophy (Pearson, 1973).
Feinberg, Joel, Sua Culpa, in Doing & Deserving: Essays in the Theory of Responsibility 187 (Princeton, 1970).
Fleming, John G., The Law of Torts (LBC Information Services, 9th ed., 1998).
Freeman, Samuel, Private Law and Rawls' Principles of Justice, in Liberalism and Distributive Justice 167 (Oxford, 2018).
Fried, Charles, An Anatomy of Values (Harvard, 1970).
Gardner, John, Backward and Forward with Tort Law, in Law and Social Justice 255 (Joseph Keim Campbell ed., Bradford, 2005).
Gardner, John, It's Not about the Money, in From Personal Life to Private Law 88 (Oxford, 2018).
Gardner, John, Obligations and Outcomes in the Law of Torts, in Relating to Responsibility: Essays for Tony Honoré on His 80th Birthday (Peter Cane & John Gardner eds., Hart, 2001).
Gardner, John, Some Rule-of-Law Anxieties about Strict Liability in Private Law, in Torts and Other Wrongs 173 (Oxford, 2019).
Gardner, John, The Mysterious Case of the Reasonable Person, in Torts and Other Wrongs (Oxford, 2019).
Gardner, John, The Negligence Standard: Political not Metaphysical, in Torts and Other Wrongs (Oxford, 2019).
Gardner, John, Tort Law and Its Theory, in The Cambridge Companion to the Philosophy of Law (John Tasioulas ed., Harvard, 2020).
Gardner, John, Torts and Other Wrongs, in Torts and Other Wrongs (Oxford, 2019).
Geertz, Clifford, Thick Description: Toward an Interpretive Theory of Culture, in The Interpretation of Cultures 3 (Basic Books, 1973).
Giliker, Paula, A Revolution in Vicarious Liability: Lister, the Catholic Child Welfare Society Case and Beyond, in Revolution and Evolution in Private Law 121 (Sarah Worthington et al. eds., Hart Publishing, 2017).
Goffman, Erving, Stigma (Penguin, 1963).
Goldberg, John C.P. & Zipursky, Benjamin C., Recognizing Wrongs (Harvard, 2020).
Goldberg, John C.P. & Zipursky, Benjamin C., Tort Law and Responsibility, in Philosophical Foundations of the Law of Torts 17 (John Oberdiek ed., Oxford, 2014).

Goldberg, John C.P., & Zipursky, Benjamin C., The Oxford Introductions to U.S. Law: Torts (Oxford, 2010).
Grey, Thomas C., Holmes on Torts (unpublished manuscript) (on file with author).
Groce, Nora Ellen, Everyone Here Spoke Sign Language: Hereditary Deafness on Martha's Vineyard (Harvard University Press, 1988).
Harsanyi, John C., Morality and the Theory of Rational Behavior, in Utilitarianism and Beyond 103 (Amartya Sen & Bernard Williams eds., Cambridge, 1982).
Hart, H.L.A., Natural Rights: Bentham and John Stuart Mill, in Essays on Bentham 79 (Oxford, 1982).
Hart, H.L.A., The Concept of Law (Oxford, 1961).
Hart Jr., Henry M. & Sacks, Albert M., The Legal Process: Basic Problems in the Making and Application of Law (William N. Eskridge Jr. & Philip P. Frickey eds., Foundation, 1994).
Henderson, James A., Pearson Richard N., & Siliciano, John A., The Torts Process (Wolters Kluwer, 4th ed., 1994).
Herman, Barbara, The Practice of Moral Judgment (Harvard, 1993).
Hershovitz, Scott, Tort as a Substitute for Revenge, in Philosophical Foundations of the Law of Torts 86 (John Oberdiek ed., Oxford, 2014).
Hirshleifer, Jack, Price Theory and Applications (Cambridge, 3d ed., 1984).
Holmes, Oliver Wendell, The Common Law (Sheldon Novick ed., Dover, 1991) (1881).
Holmes, Oliver Wendell, The Path of the Law, in Collected Legal Papers 167 (Peter Smith 1952) (1920) (originally presented 1897).
Honoré, Tony, Responsibility and Fault (Hart, 1999).
Honoré, Tony, The Morality of Tort Law—Questions and Answers, in Responsibility and Fault (Hart, 1999).
Kamm, Frances, The Use and Abuse of the Trolley Problem, in Ethics of Artificial Intelligence 79–108 (S. Matthew Laio ed., Oxford, 2020).
Kant, Immanuel, Groundwork for the Metaphysic of Morals (Early Modern Texts, Jonathan Bennett ed., 2017) (1785).
Kaplow, Louis & Shavell, Steven, Fairness Versus Welfare (Harvard, 2002).
Keating, Gregory C., The Ambiguous Standing of Suffering in Negligence Law, in Knowing the Suffering of Others 78–121 (Austin Sarat ed., University of Alabama Press, 2014).
Keating, Gregory C., When Is Emotional Distress Harm?, in Tort Law: Challenging Orthodoxy 273–307 (Stephen G.A. Pitel, Jason W. Neyers, & Erika Chamberlain eds., Hart, 2013).
Keeton, Robert E. et al., Teacher's Manual to Accompany Tort and Accident Law: Cases and Materials (West, 1998).
Keeton, Robert E. et al., Tort and Accident Law (West, 4th ed., 2004).
Keeton, W. Page et al., Prosser and Keeton on Torts (West, 5th ed., 1984).
Kumar, Rahul, Contractualism on the Shoal of Aggregation, in Reasons and Recognition: Essays on the Philosophy of T.M. Scanlon (R. Jay Wallace, Rahul Kumar, & Samuel Freeman eds., Oxford, 2011).
Kumar, Rahul, Contractualism and the Roots of Responsibility, in New Essays on Moral Responsibility 251 (Randolp Clarke, Michael McKenna, and Angela M. Smith eds., Oxford, 2015).
Landes, William M. & Posner, Richard A., The Economic Structure of Tort Law (Harvard, 1987).

MacCormick, Neil, The Obligation of Reparation, in Legal Right and Social Democracy (Clarendon, 1982).
McMahan, Jeff, Killing in War (Oxford, 2009).
Mehr, Robert I. et al., Principles of Insurance (Irwin, 8th ed., 1985).
Mill, John Stuart, On the Connection between Justice and Utility, in Utilitarianism (Hackett, 1979) (1861).
Mill, John Stuart, Utilitarianism (Hackett, 1979) (1861).
Mill, John Stuart, Utilitarianism, in Utilitarianism and on Liberty (Mary Warnock ed., Blackwell, 2003) (1861).
Mishan, E.J., Introduction to Normative Economics (New York, 1981).
Nagel, Thomas, Equality and Partiality (Oxford, 1991).
Nolan, Virginia E. & Ursin, Edmund, Understanding Enterprise Liability: Rethinking Tort Reform for the Twenty-first Century (Temple, 1995).
Nozick, Robert, Anarchy, State, and Utopia (Basic, 1974).
Oberdiek, John, Imposing Risk: A Normative Framework (Oxford, 2017).
Parfit, Derek, Moral Concepts, in On What Matters, Vol. 1 (Oxford, 2011).
Polinsky, A. Mitchell, An Introduction to Law and Economics (Little, Brown, and Co., 2d. ed., 1989).
Posner, Richard A., Economic Analysis of Law (Aspen, 7th ed., 2007).
Posner, Richard A., Economic Analysis of Law (Little, Brown and Co., 4th ed., 1992).
Posner, Richard A., The Problems of Jurisprudence (Harvard, 1990).
Priest, George L., Products Liability Law and the Accident Rate in Liability: Perspectives and Policy (Robert E. Litan & Clifford Winston eds., Brookings Institute, 1988).
Rawls, John, A Theory of Justice (Harvard, 1999).
Rawls, John, Collected Papers 117–29 (Samuel Freeman ed., Harvard, 1999).
Rawls, John, Justice as Fairness: A Restatement (Harvard, 2001).
Rawls, John, Legal Obligation and the Duty of Fair Play, in Law and Philosophy 3 (Sidney Hook ed., NYU, 1964).
Rawls, John, Political Liberalism (Columbia, 1993).
Rawls, John, Political Liberalism (Columbia, rev. ed., 2005).
Rawls, John, Social Unity and Primary Goods, in Utilitarianism and Beyond (Amartya Sen & Bernard Williams eds., Cambridge University Press, 1982).
Rawls, John, Two Concepts of Rules (1955), in Collected Papers 20 (S. Freeman ed., Harvard, 1999).
Raz, Joseph, Personal Practical Conflicts, in Practical Conflicts: New Philosophical Essays 172 (Peter Baumann & Monica Betzler eds., Cambridge, 2004).
Raz, Joseph, The Morality of Freedom (Oxford, 1986).
Ripstein, Arthur & Zipursky, Benjamin C., Corrective Justice in an Age of Mass Torts, in Philosophy and the Law of Torts 214 (Gerald J. Postema ed., Cambridge, 2001).
Ripstein, Arthur, Equality, Responsibility, and the Law (Cambridge, 1998).
Ripstein, Arthur, Force and Freedom: Kant's Legal and Political Philosophy (Harvard, 2009).
Ripstein, Arthur, Private Wrongs (Harvard, 2016).
Rousseau, Jean-Jacques, Emile, in Oeuvres Complètes 320 (B. Gagnebin & M. Raymond eds., Gallimarde, 1959) (1762).
Rousseau, Jean-Jacques, The Social Contract (Lester G. Crocker trans., Pocket Books, 1967) (1761).
Rousseau, Jean-Jacques, The Social Contract and the Discourses (G.D.H. Cole trans., Dutton, 1979).

Samuelson, Paul A., Foundations of Economic Analysis (Harvard, enlarged ed., 1983).
Sangiovanni, Andrea, Rights and Interests in Ripstein's Kant, in Freedom and Force: Essays on Kant's Legal Philosophy 77 (Sari Kisilevsky & Martin J. Stone eds., Hart, 2017).
Scanlon, T.M., The Significance of Choice, in 8 The Tanner Lectures on Human Values 149 (Sterling M. McMurrin ed., Utah, 1988).
Scanlon, T.M., Contractualism and Utilitarianism, in Utilitarianism and Beyond 103 (Amartya Sen & Bernard Williams eds., Cambridge, 1982).
Scanlon, T.M., Rights and Interests, in Arguments for a Better World, Essays in Honor of Amartya Sen, Vol. I, at 68 (Kaushik Basu & Ravi Kanbur eds., Oxford, 2009).
Scanlon, T.M., Rights, Goals, and Fairness, in The Difficulty of Tolerance 26 (Cambridge, 2003).
Scanlon, T.M., What We Owe to Each Other (Harvard, 1998).
Scanlon, T.M., The Moral Basis of Interpersonal Comparisons, in Interpersonal Comparisons of Well-Being 17 (Jon Elster & John E. Roemer eds., Cambridge, 1993).
Scanlon, T.M., Value, Desire, and Quality of Life, in The Quality of Life 185 (Martha Nussbaum & Amartya Sen eds., Oxford, 1993).
Schelling, T.C., The Life You Save May Be Your Own, in Problems in Public Expenditure Analysis 127 (Samuel B. Chase Jr. ed., Brookings, 1968).
Schelling, Thomas C., The Strategy of Conflict (Harvard, 1980).
Schuck, Peter, Why Government Fails So Often: And How It Can Do Better (Princeton, 2014).
Shapo, Marshall S., Tort and Injury Law (Carolina Academic Press, 1990).
Shavell, Steven, Economic Analysis of Accident Law (Harvard, 1987).
Shiffrin, Seana, The Moral Neglect of Negligence, in 3 Oxford Studies in Political Philosophy 197 (Steven Wall et al. eds., Oxford, 2017).
Sinnott-Armstrong, Walter, Consequentialism, in Stanford Encyclopedia of Philosophy (Edward N. Zalta ed., Stanford, 2019).
Smith, Steven, Rights, Wrongs, and Injustices: The Structure of Remedial Law (Oxford, 2020).
Stevens, Robert, Torts and Rights (Oxford, 2007).
Stone, Martin, The Significance of Doing and Suffering, in Philosophy and the Law of Torts 131 (Gerald J. Postema ed., Cambridge, 2001).
Strawson, P.F., Freedom and Resentment, in Studies in the Philosophy of Thought and Action 71 (Oxford, 1968).
Sunstein, Cass R., Risk and Reason: Safety, Law, and the Environment (Cambridge, 2002).
Sunstein, Cass R., The Cost-Benefit Revolution (MIT Press, 2018).
Sunstein, Cass R., The Cost-Benefit State (ABA, 2003).
Thomson, Judith Jarvis, Remarks on Causation and Liability, in Rights, Restitution, & Risk: Essays in Moral Theory 192 (William Parent ed., Harvard, 1986).
Thomson, Judith Jarvis, The Realm of Rights (Harvard, 1990).
Viscusi, W. Kip, Regulating Health and Safety in the Workplace (Harvard, 1983).
Viscusi, W. Kip, The Value of Life, 2 New Palgrave Dictionary of Economics and the Law (Palgrave MacMillan, 2005).
Waldron, Jeremy, A Right to Do Wrong, in Liberal Rights: Collected Papers 1981–1991, at 63 (Cambridge, 1993).
Waldron, Jeremy, Moments of Carelessness and Massive Loss, in Philosophical Foundations of Tort Law 387 (David G. Owen ed., Oxford, 1995).
Waldron, Jeremy, Rights in Conflict, in Liberal Rights: Collected Papers 1981–1991, at 203 (Cambridge, 1993).

Watson, Gary, Two Faces of Responsibility, in Agency and Answerability: Selected Essays (Oxford, 2004).
Weinrib, Ernest J., The Idea of Private Law (Oxford, rev. ed., 2012).
White, G. Edward, Tort Law in America: An Intellectual History (Oxford, 1985, expanded ed., 2003).
Witt, John Fabian, The Accidental Republic (Harvard, 2006).

Articles (Scholarly)

1959 Joint Committee on Continuing Legal Education of the A.L.I. and the A.B.A. 116, 119. Reprinted in The Spirit of Liberty: Papers and Addresses of Learned Hand 302, 307 (Knopf, 3d ed., 1974).

Abraham, Kenneth S. & Rabin, Robert L., Automated Vehicles and Manufacturer Responsibility for Accidents: A New Legal Regime for a New Era, 105 Va. L. Rev. 127 (2019).

Abraham, Kenneth S., Strict Liability in Negligence, 61 DePaul L. Rev. 271 (2012).

Abraham, Kenneth S. & White, G. Edward, Conceptualizing Tort Law: The Continuous (and Continuing) Struggle, 80 Md. L. Rev. 293 (2021).

Akerlof, George A., The Market for "Lemons": Quality Uncertainty and the Market Mechanism, 48 Q. J. Econ. 488 (1970).

Anderson, David A., Is Libel Law Worth Reforming?, 140 U. Pa. L. Rev. 487, 489 (1991).

Ardia, David S., Reputation in a Networked World: Revisiting the Social Foundations of Defamation Law, 45 Harv. C.R.-C.L. L. Rev. 261 (2010).

Arlen, Jennifer H., Reconsidering Efficient Tort Rules for Personal Injury: The Case of Single Activity Accidents, 32 Wm. & Mary L. Rev. 41 (1990).

Arneson, Richard J., The Principle of Fairness and Free-Rider Problems, 92 Ethics 616 (1982).

Avraham, Ronen & Yuracko, Kimberly, Torts and Discrimination, 78 Ohio St. L.J. 661 (2017).

Ayres, Ian & Gertner, Robert, Filling Gaps in Incomplete Contracts: An Economic Theory of Default Rules, 99 Yale L.J. 87 (1989).

Baker, Tom, Uncertainty > Risk: Lessons for Legal Thought from the Insurance Run-Off Market, 62 B.C.L. Rev. 59 (2021).

Beever, Allan, The Form of Liability in the Torts of Trespass, 40 Common L. World Rev. 378 (2011).

Beitz, Charles R., The Moral Rights of Creators of Artistic and Literary Works, 13 J. Pol. Phil. 330 (2005).

Benson, Peter, The Basis of Corrective Justice and Its Relation to Distributive Justice, 77 Iowa L. Rev. 515 (1992).

Bishop, W., Economic Loss in Tort, 2 Oxford J. Legal Stud. 1 (1982).

Bohlen, Francis H., Incomplete Privilege to Inflict Intentional Invasions of Interests of Property and Personality, 39 Harv. L. Rev. 307 (1926).

Bohlen, Francis H., The Basis of Affirmative Obligation in the Law of Tort, 53 Am. L. Reg. 209 (1905).

Bohlen, Francis H., The Rule in Rylands v. Fletcher: Parts I–III, 59 U. Pa. L. Rev. 298, 373, 423 (1911).

Brickman, Philip et al., Lottery Winners and Accident Victims: Is Happiness Relative?, 36 J. Personality & Soc. Psychol. 917 (1978).

Broome, John, Fairness, 91 Proc. Aristotelian Soc'y 87 (1990–1991).
Buchanan, James M., In Defense of Caveat Emptor, 38 U. Chi. L. Rev. 64 (1970).
Calabresi, Guido & Hirschoff, Jon T., Toward a Test for Strict Liability in Torts, 81 Yale L.J. 1055 (1972).
Calabresi, Guido & Melamed, Douglas, Property Rules, Liability Rules and Inalienability: One View of the Cathedral, 85 Harv. L. Rev. 1089 (1972).
Calabresi, Guido, An Exchange: About Law and Economics: A Letter to Ronald Dworkin, 8 Hofstra L. Rev. 553 (1980).
Calabresi, Guido, Concerning Cause and the Law of Torts, 43 U. Chi. L. Rev. 69, 96 n.39 (1975).
Calabresi, Guido, Some Thoughts on Risk Distribution and the Law of Torts, 70 Yale L.J. 499 (1961).
Calabresi, Guido, The Decision for Accidents: An Approach to Nonfault Allocation of Costs, 78 Harv. L. Rev. 713 (1965).
Cannon, Jonathan, The Sounds of Silence: Cost-Benefit Canons in Entergy Corp. v. Riverkeeper, Inc., 34 Harv. Envtl. L. Rev. 425 (2010).
Coase, Ronald, The Problem of Social Cost, 3 J.L. & Econ. 1 (1960).
Coleman, Jules & Ripstein, Arthur, Mischief and Misfortune, 41 McGill L.J. 91 (1996).
Coleman, Jules, The Economic Structure of Tort Law, 97 Yale L.J. 1233 (1988).
Cooter, Robert & Rappoport, Peter, Were the Ordinalists Wrong about Welfare Economics?, 22 J. Econ. Literature 507 (1984).
Cooter, Robert D., The Best Right Laws: Value Foundations of the Economic Analysis of Law, 64 Notre Dame L. Rev. 817 (1989).
Craswell, Richard, Contract Law, Default Rules, and the Philosophy of Promising, 88 Mich. L. Rev. 489 (1989).
Craswell, Richard, Passing on the Costs of Legal Rules: Efficiency and Distribution in Buyer-Seller Relationships, 43 Stan. L. Rev. 361 (1991).
Croley, Steven P. & Hanson, Jon D., The Nonpecuniary Costs of Accidents: Pain and Suffering Damages in Tort Law, 108 Harv. L. Rev. 1785 (1995).
Cross, Frank B., Tort Law and the American Economy, 96 Minn. L. Rev. 28 (2011).
De Geest, Gerrit, Who Should Be Immune from Tort Liability?, 41 J. Legal Stud. 291 (2012).
Dworkin, Ronald, Why Efficiency?—A Response to Professors Calabresi and Posner, 8 Hofstra L. Rev. 563 (1980).
Encarnacion, Erik, Resilience, Retribution, and Punitive Damages, 100 Tex. L. Rev. 1025 (2021).
Engstrom, Nora Freeman, An Alternative Explanation for No-Fault's "Demise," 61 DePaul L. Rev. 303 (2012).
Epstein, Richard A., A Theory of Strict Liability, 2 J. Legal Stud. 151 (1973).
Epstein, Richard A., Common Law, Labor Law, and Reality: A Rejoinder to Professors Getman and Kohler, 92 Yale L.J. 1435 (1983).
Epstein, Richard A., Products Liability as an Insurance Market, 14 J. Legal Stud. 645 (1985).
Epstein, Richard A., The Unintended Revolution in Product Liability Law, 10 Cardozo L. Rev. 2193 (1988).
Fallon, Richard H., Bidding Farewell to Constitutional Torts, 107 Cal. L. Rev. 933 (2019).
Farber, Daniel A., Toxic Causation, 71 Minn. L. Rev. 1219 (1987).
Fennell, Lee Anne, Forcings, 114 Colum. L. Rev. 1297 (2014).

Fletcher, George P., Fairness and Utility in Tort Theory, 85 Harv. L. Rev. 537 (1972).
Frank, Robert H., Why Is Cost-Benefit Analysis So Controversial? 29 J. Legal Stud. 913 (2000).
Fried, Barbara, Is Wealth a Value, 9 J. Legal Stud. 191 (1980).
Fried, Barbara, The Limits of a Nonconsequentialist Approach to Torts, 18 Legal Theory 231 (2012).
Friedmann, Daniel, The Performance Interest in Contract Damages, 111 L.Q.R. 628 (1995).
Fuller, L.L. & Perdue Jr., William R., The Reliance Interest in Contract Damages: I, 46 Yale L.J. 52 (1936).
Gardner, John, Damages without Duty, 69 U. Toronto L.J. 412 (2019).
Gardner, John, Torts and Other Wrongs, 39 Fla. St. U. L. Rev. 43 (2011).
Gardner, John, What Is Tort Law For? Part I: The Place of Corrective Justice, 30 Law & Phil. 1 (2011).
Geistfeld, Mark A., The Principle of Misalignment: Duty, Damages, and the Nature of Tort Liability, 121 Yale L.J. 142 (2011).
Gergen, Mark P., The Jury's Role in Deciding Normative Issues in the American Common Law, 68 Fordham L. Rev. 407 (1999).
Gibbard, Allan, Constructing Justice, 20 Phil. & Pub. Aff. 264 (1991).
Gilles, Stephen G., The Invisible Hand Formula, 80 Va. L. Rev. 1015 (1994).
Goldberg, John C.P. & Zipursky, Benjamin C., Civil Recourse Revisited, 39 Fla. St. U. L. Rev. 342 (2011).
Goldberg, John C.P. & Zipursky, Benjamin C., The Strict Liability in Fault and the Fault in Strict Liability, 85 Fordham L. Rev. 743 (2016).
Goldberg, John C.P. & Zipursky, Benjamin C., Torts as Wrongs, 88 Tex. L. Rev. 917 (2010).
Goldberg, John C.P., The Constitutional Status of Tort Law: Due Process and the Right to a Law for the Redress of Wrongs, 115 Yale L.J. 524 (2005).
Goldberg, John C.P., Two Conceptions of Tort Damages: Fair v. Full Compensation, 55 DePaul L. Rev. 435 (2006).
Gordon, Wendy T., Of Harms and Benefits: Torts, Restitution, and Intellectual Property, 21 J. Legal Stud. 449 (1992).
Grady, Mark F., Untaken Precautions, 18 J. Legal Stud. 139 (1989).
Green, Michael D., Negligence = Economic Efficiency: Doubts, 75 Tex. L. Rev. 1605 (1997).
Gregory, Charles, Trespass to Negligence to Strict Liability, 37 Va. L. Rev. 359 (1951).
Grey, Thomas C., Accidental Torts, 54 Vand. L. Rev. 1225 (2001).
Grossman, Igor et al., Folk Standards of Sound Judgment: Rationality Versus Reasonableness, 6(2) Sci. Adv. (2020).
Hacker, Jacob S. & Pierson, Paul, Making America Great Again: The Case for the Mixed Economy, 95 Foreign Aff. 69 (2016).
Hampton, Jean, Correcting Harms versus Righting Wrongs: The Goal of Retribution, 39 UCLA L. Rev. 1659 (1992).
Hand, Learned, Address at the National Conference on the Continuing Education of the Bar, in Continuing Legal Education for Professional Competence and Responsibility: The Report on the Arden House Conference (Dec. 16, 1958).
Hanser, Matthew, The Metaphysics of Harm, 77 Phil. & Phenomenological Res. 421 (2008).
Hanson, Jon D. & Logue, Kyle D., The First-Party Insurance Externality: An Economic Justification for Enterprise Liability, 76 Cornell L. Rev. 129 (1990).

Hart, H.L.A., American Jurisprudence through English Eyes: The Nightmare and the Noble Dream, 11 Ga. L. Rev. 969 (1977).
Hart, H.L.A., Are There Any Natural Rights?, 64 Phil. Rev. 175 (1955).
Henderson Jr., James A., Judicial Review of Manufacturers' Conscious Design Choices: The Limits of Adjudication, 73 Colum. L. Rev. 1531 (1973).
Henderson Jr., James A., Judicial Reliance on Public Policy: An Empirical Analysis of Products Liability Decisions, 59 Geo. Wash. L. Rev. 1570 (1991).
Henderson Jr., James A., The Boundary Problems of Enterprise Liability, 41 Md. L. Rev. 659 (1982).
Hershovitz, Scott, Corrective Justice for Civil Recourse Theorists, 39 Fla. St. U. L. Rev. 107 (2011).
Hershovitz, Scott, Harry Potter and the Trouble with Tort Theory, 63 Stan. L. Rev. 67 (2010).
Hershovitz, Scott, The Search for a Grand Unified Theory of Tort Law, 130 Harv. L. Rev. 942 (2017).
Hershovitz, Scott, Two Models of Tort (and Takings), 92 Va. L. Rev. 1147 (2006).
Herstein, Ori J., A Legal Right to Do Wrong, 34 Oxford L.J. 21 (2014).
Herstein, Ori J., How Tort Law Empowers, 65 U. Toronto L.J. 99 (2014).
Holmes, Oliver Wendell, Book Review, 5 Am. L. Rev. 340 (1871).
Holmes, Oliver Wendell, The Theory of Torts, 7 Am. L. Rev 652 (1873).
Johnson, Conrad D., On Deciding and Setting Precedent for the Reasonable Man, 62 Archiv Rechts & Sozialphil. 161 (1976).
Jones, William K., Strict Liability for Hazardous Enterprise, 92 Colum. L. Rev. 1705 (1992).
Kahneman, Daniel et al., Anomalies: The Endowment Effect, Loss Aversion, and Status Quo Bias, 5 J. Econ. Persp. 193 (1991).
Kaplow, Louis & Shavell, Steven, Should Legal Rules Favor the Poor? 29 J. Legal Stud. 821 (2000).
Kaplow, Louis & Shavell, Steven, Why the Legal System Is Less Efficient than the Income Tax System in Redistributing Income, 23 J. Legal Stud. 667 (1994).
Keating, Gregory C., Fidelity to Preexisting Law and the Legitimacy of Legal Decision, 69 Notre Dame L. Rev. 1 (1999).
Keating, Gregory C., Is Negligent Infliction of Emotional Distress a Freestanding Tort?, 44 Wake Forest L. Rev. 1131 (2009).
Keating, Gregory C., Is There Really No Liability Without Fault? 85 Fordham L. Rev. Res Gestae 24 (2017).
Keating, Gregory C., Must the Hand Formula Not Be Named?, 163 U. Pa. L. Rev. 367 (2015).
Keating, Gregory C., Nuisance as a Strict Liability Wrong, 4(3) J. Tort L. [ii] (2012).
Keating, Gregory C., Products Liability as Enterprise Liability, 10 J. Tort L. 41 (2017).
Keating, Gregory C., Recovering Rylands: An Essay for Robert Rabin, 61 DePaul L. Rev. 543 (2012).
Keating, Gregory C., The Theory of Enterprise Liability and Common Law Strict Liability, 54 Vand. L. Rev. 1285 (2001).
Keeton, Robert E., Conditional Fault in the Law of Torts, 72 Harv. L. Rev. 401 (1959).
Kelley, Patrick J. & Wendt, Laurel A., What Judges Tell Juries About Negligence: A Review of Pattern Jury Instructions, 77 Chi.-Kent L. Rev. 587 (2002).
Kelly, Erin I., Desert and Fairness in Criminal Justice, 40 Phil. Topics 63 (2012).

Kennedy, Duncan, Distributive and Paternalist Motives in Contract and Tort Law, with Special Reference to Compulsory Terms and Unequal Bargaining Power, 41 Md. L. Rev. 563 (1982).

Kennedy, Duncan, Distributive and Paternalist Motives in Contract and Tort Law with Special Reference to Compulsory Terms and Unequal Bargaining Power, 41 Md. L. Rev. 563 (1982).

Kennedy, Duncan, The Stages of the Decline of the Public/Private Distinction, 130 U. Pa. L. Rev. 1349 (1982).

Klepper, Howard, Torts of Necessity: A Moral Theory of Compensation, 9 Law. & Phil. 223 (1990).

Kordana, Kevin A. & Blankfein Tabachnick, David H., Rawls and Contract Law, 73 Geo. Wash. L. Rev. 598 (2005).

Kordana, Kevin A. & Blankfein Tabachnick, David H., The Rawlsian View of Private Ordering, 25 Soc. Phil. & Pol'y 288 (2008).

Korsgaard, Christine, The Reasons We Can Share: An Attack on the Distinction Between Agent-Relative and Agent-Neutral Values, 10 Soc. Phil. & Pol'y 24 (1993).

Kronman, Anthony T., Specific Performance, 45 U. Chi. L. Rev. 351 (1978).

Kronmant, Anthony T., Contract Law and Distributive Justice, 89 Yale L.J. 472 (1980).

Laycock, Douglas, The Death of the Irreparable Injury Rule, 103 Harv. L. Rev. 687 (1990).

Levmore, Saul, Explaining Restitution, 71 Va. L. Rev. 65 (1985).

Liao, Yu-Ping & White, Michelle J., No-fault for Motor Vehicles: An Economic Analysis, 4 Am. L. & Econ. Rev. 258 (2002).

Livermore, Michael A. & Revesz, Richard L., Rethinking Health-Based Environmental Standards and Cost-Benefit Analysis, 46 Envtl. L. Rep. 10674 (2016).

Livermore, Michael A. & Revesz, Richard L., Rethinking Health-Based Environmental Standards and Cost-Benefit Analysis, 89 N.Y.U. L. Rev. 1184 (2014).

Malone, Wex, The Genesis of Wrongful Death, 17 Stan. L. Rev. 1043 (1965).

Martins, Ryan, Price, Shannon, & Witt, John, Contract's Revenge: The Waiver Society and the Death of Tort, 41 Cardozo L. Rev 1265 (2020).

Massey, Calvin R., The Excessive Fines Clause and Punitive Damages: Some Lessons from History, 40 Vand. L. Rev. 1233 (1987).

Masur, Jonathan S. & Posner, Eric A., Against Feasibility Analysis, 77 U. Chi. L. Rev. 657 (2010).

McClurg, Andrew J., Dead Sorrow: A Story about Loss and a New Theory of Wrongful Death Damages, 85 B.U. L. Rev. 1 (2005).

Miller, Richard S., An Analysis and Critique of the 1992 Changes to New Zealand's Accident Compensation Scheme, 52 Md. L. Rev. 1070 (1990).

Morris, Herbert, Persons and Punishment, 52 Monist 475 (1968).

Murphy, Liam B., Institutions and the Demands of Justice, 27 Phil. & Pub. Aff. 251 (1998).

Oberdiek, John, The Wrong in Negligence, 41 Oxford J. Legal Stud. 1 (2021).

Perry, Stephen R., The Impossibility of General Strict Liability, 1 Can. J.L. & Juris. 147 (1988).

Perry, Stephen R., The Moral Foundations of Tort Law, 77 Iowa L. Rev. 449, 506–07 (1992).

Pierce Jr., Richard, Encouraging Safety: The Limits of Tort Law and Government Regulation 33 Vand. L. Rev. 1281 (1980).

Pogge, Thomas, Three Problems with Contractarian-Consequentialist Ways of Assessing Social Institutions, 12 Soc. Phil. & Pol'y 221 (1995).

Posner, Richard A., A Theory of Negligence, 1 J. Legal Stud. 29 (1972).

Posner, Richard A., The Concept of Corrective Justice in Recent Theories of Tort Law, 10 J. Legal Stud. 187 (1981).
Priest, George L., Modern Tort Law and Its Reform, 22 Val. U. L. Rev. 1 (1987).
Priest, George L., The Current Insurance Crisis and Modern Tort Law, 96 Yale L.J. 1521 (1987).
Priest, George L., The Invention of Enterprise Liability: A Critical History of the Intellectual Foundations of Modern Tort Law, 14 J. Legal Stud. 461 (1985).
Rabin, Robert L., Some Thoughts on the Ideology of Enterprise Liability, 55 Md. L. Rev. 1190 (1996).
Rabin, Robert L., The Historical Development of the Fault Principle: A Reinterpretation, 15 Ga. L. Rev. 925 (1981).
Rabin, Robert L., The September 11th Victim Compensation Fund: A Circumscribed Response or an Auspicious Model?, 53 DePaul L. Rev. 769 (2003).
Radin, Margaret Jane, Compensation and Commensurability, 43 Duke L.J. 56 (1993).
Radin, Margaret Jane, Property and Personhood, 34 Stan. L. Rev. 957 (1982).
Rapaczynski, Andrzej, Driverless Cars and the Much Delayed Tort Law Revolution (Colum. L. & Econ., Working Paper No. 540, 2016), http://papers.ssrn.com/sol3/papers.cfm?abstract_id=2764686.
Ripstein, Arthur, Beyond the Harm Principle, 34 Phil. & Pub. Aff. 215 (2006).
Ripstein, Arthur, Self-Defense and Equal Protection, 57 U. Pitt. L. Rev. 685 (1996).
Ripstein, Arthur, The Division of Responsibility and the Law of Tort, 72 Fordham L. Rev. 1811 (2004).
Ripstein, Arthur, Tort, The Division of Responsibility and the Law of Tort, 72 Fordham L. Rev. 1811 (2004).
Scanlon, T.M., Preference and Urgency, 72 J. Phil. 655 (1975).
Scanlon, Thomas, Promises and Practices, 19 Phil. & Pub. Aff. 199 (1990).
Scheffler, Samuel, Distributive Justice, the Basic Structure and the Place of Private Law, 35 Oxford J. Legal Stud. 213 (2015).
Schroeder, Christopher H., Corrective Justice and Liability for Increasing Risks, 37 UCLA L. Rev. 439 (1990).
Schwartz, Alan, Products Liability Reform: A Theoretical Synthesis, 97 Yale L.J. 353 (1988).
Schwartz, Alan, The Case Against Strict Liability, 60 Fordham L. Rev. 819 (1992).
Schwartz, Gary T., Contributory and Comparative Negligence: A Reappraisal, 87 Yale L.J. 697 (1978).
Schwartz, Gary T., Reality in the Economic Analysis of Tort Law: Does Tort Law Really Deter?, 42 UCLA L. Rev. 377 (1994).
Schwartz, Gary T., The Myth of the Ford Pinto Case, 43 Rutgers L. Rev. 1013 (1991).
Schwartz, Gary T., The Vitality of Negligence and the Ethics of Strict Liability, 15 Ga. L. Rev. 963 (1981).
Seavey, Warren A., Nuisance: Contributory Negligence and Other Mysteries, 65 Harv. L. Rev. 984 (1952).
Seo, Sarah A. & Witt, John Fabian, The Metaphysics of Mind and the Practical Science of Law, 26 Law & Hist. Rev. 161 (2008).
Sharkey, Catherine M., Preventing Harms, Not Recognizing Wrongs, 134 Harv. L. Rev. 1423 (2021).
Shavell, Steven, Strict Liability versus Negligence, 9 J. Legal Stud. 1 (1980).

Shavell, Steven, The Mistaken Restriction of Strict Liability to Uncommon Activities, 10 J. Legal Analysis 1 (2018).
Sheinman, Hanoch, Tort Law and Corrective Justice, 22 Law & Phil. 21 (2003).
Shiffrin, Seana, Harm and Its Moral Significance, 18 Legal Theory 357 (2012).
Shiffrin, Seana, Wrongful Life, Procreative Responsibility, and the Significance of Harm, 5 Legal Theory 117 (1999).
Shulman, Harry, The Standard of Care Required of Children, 37 Yale L.J. 618 (1928).
Sibley, W.M., The Rational versus the Reasonable, 62 Phil. Rev. 554 (1953).
Siegel, Reva B., The Modernization of Marital Status Law: Adjudicating Wives' Rights to Earnings 1860–1930, 82 Geo. L.J. 2127 (1994).
Simons, Kenneth W., Tort Negligence, Cost-Benefit Analysis, and Tradeoffs: A Closer Look at the Controversy, 41 Loy. L.A. L. Rev. 1171 (2008).
Simons, Kenneth W., Rethinking Mental States, 72 B.U. L. Rev. 463 (1992).
Smith, Jeremiah, Sequel to Workmen's Compensation Acts, 27 Harv. L. Rev. 235 (1914).
Smith, Jeremiah, Tort and Absolute Liability—Suggested Changes in Classification, 30 Harv. L. Rev. 241 (1917).
Smith, Lionel, Corrective Justice and Public Law (Paper presented at the Obligations V Conference: Rights and Private Law, University of Oxford, July 14–16, 2010).
Smith, Stephen A., Duties, Liabilities, and Damages, 125 Harv. L. Rev. 1727 (2012).
Smith, Young B., Frolic and Detour, 23 Colum. L. Rev. 444 & 716 (1923).
Solow, Robert M., Defending Cost-Benefit Analysis, 5 Regulation 40 (1981).
Stapleton, Jane, Tort, Insurance and Ideology, 58 Mod. L. Rev. 820 (1995).
Steel, Sandy & Stevens, Robert, The Secondary Legal Duty to Pay Damages, 136 L.Q.R. 283 (2020).
Steel, Sandy, Compensation and Continuity, 26 Legal Theory 250 (2020).
Sugarman, Stephen D., Judges as Tort Law Un-Makers: Recent California Experience with "New" Torts, 49 DePaul L. Rev. 455 (1999).
Sunstein, Cass & Stewart, Richard, Public Programs and Private Rights, 95 Harv. L. Rev. 1193 (1982).
Sunstein, Cass R., Humanizing Cost-Benefit Analysis, Remarks Prepared for American University's Washington College of Law Administrative Law Review Conference 13 (Feb. 17, 2010).
Sunstein, Cass R., The Real World of Cost-Benefit Analysis: Thirty-Six Questions (And Almost as Many Answers) 114 Colum. L. Rev. 167 (2014).
Thomson, Judith Jarvis, More on the Metaphysics of Harm, 82 Phil. & Phenomenological Res. 436 (2011).
Twerski, A.D., Weinstein, A.S., Donaher, V.A. , & Piehler, H.R., The Use and Abuse of Warnings in Product Liability-Design Defect Litigation Comes of Age, 61 Cornell L. Rev. 495 (1976).
Twerski, Aaron D., An Essay on the Quieting of Products Liability Law, 105 Cornell L. Rev. 101 (2020).
Vandall, Frank, The Restatement (Third) of Torts, Products Liability, Section 2(b): Design Defect, 68 Temple L. Rev. 167 (1995).
Vermont, Samson, The Golden Hand Formula, 11 Green Bag 2d 203 (2008).
Viscusi, W. Kip & Gayer, Ted, Rational Benefit Assessment for an Irrational World: Toward a Behavioral Transfer Test, 30 J. Benefit-Cost Analysis 1 (2016).
Viscusi, W. Kip, Corporate Risk Analysis: A Reckless Act?, 52 Stan L. Rev. 547 (2000).
Viscusi, W. Kip, How Do Judges Think About Risk?, 1 Am. Law Econ. Rev. 26 (1999).

Viscusi, W. Kip, Jurors, Judges, and the Mistreatment of Risk by the Courts, 30 J. Legal Stud. 107 (2001).
Waisman, Dov A., Reasonable Precaution for the Individual, 88 St. John's L. Rev. 653 (2014).
Warren, Samuel D. & Brandeis, Louis D., The Right to Privacy, 4 Harv. L. Rev. 193 (1890).
Weinrib, Ernest J., Law as a Kantian Idea of Reason, 87 Colum. L. Rev. 472 (1987).
Weinrib, Ernest J., Understanding Tort Law, 23 Val. U. L. Rev. 485 (1989).
Wells, Catharine Pierce, Tort Law as Corrective Justice: A Pragmatic Justification for Jury Adjudication, 88 Mich. L. Rev. 2348 (1990).
Wells, Catherine Pierce, Tort Law as Corrective Justice: A Pragmatic Justification for Jury Adjudication, 88 Mich. L. Rev. 2348 (1990).
Wells, Michael, Scientific Policymaking and the Torts Revolution: The Revenge of the Ordinary Observer, 26 Ga. L. Rev. 725 (1992).
White, G. Edward, The Unexpected Persistence of Negligence, 1980–2000, 54 Vand. L. Rev. 1337 (2001).
Wiley, Jerry, The Impact of Judicial Decisions on Professional Conduct: An Empirical Study, 55 S. Cal. L. Rev. 345 (1981).
Williams, Sean, Self-Altering Injury: The Hidden Harms of Hedonic Adaption, 96 Cornell L. Rev. 535 (2011).
Witt, John F., From Loss of Service to Loss of Support: The Wrongful Death Statutes, the Origins of Modern Tort Law, and the Making of the Nineteenth Century Family, 25 Law & Soc. Inquiry 717 (2000).
Wright, Richard W., Actual Causation. Probabilistic Linkage: The Bane of Economic Analysis, 14 J. Legal Stud. 435 (1985).
Zipursky, Benjamin C., A Theory of Punitive Damages, 84 Tex. L. Rev. 105 (2005).
Zipursky, Benjamin C., Civil Recourse, Not Corrective Justice, 91 Geo. L.J. 695 (2003).
Zipursky, Benjamin C., Reasonableness In and Out of Negligence Law, 163 U. Pa. L. Rev. 2131 (2015).
Zipursky, Benjamin C., Sleight of Hand, 48 Wm. & Mary. L. Rev. 1999 (2007).

Articles (Journalistic)

Boudette, Neal E., Auto Safety Regulators Seek a Driver Mode to Block Apps, N.Y. Times (Nov. 22, 2016), https://www.nytimes.com/2016/11/22/business/auto-safety-regulat ors-seek-a-driver-mode-to-block-apps.html.
Chung, Helier & Wong, Tessa, The Full Story of Thailand's Extraordinary Cave Rescue, BBC News (July 14, 2018), https://www.bbc.com/news/world-asia-44791998.
Finnegan, William, A Theft in the Library, The New Yorker (Oct. 17, 2005), https://www.newyorker.com/magazine/2005/10/17/a-theft-in-the-library.
Glionna, John M., Trestle-Jumping Fad Puts Youths in Path of Danger, L.A. Times (Aug. 10, 1992), https://www.latimes.com/archives/la-xpm-1992-08-10-mn-4791-story.html.
Hitzig, Zoë, Objectivity as a Blanket, The New Yorker (Mar. 17, 2017), https://www.newyorker.com/magazine/2017/03/20/objectivity-as-blanket?mbid=social_twit ter&mbid=social_facebook&fbclid=IwAR3nk7atmBjtH5jlAYqehaUNgvESvs9Xnn caXQJ4NPume-711rc9eQVfDoc.
Jeff McLaughlin, Diver's Body Found at Andrea Doria Wreck, Boston Globe (July 14, 1993).

Krugman, Paul, Mornings in Blue America, New York Times (Mar. 27, 2015).
Pierson, Brendan, Factbox: U.S. Lawsuits Take Aim at Vaping, Reuters (Sept. 25, 2019), https://www.reuters.com/article/us-health-vaping-lawsuit-factbox/factbox-u-s-lawsuits-take-aim-at-vaping-idUSKBN1WA250.
Penn, Ivan, PG&E Aims to Curb Wildfire Risk by Burying Many Power Lines, N.Y. Times (July 21, 2021), https://www.nytimes.com/2021/07/21/business/energy-environment/pge-underground-powerlines-wildfires.html.
Richtel, Matt, Phone Makers Could Cut Off Drivers. So Why Don't They? N.Y. Times (Sept. 24, 2016), https://www.nytimes.com/2016/09/25/technology/phone-makers-could-cut-off-drivers-so-why-dont-they.html.
Rose Bird Deserved to Be Removed, Chicago Tribune (Nov. 9, 1986), https://www.chicagotribune.com/news/ct-xpm-1986-11-19-8603270146-story.html.
Sunstein, Cass R., Thanks, Justice Scalia, for the Cost-Benefit State, Bloomberg Opinion (July 7, 2015), https://www.bloomberg.com/opinion/articles/2015-07-07/thanks-justice-scalia-for-the-cost-benefit-state.
Tamburin, Adam & Barchenger, Stacey, Erin Andrews Awarded $55 Million in Civil Case over Nude Video, The Tennessean (Mar. 7, 2016), https://www.tennessean.com/story/news/crime/2016/03/07/erin-andrews-awarded-55-million/81367588/.
Wilson, John Morgan, Op-Ed: Texting While Driving Is as Dangerous as Driving Drunk. We Need to Treat It Accordingly, L.A. Times (Apr. 4, 2018), latimes.com/opinion/livable-city/la-oe-wilson-texting-while-driving-20180404-story.html.
Winton, Richard et al., DWP Power Lines Hit by Tree Branch Sparked Getty Fire that Destroyed Homes, L.A. Times (Oct. 29, 2019), https://www.latimes.com/california/story/2019-10-29/getty-fire-arson-investigation.

Cases

Ackison v. Anchor Packing Company, 120 Ohio St. 3d 228 (2008).
Acosta v. Honda Motor Co., 717 F.2d 828 (3d Cir. 1983).
AFL-CIO v. Marshall, 617 F.2d 636 (D.C. Cir. 1979).
Agis v. Howard Johnson Co., 355 N.E.2d 315 (Mass. 1976).
Albers v. County of Los Angeles, 62 Cal. 2d 250 (1965).
Alcorn v. Mitchell, 63 Ill. 553 (1872).
Altman v. Aronson, 121 N.E. 505 (Mass. 1919).
Am. Iron & Steel Inst. v. Occupational Safety & Health Admin., 577 F.2d 825 (3d Cir. 1978).
Am. Textile Mfrs. Inst. v. Donovan, 452 U.S. 490 (1981).
Amoco Transport Co. v. SIS Mason Lykes, 768 F.2d 659 (5th Cir. 1985).
Amphitheaters, Inc. v. Portland Meadows, 198 P.2d 847, 851 (Or. 1948).
Anderson v. W.R. Grace & Co., 628 F. Supp. 1219 (D. Mass. 1986).
Ayers v. Township of Jackson, 525 A.2d 287 (N.J. 1987).
Baltimore Transit Co. v. Young, 56 A.2d 140 (Md. 1947).
Barber Lines NS v. MN Donau Maru, 764 F.2d 50 (1st Cir. 1985).
Barber Lines v. Donau Maru, 764 F.2d 50 (1st Cir. 1985).
Barker v. Lull Engineering Co., 573 P.2d 443 (Cal. 1978).
Belair v. Riverside County Flood Control Dist., 47 Cal. 3d 550 (1988).
Berg v. Reaction Motors Div., Thiokol Chem. Corp., 181 A.2d 487 (N.J. 1962).
Bigelow v. RKO Radio Pictures, 327 U.S. 251 (1946).

Blyth v. Birmingham, 11 Ex. Welsh. H. & G. 781 (1856).
Bolton v. Stone, A.C. 850 (1951).
Boomer v. Atlantic Cement Co., 257 N.E.2d 870 (N.Y. 1970).
Boomer v. Atlantic Cement Co., 287 N.Y.S.2d 112 (Sup. Ct. 1967).
Breunig v. American Family Ins. Co., 173 N.W.2d 619, 624 (Wis. 1970).
Brillhart v. Edison Light & Power Co., 82 A.2d 44, 47 (Pa. 1951).
Brown v. Collins, 53 N.H. 442 (1873).
Brown v. Kendall, 60 Mass. 292 (1850).
Browning-Ferris Indus. of Vermont, Inc. v. Kelco Disposal, Inc., 492 U.S. 257 (1989) (O'Connor, J., dissenting).
Bryant v. Lefever, 4 C.P.D. 172 (1878–79).
Brzoska v. Olson, 668 A.2d 1355 (Del. 1995).
Burns v. Jaquays Mining Corp, 752 P.2d 28, 30 (Ariz. Ct. App. 1987).
Caplan v. Atas, 2021 ONSC 670 (Ont. Super. Ct. Mar. 20, 2021).
Carolina Environmental Study Group v. U.S. Atomic Energy Commission, 431 F. Supp. 203, 225 (W.D.N.C. 1977).
Charbonneau v. MacRury, 153 A. 457 (N.H. 1931).
Cleveland Park Club v. Perry, 165 A.2d 485 (D.C. 1960).
Conway v. O'Brien, 111 F.2d 611 (2d Cir. 1940), rev'd 312 U.S. 492 (1941).
Coomer v. Kan. City Royals Baseball Corp., 437 S.W.3d 184 (Mo. 2014).
Cotton v. Buckeye Gas Prod. Co., 840 F.2d 935, 937–39 (D.C. Cir. 1988).
Crawn v. Campo, 643 A.2d 600 (N.J. 1994).
Cullison v. Medley, 570 N.E.2d 27 (Ind. 1991).
Cusick v. Clark, 360 N.E.2d 160 (111 App. Ct. 1977).
Daly v. Liverpool Corporation [1939] 2All ER 142.
Daniels v. Evans, 224 A.2d 63, 64 (N.H. 1966).
Davis v. Consolidated Rail Corp., 788 F.2d 1260 (7th Cir. 1986).
De Martini v. Alexander Sanitarium, Inc., 13 Cal. Rptr. 564 (Cal. Dist. Ct. App. 1961).
Delair v. McAdoo, 188 A. 181, 184 (Pa. 1936).
Dellwo v. Pearson, 107 N.W.2d 859, 863 (Minn. 1961).
Denny v. Ford Motor Co., 87 N.E.2d 730 (N.Y. 1995).
Dillon v. Legg, 441 P.2d 912 (1968).
Duckworth v. Franzen, 780 F.2d 645 (7th Cir. 1985), cert. denied, 479 U.S. 816 (1986) (Posner, J.).
Duke Power Co. v. Carolina Environmental Study Group, 438 U.S. 59 (1978).
East River S.S. Corp. v. Transamerica Delaval, Inc., 476 U.S. 858 (1986).
Eckert v. Long Island R. Co., 43 N.Y. 502, 506 (N.Y. 1871).
Eckert v. Long Island R.R. Co., 57 Barb. 555 (N.Y. 1870).
Edwards v. Lee's Adm'r, 96 S.W.2d 1028, 1029 (Ky. 1936).
Entergy Corp v. Riverkeeper, Inc., 556 U.S. 208 (2009).
EPA v. Nat'l Crushed Stone Ass'n, 449 U.S. 64 (1980).
Escola v. Coca Cola Bottling Co., 150 P.2d 436 (Cal. 1944) (Traynor, J., concurring).
Exner v. Sherman Power Construction Co., 54 F.2d 510 (2d Cir. 1931).
Farwell v. Boston & Worcester Rail Road Corp., 45 Mass. 49 (1842).
Fletcher v. Rylands, 159 Eng. Rep. 737 (Ex. 1866).
Fletcher v. Rylands, I L.R.-Ex. 265 (Ex. Ch. 1866) (Blackburn, J.).
Fontainebleau Hotel Corp. v. Forty-Five Twenty-Five, Inc., 114 So.2d 357 (Fla. 3d Dist. App. 1959).

Forcier v. Grand Union Stores, Inc., 264 A.2d 796 (Vt. 1970).
Foster v. City of Keyser, 501 S.E.2d 165 (W. Va. 1997).
Friedman v. State, 282 N.Y.S.2d 858 (N.Y. Ct. CI. 1967).
Galligan v. Blais, 364 A.2d 164, 166 (Conn. 1976).
Gardner v. National Bulk Carriers, Inc., 310 F.2d 284, 286 (1962).
Garratt v. Dailey, 279 P.2d 1091 (Wash. 1955).
Green v. Smith & Nephew AHP, Inc., 629 N.W.2d 727 (Wis. 2001).
Grimshaw v. Ford Motor Co., 174 Cal. Rptr. 348 (Cal. App. 1981).
Hammontree v. Jenner, 97 Cal. Rptr. 739 (Cal. App. 1971).
Hattori v. Peairs, 662 So.2d 509 (La. App. 1995).
Heddles v. Chi & Nw. Ry., 42 N.W. 237 (Wis. 1889).
Helling v. Carey, 519 P.2d 981 (Wash. 1974).
Henningsen v. Bloomfield Motors, Inc., 161 A.2d 69 (N.J. 1960).
Horton v. Oregon Health and Science University, 373 P.3d 1158 (Or. 2016).
Hughey v. Lennox, 219 S.W. 323, 325 (Ark. 1920).
Hustler Magazine v. Falwell, 485 U.S. 46 (1988).
I. de S. and Wife v. W. de S., At the Assizes, coram Thorpe, C.J., 1348 or 1349 Year Book, Liber Assisarum, folio 99, placitum 60.
In re Hawaii Federal Asbestos Cases, 734 F. Supp. 1563 (D. Haw. 1990).
In re PG & E Corp., 611 B.R. 110 (Bankr. N.D. Cal. 2019).
Ira S. Bushey & Sons, Inc. v. United States, 398 F.2d 167 (2d Cir. 1968).
Jacque v. Steenberg Homes, Inc., 563 N.W.2d 154 (Wis. 1997).
Jolley v. Powell, 299 So.2d 647 (Fla. 2d Dist. App. 1974).
Keel v. Banach, 624 So.2d 1022 (Ala. 1993).
Keene v. Brigham & Women's Hosp., Inc., 775 N.E.2d 725 (Mass. App. Ct. 2002).
Kennedy v. Parrott, 90 S.E.2d 754 (N.C. 1956).
Knight v. Jewett, 834 P.2d 696 (Cal. 1992).
Konradi v. United States, 919 F.2d 1207 (7th Cir. 1990).
Kremen v. Cohen, 337 F.3d 1024 (9th Cir. 2003) (Kozinski, J.).
Kubert v. Best, 75 A.3d 1214 (N.J. Super. Ct. App. Div. 2013).
La Marra v. Adam, 63 A.2d 497 (Pa. 1949).
Lamson v. American Ax & Tool Co., 177 Mass. 144 (1900) (Holmes, C.J.).
Lange v. Hoyt, 159 A. 575 (Conn. 1932).
Latimer v. A.E.C. Ltd., [1952] 2 Q.B. 70 I, 711 (Denning, L.).
Longenecker v. Zimmerman, 267 P.2d 543 (Kan. 1954).
Losee v. Buchanan, 51 N.Y. 476 (1873).
Lubin v. Iowa City, 131 N.W.2d 765 (Iowa, 1964).
Lucchese v. San Francisco–Sacramento R. Co., 289 P. 188 (Cal. 1930).
MacPherson v. Buick Motor Co., 111 N.E. 1050 (N.Y. 1916).
Magee v. West-End St. Ry., 23 N.E. 1102 (Mass. 1890).
Mansfield v. City of Philadelphia, 42 A2d 549 (Pa. 1945).
Marshall v. Ranne, 511 S.W.2d 255 (Tex. 1974).
Martin v. Herzog, 126 N.E. 814 (N.Y. 1920).
Mattyasovszky v. West Towns Bus Co., 61 Ill.2d, 31 (1975).
McCormick v. Carrier, 795 N.W.2d 517 (Mich. 2010).
McGuire v. Almy, 8 N.E.2d 760, 762 (Mass. 1937).
Michigan v. EPA, 135 S. Ct. 2699 (2015).
Miller v. State, 306 N.W.2d 554 (Minn. 1981).

Modisette v. Apple Inc., 30 Cal. App. 5th 136 (2018).
Mohr v. Williams, 104 N.W. 12 (Minn. 1905).
Moisan v. Loftus, 178 F.2d 148, 149 (2d Cir. 1949).
Moorman Mfg. Co. v. Nat'l Tank Co., 435 N.E.2d 443 (Ill. 1982).
Morris v. West Hartlepool Steam Navigation Co., 1956 App. Cas. 552, 574 (appeal taken from C.A.) (Reid, L.).
Morson v. Superior Court, 109 Cal. Rptr. 2d 343 (Cal. Ct. App. 2001).
Myhaver v. Knutson, 942 P.2d 445 (1997).
Nelson v. State, 181 N.E. 448 (Ohio Ct. App. 1932).
New York Times Co. v. Sullivan, 376 U.S. 254 (1964).
Norfolk & W. Ry. Co. v. Ayers, 538 U.S. 135, 150 (2003).
O'Brien v. Cunard Steamship Co., 28 N.E. 266 (Mass. 1891).
O'Cain v. O'Cain, 473 S.E.2d 460 (S.C. 1996).
Otani v. Broudy, 59 P.3d 126 (Wash. Ct. App. 2002).
Owens-Illinois, Inc. v. Armstrong, 604 A.2d 47 (Md. Ct. App. 1992).
Palsgraf v. Long Island Railroad 161 N.E. 99, 100 (1928).
Parrott v. Wells, Fargo, & Co., 82 U.S. (15 Wall.) 524 (1872).
Paul v. Watchtower Bible and Tract Society, 819 F.2d 875 (9th Cir. 1987).
Planned Parenthood of Mid-Iowa v. Maki, 478 N.W.2d 637 (Iowa 1991).
Porter v. City of Manchester, 849 A.2d 103 (N.H. 2004).
Portland Cement Ass'n v. Ruckelshaus, 486 F.2d 375 (D.C. Cir. 1973).
Public Serv. Co. v. Elliot, 123 F.2d 2, 6 (1st Cir. 1941).
Quiroz v. Seventh Ave. Center, 45 Cal. Rptr. 3d 222 (Cal. Ct. App. 2006).
Raim v. Ventura, 113 N.W.2d 827, 830 (Wis. 1962).
Randi W. v. Muroc Joint Unified School Dist., 929 P.2d 582 (Cal. 1997).
Roberts v. Stevens Clinic Hosp., Inc. 176 W.Va. 492 (1986).
Robins Dry Dock & Repair Co. v. Flint, 275 U.S. 303 (1927).
Rogers v. Elliot, 15 N.E. 768 (Mass. 1888).
Ryan v. N.Y. Central Railroad Co., 35 N.Y. 210, 217 (1866).
Rybachek v. EPA, 904 F.2d 1276 (9th Cir. 1990).
Rylands v. Fletcher, L.R. 3 H.L. 330 (1868).
Schloendorff v. Society of New York Hospital, 105 N.E. 92 (N.Y. 1914).
Schweitzer v. Consolidated Rail Corp., 758 F.2d 936 (3d Cir. 1985).
Scott v. Pacific West Mountain Resort, 834 P.2d 6 (Wash. 1992).
Shipley v. Fifty Associates, 106 Mass. 194 (1870).
Siegler v. Kuhlman, 502 P.2d 1181 (Wash. 1972).
Sindell v. Abbot Laboratories, 607 P.2d 924 (Cal. 1980).
Sinram v. Pennsylvania Railroad Co., 61 F.2d 767 (1932).
Soc'y of Plastics Indus. v. Occupational Safety & Health Admin., 509 F.2d 1301 (2d Cir. 1975).
Spur Indus., Inc. v. Del E. Webb Dev. Co., 494 P.2d 700 (Ariz. 1972).
State v. Ingram, 74 S.E.2d 532 (N.C. 1953).
State v. Leidholm, 334 N.W.2d 811 (N.D. 1983).
Stevenson v. East Ohio Gas Co., 73 N.E.2d 200 (Ohio Ct. App. 1946).
Summer J. v. United States Baseball Federation, 258 Cal. Rptr. 3d 615 (Ct. App. 2020).
Summers v. Tice, 199 P.2d 1 (Cal. 1948).
Taber v. Maine, 45 F.3d 598 (2d Cir. 1995) (Calabresi, J.).
Tarasoff v. Regents of the University of California, 529 P.2d 553 (Cal. 1974).

Telda v. Ellman, 19 N.E.2d 987 (N.Y. 1939).
Theisen v. Milwaukee Auto. Mut. Ins. Co., 118 N.W.2d 140, 144 (Wis. 1962).
Thing v. La Chusa, 771 P.2d 814 (Cal. 1989).
Tiller v. Atlantic Coast Line Railroad Co., 318 U.S. 54 (1943) (J. Black).
Troppi v. Scarf, 187 N.W.2d 511 (Mich. Ct. App. 1971).
Tuchkashinsky v. Lehigh & W. Coal Co., 49 A. 308 (Pa. 1901).
Union Elec. Co. v. EPA, 427 U.S. 246, 258 (1976).
United States Fid. & Guar. Co. v. Jadranska Slobodna Plovidba, 683 F.2d 1022, 1026 (7th Cir. 1982).
United States v. Carroll Towing Co., 159 F.2d 169 (2d Cir. 1947).
United Steelworkers of Am., AFL-CIO-CLC v. Marshall, 647 F.2d 1189 (D.C. Cir. 1980).
Van Skike v. Zussman, 318 N.E.2d 244 (Ill. App. Ct. 1974).
Vaughan v. Menlove, 3 Bing. (N.C.) 467, 132 Eng. Rep. 490 (Court of Common Pleas 1837).
Verbryke v. Owens-Corning Fiberglas Corp., 84 Ohio App. 3d 388 (1992).
Victorson v. Bock Laundry Mach. Co., 335 N.E.2d 275 (N.Y. 1975).
Villanova v. Abrams, 972 F.2d 792, 796 (7th Cir. 1992).
Vincent v. Lake Erie Transportation Co., 124 N.W. 221 (Minn. 1910).
Vosburg v. Putney, 50 N.W. 403 (Wis. 1891).
Wagner v. Int'l Ry., 133 N.E. 437 (1921).
Warren v. Mendenhall, 79 N.W. 661 (Minn. 1899).
Weinberg v. Dinger, 524 A.2d 366 (N.J. 1987).
Wheat v. Freeman Coal Mining Corp., 319 N.E.2d 290 (Ill. App. Ct. 1974).
Whelan v. Whelan, 588 A.2d 251 (1991).
White v. University of Idaho, 797 P.2d 108 (Idaho 1990).
Whitman v. American Trucking Associations, 531 U.S. 457 (2001).
Zaslow v. Kroenert, 176 P.2d 1 (Cal. 1946).
Zibell v. S. Pac. Co, 160 Cal. 237 (Cal. 1911).

Statutes, Constitutions, and Legislative Materials

33 U.S.C. § 1311(b)(1)(A).
33 U.S.C. § 1311(b)(2)(A).
33 U.S.C. § 1311(b)(2)(A).
33 U.S.C. § 1314(b)(2)(B).
33 U.S.C. § 1317(a)(2) (2012).
42 U.S.C. § 7412.
Accident Compensation Act 1972 (N.Z.).
Accident Compensation Act 1982 (N.Z.).
Accident Insurance Act 1998 (N.Z.).
Accident Rehabilitation Compensation and Insurance Act 1992 (N.Z.).
Act to Amend the Clean Air Act, Pub. L. No. 101-549, 104 Stat. 2399 (codified as amended at 42 U.S.C. §§ 7401–7671).
Black Lung Benefits Act of 1972, 30 U.S.C. §§ 901–945 (2000).
California Civil Code § 1714(a) (West 2002) (enacted 1872).
California Constitution, Art. I, § 19(a).
California Vehicle Code § 22352(a)(2) (2015).
Exec. Order No. 12,291, 3 C.F.R. 127 (1982) (repealed 1993).

Federal Coal Mine Health and Safety Act of 1969, Pub. L. No. 91-173, §§ 401–426, 83 Stat. 742 (1969).
Food Quality Protection Act of 1996, Pub. L. No. 104-170, §§ 405, 408(b)(2)(A)(ii), 110 Stat. 1489, 1516 (codified as amended at 21 U.S.C. § 346a (2012).
Injury Prevention, Rehabilitation, and Compensation Act 2001 (N.Z.).
MCL 500.3135(1).
National Childhood Vaccine Injury Act of 1986, 42 U.S.C. §§ 300aa-10 to 300aa-34 (2000).
Occupational Exposure to Hexavalent Chromium, 71 Fed. Reg. 10 (Feb. 28, 2006).
Price-Anderson Act, Pub. L. No. 85-256, 71 Stat. 576 (1957).
Report of the Royal Commission of Inquiry, Compensation for Personal Injury in New Zealand (1967).

Restatements and Principles of the Law

1 Blackstone, Commentaries *125, *129, *134, *138 (1766).
1 Blackstone, Commentaries *54 (1766).
13 Am. Jur. Proof of Facts 3d 219 (1991).
14 Larson's Workers' Compensation Law §§ 150.01, 150.05 (2019).
3 Blackstone, Commentaries *1–*2 (1766).
3 Blackstone, Commentaries *116 (1766).
3 Blackstone, Commentaries *123 (1766).
Coke, Edward, The Second Part of the Institutes of the Laws of England (1797 ed.).
Restatement (First) of Torts § 15 (1934).
Restatement (First) of Torts, P.D. No. 1, at 3, December 10, 1923 (Francis H. Bohlen, Reporter).
Restatement (Second) of Agency § 228 (1958).
Restatement (Second) of Torts § 1 (1965).
Restatement (Second) of Torts § 13 (1965).
Restatement (Second) of Torts § 15 (1965).
Restatement (Second) of Torts § 158 (1965).
Restatement (Second) of Torts § 19 (1965).
Restatement (Second) of Torts § 282 (1965).
Restatement (Second) of Torts § 283 (1965).
Restatement (Second) of Torts § 291 (1965).
Restatement (Second) of Torts § 329 (1965).
Restatement (Second) of Torts § 402A (1965).
Restatement (Second) of Torts § 519 (1977).
Restatement (Second) of Torts § 652B (1977).
Restatement (Second) of Torts § 7 (1965).
Restatement (Second) of Torts § 821D (1979).
Restatement (Second) of Torts § 826 (1979).
Restatement (Second) of Torts § 903 (1979).
Restatement (Second) of Torts §§ 292–93 (1965).
Restatement (Third) of Torts: Liability for Physical and Emotional Harm § 8(b) (2010).
Restatement (Third) of Agency § 7.07 (2006).
Restatement (Third) of Torts: Intentional Torts to Persons § 103 Discussion Draft (2014).
Restatement (Third) of Torts: Liability for Physical & Emotional Harm § 4 (2010).

Restatement (Third) of Torts: Liability for Physical and Emotional Harm § 7(a) (2010).
Restatement (Third) of Torts: Liability for Physical and Emotional Harm § 18 (Am. Law Inst., Council Draft No. 2, 2000).
Restatement (Third) of Torts: Liability for Physical and Emotional Harm § 3 (2010).
Restatement (Third) of Torts: Physical & Emotional Harm § 10 (2010).
Restatement (Third) of Torts: Physical & Emotional Harm § 20 (2010).
Restatement (Third) of Torts: Physical & Emotional Harm § 3 (2010).
Restatement (Third) of Torts: Physical & Emotional Harm § 4 (2010).
Restatement (Third) of Torts: Physical & Emotional Harm § 47 (2010).
Restatement (Third) of Torts: Physical & Emotional Harm § 6 (2010).
Restatement (Third) of Torts: Physical & Emotional Harm § 7 (2010).
Restatement (Third) of Torts: Physical & Emotional Harm 4 Scope Note (2010).
Restatement (Third) of Torts: Physical and Emotional Harm § 11(e) (2010).
Restatement (Third) of Torts: Products Liability § 1 (1998).
Restatement (Third) of Torts: Products Liability § 2(a) (1998).

Reports

Center for Disease Control, About DES, https://www.cdc.gov/des/consumers/about/index.html.
Consumer Reports, How Safe Is Safe Enough? (Apr. 2017).
National Highway Traffic Safety Administration, Federal Automated Vehicles Policy (2016).
National Highway Traffic Safety Administration, Traffic Safety Facts Annual Report Tables (2018).
U.S. Department of Transportation, Automobile Insurance and Compensation Study (1970).

Films

Black Hawk Down, directed by Ridley Scott (Columbia Pictures, 2002).
Free Solo, directed by Elizabeth Chai Vasarhelyi & Jimmy Chin (National Geographic, 2018).
Minority Report, directed by Stephen Spielberg (20th Century Fox, 2002).

Internet Sources

The Cost-Benefit Revolution, MIT Press, https://mitpress.mit.edu/books/cost-benefit-revolution.

Index

For the benefit of digital users, indexed terms that span two pages (e.g., 52–53) may, on occasion, appear on only one of those pages.

Abraham, Kenneth, 301
absolute liability, 271–72
adjudication (tort), 22–23, 22–23n.9, 28n.18, 58–59
administrative schemes
   enterprise liability and, 267, 291–96
   irreparable injury and, 192–93
   loss insurance and, 293–94
   New Zealand accident scheme and, 75, 75n.17, 77–78, 104–5, 110, 117–20, 295–96
   no-fault automobile insurance and, 292–93, 294, 295–96
   private law theory and, 43–45, 70–71, 104–11, 303, 304
   workers' compensation, 105–6, 108–10
agency
   corrective justice and, 30–31
   defamation and, 65–66
   harm and, 63–65, 143–44
   harm-benefit asymmetry and, 11, 198
   law of security and, 66
   other bodies of law and, 66
   physical harm and, 70, 148
   role of the state and, 196–97
   tort law and, 61–63, 306–7
agency law, 274–75
Alcorn v. Mitchell, 240–41
American Iron & Steel Institute v. Occupational Safety & Health Administration, 204
American Textile (multiple cases), 207
Amphitheaters, Inc. V. Portland Meadows, 91
Andrews, Erin, 90
ARP doctrine. *See* average reasonable person (ARP) doctrine
autonomy, 65–66, 70–71, 85, 92–93, 150, 198, 231–32, 234, 240–46. *See also* agency; sovereignty
average reasonable person (ARP) doctrine
   adjudicative form, 177–79
   due care and, 179–81
   legislative form, 177–79
   normalizing assumptions and, 173–74

   reasonable care and, 139, 164–67
   reasonableness and, 175–79
   subjective valuation and, 167–73

background justice. *See* justice
Barker v. Lull Engineering, 211–12
battery, 88–91, 151, 234
benefit
   agency and, 11, 198
   enterprise liability and, 265, 270, 272, 278–79, 282, 284, 288–89, 290, 297
   harm and, 9–13, 15–16, 143–44, 160
   obligations and, 9–10
   power of, 10–11
   strict liability and, 253–55, 260–61, 263
   Vincent and, 217–18, 253
   See also cost-benefit analysis; harm
Bezos, Jeff, 280–81
Black Lung Benefits Act, 295–96
Blackstone, William, 1–2, 66
Blyth v. Birmingham, 96–97
Boomer v. Atlantic Cement, 233–34, 236–37, 247, 248–49, 256–57, 268
boundary crossings, 242
Bramwell, George (Baron), 297
Brown v. Kendall, 286–87

Calabresi, Guido, 6, 127, 195, 210–11
California Supreme Court, 53, 269n.16, 273–74
Caputo, Philip, 216
cardinal utility, 135–36
Cardozo, Benjamin, 152–53
care, 96–97. *See also* due care; reasonable care
cheapest cost-avoiders, 7, 29–30, 32, 34, 38–39, 59–60, 303
children, 165–67, 168–69, 174
civil recourse. *See* corrective justice theory
Clean Air Act, 200, 201–3, 205
Clean Water Act, 205–6
Coase, Ronald, 6, 271–72, 277
Coast Guard, 274–75, 277–78

Coke (beverage), 278
Coke, Edward, 1–2
Coleman, Jules, 26–29, 30–31, 42–43, 54, 55–56, 236, 247–48, 259–60, 301–2
Commentaries on the Laws of England (Blackstone), 1–2
commutative justice, 263
conditional privilege, 55, 102–3, 251–52, 253–54, 302
consumer-expectation test, 211–12, 214
Consumer Reports, 193–94
continuity thesis, 45–46
contract law, 43, 66
corpses, 216–17
corrective injustice, 53–54
corrective justice theory
  agency and, 30–31
  backward-looking repair and, 7, 32–33
  conceptions of, 25–30, 31–32
  continuity thesis and, 45–46
  corrective injustice and, 53–54
  distributive justice and, 24–25
  economic analysis and, 7, 21, 24–35, 303
  enterprise liability and, 270
  forward looking remedies and, 58–59
  intrinsic justification for, 32
  irreparable injuries and, 48–50
  priority of responsibilities and, 7
  shortcomings of, 50–51, 67–68
  strict liability and, 55–57, 59, 234–36, 237–39, 247–48, 250–51, 257–60
  wrongfulness and, 46–48
  wrongs without losses and, 48–50
correlativity, 31–32
cost-benefit analysis, 9–10, 16–18, 48, 194–96, 218–20, 222–23
cost-justified precaution, 9–10, 307
The Cost of Accidents (Calabresi), 4–5
criminal law
  moral wrongness and, 255–56
  primary concerns of, 2; tort law and, 2
customary care, 97. *See also* care

damages. *See* reparation
Davis v. Consolidated Rail, 124, 131, 152–53
deafness, 12n.32
death. *See* wrongful death
Death Statutes, 190–91
defamation, 65–66
Delair v. McAdoo, 176, 179
Denny v. Ford Motor Co, 213
difference principle, 81
direct risk regulation. *See* administrative schemes

discrimination, 82
disproportionality, 157–59
distributive justice, 24–25
driving, 175–76
due care, 130, 133, 136, 138–39, 147–48, 179–81. *See also* care; Hand Formula; reasonable care; reasonableness
duty
  continuity thesis and, 45–46
  of reasonable care, 53
  successive waves of, 44–45
  See also responsibility
duty-continuity, 45–46

economic analysis
  adjudication and, 60
  cheapest cost-avoiders, 32
  corrective justice critique of, 59–60, 303
  corrective justice theory and, 7
  liability rules and, 21
  strict liability and, 234–35, 240
efficiency, 197
eminent domain, 252, 259–60
emotional distress, 146–47, 149–50
enterprise liability
  accident avoidance and, 278–81
  administrative schemes and, 267, 291–96
  boundary problem in, 278
  causation and, 290–91
  corrective justice and, 270
  critique to, 275–78
  definition of, 271–73
  essential risk and, 299–300
  fairness and, 276–77, 278–79, 298
  the fairness rationale and, 281–82
  fairness to actual and potential injurers and, 289
  fairness to injurers and, 289
  fairness to victims and, 288–89
  features of, 272–73
  limits of, 297–98
  loss-spreading and, 278–81
  property rights and, 298–99
  risk and, 282–85
  significance of, 267–68
  strict liability and, 249–50, 273–75, 276–77
  theory of, 265–66
  waning of, 268–69
enterprise responsibility, 119
Environmental Protection Agency, 210
Epstein, Richard, 276–77

Fairness
  enterprise liability and, 276–77, 278–79

New Zealand accident scheme and, 117–18
reasonable care and, 152–54
strict liability and, 253–54, 256–57
Fairness versus Welfare (Kaplow and Shavell), 195
false-target, 30
"Fate" and "Fortune," 117–18, 290
fault liability
  avoidable harm and, 123
  corrective justice and, 247–48
  private law and, 94, 101–4, 106, 119–20
  Ripstein and, 101–2, 103–4
  strict liability and, 229–33, 237, 240, 246, 247–48, 259–60
  tort law and, 43–44, 56, 71
  workers' compensation and, 106
fault principle, 106–7
First Restatement of Torts, 13, 64, 92
Fletcher, George, 283–87
Fontainebleau Hotel Corp. v. Forty-Five Twenty-Five Inc., 253, 254
Food Quality Protection Act (1996), 200, 210
free contract, 72
Friendly, Henry, 249, 277–78, 281–82

Gardner, John, 95–96, 185, 243–44
Geistfeld, Mark, 155
glaucoma, 158–60
Goldberg, John, 237–38, 247–48, 259
good, 70n.6, 193–99, 226
Green v. Smith & Nephew AHD, Inc., 213–14
Grey, Tom, 304–5
Gutenberg Bibles, 222

Hand Formula, 97–98, 127–28, 129–38, 137n.38, 137n.40, 150–60, 163–64, 182, 235
harm
  agency and, 11, 63–65
  avoidance of, 10, 144, 310
  economic perspective and, 15
  emerging forms of, 108
  emotional distress and, 146–47, 149–50
  fault liability and, 123
  forms of, 13n.38, 92–93
  harm-benefit asymmetry and, 15n.45, 143–44, 198
  impaired condition conception of, 11–15, 64
  irreparable, 48–50, 189–93, 228, 307
  justification of tort law and, 16
  meaning of, 1
  moral significance of, 9, 74–75, 236–37
  physical, 74–75, 144–50, 154–55
  proportionality of precautions and, 155–60

  psychological, 14n.43
  See also wrongful death
Helling v. Carey, 158–62, 163–64
Henderson, James, 147–48
Holmes, Oliver Wendell, 3–4, 107, 110–11, 127

The Idea of Private Law (Weinrib), 69–70
impairment of normal functioning. *See* harm
inalienability, 149–50
injunctive relief, 185–86, 188, 248–49
injury. *See* harm
Institutes of the Laws of England (Coke), 1–2
intentional torts, 62
interests
  balancing liberty and security and, 99–101
  inquiry into, 88–92, 98–99
interpersonal comparison, 136, 141
intrusion upon seclusion, 90–91

jury adjudication, 162–64, 180–81
justice
  background, 113, 114–20
  commutative, 263
  distributive, 80–81
  as fairness, 111–12
  foreground, 110–11, 114–20
  personal property and, 145–46
  private law and, 79–82, 111–20
justification, 123–24

Kaldor Hicks efficiency, 134–35, 142
Kant, Immanuel, 72–73, 220, 222–23
Kaplow, Louis, 195
Krugman, Paul, 193–94

latex, 213–14
law of accidents, 3–4
Levmore, Saul, 143–44
liability
  economic analysis and, 21, 33–34
  negligence and, 33
  sovereignty-based, 56–57
  strict, 55–57
  vicarious, 274–75
libertarianism, 72–73
liberty, 143
Longenecker v. Zimmerman, 245–46
Lord Campbell's Act, 190–91
Lubin v. Iowa City, 287
Lucchese v. San Francisco-Sacramento Railroad, 52

Marshall v. Gotham Co., 158
Martin v. Herzog, 177–78

336　INDEX

Masur, Jonathan, 194–95
means, 75–76, 82–83, 116
Mill, John Stuart, 306–7
misfortune, 236
Mohr v. Williams, 57, 239–40
morality
　harm and, 236–37
　harm-based strict liability and, 262–63
　private law and, 69–70
　rescues and, 214–17
　standards of precaution and, 197
Morris, Herbert, 255

National Childhood Vaccine Injury Act, 267, 268–69, 294, 295–96
negligence law
　average reasonable person (ARP) doctrine and, 139, 175–79
　balancing character of, 99–101, 128–29
　complete negligence and, 152–53
　disproportionality and, 156–59
　due care and, 130, 133, 136, 138–39, 179–81
　economic understanding of, 9–10, 182
　enterprise liability and, 273–74, 275–76, 283, 288, 289, 290
　Hand formula and, 129–38, 150–60
　interpersonal comparison and, 136, 141
　irreparable injury and, 48–50, 189–93, 228
　jury adjudication and, 162–64
　liability and, 33
　modern English, 157–58
　paternalism and, 160–62
　physical harm and, 144–50
　Posner and, 73–74
　reasonable conduct and, 123–25, 126–27, 129
　reasonable person test and, 95–96
　regime of responsibility and, 182–83
　Ripstein and, 96–99, 128–29
　standard of care and, 96–97
　See also enterprise liability; reasonableness
New Zealand Accident Compensation Scheme, 75, 75n.17, 77–78, 104–5, 104n.112, 110, 117–20, 295–96. *See also* administrative schemes
Nozick, Robert, 276–77
nuisance, 79

objective fault liability, 231. *See also* strict liability
Occupational Safety and Health Act (1970), 203
Occupational Safety and Health Administration, 204–5, 206–9, 210
ordinal utility, 135–36
Oregon Supreme Court, 1, 91

Palsgraf v. Long Island Railroad, 131–32, 152–53
Pareto Superior, 134–36
Parfit, Derek, 243–44
paternalism, 160–62
Peeping Tom, 90
Perry, Stephen, 276–77
Pogge, Thomas, 113
Portland Cement Association v. Ruckelshaus, 205
Posner, Eric, 194–95
Posner, Richard
　corrective justice and, 27–29
　Hand formula and, 127–28, 130–32
　precautions and, 156–57
　private law and, 73–74
precaution
　as a consumer choice, 220–22
　cost-benefit analysis and, 194–96, 218–19
　cost-benefit standard and, 209, 218–19
　efficient, 27–28, 32, 125, 155–60, 193, 195–96, 202, 217–18, 225–27
　feasibility standard, 202–9, 227
　irreparable injury and, 192–93, 218–19
　morality and, 197–98
　paternalism and, 160–62
　private necessity and, 217–18
　product liability law and, 211–14
　proportionality of, 155–60, 182
　Reagan administration and, 210
　rescues and, 214–17
　safe-level standard and, 200–2, 226
　standards of, 199–200, 218
　See also risk
precedent, 58–59
Price-Anderson Act, 295–96
Priest, George, 229–30, 265–66, 271–72, 271n.21, 276
primary goods, 193–99
primary obligations
　centering of, 61, 67–68
　omnilaterality of, 51–53
primary responsibilities
　adjudication and, 59
　corrective justice theory and, 7, 32
　in relation to secondary, 36–39
　shifts in, 19–20
privacy tort, 90–91
private law (theory)
　administrative alternatives and, 104–11
　background justice and, 115
　equal right and, 69–70, 77
　form and, 70–71, 73–76
　interest and, 78–79, 83–104
　justice and, 79–82, 111–15

INDEX 337

libertarianism and, 72–73
means and, 75–76, 82–83
Posner and, 73–74
public-private distinction and, 71–72, 77–78, 83
See also Ripstein, Arthur
Private Wrongs (Ripstein), 69, 104–5, 114–15, 301–2
privilege, 217
The Problem of Social Cost (Coase), 6, 271–72
product liability law, 116–17, 211–14, 265–66, 268–69. *See also* enterprise liability
property law, 43, 298–99
Prosser, William, 3–4
public law, 73–74

Rabin, Robert, 273–74
rationality, 5–6, 125–28, 182
Rawls, John, 73, 74, 79–80, 81–82, 110–12, 119, 142, 145–46, 254–55
Reagan administration, 210
reasonable care
  cost-justified care and, 125
  demands of, 175–79
  Hand formula and, 97–98, 127–28, 129–38, 150–60, 163–64
  impartiality and, 142
  interpersonal fairness and, 152–54
  jury adjudication and, 162–64
  moral frameworks and, 125–26
  mutuality, 142
  natural duties and, 178
  ordinary care and, 128–29
  rights and, 151
  standards of, 97
  See also average reasonable person (ARP) doctrine; care
reasonableness
  average reasonable person (ARP) doctrine and, 175–79
  continuity thesis and, 45–46
  excuse and, 124–25
  justifiability and, 5–6
  Pareto superiority and, 134–36
  rationality and, 127–28, 182
  risk and, 123–24, 125–27, 223–26
  See also average reasonable person (ARP) doctrine; care; Hand Formula; reasonable care
reasonable person test, 95–96. *See also* average reasonable person (ARP) doctrine
reasons-continuity, 45–46
reciprocity, 142
regulation, 193
remedial responsibilities. *See* reparation; secondary responsibilities
remedies
  definition of, 1
  diversity of, 41–42
  rights and, 39–41
reparation
  adequacy of, 185–88, 189, 191–92
  injunctive relief and, 188
  money damages and, 185–86, 187–88
  punitive damages and, 187–88
  reparative damages and, 185–86, 187–88, 189
  traditional remedies doctrine and, 188
  wrongful death and, 189–93
  See also secondary responsibilities
respondeat superior, 103, 106, 274–75, 282, 302
responsibility
  bilateral principles of, 75
  distinguishing between, 35–36
  priority of, 36–39
  tort law and, 71
  See also primary responsibilities; secondary responsibilities
Restatement of Agency, 274–75
rights
  battery and, 151
  continuity thesis and, 45–46
  distributive justice and, 80–81
  enforcing, 39–41
  public law and, 42–43n.56
  reasonable care and, 151
  secondary responsibilities and, 37–39
  strict liability and, 253–54
  tort law and, 8, 36–37, 70, 245
rights-continuity, 45–46
Ripstein, Arthur
  administrative schemes and, 104–11
  fault and, 101–3
  harm and, 92–93
  interests and, 88–92, 98–99
  justice and, 111–20
  means and, 75–76, 82–83
  misfortune and, 236
  negligence and, 93–94, 128–29
  private law and, 77–78, 79–82, 302
  Private Wrongs and, 69–70
  reasonable care and, 97–98, 152–53
  strict liability and, 237, 283–84
  See also private law (theory)
risk
  activity and, 142–43
  background level of, 226–27, 297

risk (*cont.*)
  characteristic, 274, 276, 277–78, 297
  as a consumer choice, 220–22
  cost-benefit analysis and, 16–18, 194–96
  distinction between persons and, 223–26
  efficiency and, 27–28, 32, 125, 155–60, 193, 195–96, 197, 202, 217–18, 225–27
  enterprise liability and, 282–85
  Hand formula and, 155–60, 182
  justification and, 123–24
  Pareto superiority and, 134–36
  paternalism and, 160–62
  precaution standards and, 199–209
  product liability law and, 211–14
  proportionality of precautions and, 155–60
  Reagan administration and, 210
  reasonableness of, 123–24, 223–26
  reciprocity of risk theory and, 285–88
  rescues and, 214–17
  significance and, 200–2
  workers' compensation and, 106
  world of activities and, 286–88
  world of acts and, 286–88
  See also cost-benefit analysis; precaution
risk-utility test, 211–12, 213–14
Rylands v. Fletcher, 94, 101, 103n.109, 282–83

safety, 8, 95–96, 143, 147–49, 157, 193–99, 226, 310–11
Schelling, Thomas, 175, 220, 223–24
Schwartz, Gary, 163–64
secondary responsibilities
  corrective justice theory and, 7, 31
  injunctive relief and, 185
  in personam remedial obligations and, 53
  in relation to primary, 36–39
  reparative damages and, 185–86
  rights and, 37–41
Second Restatement of Torts, 13, 64, 92, 153–54, 187–88, 211–12
security, 143
Shavell, Steven, 140–41, 195
Siegler v. Kuhlman, 235–36
Smith, Jeremiah, 106
social insurance, 119
society
  accidental injury and, 117
  private law and, 115–17
  socially rational care and, 125–26
solidarity, 216–17
Solow, Robert, 209
sovereignty
  sovereignty torts and, 242–43

strict liability and, 56–57
tort law and, 49–50, 62–63, 65
strict liability
  conduct-based wrongs and, 239–40
  corrective justice and, 234–36, 237–39, 257–60
  definition of, 229
  economic analysis and, 234–35, 240
  eminent domain and, 252, 259–60
  enterprise liability and, 249–50, 267, 273–75, 276–77, 288
  fact-relative wrongs and, 244–45
  fairness and, 253–54, 256–57
  fault liability and, 102–3, 230–31
  forms of, 231–33
  harm-based, 55–56, 233–34, 247–57, 259–60
  history of, 229–30
  indeterminacy of harm-based, 260–62
  interests and, 88–89
  morality of harm-based, 262–63
  responsibility for harm and, 4
  rights and, 253–54
  rule of law and, 245n.45
  secondary conduct and, 250–52, 258
  sovereignty-based, 56–57, 233, 234, 243–44, 246, 250–51
  types of, 55, 57
  unreasonable harm and, 5–6
  workers' compensation and, 106
  wrongful conduct and, 55
substantive responsibilities. *See* primary responsibilities
Sunstein, Cass, 194–95
Supreme Court, 195, 207
Survival Statutes, 190–91

Tarasoff v. Regents of the University of California, 273–74
Tedla v. Ellman, 177–78
telishment, 29n.20
Teslas, 280–81
Third Restatement of Torts, 13, 64, 92, 127–28, 212
tort law
  accidental injury and, 4–5
  administrative alternatives to, 43–45, 70–71, 75, 77–78, 104–11, 117–19, 192–93
  distinguishing features of, 42–45
  evolution of, 2–3, 19–20, 61, 106–7, 123
  fault principle and, 106–7
  form and, 70–71, 240
  heterogeneity of, 4, 301–11

irreparable injuries and, 48–50, 189–93, 228, 307
justice among persons and, 8
liability rules and, 21
minimizing costs and, 21–22
norms in, 53, 71
primary concerns of, 2
public law and, 73–74
regulation and, 193
rights and, 8, 19–68, 70, 245
as a shadow price system, 6, 301–2
sovereignty torts and, 242–43
traditional definitions of, 3–4, 301–2
See also adjudication (tort); corrective justice theory; economic analysis; private law (theory); rights
traditional remedies doctrine, 188
Traynor, Roger, 230–31, 310
trespass, 88–89, 90, 91, 234, 245–46
Twerski, Aaron, 212–13

United Steelworkers of American, AFL-CIO-CLC v. Marshall, 204–5
utility, 135–36

value
of human life, 214–15n.115, 215n.117, 220–23
judgements of, 16–18, 218–20
Van Skike v. Zussman, 155–56
vicarious liability, 274–75
Vincent v. Lake Erie Transportation Co., 55–56, 217–18, 225, 248–49, 251–52, 253, 254, 258, 261–62

Waldron, Jeremy, 44–45, 117–19, 290
warning regime, 161–62

Weinrib, Ernest
corrective justice and, 24–25, 28–29, 53
fault and, 101, 103
private law and, 69–70, 75, 112–13, 302
welfare, 195–97
White, Edward, 20–21
White, G. Edward, 301
willingness-to-pay, 137
workers' compensation, 105–6, 108–10, 268–69. *See also* administrative schemes
workplace safety, 116–17
world of activities, 285–88, 308–9
world of acts, 286–88, 308–9
Wright, J. Skelly, 204–5, 206, 207
wrongful death, 189–93. *See also* harm
wrongfulness, 31, 46–48
wrongs
accidental, 2–3
bilateral, 74, 75
conditional, 55–56
contempt and, 240–41
corrective injustice and, 53–54
corrective justice theory and, 46–48
fact-relative, 244–45
forms of, 240
innocent, 241
intentional, 240–42, 243–45
irreparable, 48–50
remedial obligations and, 53
sovereignty torts and, 242–43, 246
tortious, 53–55
without losses, 48–50

Yale University, 222

Zipursky, Ben, 237–38, 247–48, 259